HITLER'S WAR
1942-1945

David Irving is the son of a Royal Navy commander. Educated at Imperial College of Science and Technology and at University College, London, he subsequently spent a year in Germany working in a steel mill and perfecting his fluency in the language. His best-known works include *The Destruction of Dresden, Accident – The Death of General Sikorski, The Rise and Fall of the Luftwaffe* and *The Trail of the Fox: The Life of Field Marshal Erwin Rommel.* He has translated *The Memoirs of Field Marshal Keitel* and *The Memoirs of General Reinhard Gehlen.* The companions to this volume, *Hitler's War 1939–1942* and *The War Path: Hitler's Germany 1933–1939,* are also published by Papermac.

HITLER'S WAR
1942-1945

David Irving

Unabridged

M
PAPERMAC

This volume is the second part of *Hitler's War* first published
as a single volume under that title 1977 by Hodder & Stoughton Limited

First published in paperback in this two-volume edition 1983 by
PAPERMAC
a division of Macmillan Publishers Limited
4 Little Essex Street London WC2R 3LF
and Basingstoke

Associated companies in Auckland, Delhi, Dublin, Gaborone, Hamburg, Harare, Hong Kong, Johannesburg, Kuala Lumpur, Lagos, Manzini, Melbourne, Mexico City, Nairobi, New York, Singapore and Tokyo

ISBN 0-333-49589-6

Reprinted 1985, 1986, 1987, 1988, 1989

Printed in Hong Kong

The cover illustration of Hitler decorating a member of the Hitler Youth Movement in 1945 is the last photograph of the Führer and is reproduced by kind permission of Ullstein Bilderdienst, West Berlin.

Contents

Publisher's Note

This is the second of the two books originally published in a single volume as *Hitler's War*. The page numbering, and the numbering of the parts of the book, reflects the division that has been made for this edition: parts 1–3, pages 1–450, are published as *Hitler's War 1939–1942*.

6 ENDKAMPF

Acknowledgments

I like to think that I chose precisely the right ten years to work on Hitler. Any earlier, and the archives would not have begun to disgorge their captured papers; any later, and those who came closest to enjoying Hitler's confidence would have died. Hitler's secretaries and adjutants were without exception of the utmost help. Traudl Junge and Christa Schroeder provided unpublished manuscripts and letters of the period; his adjutants Admiral Karl-Jesco von Puttkamer (navy), General Gerhard Engel (army), and Colonel Nicolaus von Below (Luftwaffe) did the same, and labored through much of the resulting manuscript. Without the memories of Colonel Erik von Amsberg, Max Wünsche, Fritz Darges, and Otto Günsche, many a gap in our knowledge would have remained unfilled. But many other adjutants attending Hitler's conferences also assisted—of whom I must single out for mention Major General Ottomar Hansen, Lieutenant Colonel Ernst John von Freyend, Admiral Kurt Freiwald, and Captain Herbert Friedrichs, and particularly Johannes Göhler and Wolf Eberhard for the important diaries and letters they made available to me for the first time.

The most important documents were provided by Professor Hugh Trevor-Roper and by Lev Besymenski. Dr. Cortez F. Enloe, Washington, D.C., furnished medical records on Hitler. François Genoud, Lausanne, Switzerland, supplied key extracts from Bormann's personal files; Frau Asta Greiner, Wiesbaden, Germany, her husband's unpublished diaries and private correspondence; the stenographer Karl Thöt, Bonn, his war diary; the late Colonel Karl-Heinz Keitel, papers from his father's collection; Albert Speer, Heidelberg, Germany, his office Chronik and other papers; Reinhard Spitzy, Austria, certain letters; Günter Peis, Munich, selected items from his unique collection; and Dr. Heinrich Heim, Munich, papers originating from his period as Martin Bormann's adjutant; furthermore Hitler's doctors Professor Hanskarl von Hasselbach, Dr. Erwin Giesing, and Dr. Richard Weber provided papers or other aid.

Many of the collections deposited in the archives would have remained closed to me without the kindness of the following: Isabella Adam, Ursula Backe, Anni Brandt, Ilse Dittmar, Friedl Koller, Paula Kubizek, Baroness Jutta von Richthofen, the late Lucie Rommel, Anneliese Schmundt, Gertrud Seyss-Inquart, Ruth von Vormann, Elisabeth Wagner, Elisabeth Todt, Margarete von Waldau, Baroness Marga von Weichs, Baroness Marianne von Weizsäcker—all of whom either permitted me to see or provided me with direct access to their husbands' papers, letters, and diaries. (The Weizsäcker diaries have been expertly transcribed by my colleague Professor Leonidas E. Hill.) Frau Blanda Benteler allowed me the diaries of her husband Walther Hewel; Liselotte von Salmuth those of her husband, the Colonel General; Else Renate Nagy the manuscripts and papers of her late husband Dr. Wilhelm Scheidt—adjutant of Hitler's court historian General Walter Scherff; Frau Gerta von Radinger the private letters of her late husband, Alwin-Broder Albrecht (whom she had married in 1940). Frau Anneliese Schmundt gave me her private war diary. I am also grateful to Dr. Peter von Blomberg, Manfred Brückner, General Heinz-Günther Guderian, Joachim Hoepner, Hermann Leeb, Fritz von Lossberg, Rüdiger von Manstein, and Roland Schaub for permission to use the private papers of their fathers. The late Karl-Otto Saur, Field Marshal Erhard Milch, Major General Ivo-Thilo von Trotha, General Walter von Seydlitz-Kurzbach, Ambassador Dr. Hasso von Etzdorf, and the late Ludwig Krieger, stenographer, all made diaries and papers available to me.

Of those who gave up their time for long conversations or to write letters I must mention these: Ludwig Bahls, Werner Best, Karl Bodenschatz, Herta Berger—widow of the stenographer killed on July 20, 1944—Herbert Büchs, Eugen Dollmann, Peterpaul von Donat, Xaver Dorsch, Baron Sigismund von Falkenstein, Ambassador André François Poncet, Reinhard Gehlen, Otto-Heinz Grosskreutz, Werner Grothmann, Hedwig Haase, Ernst "Putzi" Hanfstaengl, Heider Heydrich, Ralph Hewins, Ambassador Hans von Herwarth, Professor Andreas Hillgruber, Professor Raul Hilberg, Gebhard Himmler, Walter Huppenkothen, Professor Hans-Adolf Jacobsen, Elisabeth Kaltenbrunner, Hans Kehrl, Werner Koeppen, Marlene Kunde (née Exner), Dr. O. H. Schmitz-Lammers, Helmut Laux, Heinz Linge, Field Marshal Friedrich List, Heinz Lorenz, Colonel J. L. McCowen, Johanna Morell, Josef Müller, Pastor Martin Niemöller, Max Pemsel, Leo Raubal, the late Anneliese von Ribbentrop, Walter Rohland, Jürgen Runzheimer, Professor Ernst-Günther Schenck, Henriette von Schirach, Richard Schulze-Kossens, Dietrich Schwencke, former Federal Chancellor Dr. Kurt von Schuschnigg, General Curt Siewert, Otto Skorzeny, Gertrud and Friedrich Stumpfegger, the late Helmut Sündermann, Admiral Gerhard Wagner, Winifred Wagner, Karl Wahl, Walter Warlimont, and Karin Weigl. Walter Frentz placed his photographic collection at my disposal; Peter Hoffmann his expertise; Frau Luise Jodl her husband's papers.

For most of the ten years I also plagued archives and institutes with my inquiries. I am most indebted to the exemplary Institut für Zeitgeschichte in Munich, and to its then director Professor Helmuth Krausnick and above all its head of archives Dr. Anton Hoch, who guided me as friend and mentor with great objectivity and ability from October 1966 onward; Frau Karla Götz, Hermann Weiss, and Anton Zirngibl fulfilled my often immodest demands, and Dr. Wolfgang Jacobmeyer permitted me to use his prepared edition of the Hans Frank diaries. In transferring to the Institut my entire Hitler document collection, including the interview and interrogation records, Hitler's armament decrees, the Canaris/Lahousen fragments, a correct transcription of Greiner's war diary notes, the Scheidt papers, and much else, I hope to have recompensed in part for the assistance given me. Much of the material was microfilmed by the Imperial War Museum, London S.E. 1, before I transferred it to Munich; these films are available from the museum's Foreign Documents Centre. I also transferred my collection of records on Hitler's medical history to the Bundesarchiv in Koblenz, Germany (where it is filed as item *Kl. Erw. 525*). I placed a copy of the Fritzsch Papers, 1938–39, in the Bundesarchiv-Militärarchiv in Freiburg, Germany, where Dr. Friedrich-Christian Stahl, Alfred Bottler, and Colonel Helmuth Vorwieg aided me. At the neighboring Militärgeschichtliches Forschungsamt (of the German Defense Ministry) I was guided by Colonels Karl Gundeslach, Manfred Kehrig, Rolf Elbe, and Dr. Georg Meyer through the intricacies of their own archives. At Nuremberg's State Archives Dr. Puchner and Dr. Schuhmann aided me; and at the Führungsakademie der Bundeswehr in Hamburg Colonel Helmuth Technau was kind enough to allow me to carry volumes of original records—including the important Koller diaries—to London with me to put on microfilm. In the Operational Archives Branch at Washington Navy Yard I met with the fullest cooperation of Dr. Dean C. Allard and Mrs. Mildred D. Mayeux; and Robert Wolfe, John E. Taylor, Thomas E. Hohmann, and their colleagues provided assistance at the National Archives. I must also mention Mrs. Agnes F. Peterson of the Hoover Library, Stanford, California; Detmar Finke of the Office of the Chief of Military History (OCMH), Washington D.C.; and Mr. George E. Blau, chief historian of USAEUR headquarters, Heidelberg, Germany. The U.S. Mission's Berlin Document Center provided speedy and efficient assistance while under its director Richard Bauer, as did the heads of archives of the German, French, Finnish, and British foreign offices. In London I encountered particularly useful help from Dr. Leo Kahn of the Imperial War Museum; Squadron Leader L. A. Jackets of the Air Historical Branch; Mr. Brian Melland, Mr. Clifton Child, and Mrs. Nan Taylor of the Cabinet Office Historical Section; and Mr. K. Hiscock at the Foreign Office Library. World War II researchers will find many of the special microfilms of materials prepared by me while researching this book available now from E. P. Microform Ltd., East Ardsley, Wakefield, Yorkshire, England.

This book would have been impossible without the patience and generosity of the many publishers who waited long years for the scaffolding to be removed from this *monumentum aeris* which I have erected. My editors, Alan Williams of the Viking Press and Stanley Hochman, provided me with many a stimulus and useful reproof. Without the indulgence of my wife, Pilar, in putting up with the years of turmoil and inconvenience the book might not have appeared. Nor shall I forget the nameless legions who typed, translated, or trudged the archives with me: Mrs. Jutta Thomas, the only one of my secretaries to survive the full marathon, and my colleague Elke Fröhlich, who encouraged me to persist and helped me to scale the mountains of records in Berlin, Munich, London, Freiburg, and Bonn that had daunted and dissuaded other writers and would otherwise have discouraged me.

Introduction

"To historians is granted a talent that even the gods are denied—to alter what has already happened!"

I bore this scornful adage in mind when I embarked on this study of Hitler's war years late in 1964. I saw myself as a stone-cleaner—less concerned with a wordy and subjective architectural appraisal than with scrubbing years of grime and discoloration from the facade of a silent and forbidding monument, uncertain whether the revealed monument would prove too hideous to be worthy of the effort.

In earlier books, I relied on the primary records of the period rather than published literature; I naïvely supposed that the same technique could within five years be applied to a study of Adolf Hitler, little realizing that it would be eleven years before I would lay bare the factual bedrock on which the legend of Hitler had been built. But I believe that hard rubbing has disclosed a picture of the man that nobody until now had suspected.

My conclusion on completing the research startled even me: while Adolf Hitler was a powerful and relentless military commander, the war years saw him as a lax and indecisive political leader who allowed affairs of state to rot. In fact he was probably the weakest *leader* Germany has known in this century. Though often brutal and insensitive, Hitler lacked the ability to be ruthless where it mattered most, *e.g.,* he refused to bomb London itself until the decision was forced on him in the late summer of 1940. He was reluctant to impose the test of total mobilization on the German "master race" until it was too late to matter, so that with munitions factories crying out for manpower, idle German housewives were still employing half a million domestic servants to dust their homes and polish their furniture. His military irresolution also showed through, for example, in his panicky vaccillation at times of crisis like the Battle for Narvik in 1940. He took ineffectual measures against his enemies inside Germany for too long, and seems to have been unable to take effective action against strong opposition at the very heart of his High Command. He suffered incompetent ministers and generals far longer than the Allied leaders did. He failed too to unite the feuding Party and Wehrmacht factions in fighting for the common cause, and he proved incapable of stifling the OKH' (War Department's) corrosive hatred of the OKW (the Wehrmacht High Command). I believe I show in this book that the more hermetically Hitler locked himself away behind the barbed wire and minefields of his remote military headquarters, the more his Germany became a Führer-Staat without a Führer. Domestic policy was controlled by whoever was most powerful in each sector—by Hermann Göring as head of the powerful economics office, the Four-Year Plan; by Hans Lammers as chief of the Reich Chancellery or by Martin Bormann, the Nazi party boss; or by Heinrich Himmler, minister of the interior and "Reichsführer" of the black-uniformed SS.

The problem is that Hitler was a puzzle even to his most intimate advisers. Joachim Ribbentrop, his foreign minister, wrote in his Nuremberg prison cell in 1945:

> I got to know Adolf Hitler more closely in 1933. But if I am asked today whether I knew him well—how he thought as a politician and statesman, what kind of man he was—then I'm bound to confess that I know only very little about him; in fact nothing at all. The fact is that although I went through so much together with him, in all the years of working with him I never came closer to him than on the first day we met, either personally or otherwise.

As a historian I have resorted to the widest possible spectrum of source materials. I have not only used the military records and archives; I have burrowed deep into the contemporary writings of his closest friends and personal staff, seeking clues to the real truth in their diaries or in the private letters they wrote to their wives and friends. In this way I have tried to understand the intricacies and contradictions in Hitler's last years.

The sheer complexity of that character is evident from a comparison of his extreme brutality in some respects and his almost maudlin sentimentality and stubborn adherence to long-abandoned military conventions in others. In the chapters that follow, we shall find Hitler cold-bloodedly ordering the execution of fifty or a hundred hostages for every German occupation-soldier killed; dictating the massacre of Italian soldiers who turned their weapons against the German troops in 1943; ordering the systematic liquidation of Red Army commissars, Allied Commando troops, and—in 1945—even captured Allied aircrews; in 1942 he announces to the General Staff that the entire male populations of Stalingrad and Leningrad will eventually be exterminated, and he justifies these orders to himself and to his staff by political doctrines and the expediencies of war. Yet the same Adolf Hitler indignantly exclaimed, in one of the last war conferences of his life, that Soviet tanks were flying the Nazi swastika as a ruse during street fighting in Berlin, and he flatly forbade his Wehrmacht to violate flag rules! In an age in which the governments of the democracies, both during World War II and in later years, unhesitatingly attempted, engineered, or condoned the assassination of the inconvenient—from General Sikorski, Admiral Darlan, Field Marshal Rommel, and King Boris to Fidel Castro, Patrice Lumumba, and Salvador Allende—we learn that Hitler, the unscrupulous dictator, not only never resorted to the assassination of foreign opponents, but flatly forbade the Abwehr (Intelligence Agency) to attempt it (in particular he rejected Admiral Canaris's plans to assassinate the Red Army General Staff).

The negative is traditionally always difficult to prove; but it seemed well worth attempting to discredit accepted dogmas if only to expose the "unseaworthiness" of many current legends about Hitler. The most durable of these concerns the Führer's involvement in the extermination of the Jews. My analysis of this controversial issue serves to highlight two broad conclusions: that in wartime, dictatorships are fundamentally weak—the dictator himself, however alert, is unable to oversee all the functions of his executives acting within the confines of his far-flung empire; and that in this particular case, the burden of guilt for the bloody and mindless massacre of the Jews rests on a large number of Germans, many of them alive today, and not just on one "mad dictator," whose order had to be obeyed without question.

I had approached the massacre of the Jews from the traditional viewpoint prevailing in the mid-1960s. "Supposing Hitler was a capable statesman and a gifted commander," the argument ran, "how does one explain his murder of six million Jews?" If this book were simply a history of the rise and fall of Hitler's Reich, it would be legitimate to conclude: "Hitler killed the Jews." He after all created the atmosphere of hatred with his anti-Semitic speeches in the 1930s; he and Himmler created the SS; he built the concentration camps; his speeches, though never explicit, left the clear impression that "liquidate" was what he meant. For a full-length war biography of Hitler, I felt that a more analytical approach to the key questions of initiative, complicity, and execution would be necessary. Remarkably, I found that Hitler's *own* role in the "Final Solution of the Jewish Problem" has never been examined. German historians, usually the epitome of painstaking essaying on every other subject, to whom no hypothesis is acceptable unless scrutinized from a thousand angles, suddenly developed monumental blind spots when Hitler himself cropped up: bald statements were made, legends were created, blame was laid, without a shadow of historical evidence in support. British and American historians followed suit. Other writers quoted them. For thirty years, our knowledge of Hitler's part in the atrocity has rested on inter-historian incest.

Many people, particularly in Germany and Austria, had an interest in propagating the accepted version that the order of one madman originated the entire massacre. Precisely when the order was given and in what form has, admittedly, never been established. In 1939?—but the secret extermination camps did not begin operating until December 1941. At the January 1942 "Wannsee Conference"?—but the incontrovertible evidence is that Hitler ordered on November 30, 1941, that there was to be "no liquidation" of the Jews (without much difficulty, I found in Himmler's private files his own handwritten note on this). On several subsequent dates in 1942 Hitler made—in private—statements which are totally incompatible with the notion that he knew that the liquidation program had in fact begun. In 1943, and again in early 1944, I find that documents being submitted to Hitler by the SS were tampered with so as to camouflage the truth about the pogrom: sometimes the files contain both the original texts and the "doctored" version submitted to Hitler. Small wonder that when his closest crony of all those years, SS General Josef ("Sepp") Dietrich, was asked by the American Seventh Army for an opinion on Hitler on June 1, 1945, he replied, "He knew even less than the rest. He allowed himself to be taken for a sucker by everyone."

My own hypothesis, to which I point in the various chapters in which I deal in chronological sequence with the unfolding persecution and liquidation of the European Jews, is this: the killing was partly of an *ad hoc* nature, what the Germans call a *Verlegenheitslösung*—the way out of an awkward dilemma, chosen by the middle-level authorities in the eastern territories overrun by the Nazis—and partly a cynical extrapolation by the central SS authorities of Hitler's anti-Semitic decrees. Hitler had unquestionably decreed that Europe's Jews were to be "swept back" to the east; I describe the various phase-lines established by this doctrine. But the SS authorities, Gauleiters, and regional commissars and governors in "the east" proved wholly unequal to the problems caused by this mass uprooting in midwar. The Jews were brought by the trainload to ghettos already overcrowded and underprovisioned. Partly in collusion with each other, partly independently, the Nazi agencies there simply liquidated the deportees as their trains arrived, on a scale increasingly more methodical and more regimented as the months passed.

A subsidiary motive in the atrocity was the animal desire of the murderers to loot and plunder the Jewish victims and conceal their traces. (This hypothesis does not include the methodical liquidation of Russian Jews during the "Barbarossa" invasion of 1941, which came under a different Nazi heading—preemptive guerrilla warfare; and there is no indication that Hitler expressed any compunctions about it.) We shall see how in October 1943, even as Himmler was disclosing to audiences of SS generals and Gauleiters that Europe's Jews had virtually been exterminated, Hitler was still forbidding liquidations—*e.g.*, of the Italian Jews in Rome—and ordering their internment instead. (This order his SS also disobeyed.) Wholly in keeping with his character, when Hitler was confronted with the facts—either then or, as Kaltenbrunner later claimed, in October

1944—he took no action to rebuke the guilty. His failure or inability to act in effect kept the extermination machinery going until the end of the war.

It is plausible to impute to Hitler that not uncommon characteristic of Heads of State who are overreliant on powerful advisers: a conscious desire "not to know." But the proof of this is beyond the powers of any historian. What we *can* prove is that Himmler several times explicitly accepted responsibility for the liquidation decision.

Given the brutality of Hitler's orders to "dispose of" the entire male populations of two major Soviet cities, his insistence on the execution of hostages on a one hundred to one basis, his demands for the liquidation of Italian soldiers, Polish intellectuals, clergy and nobility, and captured Allied airmen and Red Army commissars, his apparent reluctance to acquiesce in the extermination of Europe's Jews remains a mystery. His order in July 1944, despite Himmler's objections, that Jews be "sold" for foreign currency and supplies suggests to some that like contemporary terrorists he saw these captives as a potential "asset," a means by which he could blackmail the civilized world. In any case, by April 1945 whatever inhibitions he may have felt were overcome, and we find him ordering Himmler to liquidate any unevacuated prisoners from concentration camps that were in danger of being overrun by American troops.

My central conclusion, however, is that Hitler was a less than omnipotent Führer and that his grip on his immediate subordinates weakened as the war progressed. Hitler certainly realized this, but too late—in the final days, in his Berlin air raid shelter. In the last two chapters we see him struggling vainly to turn the clock back, to reassert his lost authority by securing one last tactical victory over his enemies. But there are few generals—either Wehrmacht or SS —who now heed him.

I also found it necessary to set very different historical accents on the doctrinaire foreign policies Hitler enforced—from his apparent unwillingness to humiliate Britain when she lay prostrate in 1940 (as I believe I establish on pages 152–53, for example), to his damaging and emotional hatred of the Serbs, his illogical and over-loyal admiration of Benito Mussolini, and his irrational mixtures of emotions toward Josef Stalin. For a modern English historian there is a certain morbid fascination in inquiring how far Adolf Hitler really was bent on the destruction of Britain and her Empire—a major raison d'être for her ruinous fight, which in 1940 imperceptibly supplanted the more implausible one proffered in August 1939: the rescue of Poland from outside oppression. Since in the chapters that follow evidence extracted again and again from the most intimate sources—like Hitler's private conversations with his women secretaries in June 1940—indicates that he originally had neither the intention nor the desire to harm

Britain or destroy the Empire, surely British readers at least must ask themselves: What, then, were we fighting for?

Given that the British people exhausted their assets and lost their Empire in defeating Hitler, was he after all right when he noted that Britain's essential attitude was "Après moi le déluge—if only we can get rid of the hated National Socialist Germany?"

Unburdened by ideological idealism, the Duke of Windsor suspected in July 1940 that the war continued solely in order to allow certain British statesmen to save face, even if it meant dragging their country and the Empire into financial ruin. Others pragmatically argued that there could be no compromise with Adolf Hitler and the Nazis. But did Britain's leaders in fact believe this?

Dr. Bernd Martin of Freiburg University has revealed that secret negotiations on peace continued between Britain and Germany in October 1939—negotiations on which, curiously, Sir Winston Churchill's files have officially been sealed until the twenty-first century! Similar negotiations were carried on in June 1940, when even Churchill showed himself in Cabinet meetings to be willing to make a deal with Hitler if the price was right.

Of course, in assessing the real value of such negotiations and of Hitler's publicly stated intentions it is salutary to know that in 1941 he confidentially admitted to Walther Hewel (as the latter recorded in his diary): "For myself personally I would never tell a lie; but there is no falsehood I would not perpetrate for Germany's sake!" It is also necessary to take into account a string of broken promises that kept Europe in paralyzed inactivity for the better part of a decade.

Nevertheless, one wonders how much suffering the (Western) world might have been spared if both sides had pursued this line. But modern historiography has chosen to ignore this possibility as heresy.

The facts revealed here concerning Hitler's recorded actions, motivations, and opinions should provide a basis for fresh debate. Americans will find much that is new about the months leading up to Pearl Harbor. The French will find additional evidence that Hitler's treatment of their defeated nation was more influenced by memories of France's treatment of Germany after World War I than by his respect for Mussolini's desires. Russians can try to visualize the prospect that could conceivably have unfolded if Stalin had accepted Hitler's offer in November 1940 of inclusion in the Axis Pact; or if, having been defeated in the summer of 1941, Stalin had accepted Hitler's offer to rebuild Soviet power beyond the Urals; or if Hitler had taken seriously Stalin's alleged peace offer of September 1944.

In each case, this book views the situation as far as possible through Hitler's eyes, from behind his desk. This technique was bound to yield different perspectives, while answering many questions that arose in the past as to the motives for his actions and decisions. For example, I have devoted great effort to accumulating the same Intelligence material that was presented to Hitler—like the rare intercepts of Göring's *Forschungsamt* (literally, "Research Office"), which monitored telephone lines and decoded international radio signals; these explain, for instance, Hitler's alarm in July 1940 over Stalin's intentions.

Because this tragic moment in history is told from Hitler's point of view, we inevitably *see* the sufferings of the Germans, whereas the destruction and death inflicted on other nations remains somewhat more abstract. However, it is well to keep in mind that conservative estimates are that Hitler's War resulted in 40,000,000 military and civilian deaths. Of this number approximately 2,500,000 were Germans.

In modern Germany, some of my conclusions proved unpalatable to many. A wave of weak, repetitive, and unrevealing Hitler biographies had washed through the bookstores two or three years before my manuscript (running to over three thousand pages in the first draft) was published. The most widely publicized was that written by Joachim Fest; but he later told a questioner that he had not even visited the magnificent National Archives in Washington, which houses by far the largest collection of records relating to recent European history. Stylistically, Fest's German was good; but the old legends were trotted out afresh, polished to an impressive gleam of authority. The same Berlin company also published my book shortly after, under the title *Hitler und seine Feldherren*; their chief editor found many of my arguments distasteful, even dangerous, and without informing me, suppressed or even reversed them: in *their* printed text Hitler had not told Himmler there was to be "no liquidation" of the Jews (on November 30, 1941); he had told him not to use the word "liquidate" publicly in connection with their extermination program. Thus history is changed! (My suggestion that they publish Himmler's note as a facsimile had been ignored.) I prohibited further printing of the book, two days after its appearance in Germany. To explain their actions, the Berlin publishers argued that my manuscript expressed some views that were "an affront to established historical opinion" in their country.

The biggest problem in dealing analytically with Hitler is the aversion to him as a person created by years of intense wartime propaganda and emotive postwar historiography. My own impression of the war is limited to snapshot memories of its side effects: early summer picnics around the wreckage of a Heinkel bomber on the fringe of the local Bluebell Woods; the infernal organ note of the V-1 flying bombs awakening the whole countryside as they passed overhead; convoys of drab army trucks rumbling past our country gate; counting the gaps in the American bomber squadrons straggling back from Germany in formation after the day's operations; the troopships sailing in June 1944 from Southsea beach, heading for Normandy; and of course VE-Day itself, with the bonfires and beating of the family gong. Our knowledge of the Germans responsible for all this was scarcely more profound. In *Everybody's* magazine, long defunct, I recall "Ferrier's World Searchlight" with its weekly caricatures of a club-footed dwarf called Goebbels and the other comic Nazi heroes.

The caricatures of the Nazi leaders have bedeviled the writing of history ever since. Writers have found it impossible to de-demonize them. Confronted by the phenomenon of Hitler himself, they cannot grasp that he was an ordinary, walking, talking human weighing some 155 pounds, with graying hair, largely false teeth, and chronic digestive ailments. He is to them the Devil incarnate. The process flourished even more after his death: at the Nuremberg Trials, the blame was shifted from general to minister, from minister to Party official, and from all of them invariably to Hitler. Under the system of "licensed" publishers and newspapers enforced by the Allies in postwar Germany, the legends prospered. No story was too absurd to gain credence; the authority of the writers who created them passed unchallenged.

Among these creative writers the German General Staff must take pride of place. Without Hitler, few of them would have risen higher than to the rank of colonel; they owed him their jobs, their medals, their estates, their endowments. Often they owed him their military victories too—the defeat of France in 1940 (see pages 44–45, 80–81, 114, 116–18), the Battle of Kharkov in 1942 (pages 387–88), to mention just two. After the war those who survived—which was not infrequently because they had been dismissed, and thus removed from the hazards of the battlefield—contrived to divert the blame away from themselves to the erstwhile Führer and Supreme Commander. I have exposed the frauds and deceptions in their biographies. Thus in the secret files of the Nuremberg prosecutor Justice Robert H. Jackson, I found a note addressed to his investigator warning about the proposed tactics of General Franz Halder, the former German Army Chief of Staff: "I just wanted to call your attention to the CSDIC intercepts of Halder's conversations with other generals. He is extremely frank on what he thinks should be suppressed or distorted, and in particular is very sensitive to the suggestion that the German General Staff was involved in anything, especially planning for war." Usually, these tactics involved labeling Hitler a "madman" —although the medical experts who treated him are unanimous that clinically speaking he remained quite sane to the very end.

Fortunately, this embarrassed adjusting of consciences and memories was more than once, as above, recorded for posterity by the hidden microphones of the Combined Services Detailed Interrogation Centers. When General Heinz Guderian—one of Halder's successors as Chief of Staff—and the arrogant, supercilious General Leo Geyr von Schweppenburg were asked by their American captors to write their history of the war, they felt obliged to obtain the permission of Field Marshal Wilhelm von Leeb as senior officer at the Seventh Army CSDIC. Leeb replied:

> Well, I can only give you my personal opinion: . . . You will have to weigh your answers carefully when they pertain to objectives, causes, and the progress of operations in order to see where they may affect the interests of our Fatherland. On the one hand we have to admit that the Americans know the course of operations quite accurately; they even know which units were employed on our side. However, they are not quite as familiar with our motives. And there is one point where it would be advisable to proceed with caution, so that we do not become the laughingstock of the world. I do not know what your relations were with Hitler, but I do know his military capacity. . . . You will have to consider your answers a bit carefully when approached on this subject, so that you say nothing that might embarrass our Fatherland. . . .
>
> *Geyr von Schweppenburg:* The types of madness known to psychologists cannot be compared with the one the Führer suffered from. He was a madman surrounded by serfs. I do not think we should express ourselves quite as strongly as that in our statements. Mention of this fact will have to be made, however, in order to exonerate a few persons. The question is whether now is the right time to mention all this.

After an agonized debate on whether and which German generals advocated war in 1939, Leeb suggested: "The question is now, whether we should not just admit openly everything we know." The following discussion ensued:

> *Geyr von Schweppenburg:* Any objective observer will admit that National Socialism raised the social status of the worker, and in some respects even his standard of living as long as that was possible.
>
> *Leeb:* This is one of the great achievements of National Socialism. The excesses of National Socialism were in the first and final analysis due to the Führer's personality.
>
> *Guderian:* The fundamental principles were fine.
>
> *Leeb:* That is true.

I was startled and, as a historian, depressed by the number of "diaries" which close scrutiny proved to have been faked or tampered with—invariably to Hitler's disadvantage. Two different men claimed to possess the entire diaries of Admiral Wilhelm Canaris—the legendary Abwehr chief hanged by Hitler as a traitor in April 1945. The first produced "documents of the postwar German Intelligence Service (BND)" and original papers "signed by Canaris" in his support; the second, a German High Court judge, announced that his set of the diaries had recently been returned by Generalissimo Francisco Franco to the West German government. Forensic tests on the paper and ink of a "Canaris" document supplied by the first man, conducted for me by a London laboratory, proved them to be forgeries. An interview with Franco's chef de bureau—his brother-in-law Don Felipe Polo Valdes—in Madrid disposed of the German judge's equally improbable claim. Neither ever provided the actual diaries for inspection. The Eva Braun diaries published by the film actor Luis Trenker were largely forged from the "memoirs" written decades earlier by Countess Irma Larisch-Wallersee; the forgery was established by the Munich lawcourts in October 1948. (Eva Braun's genuine diaries, and her entire correspondence with Hitler, were acquired by a CIC team based on Stuttgart-Backnang in the summer of 1945; they have not been seen since. I identified the team's commander and visited him in New Mexico; he admitted the facts, but I failed to persuade him to make the papers available for historical research—perhaps he has long since sold them to a private dealer.) The oft-quoted "diaries" of Himmler's masseur Felix Kersten are equally fictitious, as for example the "twenty-six-page medical dossier on Hitler" described in them shows. Oddly enough Kersten's real diaries—containing political dynamite on Sweden's elite—do exist and have not been published. Similarly, the "diaries" published by Rudolf Semmler in *Goebbels—the Man Next to Hitler* (London, 1947) are phony too, as the entry for January 12, 1945, proves: it has Hitler as Goebbels's guest in Berlin, when the Führer was in fact still fighting the Battle of the Bulge from his HQ in West Germany. And there are no prizes for spotting the anachronisms in Count Galeazzo Ciano's extensively quoted "diaries": for example Marshal Rodolfo Graziani's "complaints about Rommel" on December 12, 1940—two full months *before* Rommel was appointed to Italy's North African theater! In fact Ciano spent the months after his dismissal in February 1943 rewriting and "improving" the diaries himself, which makes them very readable but virtually useless for the purposes of history. Ribbentrop warned about the forgery in his prison memoirs—he claimed to have seen Ciano's real diaries in September 1943—and the Nazi interpreter Eugen Dollmann described in his memoirs how the fraud was actually admitted to him by a British officer at a prison camp. Even the most superficial examination of the handwritten original volumes reveals the extent to which Ciano doctored them and interpolated material—yet historians of the highest repute have quoted them without question as they have Ciano's so-called "Lisbon Papers," although the latter too bear all the hallmarks of subsequent editing. They have all at some time been retyped on the same typewriter, although ostensibly originating over six years (1936–42).

Other diaries have been amended in more harmless ways: the Luftwaffe Chief of Staff Karl Koller's real shorthand diary often bears no resemblance to the version he published as *Der letzte Monat* (Mannheim, 1949). And Helmuth Greiner, keeper of the official OKW operations staff war diary until 1943, seized the opportunity in 1945, when asked by the Americans to retranscribe his original notes for the lost volumes from August 1942 to March 1943, to excise passages which reflected unfavorably on fellow prisoners like General Adolf Heusinger—or too favorably on Hitler; and no doubt to curry favor with the Americans, he added lengthy paragraphs charged with pungent criticism of Hitler's conduct of the war which I found to be missing from his original handwritten notes when I compared them with the published version. This tendency—to pillory Hitler after the war—was also strongly evident in the "diaries" of General Gerhard Engel, who served as Hitler's army adjutant from March 1938 to October 1943. Historiographical evidence alone—*e.g.*, comparison with the 1940 private diaries of Reichsminister Fritz Todt or the wife of General Rudolf Schmundt, or with the records of Field Marshal von Manstein's Army Group Don at the time of Stalingrad—indicates that whatever they are, they are *not* contemporaneous diaries (regrettably, the well-known Institut für Zeitgeschichte in Munich has nonetheless published them in a volume, *Heeresadjutant bei Hitler 1938–1943* [Stuttgart, 1974], rather feebly drawing attention to the diaries' inconsistencies in a short Introduction).

My exploration of sources throwing light on Hitler's inner mind was sometimes successful, sometimes not. Weeks of searching with a proton-magnetometer—a kind of supersensitive mine-detector—in a forest in East Germany failed to unearth a glass jar containing stenograms of Goebbels's very last diaries, although at times, according to the map in my possession, we must have stood right over it. But I did obtain the private diaries written by Walther Hewel, Ribbentrop's liaison officer on Hitler's staff, and by Baron Ernst von Weizsäcker, Ribbentrop's state secretary. Field Marshal Wolfram von Richthofen's widow made available to me the two thousand-page original text of his unpublished diaries too; in fact every officer or member of Hitler's staff whom I interviewed seemed to have carefully hoarded diaries or papers, which were eventually produced for my exploitation here—mostly in German, but the research papers on the fringe also came in a Babel of other languages: Italian, Russian, French, Spanish, Hungarian, Romanian, and Czech; some cryptic references to Hitler and Ribbentrop in the Hewel diaries defied all my puny codebreaking efforts, and then proved to have been written in Indonesian! For the sake of completeness, I would add that Field Marshal Fedor von Bock's diary was pruned by him, but he does not seem to have interpolated fresh material; and that General Halder's diary is completely trustworthy (having been originally transcribed from the shorthand by the British) but is best employed *without* reference to Halder's postwar footnotes.

Many sources of prime importance are still missing, although enterprising West German publishers have now obtained the full text of Goebbels's diaries. That those of Hewel and Weizsäcker remained hitherto unexplored by historians is a baffling mystery to me. They only had to ask the widows, as I did. The diaries of Hans Lammers, Wilhelm Brückner, Karl Bodenschatz, Karl Wolff, and Professor Theo Morell are missing, although known to have fallen into Allied hands in 1945. Nicolaus von Below's are probably in Moscow. Himmler's missing pocket notebooks certainly are. Alfred Rosenberg's remaining diaries are held by an American lawyer in Frankfurt. The rest of Field Marshal Erhard Milch's diaries—of which I obtained some five thousand pages in 1967—have vanished, as have General Alfred Jodl's diaries covering the years 1940 to 1943; they were looted with his private property by the British 11th Armored Division at Flensburg in May 1945. Only a brief fragment of Benito Mussolini's diary survives (see pages 541–42): the SS copied the originals and returned them to him in January 1945, but both the originals and the copy placed in Ribbentrop's files are missing now; a forgery perpetrated by two Italian nuns temporarily and expensively deceived the London *Sunday Times* some years ago, before it was exposed by the same laboratory that tested the "Canaris" document for me. The important diaries of Schmundt were unhappily burnt at his request by his fellow adjutant Admiral Karl-Jesco von Puttkamer in April 1945, along with Puttkamer's own diaries. The diary of Dr. Stephan Tiso, the last Slovak premier (from August 1944), is regrettably held in the closed files of the Hoover Institution.

As for autobiographical works, I preferred to rely on the original manuscripts rather than the published texts, as in the early postwar years apprehensive publishers (especially the "licensed" ones in Germany) made changes in them—for example in the memoirs of Karl-Wilhelm Krause, Hitler's manservant. Thus I relied on the original handwritten memoirs of Himmler's Intelligence chief, Walter Schellenberg, rather than on the mutilated and ghostwritten version subsequently published. I would go so far as to warn against the authoritativeness of numerous works hitherto accepted as "standard" sources on Hitler—particularly those by Konrad Heiden, Dr. Hermann Rauschning, Dr. Hans Bernd Gisevius, Erich Kordt, and by Hitler's dismissed adjutant Fritz Wiedemann. (The latter unashamedly explained in a private 1940 letter to a friend: "It makes no difference if exaggerations and even falsehoods do creep in.")

With the brilliant exception of Professor Hugh Trevor-Roper, whose book *The Last Days of Hitler* was based on the records of the era and is therefore virtually unassailable even today, each successive biographer has repeated or engrossed the legends created by his predecessors, or at best consulted only the most readily available works of reference themselves. Since it proved impracticable to study in detail such a dictator's whole life within this one volume, I limited myself to his war years; I eschewed as far as possible all *published* literature, since by 1964 when I began the research it was possible to speculate that "books on Hitler" outnumbered page for page the total original documentation available. This proved a sad underestimate.

Idle predecessors had gratefully lamented that most of the documents had been destroyed. They had not—they survived in embarrassing superabundance. The official papers of the Luftwaffe Field Marshal Milch, Göring's deputy, were captured by the British and total over 60,000 pages (not that Göring's most recent biographer consulted even one page of them). The entire war diary of the German naval staff, of immense value far beyond purely naval matters, survived; it took many months to read the 69 volumes of main text, some over 900 pages long, in Washington, and to examine the most promising of the 3,900 microfilm rolls of German naval records held there too.

And what is the result? Hitler will long remain an enigma, however hard the historians burrow and toil. Even his intimates realized they hardly knew him. I have already quoted Ribbentrop's puzzlement; but General Alfred Jodl, his closest strategic adviser, also wrote in his Nuremberg cell on March 10, 1946:

> . . . But then I ask myself, did you ever really know this man at whose side you led such a thorny and ascetic existence? Did he perhaps just trifle with your idealism too, abusing it for dark purposes which he kept hidden deep within himself? Dare you claim to know a man, if he has not opened up the deepest recesses of his heart to you—in sorrow as well as in ecstasy? To this very day I do not know what he thought or knew or really wanted. I only knew my own thoughts and suspicions. And if, now that the shrouds fall away from a sculpture we fondly hoped would be a work of art, only to reveal nothing but a degenerate gargoyle—then let future historians argue among themselves whether it was like that from the start, or changed with circumstances.
>
> I keep making the same mistake: I blame his humble origins. But then I remember how many peasants' sons have been blessed by History with the name, The Great.

"Hitler the Great"? No, contemporary History is unlikely to swallow such an epithet.

From the first day that he "seized power," January 30, 1933, Hitler knew that only sudden death awaited him if he failed to restore pride and empire to post-Versailles Germany. His close friend and adjutant, Julius Schaub, recorded Hitler's jubilant boast to his staff on that evening, as the last celebrating guests left the Berlin Chancellery building: "No power on earth will get me out of this building alive!"

History saw this prophecy fulfilled, as the handful of remaining Nazi faithfuls trooped uneasily into his underground study on April 30, 1945, surveyed his still warm remains—slumped on a couch, with blood trickling from the sagging lower jaw, and a gunshot wound in the right temple—and sniffed the bitter-almonds smell hanging in the air. Wrapped in a gray army blanket, he was carried up to the shell-blasted Chancellery garden. Gasoline was slopped over him in a reeking crater and ignited while his staff hurriedly saluted and backed down into the shelter. Thus ended the six years of Hitler's War. We shall now see how they began.

— David Irving,
London, January 1976

Hitler's People

As an aid to following the narrative, brief biographical details follow of the principal German personalities referred to in the text.

ALBRECHT, Alwin-Broder: Until June 1939 Hitler's naval adjutant, his replacement was demanded by Raeder after an unfortunate marriage; Hitler demurred and made him a personal adjutant instead. He is presumed to have died in the last days in Berlin.

AMSBERG, Colonel Erik von: A former adjutant of Keitel's, he stepped in as Hitler's Wehrmacht adjutant after Below, Puttkamer, and Schmundt were injured in the July 20, 1944, bomb explosion.

ASSMANN, Admiral Heinz: Jodl's naval staff officer, who frequently attended Hitler's war conferences from 1943 to 1944.

BACKE, Dr. Herbert: The very capable state secretary in the food ministry, who virtually supplanted the minister, Richard Walter Darré, in 1942.

BECK, General Ludwig: Was Army Chief of Staff until August 1938, when he was replaced by Halder and began to intrigue against Hitler; after the July 20, 1944, bomb plot failed, he committed suicide.

BELOW, Colonel Nicolaus von: Genteel and educated, Below served as Hitler's Luftwaffe adjutant from 1937 until the Führer's suicide.

BERGER, SS General Gottlob: Chief of Himmler's SS Main Office *(Hauptamt).*

BEST, Dr. Werner: A department head in the Gestapo, he was appointed Hitler's Plenipotentiary in Denmark in 1942.

BLASCHKE, Professor Johannes: Hitler's principal dentist—his postwar interrogation by the Americans provides the main evidence that Hitler's was the corpse found by the Red Army in Berlin.

BLOMBERG, Field Marshal Werner von: The first field marshal created by Hitler—in 1937—Blomberg was fired as war minister in early 1938 after marrying way, way below his station; but Hitler had a soft spot for him until the very end.

BOCK, Field Marshal Fedor von: One of Hitler's toughest and most successful soldiers in France (1940) and Russia (1941–42), he died in an air raid in 1945.

BODENSCHATZ, General Karl: Officially Göring's chef de bureau, Bodenschatz became his permanent representative at Hitler's HQ.

BONIN, Colonel Bogislaw von: Latterly the chief of operations in the German General Staff.

BORGMANN, Colonel Heinrich: Succeeded Engel as Hitler's army adjutant in 1943; killed by air attack on his car in April 1945.

BORMANN, Albert: Younger brother of Martin Bormann, but not on speaking terms with him; Albert was an adjutant in Hitler's Private Chancellary.

BORMANN, Martin: Rose from relative obscurity as Hess's right-hand man to position of vast personal power upon Hess's defection in May 1941. Head of the Nazi Party Chancellery, and from 1943 the "Führer's secretary" as well. He was the dynamo inside the Nazi machine, converting Hitler's half-spoken thoughts into harsh reality. Hard working, hard living—condemned to death at Nuremberg in absentia, his lawyer's appeal for clemency is still on the case file, undecided.

BOUHLER, Reichsleiter Philipp: As Chief of the Chancellery of the Führer of the Nazi party, Bouhler handled the incoming mail of German citizens; as such his office dealt with applications for clemency and thus became involved in the murderous euthanasia projects and the technicalities of the liquidation of Jews and other "undesirables." He took his own life in May 1945.

BRANDT, Dr. Karl: Hitler's accompanying surgeon from the mid-Thirties onward, he was dismissed in October 1944 by Martin Bormann; the Americans hanged him in 1947 for his part in the euthanasia planning.

BRAUCHITSCH, Field Marshal Walther von: Appointed Commander in Chief, Army, by Hitler in 1938 for want of a better general; Hitler tolerated him only reluctantly until his ill-health provided sufficient cover for his retirement in December 1941. He died in British captivity in 1948.

BRAUN, Eva: Hitler's only known mistress from 1931 onward; she provided conversation and company, and according to Hitler's secretaries, developed from the humble laboratory assistant she had been before then into a woman of great poise and charm. He formally married her thirty-six hours before their joint suicide in April 1945.

BRÜCKNER, SA Gruppenführer Wilhelm: A chief adjutant of Hitler's, dismissed in October 1940—having, like Albrecht and Blomberg, contracted a much-criticized marriage.

BURGDORF, General Wilhelm: Succeeded Schmundt as Hitler's chief Wehrmacht adjutant and chief of the army personnel branch after Schmundt was wounded in the July 20, 1944, bomb explosion; previously Schmundt's deputy. A rough diamond and heavy drinker, he committed suicide soon after Hitler.

CANARIS, Vice Admiral Wilhelm: Chief of the Abwehr—the OKW Intelligence

Branch—until its absorption by the SS in 1944, Canaris weathered many storms. A man of few friends, with Indian manservants, Greek blood, and a liking for warm champagne for breakfast, he slipped off his tightrope between the traitors and the SS in 1944 and was hanged in the last month of the war.

CHRISTIAN, General Eckhard: He had been Jodl's chief staff officer until he married Hitler's personal secretary Gerda Daranowski in November 1942; then he rose rapidly until he was the chief of the Luftwaffe operations staff.

CHRISTIAN, Frau Gerda: One of Hitler's four private secretaries, and certainly the most attractive—as the Führer is known to have appreciated. She joined his staff before the war, retired on her marriage in November 1942, but returned a year later and stayed with Hitler until the end.

DARGES, Fritz: Martin Bormann's adjutant until 1939, he became Hitler's personal adjutant from March 1943—until Hitler sacked him in July 1944, ostensibly because of an incident with an insect during a war conference, more probably because Darges had jilted Eva's sister Gretl Braun. He was sent to the Russian front.

DIETRICH, Dr. Otto: Hitler's press spokesman.

DIETRICH, SS General Josef "Sepp": One of the Party Old Guard, he commanded the SS Leibstandarte (Life Guards) and then the SS Sixth Panzer Army.

DÖNITZ, Grand Admiral Karl: Commander in Chief of the German U-boat service until 1943, he stepped into Raeder's shoes when the latter resigned as Commander in Chief, Navy, that January. Dönitz supported Hitler's bolder strategic decisions—*i.e.,* to hold on to the Crimea and the eastern Baltic provinces—and satisfied Hitler that he was the best successor as Führer in April 1945.

DORSCH, Dr. Xaver: After Fritz Todt, one of the Reich's most outstanding civil engineers; became head of the Todt Organization building military sites in Reich-occupied countries.

EICHMANN, SS Colonel Adolf: A minor official in Kaltenbrunner's Reich Main Security Office, Eichmann was responsible for the smooth running of the Jewish deportation programs; he was one of the driving forces behind the extermination of the Jews.

EICKEN, Professor Carl von: The ear, nose, and throat specialist who operated on Hitler's throat in 1935 and again in November 1944.

ENGEL, Colonel Gerhard: Hitler's army adjutant from 1938 to 1943, he then distinguished himself as a division commander.

ETZDORF, Major Hasso von: Liaison officer between the General Staff and Ribbentrop's foreign ministry, his often cryptic penciled notes were deciphered by the Americans postwar and present vital information on Hitler's foreign strategy.

FALKENHAUSEN, General Alexander von: The aristocratic Nazi Military Governor of Belgium, he entered into a liaison with an equally aristocratic Belgian lady which resulted in his dismissal in July 1944; this probably spared him from the hangman's noose some weeks later, as his implication in the bomb plot escaped the attention of the Gestapo.

FEGELEIN, SS General Hermann: Himmler's representative at Hitler's HQ from 1944 to the end; married Gretl Braun (*see also* Darges) but left her a widow, as he was shot for attempted desertion in the last days.

FELLGIEBEL, General Erich: Chief of the Wehrmacht's and Army's Signals Branches, he was executed after the failure of the 1944 bomb plot in which he was implicated.

FRANK, Dr. Hans: One of Hitler's oldest friends and his personal legal adviser in the Thirties. Hitler appointed him Governor General of rump Poland after that country's defeat in 1939.

FRANK, Karl-Hermann: Deputy Protector of Bohemia-Moravia.

FRICK, Dr. Wilhelm: Minister of the Interior, until Himmler supplanted him in August 1943.

FROMM, General Friedrich: A deadly enemy of Keitel, Fromm commanded the Replacement Army—divisions being raised and trained in Germany; he was implicated in the July 20, 1944, conspiracy, but only vaguely—the People's Court found no evidence, for example, that he had known of the plot, but condemned him to death for cowardice in not having acted more energetically against his Chief of Staff, Stauffenberg, that afternoon.

GIESING, Dr. Erwin: Army ENT-specialist summoned from Rastenburg hospital after July 20, 1944, bomb explosion to treat Hitler's head injuries.

GLOBOCNIK, SS Brigadier Odilo: Formerly police commander in occupied Polish district of Lublin, he ranked with Eichmann as one of the Nazis behind the massacre of the Jews.

GOEBBELS, Dr. Joseph: one of the Party's Old Guard; Gauleiter of Berlin, and after 1933 Reich propaganda minister—an outstanding speaker and master of dialectics, but undoubtedly one of the evil geniuses behind the Führer. Took his own and his family's lives after Hitler's suicide.

GOERDELER, Dr. Carl: Former mayor of Leipzig, Goerdeler was political leader of the anti-Hitler conspiracy culminating in the July 20, 1944, bomb explosion.

GÖRING, Reichsmarschall Hermann: A man of many titles, but principally important as Commander in Chief of the Luftwaffe and head of the Four-Year Plan office. Alternating between bouts of laziness and spasms of intense activity, he was most closely identified by the German public with their eventual misery and defeat—but somehow his popularity remained virtually unimpaired until his October 1946 suicide.

GUDERIAN, General Heinz: Ranks as one of World War II's leading tank commanders; was dismissed by Hitler in December 1941 to satisfy Kluge and remained in a command limbo until Hitler appointed him his personal Inspector of the Panzer Service in February 1943. Even then Guderian wavered in his loyalty; he certainly had advance warning of the July 20, 1944, bomb explosion and prudently absented himself from the Führer's HQ that day—to return only hours later, to his own surprise, as the army's new Chief of General Staff until March 1945.

GÜNSCHE, SS Colonel Otto: Formerly a private in Hitler's escort squad, Günsche—a big, blond bulldog of an officer—became his personal adjutant and bodyguard, and was entrusted by the Führer with burning his corpse after his suicide in April 1945—and with giving him a coup de grâce with his pistol if necessary.

HAASE, Professor Werner: Had treated Hitler before the war, became his doctor again briefly in the last days in Berlin.

HALDER, General Franz: Succeeded Beck as the army's Chief of General Staff in 1938; generally acknowledged to have been a good tactician, Halder retained this post until Hitler could stand him no longer—in September 1942.

HASSELBACH, Dr. Hanskarl von: Dr. Karl Brandt's deputy as Hitler's accompanying surgeon until October 1944.

HESS, Rudolf: Hitler's official "deputy" until his flight to Scotland in May 1941.

HEWEL, Ambassador Walther: He had joined the Nazi party as a student in the early Twenties, shared Hitler's Landsberg imprisonment briefly in 1923, then emigrated as a planter to Java; he returned to become a member of Ribbentrop's staff—serving through the period of this book as liaison officer at Hitler's HQ.

HEYDRICH, SS General Reinhard: Kaltenbrunner's predecessor as chief of the Reich Main Security Office of the SS; as such he was more interested in the "executive" side—the building of a formidable police organization throughout Germany. Appointed "Reich Protector" of occupied Czechoslovakia in October 1941, embarked on reforms there, assassinated by British-trained agents in May 1942. As he was the brain behind the extermination camps, he merits no sympathy.

HIMMLER, Heinrich: SS Reichsführer, chief of police, and—after August 1943—Minister of the Interior. "Himmler," said the Nazi party newspaper chief Max Amann, "considered it his duty to eliminate all enemies of the Nazi ideology and he did so calmly and impersonally, without hate and without sympathy." A rare mixture of crackpot and organizational genius.

JESCHONNEK, General Hans: A lieutenant at sixteen in World War I, he seemed marked out for a brilliant career; by 1939 he was Luftwaffe Chief of Staff—by August 1943 he was dead, a suicide.

JODL, General Alfred: A pure soldier, of unquestionable loyalty to his Führer, Jodl served as chief of the OKW operations staff *(Wehrmachtführungsstab)* from August 1939 to the very end. His strategic insight was profound. He was hanged at Nuremberg in 1946.

JUNGE, Frau Traudl: Youngest of Hitler's secretaries, she joined his staff when Gerda Daranowski married in 1942; she herself married Hitler's manservant Hans Junge, was widowed by 1944, and stayed with Hitler to the end. (Née Traudl Humps.)

JUNGE, Captain Wolf: Jodl's naval staff officer until August 28, 1943, then again from summer 1944 onward while Assmann recovered from injuries sustained on July 20, 1944.

KALTENBRUNNER, SS General Dr. Ernst: Heydrich's successor as chief of the Reich Main Security Office—but personally more interested in the Intelligence side and less in the police and executive aspects, in which "Gestapo" Müller grew in influence.

KEITEL, Field Marshal Wilhelm: Chief of OKW (German High Command) in title only; he exercised his ministerial functions well; the military and strategic side he—wisely—left to Jodl. Loyal and hardworking, Keitel shared Jodl's fate at Nuremberg.

KESSELRING, Field Marshal Albert: He held important air commands during the invasions of Poland, France, and Russia. Supreme commander of German forces in Italy (1943–1945), in March 1945 he took over from Rundstedt as Commander in Chief West. In 1947 he was condemned to death for war crimes against Italian civilians, but this sentence was later commuted to life imprisonment. He was pardoned in 1952.

KLUGE, Field Marshal Günther Hans von: A good commander of men, like Rommel—always in the battle line with his troops, but politically ambitious too. Lent an ear to various groups of plotters, but would not commit himself. Fearing implication in the failed July 20, 1944, plot, Kluge took cyanide and closed his "big blue, patrician eyes" for the last time on August 18, 1944, his personal admiration for Adolf Hitler undiminished.

KOCH, Erich: Gauleiter of East Prussia, he was appointed Reich Commissioner in the Ukraine in 1941, pursuing policies of such brutality as to achieve the impossible—a pro-Soviet Ukraine.

KOEPPEN, Dr. Werner: Rosenberg's representative at Hitler's HQ, he recorded the Führer's political Table Talk for some months in 1941.

KOLLER, General Karl: Luftwaffe Chief of Staff from November 1944 to the end; Bavarian, dour but capable, having risen from the enlisted ranks.

KORTEN, General Günther: Luftwaffe Chief of Staff following Jeschonnek's 1943 suicide, he died an agonizing death when a fragment of table pierced him after Stauffenberg's bomb exploded beneath it in July 1944. Korten was the first to campaign for a strategic bomber force in the Luftwaffe.

KRANCKE, Vice Admiral Theodor: Permanent representative of the Commander in Chief, Navy, at Hitler's HQ after September 1942.

KREBS, General Hans: Last Army Chief of Staff, he negotiated with the Russians in Berlin following Hitler's death, then committed suicide.

KREIPE, General Werner: Luftwaffe Chief of Staff from August 1 to September 21, 1944, when Hitler banished him from war conferences at his HQ.

LAMMERS, Dr. Hans Heinrich: A legacy of the Hindenburg regime, Lammers was an expert on constitutional law and, as chief of the Reich Chancellery, the most important civil servant of the Third Reich.

LEY, Dr. Robert: Party Organization chief, he took over the trade unions in 1933 and molded them into the monolithic German Labor Front (DAF).

LINGE, Heinz: Hitler's manservant until the very end in Berlin.

LOSSBERG, Colonel Bernhard von: Jodl's army staff officer.

LUTZE, Victor: Succeeded the murdered Ernst Röhm as chief of the SA brownshirt army in 1934. A heavy drinker and loose talker, he engaged Himmler's displeasure by remarks about the SS, and died in a car crash in 1943.

MAISEL, General Ernst: Burgdorf's deputy in the Army Personnel Branch—a quiet, intelligent officer manhandled by postwar writers for his unfortunate part in Rommel's death.

MANSTEIN, Field Marshal Erich von: Universally acclaimed as Germany's most outstanding General Staff product, as he displayed in offensive operations in Poland (1939), the west (1940), and the Russian campaign.

MEISSNER, Dr. Otto: Like Lammers, a leftover of the Hindenburg era; head of the Presidential Chancellery *(Präsidialkanzlei).*

MILCH, Field Marshal Erhard: Founder of Lufthansa airline, Milch was called upon by Hitler and Göring to build the secret Luftwaffe in 1933. After years of intense rivalry with Göring, Milch—who had labored to conceal a serious defect in his family tree (he was pure Aryan, but accepted popular legend to the contrary to conceal the fact that he was the product of the illicit relationship between his mother and her mother's brother)—was sacked in 1944.

MODEL, Field Marshal Walter: Monocled, highly schooled, modern in outlook, he was the antithesis of Manstein; when a front line needed holding or restoring, Hitler sent for Model.

MORELL, Professor Theo: Morell alone had been able to cure Hitler of a gastric disorder in 1936; he appointed him personal physician and turned a deaf ear on all his critics until the very end.

MÜLLER, SS General Heinrich: Chief of *Amt IV* (the Gestapo) under Kaltenbrunner, he vanished in the last days of the war and has not been positively seen since.

PAULUS, Field Marshal Friedrich: Led his Sixth Army into Soviet captivity after the Battle of Stalingrad, 1943.

PUTTKAMER, Admiral Karl-Jesco von: Hitler's naval adjutant from March 1935 to June 1938, then again from August 1939 to the end—one of the most important witnesses still surviving from Hitler's circle.

RAEDER, Grand Admiral Erich: Was already Commander in Chief, Navy, when Hitler came to power in 1933, and forcefully resigned exactly ten years later.

RATTENHUBER, SS Brigadier Hans: Chief of Hitler's police bodyguard at HQ, responsible for his security, he sought to conceal his brutal and intriguing nature beneath a veneer of Bavarian charm.

RIBBENTROP, Joachim von: Reich foreign minister after 1938, he realized that many of Hitler's foreign policies were doomed to failure but allowed the Führer to overrule him every time; hanged at Nuremberg in 1946.

RICHTHOFEN, Field Marshal Wolfram von: Perhaps the toughest Luftwaffe strike commander, Richthofen commanded first an air corps, then an air force (Luftflotte); Hitler always committed Richthofen where the battle was fiercest, and listened readily to the field marshal's extravagant complaints about his army counterparts.

ROMMEL, Field Marshal Erwin: Commandant of Hitler's HQ 1939–40, he secured command of a panzer division in time for the attack on France, fought a brilliant if reckless campaign there, and repeated his triumphs on a larger scale in North Africa, until the lack of supplies and the Allied superiority in tanks and aircraft beat him back; his loyalty to Hitler remained unchanged, but his hatred of the OKW and Jodl reached pathological proportions in 1944. Implicated by others in the July 20, 1944, conspiracy, he took the consequences —poison—in October that year.

ROSENBERG, Alfred: Verbose Party philosopher; bitter opponent of Koch, particularly after Rosenberg as Minister for the Occupied Eastern Territories had to deal with him; notorious anti-Semite.

RUNDSTEDT, Field Marshal Gerd von: Blunt, chivalrous, loyal, but elderly and easygoing in later years, Rundstedt was the senior serving German soldier; Hitler was fond of him and rightly trusted him—thrice appointing him to high commands, and thrice relieving him when expediency demanded. From 1942 to 1945 Rundstedt was—with a brief interval in the summer of 1944—Commander in Chief West.

SAUCKEL, Fritz: Gauleiter of Thuringia, Sauckel was appointed by Hitler in 1942 to take charge of the manpower procurement program of the Reich; this Sauckel achieved by contracts, inducements, or slave labor. Hanged at Nuremberg.

SAUR, Karl-Otto: Outwardly the typical Nazi—stocky, forceful, crude—Saur was first Todt's, then Speer's right-hand man in the munitions ministry; his phenomenal memory for dates and statistics made him one of Hitler's favorites.

SCHAUB, Julius: Joined the Nazi party in 1925, served as Hitler's personal adjutant and factotum until the end; of too limited an intellect to intrigue—hence valued highly by the Führer in his entourage.

SCHEIDT, Dr. Wilhelm: Adjutant to Hitler's court historian Scherff. After Scherff's injury on July 20, 1944, Scheidt took his place for many months at Hitler's war conferences. But through his friendship with Beck, Goerdeler, and Kurt von Hammerstein, Scheidt was the source (unwittingly perhaps?) of much secret Intelligence that reached the enemy, direct from Hitler's HQ.

SCHERFF, General Walter: Chief OKW historian, appointed by Hitler in 1942 to write the Reich war history; but he never got around to it—and on his orders the shorthand records of most of Hitler's war conferences were burned in May 1945.

SCHMUNDT, General Rudolf: Hitler's chief Wehrmacht adjutant after 1938, and chief of the army personnel branch after October 1942 as well; his role as private adviser to Hitler needs intensive research. He died a lingering death, blind and burnt, after the July 20, 1944, bomb blast.

SCHÖRNER, Field Marshal Ferdinand: Like Model, Schörner was usually assigned to sectors where other generals had failed, and he usually succeeded.

SCHROEDER, Christa: Hitler's private secretary after 1933, she stayed with him until ordered to leave Berlin on April 20, 1945. Hitler warmed toward her, despite her sharp tongue and feline comments on the war's progress.

SEYSS-INQUART, Dr. Arthur: A quiet-spoken Austrian lawyer, propelled by the 1938 union between Germany and Austria into high office in Vienna as a Nazi sympathizer, Seyss-Inquart was Hans Frank's deputy in Poland until May 18, 1940, when he was appointed Hitler's viceroy in the Netherlands. Hanged at Nuremberg.

SONNLEITNER, Dr. Franz von: diplomat, stood in for Hewel during his recovery from air crash injuries in 1944.

SPEER, Albert: Nominated by Hitler as architect for Berlin, despite his youth; ambitious, vain, publicity-conscious, but possessing—like Göring—undoubted *presence* and organizing ability. Hitler shrewdly appointed him Todt's successor as munitions minister in February 1942, but became disillusioned with him in the last weeks of his life.

STUMPFEGGER, Dr. Ludwig: A well-known surgeon on Himmler's staff, who began treating Hitler in October 1944.

TODT, Dr. Fritz: Hitler's main civil engineer, who had built the autobahn network on his orders, and then the West Wall in 1938–39; in March 1940 Hitler nominated him to head a new munitions ministry. When Todt was killed in a plane crash in February 1942, Speer succeeded him.

VORMANN, General Nikolaus von: Appointed by Brauchitsch to act as army representative at Hitler's HQ in August and September 1939.

VOSS, Vice Admiral Hans-Erich: Succeeded Krancke as naval representative at Hitler's HQ on March 1, 1943.

WAGNER, General Eduard: Quartermaster General of the German army—until his suicide after the July 20, 1944, bomb plot failed.

WARLIMONT, General Walter: *De facto* deputy to Jodl in the OKW operations staff, Warlimont deeply felt that he should have held Jodl's position (which by rights was his).

WEIZSÄCKER, Baron Ernst von: Ribbentrop's state secretary at the foreign ministry after 1938; from early 1943 onward he was German ambassador to the Vatican.

WOLF, Johanna: Oldest of Hitler's private secretaries.

WOLFF, SS General Karl: Chief of Himmler's personal staff, SS representative at Hitler's HQ until early 1943—when he was involved in a marriage scandal—and from September 1943 chief of police in Nazi-occupied Italy.

ZEITZLER, General Kurt: Dubbed "Thunderball" *(Kugelblitz)* because of his intensive energy as Chief of Staff to a panzer corps in Russia, 1941–42; Hitler fetched him from his position as Rundstedt's Chief of Staff in France (1942) to succeed Halder as Army Chief of Staff. Zeitzler put up with Hitler's tantrums until June 30, 1944, when he simply vanished and reported sick.

NORWEGIAN SEA
Narvik
Namsos
Trondheim
Andalsnes
NORWAY
Bergen
Oslo
SWEDEN
Stavanger
Stockholm
Kristiansand
ATLANTIC OCEAN
UNITED KINGDOM
SCOTLAND
Glasgow
Edinburgh
Belfast
EIRE
Dublin
NORTH SEA
DENMARK
Copenhagen
BALTIC SEA
Libau
Königsberg
Liverpool
Manchester
Flensburg
Wilhelmshaven
Lübeck
Hamburg
Gdynia
Danzig
Elblag
Birmingham
ENGLAND
Bristol
London
Portsmouth
HOLLAND
Amsterdam
Rotterdam
Nijmegen
Arnhem
Bremen
Prenzlau
Eberswalde
Oranienburg
Potsdam
Berlin
Szczecin (Stettin)
Stargard
Rastenburg
Thorn
Poznań
Kutno
Vistula
ENGLISH CHANNEL
Le Havre
Cherbourg
Caumont
Brest
Dieppe
Arras
Amiens
Soissons
Antwerp
Brussels
BELG.
Liege
Aachen
Essen
Dortmund
Duisburg
Kassel
GERMANY
Cottbus
Spremberg
Leipzig
Dresden
POLAND
Lodz
Wroclaw
Pilica
Caen
Avranches
Lorient
Mortain
Argentan
Alençon
Paris
LUX.
Luxembourg
Echternach
Saarbrücken
Frankfurt
Metz
Nancy
Strasbourg
Mannheim
Nuremberg
Stuttgart
Prague
Plzen
Katowitz
Ostrau (Ostrava)
CZECHOSLOVAKIA
Saint-Nazaire
Nantes
Montoire
FRANCE
Munich
Zisterdorf
Bratislava
Salzburg
Vienna
AUSTRIA
Budapest
HUNGARY
La Rochelle
Zurich
Bern
SWITZ.
Geneva
Vichy
Lyons
St.-Étienne
Bordeaux
Nagykanizsa
LAKE BALATON
Szeged
Tarvisium
Turin
Milan
Venice
Trieste
Zagreb
Drava River
Tisza
Bilbao
Hendaye
Toulouse
Monaco
Marseilles
Nice
Genoa
Po River
La Spezia
Florence
Leghorn (Livorno)
Belgrade
YUGOSLAVIA
Sarajevo
Oporto
PORTUGAL
SPAIN
Madrid
Toledo
Lisbon
ADRIATIC SEA
CORSICA
ITALY
Dubrovnik
Rome
Gaeta
Cassino
Foggia
Tirane
ALBANIA
Naples
Salerno
Taranto
Valencia
Seville
Cordoba
SARDINIA
Granada
Cadiz
Malaga
Gibraltar
MEDITERRANEAN
SP. MOROCCO
Palermo
SICILY
Algiers
Bizerte
Tunis
Rabat
Casablanca
PANTELLERIA
MALTA
MOROCCO
ALGERIA
TUNISIA
Tripoli
Benghazi
LIBYA
------- Eastern Front, late 1942
—— Eastern Front, 1945

EUROPE 1942-1945
UNION OF SOVIET SOCIALIST REPUBLICS
Dvina River
LAKE LADOGA
Kronstadt
Petrokrepost
Leningrad
Tikhvin
Narva
Volkhov River
LAKE ILMEN
Demyansk
Kalinin
Rzhev
Moscow
Velikiye Luki
Nevel
Vyazma
Vitebsk
Smolensk
Orsha
Gorki
Sukhinichi
Minsk
Bryansk
Orel
Voronezh
Kursk
Desna River
Belgorod
Kharkov
Stalingrad
Volga River
Kovel
Kiev
Zhitomir
Fastov
Poltava
Izyum
Berdichev
Cherkassy
Dnieper River
Kotelnikovo
Astrakhan
Tarnopol
Vinnitsa
Uman
Dnepropetrovsk
Zaporozhye
Stalino
Rostov
Dniester River
Krivoi Rog
Taganrog
Mariupol
Prut River
Melitopol
Nikolaev
Odessa
Kherson
SEA OF AZOV
Kerch
Krasnodar
Armavir
Kuban R.
Maykop
Grozny
Ordzhonikidze
Novorossisk
CRIMEA
Sevastopol
CASPIAN SEA
Gudauta
Sukhumi
Baku
Galatz
Bucharest
Constanta
BLACK SEA
Nikopol
BULGARIA
Istanbul
Teheran
Ankara
TURKEY
DARDANELLES
AEGEAN SEA
Izmir
IRAN
SYRIA
Baghdad
IRAQ
RHODES
Nicosia
CYPRUS
CRETE
Damascus
S E A
PALESTINE
Amman
TRANS-JORDAN
Bardia
Mersa Matruh
Alexandria
Sollum
Fûka
El Alamein
Suez
Cairo
EGYPT
Nile River
0 100 200 300 400 500 miles
Paul J. Pugliese

PART 4

TOTAL WAR

Trauma and Tragedy

Few events in World War II were to rouse greater controversy than Stalingrad; around even fewer was to be woven a more intricate, yet durable, fabric of lies and legends in the postwar years. This is, however, understandable, for Stalingrad marked the end of German military initiative in the east; it cost perhaps two hundred thousand German lives, and it exploded the dream of empire which had fired Hitler when he came to power ten years before.

German army Intelligence had consistently reported that the Red Army was on its last legs, yet Stalin continued producing unsuspected masses of tanks and infantry out of thin air. Jodl was seen, white-faced, exclaiming, "The Russians are stronger than in 1941!" Hitherto the Russian command had been wooden, hesitant, and bureaucratic. Now suddenly it was flexible, deliberate, and far-sighted, operating its tank forces as the Germans had in 1939, but with the entire might of the Soviet war potential behind them.

The blame for the disaster was diverted onto Hitler. In later years memoirs were fudged by field marshals, fake diaries were concocted, guilty sentences were expunged from the OKW's war diary, and "contemporary" judgments on Hitler's leadership were slotted in.[1]

Nobody had expected the Soviet offensive to begin so soon.

The Russians achieved tactical surprise as well through an uncharacteristic display of cunning. The very first word to reach Hitler was of two infantry assaults on the Romanian Third Army's sector—seemingly the usual enemy

[1]Thus in the published war diary of the OKW an account of a crucial argument between Hitler, Jeschonnek, and Zeitzler on December 21, 1942, at the height of the Stalingrad crisis, includes the following sentences: "As usual, however, again no bold decisions are taken. It is as though the Führer is no longer capable of doing so." These sentences are a 1945 fabrication not included in the 1942 text.

"spattering" without either tanks or artillery preparation; the Romanians were confident, even when a gradual artillery barrage did begin. No use was made of the panzer corps stationed in reserve behind them and commanded by General Ferdinand Heim. At 5 A.M. on November 19, however, a colossal Russian artillery barrage suddenly began, and at 7 A.M. wave upon wave of tanks laden with infantry assailed the Romanians. They fought heroically—three of the four Romanian generals were killed in enemy bayonet charges, and every Romanian company commander fell in the ensuing battle—but their military equipment was not good enough. A rout began. At 10:10 A.M. General von Weichs's Army Group B ordered Heim (Forty-eighth Panzer Corps) to counterattack to seal the worst breach, but by midnight it was clear that he could not. He had begun the day with the 22nd Panzer Division, the 1st Romanian Panzer Division, and a battlegroup of the 14th Panzer Division under his command: but the 22nd was still exhausted from the battle for Stalingrad itself; the battlegroup of the 14th was removed from his control during the day; and the Romanian 1st Panzer Division had evidently abandoned the field of battle—Heim had no idea where it was, because all attempts to raise it by radio remained unanswered.

Barely trained, and totally inexperienced of battle, the Romanians in the front line itself had no hope. Half their tanks were immobilized because field mice had made a meal of their wiring. The enlisted ranks lacked discipline, tending to stop work most afternoons at four. Weichs had hoped that they would hold the front long enough for Heim's corps to arrive, but they did not, and their headlong flight barred the advance of Heim's tanks. Still searching for his own missing 1st Romanian Panzer Division, Heim was further beset by appalling weather—by freezing fog and rain, by sleet and snow. Weichs ordered him to go over to the defensive that evening.

Zeitzler, calling from East Prussia, had scarcely been off the telephone to Hitler at the Berghof since the crisis began. Hitler clearly realized it as such, although the General Staff situation reports painted it in a misleadingly pastel hue. By 9:30 P.M. he had authorized Weichs to abandon all further assault operations in the city of Stalingrad so as to release forces to patch up the main front line. He also ordered Field Marshal von Manstein to abandon the planned attack at Velikiye Luki and to establish a new army group on the Don, between Army Groups A and B, thus relieving Weichs of direct responsibility for the two Romanian armies, and for the Fourth Panzer Army and the Sixth Army at Stalingrad. He was furious at Heim's "delay" in launching the counterattack, and during the night he ordered him to attack again regardless of any risk to his flanks and rear. On Hitler's charts the panzer corps was a thick blue circle boasting of over a hundred tanks. Again Heim failed. This time his corps was engulfed in the Russian flood and extricated its few remnants only with difficulty.

The Romanian Third Army evaporated. From Bucharest came the most indignant sounds. Hitler needed an immediate scapegoat; he ordered Keitel: "Send for General Heim at once. Strip him of his insignia and arrest him. He is to blame!" To appease Antonescu, Heim was sentenced to death some months later, but when Schmundt, Hitler's chief Wehrmacht adjutant, reasoned with him, the Führer relented and commuted the sentence to a term of imprisonment.[2]

Such were the shocking events northwest of Stalingrad. To the south of the city, a Russian bridgehead of equal menace had spewed forth hundreds of tanks on November 20. The enemy's preparations here had totally escaped detection until two days before. The eastern flank of the Fourth Panzer Army had withstood the blow, but three adjacent Romanian divisions crumpled with scarcely a sigh. By the twenty-first it was clear that the two great pincer arms of the Red Army offensive would join around Stalingrad the next day unless the weather cleared long enough for the Luftwaffe to strike.

It was natural that the endangered Sixth Army should see its survival as depending on an airlift. When he arrived at Berchtesgaden on November 20 from his headquarters in East Prussia, the Luftwaffe's Chief of Staff, Jeschonnek, certainly did not reject the idea—if he had, Hitler would subsequently have acted very differently in the view of his Luftwaffe adjutant Major von Below. A hundred thousand men had been successfully sustained in the Demyansk pocket for many months the previous winter by such an airlift; in addition, Richthofen's squadrons had regularly airlifted fuel to the southern front during the summer—as well as engineer battalions and antiaircraft batteries to the Sixth Army—to compensate for the inadequate railroad supplies. On the afternoon of the twenty-first, Hitler therefore decided the Sixth Army must stand fast "despite the danger of its temporary encirclement"; the railroad line was to be held open as long as possible. "As to airlift, orders will follow." With Jodl he meanwhile discussed ways and means of rushing reinforcements to Weichs's army group.

Loud and weighty objections were raised against the airlift idea. Richthofen telephoned Göring, Zeitzler, and Weichs that there were not nearly enough transport aircraft for an airlift. (Transport squadrons were heavily committed in the Mediterranean.) His subordinates seconded his objections. The Sixth Army would need many hundreds of tons of food, oil, and ammunition airlifted to it every day. Ever since July it had been living from hand to mouth; it needed nine or ten supply trains daily, but in the twenty-four hours before the only railroad

[2]In 1944 Hitler authorized Heim's "rehabilitation" as commandant of a beleaguered Channel port; to his chagrin the general surrendered the port to the Allies without much ado, and Hitler decided not to allow other army "delinquents" a second chance in the future.

line was cut not one train had got through. Hitler, however, neither saw nor sought any alternative: in his speeches of September 30 and November 8 he had committed himself before the entire German nation—he could not relax his grip on Stalingrad and the Volga now. Late on the twenty-first he again ordered Paulus to hold on.

At what stage Hitler consulted Göring on an airlift is uncertain. Jeschonnek, prompted by Richthofen's remonstrances and the gloomy calculations of his own staff, very shortly reversed his opinion. But Hitler telephoned Göring, and the Reichsmarschall assured him the Luftwaffe would do all in its power to meet the army's needs. (Göring later explained to Richthofen: "The Führer was optimistic. What right had I to be the pessimist?") It is improbable that Göring gave his assurance unconditionally; but then Hitler himself expected the encirclement to last only temporarily—until the damaged army group front had been repaired and the infiltrating enemy annihilated. Late on the twenty-second, Paulus radioed that the Sixth Army was encircled: his ammunition and food stocks would soon be exhausted, and his fuel would last only six more days. (Since his trapped army was to survive for two more months, Paulus seems to have painted a deliberately dark picture; Hitler may have taken this into account.)

At midday on November 22 Hitler had realized he could postpone his return to East Prussian headquarters no longer. At five to ten that evening his train left Berchtesgaden station. Keitel, Jodl, Jeschonnek, and the adjutants accompanied him. Foul weather evidently prevented him from taking his plane at Leipzig, and for a whole day he was confined to the train as it headed for the Wolf's Lair. Every four hours or so the train was halted for brief telephone contact to be established with General Staff headquarters. While Hitler strolled about or looked gloomily out of the windows, Keitel and Jodl inked the latest grim details onto the Stalingrad chart; as soon as the train jolted into motion again, Hitler came to see and hear the worst for himself. Hitler and Jodl began elaborating a daring plan for General Hoth's Fourth Panzer Army to attack the encircling ring and thus relieve Stalingrad. It would take about ten days to prepare, but might inflict on the Russians just the defeat Hitler now gravely needed. When Zeitzler telephoned him during their next halt, imploring him to instruct the Sixth Army to abandon the Volga and break out westward before it was too late, Hitler rebuffed him. "We have thought of a new way out. Jodl will tell you. We will discuss it in person tomorrow."

Hitler arrived at his East Prussia headquarters late on November 23. Zeitzler was waiting outside his concrete bunker. The Führer stepped forward, his hand outstretched in welcome and a forced smile on his lips. "You have done all you could. I could not have done more myself had I been here." With calculated pathos he added, "One finds one's own true greatness in the hour of deepest misfortune—like Frederick the Great." Zeitzler was unimpressed and reported that the army group commander, Weichs, now shared his view that the Sixth Army was doomed if it held fast.[3] Hitler thumped his desk. "We are not budging from the Volga!" During the night Paulus radioed to Hitler a frantic appeal in the same sense: unless every division was withdrawn from Stalingrad, the army was doomed to "abrupt destruction." They would certainly lose most of their equipment, but at least they would save their troops. Hitler's reply was transmitted to Paulus in the early hours of the twenty-fourth: the Sixth Army was to stay where it was because an "airlift by a hundred more Junkers is getting under way."

The week that followed was ruled by Hitler's unshakable conviction that he was right; it would not be the first time that he alone had kept his head in a crisis. But optimism also prevailed around him—an optimism that has been effectively masked by postwar alteration of the few headquarters records that survive. Firstly, the military situation was not all but hopeless: reserves were moving up, ready for the relief offensive Manstein was to direct. Secondly, according to army Intelligence, Russian prisoners said that their officers were disconcerted by their own success so far and were wavering about how to proceed. Thirdly, the Sixth Army's supply position, on which the crisis hinged, was not as bad as feared (though the statistics on its needs, and even on its fighting strength, varied). On November 24 the army's quartermaster asked for 200 tons of fuel and 200 tons of ammunition a day, with an unspecified quantity of flour after the twenty-seventh. But on the twenty-fifth the OKW historian wrote that Paulus's "demand for 700 tons" was evidently exaggerated;[4] gradually the figure of 300 tons a day was accepted. Richthofen's objections that there were not enough Junkers available were disbelieved. His telephoned advice that the Sixth Army must break out to the southwest was discounted. "Führer gives me a good hearing," he wrote in his diary, "but decides against, as he believes army can hold on and does not think we would reach Stalingrad again." Richthofen's attempts to reach Göring failed: the Reichsmarschall was in Paris.[5] The air staff was evidently optimistic, for twice the OKW historian noted that 298 Junkers transport aircraft were available, with a daily capacity of 600 tons.[6] Admittedly few were reaching Stalingrad yet—only some 20 or 30 a day—but once the weather improved and the airlift got under

[3]According to Weichs's Chief of Staff, General von Sodenstern, in 1950, Zeitzler telephoned him at about 2 A.M. that he had at last managed to persuade Hitler to let the Sixth Army break out. But the promised order never came; Zeitzler had probably misinterpreted a remark by Hitler.

[4]Greiner, author of the OKW war diary, removed this sentence in 1945, and it does not appear in the text subsequently published.

[5]In his "diary" entry of November 25, 1942, Major Engel nonetheless transplanted Göring to the Wolf's Lair for a dramatic conference with Hitler!

[6]Greiner "improved" his record—with hindsight—in 1945 to read: "Only 298 transport planes are with the Fourth Air Force; about 500 are needed."

way things would be different; so Hitler was assured. On November 27 the OKW's note on Hitler's afternoon conference read: "Enemy's dispositions around Stalingrad could hardly be more favorable for Sixth Army's intentions. The Stalingrad food situation is better than we thought." Paulus's planned withdrawal of his northwestern front was going well. On the twenty-ninth, the conference record referred to Field Marshal von Manstein's appreciation of the situation: "Arrives at same conclusion as Führer."[7]

Manstein's opinion was highly valued by Hitler and unquestionably strengthened his determination here. On November 24, arriving at Weichs's operations room, Manstein had emphatically rejected the general's judgment that Paulus had no alternative but to abandon Stalingrad and break out; obviously a breakout was still possible and "the surest way"—Manstein's report said—and staying put was highly risky in view of the ammunition and fuel situations, but

> Nonetheless I am unable to share Army Group B's enthusiasm for a breakout as long as there are still adequate supplies—at least of armor-piercing ammunition, infantry ammunition, and fuel. This is vital.[8]

Manstein added that a relief operation would be possible with the reinforcements being moved up by the beginning of December; only if these latter movements were blocked by the enemy might a breakout by the Sixth Army become necessary; but he would ask for this only if "worse comes to worst." At the same time he radioed Paulus: "We shall do everything to hew you out of there." In a further report four days later Manstein added that the Sixth Army would need at least four hundred tons of supplies a day. But by this time Hitler's mind had long been made up.

Manstein himself was engrossed in planning a relief offensive by General Hoth from Kotelnikovo toward Stalingrad, but the forces placed at his disposal were steadily whittled away to buttress the vulnerable Italian and Hungarian sectors of the Don front north of Stalingrad. From November 28 onward the storm signs there multiplied—it was here that ever since mid-August Hitler had expected Stalin's strategic push toward Rostov to develop. Richthofen uncomfortably observed: "It seems the Russians are going to attack the Italian sector too—a bad thing, as they will probably run faster than the Romanians." He blamed Weichs's army group—and its Chief of Staff Sodenstern in particular—for treating these allies like the Cinderellas of the eastern front. Hitler, anxiously investigating the fighting fitness of the Italians and Hungarians, now observed that their provision

[7]This compromising sentence was omitted altogether by Greiner from his improved 1945 text.

[8]The original document has survived. In his published memoirs Manstein "improves" the damning wording I have quoted: Sixth Army should wait to be relieved, since its best chance of breaking out had passed, but *"only if"* it could be adequately supplied by air.

with antitank guns had been badly neglected; he ordered this omission repaired immediately from captured French stocks. Manstein, meanwhile, was optimistic. On December 9 he announced that the relief offensive would begin two or three days later; by the seventeenth it should have restored contact with Paulus's Sixth Army. Jodl's deputy dictated into the OKW war diary that day: "The Führer is very confident and plans to regain our former position on the Don. The first phase of the Russian winter offensive can be regarded as finished, without having shown any decisive successes." Jodl himself depicted Hitler's grand strategy in the east as to stabilize the front line for the winter so that he could resume the offensive in at least one sector in the spring of 1943.

Hitler contemplated minor losses of ground in the east philosophically. It would matter little in the end if his armies there were pressed back forty or eighty miles; but for the Axis to lose comparable ground in Europe would be catastrophic. This was why North Africa—as Europe's "outfield"—was significant. This was why he was pouring troops and armor, including the very latest Tiger tanks, into Tunis. No longer did he envisage an offensive by Rommel across the Suez Canal; Rommel was a write-off, a nervous wreck in need of rest and recuperation. To General Hans-Jürgen von Arnim, commanding the new Fifth Panzer Army in Tunisia, Hitler confided that eventually he planned to throw the enemy right out of Algeria and French Morocco. Early in December the Germans inflicted a convincing defeat on the British armor attempting to seize Tunisia. Here at least Hitler had the initiative. Seven months later he was to brag: "By occupying Tunisia we succeeded in postponing the invasion of Europe by half a year; and even more important, Italy has stayed in the Axis."

These were political considerations of which his generals had little understanding. On November 28, Rommel had arrived unannounced at the Wolf's Lair—with neither the knowledge nor consent of his Italian supreme commanders—and hinted bluntly that Hitler had best brace himself for the loss of Africa altogether. Hitler's reaction to this fresh insubordination was to humiliate the field marshal: when Rommel described the desperate retreat his men had fought across eight hundred miles of North Africa since El Alamein, and how his fifteen thousand combat troops had only five thousand rifles among them, Hitler shouted at him that the troops had thrown the other rifles away. When Rommel bitterly criticized the Italian supply shortcomings, particularly of gasoline, Hitler ordered Göring to escort him personally to Rome to speed up the shipments. He flatly refused Rommel's suggestion that his present stronghold at El Agheila be abandoned. He disbelieved Rommel's claim that he lacked the gasoline to fight on. "A giant army drove back on gasoline from El Alamein to here [El Agheila]," commented Hitler sarcastically later. "They didn't drive on water!"

Göring's visit to Rome was not an unqualified success. Mussolini accepted Rommel's opinion that in view of the two hundred miles of waterless desert behind it El Agheila could not be held for long. Kesselring, the German Commander in Chief South, was as optimistic as Rommel was pessimistic—indeed the latter openly wept on the shoulder of Milch, whom Göring had brought to Rome as well. The Reichsmarschall evidently spared no detail in his report to Hitler, but Hitler understood the strain that a long series of retreats—however brilliantly executed—had placed on Rommel's nerves. "Perhaps we should have recalled him right away and put a proper bulldog in his place with the strict order, 'You are to hold this position!' " As it happened, it was fortunate that Rommel did not stand and fight when the British assault on El Agheila began, for the enemy plan was to ambush him from the rear; but Rommel's army escaped in time and lived to fight another day.

Göring reported back to Hitler on December 11, but he had evidently telephoned the Führer the burden of his Rome impressions several days before. Mussolini was wallowing in despair—he had advised the Germans to wind up their pointless Russian campaign as best they could, to husband their depleted armies for what really mattered: the war in the Mediterranean. Hitler knew how precarious his ally's personal position now was. A series of enemy air raids had inflicted heavy casualties in Naples and Turin; but the population in West Germany had put up with far worse for far longer. But that he was clearly worried that Italy might make a deal with the enemy even now is indicated by the fact that he ordered Kesselring to start stockpiling maps of Italy in case Germany had to take over her defense. And on December 6, SS channels had warned him of the latest secret peace deal offered by Myron Taylor, the American ambassador to the Vatican. Hitler decided to bluff. Kesselring was instructed to draw the Italian *comando supremo*'s attention to the grave disparity between the enemy's shipping effort to North Africa, and the Italians' effort, on which both Arnim and Rommel depended. On the "binding answer" the Italians gave would depend "far-reaching decisions" the Führer proposed to take—a clear hint that he might abandon North Africa entirely.

Hitler began planning on the ninth a lengthy sojourn at the Berghof "to clear his head for fresh decisions"; as soon as Manstein's relief-offensive had begun, he would leave for Berlin, where he would see Laval on the fifteenth, and then go to the Obersalzberg, where he would see Mussolini and Antonescu. Events in Russia were to disrupt this plan.

Consideration for Mussolini's feelings—the staple of all German diplomacy—was to cost Hitler dearly. A hundred sorely needed heavy antiaircraft batteries had been sent to northern Italy. The six hundred thousand tons of French shipping captured at Marseilles was transferred to the Italian merchant marine. Tunisia was declared an Italian sphere of interest—although in private Hitler scoffed, "If we ever go over to the offensive there, you can bet your boots the Italians won't join in with us." On December 5 five hundred expert saboteurs of Admiral Canaris's "Brandenburg" commando regiment had disembarked in Tunis, for operations behind enemy lines; these too were placed under the Italian supreme command. But when the Grand Mufti of Jerusalem offered to stir up a pro-Axis insurrection of his Mohammedan subjects throughout Tunisia, Algeria, and French Morocco, Hitler turned him down. The Mufti's condition was that North Africa must be promised its eventual freedom, and even a secret letter to the Bey of Tunis couched in these terms would have been totally incompatible with Hitler's loyalty toward Mussolini.

Before returning to the doleful events of December 1942 on the eastern front, we can review the possible sources of fresh danger to the Axis in the Mediterranean now that the enemy had secured a firm base at its western end. Hitler himself undertook such *tours d'horizon* more than once that December.

Initially he deduced that if the Axis did lose North Africa, the enemy's next thrust would be into the Balkans. They would probably bypass Crete, as it was such a bulwark of German military strength as to make its capture a most formidable proposition. But the islands of Rhodes or the Peloponnesus might seem more attractive, particularly if Churchill planned to rehash the old Salonika campaign. Since Germany's eastern campaign was again halted, Turkey's friendship had cooled perceptibly; Hitler therefore deemed it expedient to furnish fresh arms to the neutral Bulgarians to dissuade Turkey from any hostile adventures. He set out a list of priorities among the recipients of Germany's scarce arms exports: first and foremost Italy's forces in the Dodecanese, Crete, and Greece; then Bulgaria; then Romania's shattered armies and Italy's other forces; and finally Spain and Hungary.

His anxiety about Spain had grown in December. At first he had turned a deaf ear on Franco's plea for modern weapons in case the enemy swept from North Africa into Spain or her African possessions. Hitler believed that the Spanish were too tenacious an opponent, and their country possessed too few advantages, for that; but the admiralty pointed out that if the enemy occupied northern Spain, this would spell the end of Germany's submarine campaign in the Atlantic. In addition, evidence that the Americans had trained Spanish Communists in Mexico and shipped them to North Africa roused Hitler's fears anew. Instructing the Abwehr to step up its Intelligence activity throughout Spain and Portugal, Keitel explained to Canaris, "The Führer is particularly alert as to Spain, because Britain has already begun a 'Stop Thief!' propaganda campaign such as usually precedes her own military operations." Hitler was in a quandary; he could ill-afford the antitank, antiaircraft, and other guns and armament Franco was appealing for. Despite the advice of Raeder and some of his own staff, his instinct told him that Spain would be better neutral. But arms deliveries would be useless if they came too late for the Spanish to install and train with them. "If Spain's only aim is to remain neutral, let her procure the arms from America," he told General Muñoz Grandes. Nonetheless he agreed to entertain the Spanish needs, provided that Franco solemnly undertook to use the weapons to ward off any British or American aggression.

Neither Hitler nor his advisers could understand why the British had so willingly allowed Roosevelt to lay hands on the eastern hemisphere. "Any sensible Englishman must say to himself that Britain is going to have to pay the bill," he told the Dutch Fascist leader Anton Mussert in mid-December. "We have not the slightest reason to fight Britain. Even if we win we gain nothing from Britain. . . . Britain ought to be glad to have in Germany a bulwark against Russia." The day when Germany and Britain would join to rise up against American imperialism seemed farther away than ever.

The uncertainty about France's loyalties was, however, banished now forever. New Forschungsamt intercepts revealed the full extent of Darlan's long-planned treachery and even hinted that Pétain had been a willing party to it. Henceforth Hitler would exploit France ruthlessly for the Axis cause. De Gaulle's supporters would be transported to the eastern front, compelled to perform the most menial tasks. British, American, and Spanish "Communists" in France would be arrested and brought to Germany. General Weygand—hero of the Battle for France—was already in German custody, bitterly protesting at being treated like a criminal.[9] General Maurice Gamelin, Léon Blum, and Édouard Daladier would have to follow. When Heinrich Himmler came to headquarters on December 10, Hitler authorized him to remove the six or seven hundred thousand Jews from France as well; at Himmler's suggestion those with influential relatives in America were to be held in a special camp "under conditions that will keep them alive and well." (Himmler's notes do not indicate that he mentioned to Hitler the alternative fate of the others.) Hitler ordered the occupation costs paid by the French increased to the maximum that the French economy would bear. The

[9]Weygand informed his SS captors that he had been *adoré* by the Arabs as French high commissioner in Syria; the British never got on with them, while the Americans in Africa were committing one *bêtise* after another. He particularly condemned the Americans for repealing the French government's anti-Jewish laws there. "I myself am an anti-Semite. I had a lot to do with the Jews in Syria too. But I must stress I never had problems with the local Jews. The other kind of Jews, the political ones, the Zionists, were even fought by the local Jews: they often came to me for help and protection against the monied Jews spreading across the country buying everything up and ruining the Arabs in the process." Himmler sent Weygand's remarks to Hitler in January 1943.

spirit that had restrained his demands at Compiègne was dead. Apart from a possible later *phalange africaine* to recapture France's lost colonies, her armed forces would be limited to an enlarged police force and *garde mobile.* "The French police are good," cackled Hitler. "We'll harness them, we'll work only with the police. Himmler knows his policemen! He employs the most reprehensible methods himself, so this will make them all partners in crime. It will be a police alliance!"

Hitler relished his private conferences with Himmler. The SS chief was always bringing something new. It was Himmler who was most assiduously propagating the new "European" spirit: in the SS panzer division "Viking," now fighting in the Caucasus, the young men of Scandinavia and the Netherlands were united with the finest German troops. He was purging occupied Europe of its undesirables. He was keeping potential dissidents like Halder and Brauchitsch under discreet surveillance. But at the same time he offered an ear to malcontents within such rival departments as the army or the foreign office. It was Himmler who first secured access to Hitler for the rocket scientists of Peenemünde. Through high officials in the Wilhelmstrasse, Himmler was also working toward the overthrow of Ribbentrop. "For your information," Himmler cabled his Intelligence chief on December 5, "the Führer is very satisfied with our reports." Ribbentrop could not make the same claim after the fiascos in the Mediterranean.

Among Himmler's reports to Hitler three deserve mention here. On December 4, 1942, the Gestapo secretly announced the "taking out" of a major arsenal of the Polish underground in Warsaw: the four-room house harbored not only the usual quantities of explosives and detonators, but also "three flasks of typhus bacilli, seventeen sealed rubber tubes presumably containing bacteria, and one fountain pen with instructions for use for spreading bacteria"; captured documents revealed that twenty pounds of arsenic had also passed through the house. A few days later Himmler produced a year-old NKVD order covering instructions to the indigenous Russian population on the poisoning—again with arsenic—of German occupation troops. A more enigmatic Himmler document is a letter to the Gestapo chief Heinrich Müller, in which he stated that "the Führer has authorized the transmission of such Intelligence data as the OKW and foreign minister agree to, in order to keep up the 'radio game' with Moscow, even though this would be *prima facie* tantamount to treason normally."[10]

[10]This may have been the origin of the suspicious radio messages to Moscow which led Gehlen and Canaris to suspect there was a traitor operating from Hitler's headquarters. See Gehlen's memoirs, U.S. edition, pages 70–71.

It was the night of December 11–12, 1942; for the first time in many months Hitler's insomnia had returned. He lay in his sparsely furnished bunker bedroom, sleepless with worry about the coming week. He knew that rumors were sweeping Germany that an entire army, the Sixth, had been encircled by the enemy at Stalingrad. Manstein's relief offensive was slated to begin in a few hours' time. But the Sixth Army's supplies were running out—the eighteenth was the last possible day for the offensive to succeed. Göring had kept his promise by marshaling a huge armada of transport aircraft for the airlift; and yet the airlift was clearly failing. On December 1, Richthofen had controlled 221 Junkers transports and 95 Heinkel 111s; but only 15 Junkers and 25 Heinkels had actually reached the besieged city, while two days later none flew in at all because of the icing and fog.[11] Were it not for the Italians Hitler might still have snatched some sleep, but during the eleventh a Russian infantry attack had developed on the Italian Eighth Army sector northwest of Stalingrad; though it was still moderate in strength, and although the terrain and their superiority in artillery favored the Italians, Hitler had steeled himself against the inevitable catastrophe the moment the Russians began the main assault. He guessed they were only waiting for the Luftwaffe to be grounded by foul weather. There were virtually no reserves behind the Italian front. Fearing the worst, he had ordered the 17th Panzer Division unloaded there, although it might make the difference between success and failure for Manstein's relief operation that it must now begin with only the 6th and 23rd panzer divisions in its spearhead.

Was it the right decision? Manstein felt it was not—he feared that his two divisions would not get through the iron Russian ring; nevertheless, between them they had 233 good tanks, more than the Russian divisions opposing them. "We've got enough tanks," Hitler told Zeitzler the next day. "But what might of course happen is this: the rogues might rapidly dismantle in front"——the general completed the Führer's thought——"and pinch us off with one group here, this side, and one group there, on that side." "The armored divisions *ought* to manage it," Hitler reemphasized. Jodl reassured them both. "He'll manage everything," meaning Manstein. "It is just that the area is so vast and our divisions so few. The enemy just flows around behind them again." Zeitzler said, "The attack mustn't get bogged down. Time is of the essence."

It was the sense of uncertainty that kept Hitler awake. Should they have

[11]Engine freeze-ups caused the greatest problems, until Milch's technical experts reminded the local air commanders late in January 1943 of the simple basic "cold-start" procedures—thinning lubricating oil with gasoline. By then it was too late.

abandoned Stalingrad three weeks ago? But they would never have recaptured it if they had. They would have had to leave huge quantities of army artillery in the city. In addition, the whole point of the Russian campaign would have been lost. "We have shed too much blood for that." "Barbarossa" had now cost the German army 371,000 dead—and Hitler did not expect many of the 86,000 missing to survive Russian captivity. But might not a wrong decision now cost the 300,000 men in Stalingrad their lives? Two days earlier Bormann had recorded Hitler as saying he would never capitulate; he would keep fighting even if he had to draft fourteen- and sixteen-year-olds into the battle. "It would still be better for them to die fighting the East than for us to lose the war and see them tortured and sold into slavery." In his mind's eye Hitler could already see the glorious moment six days hence when the siege of Stalingrad would be lifted. First a narrow corridor—and the taut-faced columns of Manstein's troops, disheveled from battle, would come pouring through with food- and gasoline-laden trucks bringing up the rear. In the city itself the word would pass from starving mouth to mouth that salvation was there. This was the vision that sustained him. The uglier possibility was banished from his mind. He could not believe that Manstein would fail—unless, of course, the Italian front caved in first. He bitterly reproached himself for not having swept straight through Stalingrad that summer. "Things would have gone faster if we hadn't got bogged down in Voronezh." Lastly, he tormented himself with the question of whether or not he could now risk going to the Berghof to see Mussolini; during the train journey they would be in touch with the outside world only every two or three hours, and there was no way he could receive *pictures* of a sudden crisis developing. "We will just have to see how things go today and tomorrow," he told Zeitzler.

The attack began well the next morning. An atmosphere of euphoria pervaded the OKW. "Little worry about carrying attack through as the enemy's tank strength is strongly reduced," noted their official historian. Nonetheless, Hitler decided to let Manstein have the 17th Panzer Division after all. The field marshal even suggested the Russians were only feinting toward the Italian front to tie down Hitler's reserves. Hitler, however, refused to be led astray by the OKW's impatient optimism.[12] Stalin was after a far bigger prize: he also wanted to cut off the retreat of the entire army group in the Caucasus, half a million men.

Russian resistance stiffened as Manstein's relief attack pushed closer to Stalin-

[12]In the OKW war diary, Greiner's *original* note for December 15, 1942, read: "The major attack anticipated against the Italian Eighth Army has not yet begun. It seems the enemy just intends to tie down our reserves by repeated feeler-operations. The Führer, however, has not yet drawn any conclusion from this." (In the published text the word "however" has been excised.)

grad. On the fourteenth, the 6th Panzer Division destroyed forty-one tanks, but Richthofen warned that the main Russian force still lay ahead; soon the 17th Panzer Division would be joined to the attack. Already it was halfway to Stalingrad. Then, on the sixteenth, came the event Hitler had feared, as the Russians hurled three armies at the narrow sector of the Don front he had entrusted to his Italian allies northwest of Stalingrad. Two bomber wings were diverted from Richthofen's support operations for the relief attack, to help the Italians—a diversion Richthofen angrily labeled "abandoning the Sixth Army—it's murder." Manstein agreed, but both Jeschonnek and Zeitzler bowed to Hitler's decision that the Italians must be saved.

How well would even German troops have fought against such odds? The Italian Eighth Army had been ill-trained, it deployed its heavy weapons wrongly, and it lacked tough officers. After two days of plucky fighting it took to its heels, tearing an immense breach between Manstein's and Weichs's army groups and leaving nothing between the Russians and Rostov but open countryside.

Foreign Minister Count Galeazzo Ciano encountered a forbidding atmosphere at the Wolf's Lair when he arrived with Marshal Cavallero at noon on December 18. Hitler had abandoned all thought of going to the Berghof. He determined to speak bluntly with the Italians. No reference was made to the Italian Eighth Army's inglorious dissolution, but he used plain language in demanding that Italy make sacrifices to keep supplies flowing into North Africa. Germany was preparing to send her four finest divisions over to Tunis. He asked that Italy's civil transport and indeed her navy make a comparable effort. Neither Ciano nor Cavallero commented on this. Ciano's main purpose in coming was to deliver Mussolini's "hypothetical" question: given that 1943 would probably see major enemy operations in North Africa, southeastern Europe, and the west, would it not even now be possible to reach a *political* settlement with Russia à la Brest-Litovsk? Hitler patiently replied that this would be irreconcilable with his objective of Lebensraum. Besides, after six months of truce Germany would have to fight Russia all over again—a Russia immensely refreshed and reinforced. It was a false illusion for Mussolini to believe that Germany could ever abstract divisions from the east to ward off possible defeat in the Mediterranean.

Hitler sugared the pill with caustic references to the French. He revealed that he was maintaining the fiction of a "French government" under Pétain only because the unbelligerent French colonials in North Africa willingly accepted Pétain's order not to fight for the Allies.[13] He no longer had any trust

[13]According to an (unpublished) note by Greiner on January 7, 1943, Hitler ordered all French prisoners taken in Tunis to be released in France and paid a French government pension.

in the French. Not that he trusted the Italians now either. As the Italians left, Keitel instructed Admiral Canaris to keep an eye on Italy ("even though it is not to be anticipated that she will defect"). A member of Ciano's entourage inquired of the OKW whether the Italian Eighth Army had suffered heavy casualties; he was told: "None at all. They never stopped running."

With the collapse of the Italian army, a terrible new situation confronted Germany's Sixth Army in Stalingrad. Only two alternatives were left to it: to push a battle group southwest to meet the relieving panzer divisions, while still retaining the strategic stranglehold on Stalingrad and the Volga; or to implement "Thunderclap," a breakout by the entire Sixth Army—abandoning its heavy equipment and tens of thousands of wounded troops to the mercies of the enemy. Zeitzler put Manstein's case for "Thunderclap" to Hitler during the war conference late on December 18. As their expert scrutiny switched from one sector of the front to the next, an adjutant spread maps across the table, while Hitler, clutching a bunch of colored pencils in one hand, watched the ominous red arrows of the Red Army's offensive plunge ever closer to the airfields from which the Luftwaffe was mounting its airlift into Stalingrad. The logistic difficulties of launching "Thunderclap" seemed insuperable: Paulus demanded no less than 1,800 tons of food and 4,000 tons of fuel first; although the Luftflotte managed to fly in all of 270 tons that day, this was twice the average so far. Richthofen telephoned Zeitzler that evening saying he would need enormous reinforcement of his improvised air transport fleet.

By December 19 the three divisions of Manstein's relief force had reached the Myshovka River, some forty miles from Paulus's perimeter. The next day, one last push was made, only to be firmly blocked by the Russians. Hitler had ordered three more divisions rushed east from France, but it would take three weeks even to get them moving. (On December 19 he ordered Himmler to raise two new crack SS panzer-grenadier divisions—the 9th and 10th—in France by mid-February to replace them.)[14]

At 6 P.M. on December 19, Manstein radioed to the Sixth Army an order to begin "Operation Winter Storm"—an attempt to extend the southwestern perimeter by a limited tank attack under General Hube, thus linking up with the relief force outside. Paulus was also directed to stand by for "Thunderclap" in case Hitler gave permission. During the afternoon Manstein asked Zeitzler to secure Hitler's permission. But time was already running out. Paulus could not disen-

[14]Hitler kept a close eye on the raising of these divisions, telephoning his liaison officer SS General Karl Wolff twice on January 13, 1943, to stress that they "must work night and day on completing them as fast as humanly possible." The divisions fought historic battles in 1944 on the eastern front and in Normandy.

gage enough forces for "Winter Storm" without losing his grip on Stalingrad altogether; and he would need five days at least to prepare for "Thunderclap," as he had eight thousand casualties to fly out and the fuel would first have to be flown in. At present his tanks had fuel for less than fifteen miles. Paulus himself referred to "Thunderclap" as a "catastrophic solution."

It was a heartrending situation and one that the lesser commanders were glad to pass to Hitler for decision. He knew that Paulus's army was already tying down over seventy Russian divisions and brigades. On December 21 Manstein made it clear that the relief offensive could bring help no nearer to Stalingrad. If the Sixth Army pulled out now, the enemy might move to cut off the entire southern front. On the twenty-third Manstein had to take the 23rd Panzer Division out of the relief force to plug gaps west of the Don. Two days later Russian tanks overran one of the two vital airfields, and a powerful counterattack pushed the rest of the German relief force back to the Akssai River. All prospects of relieving Stalingrad that winter faded.

Hitler steeled himself against the noisy counsels of his commanders. Göring and Jeschonnek supported him; Manstein impertinently remarked to Zeitzler that if the Reichsmarschall was so sure the Stalingrad situation was not grave, then he should himself take command of the army group and its associated Luftflotte! Hitler refused to speak on the telephone with Manstein or to see him personally. Zeitzler and Manstein nonetheless argued loudly that only the immediate withdrawal of Kleist's Army Group A from the Caucasus would release enough reserves to prevent a catastrophe. When Zeitzler returned to his demand that the whole Sixth Army be ordered to break out, Hitler irritably replied, "The Sixth Army must stand fast. Even if I cannot lift the siege until spring." Göring assured him the airlift was working well. Keitel and Jodl supported Hitler with varying degrees of enthusiasm. Zeitzler accused the Reichsmarschall of lying about the Luftwaffe's capabilities and afterward reported the true airlift tonnage daily to Hitler each morning. On December 21 over 360 tons had been flown in, but now that the two closest airfields had been overrun, and the figure was soon barely a tenth of that amount. General Martin Fiebig, whose Eighth Air Corps was now wholly engaged in the airlift, wrote: "One wonders whether the Führer has got the picture—whether he really knows the state of our men and their capacity for effort, and whether the Russian strength isn't being underestimated once more."

In this atmosphere of despondency Hitler kept his nerve; but this time nerve alone was not enough. A year later he explained his grim philosophy thus in a secret speech to his downhearted generals: "Let this much be understood—nothing shocks me, whatever may happen. Some may think me heartless to insist on fighting to the last man just because the enemy will also let more blood that way, rather than to undertake this maneuver or that. It has nothing to do with heartlessness, only with my realization and conviction that *this* is the action to be taken. . . . It is a matter of supreme indifference to me what posterity may think of me."

At the time of Stalingrad, Hitler radiated outward confidence that the Sixth Army would shortly be liberated, though his private feelings may have been somewhat different. His generals trusted him—had he not proved them all wrong as recently as the Battle of Kharkov in May? Richthofen consoled the mutinous Luftwaffe generals with this argument: the Führer had been right before, even though his experts had advised otherwise, and nobody had understood him then either. "Perhaps we will all be chuckling over this crisis when May comes!" But Fiebig for one was unconvinced. "Richthofen mentioned yesterday that entire armies are often lost without any effect on the outcome of the war. But what can the Führer himself be thinking? It is a matter of two hundred fifty thousand human beings—we can't just sacrifice them, as there are no replacements. What will the Russians do with this quarter-million? They can but kill them, they haven't the food for them. Death will take a huge toll. Each man one last bullet for himself!—What does the Führer want to document with the fate of this army? There must be some purpose, otherwise one might lose faith."

Throughout December General Zeitzler pressed for the evacuation of Kleist's army group from the Caucasus in good time. Hitler at first refused. "First wait and see the outcome of our relief operation against Stalingrad. That will change the whole picture at one stroke." The prophecy had been fulfilled, but the outcome was not what Hitler had expected. On December 27 when issuing instructions to the army for the coming months, Hitler decreed that Kleist was to defend his existing line. The eventual liberation of the Sixth Army must guide all other considerations; thus the town of Kotelnikovo must be held too, as a starting point for that offensive. Meanwhile the SS panzer division "Viking" would be moved up from the Caucasus and the 7th Panzer Division brought from France early in January. A new battalion of Tiger tanks would also be provided. But these instructions were overtaken by events: the Romanian divisions guarding the flanks of the relieving force which had attacked on December 12 collapsed, and its depleted armored spearhead barely managed to extricate itself.

That evening, December 27, Zeitzler ambushed Hitler by arriving unannounced at the Wolf's Lair and bearding the Führer in his private bunker despite his adjutants' protests. He was moodily listening to records of Beethoven. The general spoke earnestly, and ended with the words: "If you do not order the withdrawal of the Caucasus front now, you will have a second Stalingrad on your hands." Hitler brooded, then curtly told him: "Very well, do as you wish!" But he regretted this almost immediately and telephoned the General Staff's nearby headquarters several times to try to intercept Zeitzler on his return. Eventually Zeitzler himself came to the phone. Hitler said, "About the withdrawal from the Caucasus—wait a bit. We'll have another talk about it." Zeitzler's voice came back: "Too late—the order has already gone out." Hitler paused, said, "Very well, then," and irritably replaced the receiver.

Given the collapse of the Romanian and Italian armies it was undoubtedly the right decision, but he may have sensed that now a retreat from Russia was beginning that would not be halted at the frontiers of Germany.

Retreat

Hitler saw in the New Year, 1943, sitting alone in his bunker with Martin Bormann, his Party secretary, until after 4:00 A.M. This itself presaged the coming times: in the year that followed a significant part of Hitler's domestic authority was delegated to a three-man cabal—Bormann, Keitel, and Lammers—convening significantly in what had been the Cabinet Room of the Berlin Chancellery, while Goebbels hovered like a predator calling impatiently for the mantle of "Führer of the home front" to descend on him.

Hitler was rarely in Berlin. He dedicated himself to his war, sustained by the prospect of coming offensives, of the growing U-boat campaign, of increased panzer and aircraft production, and by "evidence" that Stalin's manpower reserves were at last declining. Victory would surely go to the combatant with the strongest nerves, with the greatest resilience. His troubled conscience over Stalingrad he kept to himself—betraying his true feelings only by chance remarks to his secretaries or doctors. At night he could not sleep, for before his eyes there danced the arrow-covered maps of the evening's war conference, crowding in on him like childhood nightmares until at last the sedatives he had taken dragged him down into unconsciousness. For the next six months he proved more accessible to the advice of the General Staff. His tactical decisions were sound, and the retreats that marked these months were considerable military achievements. But he had lost forever the venturesome spirit that was his forte. Only at Stalingrad and in the first disordered retreat to the Donets did the army lose equipment of any consequence. Thereafter the withdrawals were planned and fought so as to inflict the maximum hardship and casualties on the enemy. Still sure of their superiority, the German soldiers felt that they were being overwhelmed by circumstance, not the Russian army: by lack of oil, by inclement weather, by unreliable allies. Their trust in Hitler remained unshaken,[1] but the security service

[1]As the generals showed on March 13, 1943. See pages 498–99, based on an unpublished note by Greiner.

reports indicated that at home the first mutterings of popular discontent were becoming audible.

General Eberhard von Mackensen's First Panzer Army began its withdrawal from the Caucasus on January 1, 1943, and completed it thirty days later, having covered over four hundred miles under appalling conditions for infantry and artillery alike—eighteen-horse teams struggled to haul the heavy guns through the mountains. Some 25,000 casualties were evacuated in time from the field hospitals; all the equipment except for about a hundred guns was saved. Simultaneously General Ruoff's Seventeenth Army withdrew from the western Caucasus. Thus at a cost of 226 lives an entire army group, some 700,000 men, was saved from the fate currently befalling those in Stalingrad. Against Zeitzler's advice, however, Hitler directed only four of Mackensen's divisions to Rostov; the rest were added to Ruoff's army, which was ordered during January to hold a bridgehead on the Taman peninsula—just over the narrow straits from the Crimea. This would have psychological value, argued Hitler; it would show friend and foe alike that in 1943 he again intended to go over to the offensive. With Albert Speer he even adumbrated plans to build across the Strait of Kerch a giant bridge linking the Crimea to the "Goth's Head," as the Taman bridgehead was termed.

Meanwhile, in the dying days of the old year Hitler had conceived a grand operational design to relieve the starving Sixth Army and turn the Russian onslaught into a rout. He would speedily transfer the three most powerful SS divisions—Sepp Dietrich's "Adolf Hitler Life Guards," "Das Reich," and "Death's Head"—from France and the crack "Gross Deutschland" infantry division from Army Group Center, assemble them southeast of Kharkov, and strike north of the Don toward Stalingrad as soon as the weather improved. That would be mid-February. Paulus's spirits were raised by Hitler's convincing assurances. When the one-armed panzer general Hube arrived at the Wolf's Lair from Stalingrad with word that the army's meat supplies would not last beyond January, Hitler ordered Quartermaster General Wagner to furnish concentrated foodstuffs such as were provided to Polar expeditions. When Paulus reported that bad weather sometimes prevented any airlift operations at all, Hitler promised that the Luftwaffe would carry 750 tons of supplies in on days when the weather was good. Göring did his best: already 480 Junkers and Heinkels were committed solely to the airlift; but the frontline squadrons, particularly of the Junkers, found their spirit cruelly assailed by the cold and by their inadequate leadership, and only a fraction of the available planes were actually flying each day. This was not realized at Hitler's headquarters, and still more planes were sent to the airlift—100 more Junkers, 10 Focke-Wulf Condors, and several of the troublesome Heinkel 177 heavy bombers too. A visit by a responsible Luftwaffe commander would have been more fruitful, but Jeschonnek could not spare the time and Göring averted his gaze from the seemingly inevitable disaster. The local air commander,

Fiebig, wrote that somehow the supply rate had to be maintained for six more weeks until the new relief operation got through. "If all goes well then, we have won the battle for Stalingrad and perhaps the war. We just don't know the potential strength of the other side."

Within Hitler the sense of public relations still stirred. Despite his Stalingrad worries, he telephoned Frau Troost in person from East Prussia to congratulate her on the solid gold cassette she had designed for Göring's warrant as Reichsmarschall—correctly speculating that this female *arbiter legendarium* would noise his evident well-being abroad. But his misgivings in fact were multiplying. Below, his Luftwaffe adjutant, had shown him a private letter from a relative trapped in Stalingrad, and its references to the Sixth Army's commanders were not encouraging. A question mark was placed against Paulus's name; General Arthur Schmidt and General Walter von Seydlitz were marked "sack 'em," but Hube was praised: "He's the man!" On January 8 the General Staff reported that General Konstantin Rokossovski had publicly called on Paulus to surrender. "Paulus asks what he should do now!"

The year had opened with an exasperating series of errors over an Allied convoy to North Russia. According to naval Intelligence it was escorted only by destroyers when it was sighted by a U-boat south of Bear Island early on December 30. Raeder's naval liaison officer, Admiral Theodor Krancke, asked Hitler for his blessing for a sortie by the *Hipper,* the *Lützow,* and six destroyers to attack the convoy; the pocket battleship *Lützow* would afterward break out into the Atlantic —"Operation Aurora." Throughout New Year's Eve the Führer was left in virtual ignorance of the progress of the battle. Under his impatient pressure Krancke somewhat tactlessly showed him the only two radio messages bearing on the battle's outcome. Admiral Kummetz had merely radioed: "Break off attack, no enemy cruiser with convoy, not possible to detach *Lützow* for 'Aurora.' " But the shadowing U-boat had radioed as the Arctic dusk engulfed the scene: "I see just red!"

Hitler badly needed a morale booster and interpreted the above messages optimistically. Evidently the enemy warships were ablaze. When Ribbentrop telephoned at midnight with New Year felicitations, Hitler bragged that the navy had just won a "magnificent victory." Not until next afternoon did he learn the woeful truth: British cruisers had been lurking nearby, his own task force had fumbled and run for cover, the cruiser *Hipper* was so badly damaged that at times she could make little more than fifteen knots. A German destroyer had mistakenly joined the enemy and paid dearly for her error. The convoy itself had escaped unscathed. Hitler raged at the incompetent navy radiomen and the inadequate naval spirit. The least his big ships could do was fight with as much determination as the U-boat crews or common soldiers in the east. He announced that he was going to lay up all the big ships, and he ordered Krancke to inform Raeder of this by telephone. The navy Commander in Chief was to come to the Wolf's Lair at once, but Raeder asked for time to conduct a postmortem on the fiasco first.

His stock with Hitler was already low. He had been a less frequent visitor to the Führer than his critics, of whom Speer and Göring were the most vociferous. Out of jealousy, Göring had furnished Hitler with a string of complaints about the admiralty. Speer had done the same, to further his own causes; he had picked holes in Raeder's tradition-based claim to the flotsam left on the beaches of Dieppe after the British raid—in error, as it turned out. As recently as January 4, Speer had reported the navy to Hitler for hoarding sixty oil-paper-wrapped 105-millimeter antiaircraft guns in a depot. (He had been unaware that they were there for ranging and calibration tests.) Speer also insidiously declared to Hitler that Raeder was hated throughout the U-boat arm for his attempts to suppress Dönitz's popularity. Raeder's true shortcoming, in Speer's eyes, was his refusal to abrogate control over naval armament to the Speer munitions ministry. Now Speer's campaign paid dividends.

The admiral arrived late on January 6. Hitler berated him for ninety minutes on the big ships' failure ever since 1864 to fight a single naval action right through. Neither its mutiny in 1918 nor its scuttling in 1919 were exactly glorious episodes. He wanted the ships laid up, their crews transferred to the smaller, more active vessels, and the armament built into the coastal defenses. At Raeder's request, Keitel and the two stenographers withdrew; the admiral then tendered his resignation—offering to postpone it until the Party's tenth anniversary in power at the end of January to stifle any further scandal. Hitler asked him to submit the names of two possible successors. Raeder suggested Admiral Rolf Carls or alternatively —though with marked distaste—Dönitz. But Carls was himself a champion of the big ships and was turned down. On January 14, Raeder also submitted the written reply Hitler had requested, predicting "shrieks of triumph" from the enemy when they learned that the Germans had mothballed their own biggest ships. Hitler heaped sarcasm on the document, but Krancke could see that he was impressed nonetheless.

The next months in the east would be crucial, but the idea of seeking even a conditional armistice did not enter his head. As he told Marshal Antonescu on January 10, the day the Russians opened their all-out offensive at Stalingrad, neither in the Punic wars nor in the Thirty Years' War nor in the Seven Years' War had any of the statesmen been able to predict how it would all end; yet their fanatical resolve and single-minded purpose had brought them victory.

Two days later the Russians weighed into the Hungarian Second Army, toward

Svoboda, just as Hitler had also predicted. Army Intelligence was also reporting rumors of enemy plans to invade the Crimea. In the north a major Soviet relief attack designed to lift the siege of Leningrad began. The Hungarians south of Voronezh suffered a defeat no less complete than that of the Romanians and Italians: 30,000 dead and 50,000 captured within days; as a result the German Second Army was threatened with encirclement and a similar catastrophe.

Hitler's tactical measures—rushing antitank guns to the Hungarians and calling in three more divisions from France—came too late. But strategically he was already thinking of 1944 and attending to the interlocking problems of raising fresh divisions and providing them with weapons and ammunition to replace those lost in this new winter of disaster. On the entire eastern front, he learned later in January, he had less than five hundred tanks; the Russians had five thousand.[2] With the help of Goebbels and Bormann he himself planned to wring a million troops out of the German population by mid-1943: in December he ordered German industry to release two hundred thousand men for call-up by the end of March; a month later the demand was stepped up to eight hundred thousand men. But who could replace the skilled aircraft workers or electronics engineers thus thrust into uniform, and even worse how would the German madam survive without her servants? Germany, which Hitler had made a world power by cunning and lightning wars, had too much domestic inertia to combat the manpower potential of the United States or the massive forces of Stalin's Soviet Union.

Providing the extra tanks and artillery was no less urgent, particularly now that he could no longer ignore American armament capacity. Twice in January Speer was called to the Wolf's Lair. Hitler wanted bigger, better, and more tanks. On the seventeenth he telephoned Walter Rohland, the tank production expert, secured his agreement to increase assault-gun, Panzer IV, Panther, and Tiger tank production from May, and decided to launch a new production program, the "Adolf Hitler Tank Program." He buttonholed Admiral Krancke after the conference and unemotionally told him that all warship construction larger than destroyers was to cease forthwith so that Speer could have the manpower he would now need for tanks. "Even if it is only five thousand men it will help," Hitler noted. The military crisis in the east was so grave that all else must bow to the tank program's needs. When Krancke protested, Hitler again harked back to the inconsequential naval action off Bear Island—the navy should have finished the job and annihilated that convoy whatever the toll in sailors' lives. "The tanks

[2]On January 23, 1943, Army Group A had 34 serviceable tanks, Army Groups Don and B had 291 between them, Center had 167, and Army Group North only 3. In early December the Germans had had about 1,300 and the Russians about 4,800.

it brought through have now probably cost many more soldiers their lives south of Lake Ladoga." (The next day the Russians announced the recapture of Petrokrepost on Lake Ladoga, thus restoring land contact with Leningrad.) Krancke reminded Hitler of his standing orders against risking the big ships against any superior enemy; but Hitler referred to the *Graf Spee* and *Bismarck* episodes as proof that it was the spirit of their crews that was wanting. Speer arrived on the night train from Berlin, drafted a decree for the tank program, and issued it over Hitler's signature together with the Führer's dramatic appeal to the workers not to let the army down. Not long afterward, Dönitz stood before Hitler, eagerly conniving at the consignment of the big ships to the wreckers'; but soon he too recognized the folly of such a decision and effortlessly persuaded Hitler to leave the ships in service. Before Raeder retired into obscurity, he begged Hitler to protect the navy from Göring, and he warned his successor not to put his trust in Speer.

The high point in Hitler's affection for Göring was reached on January 12, the Reichsmarschall's fiftieth birthday. Thereafter a series of Allied night air raids on the German and French population affected Göring's prestige. In mid-January Hitler sent for Göring's deputy, Milch, and put him in personal charge of the airlift to Stalingrad—a step which the jealous Göring had urgently counseled against, and with good cause, for Milch embarrassed the Reichsmarschall by achieving the near impossible in the two weeks that remained.

Along the southern front as far north as Voronezh a Soviet avalanche of troops and tanks was pouring through the breach created by the Romanian, Italian, and Hungarian collapse. Hitler's object was to keep Paulus's army fighting for six more weeks at least—until it could be relieved by Paul Hausser's SS panzer corps—or at least long enough to preoccupy the enemy. But what then? General von Weichs cabled him that his army group was left with barely seven divisions—mostly exhausted, dispirited, and improvised—along a two-hundred-mile front; he saw no possible way of holding up the enemy's relentless march westward. At any moment the Russians might encircle the Second Army. From within Stalingrad strong protests were now emanating from the Sixth Army, too. "Mein Führer!" Paulus radioed on the seventeenth. "Your orders on the supply of my army are not being obeyed." The planes were no longer landing at Gumrak airfield; they were just throwing out their loads in midair. The loads were thus largely wasted, and the thousands of injured waiting to be flown out were left to suffer. The Luftwaffe generals denied Paulus's allegations. Göring later bitterly accused Paulus—at the time no doubt to Hitler himself—of being too soft a commander; he was feeding thousands of Russian civilians and useless injured German soldiers. "One can't burden oneself with wounded men beyond hope of recovery; they must be left to lapse into the hereafter." The army generals did not share this attitude. General Hube, again flown out of Stalingrad, feelingly reproached Hitler. "The Luftwaffe airlift has failed. Somebody must be to blame for that. Why don't you kill off some of your Luftwaffe generals—it's always the army generals who go to the wall!" Hitler replied in level terms, "I know the grim position you are in at Stalingrad. But soon things will get better. I have got it all in hand." But Hube's reproach nettled the Führer, and he quoted it to Göring with equal feeling later. Hube was assigned to Milch's emergency staff.

Hitler turned a deaf ear on Hube's advice to appoint a Commander in Chief East, suspecting as he did that the advice had come from Manstein. Richthofen has painted a vivid portrait of Manstein in this month of crisis. "In my view Manstein is a write-off, trembling in every limb and looking years older. . . . He has been deprived of all possibility of command, as every single battalion is still being directed from On High.[3] Again and again the mistrust from above is blazoned forth against army- and army-group commanders alike. An excruciating war." Disaster seemed inevitable; already Richthofen was blaming Manstein and Göring, Göring was blaming Manstein and Paulus—for allowing the airlift's airfields to be overrun—and Paulus and his Chief of Staff were blaming the Luftwaffe. Within the Luftwaffe, Milch was not talking to Jeschonnek, and Jeschonnek was not on speaking terms with the quartermaster general; all three were responsible for the airlift.

At Hitler's headquarters, Zeitzler pointedly introduced "Stalingrad" rations for his staff, and he visibly lost weight. Milch had now discovered that the ignorance and negligence of the local air transport commanders—particularly of the Junkers 52 squadrons—accounted for most of the disappointing serviceability of their planes. On January 22 the enemy again called on Paulus to surrender. Manstein and Zeitzler both now argued that he should comply, but Hitler replied that the Russians would abide by no conventions—no prisoners would survive long; on the other hand, every day the Sixth Army fought on, no matter how hopelessly, would help stabilize the other fronts. Paulus radioed a dignified response to Hitler's instructions: "Your orders are being executed. Long live Germany."

Hitler deemed that the word of his soldiers' heroism at Stalingrad would itself be worth many divisions in the months to come. Whenever in the future Hitler's soldiers were encircled, they would fight with like tenacity. The legend of Stalingrad would enhance each later fortress's invincibility in enemy eyes. Thus, when Goebbels came to map out their propaganda on the coming total war campaign, Hitler instructed that absolute frankness be observed by the press in describing

[3] "*Von allerhöchster Stelle.*" See page 391 above.

the situation of German soldiers in Stalingrad. In this way, Hitler hoped to mobilize in Germany the same latent strength that Churchill had called on in England after Dunkirk. Above all, the coming Bolshevik victory communiqués were to pass unchallenged—the better to bring a bracing shiver of apprehension to the peoples of the West. On January 24, German newspapers for the first time revealed the death throes of the Sixth Army. Speer, arriving in Berlin that day from the Wolf's Lair, telephoned Milch that Hitler sorely regretted not having called in Milch to run the airlift from the start. Twenty-nine thousand injured troops had been evacuated by the time Paulus's last airfield was overrun. His soldiers had been allowed to write one last letter home. When the last Heinkel took off, it brought out nineteen injured soldiers and seven bags of mail.

In Stalingrad, Paulus's ragged army had been severed into two pockets. In the smaller, southern pocket, Paulus despondently predicted defeat on the twenty-fifth, but his men fought on, the swastika banner still flying symbolically from the ruins of the highest building. Twenty thousand untended injured were lying in the streets. Paulus ordered the dwindling food supplies issued only to those still fit enough to fight. The Luftwaffe crews matched the courage being demanded of the soldiers, flying two and sometimes even three sorties a night to discharge food and ammunition over Stalingrad. "On the anniversary of your assumption of power," Paulus radioed Hitler, "the Sixth Army sends greetings to the Führer. The swastika still flutters over Stalingrad. May our struggle stand as an example to generations as yet unborn, never to surrender no matter how desperate the odds. Then Germany will be victorious. Heil, mein Führer!" Hitler's reply was a proclamation broadcast to the German nation as long-range Luftwaffe fighters arrived over Stalingrad for the first time. It ended: "In this fight we will have the Almighty on our side. We will not shy from shedding our own blood, because one day a new land will blossom from the sacrifices of the fallen. And our teutonic state, our German nation, shall emerge victorious!"

This was his rejoinder to the call for unconditional surrender just raised by Roosevelt at Casablanca.[4]

At Zeitzler's instance—though not without misgivings—Hitler telegraphically promoted Paulus to field marshal. Since no German field marshal had yet sur-

[4]On January 24, 1943. Not until later did Goebbels seize on it as a propaganda weapon. It certainly stiffened the German people's resolve to fight on under Hitler. In an April 1944 memorandum Churchill wisely—though mendaciously—disowned unconditional surrender. "This matter is on the President. He announced it at Casablanca without any consultation and I backed him up in general terms. Subsequent correspondence with the President has shown him very much disinclined to remodel his statements now." (A doctored version of the memorandum is in his memoirs.)

rendered he thus pressed the pistol into Paulus's hand. At 7:35 A.M. on the thirty-first Sixth Army headquarters radioed: "In our bunker we listened to the Führer's Proclamation and saluted the national anthem for perhaps the last time." Almost at once they added, "The Russians are outside the door," and then, "We are destroying . . ." The radio went dead.

Hitler probably spared little attention for Stalingrad that day, for alarm bells were ringing throughout his domain. In Italy, Keitel's counterpart, Marshal Ugo Cavallero, had been replaced by General Vittorio Ambrosio without explanation; English newspapers hinted that he had been at the center of an anti-Fascist clique. Ciano was retired as foreign minister. In North Africa Rommel was retreating toward Tunisia, outnumbered eight to one by the enemy; Tripoli—and thus Libya itself—had been abandoned by the Axis. In northwest Germany, American heavy bombers had just attacked Wilhelmshaven in broad daylight; and on January 30 fast British bombers had penetrated to Berlin at noon.

Long before the war Hitler had called for Luftwaffe bombers just like these—and now the enemy had them but not he. "An impertinence! It's called the Mosquito! And it's made of wood!" The Luftwaffe's own heavy bomber, the Heinkel 177, which should have been available in time to bomb Moscow when "Barbarossa" began in June 1941, was still not perfected. Nineteen sorties had been flown to Stalingrad: no Heinkel 177 had been lost to enemy action, but six had been destroyed by engine fires in midair: the bomber's engines were coupled in pairs onto one propeller shaft—a technical monstrosity conceived by General Udet, who had put a bullet in his brain in connection with Luftwaffe production failures. How Hitler would have liked to send thirty Heinkel 177s—each with a ton of bombs—to smash Stalin's war plants at Sverdlovsk and even farther afield!

It was infuriating. Here was Germany, with her magnificent corps of commanders, her outstanding soldiers, and her vaunted weapons technology—yet compelled to retreat along the entire eastern front. Kharkov itself was in danger; Hausser's SS panzer corps must move in. In the Demyansk pocket south of Leningrad, so jealously defended by Hitler these many months, supplies were running low; it would have to be given up at last. There seemed to be concrete evidence that the Allies would soon invade Portugal; thus divisions were tied down in the west. Equally disturbing for Hitler was the persistent incompetence of his Intelligence agencies. Unconditional surrender perturbed him far less than the failure of both Canaris and the SS to advise him that Churchill and Roosevelt were meeting at Casablanca (the SS placed them both in Washington).

Hitler had turned in at 2:30 A.M., earlier than usual, that first day of February. He was shortly awakened with word from Moscow: Paulus had meekly surrendered, and was thus still alive—as were eleven German and five Romanian generals. Hitler's chagrin was huge. That his field marshal should have chosen the Tartarus of Soviet captivity to the Valhalla that Hitler had opened unto him, that he had lacked the routine courage of every captain who had gone down with his ship, that he had not mustered the same bravery as had a score of Soviet commissars and commanders in identically hopeless situations—this he could never forgive Paulus. He instructed his naval adjutant, Puttkamer, to find out if it was too late to cancel Paulus's promotion, but it was already in the newspapers. "The others stick together, form a phalanx, and keep the last bullet for themselves. Imagine, even a woman with an ounce of pride in her will lock herself in and put a bullet in her brain just because she has heard a few insulting words! . . . Here is a man who can look on while fifty or sixty thousand of his troops are dying and defending themselves with courage to the end—how can he give himself up to the Bolsheviks?" When Speer's deputy, Karl Saur, telephoned the Führer at 3 A.M. with the January production figures, for the first time Hitler did not want to hear them.

Throughout February appalling crises gripped the eastern front. Weichs was removed—his army group had virtually dissolved. Through the yawning gap thundered the Soviet avalanche. "I won't be able to sleep again without sedatives until the breach is plugged," declared Hitler. Only his staff stenographers shared his awful, all-embracing knowledge of the true picture. The diary of one of them reveals that a stenographer who had arrived as recently as December had suffered a nervous breakdown by mid-February. He was apprehended just as he was about to burst into the Führer's bedroom, screaming, "The Führer wants to speak to me. I must see him!" Martin Bormann rushed him off to a Berlin hospital. Meanwhile, frightened of fresh bloody nightmares, Hitler postponed retiring to his camp bed longer every night—wearying his obedient secretaries and physicians with endless somber monologues in an atmosphere that reminded the youngest secretary, newcomer Traudl Humps, of a cemetery on a wet November day. Hitler explained to an army doctor two years later: "I have to relax and speak about something else, otherwise I keep seeing the staff maps in the dark, and my brain goes grinding on and it takes me hours on end to drop off. If I then switch on the light, I can sketch exactly where every division was at Stalingrad. Hour after hour it goes on, until I finally drop off around five or six."

In two months the Red Army had demolished five armies—German, Romanian, Italian, and Hungarian. By the end of February the Russians had recaptured Kursk, Belgorod, Kraznodar, Demyansk, and even Rostov and Kharkov. Hitler might yet even have to abandon the Donets Basin, on whose coal and iron resources he and Speer had planned to hinge the expansion of the arms industry for the final overthrow of Russia. "I will have to think it over," he declared on February 1—referring to abandoning the Donets Basin. "But one thing I can say now: if I do, there will be no further possibility of bringing the war in the east to an *offensive* conclusion. Let's make no mistake about that!" Four days later he was quoted in Greiner's private diary to this effect: "I can't abandon the Donets Basin. If I do, I can't continue the war any longer."

Nor would Hitler as yet contemplate a political solution with Stalin. Japan's Ambassador Oshima had called on January 20 and left disappointed in this respect; indeed, Hitler now reversed his earlier stand and urgently demanded a Japanese attack on Stalin in the Far East. As for the public clamor, Goebbels successfully steered it into more productive channels—toward the totalization of the national war effort. Ribbentrop favored an appeal to the rest of Europe—a Hitler proclamation which would promise the western Europeans a degree of independence, and the eastern Europeans the same, though rather less: Poland would become a Protectorate, the Baltic states would be kept in tow like Slovakia, and Italy would make parallel concessions to Croatia, Greece, Albania, and Serbia. But Hitler still wanted Germany to go it alone. When Hewel brought him Ribbentrop's renewed proposal for peace feelers toward Moscow, Hitler refused even to read it. "First we must win a major military victory," he told Ribbentrop afterward. "Then we can see."

In presenting his plans to mobilize the native populations against Stalin, Rosenberg fared no better than Ribbentrop. By early 1943 the Germans had over 130,000 "Eastern troops" organized in battalions ready to fight for them, and there were Russian generals willing to lead them against Stalin; but Hitler could still not bring himself to accept this aid; in addition, he suspected it would be playing with dynamite, for it would merely be a rekindling of Russian nationalism under a different management. Now that the great retreat had begun, he temporized—ordering his armies to evacuate the anti-Stalin population of the Caucasus to spare them Soviet reprisals for collaborating with the Axis, but still unwilling to accept Rosenberg's appeal for a major propaganda offensive to win over Stalin's other subjects.[5] Rosenberg's blunders in the Ukraine and elsewhere had lowered him in Hitler's eyes. When in February 1943 Rosenberg read him a lengthy proposal for replacing the Soviet collective system with private enterprise and property again, raising legions from all the Soviet Union's ethnic groups (not just the Russians), restoring their freedom of religion, and issuing a suitable political proclamation to them, Hitler remarked that all this seemed inopportune at present. He would perhaps return to some of the proposals "after the coming spring

[5]On February 13, 1943, "for humanitarian reasons" Himmler ordered his police commanders in Russia to evacuate all able-bodied men and women—together with their children—from the regions being abandoned by the army; if they did not afford to the public that had collaborated this protection from Soviet wrath and reprisal, they would forfeit the public's trust in the future. A similar Hitler Order was issued the next day. Thus in one February day 1,500 German troops and 780 Russian civilians were evacuated from the Caucasus to the Crimea.

offensive began." When Zeitzler mentioned to him that the captured Russian general Andrei Andreyevich Vlasov was willing to lead a "National Army of Liberation" against Stalin, Hitler saw in the general only a useful propaganda tool. "What a swine Vlasov must be," he commented to his own staff. "He owes everything to Stalin. It was Stalin who made a general out of him. Now he bites the hand that fed him." Not that he expected Paulus to act any differently. A few weeks in the Lubyanka prison and he would say anything. "Just wait and see. . . . It won't be long before he's speaking on Moscow radio."

The cost of Stalingrad had been high. Göring's Luftwaffe had lost 488 aircraft and about a 1,000 airmen in the airlift, the equivalent of an entire air corps. Only 108,000 of Paulus's troops had survived to enter Soviet captivity, of which only 6,000 were ever to see Germany again. But on February 4, Gehlen's Intelligence division estimated that 107 Soviet divisions and brigades had been tied down by the battle for the city, together with 13 tank regiments.[6] This and the blocking of the rail and road links through the city had hampered all enemy operations on the southern front. In consequence a noticeable indecision marked the enemy's next moves; Gehlen could do little more than guess at where Stalin's next offensive would begin. Admittedly he had detected an increase in the enemy reserves early in January, but these were not new troops—merely divisions taken out of the front line for rehabilitation. Hitler was still optimistic that shortages of food and raw materials would defeat Stalin. His agencies had captured a Russian document listing their casualties by now as 11,200,000 dead, missing, and injured. It seemed well worth fighting on.

Hitler spent February 1943 mending the fences torn by the winter's storms. On Sunday February 7 he invited the Gauleiters to his headquarters and briefed them on the disaster. Herbert Backe dictated this summary to his wife the next day:

> Sunday with the Führer. The Führer spoke. First words were: "What you are witnessing is a catastrophe of unheard-of magnitude. The Russians broke through, the Romanians gave up, the Hungarians didn't even put up a fight, for five days German troops from the rear held the front in a thin line thrown across the breakthrough locations. We've lost four armies in and around Stalingrad." Compares our situation with Kolin and Kunersdorf, says that if Frederick had had weapons like ours, they'd never have called him The Great because

[6]Greiner's war diary note for the OKW was, despite its obvious significance, not included in the text published in 1963.

then his Seven Years' War would have been over in two months. The Führer again praised Speer. . . .

The Führer also said: "If the German people fails, then it does not deserve that we fight for its future; then we can write it off with equanimity." Not the right attitude of mind.

The Gauleiters were satisfied by Hitler's speech. But the damage to the generals' confidence in him was not so easily repaired. It took all his cunning and eloquence to play them off against each other during February, until Manstein's successful spring campaign quieted them again. General Schmundt, whom he had sent on a fact-finding tour of Army Group Don just before Stalingrad fell, must have faithfully reported the ugly mood brewing there—that Manstein, Milch, and Richthofen were unanimous that so long as Hitler directed each battalion in person the army would always lack the rapid, incisive direction from above that it needed for victory; in short, that Hitler should at least appoint a Commander in Chief East. They clearly favored Manstein, but though Hitler accepted him as their greatest military commander when on the offensive, in their present dilemma he felt they needed a tough, tenacious bulldog of a man—though with a flair for improvisation—such as Admiral von Schroeder, the legendary "Lion of Flanders" who had dominated the bloody battlefield in World War I; and Hitler knew of no such general now. In this outlook he was strengthened by Göring—jealous of Manstein's warlord aura—and by Keitel and Jodl too, who had sour memories of Manstein's hostility toward the OKW principle of a unified Wehrmacht command.

Milch, who flew straight in from the Stalingrad front with Hube on February 3, deserved a close hearing, for he had performed consistently well both in expanding aircraft production and in boosting the flagging airlift to Stalingrad. But Hitler fobbed him off until March: admittedly Göring had just bragged that two thousand new aircraft had been manufactured in January, an all-time record. Hitler snubbed Milch: "Let's see if you can keep it up!" Changing the theme of their talk, he stressed the need for the Luftwaffe to mass-produce a cheap, primitive transport plane capable of making the return flight of Africa without refueling. Milch was so severely rebuked for the calamitous record of the Heinkel 177 bomber project that a few days later the field marshal gasped, "I stood in front of the Führer like a very small boy who has not done his sums properly." Manstein and Kluge, summoned to the Wolf's Lair on the sixth, fared no better. No doubt through Göring, Hitler had prior knowledge of Manstein's intention of demanding his resignation as Supreme Commander of the army. Göring evidently advised Manstein against even broaching such heresy. Hitler himself charmed the field marshal with a frank admission that he alone was responsible for Stalingrad—not Göring. "He is the man I have chosen as my successor, and that is why I cannot burden him with the blame for Stalingrad." And after a four-hour display of obstinacy, he flattered Manstein by agreeing to his demand that the eastern Donets region should be abandoned to release the Fourth Panzer Army for the coming German offensive on his army group's western flank. His batteries visibly recharged, the field marshal flew back to the eastern front. Kluge fared no better. Hitler would make no adjustments in his leadership—only in the front line. At long last he bowed to Zeitzler's recommendation that the uneconomical three-hundred-mile-long salient around Rzhev and Vyazma should be abandoned in favor of the far shorter chord-line in the rear; but Kluge had to promise to make the twenty-one divisions thus released available for a great spring offensive. The fighting retreat from Vyazma and Rzhev—code-named "Buffalo"—began in March, the first German tactical triumph of 1943.

The field marshals were putty in Hitler's hands. Once when an English newspaper mentioned one of them as the kingpin of the anti-Hitler movement, he guffawed to his staff: "The British are living in the past if they imagine a field marshal really is something nowadays. The moment he lifts his arm in salute he is just another wretched sausage to me!"

General von Richthofen, the choleric, restless Fourth Air Force commander, was an admirer of Hitler's, but educated and critical. He arrived at the Wolf's Lair with Göring on February 11. A tougher nut to crack, Richthofen refused to allow Hitler to sidetrack him with tactical issues but said bluntly that now that this *Schweinerei* had occurred they must get a grip on the ground organization of the army. Of course they would be short of men as long as divisions twelve thousand-strong still put only six hundred actual combat troops into the line. "The Führer asked me point-blank what I think of Manstein," Richthofen wrote in his diary. "I said he is the best tactician and combat commander we have . . . but that Manstein, like all army commanders, is only really interested in operations and tactics." An iron hand was needed in the rear zones. "I stressed to the Führer that the army commanders were all right . . . but must be given tactical freedom to act as their own local experience dictated. Leading them by the scruff of the neck as though they were children just did harm. The Führer said if he hadn't led them like that they would have been fighting in Germany by now. I flatly contradicted him and said that if he didn't trust his top men, he should replace them. . . . Above all I suggested that it was absolutely essential for him to have personal contact with them. If—and this particularly concerned him as Führer—he couldn't visit the armies for some reason or other I was not aware of, then they must be summoned at least once a month to talk over plans and possibilities with him. . . . The Führer cursed his immediate advisers; he tells them everything but they brief him falsely and do nothing. He took it calmly when I retorted that this wasn't of the slightest importance either to us at the front or to future historians. He alone is answerable. There is no point in cursing anybody."[7] Hitler decided it was time Richthofen was made a field marshal too.

Much of the advice given Hitler did sink in, however. He accepted that 1943 would be a "year of clenched teeth," of strategic defense everywhere until production of Speer's tanks, Milch's aircraft, and Dönitz's U-boats increased. When the Gauleiters mustered at the Wolf's Lair for lunch on February 7, Hitler congratulated Goebbels on the post-Stalingrad propaganda but warned that on no account was the failure of "certain allies" to be revealed as the cause of the three-hundred-mile-wide breach torn in the eastern front. He now unconditionally approved the propaganda minister's oft-stated demand for total war. It was what "the people" wanted. To Hitler the opposition was an infinitesimal, misguided minority that had to be dealt with ruthlessly. When a handful of Munich students scattered mimeographed leaflets calling for Hitler's overthrow, the ringleaders were arrested and—young though they were—condemned to death by the People's Court. "Perhaps there are those who say it is incomprehensible that the People's Court acts so ruthlessly," Hitler thundered in a secret speech to his generals later. "A man who just distributed leaflets—and a senior civil servant at that—is condemned to death; or another, a university professor, and two students, who also distributed leaflets are also executed. But if the professor and students responsible had been at the front, they might be just as dead now, who knows? It's a risk every soldier takes all the time. I took it myself, and if need be today I would do so again. . . . But at a time when I expect young girls at home to buckle on their steel helmets and do their duty under heavy air raids, I will have any person making even the slightest attempt to stab my soldiers in the back stood before the People's Court and liquidated. Let that be known." The generals applauded.

Manstein's newly created Army Group South had its headquarters at Zaporozh'ye on the Dnieper. The huge hydroelectric power station there had just been rebuilt by AEG, a major German electric corporation, and electricity was again flowing to the coal mines and munitions plants of the surrounding Ukraine. Speer had recently shown Hitler the completion dates of his Project Ivan—the rapid expansion of the heavy chemical, nitrogen, and explosives industries of the Donets region. Hitler had anxiously ordered extra antiaircraft batteries and ground

[7]Hitler believed that the failure of the army's organization branch to implement a number of his orders was partly to blame for Stalingrad. (See page 413 in this respect.)

Over lunch, Richthofen observed Hitler's method of dealing with Göring: when the Reichsmarschall raised an unwelcome topic, he began reminiscing about the old Vienna Burg Theater—to which "only Munich's Residenz Theater" was now comparable. (Göring was responsible for actor-director Gustav Gründgens's State Theater and sulked in silence.)

defenses to protect the power station, but unless Manstein's sluggish counteroffensive in the Ukraine gathered momentum, it was clear that the whole region would soon be overrun. To the consternation of Hitler's staff, Zeitzler suggested Hitler should fly out to Zaporozh'ye in person. Göring indignantly objected, as did Keitel, to the risk; but Zeitzler sardonically pointed out: "The Reichsmarschall will be able to darken the skies with fighter squadrons. There's no risk!" Hitler did not agree with this estimate of the situation, but that night his staff stenographer wrote in his diary: "At this evening's conference the Führer announced his decision to go to the front and take over command of Army Group South; this means breaking camp here."

The next day, February 16, Bormann explained in a letter: "Our southern sector is by no means a 'front' even now. Over vast areas we have just a void. To master this extremely tricky and dangerous situation the Führer . . . is going to fly out there with a small escort of intimates." Hitler in fact decided to take just Zeitzler and Jodl—to whom he had once again extended his hand on January 30—with him, together with Schmundt, Hewel, and Dr. Morell. Keitel, Bormann, and the other adjutants stayed behind at the Wolf's Lair. Puttkamer was sent ahead to open up Werewolf, the old summer HQ in the Ukraine. The long flight south began as soon as it was light on February 17, 1943.

"By afternoon the Führer's bunker was deserted," wrote a newly arrived private secretary. "It was strange, the hush that suddenly descended on the whole compound. It was as if the main dynamo of the concern had stopped. This was the first time I sensed how much Hitler's personality acted as a mainspring for all these men—the puppet-master, who held all the marionettes' strings in his hands, had suddenly let them fall."

No secret was made of Hitler's arrival at Manstein's Zaporozh'ye headquarters. Field Marshal von Richthofen arrived shortly, driving a Volkswagen. "There were cordons everywhere," he wrote in his diary. "Everybody that I asked in the streets where army group HQ was smiled scornfully, 'You won't get near it—the Führer's there!' . . . Found the Führer in thick of big war conference. I reported to him. Much beating about the bush, no real opinions, mutual tension, an atmosphere you could cut with a knife. Führer then withdrew to his quarters without reaching any decisions. . . . I saw Field Marshal von Manstein, who shares my view on situation and intentions.—Manstein against all innovations: systems of government, personalities, Luftwaffe devices, and anything else he didn't learn in his youth. . . . Führer very pleasant to me, placid, clear-thinking: question is, has he the necessary implements and ability to convert his clear thoughts into orders?" Hitler directed the Luftwaffe to concentrate on a few hot-spots in the coming offensives. Richthofen and General Otto Dessloch, a local Luftwaffe commander, arranged for two hundred antiaircraft guns to be arrayed as a last-ditch defense against the unceasing Russian tank onslaught, with orders to fight to the last shell.

The next evening, February 18, German radio broadcast throughout occupied Europe Goebbels's defiant Sportpalast speech, whipping his vast audience of Berliners—everybody from the government to the munitions workers—into a frenzy with his proclamation of total war. Now every able-bodied person in the Reich would be harnessed to the war machine; no pleas for exemption would be heeded. Hitler, too busy to listen in person, thoroughly endorsed the extracts he had read. Next morning he himself addressed an effective proclamation to Manstein's and Richthofen's troops on the eve of their counteroffensive between the Dnieper and Donets rivers, on which so much depended:

> Soldiers of Army Group South, airmen of the Fourth Air Force! The outcome of a crucial battle depends on you! A thousand kilometers away from the Reich's frontiers the fate of Germany's present and future is in the balance. . . . The entire German homeland has been mobilized. Everybody down to the last man and woman is being called to serve your battle's needs. Our youth are manning the antiaircraft defenses around Germany's cities and workplaces. More and more divisions are on their way. Weapons unique and hitherto unknown are on the way to your front. . . . This is why I have flown to you, to exhaust every means of alleviating your defensive battle and to convert it into ultimate victory. If every one of you will help, we shall once again succeed, with the Almighty's aid.

At noon Hitler called a further war conference. It was obvious that Manstein and Kleist could not stand each other. Richthofen wrote: "Each is always trying to score over the other in the Führer's eyes. After a final summing up and after due deliberation, the Führer announced in favor of Kleist. Everybody grinning except Manstein, who was furious." By this time Russian tanks were approaching Zaporozh'ye; there was nothing between them and the Luftwaffe airfields. Hitler was loath to leave, but valued his person too highly to stay too long. Richthofen privately suggested that it would make a bad impression if the Führer had to make a hasty exit under the Russian guns, and when Hitler mentioned that he had ordered General Guderian to meet him soon at Vinnitsa—he had given in to Schmundt's badgering and decided to make the truculent general his inspector of panzer troops—Richthofen recommended that Hitler immediately fly there for a couple of days and return to Zaporozh'ye if the Russian threat was thwarted. It was a diplomatic solution.

The gunfire of the Russian tanks was audible from the airfield. Hitler took off for Werewolf immediately. However, in Warlimont's opinion the Führer's presence at the front was certainly to contribute to the great success of the German offensive that now followed.[8] The First and Fourth panzer armies struck northward on February 22, destroying, encircling, and capturing the enemy units in

[8]Warlimont confidentially made this observation in a 1945 study for the Americans. In his published work *Im Hauptquartier der Wehrmacht,* page 328, he adopted the more fashionable opposite view.

their path. A bridgehead was soon thrown across the Donets at Balakleya, and by early March a fourth battle for Kharkov was about to begin. The Führer's confidence in Manstein was restored—he was heard to comment privately in admiring language on both the field marshal and General Zeitzler. At last the huge breach wrought that winter in the Axis lines had been plugged; the eastern front had been stabilized—now Hitler could turn his attention to his other affairs of state.

Strychnine

Until mid-March 1943 Hitler remained in the Ukraine, seven hundred miles from Berlin. Werewolf in winter was a bleak and dreary site. Battle-scarred aircraft stood around the local airfield; the countryside was neglected; impoverished Ukrainian peasants with starving horses trudged the fields and forests collecting wood to warm their wretched hovels. The thaw was coming—blessed by the soldiers for the respite it afforded, but turning field and road alike into the now familiar bottomless muddy swamps.

In the bare wooden hutments Hitler contracted first influenza and then a more serious complaint which Morell diagnosed as a brain inflammation; according to medical authorities, this could have resulted from the severe mental strain of Stalingrad, and normally several weeks of rest would have been imperative. Hitler could not afford the time. Soon he was experiencing splitting headaches on one side, and one arm developed a tremor to which he drew Morell's attention; Morell suspected it was of hysterical origin, and he noticed Hitler was dragging one leg slightly too. Hitler sat in his badly ventilated quarters, brooding and worrying; his staff were anxious about his lack of exercise. He was seized by moods of black depression, which Morell tried to combat with injections of Prostakrinum hormones (an extract of young bulls' seminal vesicles and prostate) every other day. As the daily appointment book maintained by his SS orderlies clearly establishes, from now on Morell was nearly always the first visitor to Hitler after his private staff had awakened him each morning. He could not sleep without sedatives; for a time he tried to induce sleep by secretly drinking a glass or two of beer, but fearing fatness even more than insomnia, he soon stopped.

Stalingrad had left deep scars within him. Outwardly he was callous, ordering a new Sixth Army created forthwith and obliterating all trace of the old. But he also ordered Schmundt to arrange for the most generous provision for the next-of-kin. The most delicate problem was raised by the letters the survivors were now writing from Soviet captivity—and indeed by the "last letters" that the Luftwaffe had flown out of the "fortress" itself. The latter were duly delivered, but not those from the Soviet prison camps. Of 1,900 letters that had arrived by mid-February only 45 slipped through to contaminate the German public's already frail belief in ultimate victory. Hitler's rationalization for ordering the letters to be intercepted was that few of the letter-writers were still alive. Why rouse false hopes among their families? and why afford Stalin gratuitous support for his propaganda tactics? Thus the letters were destroyed, adding to the guilty pressure on Hitler's mind. Guderian, who had not seen him since December 1941, found a changed man at Vinnitsa on February 21, 1943. "His left hand trembled, his back was bent, his gaze was fixed, his eyes protruded but lacked their former luster, his cheeks were flecked with red. He was more excitable, easily lost his composure, and was prone to angry outbursts and ill-considered decisions in consequence." For this, however, his self-medication bore much blame.

Even deeper were the scars that had been left in the Axis alliances and within the Axis itself—symbolized at their ugliest by the hand grenade tossed with fatal consequences at a German panzer general as he drove past a surly column of Italian troops marching back from the southern sector of the eastern front. These rifts tested Hitler's diplomacy to the utmost. His immediate reaction had been to "hand back the Eighth Army" to Italy and "write off" the Romanians altogether. But he learned to stifle his anger at these fitful allies. "I never want to see another soldier of our allies on the eastern front," he growled in private to Goebbels. "We can only finish off the Bolsheviks with our own soldiers—and particularly the SS." When Mussolini offered another seven hundred thousand men, Hitler disdainfully commented that there was no point in equipping them with scarce German arms which they would surrender at the first opportunity. "They can't even be assigned 'defensive' combat duties." The Italian Eighth Army, which had gone to battle with a truly splendid artillery, had proved to be incapable from the head down.

Yet when he learned in February that the bedraggled remnants of the Hungarian, Romanian, and Italian armies were being insulted and reviled, and that the Italian ambassador had complained that German units had refused any succour to the unarmed, dispirited, and hungry retreating troops, Hitler piously reminded his generals of the need for common decency and cameraderie—besides which the Reich had a powerful interest in preventing their total disintegration. In an internal policy conference with Keitel and court historian Scherff on May 31, Hitler ruled against any overall communiqué on the winter campaign. "He particularly stressed," wrote Scherff, "that the Stalingrad operation cannot be depicted without passing judgment on our allies. However, for political reasons this historical fact would have to be stood on its head, and then our allies would be able to use this in their favor later on."

Hitler's respect for the Romanian contingent was less affected by their defeat; some of their generals had fought with great distinction, and he was pleased that Antonescu permitted eight divisions to remain in the Crimea and the bridgehead across the Kerch strait. But Hungary's attitude was more ambivalent. On January 22 Germany had invited both her and Italy to withdraw their armies from the eastern front. Hungary had, it must be said, suffered the bloodiest casualties, for her army was less than four years old; 80,000 Hungarian soldiers were dead or missing since the January 12 offensive, and another 63,000 had been injured. Hitler had at once ordered the Reich air ministry to increase its industrial and antiaircraft support for Hungary. Though the murmurs of Magyar discontent grew menacing and insistent, Horthy's military remained largely loyal to the Axis cause. The Second Army's commander, General von Jány, rebuked his men with a famous document (of which Himmler's agents later obtained a photocopy for Hitler), beginning: "The Hungarian Second Army has lost its honor, for only a few men did the duty that was expected of them under their oath. . . ." And General Szombathelyi, the Chief of Staff, accepted Hitler's suggestion that the Hungarian army's new purpose should be to defend the Balkans from Anglo-American invasion.

But though Horthy's generals seemed loyal, his diplomats were more devious. The Forschungsamt and Ribbentrop's cryptographers decoded foreign radio messages that established beyond doubt that the Hungarian prime minister, Miklas von Kállay, was attempting through intermediaries in Turkey, Switzerland, and the Vatican to open secret negotiations with Britain and the United States, and that Kállay had eagerly grasped at Churchill's bumbling proposal to the Turkish government for a new Balkan League (consisting of Turkey, Hungary, and Romania) aligned against both the Soviet Union and the Axis powers. Himmler's agents had obtained word of Kállay's recent secret speech to the foreign policy committee of his Parliament, a speech which proved that he was not to be trusted. Impregnable though Crete now was, Hitler feared that the enemy might land somewhere in the Balkans that spring. He decided personal pressure must be brought to bear on Horthy to rid himself of Kállay and his dangerous doctrines.

So effective was the smokescreen of spurious Intelligence being laid down before both Canaris's Abwehr and Himmler's agencies that Hitler had only his vaunted strategic intuition to rely on in guessing where the war in the Mediterranean would turn next. Spain and Portugal were particularly vulnerable targets; their occupation would prevent Hitler from seizing Gibraltar, impede his U-boat offensive in the Atlantic, and deprive him of their iron, tungsten, lithium, and tin. Canaris was twice sent to Madrid but reported unenthusiastically. Spain neither could nor would voluntarily enter the war unless her neutrality were directly threatened. Hitler decided to furnish Franco with the weapons he would need. He may also have been the source of Franco's information that in August 1942 Churchill had "promised Russia predominant influence in Europe east of the Rhine."[1] On January 16 Himmler's report on an agent's long confidential talk with Franco was in Hitler's hands, and it showed how worried Franco was about both the bolshevik peril looming over Europe and the hardly less disconcerting shadow of American imperialism over North Africa. Conversely, there was also evidence that Churchill had secretly promised Franco a slice of French Morocco.

By February it seemed clear that the British and Americans were in fact massing strength near the border of Spanish Morocco, even at the expense of their front in Tunisia. Through Stockholm came fresh agents' warnings of an early invasion of the Iberian peninsula. Canaris went to Hitler's headquarters on the ninth and tried to kill these rumors, but Hitler ordered divisions moved up to the Spanish frontier ready for an immediate occupation of northern Spain should an enemy invasion occur. At a war conference on the tenth he predicted that it would be coupled with simultaneous invasions of the Channel and Atlantic coastlines, where his Atlantic Wall was still some months short of completion. He warned the defenses to stand by for possible mass parachute landings in the rear. A naval participant wrote after the conference: "As to Spain's attitude, the Führer's mind was suddenly completely at ease. He had certain information, I don't know where from. At any rate he said everything had been cleared up to our satisfaction." Hitler and Göring positively exuded optimism that Spain would now fight to defend herself, but Richthofen, meeting them the next day, was less sure. "I said we shouldn't expect any gratitude for the help we rendered from 1936 to 1939. The Spanish always only think of Spain; they are utterly selfish—which is natural enough—and they regard us as God-damned heretics." What Hitler and Göring knew was that one of the war's most secret treaties had just been signed in Madrid: in return for modern German weapons in sufficient quantities, Franco now committed his country in writing to fighting the British and Americans the moment they set foot in Spain, Portugal, or any Spanish possessions in the Mediterranean, Atlantic, and Africa.

The enemy might equally well exploit the partisan chaos in the Balkans; an Allied invasion there would bring the Romanian oil fields within bomber reach. Despite

[1]On January 19, 1943, Franco warned Churchill in a secret message that "the longer the war goes on, the more Britain will be obliterated by her Allies—Russia and the United States." He advised Britain to negotiate with non-Nazi elements in Germany while there was still time. Churchill did not welcome Franco's message, though the Caudillo's claim to have seen detailed accounts of his talks in Moscow may have roused his curiosity.

the mounting bomber offensive against Germany, Hitler therefore ordered fresh antiaircraft defenses supplied to Romania. He arranged for Bulgarians in German uniforms to police the more restless areas of Greece. He eloquently directed his military commander in the southeast, General Löhr, to restore peace there—"the peace of the graveyard, if need be."

In Croatia as elsewhere Italy was at the root of Hitler's troubles. General Roatta's Second Army had persistently pursued policies dramatically athwart both Hitler's and Mussolini's. When Tito's partisan forces had become too powerful, the Italians had merely ignored Germany's protests and abandoned territory wholesale. Roatta had continued to arm the Četnik (Serbian) irregulars against the partisans even though many a Četnik bullet now winged toward a German or Croatian soldier. Though in December Ciano had unenthusiastically agreed to Hitler's demand that the Četniks be disarmed, the army ignored Mussolini's directive to that effect. Soon the vital bauxite mines of Mostar were abandoned to the partisans. Every joint Italian-German sweep against them failed, the Germans felt, because of Italian sloth and ineptitude. Tito escaped time after time, until gradually Hitler came to extend to him an admiration he had previously reserved for Stalin. Late in February, he sent Ribbentrop to Rome with a strongly worded letter demanding more active Italian support, particularly against the Četniks; he furnished dozens of radio messages intercepted and decoded by his agencies, proving beyond doubt that the Četnik irregulars were fighting for General Draža Mihajlovič and thus for London. But while the Duce was willing to accept German demands, his soldiers were not. The new Chief of Staff, General Ambrosio, furnished various excuses for not proceeding against Mihajlovič: for example, the Italian troops were needed for the defense of Italy. Löhr came to Vinnitsa and asked for a saturation air raid on Mihajlovič's headquarters at Collasin in Montenegro, and he proposed pacifying Croatia by installing at every level a German civil administration backed by local gendarmes to be supplied by Himmler. Hitler's patience with the Italians was exhausted; he ordered Mostar and the bauxite mines recaptured, and he began planning a short, sharp war of annihilation against Mihajlovič and the Četniks. "On account of the intimate relations between the Mihajlovič commanders and the Italian authorities, the Führer attaches particular importance to camouflaging our object and all the preparations." But not until mid-May would this operation, code-named "Black," begin.

If it were not for the political effect the loss of Tunisia would have had on Italy, Hitler would have long since withdrawn his divisions there and made more profitable use of them—just as Mussolini had urgently requested the repatriation of 290,000 Italian workers in Germany. His own interest in this distant desert war was negligible. He considered that Rommel had missed his chance, a view shared by Kesselring and Göring. "Without optimism, military command is impossible," Hitler meditated afterward. "I see Rommel—though he has limitations—as an extraordinarily bold and clever commander, but he lacks staying power; everybody thinks so." Given the Italian inability to protect supply ships—during January alone 22 out of 51 had been sunk—it was obvious the holding action in Tunisia would not last much longer.

In Tunisia Rommel was a sick man, and his future was uncertain. But General von Arnim's Fifth Panzer Army, facing westward, was in better shape. Warlimont returned from Tunis in mid-February quoting Rommel's description of the bridgehead as a "house of cards" which would collapse the moment Montgomery attacked—presumably one month hence, when the moon was full. Ominously, the Allies had a new 57-millimeter shell capable of piercing the Tiger tank, the pride of Hitler's armor.[2] But Arnim detected a weak spot facing him, the American Second Corps; on February 14 General Heinz Ziegler struck at these inexperienced soldiers and drove a big salient toward the vital Kasserine Pass, taking hundreds of American prisoners. German interrogators claimed that a surprising number of Americans were ex-convicts, adventurers, and mercenaries. "Politically speaking they are naïve," remarked Hewel to Hitler. "They are rowdies who take to their heels rather than stand fast at a crisis. . . . You really ought to see their war posters, quite incredible."—"I don't doubt," replied Hitler, "that of the Anglo-Saxons the British are the best." But the German offensive failed, and Canaris quoted Arnim as saying, "With the supply position as it is" —twenty-five thousand tons instead of the requisite eighty thousand tons had arrived in February—"you can work out with pencil and paper when the end will come." Canaris reported that nobody knew whether Kesselring or Rommel was in overall command of the newly created Army Group Africa.

Exactly why Rommel was given the army group, and not Arnim as had been planned, is not evident from the records. A specialist had checked Rommel's health and reported to Hitler that he would have to go on leave by February 20 at the latest; but the moment he was given the army group, with one German and one Italian army to defend Tunis, his illness mysteriously cleared up. Rommel was also cheered by word from Schmundt that the Führer was deeply concerned about him; Hitler evidently hoped that if properly pepped up, this petulant commander would put his heart into the final decisive strike at Montgomery's Eighth Army before departing for his convalescent leave. But Rommel did not gain heart. He took counsel of his two army commanders, Arnim and Messe, and on March 4 Hitler was handed his discouraging opinion: the present Tunis

[2]The Tiger was still having teething troubles. Hitler jealously called for details of the training of every Tiger tank crew whose tank was knocked out in Africa. The results were embarrassing for the army. Himmler hastily ordered that only the best crews were to man the Tigers allocated to the SS panzer corps.

battlefront was over 400 miles long, the enemy had 1,600 tanks, 1,100 antitank guns, and about 210,000 combat troops; unless Hitler would authorize Rommel to withdraw to a far shorter front, of about 100 miles, the two armies under his command would be overwhelmed. Not without justification Hitler noted: "That is a complete contradiction of his earlier contention"—namely that a retreat to Tunisia would solve their strategic shortcomings. Jodl pointed out that Rommel's plan would make a gift of vital airfields to the enemy and allow Montgomery and Alexander to join forces against the bridgehead. With 140,000 German troops alone, Rommel was not numerically all that inferior to the enemy. Hitler refused to allow the withdrawal. "This is the end," he predicted nonetheless. "They might just as well be brought back."

Hitler particularly wanted the final enemy offensive fought off long enough for the rest of the German divisions to arrive and the mass production of small transport ships to take effect. "On superior orders," as Rommel querulously wrote, he launched his last attack on March 6, on Montgomery. But that same day he returned to the line fortified at Mareth, outfought and outgunned by the British army. As Hitler had predicted, it was the end. From all appearances—arranged by the British secret service, which had read Rommel's cipher telegrams—captured Italian officers had betrayed Rommel's plans to Montgomery, so Hitler did not reproach him. He decided on the eighth to recall "the Desert Fox" before he could be tarnished by the eventual defeat in Tunis; for the time being, however, Rommel's recall remained a closely guarded secret—the *reputation* of Rommel would soldier on, *in absentia.*

He flew into Vinnitsa late on March 9 and spent the evening alone with Hitler. Again Hitler turned a deaf ear on the idea of shortening the bridgehead's battlefront; he betrayed his obvious conviction that Rommel had become a defeatist. Hitler intended to retain Tunis at all costs: he would increase the supply rate to 150,000 tons a month, he said, and when Rommel's health was better he was to return to Africa and direct the offensive westward to Casablanca. The next day Reichsmarschall Göring, summoned by Hitler, arrived in his special train from Rome and eagerly lent his not inconsiderable weight to Hitler's optimism—as did Kesselring on the fourteenth. Kesselring and Dönitz were flown immediately to Rome to put pressure on the Italians to increase the rate of supply across the Strait of Sicily. Dönitz was instructed not to mince words with the Duce; and Kesselring was to hand Mussolini a stinging written reproach by Hitler on the supply problem. It read in part:

> . . . for whatever posterity may think of Field Marshal Rommel, he has been well loved by his troops and of course by all the German troops in every one of his commands. To his enemies he was a feared opponent, and still is. It is

a tragedy that this man, one of my most courageous officers and distinguished by exceptional capability, should have come to grief on the problem of logistics —a problem which can only be solved by stepping up the sea transports to a maximum.

To Rommel, the "has-been," Hitler secretly awarded the diamonds for his Knight's Cross; the Italians refused to emulate this distinction.

Göring's prestige was plummeting with every fresh ruinous air attack on Germany's proud and ancient cities. That was why Hitler had rudely ordered his return from Rome. On March 1 hundreds of night bombers had rained high explosives and incendiaries on Berlin, leaving thirty-five thousand people homeless and over seven hundred dead. Hitler's doctors and staff reported that far into the nights that followed, he was troubled by anguished images of humble Berlin families who had lost not only their homes but two or three children before their eyes as well. The finest fighter aircraft or antiaircraft defenses were of no avail against bomber hordes like these! Only counterterror would deter the British! But Field Marshal Sperrle's emasculated Third Air Force could stage only the weakest retaliatory raids, and London barely noticed them. "The British write that our latest raid was a mere phantom," fumed Göring to his staff, "and that the lot fell in open countryside. It drives you mad! Bombing through dense cloud, *they* can hit an egg in a railroad station—yet our fellows can't even find London." A low-level Luftwaffe fighter-bomber attack on London on March 5 had been scrubbed, as Hitler was apologetically told, because of fog and the "dead calm sea"—evoking Hitler's natural astonished query: "Do our planes *swim* over, then?" (In fact without visible waves to guide them the low-flying pilots *were* in danger of crashing.) Hitler blamed the indolent and sybaritic Sperrle and called for a younger man to direct the attack on Britain. "When does the Reichsmarschall get back?" he had demanded. "Things can't go on like this; we will never wear down the British like this."

That night, March 5, a crippling attack was made on Essen, heart of the Ruhr's steel industry, destroying three thousand houses and buildings and killing hundreds of workers. When Goebbels arrived on March 8 with Speer, Hitler was still furiously inveighing against the complete failure of the Luftwaffe in comparison to the army now that Zeitzler was in charge. Göring was less to blame than the mendacious and incompetent generals around him, said Hitler, but the next six months might see many of their cities in ruins and thousands of civilians dead. Toward midnight, sitting in his bunker with Speer and Goebbels, Hitler was just saying sourly that he only had to picture his generals in mufti to lose every shred of respect for them when he heard that a colossal air raid had just been launched against Nuremberg—the medieval gem of Bavaria and seat of the Party's affairs.

Hitler had General Bodenschatz, Göring's cynical lieutenant, roused from his sleep, and rasped that the Reichsmarschall must return from Rome forthwith.

Hoping to preserve him as the vehicle of their political ambitions, Speer and Goebbels both defended Göring that night; this alone had warded off Hitler's wrath, for he had hinted to Bodenschatz that he might even assume overall command of the Luftwaffe himself. How many orders he had given the Luftwaffe both before 1939 and after—and how few had been carried out! "The generals always knew better than I; now the German public is paying the price." Göring —when he arrived on the eleventh—gratefully adopted the same line. "I told the Führer I am not an aircraft designer or technician, so I can't build the planes myself, nor can I develop new engines or equipment," he said a week later. His generals and experts had always bluffed him; his radar specialists had even excused their inability to test blind-bombing devices by pleading bad weather. Over the next nights Munich and Stuttgart were the bombers' targets. Now Hitler overrode Göring; he ordered the air war against Britain stepped up, and he appointed the youthful Colonel Dietrich Peltz "Attack Commander, England" —responsible not to the sluggish Sperrle but to Jeschonnek (and hence to Hitler) alone.

A naïve plan by Goebbels, Speer, and a handful of their disgruntled contemporaries to use Göring and his Reich Defense Committee as a front whereby they could divert absolute power from Lammers, Keitel, and Bormann to themselves was temporarily placed in limbo.

Hitler flew for the morning of March 10 to Manstein's headquarters at Zaporozh'ye, for he was well satisfied with events on the southern front. His high hopes in the SS panzer divisions had proven justified. Here he awarded Manstein the Oak Leaf Cluster for his Knight's Cross in recognition of his achievements. Manstein's two panzer armies had left 23,000 Russian dead on the first battlefield between the Donets and Dnieper rivers; 615 tanks, 354 guns, and enormous quantities of other equipment had fallen into his hands. Thereupon, an offensive against Stalin's Voronezh army group had resulted in the destruction of the enemy's Third Tank Army southwest of Kharkov. In this operation, some 12,000 of the enemy were killed. Now Manstein's Fourth Panzer Army, with its powerful SS panzer corps, was embarking upon the fifth battle fought over Kharkov since "Barbarossa" began. Meanwhile Hitler had issued detailed orders for defensive lines to be excavated and built everywhere to the rear of the eastern front. To do this, he made ruthless use of forced labor, just as the Russians had in similar circumstances.

Thus the mood at Zaporozh'ye was one of elation, for the generals' morale was again high. Richthofen noted:

> The Führer lands at 10:40 A.M. Manstein and I drive in Führer's car to army group HQ, with Führer in pretty good mettle. Fiebig at last gets the Oak Leaves.—Every army commander from both army groups and my own [Luftwaffe] corps commanders present. Army commanders deliver briefings on their situation, which tell me nothing new. Then the Führer on the coming operations and Manstein on his own intentions; nothing new either. . . . Manstein keeps up a hate campaign against Kleist [commander of Army Group A] the whole time, and Führer prompts Manstein to make hostile comments about Kleist and Kluge, his two neighbors. Führer enjoying every minute. Ribs me mercilessly but kindly; for some reason addresses everybody as "Herr Feldmarschall" today as a joke. . . . Says he never wants to hear of the Romanians or our other gallant allies again: if he relies on them he only gets worked up because they don't stand firm; and if he arms them but *doesn't* use them, he gets just as worked up to see them standing around doing nothing.

The snows were melting, turning the eastern front into its seasonal morass. The three-hundred-mile nightmare breach had almost been stitched together, proof in Hitler's eyes that the Red Army had no reserves up its sleeve after all. Already the Russians were drafting their seventeen-year-olds; perhaps the great collapse was in sight at last. Admittedly the eight-hundred-thousand-man call-up he had himself projected was proceeding less smoothly than he had hoped, and a new Russian thrust between the Second Panzer and Second Armies at Kursk and Orel was still causing concern. But in the south the recapture of Kharkov was now certain. And west of Moscow "Operation Buffalo"—the careful withdrawal of two armies to a well-fortified new line between Spass Demensk and Byelyi—was drawing to its brilliant conclusion. The Red Army, puzzled at this uncharacteristic retreat, had followed only hesitantly, stumbled upon well-laid minefields and booby-traps, and suffered heavy casualties at no cost to the Germans. The retiring Germans had destroyed or dismantled everything of value to the enemy. "A battle won," concluded Kluge's army group.

On March 13, Hitler flew back from Vinnitsa to the Wolf's Lair, calling first that afternoon at Smolensk, headquarters for Kluge's Army Group Center. Three days before, on March 10, Himmler had telephoned to Hitler's police bodyguard a warning to be on the lookout for parcel bombs.[3] Hitler showed no concern. He

[3]In fact Kluge's Intelligence officer, Colonel Rudolf von Gersdorff, and others claimed after the war that they planted a parcel bomb in Hitler's aircraft before it left Smolensk on March 13, 1943. (If they did, it failed to go off.) Admiral Canaris, one of the plotters, wrote in his own notes of the flight he made to Smolensk on March 8: "I conveyed time fuses and explosives in my plane to the Army Group's Abwehr II sabotage unit." Since Canaris dined for two hours with Himmler on March 10, shortly *before* Himmler put through his telephone warning to Hitler's police bodyguard, it is tempting to assume that Canaris made an incautious remark to him about the bomb plot; but Himmler's files show that since March 3 parcel bombs posted by the Polish underground were causing some concern, and his phone call to SS Brigadeführer Hans Rattenhuber, chief of Hitler's bodyguard, was probably

was inspired by the buoyant mood of Kluge's officers at Smolensk. They were delighted at the tactical victory of the Fourth and Ninth armies, which had succeeded beyond all their expectations in disengaging from the enemy and withdrawing without any loss of men or equipment, while at the same time carrying out extensive demolitions in their wake. Initially the Russians had whipped their armies into hot pursuit—with consequent heavy casualties in the intricate and well-planned minefields the Germans had laid. The Russians captured only their own wrecked equipment. The new "Buffalo" line was already built—a formidable line of barbed wire entanglements, bunkers, and antitank ditches. When Kluge asked if the objective of their coming summer campaign could be disclosed to them, Hitler astonished both Kluge and his staff with its modesty: "To hold the eastern front just as it is." That evening he was back in East Prussia.

Yet the prospect of a year on the defensive galled him. "I can't just let a whole year go to waste," he said. All the indications were that the Soviet Union might yet be about to collapse. Zeitzler agreed; the new East Wall was all very well, but "they will flatten us first, before we can finish it." Hitler responded, "They are in such a state now that we would be lunatic not to exploit it." The fragmentary records of his war conferences reveal him already plotting with Zeitzler a partial resumption of the offensive in order to regain the initiative in the central front. Zeitzler hinted at April 15 as a suitable date, though Manstein thought that too early. "One thing we must *not* say," insisted the Führer, "is—this year just a few prods at the enemy, next year the Big Push. Perhaps *this* year we can win the war!" Before March 13 was over Hitler had signed Zeitzler's order laying the foundations of "Citadel," a combined attack by Kluge's and Manstein's army groups on a tempting enemy salient at Kursk.

The next day Sepp Dietrich's SS troops retook Kharkov. Hitler exuberantly telephoned Goebbels, but the canny propaganda minister was against any special radio fanfare—it would undermine the very "Dunkirk spirit" he had labored to contrive in Germany. Hitler, however, wanted the gallantry of his SS Life Guards properly recognized, and insisted; half an hour later he heard the announcement on the radio, though preceded by the less pompous Horst Wessel fanfare this time rather than the one from Liszt's *Préludes.*

That evening Goebbels appealed to be allowed to revive the anti-Jewish propaganda motif and pestered him to complete displacing Jews from the entire Reich

---

just a reprimand for not having issued warnings to the Reich ministries yet. A remarkable coincidence nonetheless.

as soon as possible. Hitler indulgently agreed that Goebbels could go ahead, but when Himmler himself arrived at the Wolf's Lair on the seventeenth, with the creation of fresh SS corps and divisions on his agenda, the Führer apparently felt it necessary to speak a word of restraint, for the next day Himmler telephoned Gestapo Chief Müller in Berlin that there was to be "no deportation of the privileged Jews*" from France. Again it does not behoove the historian to speculate or embroider on the precise significance of the words employed.

For the first time in six years, Hitler's stomach spasms had begun to recur. The doctors advised him to retire for a week or two to the Obersalzberg. With the eastern front now paralyzed by the thaw, Hitler bowed to their advice. Besides, he wanted to speak in Berlin on March 21, Memorial Sunday, to kill the persistent rumors that he was gravely ill; and at the Berghof he would be closer to the Mediterranean theater. While the invasion of Spain and Portugal predicted by Jodl for February 22 had failed to materialize, Admiral Canaris had twice warned that the enemy would occupy Sicily, Sardinia, and Corsica during March, and Zeitzler's Intelligence officers agreed. (Thus convincingly had they been hoaxed by the Allies.) In Tunis, General Montgomery had just begun the offensive against the Mareth line. It seemed high time for Hitler to meet the Duce—and his other coalition partners too.

He had himself lighted on a cure for his stomach pangs. In 1936 his SS doctor, SS General Dr. Ernst-Robert Grawitz, had prescribed "Dr. Koester's Antigas Tablets," a German patent medicine, for his tender gastrointestinal tract, and at his request Dr. Morell supplied several gross of these. Hitler was relieved to experience the same well-being these apparently harmless black pills had given him six years earlier and began to consume them regularly—from eight to sixteen every day—until an appalled visiting doctor examined them in October 1944 and read the legend on the small flat aluminum tin: "Extr.nux.vomic. 0.04; Extr. bellad. 0.04." The doctor then announced that they were principally based on the poisons strychnine and atropine, and that Hitler had from time to time been imbibing nearly lethal doses. Only then were relevant entries in the poisons manual read out to a chastened Führer. "Atropine acts on the central nervous system first as a stimulant, then as a paralyzer. In humans it primarily affects the forebrain, manifesting itself in a state of psychic exaltation. A state of cheerfulness develops, coupled with vivid flights of ideas, talkativeness, and restlessness, visual and aural hallucinations, and fits of delirium which may be peaceful and serene but may equally degenerate into acts of violence and frenzy." Strychnine, on the

*Those with influence in the United States. See page 462.

other hand, accumulated in the body, acting on the nervous system to increase all the senses' acuteness. "After heavy doses the accentuated sensitiveness to light may turn into downright aversion to light; and the other senses show similar changes. The senses of hearing and touch are accentuated, and for a time the senses of smell and taste may become more acute." So dramatically could strychnine amplify the reactions of the nervous system that lockjaw could result from a normally harmless stimulus. The significance of Hitler's self-medication beginning in the spring of 1943 should not be scanted.

Thus Hitler left the Wolf's Lair, though for many weeks longer than he originally planned. His car brought him to the local railroad station, where his special train was waiting, and as soon as he, his servants, and his Alsatian bitch Blondi were aboard it began to move. His compartments were of a luxury strange to him after the strenuous bunker life of Rastenburg—there were silken sheets for all his staff, highly polished woodwork and brass lamps, and a soft carpet on the floor. Surrounded by his private staff, he took dinner in the dining car with its red-leather-covered chairs. At his command the three secretaries joined him—Johanna Wolf, the most senior and self-effacing; the forthright Christa Schroeder, who had served her apprenticeship with Bormann; and Traudl Humps, the newcomer. Schaub, Hewel, Bormann, and Morell sat in as well—the portly doctor wading into the meal with an appetite that was as audible as it was evident. Hitler contented himself with mashed potato, an egg, and a dry biscuit.

Traudl Humps later wrote: "I was taken aback by the informal nature of the conversation. Bormann above all was gentle and friendly. . . . The Führer spoke softly and with restraint. After the meal he asked for the ceiling lights to be switched off. He preferred subdued light as his eyes were rather sensitive." A pot of caraway tea was served. "Delicious," exclaimed Hitler, but nobody accepted his offer of a cup. At intervals the train halted, and telephone messages were received. Hitler summoned a manservant: "Take Blondi for a walk outside." Then the train began again, the dining car gently swaying, Morell snoring lightly, and the one small table lamp casting a dim glow.

At Rügenwalde in Pomerania the next morning he stayed for a few hours to inspect Krupp's new giant gun, "Long Gustav," and various new tank prototypes undergoing trials on the ranges. Here at last was the new Ferdinand tank, a seventy-ton monster powered by two diesel-electric sets, all but impregnable with its eight-inch-thick armorplate and formidable 88-millimeter gun. These and the Tigers would surely overwhelm the Russians when "Citadel" began. Speer and his dynamic Nazi deputy Karl-Otto Saur boarded the train for an informal conference on the new weapons programs, as it continued toward Berlin. Hitler was undaunted by the prevailing fear of Russian "armies" that were a mere shadow of their name. "I am convinced the rogues are so weak . . ." the stenographers heard him say; and "All they have against us are 'formations,' but . . ." (The fragments alone exist, but they seem clear enough.) He invited Speer and Goebbels to dinner in the Chancellery, showed them the damage survey of Munich after the last British air raid, and mentioned the high hopes he vested in Dönitz's U-boat war. Goebbels recommended that the Luftwaffe bomb London's plutocratic districts rather than the slums. When he channeled the conversation around to the Jews, Hitler congratulated him on having evacuated most of them from Berlin. "The war is enabling us to deal with a whole series of problems we could never have dealt with in normal times," Goebbels quoted him as saying. Yet Hitler obviously found the propaganda minister's company distasteful, for he refused to make time available for a further private meeting with him until May. Thus far had Martin Bormann's influence over Hitler progressed.

Half an hour after midnight on March 22 his train left Berlin for Munich. He spent the day with Frau Troost, lunched in the Osteria, and looked at the latest paintings. That evening Eva Braun joined the train for the short journey to Berchtesgaden; a long column of Mercedes cars brought them up the mountain to where the Berghof lay, its Great Hall window palely reflecting the moonlight and the snow; Frau Mittelstrasser, the housekeeper, welcomed the couple; Hitler's coat and cap were hung up in the vestibule, and he withdrew to his quarters.

Few records survive of his conferences and decisions of the following weeks. A minute-by-minute logbook of his movements, kept by his manservants, shows him rising regularly around noon, lunching at two or three, and going to bed far into the night; supper was a very movable feast indeed. Apart from "Citadel," we know that Hitler was looking ahead to a further offensive against Leningrad in the summer. But he was also casting around for some way of regaining the initiative in the west too: "Gisela," a Nazi occupation of northern Spain, was one; but he had begun to reconsider a lightning invasion of Iceland too—"Operation Ikarus," which Raeder had barely talked him out of in 1940. Mussolini was not due to come until April 7; before then Hitler had only a little-publicized meeting with King Boris, one of his trustier allies; the monarch confirmed that Bulgaria would fight on Hitler's side if Britain and Turkey should invade the Balkans. No record was made of the meeting; it was so informal that at one stage one of Hitler's secretaries made an unheralded appearance munching an apple and clutching a pair of tennis rackets. "Don't worry yourself," Hitler consoled her afterward; "even kings are only human."

In these weeks at the Berghof, Hitler looked briefly into some Third Reich problems he had too long ignored. Others he studiously avoided, but many more were kept deliberately from him. Thus when Reichsführer Himmler came on

March 30 the discussion revolved solely around the military affairs of the SS, according to Himmler's note—and no mention was made of the Black Chapel scandal which was about to disclose the dubious loyalties of Admiral Canaris's Abwehr.[5] An Intelligence chief who had produced as little hard information as Canaris had, should long since have been dispensed with. His predictions had invariably proven wrong. For example, initially he had prophesied that Britain and France would march at the time of Munich and that France was about to attack Germany in mid-September 1939. In addition, he had known nothing of Stalin's huge tank production in 1941, of the North African invasion plan in 1942, or of the Roosevelt-Churchill Casablanca meeting more recently. But so long as Keitel shielded Canaris, his subordinate, Himmler was loath to burn his fingers by impeaching him for treason. Canaris knew of this—perhaps he had some hold over Himmler. We can imagine with what concealed contempt Canaris recorded, after a heart-to-heart talk with the visibly dejected field marshal in 1941, that Keitel had ("verbatim") confided to him: "If I did not have such loyal friends in my department as you, my dear Canaris, I would have chucked it all up long ago. Only the knowledge that I have such reliable colleagues consoles me and keeps me going."

Nor did Himmler evidently raise with Hitler the progress made on the "Jewish problem" during their two-hour mountain stroll on March 30—Hitler wearing a soft peaked cap to shade his eyes against the Alpine glare. Earlier in 1943 Himmler had submitted to him a statistical report on a similar topic—the population migrations he had sponsored since Hitler's written order of October 1939; the report[6] was typed on the special large-face typewriter and clearly went to the Führer. But did Hitler ever see the statistical report the Reichsführer had commissioned at the same time on the "Final Solution of the Jewish Problem in Europe"? In dry tones, Himmler's chief statistician, Dr. Richard Korherr, had analyzed the fate of the world's estimated 17,000,000 Jews: Europe's 10,000,000 had dwindled by 45 percent since 1937, owing to emigration, the high natural mortality rate, and the enforced "evacuation" that had begun with the prohibition of emigration late in 1941. To Himmler's annoyance, on reading the sixteen-page document on March 23 he found that it stated *expressis verbis* on page 9 that of

[5]Following the routine arrest of a Munich Abwehr agent involved in a sordid currency racket, the Gestapo had uncovered evidence linking Canaris's principal officials with treasonable communications to the Vatican. On March 24, 1943, Himmler had a telephone conversation with the Gestapo chief, Müller, in Berlin on the "Black Chapel complex." On April 5 the Abwehr headquarters was raided, and key Canaris aides including Dr. Hans von Dohnanyi and General Hans Oster were arrested.

[6]In three years Himmler had resettled 629,000 ethnic Germans from outside the Reich; 400,000 more were still to come. In the same period 365,000 Poles were dumped in the Generalgouvernement of Poland, and 295,000 French citizens were evicted from Alsace, Lorraine, and Luxemburg.

the 1,449,692 Jews deported from the eastern provinces 1,274,166 had been subjected to "special treatment" at camps in the Generalgouvernement and a further 145,301 similarly dealt with in the Warthegau. Himmler knew too well that the Führer had in November 1941[7] ordered that the Jews were *not* to be liquidated. On April 1 he had the report edited "for submission to the Führer"; and a few days later—lest he had not made himself plain—instructed that in the version for the Führer he "did not want there to be any mention of 'special treatment of Jews' whatever." According to the new text, the Jews would have been "channeled through" the camps to Russia—not "subjected to special treatment" at the camps. As he wrote on April 9, the report would serve magnificently for "camouflage purposes" in later years.

Mussolini arrived at Salzburg station on April 7. The sun glinted on the snow-clad mountains, the sky was postcard blue, but the Duce himself was a sick man—his eyes lusterless, his cheeks hollow, he had to be helped out of his carriage by two companions. There were rumors that he had cancer, but Hitler privately believed it was just a psychological depression. While it was understood that the fall of Tunis was probably inevitable, at least he could inspire Mussolini with the coming campaigns in the east. Mussolini and his *de facto* foreign minister, Giuseppe Bastianini, were housed at Klessheim—an enchanting baroque chateau near Salzburg which had been lavishly restored by Hitler—and here a short series of what Zeitzler contemptuously dubbed "gala war conferences" were held for Mussolini's benefit. Here Göring, Zeitzler, and Jodl rehearsed the daily situation in optimistic tones (though Zeitzler refused Hitler's suggestion that a fake map of the eastern front should be employed, as had been customary in Halder's day on such occasions). They banqueted together, Hitler consuming his vegetarian concoctions, Mussolini's meals first sampled by an unenthusiastic "taster" as in Roman times.

The conferences were short, out of regard for the Duce's health, but even so he had difficulty following them. The two dictators were moved by different purposes. Mussolini still wanted an armistice with Stalin, to enable the Axis to throw all its might against Britain and the United States; and he handed Hitler a memorandum on the possible negotiations. Given the Allies' poor showing over the Russian convoys and a Second Front, Stalin had good cause to be upset. The Duce believed Spain would voluntarily join the Axis. To Hitler all this was disappointingly naïve: from the Forschungsamt intercepts he knew just how closely the "Jewish Bolsheviks" of London, Washington, and Moscow were

[7]Page 332.

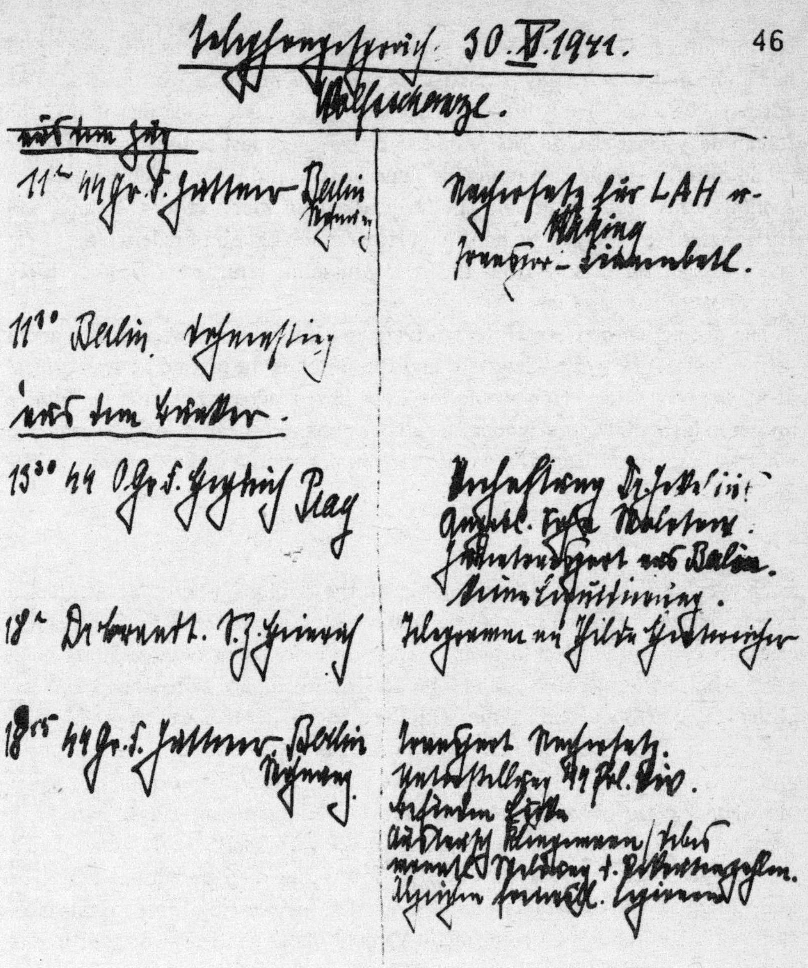

Himmler's telephone notes of November 30, 1941. At 1:30 P.M. the SS chief telephoned Heydrich in Prague from Hitler's bunker at the Wolf's Lair, ordering that there was to be "no liquidation" of Jews.

collaborating in Germany's defeat; and there were alarming signs that even Spain had come under their sway. If fascism in Italy was not to be overthrown, so he advised Mussolini, Tunis must be held if at all possible. This meant that the Italian navy must abandon its pride and throw every fast cruiser and destroyer it had into the supply operations for Tunisia. It would be impossible to salvage Arnim's army group in defeat. The Duce asked for more oil for the ships, and Hitler agreed to supply it. An hour-long Hitler monologue on Frederick the Great and Prussian steadfastness did the rest; Mussolini returned to Rome visibly improved in body and mind.

The distinction between Hitler's private and his public views was as marked as the contrast between Klessheim and the Berghof. In private he was cynical about the New Order. How would the Duce have reacted to hearing the Führer mutter to his staff: "Our neighbors are all our potential enemies. We must squeeze what we can out of them. But we neither can nor should make them any promises."

Each evening Hitler was driven back up to the Berghof, where he was greeted by the barking of Eva Braun's two untidy black scotties and by Eva herself, elegantly clad in the latest fashions. Her favorite dress was of close-fitting Nile-green wool, with long sleeves and a broad strip of leopard skin around its hem. Hitler kissed her hand and chatted with the others of her house party—her pretty sister Gretl, Frau Herta Schneider, and Frau Marion Schönmann were frequent guests, as were the wives of Below and Dr. Karl Brandt. Eva organized regular film shows in the basement bowling-alley, but Hitler piously stayed away. "In wartime, with the people called upon to make such sacrifices, I cannot watch movies.—Besides, I must save my eyesight for reading maps and dispatches." The same priggish considerations militated against his wearing more comfortable clothes. A Churchill, he noted, might gambol about the world dressed in silk blouses and cowboy hats—but not the Führer of the Reich. "As long as we are at war I will not take off this uniform. My knees are white as chalk anyway, and that looks awful in short trousers. —But the moment the war is over, I am going to hang my uniform on a nail, retire here, and let somebody else take over the government. As an old man I will write my memoirs, surrounded by clever, intellectual people—I never want to see another officer. My two elder secretaries will stay with me and do the typing . . ."

They were long evenings that spring, for Hitler refused to go to bed until the last enemy bomber had left Germany's airspace. British and American bombers had already carved black swaths far into central Europe. In March alone eight thousand tons of bombs had rained down on Germany, sometimes a thousand tons a night on single cities like Duisburg, Essen, and Berlin. On April 4, 228 civilians were killed in Paris and 221 in Naples in American air raids; on the fifth an American raid on the Belgian port of Antwerp accounted for 2,130 civilians. Göring's Luftwaffe was powerless to defend or deliver adequate reprisals. Hitler's interest in the army's long-range missile project increased, and on March 29 he approved Speer's blueprints for a huge concrete missile site on the Channel coast, from which Britain would be bombarded once missiles were available. It was the first of several "secret weapon" projects that were—however improbably—to sustain his own hope of final victory.

As Göring's prestige declined, the rivalry of the other satraps increased. Speer was an almost permanent visitor to the Berghof throughout April, but Bormann was lord of the manor here. He had secured Hitler's signature to a document appointing him his official "Secretary"—giving him express control over Hitler's security and affairs: he had the right to attend all conferences and "communicate the Führer's decisions and opinions to the Reich ministers and other departments and agencies"—a formidable prerogative. He alone would decide which nonmilitary supplicants might see Hitler and which documents would be shown to him. Bormann's powers became vast. His eyes were everywhere; his energy was prodigious; his loyalty was beyond question. When Baldur von Schirach, the thirty-five-year-old Gauleiter of Vienna whom Hitler had regarded as his possible successor, challenged Bormann's domestic policies, the Reichsleiter outmaneuvered him—summoning him to Hitler on March 26 for a tirade about his "decadent" cultural speeches and art exhibitions. Speer and Goebbels followed through. Schirach gamely accused Ribbentrop of failing to build bridges to the enemy. Hitler rejoined that since Casablanca and "unconditional surrender" there was no alternative. Afterward he angrily remarked to Bormann that the Gauleiter had become infected by Vienna: he too had contracted defeatism.

Clutching at Straws

By the spring of 1943 the Axis alliance was a myth, and Hitler knew it. In Tunisia, Montgomery's offensive had succeeded and the Axis bridgehead was being inexorably crushed. Late in February the Italians had already hinted that the loss of Tunis might bring about a new situation, and one month later Churchill had only evasively answered Parliamentary questions about possible Axis armistice feelers. Finland was already searching for a way out of the war. From the decoded messages shown to Hitler, it was clear that both the Hungarian and Romanian governments had in neutral capitals official emissaries who were sounding out the western enemy on the prospects of peace. Now Vidkun Quisling and Gauleiter Terboven—Reich Commissar for Norway—separately warned Hitler that in the event of an enemy invasion of Norway, Sweden would support the Allies. Hitler, who had just personally instructed his new envoy to Stockholm that his sole purpose must be to keep Sweden neutral—to safeguard Germany's iron-ore supplies—now resorted to more drastic measures: after one routine Berghof conference he detained Jodl and a handful of trusted advisers and instructed them to draft outline plans for a lightning invasion of Sweden should need arise. Only the success of "Citadel," regaining the initiative on the eastern front, would bring all these peripheral nations back into line.

Romania's Marshal Antonescu, invited to the Berghof on April 12, accepted Hitler's reproaches with a fatalistic air; for him as for Hitler himself there could now be no compromise between a clear victory or complete annihilation. When Hitler read him the Forschungsamt records of incriminating telephone conversations and other documents proving the disloyalty of Romanian ministers—and their clandestine negotiations with the enemy in Ankara, Bucharest, Budapest, Berne, and above all Madrid—the marshal made a convincing display of indignation (though he himself had authorized the feelers). Hitler gave the Hungarian regent, Horthy, a far rougher ride a few days later when the admiral flatly denied that the Forschungsamt records could be true; he supported Prime Minister

Kállay to the hilt and thrice denied that Hungary was in contact with the enemy. Hitler with good reason trusted neither Horthy nor Kállay. "We are all in the same boat," he said. "If anybody goes overboard now, he drowns."

Nor was the language Hitler and Ribbentrop used to prod the Hungarian regent into taking a sterner line over his Jewish citizens very delicate. The Nazis found it intolerable that eight hundred thousand Jews should still be moving freely around a country in the heart of Europe—particularly just north of the sensitive Balkans. For many months Germany had applied pressure for the Hungarian Jews to be turned over to the appropriate German agencies for deportation to "reservations in the east." It was argued that so long as they remained, they were potential rumormongers, purveyors of defeatism, saboteurs, agents of the enemy secret service, and contact men for an "international Jewry" now embattled against Germany.

Events in Poland were pointed to as providing an ugly precedent: there were reports of Jews roaming the country, committing acts of murder and sabotage. The eviction of the Jews ordered by Hitler had recentlv been intensified by Himmler's order that even those Jews left working for armaments concerns in the Generalgouvernement were to be housed collectively in camps and eventually to be got rid of as well. In Warsaw, the fifty thousand Jews surviving in the ghetto were on the point of staging an armed uprising—with weapons and ammunition evidently sold to them by Hitler's fleeing allies as they passed westward through the city. Himmler ordered the ghetto destroyed and its ruins combed out for Jews. "This is just the kind of incident that shows how dangerous these Jews are."

Poland should have been an object lesson to Horthy, Hitler argued. He related how Jews who refused to work there were shot; those who could not work just wasted away. Jews must be treated like tuberculosis bacilli, he said, using his favorite analogy. Was that so cruel when one considered that even innocent creatures like hares and deer had to be put down to prevent their doing damage? Why preserve a bestial species whose ambition was to inflict bolshevism on us all? Horthy apologetically noted that he had done all he decently could against the Jews: "But they can hardly be murdered or otherwise eliminated," he protested. Hitler reassured him: "There is no need for that." But just as in Slovakia, they ought to be isolated in remote camps where they could no longer infect the healthy body of the public; or they could be put to work in the mines, for example. He himself did not mind being temporarily excoriated for his Jewish policies, if they brought him tranquillity. Horthy left unconvinced.

What had prompted the earthier language Hitler now employed? It is possible to recognize the association in his mind of certain illogical ideas; half were unconscious or the result of his own muddled beliefs, but half had deliberately been implanted by trusted advisers like Himmler and Goebbels: the Jews had started the war; the enemy was the international Jew; the most deadly of the Bolsheviks, like Stalin's propagandist Ilya Ehrenburg, were Jews; Ehrenburg and the Jews behind Roosevelt were preaching the total extermination of the German race. The saturation bombing of German cities, their blasting and burning, was just the beginning.

In his warning to Horthy that the "Jewish Bolsheviks" would liquidate all Europe's intelligentsia, we can identify the influence of the Katyn episode—an unexpected propaganda windfall about which Goebbels had just telephoned him. Strange frozen mounds had been pointed out to German soldiers in a forest near Smolensk in February; now they had thawed and been opened to reveal the mummified remains of twelve thousand Polish army officers. The diaries and letters on the corpses were last dated April 1940—when the region was in Russian hands. They had all been shot expertly in the nape of the neck. Hitler warmly approved Goebbels's suggestion that Katyn should be linked in the public's mind with the Jewish question.

But the most poisonous and persuasive argument used to reconcile Hitler to a harsher treatment of the Jews was the bombing war. From documents and target maps recently found in crashed bombers he knew that the British aircrews were instructed to aim only at the residential areas now and to disregard the industrial targets proper. Only one race murdered, he told the quailing Horthy, and that was the Jews, who had provoked this war and given it its present character against civilians, women, and children. He returned repeatedly to this theme as 1943 progressed; in 1944 it became more insistent; and in 1945 he embodied it in his Political Testament, as though to appease his own conscience and justify his country's actions.

Nor was Hitler minded to treat even the non-Jewish Russian peoples with kid gloves. Throughout the spring of 1943 a noisy squabble raged between Alfred Rosenberg, the endlessly verbose minister for the eastern territories, and Gauleiter Erich Koch, Rosenberg's primitive and unruly minion in the Ukraine. Hitler had wanted Rosenberg's ministry to confine itself to political guidance in the east; instead he had established an unwieldy and bureaucratic executive apparatus. Rosenberg—supported by Ribbentrop, Zeitzler, and Goebbels—wanted to win the Russian peoples' support in the fight against Stalin, and he complained that Koch's brutal methods were incompatible with this. For example: to create a private hunting preserve, Koch had liquidated all the peasants in a certain forest. His pasha lifestyle was incompatible with the spirit of total war. At Christmas he had sent a special plane to Rostov to collect two hundred pounds of caviar at a time when General Paulus's soldiers were starving in Stalingrad.

Party dignitaries rose up in arms to demand Koch's expulsion from office and Party alike; yet Hitler, Bormann, and—more circumspectly—Himmler defended him. Rosenberg and his circle of Baltic emigrés might theorize about the future cultural life of the Ukraine, but Koch's harsh duty was to squeeze every ton of grain and every slave laborer he could out of the region. That was what war was about—and apparently the ability to fulfill this task excused all else.

The idea of harnessing Russians voluntarily to the war against Stalin was a chimera, said Hitler. "I have always felt there are only a handful of men who can really keep their heads in a major crisis, without being waylaid by some phantom hope or other. The saying that drowning men clutch at straws is only too true." When Ribbentrop identified himself with General Vlasov's previously mentioned idea for a Russian army of liberation, Hitler rapped his knuckles. "There are to be no such political operations. They are useless and unnecessary. They will only result in our people fraternizing with the Russians. Besides, it will be seen as a token of weakness on our part." Field Marshals Kluge and Küchler were also rebuffed when they supported the Vlasov project. Vlasov and Zeitzler's Colonel Gehlen had put their names to millions of leaflets dropped over the enemy lines; they announced that the Wehrmacht was fighting only Stalin and not the Russian people, and they spoke of a "National Committee" in Smolensk as though it were the Russian government being groomed for the post-Stalin era. To Hitler this idea was madness; as he angrily told Zeitzler, to let the Ukrainians set up their own government would be tantamount to throwing away the Nazis' entire war aim. The Russians would start off as a satellite state such as Poland had been in World War I, and Germany would end up confronting an entirely independent state all over again.

On May 19, Hitler brought Rosenberg and Koch face to face and refereed the match himself. Rosenberg firmly repeated that Koch's policies were damaging the Reich and supplying the enemy with thousands of partisans; Koch was accused of being disobedient, rebellious, and libelous about Rosenberg's "conspiring with emigrés." Koch defended himself and justified his methods. With a sense of justice worthy of a comic-opera character, Hitler adjudged that both were right, though Koch was righter. In the future only the Führer would authorize any proclamations to the peoples of Russia—"not some idiot or other in the war ministry or at the front." As for the partisan argument, if Rosenberg were right, there would be fewest partisans where the "particularly crafty generals" spoke in the most honeyed tones; this was not the case. Nor could slave labor be procured except by Koch's methods. "Only feeble-minded generals imagine we can win any manpower by sweet-talking." And as for Koch's executions in the Ukraine: "How many of our compatriots are losing their lives in air raids here at home?" Hitler laid down that in the future neither Koch nor Rosenberg was to employ foreigners as advisers. "If they work *against* their own country, they are devoid of character. If they work *for* it, they are useless as advisers to us."

The military aspects of the Vlasov "Russian army" project were analyzed in a heated session between Hitler, Keitel, and Zeitzler some weeks later. Hitler knew that the German army's Georgian and Armenian battalions had deserted en masse to the enemy, and he had little patience for this new project. He did not object to employing hundreds of thousands of Russian volunteers in noncombatant duties (General Lindemann's Eighteenth Army alone had forty-seven thousand). But he would not approve of the Vlasov project beyond its sheer propaganda value in enticing Soviet soldiers to desert: the deserters were to be transported into Germany, "decently treated," and employed in the coal mines. Vlasov himself would be needed only for his photograph and signature on the leaflets; otherwise, his activities were to be curbed. History, said Hitler, had proven that in times of crisis such nationalistic movements only rounded on the occupying power. Keitel accordingly ruled that no "National Committee" was actually to be set up in occupied Russia; the Führer would permit Vlasov's propaganda leaflets only on condition that German agencies realized that nobody must take them seriously.

General Zeitzler's prestige with Hitler had risen in the same measure as the OKW's had declined, with the crumbling of its North African theater. Hitler had given the army's General Staff a free hand in devising a plan for "Citadel" to the success of which he attached considerable importance: a modest offensive victory in Russia would inspire the neutrals and halfhearted allies too; it would stabilize the front for the rest of 1943, long enough for him to release armored divisions to thwart any enemy molestation of Italy or the Balkans; in addition, the home economy badly needed the slave labor that "Citadel" would harvest in its wake.

Even though they were half a continent apart, the interreaction of the Mediterranean and eastern theaters naturally made for a variety of difficulties. During March and early April various operational concepts for "Citadel" had been examined and cast aside. Zeitzler's final proposal was that the objective—an inviting rectangular salient 130 miles wide and thrusting 80 miles out toward the German Second Army—should be excised in a classic pincer attack by the Ninth Army from the north and the Fourth Panzer Army from the south, their spearheads meeting just east of Kursk. Zeitzler drafted a pompously worded operational order ("The victory at Kursk must shine as a beacon to the whole world") and Hitler signed it on April 15. It made grim provision for the rounding up and smooth westward dispatch of the hundreds of thousands of able-bodied Russians expected to fall into the German net. "Citadel" was set to begin on the third of May.

Once this much had been settled, Zeitzler flew back to his headquarters in East

Prussia, but a few days later he received a telephone call from Hitler: the Führer had thought "Citadel" over and now felt it would be better to abandon the idea of a pincer attack—which was so obvious that the enemy would be certain to be ready and waiting for it—and instead combine the assault forces of Army Groups South and Center in one frontal thrust, piercing the very center of the bulge and thus splitting the enemy's massed strength in two.[1] Zeitzler would not hear of it; redeploying the two armies would inflict a crippling delay on "Citadel," and he made a special flight to Berchtesgaden on April 21 with the maps and statistics to prove it. Hitler yielded. Zeitzler had proved right at Stalingrad; his own sureness of touch, his strategic instinct, had failed him then. Worse still, now that "Citadel" had become Zeitzler's baby, Hitler's heart was no longer in it.

General Model, commander of the Ninth Army, had originally asked for two days to punch through the Russian defenses, but late in April he raised this estimate to three days. His superior, Kluge, impatiently pointed out that with 227 tanks and 120 assault guns the Ninth Army was stronger than ever before, but Model claimed he still needed 100 more tanks. Zeitzler agreed to rush 50 from the west, with 20 more Tigers and 40 assault guns. But the "three-day" estimate worried Hitler: three days of uninterrupted battle against an experienced enemy would result in the massacre of the assault troops. "When Model told me before 'Citadel,' " Hitler said a year later, "that he'd need three days—that's when I got cold feet." He asked Model to fly to the Berghof. On April 27 the wiry, dark-haired general was standing before him in the Great Hall; his aerial photographs appeared to confirm the claim that twelve-mile-deep Russian fortifications with immensely powerful antitank artillery had to be overcome before the Ninth Army could advance on Kursk. Moreover, Model warned that even the Mark IV tank was vulnerable to the new Russian antitank rifle. Hitler postponed "Citadel" to May 5. On April 29 he ordered a further postponement to the ninth, to give the armies a few more days to stockpile tanks and guns.

Out of "a few days" grew weeks, then months. General Guderian, who began attending the war conferences on May 2 in his capacity as inspector of panzer troops, gave Hitler his own impression of tank production prospects if "Citadel" could be delayed long enough. At present the Tiger was plagued by gear and steering faults, and the advanced Panther tank production had repeatedly broken down. But Guderian told Hitler that during May two battalions of each of the different tank types—Panthers, Ferdinands, Tigers, and Hornets—would be activated; the existing tanks on the Russian front would be reinforced with armored

[1]In postwar captivity, General Johannes Friessner met one of Hitler's adjutants and asked why the Führer had not mounted just such an offensive. Given the comparative weakness of the Russian defenses in the center of the bulge, Friessner—who had commanded a corps under Model's Ninth Army—believed it would have succeeded.

"aprons" against antitank shells; in addition, tank output itself was increasing. The Speer ministry had promised 939 tanks in April, 1,140 in May, 1,005 in June, and 1,071 in July. In short, suggested Guderian, it was well worth holding up "Citadel" for a bit. In reality he was opposed to the offensive altogether, for he wanted to conserve German tank strength throughout 1943 in order to meet the enemy's operations in the west thereafter.

Hitler—his own mind already made up for an even longer postponement—summoned his leading generals to Munich for a three-hour conference on May 4. No stenogram survives, and recollections differ as to the standpoints adopted by each general (a common phenomenon after a defeat). However, the Chief of Air Staff, Jeschonnek, rendered a contemporary description to one diarist (Richthofen), and it throws a piquant sidelight on the personalities around the Führer.

> [On April 27] General Model declared he was not strong enough and would probably get bogged down or take too long. The Führer took the view that the attack must be punched through without fail in shortest time possible. [Early in May] General Guderian offered to furnish enough tank units within six weeks to guarantee this. The Führer thus decided on a postponement of six weeks. To get the blessing of all sides on this decision, he called a conference [on May 4] with Field Marshals von Kluge and von Manstein. At first they agreed on a postponement; but when they heard that the Führer had already made his mind up to that effect, they spoke out for an immediate opening of the attack—apparently in order to avoid the odium of being blamed for the postponement themselves.

There is nothing to be gained from referring here to the postwar versions of Manstein or Guderian. Jeschonnek, Richthofen, and Zeitzler all opposed any further delay, arguing that time would operate solely in favor of the Russians; their fortifications, minefields, and artillery emplacements would become more formidable with each passing day. Nonetheless, Hitler now postponed "Citadel" to mid-June.

Another factor now bore on his decisions: the imminent Axis defeat in Tunisia.

Starved of ammunition, food, and fuel, General von Arnim's quarter of a million troops had fought a stubborn rearguard action in its ever shrinking bridgehead. Bereft of Italian naval support, supply ships were not getting through; and enemy fighters were inflicting cruel losses on the Junkers transport planes. By the end of April, Arnim had only seventy-six tanks left and was distilling what fuel he could from low-grade wines and liquors. Dispatching General Warlimont to Rome to renew pressure on the quivering Italian navy, Hitler told him to say that tanks and divisions were just as "nice to look at" as warships. "There are no moral reasons not to fight. The only moral act is to fight and win this war. What is immoral is to lose, and then scuttle your ships without having fought." The appeal availed him naught—the Italian navy stayed in harbor; indeed, some days later Hitler heard that the battleship *Vittorio Veneto* had secretly radioed British headquarters at Malta details of German supply convoys putting to sea. On May 6, overcoming Arnim's defense of the mountain passes, the British First Army broke through to Tunis. Two days later the Luftwaffe—faced now by forty-five hundred fighter and bomber aircraft—abandoned its North African airfields. Keitel wrote that day: "The Führer and Duce are determined to continue the fight in Tunisia as long as possible," but one by one Arnim's divisions were enveloped as their last ammunition was spent.

Warlimont returned from Rome on May 7 with comforting news about Mussolini's health and his personal assessment that provided Il Duce kept a tight rein on events, the coming loss of Tunis need not spell disaster within Italy. Hitler was not so sure. "The Duce and the Fascist party are resolved to stand by Germany through thick and thin," he told his staff at noon. However "a section of the officer corps—more at the top, fewer lower down—is inclined to make peace already. Certain influential circles are capable of treachery." He announced that he planned to furnish armed support to the Fascists in Italy to bolster her powers of resisting the enemy. Meanwhile, every week Arnim could fight on was vital to the Axis cause. He asked Field Marshal Rommel to come to see him.

Hitler had slept the last three nights at Martin Bormann's villa outside Munich. On May 6 he turned his back on the Mediterranean and returned by train to Berlin. Viktor Lutze, SA Chief of Staff, had just died in an autobahn accident, and Hitler intended to use the next day's state funeral to underline his lingering nostalgia for political militias like the SA. He had had a bellyful of army generals —liars and cheats, they were reactionary and hostile to the dogmas of National Socialism.

It was a good funeral. The routine selection from *Götterdämmerung* stirred him deeply. At four o'clock, after banqueting the Party leaders, he gave them a stern if banal warning against the autobahn madness that seemed to go with high office. Then he addressed the Gauleiters on the meaning of the present war. It had begun as a fight between bourgeois and revolutionary states, in which the former had been easily overthrown. But now they were facing in the east a *Weltanschauung*-state like their own, its Jewish-Bolshevist ideology permeating its army with a zeal and spirit which only his own SS divisions could match. This was why he, Hitler, had decided that "the Jews must be thrown out of Europe." He had come to believe that in the great prewar purge Stalin had not ruined the Red Army after all; quite the contrary. And the introduction of political commissars had vastly increased the army's effectiveness. The Russian solidarity behind Stalin was complete: for twenty-five years he had ruthlessly eliminated his opposition; he had no Church elements to restrain him as Hitler had in Germany. The Führer often feared that the Herrenvolk could not forever maintain their superiority over the enormous manpower reservoirs of the east. Ghengis Khan's hordes had penetrated far into the heart of Europe—the glittering jewel—without Germandom having possessed the strength to hold them back. Now too Germany alone must bear the brunt of the struggle against Asia. Speer's gigantic tank program would ensure victory in the east, while Dönitz's U-boats kept the Jewish-fostered warmongers of the West at bay. Hitler told the Gauleiters that Stalin had lost over thirteen million troops since "Barbarossa" had started. The summer offensive would be modest in scale but carried forward by dependable German troops alone. Postwar Europe would dispense with the present "hodgepodge of small states." The time would come, announced Hitler, when Germany would dominate all Europe.

He wrote off the Tunis bridgehead in North Africa, even though small bands of Axis troops were continuing to hold out. But he had not turned his back on Mussolini. (He had never forgotten the Duce's benevolence over Austria in 1938. "I told him then 'I will never forget you for this!' And I never will," Hitler admonished his less forgiving staff.) He was worried about the Duce's health, but he worried far more that treacherous, royalist generals would betray Italy into the enemy's hands. This was why he had recalled Rommel from his convalescence to Berlin—Rommel, rather than the gullible and popular Field Marshal Kesselring, who refused to believe that the Italian generals were as dark-hearted as the Führer sensed them to be, was the one to command Hitler's troops in Italy.

Rommel flew into Berlin on May 9 and reported to Hitler at 1 P.M., looking fit and well. That he was not still in Tunis was a secret Hitler had not yet revealed to his people; now was the time to dissociate this valuable commander from the debacle in Africa. Hitler kept the ambitious field marshal on tenterhooks. Rommel wrote in his diary: "Afterward I attended the war conference. No special job as yet. Field Marshal Keitel hinted at my utilization in Italy with the Duce if things should turn sticky there." Rommel spent the rest of the day being lectured by Goebbels. The next day he recorded: "I stressed to both the Führer and Goebbels the meager fighting quality of the Italians and their reluctance to fight." On the twelfth Hitler published the news that Rommel had been in Germany since March, when he had awarded him the highest medal; but, aware that the field marshal was spurned by the Italians (as Göring and Kesselring reminded him) as "the man who lost Libya," he refrained from releasing the text of his extravagant letter of praise to Rommel. At 6 P.M. that evening, Hitler and his staff flew back to his East Prussian headquarters.

Why he did so is a mystery. Perhaps it was a blind, an attempt to deceive the enemy into believing that "Citadel" was imminent. He had no fear of an enemy invasion in the west as yet—the Atlantic Wall allayed that peril. No, he knew that the Mediterranean was still the most dangerous theater. As early as May 1 he had believed both the western Mediterranean and the Peloponnesus of Greece most vulnerable to invasion. A week later an adjutant had announced at the war conference a startling Abwehr scoop which seemed to substantiate Hitler's fears: a corpse found floating off the Spanish coast had yielded sealed envelopes bearing ostensibly genuine letters from the British war office and Lord Mountbatten to Admiral Cunningham and General Dwight D. Eisenhower, betraying the enemy's most secret plans after the capture of Tunis. Two invasion operations were to be mounted, one in the western Mediterranean and one in the Peloponnesus (code-named, apparently, "Brimstone" and "Husky"); these would be covered by dummy invasions of Sicily and the Dodecanese, respectively. The envelopes had been expertly resealed and turned over to the British by the Spanish foreign ministry. Admiral Canaris fell hook, line, and sinker for their contents. Hitler was less gullible, for at the end of the war conference he turned on his heel and spoke his thoughts to Jodl's staff officer: "Christian, couldn't this be a corpse they have deliberately played into our hands?"[2] There was no way of knowing. Both Zeitzler's Intelligence staff and Canaris ruled out the possibility, and for the next month the Peloponnesus and Sardinia—presumed to be the target of the real assault in the western Mediterranean—attracted most of Hitler's attention.

Albert Speer and his principal arms barons came to see him at the Wolf's Lair on May 13. Hitler bestowed a rare award, the "Doctor Todt Ring," on the munitions minister, for his reorganization of the armaments industry had yielded amazing results. Germany was turning out six times as much heavy ammunition as in 1941 and three times as many guns. Between February and May heavy tank production had doubled, testifying to the indomitable spirit of the workers despite the paralyzing air raids. "In the autumn," Speer reminded Hitler, "you instructed us to deliver specific quantities of arms by May 12. Today we can report that we have met every one of those figures and in some cases far exceeded them."

To Goebbels, Speer afterward commented that the Führer looked worn out with worry: it was the anxiety over Italy. What use indeed were the new weapons

[2]The stenographer—himself a close aide of the famous Intelligence chief Colonel Nicolai in World War I—recalls the scene vividly. The corpse was indeed a brilliant if gruesome ploy of the British secret service.

Speer had demonstrated within the headquarters compound the next day—the mighty hundred-ton Mouse tank, the new assault guns, and the deadly Blowpipe bazooka (Pusterohr)—if Italy changed sides, the enemy landed in the Balkans, and the Romanian oil fields were reduced to ruins?

The fighting in Tunis was now over. The Afrika Korps' last radio emission had arrived: "Ammunition spent. Arms and equipment destroyed. The Afrika Korps has fought till it can fight no more, as ordered." A hundred thousand of Hitler's finest troops were being marched into British and American captivity; some 150,000 Italians had been taken prisoner. The blow was softened in Hitler's eyes by its gradualness, its inevitability given Italian shortcomings, and the realization that these captives would at least be spared the torments that faced prisoners in Soviet hands. Yet the Italian posture now raised fresh alarm. Hitler offered Mussolini five divisions to restore the blood to Italy's anemic arteries. The Duce's reply, obviously drafted by the devious General Ambrosio—Keitel's counterpart as chief of the *comando supremo*—stated that the three German divisions left on Italian soil as a backlog of the transport movements to Tunisia were quite enough: but he wanted three hundred tanks, fifty antiaircraft batteries, and hundreds of fighter aircraft. When Admiral Dönitz reported back to Hitler on May 14 after personally grilling the Italian commanders in Rome, he could only reinforce Hitler's suspicions. Hitler responded, "A man like Ambrosio would be happy to see Italy an English dominion."

Dönitz stated that the Italians expected the British to invade Sicily next. Obviously forgetting his earlier suspicions, Hitler replied that the letters on the British corpse indicated that the target would be Sardinia; Sicily was too heavily defended, and it would take up to four weeks to sweep the Strait clear of the Axis minefields. One thing was clear—colossal enemy bombardments of the ports and railway networks of Sardinia, Sicily, and Corsica had begun. Dönitz had tried to impress on the Italians that if they did not employ every available ship—big and small—to pump troops and stores into these islands now, the dismal story of North Africa would be repeated all over again. Mussolini had weakly accepted this; Ambrosio had not—submarines and cruisers were there to fight, not act as transport vessels. When Dönitz quoted Mussolini as saying that the British press was bragging that the capture of Sicily would release two million tons of shipping presently obliged to detour around the Cape, Hitler irritably interrupted ". . .. and then our fine submarines must sink them." "And on top of that," continued Dönitz, "we are coming up to our worst U-boat crisis, since the enemy has new detecting gear which makes submarine warfare impossible for the first time." Suddenly they were losing over fifteen U-boats a month. "The losses are too high," exclaimed Hitler. "We can't go on like this."

His insomnia returned. If he lost the Balkans, he would lose his last allies, forfeit Romania's oil, and lose the bauxite, chrome, and copper mines on which

Speer's factories depended. Zeitzler, jealously husbanding his divisions massed for "Citadel," refused to release a panzer division for possible use in the Balkans; but the road and rail network in the Balkans was so primitive that Hitler knew he could not leave it until the last moment. With Italy the problem was less acute: the railways were better, and if worse came to worst he could always barricade Italy off from the Reich; but not the Balkans. He ordered the Luftwaffe field division on the Isthmus of Corinth strengthened, and a panzer division transferred to the Balkans from the west.

The next fortnight in Italy would be crucial. Rommel might have to storm the Italian frontier and go to the Duce's rescue if his generals betrayed him. After the noon conference on May 15, Hitler made a two-hour secret speech to his generals, including Rommel, on the dangerous situation left by the defeat in North Africa. It is so important that the note taken by one officer present, Captain Wolf Junge, is quoted here at length:

> The enemy's victory in Africa has not only opened up the east-west passage through the Mediterranean for him, but released eighteen to twenty divisions and considerable air and naval forces. They will also exploit the new situation for a political offensive designed to use bluster and blandishments to persuade Germany's weak allies to defect. Quite apart from the military position, this is particularly dangerous in Italy and Hungary. Bulgaria and Romania can be regarded as secure. . . .
>
> In Italy we can rely only on the Duce. There are strong fears that he may be got rid of or neutralized in some way. The royal family, all leading members of the officers' corps, the clergy, the Jews, and broad sectors of the civil service are hostile or negative toward us. Their motives are partly deliberate enmity, partly shortsighted incompetence and blind egoism. The broad masses are apathetic and lacking in leadership.
>
> The Duce is now marshaling his Fascist guard about him. But the real power is in the hands of the others. Moreover he is uncertain of himself in military affairs and has to rely on his hostile or incompetent generals (Ambrosio!!!) as is evident from the incomprehensible reply—at least as coming from the Duce—turning down or evading the Führer's offer of troops.
>
> In the present situation a neutral Italy would not be bad at all; but it could not be neutral now—it would defect voluntarily or under pressure to the enemy camp. Italy in enemy hands is the Second Front in Europe we must avoid at all costs; it would lay open the western flank of the Balkans too. Our main purpose now must be to prevent a Second Front in Europe. "Europe must be defended in its outfield—we cannot allow a Second Front to emerge on the Reich's frontiers." It is for this objective that we may have to make sacrifices elsewhere.
>
> It is good that we have not yet attacked in the east ["Citadel"] and still have forces available there; because the decision has been taken to act as soon as a

crisis breaks out in Italy. To this end, of the eighteen mobile divisions available in the east, eight armored and four infantry divisions will have to be rushed to Italy to get a firm grip on her and defend her against the Anglo-Americans (or throw them out again). No resistance of note is expected from the Italians (according to Rommel). Collaboration of the Fascist political forces is hoped for.

At the same time Hungary will be occupied.

The consequences on eastern front will be: defensive evacuation of the Orel Bend; acceptance of risk to the Donets region; if worse comes to worst even withdrawal in the north to the Luga line. Zeitzler demanded that the bridgehead on the Kuban should also be given up; but the Führer did not express an opinion on that.

Zeitzler was instructed to work out a timetable for the troop movements [from Russia to Italy]. The next one or two weeks are crucial. . . . Every week is vital to us, because after about eight weeks the newly activated "Stalingrad" divisions in the west will become operational, which would obviate the need to raid the eastern front for divisions.

Thus the main points of the Führer's remarks.

It was certainly a remarkable speech. Quite apart from the first hint at enforced German occupations of Italy and Hungary, it destroys the myth that Hitler always refused to abandon territory voluntarily in Russia, when it was strategically necessary. It also puts "Citadel," the Battle of Kursk, into its proper perspective in history: it was subordinated to the need to prop up a crumbling dictatorship in a country whose military value was nil.

All eyes turned to Italy. Hitler began planning an urgent personal meeting with Mussolini again.

Out of regard for Mussolini's feelings he scrapped the official communiqué on the Tunis fighting, which put the blame on the Italians. When British newspapers, week after week, mocked the German soldiers for surrendering, Ribbentrop begged the Führer to publish the war diaries and documents proving how heroically they had fought against impossible odds in Tunisia. Hitler's stubborn refusal was telephoned by Hewel back to Ribbentrop: "We have to be clear that we have suffered a painful defeat in Africa. If you have taken a knock, you mustn't try and talk your way out of it or pretty things up. You will soon end up like the Italians—who make a veritable saga of every defeat they suffer until the whole world laughs at them. There is only one thing to do at times like this: *Hold your tongue and prepare to counterattack.* Once the counterattack is delivered, all talk of any insufficiency in German soldiers vanishes. Stalingrad is an example: the stories that the German divisions' morale was collapsing stopped the moment we struck back hard at the Russians again, at Kharkov."

Before leaving for the Berghof again, Hitler conferred in detail with Keitel, Kesselring, and Löhr on the defense of the Mediterranean position; his aim was to prevent a "boundless bankruptcy" from loosening their stranglehold on the Balkans the moment the *Schweinerei* in Italy began. Rommel—given his deep personal hatred of them now—would be the ideal commander to confront the Italian generals with.

On May 18, Hitler ordered him to set up the skeleton staff of a new army group for what was, after all, the occupation of Italy. Rommel would report directly to him. His interim headquarters would be in Munich. The operation—code-named "Alarich"—was so secret that Hitler declined even to sign the OKW's draft directive. "This time we've got to be fanatically careful with bits of paper," he said. A similar directive, "Konstantin," provided for filling the vacuum in Greece and Croatia should the Italian army suddenly pull out. Initially, Rommel's worry was that the Alpine fortifications being hastily completed by the Italians against the Reich frontier might be manned, especially on the Brenner Pass, to keep German divisions out—thus deliberately letting Italy fall into the enemy's hands. Rarely can two ostensibly allied armies have contemplated each other with such veiled mistrust.

Zeitzler had calculated for Hitler that the first reinforcements could be flooding from the Russian front into Italy within ten days of any trouble there. Every two days would then bring a fresh infantry division, spearheaded by three SS armored divisions—the troops with the closest ideological ties to the Fascist leaders. A speech by Mussolini's Foreign Minister Bastianini early on May 20 convinced the Führer that dirty work was afoot. "We must be on our guard, like a spider in its web. Thank God I've a good nose for things like this, so I usually get wind of anything long before it breaks out."

How far Admiral Canaris reliably warned of the treason blossoming in Italy is uncertain from the records. But Himmler's officials left Hitler in no doubt. SS Specialist [*Sonderführer*] von Neurath brought hair-raising details back from Sicily: the local people hated the German troops and were making unabashed preparations for "postwar"; government officials were turning a blind eye on anti-German outrages; the Italian Sixth Army based on Sicily was now commanded by General Roatta of Balkan ill-repute, and Roatta obviously regarded defeat as certain. Perhaps he even relished the prospect. His staff were anglophiles; some had even married Englishwomen. "Crafty?" exclaimed Hitler, on hearing Roatta's name. "He is the Fouché of the Fascist revolution, a spy totally devoid of character. A spy is what he is!" Hitler's field marshals shared this view. Curiously enough, the attaché reports from Rome spoke only in the highest terms of both Roatta and Ambrosio; this may have been because one of Canaris's assistants, Colonel Emil Helfferich, was attached to the attaché's staff.

At 1 P.M. on May 21, 1943, Hitler flew from East Prussia to Berchtesgaden, after a brief treatment session with his personal surgeon, Dr. Karl Brandt. His health was still impaired: ten days earlier, a fresh electrocardiogram had revealed no improvement in the rapid progressive coronary sclerosis affecting his heart vessels. He had discussed his stomach problems with Romania's Marshal Antonescu, and the latter recommended to him a Viennese dietician, Frau Marlene von Exner. Much against her will, Dr. Morell induced her to cook exclusively for the Führer by paying her a two thousand-Reichsmark bribe and a tax-free salary of eight hundred marks a month as a reward. Young, attractive, and good-natured, she soon shared the Führer's table with the other female headquarters staff. She brought back memories of old Vienna to her new employer, and he humored her cheerful protests at the way National Socialism favored Linz above Vienna. But whereas she had been able to display her culinary talents to Antonescu in a welter of oysters, mayonnaise, and caviar delicacies, with Hitler's austere meals she was at her wit's end. A typical Berghof menu was that on June 7, 1943: orange juice with linseed gruel; rice pudding with herb sauce; crispbread with butter and nut paste. Hitler adored her.

Mussolini could not come and see him; the records do not explain why. Probably he feared to leave Italy even for a few hours.

According to Jodl's deputy, Warlimont, Himmler submitted to Hitler a detailed plan for launching an operation against Italy if need arose. Hitler's own plan was to infiltrate four divisions into Italy more or less by stealth; at least sixteen more were to follow under Rommel the moment an enemy invasion occurred. But Rommel greatly feared that enemy bombers—or for that matter Italian officer renegades—would block the Alpine frontier passes. Hitler ordered the Luftwaffe to furnish antiaircraft batteries for the Brenner Pass; if the Italians demurred, then "British air raids" were to be faked, using refurbished unexploded RAF bombs hauled out of the ruins of German cities. On June 5, Warlimont briefed Canaris on this at Berchtesgaden. Canaris offered "Brandenburg" Division commandos who would become members of the gun crews and so be in a position to combat any attempted sabotage on the Alpine passes. But Jodl's deputy warned that no measure casting doubt on Italy's will to fight must ever become public; not even the general commanding the "Brandenburgers" must know. Canaris mouthed agreement; he was willing to risk "acting disloyally" toward the Italians, but he doubted whether the "true objectives" of the military preparations could be totally concealed from them. To Keitel he suggested that OKW fears of Italian defection were exaggerated, and he persuaded the guileless field marshal to cancel the antisabotage provisions. He also asked for Hitler to attach an Abwehr representative to Rommel's top-secret working party. Then he flew to Rome.[3]

Hitler's June 1943 sojourn at the Berghof was dismal and depressing. What price victory now? Bormann brought him a seventy-six-page speech Goebbels was planning to deliver to Berlin munitions workers on the fifth. Hitler crossed out whole pages or inked in spidery alterations. Where Goebbels proclaimed that their long-suffering fellow citizens would all receive generous compensation for their sacrifices "when victory is ours," Hitler thoughtfully altered this to read "after this struggle is over."[4]

The black outlook in both the submarine campaign and the air war contributed to this subtle distinction. At the end of May, Dönitz had frankly outlined the catastrophic U-boat situation in the North Atlantic to Hitler: enemy air patrols had been stepped up, and they were evidently using some secret device to detect the U-boats; in May, 38 submarines had been lost compared with 14 in April. As recently as March submarines had been able to destroy 875,000 tons of enemy shipping, and Hitler had spoken highly of their future prospects to the Gauleiters in Berlin on May 7: but the very next day 5 U-boats had been destroyed in one convoy battle, and on the twenty-fourth Dönitz had had to call off his attack in the North Atlantic if he was not to lose his entire front line. It was a tragedy for the German navy. Their Intelligence departments were successfully cracking the enemy codes that told Dönitz precisely where the convoys would be routed; there was talk of a "Hedgehog" in some messages, but this appeared to be just a patterned release of depth charges. The Germans had learned of the enemy's advances in centimetric radar after examining the remains of a bomber shot down near Rotterdam in February. Dönitz—correctly—believed the same equipment lay behind his submarine losses, but there was no evidence. Keitel instructed Canaris to find out as a matter of urgency.

Hitler had long expected just this setback to the U-boats—he was surprised they had done so well so long. Thus he did not reproach the navy. Dönitz had immediately fitted his submarines with multiple-barreled 20-millimeter antiaircraft guns and ordered that in the future they were to stand and fight back when aircraft approached. Ten U-boats were equipped to carry only antiaircraft guns. But these were improvisations. Until the acoustic homing torpedoes entered service in October as "destroyer busters," the U-boats would be restricted in their

[3]At this point the surviving fragments of Canaris's diary end.

[4]See facsimile on page 524.

hat das mehr bedauert als wir. Aber die braven Volksgenossen, die ~~dabei~~ dadurch zunächst Beruf, Geschäft und den Genuß eines manchmal jahrzehntelangen Fleißes einbüßten, können schon heute das Bewußtsein haben, daß ihr Opfer nicht umsonst war. Sie werden dafür nach Möglichkeit jetzt schon und besonders nach dem ~~Siege~~ Ende dieses Ringens in ~~großzügigster~~ gerechter Weise entschädigt werden. Heute aber gilt es, alle Kraft auf den Sieg zu konzentrieren.

Im Rahmen dieses gigantischen Umschichtungsprozesses sind im Verlaufe der vergangenen fünf Monate fast 3 1/2 Millionen Meldungen von Arbeitskräften eingelaufen. Von diesen Meldungen sind bisher 2 1/2 Millionen bearbeitet. Hunderttausende von Männern konnten aus dem Produktionsprozess für

Hitler censors Goebbels' speech of June 5, 1943. Where Goebbels wanted to say "when victory is ours," Hitler altered it to read, "after this struggle is over." (The handwriting above Hitler's is Martin Bormann's.)

usefulness. Hitler knew that unless Dönitz could sink enemy shipping faster than it could be built, the war could not be won. He ordered Dönitz's submarine program increased from thirty to forty new boats a month, and he approved Dönitz's suggestion that all naval construction work be transferred to Speer's ministry. On June 15, however, the admiral arrived at the Berghof with a staggering demand for nearly 150,000 men to implement this naval expansion. Hitler told him: "I just don't have the men. The antiaircraft and night-fighter defenses have got to be increased to protect our cities. The eastern front has got to be strengthened. The army needs divisions for its job defending Europe."

Dönitz's energy was in stark contrast to Göring's indolence and lethargy that summer. From Gestapo morale reports, Hitler knew that his people were prey to a growing conviction that nothing could halt the enemy bombing campaign. Every night the British bombers visited a different town or city of the Ruhr, methodically heralded their arrival by chilling showers of colored pyrotechnic flares, and unloaded one or two thousand tons of bombs over the streets and houses. Their losses, sometimes thirty or forty bombers in one night, seemed not to deter them. A handful of bombers breached the Ruhr dams, unleashing the reservoirs on the sleeping populaces below. (Goebbels informed Hitler that the enemy press gave credit for this diabolical plan to a former Berlin Jew.) By day the American bomber formations completed the destruction in the ports or bombed targets in France and Italy. Sometimes the British sent small fast bombers by daylight deep into Germany, causing more insult to public morale than injury to industry. Or lone Mosquitoes, each with a one-ton sting, would circle for hours on end above Berlin, forcing its millions of inhabitants to take refuge until the all clear sounded. Though Milch warned that when Berlin's time really came, the people would no longer heed the sirens, Hitler still commanded that the sirens must sound each time, even if they saved only one or two lives thereby. Göring's solution was to propose that Germany's bombed-out citizens be evacuated to Burgundy—but this was hardly likely to commend itself to the Ruhr workers. Besides, in one night over a hundred thousand people lost their homes in Dortmund alone. Not until November could the Luftwaffe expect to strike back in force. Milch hoped to be manufacturing over three thousand fighters and bombers every month by then.

Unquestionably air superiority was the key to this war. This was why Hitler now ordered bomber squadrons transferred from the west to the Mediterranean and why he placed Field Marshal von Richthofen—his most trusted air commander—in command of the Second Air Force there. This incidentally was further proof that "Citadel" ranked lower in his order of priorities than keeping the enemy at bay in the Mediterranean. But even Richthofen could not prevent the huge enemy air onslaught that preceded each ground operation there. Six thousand tons of bombs were discharged over the tiny fortified island of Pantelleria, commanding the shipping routes in the Strait of Sicily. The Italian defenders suffered few casualties but were so demoralized that without firing a shot they offered to capitulate. On June 11 the Germans heard the island's commandant, Admiral Parvesi, radioing to the enemy in Malta: "We offer surrender; out of water." By that evening the island was firmly in Allied hands. That the Italian soldiers had been unable to withstand the kind of bombardment German civilians —men, women, and children alike—were enduring night after night certainly did not augur well for the coming Mediterranean campaigns, Hitler noted.

Correcting the Front Line

No month brought such concentrated high drama as July 1943. "Citadel" began, the enemy invaded Italian soil, the Russians sprang their own great summer offensive, and Mussolini was ousted by his monarch just as Hitler had always predicted. (Had he not written in October 1939 of the Italian monarchy: "For a pittance they would be willing to sell Italy's own birthright in the Mediterranean, in their own stupid shortsightedness, and then to join Germany's enemies as well"?) Finally, the war in the air reached a climax in prenuclear barbarism as over forty thousand civilians were burned, blasted, or poisoned to death in Hamburg.

Until the end of June Hitler had waited at the Berghof, watching events in Italy, fearing to trigger off "Citadel"—the battle for Kursk—in case Mussolini's generals staged a mass defection while his back was turned, or the enemy launched their invasion of Sardinia (which he believed must be their next target). Thrice he had ordered fresh postponements of "Citadel." On the sixteenth General Guderian had come, and explained why his earlier tank-output estimates had proved overoptimistic. With the Panther tank it was the old story: mass production had begun before its trials were completed. Guderian suggested this promising battle tank should not be put into action until at least five hundred were available. Jodl's staff also argued against executing "Citadel" in its original form, and Zeitzler probably took the same line now: he proposed staying their own hand until the Russians had pushed out westward themselves, and *then* launching a counterattack; tactically it was an attractive idea, but Hitler's objection was that Stalin had no reason to oblige him by attacking before events on the Mediterranean front compelled Germany to send divisions there, and this objection could not be faulted. On June 18, after a fresh conference with Zeitzler and Guderian, Hitler had committed himself to the offensive solution and three days later set July 3 as the date—finally postponed by two more days upon reasoned objections stated by General Model on June 25. Kluge and Manstein approved the decision.

Yet Hitler clearly anticipated failure, for he forbade the OKW to proclaim "Citadel" publicly, so that he could deny its existence if success was denied to him.

When Goebbels had come to the Obersalzberg on June 24, Hitler had lengthily justified his strategic thinking to him. He had abandoned forever his old dream of capturing the Caucasus and waging a campaign in the Middle East; the winter had swallowed up too many divisions for that. Nor could his armies contemplate advancing on the Urals. Despite the superior quality of the new Tiger and Panther battle tanks, he had decided to sit tight and conserve strength until 1944, to render the eastern front impregnable to winter crises like those of the past two years. He regarded the imminent operation only as a "minor correction" of the line, which might well rob Stalin of a few armies or even an army group but which would hardly swing neutral world opinion to a view of Germany as victor again. In the Mediterranean he expected the Allies to assail Sardinia first and then lunge toward the Peloponnesus. "The Führer believes he can hold this line," wrote Goebbels the next day. "Under no circumstances will he fall back from the Italian mainland. He has no intention of falling back on the Po River, even if the Italians do defect; in that case the war in Italy will just have to be fought by us alone." The Duce himself was old and worn out, said Hitler, and his people were limp and listless; this was why he was determined not to become too powerfully engaged in Russia—it would tie him hand and foot if Italy collapsed.

In the Generalgouvernement of Poland, in Russia, and in other regions where there was heavy partisan activity, Himmler's SS brigades fought to restore order, if not law, for the vital links between German industry and the front line were themselves under constant attack. In vain Hans Frank and his provincial governors complained that it was Himmler's own doctrinaire and muddled policies that contributed most to the unrest and fed the partisan cause. Several times since August 1942 Frank had even tendered his resignation, only to have it rejected by the Führer. Meanwhile the SS rampaged regardless of Frank's political authority, ruthlessly arresting "suspects," rounding up able-bodied Poles for labor service, or simply terrorizing and intimidating. Himmler's forced resettlement programs in the Lublin district—with whole villages being expelled overnight and repopulated with bemused German peasants as a "Germanic bulwark" against the East—caused uproar and resulted in the indignant resignation of Frank's governor at Lublin. Outwardly a strongman, Frank was weak and vacillating. He took his complaints personally to Hitler early in May 1943, but Hitler told him his problems were nothing to those of the occupied eastern territories and sent him back to Cracow. Hitler's chagrin at the lengthy April ghetto uprising in Warsaw was so great that he would dearly have liked to replace Frank by a tougher viceroy, but by whom? Only his Gauleiters were tough enough. For two hours he debated with Bormann, Ley, and Goebbels the Party's debilitating lack of first-class leadership material. He might even have to appoint a Gauleiter as the new SA Chief of Staff.

Eventually he decided that Hans Frank must stay. Frank could not help his failure, Hitler admitted; the job was beyond anybody's ability. "He has to extract food supplies, prevent the unification of his people, ship out the Jews and yet at the same time accommodate the Jews from the Reich, he has to step up arms production, refrain from rebuilding the ruined cities, and so on." Frank bitterly opposed Himmler's methods, but after a four-hour walk with the Reichsführer on the Obersalzberg on June 19, Hitler endorsed the SS position: in the future, fighting partisans and guerrillas was to be Himmler's responsibility alone; no blame was to be attached to the SS for the current increase in partisan activity in Poland or elsewhere. Himmler noted that day: "When we discussed the Jewish problem the Führer spoke in favor of the radical completion of the evacuation of the Jews, despite the unrest this will still cause over the next three or four months—that will just have to be put up with." The vicious SS General Erich von dem Bach-Zelewski took overall command of antiguerrilla warfare.

The "Jewish problem" was taboo at the Berghof. Only once was it mentioned, during an uncomfortable scene in June a few days after Himmler's visit. Baldur von Schirach and his pretty wife—court photographer Heinrich Hoffmann's daughter Henriette—were in Hitler's house party. They joined the fireside circle, slumped in the deep armchairs in the semi-darkness; the drawing room was lit only by the single floor lamp in one corner and the candles on the mantelpiece. While Hitler drank his special tea and the others their wine or cognac, Henriette exclaimed that she had just witnessed at Amsterdam the loading of Jews into trucks for deportation. "It is horrifying to see these poor people being packed into open trucks. Do you know about it? Do you permit it?" Her outburst was greeted by an icy silence. Hitler retorted, "They are being driven off to work, so you needn't pity them. Meantime our soldiers are fighting and dying on the battlefields!" Later he added, "Let me tell you something. This is a set of scales"—and he put up a hand on each side like the pans—"Germany has lost half a million of her finest manhood on the battlefield. Am I to preserve and minister to these others? I want something of our race to survive a thousand years from now." He reproached her: "You must learn how to hate!" Henriette countered with a line from Goethe's *Iphigenie:* "Man is made to love, not hate." This was probably the occasion on which Hitler irritably asked Schirach to tell his wife not to come with her "warpaint" on again: her eyelids were silvered, and her lashes heavy with mascara. It irked Hitler that Schirach had used his wife to plead his case for him.

The next evening, June 24, Goebbels wickedly brought the fireside conversation around to Vienna. Until after 4 A.M. Hitler drew savage comparisons between Schirach's Viennese and Goebbels's Berliners until tears welled up in Henriette's eyes: the Berliners were hard-working, intelligent, and politically shrewd; Vienna's musicians were either not themselves Viennese or had to die first before they were recognized. Hitler's abruptness with Henriette unsettled even Goebbels. "The behavior of Schirach and his wife charged the evening with a certain tension," Goebbels wrote. "Frau von Schirach in particular acted like a silly cow . . . and later summed up her unhappiness by saying that she wanted to go back to Munich with her husband and would the Führer send [Gauleiter] Giesler to Vienna instead." "Tell me," Hitler challenged her, "is your husband our Reich representative in Vienna—or is he Vienna's man in the Reich?" By the time the last air raid reports came in, it was long after dawn. Hitler kissed Eva Braun's hand and withdrew to his quarters—his shoulders hunched, his head sunk, his gait firm. The Schirachs departed for Vienna in a huff the same night, without seeing him again.

In the Ruhr town of Wuppertal, three thousand civilians had been killed by British bombers in half an hour that night. Over two thousand had died in the same town in a raid one month before. Hitler decided to deliver a fresh homily to Göring the next day. As Goebbels—who had just toured the blitzed Ruhr towns himself—said, the Reichsmarschall's stock had hit rock-bottom. The ravaging of these ugly Ruhr conurbations did not perturb Hitler overmuch; one day, he predicted, Germany would have ten million Volkswagens and five million other cars to contend with, and these towns would have had to be rebuilt with broad boulevards and streets anyway. But Speer was having to divert a hundred thousand men to repair the Ruhr, and the people's morale was brittle. Hitler promised to make an early surprise visit to the Ruhr. But at present grand strategy required that he turn the other cheek: the bombers were needed for "Citadel" and Italy. He had ordered the antiaircraft and night fighter defenses increased, he told Goebbels; and now at last they were getting the heavier armament that Udet and Mölders in their wisdom had thought unnecessary. One fighter armed with the new 30-millimeter cannon had recently shot down five bombers in a single night. By autumn the army's rocket missiles should be raining down on London from launching sites on the Channel coast, he assured the propaganda minister. "For the time being we've just got to be patient."

His forebearance with Göring was truly monumental. The Reichsmarschall gently let things slide and lost his grip. Hitler had arrogated direct control of the air war against Britain to himself. But the technical stagnation of the Luftwaffe was a mystery to him. Without Göring's knowledge he invited the leading aircraft manufacturers to see him. He wanted to find out the truth, but the absence of both Göring and Milch had the reverse effect. Professor Ernst Heinkel excused his failure to produce a satisfactory heavy bomber by citing Göring's persistent demand that the Heinkel 177 be a dive-bomber—although Göring had forbidden precisely that use ten months earlier. And when Hitler questioned Professor Willy Messerschmitt about the new Me-262 jet aircraft, the brilliant designer—whose vanity had been injured by Milch's closing down an obsolete piston-engined fighter project, the Me-209, in favor of the Me-262 one month earlier—pointed out that the jet aircraft's fuel consumption would be far higher than the Me-209 and thus secured a Führer Order reversing Milch's decision. (Hitler was not told that the jet used low-grade fuels which were more plentifully available than high-octane aviation fuel.) This half-truth by Messerschmitt set back jet-aircraft production in Germany by many months.

The immediate prospect for Speer's arms factories seemed grim. The Abwehr had just received a long report on a top-secret conference held by the British ministry of aircraft production at the beginning of the week. The Abwehr's agent, "Hektor," claimed to have been one of the few people present, and quoted Sir Stafford Cripps as insisting on an increase of heavy-bomber production to five hundred a month. "Cripps said almost verbatim that after talks with Portal and Harris he has the impression that Germany might be softened-up to such an extent by the present around-the-clock bombing that a costly invasion in the west could be dispensed with altogether. The main thing now, he said, is to flatten one town after another in Germany and especially the Rhine–Ruhr area. Deliberate attacks on the civilian population are also intended, as there are reports that morale in Germany is beginning to crumble."[1] All the mysterious "Hektor's" messages so far, and those of his controller in the legation in Stockholm, were unanimous in stating that the air offensive against Germany was only just beginning. Hitler at once signed orders for Speer to begin the immediate evacuation of arms production to the occupied areas of eastern Europe.

At midday on June 29, 1943, Hitler decided to transfer his headquarters back to the Wolf's Lair. He believed "Citadel" could safely begin in six days, on schedule. The Italians had handed Kesselring the text of an urgent telegram from the British naval liaison office in Washington to the admiralty in London. It was dated June 23, and taken in conjunction with remarks of a British naval officer overheard in Alexandria it appeared to show that the Allied invasion operations

[1]Sir Stafford Cripps was minister of aircraft production, Sir Charles Portal was Chief of Air Staff, and Sir Arthur Harris was Commander in Chief of RAF Bomber Command.

in the Mediterranean had been postponed and even changed: there was now explicit reference to *three* islands, and a distinction was drawn between commando assaults and the main invasion operations, which Hitler's Intelligence experts found significant. Moreover, there seemed clear proof that Stalin was as apprehensive about "Citadel" as the German General Staff was confident: on June 21, Hans Thomsen, the German envoy in Stockholm, cabled that the Soviet diplomatist A. M. Alexandrov had arrived there and "wants to meet with a gentleman from the German foreign service with whom he is acquainted." The next day Moscow again expressed dissatisfaction with the absence of an Allied Second Front—without one, "victory over Germany is impossible." On July 1 an authoritative Soviet magazine article derided the "collective guilt" theory propagated by the West against Germany and hinted that the Reich might even keep Poland and the Sudeten territories.

Hitler arrived back at the Wolf's Lair on July 1. Fresh wooden barracks had sprouted everywhere, invisible under the camouflage netting. It was unseasonably cold here. That evening he addressed a major policy speech to his "Citadel" commanders, assembled at Zeitzler's nearby HQ. He explained why he had kept postponing "Citadel"—he now had two thousand tanks ready for the battle, although admittedly half were only the older Mark III. "In a grave, clear, and confident voice he made the following points," recorded an infantry corps commander, General Friessner:

> *Our situation.* The blame for our misfortunes must be laid squarely on our allies. The Italians let us down completely. If, as the Führer repeatedly demanded, they had made timely use of their fleet to escort and transport their troops to Africa, Africa would not have been lost. Now their ships are being smashed in their harbors. Comparison with World War I, where we too conserved our fleet too long until it was too late.—Italians failed on the eastern front, in Greece, etc. Hungary likewise: . . . Romania unreliable: the marshal's brother, Prime Minister [Mihai] Antonescu, is a devious character. Finland at the end of her tether; internal troubles with Social-Democrats, fostered and fed by Sweden.
>
> *What's at stake?* Germany needs the conquered territory, or she will not exist for long. She must win hegemony over Europe. Where we are—we stay. Soldiers must see this, otherwise they'll regard their sacrifices as in vain. Balkans must not be lost whatever happens; our most vital raw materials for war are there. The Italians have pulled out of Greece and been replaced by Germans. Feel safer since then. Crete is firmly in our hands; thus we prevent enemy from getting air bases. Greater Germany and Europe must be defended far beyond our frontiers; so far we have managed this perfectly. German troops are now occupying the isles of Rhodes, Sicily, Sardinia, and Corsica—the Italians would have long surrendered them, just as they did without fighting in Pantelleria.

> *Eastern front.* We will yield nothing without a scrap. . . . The Russians are biding their time. They are using their time replenishing for the winter. We must not allow that, or there'll be fresh crises this winter. So we've got to *disrupt* them.

(The last sentence indicates how limited "Citadel's" objective was.) Hitler concluded: "The die has been cast. The attack is on. Everything must now be done to ensure its success."

The operation itself was barely discussed. General Model repeated his misgivings, and the Ninth Army's situation was examined on the map. The only moment of anger occurred when Manstein tactlessly asked for Richthofen to be recalled from Italy to restore the vigor of the Luftwaffe on the eastern front. This upset Richthofen's stand-in, General Otto Dessloch, and brought a bellow of rage from Göring, who was jealous enough of Richthofen's prestige. Göring and Manstein otherwise shared the general optimism about "Citadel." Only Jodl did not, fearing that a long-drawn-out battle lay before them. But Hitler reassured his generals that Stalin had lost up to fourteen million troops so far and was facing a crippling famine. Of course the attack was a risk, he admitted, but he felt it had to be taken.

In Hitler's words, "Citadel" had to procure a victory "to dispel the gloom of our allies and crush any silent hopes still stirring within our subjugated peoples' breasts." His field commanders had high hopes that it would. They saw Luftwaffe squadrons amassed in a strength never before witnessed on the Russian front. The armored and infantry divisions were eager and well equipped, the troops were confident and refreshed by the months of resting. Elaborate steps had been taken to deceive the Russians.

"Citadel" began early on July 5—the Russians had evidently been forewarned, for their artillery heavily bombarded the German lines shortly before. An immense and bloody battle ensued. Longing for word of great victories once more, Hitler telephoned Zeitzler and Jeschonnek repeatedly for the latest news. Zeitzler could tell him little at first, but by evening it was clear that the battle was going well. General Dessloch's and General Robert Ritter von Greim's combined Air Forces (the Fourth and Sixth) had flown 4,570 sorties, destroying 432 Russian planes. Manstein had plunged eleven miles northward into the enemy fortifications; Kluge had come seven miles south toward him. Between their spearheads lay the city of Kursk—and 3,000 tanks which Stalin—willing to stake everything on the outcome of the battle even where Hitler was not—had thrown into the defense. The familiar euphoria gripped the Wolf's Lair, though all knew it would be a hard fight: line after line of fortifications extended before the Germans, reaching up to two hundred miles eastward into enemy territory. The Soviet tanks were well dug-in and flanked by treacherous minefields. Mass rocket-launcher regiments were waiting for the invaders too. In the first three days there were 30,000 German casualties, but Zeitzler could report that tank losses were at an acceptable level. By the eighth, 460 enemy tanks had been destroyed; Hoth's Fourth Panzer Army knocked out 195 that day alone.

But in the south the technical inadequacy of the much vaunted Panther battle tank drained Manstein's offensive badly. It was to await the arrival of 200 Panthers that "Citadel" had after all been delayed until July 5; but on that first day alone, all but 40 broke down, and a week later barely more than 16 were still in action. Nonetheless, while in the north Model's Ninth Army found it could penetrate no farther, little now lay ahead of Manstein in the south. Rommel noted in his diary at the Wolf's Lair on July 9: "Noon, at war conference with Führer: attack in the east is going well."

That afternoon, however, Hitler received the first reports that a large enemy invasion operation was again under way in the Mediterranean. Luftwaffe aircraft sighted the ships after they sailed from Malta and Pantelleria. By late evening it was clear they were heading for Sicily and not Sardinia. Hitler ordered a paratroop division thrown into action as soon as it could be ferried down to Sicily. There were reports of enemy paratroop landings and a heavy naval bombardment of the island's main harbors at Syracuse, Catania, and Augusta. The next morning the invasion began. Hitler was told at his noon conference that three hundred ships were involved.

The invasion's timing was totally unexpected. As recently as July 6, Kesselring, Commander in Chief South, had considered that the reinforcement of the Italian islands with German troops would give the enemy second thoughts about attempting an early invasion. Schmundt, Hitler's chief adjutant, had gone on leave. The invasion could hardly have come at a less propitious moment for Hitler's strategy, unless the German and Italian divisions in Sicily could throw the enemy into the sea without fresh reinforcement. The enemy paratroops were mopped up during the first day, and the "Hermann Göring" Division fought well against the Americans. On July 10 the naval staff considered that "the fight now beginning offers us every chance." Much would hinge on the Italian navy's willingness to do battle with the enemy's seaborne lines of supply: it was like the Tunis position, but reversed in favor of the Axis. Admiral Dönitz ordered every German torpedo boat into the fray, and he asked his Italian counterpart, Admiral Arturo Riccardi, to do likewise; he obliquely hinted that the Italian battleships should also be "brought up in closer proximity to the battle zone." It was clear from aerial reconnaissance that the enemy had committed his entire invasion fleet to Sicily, but even now the Italians opted for a policy of conservation of their warships.

Moreover, the most disturbing accounts reached Hitler about the actions of Italian officers in Sicily. Admiral Priam Leonardi, the commandant of Augusta, had falsely reported that on July 11 enemy assault craft had landed there. According to the local German brigade commander, Colonel Wilhelm Schmalz, the Italian defenders at once blew up their guns and ammunition and set fire to their fuel dumps; the fires were still raging. The antiaircraft batteries at Augusta and Priolo had fired their entire ammunition into the sea and blown up their guns as well. "On the afternoon of July 11 there was not one Italian soldier left in Schmalz's brigade area under any kind of command. Every single officer had abandoned his troops during the morning and was heading for Catania on bicycles and motor transport. Italian troops are drifting around the countryside and roads singly or in clusters of up to five men. Many have thrown away their weapons; some have discarded their uniforms too and donned blue denims."

By July 12 the enemy had landed 160,000 men and 600 tanks on Sicily. With a few exceptions, the Italian fleet lay idle under the hands of its older-generation officers. A strategic decision, which he could no longer ignore, now confronted Hitler.

On July 12, Stalin launched his own counteroffensives.

Before, however, we proceed to analyze Hitler's strategic decisions, it will be appropriate to examine the origins of his continued buoyancy. With hindsight, we can recognize July 1943 as the month the tide finally turned against him. Why did he not see this too? Hitler felt that even if "Citadel" were called off, it would still have drawn the Soviet dragon's teeth: Manstein alone counted 24,000 prisoners by July 13; and he had also captured or destroyed 1,800 enemy tanks, 267 artillery pieces, and 1,080 antitank guns. In consequence, no Soviet counterattack of strategic significance need be feared before the autumn. The Berlin view was that if nonetheless Stalin had had to counterattack now, it was because famine and unrest were sweeping his country. This was well supported by Zeitzler's Intelligence experts, who had sorted through hundreds of bags of captured Russian mail. There were comparisons between 1943 and the disastrous Soviet killer-famine of 1921. One letter described a girl's forty-mile trek through wolf-infested country just to get fifteen eggs. "The letters often afford heartrending glimpses into human destinies," the army digest read by Hitler said. "A mother describes to her husband at the front how their children are growing up and sketches the outline of their tiny hands. A twelve-year-old girl writes to tell her father that her mother has died, and imparts to her lines all the sympathy that her suddenly grown-up heart can bestow. A young wife dispels all her husband's fears that her love won't outlast their separation, which has already gone on three years, in words of deep and powerful sensitiveness. These are no subhumans who wrote these letters." Hitler was probably more impressed by the recurring theme in them: the Soviet Union was at its last gasp.

Above all, Hitler now had the prospect of German "secret weapons" to sustain him until 1944. On July 8, Dönitz came with blueprints of the new Type XXI submarine, all-electric, with an underwater speed so high that it would frustrate all the enemy's defensive tactics. His experts hoped the first boats would be ready by November 1944, but he had discussed with Speer ways and means of producing them much faster. As for the enemy's deadly radar detection equipment, Dönitz hoped to fit out all his U-boats soon with a simple device that would give them ample warning that a radar set was homing onto them. A new antishipping mine had been developed—so potent and so difficult to combat that for the present Hitler would not even allow his navy to employ it for fear the enemy would capture one and use the device in far greater numbers against Germany. As Speer came in, Hitler turned to him. "The most vital thing is to build this new U-boat." Speer replied, "We all agree on that. We have already ordered that it is to take priority over everything else."

That same day Speer brought to him the top scientists of the army's rocket research laboratory at Peenemünde on the Baltic. Hitler knew that Göring and Milch had a team at Peenemünde developing a pilotless flying bomb, but he had been cool toward the army's A-4 rocket project. Todt had expressed dismay at the lavishness of the Peenemünde site's installations and doubted that anything practical would emerge from the complex of engine-test rigs, launching pads, and wind tunnels. But Brauchitsch had backed the A-4 project, and General Friedrich Fromm, commander of the Replacement Army, had been a dedicated benefactor; he had shown Speer over Peenemünde in June 1942 and the new minister had been captivated by the grandeur of the project and lent it his authority. Hitler frankly and realistically told Speer some months later that the A-4 would be pointless unless five thousand were available for the first salvo and production ran at the rate of three thousand a month—a cool appraisal from which he was, however, to depart in the intoxication of the hour of revenge. After all, the rocket had only a one-ton warhead, yet cost as much as one hundred of Milch's flying bombs. In June 1943 Himmler saw an A-4 being launched and learned of its impacting accurately over one hundred miles away. He also commended it to Hitler—oblivious to its disadvantages: it was fueled by such exotic substances as liquid oxygen and pure alcohol, and its fourteen-ton weight was largely aluminum and electronics equipment, both of which were needed far more urgently for the Luftwaffe's industry. But Speer turned a blind eye on this, for he was not, after all, accountable for the aircraft industry as yet. On July 8, Speer introduced to Hitler the men behind the A-4 project: Gerhard Degenkolb, the man who had revolutionized the locomotive industry in 1942 and was now to mass-produce the rockets; General Walter Dornberger, commandant of Peenemünde; and a young, flaxen-haired chief scientist, Wernher von Braun. Hitler gripped his hand. "*Professor* von Braun!" he greeted him. Both the army and the Luftwaffe assured Hitler that their missiles would be operational against England before the year was out.

Two days later, July 10, Heinrich Himmler came to the Wolf's Lair. The A-4 rocket was at the top of his agenda: the wide diversification of Himmler's interests is testified to by the fact that within a year the SS was to have complete control of rocket plants and launching batteries.

Himmler never disappointed Hitler, let alone bored him. One minute he was discussing the use of "Russian poisons in Africa," or the case of the exiled Russian Archduke Vladimir; the next it was the procurement of foreign currency, the bombing war, or the SS panzer corps. Today Himmler wanted to advocate turning the Polish underground army against Stalin. Hans Frank was also demanding a new line over Poland, and the SS was clandestinely fostering a Polish underground group, "The Sword and Plow," to ferret out the rival pro-Allied underground army. The latter was bitterly disillusioned now that Churchill had openly torn up Chamberlain's costly guarantee to Poland, and when the Gestapo captured the Polish underground's chief, General Stefan Rowecki, Himmler felt the whole army could be swung around to fight Stalin instead of the German occupation forces. Hitler read Rowecki's *vita* and admitted that he had had the same idea. But he decided against it: Rowecki was obviously a leader, and such men were dangerous. Himmler noted: "The Führer then reiterated the basis of our Polish policies. These I was aware of and fully understand."

Hitler willingly used non-Slav soldiers in the fight against Stalin. Himmler regularly reported on his SS volunteer divisions raised in the occupied countries. Hitler particularly wanted to attract British captives into joining the fight. Hewel had noted after a conversation with Hitler on November 29, 1942: "He believes that countless patriotic Englishmen must be suffering under their present regime, as they see the future danger of the Jews, and particularly the Bolsheviks, taking over the Empire. He considers it quite possible that given suitable treatment a British legion could be raised to fight in British uniforms against bolshevism. Such a legion would be more welcome to him than one of any other nationality." The problem was that while the Russian captives would, the British would not fight for Hitler; and the one legion Hitler would not even contemplate was a Russian "liberation army."

As he had told his generals on July 1, his soldiers must have the animal satisfaction of knowing that the ground they were fighting for would become theirs for all time. "When our fine peasant lads march into action now they are not thinking, 'Thank God we can liberate this soil for the wonderful Ukrainians.'

They are saying, 'What land this is! Here I come—and here I stay!' " As for the "partisan-infested" regions of the northern Ukraine and the central front, Hitler accepted Himmler's radical proposal that the entire population should be evacuated forthwith; the adults would labor for the Reich, their children would be taken away from them and housed in camps on the periphery, to work in the *Kok-sagys* rubber plantations Himmler planned to cultivate in those regions. *Kok-sagys*—a species suited to temperate climates—was another child of the Reichsführer's fertile brain.[2]

After the Russian counteroffensive began north of operation "Citadel," with Orel as its target, Hitler placed General Model in tactical command of both the Ninth and the Second panzer armies there. The northern pincer of "Citadel" could advance no farther, and on July 13, the Führer summoned both army group commanders, Manstein and Kluge, to discuss the operation's future. Kluge wanted "Citadel" called off. Manstein, still brimming with optimism, took the opposite view. His armies were on the brink of victory—if he could add the Twenty-Fourth Panzer Corps to them, it would tilt the balance finally against the defenders of Kursk; the Russians had thrown their last reserves into the battle—now Hitler must commit his. He could still encircle and destroy half the troops defending Kursk. If the battle was tamely abandoned, the enemy would be free to cause trouble later elsewhere along the front. When Kluge declared that the Ninth Army could not resume the attack either now or later, Hitler irritably exclaimed, "The Russians manage everything, and we manage nothing at all!" Thus the battle was stopped—neither defeat nor victory. Hitler had not excised the Kursk pocket and herded off its inhabitants to slave labor as he wanted; he had lost some 20,720 men, including 3,330 dead. "That's the last time I will heed the advice of my General Staff!" he proclaimed to his adjutants; but he generously shielded Zeitzler himself from the criticism that now sprang up against him. Hitler had himself agreed to the operation and issued the orders for the attack; the responsibility was, he admitted, his and his alone.

But the Russians had suffered the heavier losses in "Citadel"—17,000 dead and 34,000 prisoners. Their tactical reserves had been decimated. Accordingly, the next weeks were to see the Russian summer offensive faltering: when they launched an attack on Manstein's southern front on July 17, Mackensen's First Panzer Army and General Karl Hollidt's new Sixth Army were able to beat them back, taking 18,000 prisoners and destroying 700 tanks in two weeks. When Stalin issued his order of the day on the twenty-fourth announcing his victory at Kursk—

[2]Hitler had just appointed him Special Commissioner for all Rubber Plant Affairs.

he claimed that 70,000 Germans had died, and 2,900 German tanks been destroyed—Hitler remarked, "My feeling is: this proves he has called off his own show . . . Stalin has abandoned all hope of pushing on here in one big *furioso.*" It seemed that stability had returned to the Russian front.

In Sicily, meanwhile, there was crisis. Unless Hitler could move reliable divisions into Italy and the western Balkans, the Allies would soon land there too. The Italians were barely putting up the pretense of a fight. All the indications were that Mussolini's renegade generals and the king were plotting his overthrow. Why otherwise had Ambrosio played the familiar Italian card of raising impossible demands for modern tanks and aircraft to be supplied forthwith by Germany? He demanded two thousand planes late in June: it was like August 1939 all over again, only this time both countries were fighting a determined invader, immensely superior in arms and men, with his command unified, resolute, and nearby; as for the Axis, Mussolini was in Rome, where he was surrounded by men the Führer saw as knaves, weaklings, and intriguers, while Hitler was in East Prussia over a thousand miles away.

The American army mopped up the Italians in western Sicily, but the British Eighth Army was soon held up by a tough, predominantly German-manned line of defense forward of Mount Etna. However, unless the Italians showed more fight, Hitler was loath to risk committing more German divisions to the island. He had ordered Colonel Schmalz's report on Admiral Leonardi's behavior at Augusta to be shown to Mussolini, and Mussolini had promised an immediate investigation; but the Duce also made a perceptible effort to push the blame for what now seemed the inevitable loss of Sicily onto the Germans for having failed to meet Ambrosio's supply demands. On July 13 thirty Italian torpedo boats did sally forth to attack enemy ships off Syracuse, but they returned unscathed, lamely pleading that they had not found any Allied shipping. Richthofen, commanding the Second Air Force, sneered in his diary: "As expected, the Italian fleet has not even put to sea 'to save its honor.' " Dönitz telephoned Hitler's headquarters that if Hitler so commanded he was willing to take over the Italian navy at once, so as to bring at least the loyal destroyers and submarines into action.

While Hitler would not go as far as that yet, he did ride roughshod over Italian sovereignty elsewhere. He decided that the defense of Sicily could only be entrusted to the Germans, and he directed an army corps staff to be flown in to reconnoiter the best line forward of Mount Etna. He personally sent a major to Sicily with the top-secret oral instruction that the German corps commander was to take over the battle himself, "unobtrusively excluding" Italians from control. A German commandant was also nominated for the Strait of Messina; the Italian batteries there were if need be to be manned with German crews. Dönitz eagerly supplied 1,723 naval gunners from the 10 batteries he had lined up in France for a possible occupation of northern Spain. On the fourteenth, the OKW brought its contingency plans for a lightning German action against Italy and the Italian-occupied Balkans up to date. If the Italians did an about-face, Rundstedt would force the mountain passes between France and Italy, and General Student's paratroops would take over the Brenner Pass.

On July 14, Hitler showed Mussolini's letter—drafted by Ambrosio—demanding 2,000 aircraft to Milch. He had already ordered one fighter and four bomber squadrons added to Richthofen's air force in Italy. But the Italian ground organization would have to be overhauled. In the last three weeks 320 aircraft had been destroyed in attacks on Italian airfields; 36 fighters out of a squadron of 40 had just suffered tire damage, for the Italians had not bothered to sweep the runways clear of bomb fragments after a raid; Richthofen had had to turn down the Luftwaffe's finest antishipping squadron because the Italian runways were too short and primitive to handle it. "Otherwise," Milch assured the Italian ambassador, "the Führer could hardly have provided better air support for Germany than he is providing for Italy. Hundreds of aircraft are already on their way to Italy and hundreds more are on their way at the expense of the night-fighter defenses of our own western air space." The navy and Luftwaffe were both contributing their heaviest gun batteries—literally hundreds of guns—to the defense of the Strait of Messina. But Hitler rightly hesitated to commit his armored divisions to Sicily. As Jodl warned, it seemed likely that Ambrosio was plotting to lure as many elite German divisions as possible to the south, where they could be cut off and turned over to the enemy on a platter when the time came. Hitler agreed with this stark appraisal of their allies' ulterior intentions. Somehow he had to prevail on Mussolini to rid himself of General Ambrosio, his own appointed gravedigger; German generals had to take over the most endangered areas. Dönitz supported Jodl's view and asked that the Italian admiralty also be frozen out, to reduce its present unholy influence on the campaign.

Hitler decided to meet Mussolini again. Meanwhile he picked General Hube, the veteran of Stalingrad, to command all ground troops in Sicily. Göring tried hard to get his own Luftwaffe's General Rainer Stahel appointed, but Rommel outargued him. Hitler had intended giving Rommel overall command in Italy, but now Göring got his revenge. On July 18, Rommel wrote in his diary: "At midday with the Führer. Field Marshal Kluge also there . . . I learn that the Führer has been advised not to make me Commander in Chief in Italy, as I am supposed to be hostile toward the Italians. I assume the Luftwaffe is behind this. Thus my employment in Italy recedes into the dim and distant future again.—Apparently the Führer's going to meet the Duce."

Two new army groups were now created: B, to be commanded by Rommel from Salonika, covering Greece, Crete, and the Aegean; and E, commanded by General Löhr from Belgrade to control the rest of the Balkans. In the event, Rommel's new appointment lasted just one week.

On July 18, Hitler flew down to the Berghof. He sat just behind the cockpit, his papers spread out on the folding table, meditating that it was all turning out just as he had feared. "This was precisely why I was so apprehensive about launching our offensive in the east too early," he said a few days later. "I kept thinking that at the same time we'd find our hands full down south."

His strategy now was this: somehow they must tempt the enemy to pour huge reinforcements into the island of Sicily—then the Luftwaffe would bomb the supply ships to pieces and starve the invader into submission; what he wanted was Tunis in reverse. He had therefore resolved to confront Mussolini with a personal ultimatum: either Sicily must be effectively defended—with a view to reverting to the offensive later on—or it should be abandoned, and the decisive battle fought on the Italian mainland. But first the Duce would have to tighten his grip over the Italians and his armed forces.

The one-day meeting between the Axis leaders had been planned for later but advanced to July 19 by events in Sicily. Mussolini—who had originally wanted several days with Hitler as he had had in April—probably wanted to impart to the Führer that his country could no longer fight on. But Hitler did not give him a real opportunity to speak his mind—not even during the time they spent together in the Duce's shabby, old-fashioned train with its jostling staff in comic-opera costumes. The account rendered in Mussolini's later diary describes how things went from the moment Hitler arrived at the Treviso airfield:

> Punctually at nine the Führer landed. He inspected the guard of honor and we proceeded to the railroad station. After about an hour the train left us at a station outside Feltre. An automobile bore us onward to the villa selected for our meeting, the house of Senator Gaggia, a veritable labyrinth of rooms and salons which are still a nightmare in my memory. We arrived there after an hour's drive in an open car under a scorching sun, during which I merely exchanged polite small talk with the Führer.
>
> The actual meeting began at noon. . . . The Führer began the talking, and continued for two hours. His words were taken down in shorthand and the complete text of his speech is in foreign ministry files. Scarcely had he begun when my secretary came in with a telephone message from Rome: "Since 11 A.M. Rome has been under intense air bombardment." I informed the Führer and the others. The news charged the atmosphere with tragedy—the atmosphere crowded in on us with each fresh telephone message reporting the exceptional length of the raid, the number of bombers employed, and the

severe damage (including the university and the church of San Lorenzo).

When the Führer had concluded his speech, a first confidential exchange of opinions took place between the two of us. He imparted two important facts to me: firstly, the U-boat war was about to be resumed with other means; and secondly that at the end of August the German Luftwaffe would begin reprisal attacks on London, razing it to the ground within a week. I replied that in anticipation of the reprisals this would provoke, Italy's air defenses would have to be [strengthened].[3]

I was then called away to receive fresh reports, whereupon it was time to return. Only during the hour-long train journey could I make one thing plainly understood to him: that Italy is now withstanding the entire weight of two empires—Britain and the United States—and there is a very real and growing danger of her being crushed beneath them. The bombing of our cities damages not only our public's morale and powers of resistance, but also our main war production. I told him again that the campaign in Africa would have ended very differently had we been at least equal, if not superior, to the enemy air force. I also warned that the nervous tension within my country is now at an extreme and dangerous pitch.

He told me the Italian crisis was a leadership crisis, and hence a human one. He would send reinforcements for the air force and new divisions to defend the peninsula. He declared that the defense of Italy is also in Germany's highest interests. His choice of words was friendly at all times, and we parted on the best of terms. The Führer's aircraft took off soon afterward.

Hitler was curiously satisfied with the outcome of this—as it happened, his last—visit to Italy. He believed he had revitalized the Italian war effort. His generals were unimpressed. Field Marshal Richthofen wrote that day: "Landed at Treviso at five to nine. As is right and proper, the Duce and Kesselring met me there. . . . At the villa the Führer delivered a two-hour speech without a break to the Duce, his military staff, and other companions on how to fight wars and battles. Nobody apart from the Duce understood a word. Afterward, Ambrosio observed with a smirk that it was not so much a *coloquio* as a *disloquio*. . . . The Führer was tired from so much energetic speaking, but looked well, much better than the Duce. Then the same trek back to Treviso. The whole show has probably produced less than one could conceal under a little fingernail."

"On parting," Richthofen wrote, "the Führer was again most cordial. The routine query as to my well-being. Particularly pressed me not to risk my health

[3]Mussolini omitted the word *assicurare*.—The German record indicates that Hitler told him of the radar warning-devices being fitted to the submarines and of the decoy buoys and new U-boat types arriving early in 1944. "Finally the Führer also mentioned a weapon on which he did not want to impart precise details, but which would enter service against the British when the winter began and against which there was no defense"—evidently meaning the A-4.

or myself—saying I would make a fine trophy for the British if they could get their hands on me. I could only respond that I would look even more unsightly stuffed than I do now."

As he flew back from the Berghof to East Prussia on July 20, Hitler was despondent about Mussolini's future. The previous evening Martin Bormann had shown him an Intelligence report cabled by Himmler to the Berghof; it contained clear evidence that "a coup d'etat is being planned to get rid of the Duce and install Marshal Badoglio to form a war cabinet." Himmler's report said: "B[adoglio] is known to be a leading Freemason in Italy. His aim is said to be to commence immediate peace talks the moment the Anglo-American troops have completed their occupation of Sicily." The cable was long and circumstantial. There was no point in warning Mussolini—he was of an almost childlike naïvete. On the railroad station he had blurted out to the Führer: "I just don't know what my generals can be thinking of, stationing such strong forces up here in the north. They are supposed to be defending Italy!"

Shortly afterward, German railroad officials on the border tipped off the OKW to the fact that the Italians were steadily stockpiling ammunition in the fortifications facing the Reich, for example at Tarvisio.

Rommel was summoned to see Hitler on July 20 and entered in his diary: "At Führer's evening conference: major breach in the eastern front at Army Group Center, aimed at Orel. All quiet in Sicily. His talk with Duce yielded no real clear decisions. Duce unable to act as he would wish. I am to take command over Greece, including the islands, for the time being, so that I can pounce on Italy later." The next day he wrote: "Morning conference: eastern front somewhat firmer, but big breach at Orel. Russians still have 8,700 tanks operational." That afternoon he saw Jodl: "The Duce is aware of his colleagues' political intentions." On July 22, Rommel wrote: "At the Führer's midday conference: eastern front now stable apart from Orel." He flew off the next day to begin his thankless task in Greece, where apart from the questionable Italian Eleventh Army he would command only one German panzer division and three German infantry divisions. Admiral Canaris's Abwehr still maintained that the main Allied invasion was not that in Sicily, but still to come in the Balkans.

Meanwhile, an ominous calm had overtaken the murderous bombing war. The Luftwaffe had abandoned its costly and ineffective raids on London and provincial cities, as the bomber squadrons were needed in Italy. Since mid-June long-range German night fighters had begun harassing Allied bombers over their own English airfields, but Hitler disapproved of such intruder-operations: the German public wanted revenge for their own dead and maimed—what did it care for minelaying operations or pinpricks against enemy airfields? When Göring and

Milch came to see him on July 23, he emphasized: "You can only break terrorism by counterterrorism. We have got to counterattack—anything else is useless!" When Colonel Peltz defended the intruder-operations, Hitler variously replied, "At present we can be pleased with ourselves if our crews even find London!" "Can't find London—a disgrace!" "If this goes on, the German public will go raving mad!" "The British will only stop bombing if their own cities are being flattened, and not otherwise!"

The next day, July 24, the first storm signals were hoisted over southern Europe. Unsettling and indeterminate news reached Hitler that the Fascist Grand Council was being convened that evening in Rome for the first time in many years. Roberto Farinacci, a radical and independent Fascist agitator, evidently intended thereby to force Mussolini to adopt more extreme measures against his opponents; but this was in fact playing straight into his critics' hands. As midnight passed without fresh word from Rome, Hitler grumbled that if a Farinacci had pulled a trick like that on him, he would have had Himmler haul him off straight away. "What good can possibly come of such a meeting? Just empty chatter!" At 3 A.M., the *consiglio* was still in session. Before Hitler retired for the night, word reached him that the British had attacked Hamburg with up to a thousand heavy bombers, that the port city was a blazing inferno, and that for some as yet undetermined reason the radar defenses had failed to function.

The first photographs of the hideous scenes there were shown to him the next morning. Corpses of men, women, and children littered the streets—the women with their hair in curlers, the men clutching suitcases, the children seeking shelter in the arms of fire-fighters. In one parish alone eight hundred civilians had died. At his noon conference Hitler learned that the enemy had begun jamming the ground and airborne radar sets by the very means the experts had feared all along: "They have released cascades of hundreds of thousands of strips of metal foil into the sky." The antiaircraft gunners and fighter pilots were fighting blind from now on; the bombers could maraud everywhere with virtual immunity. During the week that followed, Hamburg was to suffer three more night attacks. In one, an immense firestorm began, the huge fires creating hurricane-strength winds that sucked trees, rooftops, debris, and people into their flames; the tens of thousands sheltering in the massive concrete bunkers were incinerated alive, poisoned by monoxide fumes, or drowned by the flood of bursting water mains. Part of Hamburg's antiaircraft batteries had been sacrificed for the defense of Italy.

Even the terror of the first night failed to presage the fact that over forty thousand more people would be killed there in the week to come. But Hitler steeled his heart. For the present, Rome was more important. He swung around on Ribbentrop's liaison official. "See that you find out what you can, Hewel!"

Hewel replied, "They adjourned their *consiglio* at three this morning. I will find out the moment anything else comes through." But by the time the conference ended at 2 P.M. he could still report only that wild rumors were sweeping Rome.

Later that day word came that Marshal Badoglio had asked the German ambassador to see him. Mackensen declined, but the aged marshal insisted on a meeting. Badoglio then dropped his bombshell: Benito Mussolini had resigned. The king had asked the marshal to set up a military government. "Badoglio has taken over," exclaimed Hitler to Keitel that evening. "The blackest of our enemies!"

"Axis"

In the week immediately following Mussolini's overthrow, Hitler vacillated between two extremes: his initial instinct was to send paratroops to Rome, flush out the monarchy, the traitors, and the Vatican, and restore the "wronged" dictator to power. He refused to believe that the Duce had willingly abdicated; he assumed that his restoration alone would bring back the Fascist organization that had seemingly melted into nothingness overnight. As July 26, 1943, dawned, he even sent out orders for his troops to abandon Sicily forthwith, leaving their tanks and equipment where they were; for between Sicily and the Brenner Pass there were virtually no German troops at all, apart from Field Marshal Kesselring's headquarters staffs outside Rome and the naval detachments based in certain Italian ports. It was indeed a chilling situation: a thousand miles of Italian coastline along which the enemy might at any moment land and be positively welcomed by the new regime in Rome. Were he, Hitler, in Churchill's shoes he would have struck at once to reap such a rich reward. Yet as the days passed and more moderate advisers came to the Wolf's Lair, reason prevailed; the enemy was as perplexed by the new situation as he was, and now time worked in Hitler's favor. Throughout August the Wehrmacht foothold in Italy was steadily strengthened, in spite of Badoglio's protests. A brilliant rearguard action was fought in Sicily after all. And when in September Badoglio and his generals finally fulfilled the Führer's gloomiest predictions and hoisted the long-prepared white flag of surrender, Hitler was ready to step in.

These weeks of drama were not devoid of comedy or bereft of bitterness. The stenographic records of Hitler's first conferences after word came from Rome show how effectively he could grapple with major crises. Sepp Dietrich's SS Life Guard Division must be rushed from the eastern front to Italy at once; the seventy thousand German troops in Sicily must be brought back to the mainland—abandoning their heavy equipment if need be. "Their pistols are all they'll need. . . . they can make short work of the Italians with pistols too"; there must be an evacuation of Sicily "like Dunkirk" in 1940. The 3rd Panzer-Grenadier Division must seize Rome, arrest the government, and kidnap the king and above all the crown prince, who would be retained as hostages to guarantee that Italy abide by her pact with Germany; Badoglio must be captured dead or alive; Mussolini must be found and rescued, if he had not already been put to death, in which case his body must be recovered to prevent the enemy from putting it on public display. And Rommel! "Find out where Rommel is!" The field marshal was run to earth in Salonika: at 11:15 P.M. on July 25 the OKW telephoned him to return to the Führer's headquarters at once.

From all over Germany they flew in to the Wolf's Lair—Himmler, Guderian, Goebbels, Göring; Speer was already there; Ribbentrop, convalescing from a lung ailment, arrived looking pale and drawn; Dönitz decided to come with several of his staff; Schmundt was ordered back from leave; Roberto Farinacci was flown up from Munich, whither he had escaped from Rome. (Hitler contemplated using him—pending Mussolini's rescue—to set up a puppet Italian government to rival Badoglio's, but he abandoned the notion the moment he talked with the weedy Italian—indeed, he began to suspect that Farinacci had been bribed by Badoglio to convene the *consiglio* which had brought about the Duce's downfall.) What disturbed all the Party leaders most was this vivid proof that dictatorships could be toppled with such ease. As Jodl bluntly put it, ruminating out loud to Hitler: "The fact is, the whole Fascist movement went pop, like a soap bubble!" Hitler directed Himmler to ensure that nothing went pop in Germany.

Yet while Hitler mastered the initial details of the crisis, his statesmanship abandoned him, swamped by the signals transmitted by his enraged emotions. For several days he was tempted to adopt rash expedients that would have put him wholly in the wrong and brought the entire Italian people solidly behind Badoglio and the king. The very existence of General Hube's soldiers in Sicily depended on the Italian railwaymen and dockers; and the longer these continued to work, the better were Hitler's chances of infiltrating additional German divisions into northern Italy.

But Hitler felt outraged; that Mussolini, a leader bound to him by destiny, should have been so ignobly deposed by traitors and vassals of the monarchy, made his blood boil. He did not doubt that Badoglio was already working hand-in-glove with the enemy. "We can be clear on one score: traitors that they are, they will of course proclaim their intention of continuing the fight. Of course! But it will be a betrayal." He smiled contemptuously. "We shall be playing the same game, leading them on until we suddenly drop like lightning on the whole bag of them and round up the entire gang." On July 26 he sent Captain Wolf Junge, Jodl's staff officer, to Kesselring with oral orders to stand by to seize Rome and prevent the Italian fleet's escape. Hitler instructed the Second Paratroop Division to fly to an airport outside Rome the next day without advance warning to either Kesselring or the Italians. The 3rd Panzer-Grenadier Division was also to move to the outskirts of the capital. Hitler would give the code word the moment Badoglio moved a muscle against Germany's interests; if that fateful twitch occurred too soon for full-scale intervention, then Kesselring and General Student would have to occupy Rome with what forces they could muster from the headquarters staffs there—the proverbial German cooks and clerk-typists who had on occasion also wrought havoc on Americans troops in Tunisia.

In the teahouse of the Wolf's Lair Himmler had lined up half a dozen Luftwaffe and army special agents as candidates for the job of rescuing the mislaid Fascist dictator, now known to have been arrested on the king's orders on leaving the palace. Otto Günsche, Hitler's bodyguard, took them into the Führer's study. Hitler asked each in turn: "What do you think of the Italians?" The last of them, a burly scar-faced Waffen SS captain, growled: "What a question, mein Führer! And me an Austrian!" Hitler picked this man, Otto Skorzeny, and assigned him a secretary to note down everything he would need. Skorzeny would leave with Student for Rome next morning. The latter parted from Hitler with the words: "A tough but particularly rewarding mission, mein Führer!"

Worn out, that evening Hitler ate alone. No less than thirty-five people packed the following war conference. Two factions were clearly crystalizing: the one, led by Dönitz and Jodl, decried precipitate action against Italy; the other, led by Hitler, wanted Student to strike as soon as he was ready. Rommel wanted the whole operation adequately thought out and prepared, but Goebbels felt that the British would hardly wait a week while Rommel was doing his thinking and preparing. Göring had already stated his opinion at midday: "Our opponents will obviously scream to the Allies for help and beg for protection." Hitler pointed out: "But it will still take them some time to get ready to invade." At first the British would be nonplussed—they always were. Everybody, particularly Goebbels and Ribbentrop, opposed Hitler's plan to sweep through the Vatican as well; "apologies afterward" would never repair the harm this would do to Germany's image abroad. Meanwhile Kesselring and Richthofen insisted from their Italian headquarters that Badoglio would stay loyal to the Axis cause; Badoglio—cunningly adjudging Kesselring's marked sense of military chivalry—had received him that evening with a copy of Napoleon's *Italian Campaigns* open on his desk. "You see, Field Marshal," he explained disarmingly, "this is the problem that gives me sleepless nights. How to lead a defeated army on to victory?" Kesselring reported innocently that Badoglio had only replaced Mussolini to provide the strong war leadership needed to restore honor to Italian arms. Hitler could only chuckle at Kesselring's gullibility.

Militarily, Hitler knew he could not defend the entire Italian mainland when Badoglio defected. "In the course of events we shall obviously have to fall back along here somewhere," he had said on July 25, tapping the map of Italy. "That is quite plain." In addition to the divisions he was already moving into northern Italy from southern France, he wanted three SS armored divisions taken out of Manstein's Army Group South: the SS divisions were most politically akin to fascism. Their transfer would in turn necessitate withdrawing the German salient at Orel to release divisions for Manstein. Kluge, brought before Hitler on the twenty-sixth, was aghast. "Mein Führer! I am bound to point out that there is nothing we can release at this moment. That is quite out of the question at present!" Only when his army group had fallen back on the new "Hagen" line, along the Dnieper, could he offer any help; but this sector of the East Wall had only just been begun and would not be ready for occupation before September. Hitler feared that Badoglio would have defected long before then. "September is quite impossible, Field Marshal!" he retorted. And he angrily commented, "The swine on the other side shovel out a line in two days, and *we* can't throw *them* out!" For the time being, however, he had to make do with Sepp Dietrich's Life Guards alone.

The next evening Field Marshal von Richthofen arrived from Rome. The crowded war conference with Hitler lasted until nearly midnight. "Everybody very rude about Kesselring," wrote Richthofen in his diary. "I counterattack. Some of his dispatches are admittedly psychologically tactless, but by and large objective and accurate. I identify myself with them. . . . Rommel knows nothing, thank God says nothing, and is just reveling in feelings of revenge against the Italians, whom he hates. Dönitz is moderate and sensible. Everybody else, especially Ribbentrop, just repeating whatever the Führer says."

Richthofen stubbornly stuck to his guns: premature action by Student would be a catastrophe. Jodl backed him up, and so did Dönitz. Richthofen did predict that Marshal Badoglio might raise impossible military demands and use their nonfulfillment as a pretext to deal with the enemy; almost on cue Ambassador Mackensen's telegram arrived from Rome, announcing just such Italian demands. Richthofen urged Hitler to appear to accept everything in order to win time to infiltrate Rommel's divisions into Italy. But Hitler's big worry was that he was missing the bus—that in silent agreement with Badoglio the British would suddenly arrive by air and sea in Italy. On this score Richthofen had to agree. Hitler ordered: "Student is to fulfill his mission as soon as possible." When Rommel left for Munich to join his new Army Group B headquarters the next morning, he had Hitler's secret instructions for the invasion of Italy in his pocket; but on no account were he or any of his more famous officers to show themselves south of the Reich frontier for the time being. Canaris's Abwehr was ordered to give Rommel every support, using its agents in Italy to find out what Badoglio and his frontier troops were up to.

It was at this moment that a blustering speech by Churchill rescued Hitler from his dilemma.[1] Speaking in the House of Commons, he said that nothing short of "wholesale unconditional surrender" would prevent Italy from being "seared and scarred and blackened from one end to the other"; he expected the new Italian government to take some time reaching a decision. "We should let the Italians, to use a homely phrase, stew in their own juice for a bit." Secretary of State Cordell Hull issued an equally intransigent statement in Washington. Badoglio and the king were evidently between the devil and the deep blue sea. They can scarcely have expected an armistice to prove so unattainable after the Allied wooing and blandishments of the past month. Now Hitler knew he would have *time* after all. A message was sent to Kesselring reminding him not to let General Student unleash "Operation Black," his plan to occupy Rome, "through any misunderstanding."

An immensely self-satisfied Führer joined his field marshals for lunch that day, July 28. By evening his mind was made up against precipitate action. Richthofen wrote: "From 9 P.M., Führer's war conference. Militarily speaking, all quiet. The sensible solution has at last won through for Italy. Obviously southern Italy will (now!) be pumped full of forces to meet the real enemy and all other eventualities. Our only purpose now is to play for time. With this in view all Italy's demands will be accepted." To the chagrin of the Italians, Hitler's divisions now began rolling singly over the Brenner into Italy.

Despite the curiously reassuring appreciations of Admiral Canaris's Abwehr and its associated Foreign Armies West branch of the General Staff, Hitler had more than enough direct evidence of Badoglio's stealthy and treacherous maneuvers. The reliability of Himmler's SS Intelligence channels cannot have failed to impress him in these weeks. It was through the SS-fostered "Post Office Research Institute" that Hitler obtained on July 29 the transcript of a radio-telephone conversation held soon after midnight between Churchill and Roosevelt. Ignoring the possibility that the enemy could unscramble this link, they had gossiped about the "imminent armistice with Italy" in language that told Hitler that Roosevelt at least was in secret contact with King Victor Emmanuel but that many days would pass before Italy would defect, because first the terms of the armistice would have to be thrashed out. Churchill wanted to prevent the sixty thousand British prisoners in Italy from being shipped to "Hunland." But by his very

[1]Since he made no reference to the speech in his memoirs, Winston Churchill evidently belatedly realized this. As the German naval staff crowed in its war diary the next day: "Churchill's speech has thrown a cold douche on patriotic circles in Italy and been a boon to us."

garrulousness he was ensuring that Hitler would propel enough divisions into Italy to do just that.

On July 30, Rommel's army group reported that the Italian defenses along the Brenner were being stealthily reinforced, and demolition charges laid. Hitler learned reliably from the Croatian Poglavnik that General Roatta, the Italian army Chief of Staff, had recently told a fellow general that Badoglio's protestations of loyalty were just a ploy to win time; indeed, on the thirty-first the Italian minister at Zagreb told the Poglavnik that Italy was not merely going to desert the Axis—she was going to join the enemy.

Nevertheless, Canaris's Intelligence agencies played all this down. When it was learned that the *comando supremo* had burnt its secret files two days before the Duce's overthrow, Colonel Alexis von Roenne (chief of Zeitzler's Foreign Armies West) swore that this did not indicate that treason was in the air. At the beginning of August, Canaris came to Hitler's headquarters and reported on a meeting he had just had with General Amé, his Italian opposite number: the Abwehr chief blandly assured Keitel that Badoglio was resolved to fight on. "There is no question of any peace negotiations."[2] During August, the discrepancy between these assessments by Canaris and Roenne and those by the SS, the foreign ministry, the Forschungsamt, and the frontier Gauleiters in Austria grew so wide that the German admiralty raised a scandalized comment in its war diary. By this time Italian obstructionism was at its height. The railways were purposefully jammed with civilian traffic to impede the entry of fresh German divisions; Hitler accordingly ordered them to enter on foot, despite the scorching Mediterranean sun. There were gunfights between Italian and German officers. At staff talks with Keitel and Ribbentrop in Tarvisio on August 6, General Ambrosio again assured the Germans that Italy "wanted to fight on at Germany's side," but his lack of interest in securing more German arms and material told Ribbentrop all he needed to know. He telephoned Hitler immediately—this was "treason, one hundred percent."

When Ribbentrop's belief was subsequently confirmed by events, this should have led to Canaris's final downfall. But he was too slippery for that. In September he trumped his SS challengers with a file of miraculously accurate Abwehr dispatches and accused Keitel of having withheld them from the Führer. Thus Canaris survived.

---

[2]General Amé has stated that Canaris met him in Venice on July 30 with the whispered congratulation: "We hope *our* July 25 will also soon come!" Canaris begged Amé to do everything to prevent the entry of more German troops. The SS learned of this, but Himmler declined to unmask Canaris to Hitler at this stage. Both Canaris and Roenne were later hanged for treason.

Under the new code word "Axis," Hitler's planning for the occupation and disarming of Italy and the seizure of her idle fleet at La Spezia continued throughout August 1943. Mussolini had still not been found by the Führer's agents. All that was known was that he was still alive, because Hitler's sixtieth birthday gift to him—a twenty-four-volume set of Nietzsche—was duly acknowledged by the deposed dictator. Meanwhile the hunt went on.

The Anglo-American air offensive had not lessened, but Hitler paid scant attention to it. After the first big Hamburg raid he had greedily signed Albert Speer's draft decree for the mass production of the army's A-4 rocket missile—the later V-2—to bombard London that autumn; heedless of the effect on the Luftwaffe's aircraft industry, Hitler had on July 25 ordered all available skilled labor, raw materials, machine tools, and electric power devoted on high priority to the rocket missile. "You can only smash terror with counterterror," he had reiterated that day. "Otherwise the time will come when the people here just lose faith completely in the Luftwaffe." Speer was as yet doing nothing to support the Luftwaffe's plea for proper emphasis on the fighter defenses. Milch had already stepped up fighter output to one thousand a month and was planning to treble this over the next year; and highly effective new night-fighter tactics had been improvised in the wake of the Hamburg catastrophe, abandoning the rigid but thin line of radar-guided fighters in favor of packs of two to three hundred at a time, fighting the enemy freelance over the actual burning target area. On August 1, Albert Speer dismally predicted to Hitler that if six more cities were given the Hamburg treatment, the war would be over. But in commending the A-4 rocket to Hitler he was mistaken, for what Germany needed were fighters for the defense of the home base.

Göring's influence over Hitler was now weak; and General Jeschonnek, the Luftwaffe Chief of Staff, had reached the end of his tether—torn between Hitler's demands and Göring's reproaches. Hitler ordered the women and children moved out of the Reich capital at once. Berlin was evacuated of one million civilians in grim anticipation of the raids to come. On August 13 the American bombing of Wiener Neustadt resulted in a four-hour row between Hitler and Jeschonnek. Four days later the Americans bombed the ball-bearing works at Schweinfurt and Messerschmitt's plant at Regensburg, killing four hundred workers. That night the British saturated Peenemünde with bombs, killing seven hundred scientists and slave laborers. Jeschonnek committed suicide, and Milch at last persuaded his successor, General Günther Korten—whom the Reichsmarschall presented to Hitler on the twentieth—to transfer fighter squadrons back to the defense of the Reich. From the British bomber-loss figures supplied to Berlin by the imaginary agent in the British air ministry, Hitler decided that the night air-war at least was tilting slowly back in Germany's favor.

On August 20 Hitler discussed with Dr. Ley and leading architects how to take care of the survivors and the bombed-out families. When Ley offered to build

350,000 homes a year, Speer interrupted: "I will not provide the materials, because I cannot." His counterproposal was for the nationalization of all homes, but Hitler would not hear of that. "I need a million new homes, and fast. Each about ten feet by twelve; it is immaterial whether they are of wood, concrete, or prefabricated slabs. I am even thinking in terms of mud huts or at worst just holes in the ground simply covered over with planks. The houses should be built singly in individual plots, around towns and villages, where possible scattered about among the trees." He did not expect each house to have a lavatory, or gas, water, or electricity—just the barest essentials in a form that even old women or children could easily erect, for their menfolk were at the front: two benches, a table, a cupboard, and nails to hang their clothes on. "We are forced to build as spartanly as possible, so there must be no distinction between them. The main thing is for these people to have a roof over their heads when winter comes; otherwise they will perish."

Speer's inability to provide materials for Ley's program to house the homeless was not unconnected with his own massive support for Hitler's secret weapons projects. On this same visit he persuaded Hitler to authorize the manufacture of an immense gunsite on the Channel coast; the guns were to have four-hundred-foot barrels and be theoretically capable of maintaining a permanent attack on London: several propelling charges were to be detonated in sequence to give each shell the necessary velocity—a principle which worked on a small scale but not when it eventually came to the test. The huge underground gun battery swallowed up hundreds of thousands of tons of urgently needed concrete, and it never fired a single shell at England. Himmler was afflicted with the same strategic blindness, having himself been intoxicated by visits to Peenemünde. He offered Speer concentration camp labor to build missile factories and man the assembly lines; he also offered him the use of the SS proving ground at Blizna, Poland, for the rocket-launching trials. Hitler ordered Speer and the SS chief to make the maximum use of caves, tunnels, and bunkers for what all three evidently considered a significant element of Germany's coming strategy.

In Berlin, Dr. Goebbels marshaled the ministers and Party officials for a pep talk to restore their battered morale; the Führer remained in East Prussia, directing the war in Russia and the Mediterranean. The German people must at all costs stand fast during the trying months to come: until the fighter and antiaircraft defenses mastered the bombing terror, until the missile attack on London could begin—and until the monolithic Anglo-American and Soviet facade began to crack.

Hitler believed that the evidence justified his hopes that one day the western Allies would turn against Moscow and decide they had committed a blunder in continuing to assail Germany. The first straw in the wind had been Stalin's rejection of General Wladyslaw Sikorski's London-based Polish exile government in April, and the creation of a puppet Polish committee in Moscow. In July, Stalin had followed this with a "Free Germany" committee consisting of exiled Communists and renegade generals captured at Stalingrad. Now British newspapers at last scented where Moscow proposed to lay the postwar boundaries of the bolshevik empire. Conversely Stalin's recall of his ambassadors from London and Washington, and his absence from Churchill's conference with Roosevelt at Quebec, indicated Soviet dissatisfaction with the Allies. There were rumors that Stalin wanted peace talks with Germany. "I fully recognize that at present a ruthless desire to destroy us has the upper hand in Britain and America," reflected Hitler. "But the British have got it all quite wrong! They declared war to preserve the 'balance of power' in Europe. But now Russia has awakened and turned into a state of the highest technical and material caliber. . . . This means that the onslaught from the east can in the future only be met by a united Europe under German leadership. That is in Britain's interest too." The time must come, in Hitler's view, when the Allies would realize their political mistake and reason would replace their present campaign of hatred and destruction against the most potent power in Europe.

Until Italy's future was more certain, however, Hitler could not speak his mind to the German people. For the same reason, he hesitated to order General Hube to evacuate his sixty thousand troops from Sicily to the mainland: on the one hand Admiral Dönitz protested that giving Sicily to the enemy would provide them with easy access to southern Italy and the Balkans; but on the other, General Jodl warned that the moment military operations were launched for the rescue of Mussolini or the capture of Rome and the Italian fleet at La Spezia, the Italians would cut off all the supply routes to Sicily and the sixty thousand men would be lost. Everything thus hinged on the loyalty of Badoglio to the Axis. Kesselring, Mackensen, and Rintelen all reported that he could be trusted. But the contrary evidence was overwhelming. From his Gauleiter in the Tyrol Hitler learned that the Italians had stealthily moved three divisions—two of them known for their anti-German inclinations—into Bolzano and Merano. "These steps were obviously taken to satisfy the Anglo-American requirement that Italy must take positive action against Germany if she is to get better peace terms."

Kesselring wanted southern Italy packed with German troops, but Hitler felt this was risky and unnecessary, as the British would be unlikely to invade a malarial zone. He told General Heinrich von Vietinghoff, whose new Tenth Army would take over the two corps stationed there, that he proposed eventually to evacuate Lower Italy and "would not be happy until all those divisions from southern Italy and Sicily were standing south of Rome." For the time being, Hitler instinctively rejected Rommel's insistent demands for Kesselring to be recalled so that he, Rommel, could exercise the supreme command in Italy—south as well as north; he anticipated that the time might well come when

Kesselring's infuriating optimism would stand Germany in good stead, and he adhered to the split command. Rommel's political plus was his blind faith in Hitler. "M[ussolini] probably won't be coming back," he wrote from his Munich headquarters. "The Fascist party was evidently very corrupt and was swept away in a matter of hours. . . . On the other hand it suits us well, as now there is only one great man to lead in Europe." Admiral Dönitz shared Rommel's sentiments about Hitler, writing with trembling hand after forty-eight hours at the Wolf's Lair: "The enormous energy the Führer radiates, his unerring conviction, his prophetic analysis of the situation in Italy—all these have very much brought home to us these last few days what poor worms we all are in comparison to the Führer!"

Rommel came up from Munich on August 11, arriving in time for the noon war conference:

> Göring, Dönitz, Student, and Himmler are at the conference. Eastern front: heavy fighting at Kharkov, big Russian breach west of the city. At Leningrad a battle of attrition, with day-long artillery barrages; offensive expected on August 12.
>
> Discussing Italy, the Führer agrees with my own views. Führer appears to intend sending me in quite soon. Like me he doesn't believe in the honesty of the Italians. . . . The Führer says the Italians are playing for time; then they will defect. The probable object of the Churchill-Roosevelt meeting is just to lure the Italians into treason, particularly since the Italians are obviously taking part in the talks. . . . The Führer evidently wants to adhere to his old plan of restoring fascism to power, as this is the only way to guarantee that Italy will unconditionally stand by us. He has sharp words of condemnation for the work of Mackensen, Rintelen, and Kesselring, as they—and particularly Kesselring—still totally misinterpret the Italian situation and blindly trust the new regime. . . .
>
> Zeitzler is very aloof toward me, and reserved. Worried about the eastern front?
>
> Lunch with the Führer. I sit on his left. A very spirited discussion, with the Führer evidently delighted I am there. Again and again I find that he has complete confidence in me. . . .
>
> Before supper I confer with Jodl. His plan, based on our proposal, was for me to take command in Upper Italy. My new draft has me in command of all Italy, with two armies (north and south), while being myself under the Italians; the army group HQ near Rome so as to exert influence over the *comando supremo* and the regime. After I refute his objections, Jodl agrees.
>
> Then supper with the Führer, and evening conference. . . . He approves my proposal to fight a delaying action in Sicily and to fall back on Italy only when forced to do so, and meanwhile to establish four lines of resistance [across the peninsula]—the first from Cosenza to Taranto, the second at Salerno, the third at Cassino, and the fourth and ultimate line along the Apennines. . . .

One last attempt was made to force the Italians to show their true intentions. Hitler ordered Rommel and Jodl to confront the Italians with a putative plan for a joint defense of Italy and to study their reactions. The meeting took place at Bologna on August 15. General Roatta took the news that Rommel would command all German forces north of the Apennines very badly. He icily submitted a map which would in effect deploy the Italian divisions in a barrier across the peninsula, where they could trap the Germans in the south; the motive was clear.[3] (On the same day the Italians declared Rome an "open city"—evidently for no other reason than to prevent the Germans from using its railway lines to the south.) Rommel wrote a twenty-page memorandum on the Bologna meeting. Jodl more succinctly cabled the OKW that evening: "Grounds for suspicion remain undiminished." Hitler ordered the evacuation of Sicily to begin.

While even the overt relations between Germany and Italy were thus deteriorating, Hitler had continued patching up his defenses in the Balkans. King Boris of Bulgaria was invited for a two-day informal visit to the Wolf's Lair. According to records kept by Hitler's manservant, they lunched together for three hours on August 14 and again the next day before Hitler himself accompanied Boris to Rastenburg airfield. He had asked the king to provide two more Bulgarian divisions for security purposes in Greece, but Boris was reluctant in view of the potential risk to his country from Turkey; besides, he wisely pointed out, the Greeks hated the Bulgars, so such a move might only increase the disturbances. Bulgaria's military position was precarious: in return for rich territorial concessions from Hitler, she had declared war on the Allies but not on Russia; but the Soviet Union was known to be grooming divisions in the Caucasus for an invasion of Bulgaria, and a powerful Communist movement was emerging in the land.

Two weeks later King Boris was struck down by a disease of mysterious suddenness. The German air attaché in Sofia provided immediate air transport for the king's German physician, Dr. Seitz, on August 24; Seitz reported that the king was dying. Ribbentrop's staff warned of the grave consequences to Bulgaria's policies. "Without the king, the Bulgarian people would be leaderless and uncertain of themselves, and they might come under the influence of the Communist and pro-British opposition." Seitz provisionally diagnosed a bladder disease, and Professor Hans Eppinger was summoned for consultation from Vienna. Complications set in, and the famous neurologist Professor Maximilian de Crinis was

[3]At that very moment an Italian general, emissary of Marshal Badoglio, was in Madrid informing the British ambassador there that if the Allies were now to land in Italy the regime was willing to make common cause with them against Germany. Not surprisingly, the main records of the Italian ministries involved in this affair remain classified in Rome to this very day.

flown in from Berlin on the twenty-eighth; but at 4:20 P.M., the king died. The government communiqué spoke of angina pectoris. Upon the doctors' return, Hitler instructed his minister of justice to discharge them from their oath of secrecy and to question them; they were unanimous that the cause of death was not angina pectoris but an exotic snake-poison. It was the characteristic "Balkan death," as Eppinger put it.

Hitler was disconsolate at the loss of this stabilizing influence in Bulgaria. Enemy radio broadcasts rejoiced at Boris's death. He ordered a powerful delegation to attend the state funeral, including Admiral Raeder, Keitel, and an impressive assembly of army generals. His instinct told him that the House of Savoy lay behind the murder: rumor had it that Boris's queen—Giovanna, third daughter of the king of Italy—was a leading figure in the Bulgarian underground; and was it not suspicious that Princess Mafalda, her sister, the wife of Prince Philipp of Hesse and "blackest carrion in the Italian royal house" (as Hitler luridly described her), had spent some weeks in Sofia quite recently? Curiously, while the Bulgarian government had agreed to allow the German doctors to perform a postmortem, the king's own family had refused. Gradually the pieces of Hitler's jigsaw puzzle were clicking into place. From the Forschungsamt he learned that Prince Philipp had recently dictated groups of ciphers over the telephone to Mafalda, evidently employing some private code. But to arrest him would be to alarm the Italian monarchy too soon. So Hitler invited the prince to be his guest at headquarters, treated him with continued hospitality—and told his guards not to let him out again.

Hitler's Intelligence agencies stubbornly contrived to distract his attention to his western front and Scandinavia—rumoring enemy invasion plans throughout August. Hitler took these threats very seriously and attributed their nonmaterialization only to the worsening weather. His edginess increased, and where a shrewder statesman would have wooed the subjected peoples with diplomacy, he resorted to brute force. This only increased the unrest and guerrilla activity.

Denmark—straddling his lines of communication to Norway—was a classic example. On the evening of August 21, Hitler had invited his staff movie cameraman, Lieutenant Walter Frentz, whose birthday it was, to take supper with him. Frentz had just returned from another tour of the Atlantic Wall project, and he mentioned that several guerrilla bomb incidents, including one at his own hotel, had marred his visit to Denmark. Hitler ordered Jodl to obtain daily reports on this "guerrilla war" in the future, and he berated Ribbentrop for being taken in by the bland dispatches of his diplomats. A few days later—alarmed by the reports the OKW commander, General von Hanneken, was now submitting—Hitler ordered Ribbentrop to issue an ultimatum to the Danish government; it was to declare a state of emergency, ban public meetings, outlaw strikes like those currently paralyzing half the country's ports, and introduce draconian measures against guerrilla activities. As Hitler evidently anticipated, the ultimatum was rejected, and the Danish forces were disarmed early on August 29 almost without a shot being fired; the generals were rounded up, the king and crown prince were placed under house arrest, and the Danish navy was surrendered to Admiral Dönitz.

Over the weeks that followed, Heinrich Himmler assumed police control of the luckless peninsula. Hitler ordered him to deport all Jews, discounting warnings that this might increase the political unrest in Denmark; several thousand Jews escaped to Sweden, but 477 were rounded up by the Germans and taken to the Theresienstadt concentration camp in October. Quixotically he ordered the release of the fifteen thousand Danish officers and men who had been interned in August, and thus the bitter pill was sugared.

Hitler's trust in Himmler and the SS was now absolute. While at the beginning of 1943 the SS chief had complained of his maltreatment by the Führer—who seemingly remembered him only when he needed fresh divisions raised—now Himmler's star was firmly in the ascendant. Hitler was sure that Germany would never forget the heroism of the Waffen SS divisions that had recaptured Kharkov in March and dispelled the gloom of Stalingrad. In his eyes the regular army was corrupt and slothful, incapable even of retreating without cramming its trucks and baggage with tons of looted property, while the SS troops could be relied on to fight well and strike terror into the enemy's heart. Himmler's pocket diary shows him attending Hitler's conferences with increasing regularity; sometimes Hitler phoned him in person; they lunched together two or three times a week or dined far into the night.

Now more than ever Hitler needed Himmler. He did not doubt the growing precariousness of his position. Events in Italy had sparked off a mood of defeatism in Germany. Himmler—in a secret January 1944 speech—epitomized the mood thus: "The Duce arrested, the Fascist party dissolved! How smoothly it went! Oh how glorious!—And then the murmurs begin: So, a Duce can be arrested. Very interesting. And many a rash mind poses the question, Why not here in Germany too! Then we'll be rid of the Nazis, we can make peace with the British, the British will guarantee Germany against Russia—and everything will be all right!"

Throughout August 1943 the Reichsführer and Gestapo rounded up German dissidents. The aged and infirm were let off with a warning. The more able-bodied, "not more than 150 in all" Himmler boasted, were put to the guillotine. The most dangerous group was, however, left at large: in March, Himmler had warned Hitler that certain nuclei of ex-ministers and dismissed army generals were beginning to plot a coup d'etat. There was General Franz Halder, whom he code-named "Reservist" ("As he's holding himself in reserve to take over the German army," Himmler sneered in August 1944); and he was also keeping watch on the former finance minister, Johannes Popitz, and his circle under the code name "Baroque" ("Because that's just what they were: baroque!"). For months Popitz had been trying to establish contact with Himmler through an intermediary, a lawyer called Carl Langbehn. The lawyer explained to the crafty Reichsführer that the war must be stopped, peace made with Britain, and the Führer pensioned off. Himmler at once told Hitler: "I'll bump him off right now—what cheek!"—meaning Popitz. But Hitler laughed. "No, not that. Hear him out first. Send for him, and if in that conversation he puts his cards straight on the table, *then* you can arrest him!" Himmler—appointed minister of the interior on August 20 in place of Dr. Wilhelm Frick, whom Hitler found infuriatingly timid and legalistic—sent for Popitz three days later and secretly recorded the entire conversation on magnetic wire. Gestapo officials stood by to arrest the man, but—Himmler ruefully admitted later—Popitz would not be lured out of his reserve and he left the building a free man.[4]

Thus Himmler was in the ascendant, and the "moderates" were on their way out. Once Frick had proposed to Hitler setting up a Reich Senate of academics and clergy as a supreme constitutional body—the very image, Hitler now remarked, of the Fascist grand council that had just proven Mussolini's undoing. Hitler appointed Frick Protector of Bohemia and Moravia in Neurath's place. At the same time he up-rated Karl-Hermann Frank's powers as deputy protector in Prague, so as to vest absolute authority in him. As Göring later disarmingly put it: "It became increasingly clear that the Führer was turning more and more to the representatives of brute force."

Jodl's account of the Bologna meeting of August 15 convinced Hitler that Italy was about to defect.

Rommel was instructed that if necessary he was to "make ruthless use of his weaponry to get his way." On August 17 an Italian general forced a German unit at gunpoint to hand over American parachutists they had taken prisoner in northern Italy. Late the next day Hitler issued a further directive to the southern front, beginning thus: "In some form or other it is expected that Italy will surrender to enemy pressure, sooner or later." He ordered Vietinghoff's Tenth

[4]Popitz was executed after the failure of the attempted assassination of Hitler on July 20, 1944; Langbehn was also executed. Halder was arrested. There is no proof for the postwar legend that Himmler ever plotted against Hitler with them—quite the reverse.

Army to move three mechanized divisions to the coastal area most in danger of invasion, the stretch between Naples and Salerno. The Italians had now assembled nearly seven divisions around Rome, leaving only one division to defend all Apulia.

Two formidable Allied convoys were sighted by agents, passing eastward through the Strait of Gibraltar. One was reported laden with seventy thousand troops and their equipment. Kesselring now assessed the enemy's total strength in the Mediterranean at twenty-five divisions, apart from those in Sicily. Hitler deduced that this was too significant a concentration for just an operation against Sardinia or Corsica: responding to Soviet pressure, the enemy must be about to invade the continental mainland. The admiralty agreed. Southern Italy was most likely, though even southern France could not be ruled out. "There is no precise evidence as to the enemy's intentions." The sentence exposed the bankruptcy of Canaris's Intelligence networks. Himmler's were working well. Early on August 26 he alerted Hitler to an agent's urgent message from Rome: "Badoglio has asked Britain for an armistice regardless of conditions. The British have promised to reply by Saturday, August 28, 1943, and want to send in a strong convoy meantime with the most up-to-date weapons to enable temporary resistance to be offered to German troops." Jodl asked the Luftwaffe to mount a rigorous air surveillance off the coasts of Italy. The tension still mounted. There were fresh clashes between the Italians and Rommel's troops in the north, now entering Slovenia with Tiger tank regiments. The Italians were detected making plans for resistance in Toulon; Hitler ordered the port's immediate occupation by his Wehrmacht.

Late on August 30, the OKW issued a revised directive for "Axis," under which Italy was to be occupied by German forces. When that code word was issued, the Germans were to disarm the Italians, seize their weapons—particularly the tanks of the "Centauro" armored division—and prepare a gradual fighting retreat northward to Rome. Northern Italy was to be pacified and a Fascist government restored. Kesselring's forces were to link up with Rommel's. The retreating troops were to burn and destroy "as though on enemy soil." Corsica was to be held (eventually General Frido von Senger und Etterlin was given command). Field Marshal Weichs would assume command of the entire southeastern front, the Balkans. Meantime, Canaris was instructed to raise a secret army of South Tyroleans to watch over the German supply routes; and he was given responsibility for ensuring that no harm came to the generating stations supplying the vital Brenner railroad. All this while, the Italian generals and government were expressing pained surprise that Hitler showed so little faith in their loyalty to the Axis cause. Hitler had replaced his two credulous diplomats in Rome—Mackensen and Rintelen—with two from a more skeptical school: Ambassador Rudolf Rahn and Colonel Rudolf Toussaint. Their dispatches spoke a more realistic language about the future.

From late September 2 on, it was plain that an invasion of southern Italy was imminent. At 6 A.M. the next day one hundred landing craft disgorged two divisions of the British Eighth Army on the southernmost point of the peninsula, at Reggio di Calabria. Hitler could do little to interfere. The Italians imposed a virtual news blackout and offered little resistance themselves. In the afternoon a British message was decoded: "Six hundred prisoners taken, including two colonels; no minefields, no Germans, civilians are friendly." The Germans had only the 29th Panzer-Grenadier Division down there; it began a fighting retreat, inflicting heavy casualties on the British all the way. Ironically, in view of what is now known,[5] the German naval commander in Italy, Admiral Wilhelm Meendsen-Bohlken, reported that day that Badoglio's government could be trusted. The report blandly assured Hitler: "They are stifling anything redolent of peace demonstrations." The Italian navy in particular had promised him that there could be no question of "a repetition of Scapa Flow or Toulon" with their fleet. Hitler marveled at the admiral's gullibility.

When Romania's Marshal Antonescu visited that day, Hitler told him to expect no gratitude from the Italian monarchy. He was convinced the king of Italy was dealing with the enemy. The Führer begged Antonescu to be on guard against poisoning attempts, and he repeated this warning to Rommel on September 4. Rommel—like Hitler—knew that the latest British operation was only the thin end of the wedge. "The thick end in the western Mediterranean has still to come. I am to have an audience of the king shortly. The Führer has forbidden me to eat anything there, out of concern for my health." In his diary that day he entered:

> Immediately after arriving at the Wolf's Lair I joined the [1 P.M.] war conference. General Glaise-Horstenau was also at the Führer's conference.
>
> Afterward lunched with Führer until 5 P.M. The Führer makes a tranquil, confident impression. He wants to send me to see the king of Italy soon. He agrees to my Italian campaign plan, which envisages a defense along the coastline, despite Jodl's objections (which don't hold water in a modern war). —The Führer considers it still too early for the countries of Europe to unite. —Himmler wants to send us Hausser in exchange for Sepp Dietrich. At my request this plan is dropped.
>
> On eastern front the situation has reached the crisis point; the Russians have managed to break through.—In Calabria the British are not going to be attacked; Calabria is to be abandoned.
>
> 8.30 P.M. Dinner with the Führer. Previously with Jodl. Führer advises me to take care when I see the king.

[5]That same day, September 3, 1943, the Italians signed their armistice with the Allies at a conference in Sicily. It was kept secret for five days, to give the enemy the maximum tactical benefit.

It was at about this time that after one war conference, Hitler was observed sketching with his colored pencils a new flag for a Republican Italy.

He had given Antonescu a reasonably forthright account of Germany's military position—although he had tended to minimize the resurgence of the Soviet threat. Instead, he referred to the disastrous Russian harvest and to Stalin's fifteen million casualties. "The first one to lose his nerves will lose the war as well," said Hitler.

During August, while Hitler was reinforcing his strength in the Mediterranean, Stalin had cleverly exploited the strategic impasse to mount a series of attacks all along the eastern front. Manstein repeatedly warned that Stalin's objective was to cut off his own Army Group South and Kleist's Army Group A in the Crimea and Kuban bridgehead, and he demanded that either at least twelve new divisions be provided him to reinforce his northern flank, or that Hitler permit him to withdraw from the coal-bearing Donets region. This would shorten his front by one-third and thus provide him with the reserves he needed. At 7 A.M. on August 27, Hitler flew down to his old headquarters in the Ukraine; Manstein told him that without reinforcements he could not prevent the Russians from sooner or later breaking through to the Dnieper River. Hitler stayed five hours, listened calmly, promised to transfer divisions to Manstein from Kluge's Army Group Center and from Army Group North; then he flew back to East Prussia. His promise to Manstein was broken within one day, for Kluge had his own enemy breakthrough to contend with; he arrived at Hitler's headquarters the next day and talked the Führer out of further weakening Army Group Center.

For several days Hitler was in the grip of indecision as he waited to see which way the cat jumped in the Mediterranean. But while Hitler hesitated, Stalin did not. On the Sea of Azov, General Hollidt's new Sixth Army was breached and a corps briefly encircled. On his own responsibility, Manstein told Hollidt to fall back—the first irrevocable step toward abandoning the rich Donets Basin. Hitler had repeatedly warned Zeitzler: "If we lose the Donets Basin, we lose the coal we need for our arms factories. And then the war will be over in eleven months." But Speer and his coal experts had assured Zeitzler that this was not so, and Hitler had no choice but to allow Manstein to withdraw. However, he ordered him to destroy anything of value to the enemy first. This decision was announced to Manstein at the Wolf's Lair on September 3.

The next day Hitler also authorized the withdrawal of General Ruoff's Seventeenth Army from the Kuban bridgehead across the Strait of Kerch. As recently as June, Speer's engineers had put into service an overhead cable railway across the four-mile-wide strait; it was capable of transporting a thousand tons of supplies a day from the Crimea to the bridgehead. For many months Stalin had confronted the bridgehead with over fifty divisions, but now he was no longer impressed by Hitler's ability to mount a new offensive and was deploying them elsewhere; Marshal Antonescu agreed with Hitler that the bridgehead had become a liability. Liquidating it would release nearly four divisions for the rest of the front. Kleist was ordered to speed up the fortification of the Crimea. How Hitler longed for the autumn rains to return!

Thus the eighth of September 1943 arrived—a hot and airless day. Hitler had slept only four hours but was awakened at 5:45 A.M. because he had to fly down to Zaporozh'ye to see Manstein again. The field marshal had cabled a frantic picture of his army group's plight the day before: over fifty-five Russian divisions were now confronting his forces, and still Hitler could offer no solution. The Russians had again pierced the Sixth Army, and at the frail weld between Manstein's and Kluge's army groups the dam had finally burst and the enemy was pouring westward toward Kiev and the middle reaches of the Dnieper.

An inexplicable restlessness gnawed at Hitler here in the Ukraine. Was it Italy? Two days before, Jodl had shown him a breakdown of the Wehrmacht's commitments and hinted that only from southern Italy could divisions possibly be spared for the eastern front. But suppose Badoglio's eighty divisions then defected to the enemy? It was a tangled web. On the seventh Hitler had suggested "unraveling it by brute force." Here at least he could take the initiative by putting a blunt political and military ultimatum to Badoglio: either provide a satisfactory explanation for his machinations, manipulations, and troop movements—or take the immediate consequences. The ultimatum was being drafted at this moment. Now, after barely ninety minutes at Manstein's headquarters, Hitler could stand the uncertainty no longer. He bolted back to his Condor aircraft, was airborne at 12:45 P.M.—leaving Russian soil for what was to prove the last time—and was back at the Wolf's Lair in conference by five.

Again his sixth sense had served him well. He found that two hours earlier an ominous SS teletype indeed had arrived—a four-day-old report by an agent on the Italian air staff. He had just overheard Ambrosio's *comando supremo* secretly telephoning this message to the air force: "Italian peace proposals by and large accepted by the British. We are trying to iron out difficulties raised by Americans." Other reports were conflicting. The Allies' morning newspapers were noisy with rumors of armistice. But the king of Italy had just assured Rahn that his country would fight on, and Badoglio had told the envoy the same: "Germany has still to learn what an Italian general's word of honor means!" Worn out by events, Hitler dozed in his room for half an hour.

Almost at once he was awakened by an adjutant. The BBC had just announced Italy's "unconditional surrender." No details were given, but shortly afterward General Eisenhower broadcast a proclamation from Algiers radio: "The armistice was signed by my representative and representatives of Marshal Badoglio and takes force immediately." At 6:30 P.M. Hitler summoned a full war conference, with Ribbentrop as well. He telephoned Goebbels to come at once on the night train. Jodl put in a direct telephone call to his generals in Rome. Both were at that very moment seeing General Roatta—and the army's Chief of Staff was hotly refuting the Allied broadcasts as wicked libels on the honor of Italy. Consternation gripped Hitler's staff, as Roatta's denial still robbed him of the freedom to issue the code word "Axis." Jodl drafted a monition alerting all commands, but before it could be teletyped, Ribbentrop learned from Rome that at 7:15 P.M. Badoglio had confessed that Italy had indeed surrendered.

The OKW acted like lightning. At 7:50 P.M. Jodl's adjutant telephoned the code word to the south. Within half an hour it was confirmed in writing. There was precious little advance warning, but as Jodl later pointed out, even the two hours' advance notice given by the BBC had given Germany some opportunity to issue orders before the Italians could react. It was unlikely that the Italian fleet could be kept from escaping; at 8:45 P.M. Admiral Cunningham was heard radioing the Italian ships to run for the nearest Allied haven.

The German admiralty commented: "The consequences of this vile act of treachery—unique in military history—will be very different from what Italy had hoped. The countryside will become a battlefield between the betrayed allies of yesterday and the ruthless conquerors of today." Alas, no record of Hitler's conversations that evening remains. Long after dawn the group disbanded. As Prince Philipp of Hesse—nephew of the Kaiser, son-in-law of the king of Italy—went out, the chief of Hitler's police bodyguard stepped forward and arrested him; he was consigned that same night by car to the Gestapo at Königsberg, and he remained in a concentration camp until the war was over.

Relieved that the clouds of uncertainty had been dispelled, Hitler fell into bed at 5 A.M. to snatch five hours' rest after a working day of twenty-three. He alone had steadfastly predicted this treachery.

Feelers to Stalin

While in the north Hitler's troops stood their ground, the Russian offensive during September and October 1943 swept over Novorossisk, Bryansk, Poltava, Smolensk, Dnepropetrovsk; and on November 6, Kiev itself fell. Army Groups South and Center had fallen back on the new "Panther" line—primarily along the Dnieper River—but Stalin rapidly built up fresh bridgeheads here as well. Hitler stormed at General Zeitzler, his Chief of Staff: "You see! I gave you permission to build the Dnieper line you were always asking for, and where is it? The troops found nothing ready for them!"

That much was true. But it is difficult to pinpoint the blame for the failure of the East Wall project. The causes are buried too deep in papers and memories to emerge with any clarity. The earliest blame attaches to Hitler and his stubborn determination to keep the fighting as far from the Reich as possible. After the winter crisis of 1941–1942 he had argued that a strongly fortified rear position would actively tempt his frontline generals to fall back on it. During 1942 he reversed this view, and he encouraged the army to fortify the stabler sectors of the front using impressed labor drawn from the local Russian population. Kluge had done little, causing Hitler to exclaim—after Mussolini's overthrow and the failure of "Citadel"—"If only he had done some construction here, instead of talking so much hot air and making explanations!" On the southern front the position was different. With his armies advancing on Stalingrad and the Transcaucasus there was no cause to construct walls far in the rear; but now that they were falling back, it was too late. While the West and Atlantic walls were built under virtually peacetime conditions, now every train in the east was needed for men, munitions, and the paraphernalia of war.

Speer's papers show Hitler repeatedly discussing with him in February and April 1943, the erection of improvised fortifications in the east. But neither Speer nor Zeitzler had set wheels in motion. Speer recorded on July 8: "Changing his earlier position, the Führer now fully agrees that the construction of the East Wall must be speeded up," but this is clearly an attempt to establish an alibi for himself before the judgment of history. The files of both Speer and the army are strongly flavored with the kind of jealous squabbling over rights and privileges that seems to have inflicted more damage on the German war effort than all the enemy's armies and bomber squadrons combined. In early September the rivalry was still raging. Zeitzler was loath to allow Speer's Todt Organization engineers to direct the East Wall project. Hitler ruled that only these engineers had the know-how to provide big, permanent fortifications, but Zeitzler favored earthworks and more primitive sites. Speer thereupon secured Hitler's signature to a decree consolidating his own absolute control of the Todt Organization throughout the Reich and occupied territories. A long feud, however, smoldered between Speer and the organization's director, Xaver Dorsch. Besides, the architect Speer had displayed in the Atlantic Wall project little of the inspiration and energy that distinguished the engineer Fritz Todt's work on the 1938 West Wall. Speer was primarily a munitions *minister,* and he had his eyes on higher targets still: his redesignation by Hitler early in September as minister of armaments and war production led to authoritative rumors that Speer was a future minister of war. He was collecting his own court around him—Goebbels, Milch, and Himmler, to whose SS General Hans Kammler he had just relinquished control of the army's A-4 missile production program.

Parallel to the high-level bickering over construction of the East Wall ran a debilitating argument over the precise route it should follow. Zeitzler had always favored following the Dnieper, as its western bank was a steep cliff towering often 150 feet above the eastern plains. In summer the river was a raging flood sometimes two miles wide and virtually unbridgeable. But it was over a hundred miles behind the lines, and initially Hitler would not agree to such a fatalistic view of the future. Now the stalling of "Citadel" and Mussolini's overthrow left him no choice. On August 12, Zeitzler ordered the army groups to start building the East Wall immediately, provisionally following the Dnieper in the central front; it was to go from the Kerch peninsula in the south to Lake Peipus and Narva in the north. The OKW, the Luftwaffe, and the navy raised immediate protests about this route. One of "Barbarossa's" original objects had been to push the closest Russian bomber airfields out of striking range of the Reich, while at the same time providing airfields from which Heinkel 177 bombers could devastate the Urals industries; the proposed East Wall route would defeat both objectives. In addition, abandoning the Black Sea naval base of Novorossisk to the enemy would not only sour Germany's political relations with Turkey, Romania, and Bulgaria but jeopardize the German sea transport to Sevastopol and the Crimea. In the south the Germans would be forfeiting the coal and grain of the Donets Basin and the Central Ukraine. If at least a bridgehead around Zaporozh'ye could not be defended, then the loss of the hydroelectric power station there would make it impossible to mine the manganese of Nikopol and the iron ore of Krivoi Rog, or operate the blast furnaces at Dniepropetrovsk. Thus Speer's plan to establish a munitions industry in the Ukraine would collapse.

Equally, both Army Group North and the naval staff objected to the proposed route of the northern section. An East Wall built from Velikiye Luki to Lake Peipus and Narva—as Zeitzler proposed—meant the final loss of Leningrad; and the Russian fleet could again maraud in the Gulf of Finland and jeopardize both the German navy's training programs in the Baltic and the iron-ore shipments from Sweden; the important oil-shales in Estonia would also have to be written off. But Zeitzler wanted a defensible East Wall built by the end of October, and on September 4 he issued orders to the army groups to that effect: east of the line, the population and property along a twenty-five-mile-wide belt was to be ruthlessly exploited for the project; a swath of total destruction in this zone must make it impossible for any enemy to survive the elements there. "The outlying area must become a desert."

Field Marshal Georg von Küchler, commander of Army Group North, came a week later to protest in person to Hitler. He agreed with Zeitzler that only his army group's withdrawal to the East Wall could release any significant reserves to the High Command—nine divisions in all. But it would be like losing a battle. His men had gained and valiantly defended their present lines at Leningrad in two years of bloody fighting; they would not like seeing the graves of thousands of their comrades abandoned to the enemy without good cause. Zeitzler would not accept his arguments, but Hitler was clearly loath to act prematurely. He could not ignore the political consequences on Finland of a withdrawal from Leningrad, but equally, he feared that Stalin was hatching a winter offensive from Velikiye Luki toward the coast at Pleskau or Riga, cutting off the whole army group's retreat. He postponed a decision.

For several days after Badoglio's capitulation there was utter confusion in Italy; not so at the Wolf's Lair. When Goebbels and his state secretary, Werner Naumann, arrived there early the next morning, September 9, 1943, the headquarters compound was bathed in an almost deathly hush. Hitler himself was calm and collected. As Martin Bormann wrote that day: "Marvelous to see the Führer's poise in face of fantastic complications in the east, the south, and elsewhere! The coming months are going to be very difficult. But now is the time to stand fast with iron determination."

Yet Hitler had not closed his mind to the possibility of an armistice with either Stalin or Churchill. A split between West and East seemed inevitable sooner or later. Ribbentrop—whose stock had fallen so sharply that Hitler could now contemptuously address him in front of his generals as "Herr Foreign Manager"—

had extended feelers to the Russians again during August. First he had sent Rudolf Likus to Stockholm to seek clues as to Stalin's peace terms. Then, in mid-August, he had ordered his subaltern, Dr. Peter Kleist, to pick up his earlier threads with a certain non-Aryan Baltic businessman in Stockholm, Edgar Klauss, known to have contacts with the Soviet embassy there. Klauss claimed that the former Russian ambassador in Berlin, Vladimir Dekanozov, was coming on September 12 and hoped to meet a German negotiator then; Kleist reported this to Ribbentrop at the Wolf's Lair on the tenth. According to Ribbentrop, Hitler proved more receptive this time; they went over to a map, and he sketched in a possible demarcation line to be agreed on with Stalin. But during the night he changed his mind and told Ribbentrop he would have to think it over more carefully. In conversation with Goebbels on the ninth he had shown a greater affinity for the British than for Stalin; but again Churchill was the obstacle. Hitler decided to wait until Dönitz could resume his submarine offensive, until the army's missile attack on London began—again provisionally postponed until the end of January 1944—and until the Allies had been dealt the kind of military reverse that, in Hitler's calculus, must always precede a secret offer of armistice.

Operation "Axis" had been smoothly completed as planned. Rome had been seized and a tough commandant, General Stahel, appointed for the city. The disarming of Italy's armed forces was proceeding rapidly. In Milan and Turin Communist rebellions had begun; in Florence the Germans were up against Italian tanks. In the Aegean, Rhodes and Corfu were still battlefields between the Germans and Italians; when the Corfu garrison was finally overwhelmed, Hitler ordered the Italian commandant's execution. Late on the tenth an ultimatum was issued to all Italian troops still resisting instructing them to lay down their arms; otherwise their commanders would be shot as francs-tireurs. Often the Italians gave their arms to the partisans—particularly to Tito's guerrillas in Dalmatia; wherever this was found to have occurred, Hitler ordered their officers to be stood before firing squads and the men to be deported to the eastern front to swell his army's labor force. The Italian fleet sailed on the ninth on a pretext: Luftwaffe bombers equipped with guided missiles sank the battleship *Roma* and injured her sister ship *Italia;* the rest defected to the enemy. In Nice, when a German officer was killed by an Italian hand-grenade, the railroad garrison was put before a firing squad in revenge. Such was the German troops' hatred of their former Italian allies.

Badoglio and his turncoat comrades had done their utmost to wound Germany. When the American Fifth Army's seaborne invasion at Salerno, south of Naples, began on September 9, the Germans realized from decoded American radio messages that their minefields had been betrayed to the enemy. There was evidence that Rome had radioed the British a warning that the ports of Trieste, Monfalcone, Bari, Metković, and Ragusa (Dubrovnik) were now in German hands. An Italian naval lieutenant put the fuel dumps in Naples to the torch—"thus possibly sealing the fate of every German soldier in southern Italy," observed Richthofen. Meanwhile Badoglio, Ambrosio, and Roatta had fled to the enemy, accompanied by the king and Crown Prince Umberto. With grim satisfaction Hitler read the latest intercept of an Anthony Eden telephone call to Winston Churchill in Washington, where he was reported by *The Times* to be waiting for a military triumph to illuminate his return to London. Eden was discussing the problems Umberto was causing by refusing to accept an English officer as aide-de-camp. Only now did the Germans learn that Badoglio had secretly concluded the armistice as early as September 3; yet the American bombing of Naples, Viterbo, and other targets had continued—no doubt as a blind. Badoglio had invited American paratroops to land on the airfields around Rome, but Hitler's troops had seized them first. Courier planes had shuttled between Badoglio and Eisenhower, while the Italian antiaircraft guns were ordered not to fire. On occasion, American officers had been driven in full uniform through Rome. As for the Duce, Badoglio had promised to relinquish him to the enemy. He would be tried forthwith. According to the Führer's secretaries, Hitler's heart went out to him, wherever he now was.

"Understandably"—Hitler was broadcasting to his people late on September 10, surrounded by Himmler, Göring, and his staff—"I am grieved by the sight of the unique injustice inflicted on this man [Mussolini] and the degrading treatment meted out to him, whose only care these last twenty years and more has been for his people, as though he were a common criminal. I was and am glad to call this great and loyal man my friend. Nor am I one to tailor my convictions to the demands of expediency, let alone disown them; some may think differently, but my belief is that in the affairs of nations as in those of men loyalty is a virtue beyond price. Without it, society must totter, and its organizations will sooner or later wither away." It sounded very much like an obituary for Mussolini.

The vultures crowded in. Hitler had appointed a National Government under Alessandro Pavolini to save what was left of fascism in Italy; SS General Karl Wolff was attached as police "adviser" to Pavolini. North of the Apennines, Italy was now officially "German occupied territory," with a military governor; to the south was the "operations zone." Kesselring was ordered on the twelfth to defeat the American divisions at Salerno if he could; if he could not, he was to fall back on Rome, blocking the enemy's advance by destroying roads, bridges, tunnels, and railway installations as he retreated. The southern Italians and Sicilians had openly abetted the enemy; now their countryside would pay the price. On the eleventh the OKW ordered that everything of value in the south—goods and raw materials—was to be stripped and shipped north "on behalf of the new Fascist government." On the twelfth, Speer persuaded Hitler to vest this power in him alone. While Hitler's order of the eleventh provided for industry in northern Italy to continue operating, Speer's superseding order of the twelfth empowered him to dismantle precious machine-tools from anywhere in Italy "in danger of air attack" and ship them back to the Reich. For Speer's purposes everywhere south of the line from La Spezia to Ancona was deemed "in danger of air attack"—the whole of the Italian "boot."

To Hitler's ministers, Mussolini's exit was something of a relief. As Goebbels wrote: "Politically speaking I do not regret it much. We must judge it all from the standpoint of expediency." On the twelfth, two of Hitler's frontier Gauleiters came for lunch—Franz Hofer from the Tyrol and Friedrich Rainer from Carinthia. Hitler signed decrees subjecting large provinces of northern Italy to their Gau administration; this was the very overture to annexation he had adopted in Alsace and Lorraine. The future Germany was intended to reach the frontiers of Venetia. By 4:40 P.M., when the conference ended, Hitler had signed all three decrees—those for the two Gauleiters and the one enabling Albert Speer to dismantle Italian industry.

At what stage Hitler learned the startling news of Mussolini's rescue is uncertain. Himmler had certainly known since 10:30 A.M. that the operation was under way, and at 2 P.M. the fallen Duce was already free. Speer suggested that under the circumstances the three decrees should be canceled, but Hitler would not hear of it and changed their date from September 12 to 13, so that there could be no doubt that the Duce's liberation had not in the least affected his decisions on Italy's future. At 9:45 P.M., as he was having supper with Himmler, an SS general telephoned from Vienna that Mussolini had just arrived there with Otto Skorzeny. Hitler spoke himself with Skorzeny, congratulated him, and awarded him the Knight's Cross for this spectacular success. According to a manservant, he exclaimed afterward, "When news of the rescue gets out, it will hit the world like a bombshell—particularly the British. That'll show them I never turn my back on a friend—that I'm a man of my word. The British will say, 'He's a friend indeed!' "

Two days later, at 2 P.M., Hitler drove from the Wolf's Lair to the local airfield to meet the plane bringing the tired Italian dictator up from Munich. Mussolini was dressed in a simple dark blue suit; gone was the bombast and the bonhomie. He was a broken man. Before they all lunched together, Hitler summoned SS General Ernst Kaltenbrunner—whose SS agents had contributed to the rescue—and Skorzeny to relate Mussolini's hair-raising escape to him. Kaltenbrunner explained that until July 28 the Duce had been imprisoned in the Carabinieri barracks in Rome; during August he had been transferred to Ponza, and then to the island of St. Maddalena. Two weeks ago he had been whisked up to the Campo Imperatore hotel high up in the Apennines. A glider-borne force of paratroops and SS agents had crash-landed around the hotel and robbed the Carabinieri of their precious charge without loss of life to either side.

It was a very different Mussolini who conferred with Hitler over the next few days. Shorn of his authoritarian powers, Mussolini was an ordinary man whose future was at best that of a glove puppet, to act as his envied friend the Führer now directed. He protested that he was still ill, and for a while Hitler believed that Mussolini had been poisoned too; but Morell took him under his scrutiny, sent for the Italian medical records, X-rayed the dictator, and found nothing wrong with him. Mussolini's moral decay and softness toward his enemies repelled Hitler, who had expected him to exact a terrible revenge on Count Ciano, Dino Grandi, and all who had betrayed the cause of fascism. A few days later Edda, Ciano's wife, who had been brought to Germany, appealed to Hitler for enough Spanish currency to enable her to emigrate with the count through Spain to South America; but Hitler gathered that Ciano planned to write his "memoirs" (which would certainly not flatter Germany), and ruled that he was to remain in German hands. Besides, his agents had intercepted a threatening letter from Edda to her father: if the Duce did not take her out of Germany, she would cause the name of her father to be cursed and hated throughout the world. For hours on end—until three in the morning—Hitler paced up and down the map room with Goebbels, speculating what Edda's stranglehold over her father could possibly be. He himself suspected that Mussolini had for months been searching for ways and means of ditching Germany: could it be that? Despite his disillusionment, Hitler advised the former dictator to put his family's affairs in order before applying himself to the new order of Italy and the Fascist party.

To Ribbentrop's astonishment, Hitler remarked to Mussolini that he planned a compromise with Stalin. But the very next day he changed his mind again and admitted to the minister in private: "You know, Ribbentrop, if I come to terms with Russia today, I would be at her throat again tomorrow—it's in my nature." Ribbentrop replied that that was hardly the way to earn respect for one's foreign policy. Hitler was torn between Stalin and the West. When Goebbels asked whether he refused to deal with Churchill on principle, he retorted: "In politics you can't let personalities and principles stand in your way. It's just that Churchill is inspired by hatred, not common sense." In one way, he would far prefer to deal with Stalin—but then Stalin could hardly grant the Reich what it was demanding in the east. On September 18 he accompanied Mussolini back to Rastenburg airfield and watched him take off for Munich, where he was to begin piecing together his new regime.

Hitler had now regretfully abandoned hope of throwing the American Fifth Army back into the sea at Salerno. Hube's four divisions had all but succeeded during the previous nine days: initially the Americans had encountered only the 16th Panzer Division, but Richthofen's rocket-firing fighters and the 88-millimeter guns of an antiaircraft regiment had wrought havoc on the invasion ships; on the thirteenth a German counterattack by two panzer and one panzer-grenadier division began, and routed two American divisions defending Salerno. But the counterattack came under heavy bombardment from Allied warships offshore—a new dimension in beachhead operations. Thus the beachhead remained; the Americans were joined by Montgomery's troops, who had landed at Taranto, and Kesselring prepared to fall back toward Rome.

Hitler's staff rejoiced at the "thrashing" meted out to the Americans. Jodl set their value far below that of Montgomery's seasoned troops. Though British and Americans had been committed in equal numbers, over nine-tenths of the prisoners who had surrendered were Americans: American paratroops were "usable," but the rest "surrender the moment the position is hopeless" and "never attack so long as a single gun is left firing from the German lines." Hitler wrote off the threat of an enemy invasion elsewhere for many months to come. "No more invasions for them! They are much too cowardly for that. They only managed the one at Salerno because the Italians gave their blessing." The bungling Allied planning comforted him greatly over the next weeks. Why did they not immediately invade the Balkans, where the natives were waiting for the Allies with open arms? Why had they not ventured a bold invasion north of Rome when Badoglio defected? Why had they not at once occupied the islands of Rhodes, Cephalonia, and Corfu? Why were they making such slow progress up Italy?

Italy's defection had profited the Reich in terms of material. Hitler rudely stripped southern Italy of every antiaircraft battery—whether German or Italian—in favor of the north and Germany. No longer did Germany have to feed Italy with coal, oil, and foodstuffs. Nearly 50,000 Allied prisoners had been removed from Italian into German custody; here they were joined by their former jailers, for by the end of September the first 268,000 Italian prisoners had already been transported to the Reich. "Operation Axis" had also yielded a big haul of Italian weaponry: 449 tanks, 2,000 guns, and 500,000 rifles. Eight hundred thousand Italians had been disarmed. But the strategic cost of "Axis" had been high, because—apart from the SS Life Guards temporarily withdrawn from Russia—the divisions pumped into Italy had drained the central reserve, which thus also indirectly weakened the eastern front. Moreover, Hitler had been duped for many weeks into expecting an early invasion of France, where the enemy had bombed ports, alerted the underground, and ostentatiously swept offshore minefields. Late in September Hitler still believed that only bad weather had stopped the invasion.

The Abwehr's remarkable agent "Josephine" now claimed that at Quebec the

Allies had agreed to postpone the invasion "of northern France" until 1944, as they lacked shipping space and the bombing offensive would not reach its climax until April. This agent seemed most reliable.[1] On August 21 he had predicted that the night-bombing offensive would resume two nights later (as it did, against Berlin). He had also reported controversy in the RAF about the value of such sporadic raids; but the British air minister, Sir Archibald Sinclair, and the war Cabinet had overruled them and demanded that the attack on Berlin begin. The British were manufacturing seven hundred four-engined bombers a month, according to "Josephine." These reports evidently reached Hitler and influenced him.

Three heavy night raids had been launched against Berlin but failed to repeat the catastrophe of Hamburg. The new freelance night-fighting tactics were proving effective. Goebbels's evacuation order had spared the lives of many thousands; in the raid on September 1 only 13 Berliners died, and in the final raid two nights later, of 346 dead only one was a child. But worse was expected: in the big cities painted arrows were to be seen everywhere—telling the people which way to flee if firestorms broke out again.

To the German people the war in the air *was* the Second Front. By September 1943, as Milch stated in a secret speech on October 6, Germany was defended by 8,876 antiaircraft guns of 88-millimeter caliber, and a further 24,500 of lighter calibers; her fighters had destroyed 48,268 enemy aircraft, and the guns a further 12,774, for the expenditure of over 26 million shells. Hitler's bombers had scattered over 35 million bombs in Europe, Africa, and Asia. But now the boot was on the other foot. By day and night the bombers ranged over Germany, sometimes as far as Danzig or East Prussia. From the newly captured airfields around Foggia in southern Italy they could reach any target in Austria and the Balkans. The American bombers now also had radar and were escorted as far as the German frontiers; soon long-range fighter escorts would appear. The bombers were heavily armored: eighteen of them, in tight formation, could concentrate 200 heavy machine-guns on any attacking fighter planes. Hitler learned that the German fighters had still not been equipped with 30-millimeter cannon, although he had seen the prototype MK 101 demonstrated in a twin-engined fighter at Rechlin in July 1939. He now ordered the fighters fitted experimentally with the

[1]Hitler and the Wehrmacht attached great importance to this Abwehr source. Not until late 1944 did Luftwaffe Intelligence deduce that "Josephine," like "Hektor" and "Ostro"—two other star agents—were the fruity product of various Abwehr attachés' imaginations, coupled with their zealous reading of the popular press. Trick questions about nonexistent British aircraft factories finally tripped them up.

50-millimeter KWK antitank gun, to enable them to open fire from well outside the bombers' defensive radius. General Adolf Galland, commander of the day fighters, opposed this, but the weapon became one of the most feared items of the day fighters' hardware.

The inadequacy of the current fighter armament sorely affected pilot morale, and this in turn was felt by the people. On October 4 the Americans bombed Frankfurt on a brilliant autumn day—their glittering squadrons droning high over the city "as ours used to, in peacetime," Hitler complained that day that the Germans had known Frankfurt would be the target, from an agent, but no fighter had challenged these bombers over the city. Hitler bitterly reproached Göring, saying that his Luftwaffe had lost the confidence of both the people and the troops. "I must insist, as spokesman of the German people, that whatever the cost, these mass daylight attacks have got to be stopped." The Reichsmarschall passed this rebuke on to General Galland: "The German public doesn't care two hoots about your fighter casualties. Try going to Frankfurt and asking what impression your fighter losses that day made on them. They'll tell you, 'You must be joking! Look at our *thousands* of dead!' "

Between them, Göring and Galland brought discipline to the fighter squadrons and inflicted savage wounds on the American bombers in October. In three days' raids up to the tenth the enemy lost 88 bombers and nearly 900 men. When they attacked the ball-bearing factories at Schweinfurt on October 14, the day fighters —each flying several sorties—brought down 60 and severely damaged 17 more.[2] Meanwhile, at night the battle ebbed and flowed: on the lakes around Berlin bobbed myriads of metal radar-reflectors intended to deceive the bombers; new radar jammers had been designed; airborne receivers enabled the night fighters to home in on the bombers' own powerful radar emissions, and their tactics were adapted to the Schwerpunkt tactics of the enemy. Germany's enemies fought back cunningly—with decoy raids, split raiding forces, and German-speaking broadcasters countermanding the orders transmitted by the German ground controllers. It was a growing nightmare. But the Nazi defenders resorted to trickery as well: unloading fake target flares over the open countryside or patrolling the enemy airfields, waiting for the exhausted bombers to return. Hitler was impatient at this unspectacular activity and demanded fresh raids on Britain's cities. Their scale was immaterial. "Aerial terrorism is only effective as a threat," he now pontificated, "not in its actual fulfillment. . . . How often these last three hundred years have entire cities or great buildings been consumed by flames? The devastation actually works in our favor, because it is creating a body of people with

[2]Galland in fact flew 882 fighters against the bombing force that day and lost 14: each side's newspapers claimed their aircraft shot down 121 of the other.

nothing more to lose—people who will therefore fight on with utter fanaticism." He ordered Speer to begin planning the reconstruction of the ruined cities—more elegant and modern than before. On October 22, a second firestorm occurred; it ravaged Kassel, and six thousand citizens died between dusk and dawn. It made no impression on Hitler; those Germans who learned of it, accepted it with a numb sense of inevitability.

Yet the brutalization of the war—the cloying smell of death clinging to the ruins of these cities—was in a way to result in new suffering for Hitler's enemies too. He intensified his pressure for the secret weapons to terrorize London—the A-4 rocket, the flying bomb, and the multiple-gun battery near Calais sinisterly known as the "High Pressure Pump." The same ruthlessness permeated his feelings toward the Badoglio Italians. When their garrison on Cephalonia was finally subdued late in September—it had held out in hope of a British invasion—Hitler ordered the four thousand Italians taken prisoner to be executed as francs-tireurs; only the deserters were to be spared their lives. A few days later he dropped a broad hint to Göring that one of the big Allied-occupied cities in southern Italy, like Brindisi or Taranto, should be stricken by a heavy Luftwaffe night attack before the enemy had time to establish a fighter defense; this would remind the Italians and Germany's other reluctant allies that allowing the enemy in was no passport to paradise.

Early in October the remaining Jews were deported from Denmark. Himmler also considered the eight thousand Jews in Rome a potential threat to public order; Ribbentrop brought to Hitler an urgent telegram from his consul in Rome reporting that the SS had ordered from Berlin that "the eight thousand Jews resident in Rome are to be rounded up and brought to Upper Italy, where they are to be liquidated." Again Hitler took a marginally more "moderate" line. On the ninth Ribbentrop informed Rome that the Führer had directed that the eight thousand Jews were to be transported to Mauthausen concentration camp in Austria instead, where they were to be held "as hostages." It was, Ribbentrop defined, purely a matter for the SS. (The SS liquidated them anyway, regardless of Hitler's order.)

Coincidentally, it was at this time that Himmler first revealed to two audiences—of SS Gruppenführer (generals) on October 4, and Gauleiters on October 6—an awful secret which he forbade them to discuss in public: by the end of 1943 the last Jews in occupied Europe would have been physically *exterminated.* That Himmler's intention was to make all his SS generals and the Gauleiters, regardless of their guilt, accessories after the fact to the massacre is strongly suggested by one curious document in his files: a name-by-name list of those who had *not* attended his speech! Against the fifty-one names were checks marking whether or not they had since read his speech or otherwise "taken cognizance of it." The shorthand record and magnetic recordings show that he did *not* yet claim to be acting on Hitler's orders.[3] Himmler clearly considered his standing with the Führer impregnable, to admit so openly that he had disregarded Hitler's veto on liquidating the Jews all along. The same Gauleiters were Hitler's guests at the Wolf's Lair on October 7; from this point on, he could no longer logically plead ignorance of what his "faithful Heinrich" had done.[4]

The SS stood high in Hitler's esteem that autumn. Between them, Himmler and his Gestapo chief, Müller, had strangled the incipient murmurings of unrest in Germany that echoed the events in Italy. Kaltenbrunner, as Heydrich's successor, had rapidly organized an Intelligence network that clearly surpassed the Abwehr's uninspiring achievements; without Kaltenbrunner's agents, Mussolini's rescue would have been impossible. Princess Mafalda had also been found and lured into German custody; even now she was languishing in a concentration camp—a useful hostage to assure the king of Italy's good behavior.[5] Himmler had inspired his Waffen SS troops, moreover, with a fanatic's loyalty to Nazi Germany. Late in October he showed Hitler a passage in a recent letter from a young SS brigadier on the eastern front: "If the others had not been there, I would so much have liked to tell the Führer how much his soldiers revere him and are devoted to him. Even if his orders sometimes seem merciless or cruel—when the order is, 'Hold on to the last man'—one feeling is supreme among the men fighting for their fatherland with rifles in their hand, that they have as their leader a man second to the Lord God alone." This was Hermann Fegelein: a few days later Hitler selected him as his liaison officer to Himmler; in June he married Eva Braun's sister; a year later he was facing Hitler's firing squad as a deserter in the ruins of Berlin.

"The Führer is confident," said Bormann in a secret speech at this time, "but he is not just an optimist; in fact, he is on principle pessimistic as far as all reports

[3]To the SS generals on October 4, 1943, Himmler praised the toughness of those who had had to carry out the massacre: "This is a page of glory in our history which has never been written and is never to be written." To the Gauleiters two days later he referred to "the Jewish problem" as the most difficult he had handled. "The Jews must be exterminated," was easier said than done. Even where women and children were concerned he, Himmler, had opted for a clear solution. "I did not consider myself justified in exterminating the menfolk—that is to kill them or have them killed—while leaving their children to grow up and take vengeance on our sons and grandsons. The hard decision had to be taken to make this race disappear from earth." He could not have been more explicit as to his own responsibility.

He first hinted at having had superior orders on May 6, 1944 (page 630).

[4]Milch, Dönitz, and several of their aides had addressed the Gauleiters on the morning of October 6; whether they stayed to hear Himmler's speech that afternoon is not clear from their diaries. Speer certainly did. Kaltenbrunner—who at Nuremberg pleaded that he had known nothing until 1944—was certainly in Berlin, and SS General Wolff was in Italy until the seventh, when he visited Hitler.

[5]Princess Mafalda died in the American bombing raid on Buchenwald concentration camp.

to him are concerned. He no longer believes what is not proven to him. He is skeptical about every cable and dispatch he receives." Even so, he was confident of the future. The very lack of communiqués from the Moscow foreign ministers' conference suggested a widening split between Russia and the West. Stalin was most probably demanding a Second Front and sidestepping all his allies' suggestions that the world's postwar frontiers should be agreed on first. Stalin was in a position of consummate strength; and thus—as Hitler had himself argued in 1933—he was in a position to dictate to the world. To this Hitler knew only one reply: "The most important thing is to keep up the fight and never falter, but spy out the enemy's weaknesses and exploit them without the least thought of capitulation or 'understanding' . . . Who can guarantee that one day a bombshell won't burst among the Allies, who will suddenly discover differences they can't plaster over anymore? . . . Just one internal collapse among our enemies and their whole enemy front might just cave in!" When fresh feelers reached Hitler now from Britain, he thrust them aside.

On October 15, Himmler's chief of foreign Intelligence, Walter Schellenberg, learned that the British trade chief in Stockholm, David MacEvan, who was known to report directly to Churchill, had offered to come secretly to Germany for a conference ostensibly on economic affairs. Schellenberg deduced there was more to it than that—that the British, fearing Russia's encroachment on western Europe and the Middle East, now wanted to start armistice negotiations. Himmler provisionally forbade MacEvan's journey and asked Ribbentrop to secure a decision from Hitler. Simultaneously, Hitler learned that the Swiss legation in London had reported to Berne in a note which—"according to Eden's private secretary"—the Americans had termed an intolerable interference in Allied strategy that Stalin had vetoed any Allied invasion of the Balkans.[6]

One reason for Hitler's rebuff to these vague Allied feelers was that under Kesselring's command the campaign in Italy was proceeding far better than he had dared to hope. Rommel, commanding Army Group B in northern Italy, had prophesied the total loss of southern and central Italy within days of Badoglio's defection; overawed by Rommel's warning, Hitler had refused Kesselring's appeal for two more divisions to be sent from Rommel's forces to the south. With these Kesselring might have routed the Allies, but even so his strategic defensive was a setback for Churchill and Roosevelt. At the end of September, Hitler had even asked Kesselring to study a German counterattack in Apulia—around the Foggia air base—to deprive the enemy of any springboard into the Balkans; but

[6]There is no record of such a note in published volumes.

Kesselring found it would be impossible to raise enough divisions. Hitler therefore ordered the line from Gaeta on one coast to Ortona on the other to be fortified and held, south of Rome. On October 9 he received at the Wolf's Lair the venerable Italian Marshal Rodolfo Graziani, who was to be Mussolini's new Commander in Chief, and he approved the activation of a small new Italian army on training grounds outside Italy.

Once again Rommel had misjudged. A year later Hitler recalled: "In Italy too he predicted our collapse as being just around the corner. It still has not occurred. Events have proved him completely wrong and thoroughly justified my decision to leave Field Marshal Kesselring there—whom I saw as incredibly naïve politically but an optimist militarily; and my view is that without optimism you cannot be a military commander." To both Hitler and General Rudolf Schmundt, chief of army personnel, it was plain that Rommel and Kesselring would always be at each other's throats; and that since Rommel was still tormented by his defeat in Africa, it would be better to give him another command far from Italy.

On October 15, Hitler sent for Rommel. At their meeting two days later, Rommel again cut a gloomy figure. A few days later Hitler gave Kesselring a fresh hearing, and on the twenty-eighth he decided in his favor. Rommel would be withdrawn from Italy and given a different assignment—as yet undecided.

On October 23, 1943, the main attack on the Sixth Army's sector of the East Wall, the southernmost portion, began: the next day Melitopol was overrun. Kleist and his commanders lost their nerve. A headlong retreat began. Farther north a gap was torn in the German lines between Dniepropetrovsk and Kremenchug that was to yawn a hundred miles wide within two weeks. Hitler appealed to Marshal Antonescu to rush Romanian divisions to help stem the Soviet flood swirling toward Bessarabia and Transnistria—the Black Sea province annexed in 1941 by Antonescu. But Antonescu feared for the seven divisions he had already committed to the Crimea, where along with two German divisions over 210,000 troops might any day be cut off from their overland supplies. In a reply received on October 27, the marshal advised Hitler to get out of the Crimea while the going was good.

Hitler demurred. Abandoning the Crimea without a fight would not impress Turkey or Bulgaria, and it would bring Stalin 250 miles closer to the Romanian oil wells and refineries on which Hitler and the Wehrmacht relied. He hoped to parry the Soviet thrust before it reached the coast at Nikolaev; but even if he could not, the Red Navy was not powerful enough to prevent him from evacuating the Crimean troops by sea after a protracted holding action. With this in mind, on the day he received Antonescu's reply Hitler summoned Göring, Dönitz, Zeitzler, and Jodl to a special war conference at 4:30 P.M. Zeitzler was optimistic that the eight divisions being supplied from other theaters would suffice to overcome the crisis. The Crimea had enough munitions to survive any immediate isolation. Admiral Dönitz agreed that a seaborne evacuation of the Seventeenth Army from the Crimea would be possible, although the job would be a long one and risky because of the powerful Russian air force. Hitler, Dönitz, and the Reichsmarschall were unanimous in believing that the Crimea must be held, and in the meantime provisioned by sea. Zeitzler "indicated his agreement." The records are plain on this score.

Only Field Marshal Kleist, commanding Army Group A, thought differently. The day before, he had—without consulting Hitler—ordered the evacuation of the Crimea to begin on the twenty-eighth. Zeitzler canceled the order that same evening. On November 1 the Russians reached the Dnieper's broad estuary into the Black Sea, thus cutting off the Crimean peninsula in the rear. How long could the 210,000 men there hold out?

The war conferences of October 27, 1943, vividly illustrated the complexities of fighting wars on many fronts—and in many mediums—with dwindling resources. Rundstedt had just submitted a horrendous account of Germany's military weakness in France. Pitched battles were being fought with Communist insurgents and guerrillas in the Balkans. At night the skies of Europe were loud with bomber engines and alight with the burning cities left behind. Speer needed workers to clear the rubble, build the new factories, and operate the machinery; Milch needed manpower for his new aircraft industry; Dönitz needed crews to man the hundreds of new submarines launched against the Allies. Above all Hitler needed fresh divisions to repair the breaches in the eastern front. With heavy heart he signed an order late in October for industry to release 210,000 German males—coincidentally the same number trapped in the Crimea—to the army over the next three months; he had already had to waive the draft deferment allowed to the sole surviving sons of families. Speer warned that declines in coal, iron, petroleum, and arms production would immediately result; but Hitler saw no alternative. On October 27, while strolling in the woods around the Wolf's Lair, Göring put in a special plea for his aircraft factories to be spared the ax, but failed to win his point.

Hitler evidently blamed bureaucracy for swallowing up industrial manpower. He told the Reichsmarschall of a British cartoon he had seen—a man told to save paper, but shown sitting at a desk throwing away sheet after sheet of it. "What on earth are you doing?" "I used too much paper, so now I've got to write a thousand times *I must save paper!*" Göring gave Hitler a concrete example of the shortage of manpower: Willy Messerschmitt, the aircraft designer, had bluntly told him a few days earlier that for want of four thousand workers his jet aircraft, the Me-262, would be held up by three or even six months. According to Göring, Hitler "almost had a heart attack" on hearing this news. Professor Messerschmitt had spoken to him of the Me-262 as a possible high-speed bomber for attacking Britain, and in his own lively imagination Hitler had already assigned this jet bomber a key role in stopping any Allied invasion attempt in France. In his mind's eye—forewarned by the newsreel film of similar events in Italy—Hitler could see the hours of utter chaos as Allied landing craft disgorged tanks, guns, and troops onto the beaches in the spring of 1944. His own troops would be pinned down in their bunkers by heavy naval and air bombardment; the air would be full of enemy fighters. At this moment his new jet bombers should appear—thundering along the beaches with cannon blazing, hurling bombs at random into the jammed invasion troops, spreading panic and confusion for vital hours until Hitler could bring up his mobile reserves. Göring promised the Führer he would get his jet bombers by May.

Hitler's strategic thinking had undergone a startling change since Italy's defection. Göring portrayed it thus to his generals on October 28: "In Russia we have won an immense outlying area in which we can resort to flexible tactics; but in doing so we must remain firmly resolved to amass sufficient troops by a certain time—this spring at the latest—to throw the Russians back out of the areas they have now regained. Seen like that, this breach [of the East Wall] is of no import: it does not affect our vital interests. Whether the Russians are at Krivoi Rog or get a hundred miles closer to us or not is not vital; what is, is that by spring at the latest we can muster enough maneuverability to stand fast in the west and stop the Second Front before it starts. Only air power can do that. The Führer made this abundantly clear yesterday in Dönitz's presence. The Führer says the [Me-262] jet fighter with bombs will be vital—because it will hurtle at top speed along the beach at just the right moment and hurl its bombs into the throngs forming there." (Göring added, "I thought to myself, 'Who knows if we'll really have the Me-262 by then?' ") If an enemy army ever set foot on French soil, concluded Göring, it would spell the end for Germany; whereas even if every German city was in ruins, the German people would still survive to fight on.

In a bulky report to Hitler, Field Marshal Rundstedt reached broadly the same conclusion: the defense of France would stand or fall at the Atlantic Wall; and, the Wall itself, he warned, was largely bluff and propaganda. But any German retreat here would provide the enemy with the harbors that he needed, and deprive Germany of her U-boat bases and coastal convoys. Besides, Rundstedt's divisions were too weak in both men and equipment to fight a war of movement against a superior enemy. At Hitler's conference on October 30, Jodl supported Rundstedt's main contention that—whatever *else* the Allies might undertake in Scandinavia or the Balkans—a spring 1944 invasion of France was a certainty, because only the loss of the Ruhr would finally defeat Germany; besides, Churchill would want to neutralize the A-4 missile sites in northern France. Given the likelihood that the Atlantic Wall would be breached eventually, Jodl demanded an immediate stop to the drain on Rundstedt's divisions for the benefit of the eastern front and a massive effort to reinforce the Channel defenses using impressed French labor for the purpose. Hitler agreed; indeed, he went further, for he now secretly ordered Rundstedt to send a team to reconnoiter a possible line to be defended along the Somme and Marne rivers down to the Swiss frontier—which implicitly assumed that all of France would be overrun by the enemy.[7]

He also found a neat solution to the Rommel-Kesselring dilemma. On November 5 he told Rommel that Kesselring alone would now command all of Italy, as Commander in Chief Southwest; Rommel's army-group staff was to inspect the western coastal defenses and suggest how they could be improved, and at the same time study ways and means of mounting counteroffensives against an enemy lodged in western Europe. He was to begin with Denmark and work his way south. Rommel was piqued by what seemed such an uninspiring mission—far from the limelight in which he had fought his famous battles. He wrote a few days later: "Nobody knows if the new job is a way of shelving me or not. Various people have taken it as that. I am loath to believe it, and the Führer spoke quite differently. The envious are legion—but these times are so grave that there is really no room for envy and strife." Only his love for Hitler spurred Rommel on. On November 8 the Führer delivered his annual address to the Old Guard in Munich's Löwenbräu beer cellar. "What power he radiates!" wrote Rommel in intoxication. "What faith and confidence he inspires in his people!"

[7]This order again dispels the legend that Hitler was loath to allow his army commanders to make timely provision for retreats. The proposed line, incidentally, still left Germany with the French provinces Hitler had decided in 1940 to annex.

"And So It Will Be, Mein Führer!"

In four years, the wheel had turned full circle, and Hitler had once again to attend to the western front. Throughout the winter it remained his constant preoccupation as he devoured Intelligence reports or enemy dispatches that had fallen into German hands, and pored over aerial photographs, trying to deduce where the Allies would set foot in Europe—and when. With his predilection for weapons technology and for designing gadgets, he began to sketch the infernal mantraps and instruments of death with which he hoped to thwart the enemy—batteries of automatic flamethrowers, impenetrable minefields, and barrels of oil that could be exploded in the sea so that the invasion troops would have to wade in through a wall of fire. More than once he was heard to exclaim that if the Allied invasion established a beachhead, the war was lost for Germany.

On November 3, 1943, he underlined this in his Directive Number 51:

> These last two-and-a-half years of tough and bloody struggle against bolshevism have strained our military strength and energy to the utmost. It was appropriate to the magnitude of the danger and the overall strategic situation. Now the danger in the east remains, but an even greater one is emerging in the west: the Anglo-American invasion! The sheer vastness of the eastern spaces allows us to countenance even a major loss of territory if the worse comes to the worst, without it striking fatally at Germany's vital arteries.
>
> Not so the west! . . . I can therefore no longer tolerate the weakening of the west in favor of other theaters of war.

Hitler expected the enemy to invade in the spring and perhaps even earlier; they would probably land near the A-4 rocket sites and the V-1 flying-bomb catapults currently being erected along the Channel coast by armies of French laborers. The political and strategic profit to the Allies of an invasion of Denmark meant that its shoreline would also have to be defended.

The Balkans cried out for reinforcements too. The Italian collapse had created pandemonium there: believing an Allied invasion was imminent, the guerrillas came out into the open; the few German divisions had to concentrate along the coastline, leaving the interior largely in guerrilla hands. Hitler's attempts to bolster the Poglavnik's tottering government in Croatia failed, even though the country now regained the Dalmatian coastline it had lost in 1941 to Italy. Several times during September and October Hitler conferred with his generals and ministers on the Balkan problem. Field Marshal von Weichs, his Commander in Chief there, toured the Balkan capitals and reported that while an Allied invasion was unlikely before the spring, "the most dangerous enemy is Tito." The partisan commander had built up within Croatia a regular Soviet state based on a solid civil administration; moreover, he had a hundred thousand men under arms, with Russian officers to organize them and British officers to tender expert advice. In his diary Weichs wrote:

> The grim partisan situation puts a completely different complexion on things. Not that you can speak of "partisans" anymore—under Tito, a powerful bolshevik army has arisen, rigidly led, acting on directives from Moscow, moving from strength to strength, and growing deadlier every day. It has strong British support. Tito's present objective is to break into Serbia and then defeat the nationalist guerrillas led by D[raža] M[ihajlovič].
>
> Seen in this light the impotence of the Croatian government is an increasing menace. Should the enemy invade Dalmatia and Albania, we can expect general Communist uprisings to break out there.

The Italian withdrawal had left a vacuum in Albania, where there was only one German battalion to defend the coastline. If the Allies had landed even one regiment here, they could have controlled the country in two weeks.

Hitler's response to this situation was a significant political realignment, since he lacked the military strength to solve the problem by force. On Himmler's advice, he had become markedly skeptical about the Croatian government's future, and supported by Weichs and Kaltenbrunner he decided to enlist the aid of the Serbs. On October 29 he vested in Ribbentrop's very able special envoy to the Balkans, Hermann Neubacher, sweeping powers to fight communism there; in particular he could make contact with the nationalist partisan leaders like Mihajlović if need be. The Serbs were tempted with the restoration of Montenegro, the removal of Göring's notoriously corrupt economic envoy Neuhausen (who landed in Moabit prison), and special favors for Prime Minister Milan Nedić —a man whom Hitler found he could trust and like.

One thing was plain: Hitler could not abandon the strategically important Balkan peninsula with its oil, copper, and bauxite. Thus he ordered its perimeter defense to be tightened, along the cordon of islands from the Peloponnesus and Crete to Rhodes. Kos was taken in October; and on November 11 a modest

German force landed on the island of Leros, held by ten thousand British and Italian troops, and recaptured it in five days' bloody fighting. Samos was taken on the twenty-second, and thus the whole Dodecanese returned to German control, one of the last German victories under Hitler's dictatorship.

Meanwhile Romania was hypnotized by Stalin's ten-mile-a-day advance on her frontier, and Hungary was already known to be longing for an armistice; but Hitler had sent Admiral Raeder to Budapest with a yacht as Horthy's birthday present, and the regent wrote back assuring Hitler of his undying loyalty. The truth was that Badoglio's humiliation by the Allies was a chastening deterrent to imitation. Besides, Hungary and Romania were busy sharpening their knives for each other's throat. In Bulgaria, meanwhile, three regents had established a pro-German government after Boris's death, but it was weak in the face of the Turkish military buildup and a pro-Russian undercurrent in the country.

Hitler hated the Balkans! "If the British said Germany's job will be to keep the Balkans in order," he said at one war conference now, "we'd be busy for the next thirty years—marching in and out and back again, banging their heads together and getting out again."

From Himmler's Intelligence sources Hitler knew that the British were applying powerful pressure on Turkey to abandon her neutrality; at present, Turkey was resisting. Himmler's principal source was the astounding "Cicero"—an Albanian manservant employed by Sir Hughe Knatchbull-Hugessen, the British ambassador in Ankara—who had contacted Franz von Papen's embassy there early in October and been equipped by the police attaché L. G. Moyzisch with a Leica camera, skeleton keys, and large sums of Turkish currency. In return, he was secretly photographing all the British ambassador's papers during the hour or so that the diplomat bathed and breakfasted. Moyzisch had already secured from the Turkish secret service a telegram in which the Turkish ambassador in Moscow reported on the foreign ministers' conference there. (The ambassador accurately stated that Stalin had reluctantly agreed that the Second Front could be postponed until 1944 provided the Allies delivered war materials and food on the largest scale.) Once he began supplying photocopies of documents from the British embassy, he was recalled to Berlin and closely questioned about Cicero—who had by now already supplied eighty films of top secret British documents. Moyzisch described how the SD Gestapo had developed this agent, who was motivated solely by greed and therefore indubitably authentic.

Moyzisch hurried back to Ankara on November 9, as the British ambassador was due back from a meeting in Cairo, where Eden had just spent three days talking with the Turkish foreign minister. By the tenth, Ribbentrop already had Cicero's dispatch. "In Cairo Eden has demanded Turkish airfields for fighter operations in view of precarious British military situation in the Aegean." Eden had added that Germany's military strength was not to be feared, and he cited her inability to do more than utter a weak formal protest to Portugal when Britain had recently established bases in the Azores. The Turkish foreign minister refused to discuss Eden's demand without consulting his government, however; and it was clear to British and Germans alike that this meant the demand would be turned down. Papen himself lunched with Hitler at the Wolf's Lair on the seventeenth. Next day German Intelligence sources in Ankara—not Cicero this time—reported:

1. The Turkish ambassador in Moscow reports, "British ambassador here told Stalin of Turkish refusal, to which Stalin replied the Turkish mistrust annoyed him and the Three Powers would shortly have to put pressure on Turkey."
2. Eden informed Hugessen in Cairo that he had formed a bad impression of the Russian army: it seems to be in confusion and at the end of its strength.

Hitler hoped that Stalin's army would not last much longer. "We must not think of it as some kind of medieval giant that gets stronger every time it topples to the ground," he rebuked his generals. "One day its strength must also fail."

On November 1, Russian troops again set foot in the north and east Crimea but were held at bay. On the third General Hoth's Fourth Panzer Army was convincingly breached; Kiev fell, and the Russians reached Fastoff, forty miles to the southwest, before slogging to a halt on the seventh—in Hitler's view, worn out by their exertions. Hitler sacked the weary Hoth. With this "Jeremiah" gone he was given details on the cancer of "defeatism" spreading among Hoth's soldiers. "His men have only just found the courage to report all this to me," complained Hitler weeks later. Zeitzler commented, "Any army is the image of its commander." Hitler agreed. "If a commander says it's pointless to try influencing his men, I can only say, 'For *you* to try influencing them is pointless because you haven't got it in you to influence men.' " This was why he admired such Party faithfuls as Koch, Sauckel, and Ley—Gauleiters who had in their time converted Communist Gaue into Nazi party strongholds. "The good Gaue were always under the good Gauleiters." He was convinced it was the same in the army.

The security service, which censored soldiers' letters home, reported that the men no longer believed in victory. Goebbels wrote with mixed feelings that morale at the front was now lower than at home. Himmler felt that Manstein was at the bottom of the eastern front's defeatism, and when Hitler sent for him on November 7 it was widely believed the field marshal would be retired. Instead, Hitler insisted that Manstein prepare a thrust from the bridgehead at Nikopol toward the Crimea—an operation he trusted would restore land contact to the vital peninsula. First the situation southwest of Kiev had to be restored, but suddenly the long-expected rains began just when they were least needed. Sepp Dietrich's Life Guards began the attack on the fifteenth, recaptured the city of Zhitomir, then slid to a halt in the mire, after killing 20,000 enemy troops and destroying or capturing 603 tanks, 300 guns, and 1,200 antitank weapons. These figures alone revealed the colossal reserves at Stalin's disposal. "Where will it ever end!" wrote Goebbels. "The Soviets have reserves of which we never dreamed in even our most pessimistic estimates."

On the northern front, squabbles between Küchler and Kluge prevented their adjacent army groups from coordinating their counterattack on the Russians at Nevel—the key city on their common boundary—whose recapture would block the enemy's further advance on Latvia. On November 8, Kluge executed a costly attack and reached his objectives, but Küchler refused to attack the next morning as arranged, and Kluge had to retire to his opening position; his casualties had been in vain. With more than a little truth Hitler complained: "The whole catastrophe of Nevel can be blamed on the petty selfishness of the two army group commanders."[1]

This was not entirely true. Fundamental to the permanent crisis of arms was the lack of reserves. In mid-November Hitler discussed with his political advisers the possibility of recruiting more Estonians and Latvians for the defense of their native soil, but Rosenberg pointed out that unless the Baltic states' autonomy was assured, they would be unwilling to spill their own blood for the German cause. Hitler "was inwardly opposed to making such far-reaching concessions in difficult times," Rosenberg wrote afterward.

He preferred to drain his own industrial labor force before making any kind of territorial concessions. His armaments chiefs were aghast. Göring insisted that the army already had a vast surplus of manpower in the rear; Milch had himself sworn that he could, given the chance, "round up 2,000,000 men from the army's rear for the battlefront within three weeks;" he complained that of the 8,000,000 German soldiers barely 260,000 were actually on the eastern front. Hitler agreed there was an imbalance and asked Göring and Dönitz to discuss with him ways

[1]On November 14, 1943, Küchler's Chief of Staff, General Eberhard Kinzel, was bluntly instructed at the Wolf's Lair that Küchler must withdraw enough strength from the army group's northernmost (Eighteenth) army to deal with Nevel. But Nevel was never recaptured.—Kinzel was, it can be remarked, the former chief of Foreign Armies East Intelligence, whose faulty appreciations had irreparably harmed the "Barbarossa" campaign until his removal in April 1942. He took his own life in April 1945.

of increasing the combat strength. But Göring felt himself so vulnerable because of his sinking prestige that when the conference began on November 24 he actually declared that he was convinced the Luftwaffe had a large number of men to spare. The army was not mentioned. Three days later Hitler signed a strongly worded command for at least 1,000,000 men to be extracted from the Wehrmacht's "fat" and sent to the front line. Theoretically it should have been possible, but the practical result, sadly recorded by Schmundt some months later, was a disappointment. "Unhappily it has not been a big success. By bureaucratic procedures the command's execution was first postponed, then not applied with the absolute harshness that was necessary. No use was made of the penal provisions laid down by the Führer. Instead of 1,000,000 men only 400,000 were extracted." During December only 20,000 troops were supplied to the eastern front, barely 10 percent of its casualties.

Göring's prestige was low because Berlin had now begun to suffer, though not on the Hamburg scale. Night after night up to a thousand heavy bombers cascaded fire bombs and demolition bombs crudely known as "blockbusters" over the capital. Often there was ten-tenths cloud, and the German night fighters could neither take off nor land; the enemy had superb radar gear, while Göring's bombers and fighters were still groping in the dark. After the big raid on November 22, the government quarter was in ruins: Speer's ministry was gutted, the admiralty was blazing, the air ministry was in ruins, and the Chancellery was badly damaged. For days on end the city had no telephones, gas, water, or electric power. The Alkett factory, where most of Hitler's self-propelled assault guns were made, was devastated. In some raids over three thousand people died, but despite the choking layers of smoke polluting the streets for days on end, the Berliners proved as tough as the people of Hamburg in July—for which Hitler repeatedly congratulated Goebbels, the city's Gauleiter. In London, some newspapers claimed that a million had died in Berlin and that the whole city was in ruins; Goebbels was careful not to deny these claims.

Hitler could only console himself with the thought of the coming reprisal attacks on Britain. Under Himmler's control, slave laborers were toiling to complete an impregnable underground factory in the Harz Mountains for the partial manufacture and assembly of the A-4 rocket—at the rate of nine hundred a month. The first big launching silo at Watten, in northwest France, had been destroyed by enemy bombers before it was complete; now Hitler accepted the recommendation of Speer's engineers that a new site be chosen at nearby Wizernes. A million-ton dome of concrete would be emplaced on the edge of a chalk quarry first, then the missile-launching complex excavated beneath it. Hitler was "unconvinced it would ever be completed," but his skepticism about the missile system was dispelled by high-pressure salesmanship from the Peenemünde team, who adroitly covered up the backwardness and costly ineffectiveness of the A-4 missile. Late in October, as Hitler was being assured that the A-4 would be operational by the end of 1943, the Luftwaffe's new Chief of Staff, General Günther Korten, had interrupted: "We are aiming at that date too"—meaning the flying bomb. But Jodl retorted that his information was more reliable than Korten's, and according to his sources the flying bomb was a long way behind the rocket. In reality, as Speer's manufacturing experts knew, the A-4 rocket had only just begun launching trials with live warheads—and these were all prematurely exploding from the heat of reentry. Speer learned on November 8 that "the research is not as complete as the development team would have people believe." Nobody told Hitler; that same day in Munich he was proclaiming: "Our hour of revenge is nigh!"

The Luftwaffe's flying bomb had meanwhile gone into mass production at Volkswagen's Fallersleben factory in September; but it was plagued by production and navigational faults, and the production line halted in November. On November 3 the Luftwaffe learned that firing trials might be complete by early February 1944. The launching organization—96 special catapult sites erected by tens of thousands of French workers and Todt engineers along the Channel coast facing England—would be ready by mid-December 1943, and the two giant launching bunkers would be operational in March. On November 26, Hitler and Göring inspected the Luftwaffe's latest secret equipment at Insterburg airfield, an hour's train journey from the Wolf's Lair. He was shown the flying bomb and asked an engineer when it would be ready. The man replied, "By the end of March!" Hitler fell abruptly silent, as the date was the latest he had yet been told (in fact the engineer was referring only to the trials, which was even worse). But at least Hitler had been told about delays on the flying bomb, while he was kept in the dark over the A-4. On December 15 he instructed Jodl that the reprisal attack on London was to begin on February 15, preferably on a foggy forenoon at 11, with a barrage of as many missiles as possible. The OKW, which had established a special corps to direct the three secret weapons' operations—the third was the long-barreled underground gun for shelling London from Calais—followed this a week later with an order to open fire in mid-*January.* The corps commander, an elderly artillery general, replied that this was out of the question: there could be no certainty about the flying bomb until January, and in his view the whole A-4 project was a costly extravaganza which should be scrapped. His lone voice of sanity was not heeded. Jodl wrote in his diary after seeing Hitler on December 25: "A-4 and [flying bomb] are dawdling." By that time the American bomber force—trounced at Schweinfurt—had diverted its attentions to the 96 catapult-launching sites for the V-1 in France; soon 73 had been destroyed, but now this mattered little, for a new system of prefabricated launchers had superseded them and the 96 were little more than decoys. Hitler drew much comfort from the fact. "Obviously the things are getting on their nerves. If they were to start erecting such things and we knew they were for wiping out Berlin, then we'd get nervous too and set *our* Luftwaffe on *them.*"

Meanwhile, on the day after the Insterburg inspection, the Reichsmarschall had sworn to Hitler that within two weeks the Luftwaffe would bomb London and take revenge for Berlin's suffering. He planned to muster 300 bombers, to fly 500 sorties during the first night, followed by 150 more sorties the next morning. Hitler and Jodl pored over the population-distribution maps of London and Birmingham, and Göring left for France to command the operation in person. However, Chief of Air Staff Korten had his heart in a different project—the creation of a long-range bomber force for strategic attacks on Soviet industrial centers such as power stations and aeroengine factories. But "two weeks" grew into two months; not until January 22 was a fleet of 462 aircraft assembled for the London attack.

After the first raid the British gloatingly announced that only thirty bombers had found their way to London. The wretched Heinkel 177 had suffered heavy losses. "That rattletrap is quite the worst junk ever manufactured," lamented Hitler. "It's a flying Panther"—referring to the equally paralytic tank—"and the Panther is the crawling Heinkel!" Hitler refused to believe that less than three hundred or four hundred had reached London. "You've got agents," he challenged Korten. "We find out the most precious secrets of their war councils, their most confidential plans and ideas! But as to whether three buildings have been burned down in London, or a hundred or five hundred—we haven't a clue!" Korten mumbled, "We've put all our star agents on to it." These agents were in fact fictitious, the product of an Abwehr attaché's imagination.

One relief to Hitler in this darkening month of December 1943 was the steadfast refusal of Turkey to declare war on Germany. The top-secret British documents being photographed by Cicero on his master's desk in Ankara revealed this and much more. Hitler, Ribbentrop, Himmler, and Papen were satisfied that the photocopies now arriving almost daily from Ankara by air courier were authentic—angry telegrams stamped "Of Particular Secrecy" from Eden and Churchill, records of the meetings with Stalin at Teheran and with Turkey's President Inönü at Cairo, and a letter from Allied headquarters in Cairo confirming that because of the German victory in the islands of Kos and Leros operations in the Aegean had come to an abrupt end. The Abwehr played no part in this Intelligence coup; it was the SS who took the credit, and Hitler trusted them.

The picture that emerged was of mounting and abrasive pressure by Britain on Turkey to live up to its alliance and enter the war on February 15. This date was to be preceded by weeks of stealthy infiltration of the country by RAF ground staffs to prepare key airfields to accommodate twenty squadrons at one swoop, airfields from which the British could command the air in the southeast. Meanwhile British submarines would enter the Black Sea to operate against the Crimea and the Romanian coastline; moreover, with Turkey in the war Bulgaria would have to withdraw her nine divisions presently policing Serbia and Greece. But the Cicero papers showed that Turkey was fearful and suspicious of Russia's still unannounced postwar plans for the Balkans; Turkey knew from Hitler that Molotov had demanded Soviet bases in the Dardanelles in November 1940, and she saw no cause to help the hangman weave the noose. In Cairo, the Turks realized that Churchill and Eden had written off the Balkans and eastern Europe to Stalin. "The President [Inönü] returned from Cairo horrified," the Turkish foreign minister told Papen, "and said that if he had seen this coming, he would never have gone there." Turkey had no desire to share Iran's fate—occupied, divided into spheres of interest, and anesthetized with a nice declaration of her independence. Soon Hitler was reading the British ambassador's enraged telegram to Churchill on the thirteenth, reporting that the Turks were demanding impossible amounts of armaments before they would agree to terms—a ploy familiar to the Führer from his dealings with the Italians. The ambassador suggested that either the talks be broken off, or a last attempt made in staff talks to secure "agreement on the deadline of February 15," or allow them to jog hopefully on *sine die.* "We have already shown the Turks the big stick," replied the British foreign office on the eighteenth; but there was no denying that if the Allies finally broke with Turkey there would be repercussions both in Germany and the Balkans. The three commanders in chief, Middle East—Air, Army, and Navy—were therefore sent to visit Ankara in person; but the Turks refused to meet them. Eden accepted temporary defeat and cabled the following to his ambassador:

> To sum up. Our object is to get Turkey into the war as early as possible, and in any case to maintain a threat to the Germans from the eastern end of the Mediterranean, until Overlord is launched. . . . We still have not given up the idea that our squadrons should fly in on 15th February.

"Overlord" was evidently the code name for the 1944 invasion in the west.[2] Hitler's conclusion from studying the Cicero papers was that it would not come until mid-February. "There's not the slightest doubt that the attack in the west will come in the spring; none whatever." As the Turkish foreign minister said to

[2]According to Hitler's Luftwaffe adjutant Colonel von Below, a further Cicero document actually identified the location of "Overlord" as the Normandy peninsula. Below can still hear Hitler's puzzled exclamation: "But why on earth should the British have found it necessary to tell their ambassador in Turkey *that?*" Late in February 1944 Hitler certainly began insisting that Normandy must be reinforced, while refusing to explain why.

Papen imploringly, "We are at the most critical pass in our recent history. But since the Balkans are to be sacrificed to the Russians . . . we have no alternative but to keep playing our hand the way we are doing, in the hope that the German eastern front holds firm."

This was the political significance of the Crimea in Hitler's eyes, a significance which Manstein either could not or would not accept. Bitter though a decision to withdraw Army Group North from the Leningrad front would be, its political effect would be mild compared with the loss of the Crimea. "The Finns can't just jump overboard; when all's said and done they will still have to defend themselves." Not so Turkey, Bulgaria, and Romania. Stalin recognized this too, for his main winter offensive when it opened on December 24 was against the Fourth Panzer Army's sector west of Kiev—the left shoulder of Manstein's army group. Manstein's new headquarters at Vinnitsa was at the very focus of the Russian offensive, and he cabled an alarmed report to the Wolf's Lair the next day, beseeching Hitler to gain twelve divisions by giving up the uneconomic "bulge" along the Black Sea and the bridgehead at Nikopol while there was still time. Politically, this would be disastrous; but even militarily Hitler doubted whether Manstein was right. He was enraged by the "white lies" in Manstein's telegram: it spoke of German "counteroperations" where it meant "decamping"; and it vaguely observed, "We might hope that the enemy . . . will attempt to strike west through Cherkassy and Kirovograd, through Krivoi Rog or across the lower Dnieper, thereby finally exhausting his strength in the frontal attack on us." Hitler angrily lectured Zeitzler: "The enemy's not going to do what we *hope,* but what will damage us the most!"

Manstein was acting as if his army group was the orphan of the eastern front. In fact, since October Hitler had sent him five first-class panzer divisions and three infantry divisions. "The ratio of his forces to the enemy's is better than anywhere else on the entire eastern front and always was. If his troops are badly demoralized, then it's because of the spirit permeating them from above." Through Party channels, and particularly from Gauleiter Koch, Hitler had learned of the defeatism infecting Manstein's headquarters. Characteristically, the field marshal warned that there were 47 Soviet infantry divisions and 9 tank corps confronting him. Hitler refused to acknowledge that these could be anything but worn-out divisions which had been "reconditioned" and fed back to the battlefields; he "knew" the enemy troops' morale was low. "How can he maintain that those are 47 brand-new divisions that nothing can stop?" Hitler asked Zeitzler. With heavy sarcasm he commented, "Our German divisions are 'all rotten formations,' the Russians are all 'fresh as a daisy.' " If the retreat shortened the German front, it would shorten the enemy front by an equal amount. "But if we retire here, then this"—presumably jabbing at the Crimea on the map—"is lost." Zeitzler blurted out: "The Crimea is as good as lost anyway sooner or later." Hitler disagreed. "I'll think it over during the night again. . . . You know, Zeitzler, we can all put on airs and say, It's as good as lost. But when the time comes and it *is* lost, it won't be Manstein who accepts the blame: the responsibility is *ours.*" It was the political effect on Turkey that alarmed him. "They [the British] are trying to blackmail Turkey into joining the war on February 15," he reminded Zeitzler. ". . . Herr Manstein won't take any responsibility for that. He'll just say, 'That's a matter for the politicians.'" In addition, if Antonescu lost his army in the Crimea, he might be overthrown. "That is why we are duty-bound to defend this second Stalingrad if at all possible."

For many nights Hitler worried over the strategic decision. If he allowed Manstein to retreat, he would lose the Crimea, the iron-ore fields of Krivoi Rog, the manganese of Nikopol, and the foodstuffs of the Ukraine. He asked Zeitzler early on December 29 to work out how many divisions Küchler could release to Manstein if Army Group North was withdrawn to the East Wall line from Narva to Lake Peipus, and soon afterward he authorized Küchler to fall back on an intermediate line. When the field marshal came to the Wolf's Lair on December 30, Hitler flatteringly noted that Küchler's was the elite army of the entire eastern front, indeed an outright provocation to Kluge and Manstein. "You are lucky the other army groups don't know your strength-ratio, otherwise we couldn't save you from them!"

Admiral Dönitz, however, voiced emphatic protests against falling back on the East Wall in the north without good cause, and on January 5, 1944, Hitler forbade any voluntary withdrawal. The consequence was that when the Russian offensive began there nine days later, Küchler's weakened army group was no longer strong enough to withstand it, and it was thrown back onto the East Wall line anyway. Küchler was replaced by General Model, Hitler's stoutest defensive expert, and he halted the Soviet onslaught. Hitler felt that Küchler had been lured into retreating by the fatal East Wall mentality. "If we are going to withdraw to it anyway, why bother to hold on!"

As for the Allies, despite Cicero, the end of 1943 saw Hitler completely ignorant of their intentions. An early cross-Channel invasion was expected, but even here an Allied bluff was not impossible. A regular participant in the war conferences, Captain Heinz Assmann, wrote on December 29:

> The questions occupying the Führer and Wehrmacht operations staff now are primarily these:
>
> 1. Is all the Anglo-American huffing and puffing about an invasion in the west —speeches, articles, new appointments, and newspaper reports—really serious or just an immense bluff to dupe Germany and perhaps Russia too? Are

they trying to lure units away from the eastern front or prevent us from reinforcing that front at the crucial moment of the Soviet winter offensive?

2. Is the invasion hubbub a diversion for a major operation in the *Balkans,* either via Crete, Rhodes, and the Aegean, or via Turkey, or both?
3. Is the invasion planned *not* for the west but perhaps in Denmark–Norway after all?
4. Is Turkey as reliable as she seems, or has she perhaps already resigned herself to the passage of British troops and the use of her airfields?
5. Can we hold on to the Ukraine, which is vital for feeding the German people? Where can we still cut back on strength to help the worst pressure points on the eastern front? Where is the first infallible clue as to their real invasion intentions?
6. Will the U-boat campaign with the new submarine types result in the desired successes?

Much would depend on the new secret submarine types. The need to train them in the Baltic was one powerful argument Admiral Dönitz had voiced against allowing Küchler's Army Group North to fall back any farther, and recent naval events had greatly enhanced Dönitz's standing at the Wolf's Lair.

Once again the navy had shown an aggressive spirit which Hitler sadly missed in his field marshals. On Sunday December 26 the battle cruiser *Scharnhorst* had attacked an Allied convoy in the Arctic. Previous experience had indicated that the enemy was prudently reluctant to fight Dönitz's big ships in the dark, and in December there would be no light at all in those northern latitudes. But at 7:35 P.M. Dönitz telephoned Hitler with the alarming news that British warships had picked up the *Scharnhorst* while they were still thirty miles off, and had evidently destroyed her. An hour earlier, the bewildered Rear Admiral Bey had signaled Berlin: "Enemy firing at us by radar at a range of over eighteen thousand meters," followed barely six minutes later by a grim farewell: "To the Führer! We fight to our last shell." Then there had only been silence, interrupted by English signals like "Finish her off with torpedoes!"—"Fire a star shell!"—"Clear the the target area except for those ships with torpedoes and one destroyer with searchlight." Hitler accepted the warship's loss philosophically. If the enemy's radar was so good—according to Dönitz the British had pinpointed in their radar every waterspout thrown up by the shells—then the *Scharnhorst* had been like a blind man boxing with a prizefighter.

Hitherto radar research had been controlled by Göring. It was a conspicuous failure. The British night bombers could bomb Berlin accurately through ten-tenths cloud, and a new 3-centimeter radar had just been found in a downed bomber, but the Luftwaffe could still not operate even a 10-centimeter radar system. Under pressure from Speer and Dönitz at the Wolf's Lair on January 2, Hitler transferred all radar and electronics research to Speer's unified control.

In a lightning war like those with Poland and France in 1939 and 1940, fought by largely professional armies, the political indoctrination of the troops was of little moment. In the bitter, protracted contest the war had now become, however, with four-fifths of the fighting men recruited from German civilian life, Hitler recognized—too late—that such indoctrination was as important as material armament. By early 1943 troop morale was already suffering, particularly from the frontline soldier's uncertainty about the fate of his wife and family after the heavy British night attacks. Hitler expected his generals to explain the purpose of the struggle to their men, and when all but a few—like Walter Model, Ferdinand Schörner, and Lothar Rendulic—proved unequal to the task he called upon the Party to instill the necessary spirit. He had addressed the generals assembled by Bormann for this purpose at the Wolf's Lair on October 16 and reassured them that he would not emulate the hated political commissar system of the Bolsheviks: he would not be putting Party lecturers into army uniform, but elevating loyal and politically conscious officers to positions in which they could influence their comrades.

There is no doubt that Hitler was finally impelled to issue his order of December 22, 1943, establishing an OKW National Socialist Leadership Staff under General Hermann Reinecke, by the uncomfortably effective subversion campaign being directed against the eastern front by the renegade German generals taken prisoner at Stalingrad. Late in August his former orderly, Hans Junge—now a Waffen SS officer in Russia—had visited him briefly. "The most dangerous developments at the front at this juncture," Hitler asserted later, "are definitely the [anti-Nazi] proclamations printed by General Seydlitz. Various people told me so, most vividly Junge, who's got his head screwed on. The proclamations arrive in black-white-and-red"—the colors of the Reich—"and the ordinary soldier can't tell what's true and what isn't. Besides our soldiers have always taken officers to be men of honor." The troops were completely taken in by trick photomontages published by these Moscow renegades. How were they to know that Stalin's League of German Officers—of which Seydlitz was chairman—was as Hitler said just "a herd of unprincipled swine who have sold their souls to the Devil"?

The December 22 order gave the Party its first bridgehead into the Wehrmacht. Early in January General Reinecke announced to Hitler that he and Martin Bormann's Party chancellery were recruiting a small fanatical leadership staff from old, experienced Party warriors and young battle-hardened army officers; in this undertaking they had Himmler's active support. Schmundt assured Hitler that the army had been clamoring for it for a long time. But while the new Party-indoctrinated "leadership officers" would undoubtedly influence the lower command levels to which they were temporarily attached, Hitler himself had to speak to the senior generals, who would otherwise remain immune. Hitler strongly wanted to crack the whip over them again, for unsettling reports had recently reached him—including one broadcast by the BBC—that certain disaffected generals were plotting his overthrow or even assassination. But he hesitated. "It would be hard to bring them all together at the same time." Bormann, however, was eager. "If it could be done, it would be the biggest success."

Keitel reminded Hitler that they needed to appoint a specially capable "leadership officer" for the army. Hitler replied without hesitation, "Schörner. He is a fanatic!" Until recently commander of the bridgehead at Nikopol, Schörner was a tough general not given to defeatism. Only recently he had ended a letter to Schmundt with the words: "You know the position here. But we will pull through." How different from the melancholy Manstein, who saw his fame as a commander withering before his eyes!

Manstein arrived in agitation on January 4, 1944, and again demanded permission to withdraw his entire southern sector—thereby abandoning Nikopol and the Crimea forever—to find the means to buttress his damaged northern sector, where the Fourth Panzer Army had now been thrown back on to the former Polish frontier. Again Hitler refused. Manstein asked for the others present to leave the room and in Zeitzler's presence alone launched a sober and forceful critique of Hitler's overall military command in the east. Hitler tried to stare him down—like "an Indian snake charmer," in Manstein's words; but the field marshal could not be charmed. He recommended that Hitler appoint a Commander in Chief East like Rundstedt in the west and Kesselring in Italy. Hitler had heard all this before. He pointed out that nobody had as much authority as he had, "and even I am not obeyed by my field marshals. Do you think they would obey *you* any better?" He could offer Manstein no fresh divisions: Dönitz had persuaded him not to shorten the front of Army Group North any further; in the west they must first wait until the invasion had been defeated, or the British had got bogged down in Portugal—his latest *idée fixe.* Hitler explained to Manstein that he was fighting to gain time—time to raise new armies, time for the U-boat campaign beginning in May 1944 to bite, time for the smoldering East-West dispute to blaze up into the open. Russia's frontier changes in Poland were already provoking near hysteria in London and Washington. In the event, Manstein's soldiers were able to withstand the winter onslaught, yielding almost no ground to the Russians; where there was a will, Hitler concluded, there was evidently a way.

During these first days of 1944, Hitler laid down the material foundations of the coming year's campaign. He personally besought Dönitz, Speer, and their submarine experts to keep to production targets. He had ordered Göring to concentrate production effort on the jet fighters and jet bombers, and—just in case the jet ran into snags—on the unique Dornier 335 fighter-bomber, which had a propellor at each end and was attaining speeds almost as high as the jet fighter. He ordered jet-engine production to be housed underground at the Central Works tunnel-factory already producing A-4 rockets near Nordhausen, and on January 4 he again told Speer and Milch how much he was relying on the new secret U-boat types and the jet aircraft. "If I get the jets in time, I can fight off the invasion with them"—and again, a few days later—"If I get a few hundred of them to the front line, it will exorcise the specter of invasion for all time."

Finally, on January 4 he applied himself to the overriding manpower problem. During 1944 Germany somehow had to raise more than four million new workers. The whole afternoon was devoted to a conference between Keitel, Speer, Milch, and Herbert Backe, agriculture minister, as the "employers" and Sauckel and Himmler as the "manpower procurers." Speer's belief was that French workers were more productive in "protected" factories in France, but Sauckel raised powerful arguments for continuing the conscription of French labor for war plants in Germany. He emphatically contended that even by taking Italian forced labor into account he could not guarantee the 4,050,000 new workers needed for 1944. Hitler was still loath to employ female workers on a scale comparable to Russia, Britain, and the United States, explaining that there was no comparison between "our long-legged, slender women" and the "stocky, primitive, and robust Russian women."

Sauckel counted heavily on Italian forced labor. But once again the "Italian problem" thwarted Hitler. To please Mussolini, he had agreed to the raising of a modest new Italian army—four divisions; the Italian internees had only to volunteer for these to escape labor service, but few of the "volunteers" ever reached the divisions. The only ray of sunshine in this darkness had been Mussolini's unexpected arrest of Count Ciano: together with his "fellow conspirators" he was tried and condemned to death by a Fascist court in Verona in January. His wife, the former Edda Mussolini, managed that very day to escape to Switzerland, having addressed this letter to Hitler:

> Führer! Twice I believed your word, and twice I have been cheated. Only the soldiers lying on the battlefields prevent me from deserting to the enemy. If my husband is not released . . . nothing but that will stop me: for some time now the documents have been held by people authorized to make use of them if anything were to happen to my husband, me, my children, or my family.

A similar letter had gone to Mussolini himself: if Ciano was not in Switzerland within three days, Edda would make use of every document she possessed. Hitler took no action to intervene, and Ciano met the Fascist firing squad at 9 A.M. the next day, January 11.

The spectacular failure of the Allies to make any headway in Italy was a huge comfort to Hitler. Since early September the enemy had managed to advance only forty kilometers—little more than six miles per month—despite immense naval and air superiority. A year later Jodl was to comment on the Allies' bad strategy. "I still cannot understand why they began right down at the bottom and fought a laborious land campaign northward instead of using their colossal naval and other strength to leapfrog northward on a huge scale." This, coupled with Hitler's stubborn defense of the Crimea, undoubtedly impressed Turkey to remain neutral. While General Jodl maintained his instinctive fear for the Balkans for some months yet, Hitler concluded correctly from the Cicero reports that he could safely draw on his Balkan contingents to strengthen the Russian front. On January 12—Cicero's microfilmed documents revealed—the British foreign office had secretly cabled in exasperation to the British ambassador in Ankara that Turkey was unlikely now to enter the war soon. "We must now concentrate our main effort on maintaining the threat to the Germans from the eastern Mediterranean. At the same time the situation on the Russian front is moving rapidly and may be followed by developments which will cause a change in the Turkish attitude." Ribbentrop advised his ambassador to disclose to the Turks that the evidence was that *provided* Turkey remained intransigent Britain could not afford to break completely with her. According to the Cicero documents, Britain's ambassador was informed that Turkey was required to enter the war at the same time as "Overlord"—the invasion from British soil—began; this finally convinced Hitler that enemy strategy in the Balkans would be limited to diversionary operations only, rather than be the main invasion assault. (Furthermore an air raid was being planned against the Romanian oil refineries at Ploesti after March 15; it was code-named "Operation Saturn.") The Turkish foreign minister, Menemencioglu Numan, meanwhile informed a furious British ambassador: "We are not so stupid as to get dragged into a war against our own interests for the second time in twenty-five years." Ribbentrop instructed that a quarter of a million gold marks was to be paid to Cicero; it was money well spent.

Despite Manstein's misgivings, his Army Group South had staged a brilliant defense of the Dnieper bend and the bridgehead at Nikopol, but as the position of the Fourth Panzer Army on his left flank grew increasingly precarious he wrote urgently first to Zeitzler and then to Hitler himself appealing for reinforcements before his entire army group was encircled. Hitler dismissed the letters as a typical attempt by Manstein to justify his inevitable failure to future historians.

Hitler next saw Manstein on January 27. At Schmundt's suggestion, he had summoned the principal generals from the Russian front to hear a two-hour secret speech designed to put fresh fire into their veins. Row upon row, the generals sat before him in the dining room of a converted inn in the OKW's Security Zone II, near the Wolf's Lair. For two days they had listened to speeches by Goebbels, Rosenberg, and other Party leaders at Posen (Poznan). Now—after a communal lunch—they heard Hitler lecture articulately and, if the shorthand record be taken as a guide, powerfully on war and nations, and on the influence of leadership and racial character on a nation's morale. He hinted at new torpedoes, new submarines, new radar equipment, and secret weapons which would turn the tide in their favor after May 1944; until then they must grimly hold out. For this, National Socialist indoctrination—that same "holy conviction" that distinguished the Reich from the merely skeletal administrative structure that had been fascism in Italy—was indispensable.

Toward the end of his speech, something incredible occurred. For the first time, he was loudly interrupted. He had just addressed this challenge to the generals: ". . . If the worse comes to the worst and I am ever abandoned as Supreme Commander by my people, I must still expect my entire office corps to muster around me with daggers drawn—just as every field marshal, or the commander of an army, corps, division, or regiment expects his subordinates to stand by him in the hour of crisis." As he paused in his rhetoric, Manstein's voice came from the front row, loud and—possibly—reproachful: "*And so it will be,* mein Führer!" The interruption created a sensation at the Wolf's Lair, where it was talked about for days. Hitler hoped at first the field marshal had meant to reassure him of their loyalty, but Bormann and the adjutants told him the generals had interpreted the outburst otherwise: that the worse would indeed come to the worst. It was an interruption of exquisite ambiguity.[3]

Shortly afterward Hitler sent for the field marshal. "Field marshal, I must forbid you ever to interrupt a speech by me to my generals again." Then he referred sarcastically to Manstein's recent letter asking for reinforcements. "No doubt you wanted it in your war diary to clear your name before the historians!" Manstein angrily retorted that his letters to the Führer never went into the diary. "Forgive me for resorting to an English expression, but *I* am a *gentleman.*" At that evening's war conference Hitler melted toward Manstein again. Perhaps it was innate respect for this outstanding commander; perhaps it was just because General Erwin Jaenecke spoke confidently of his Seventeenth Army's ability to hold the Crimea, during the conference. The other army- and army-group commanders were equally optimistic now, though none of them viewed the future exactly rosily. This was the effect of Hitler's rhetoric.

Twice that day—both in his speech and in the private evening circle—Hitler again formulated his goal as winning for Germany the "world domination" for

[3]It resulted, according to Schmundt's diary, in Manstein's eventual dismissal. See page 616.

which she was "predestined." That night he told Bormann of his unorthodox ideas for making good Germany's disastrous casualties, for otherwise in population terms she would lose the war even though victorious militarily. Hitler remarked that Germany's most important asset, the fertility of entire generations of German women—perhaps three or four million of them—would be wasted unless men could be found for them. A great campaign must begin for every sound German woman, married or not, to bear as many children as possible to safeguard Germany's future. Writers, poets, and artists must henceforth extol the unmarried mother. As in animal breeding, the finest specimens of manhood must do their bit, and German womanhood must be educated to abandon their fanatical insistence on marital fidelity—"a fetish they often ignore themselves until they are married," Hitler slyly observed. Otherwise one day Germany, and with her all Europe, would be overwhelmed by the Asiatic hordes of which the current Russian plague was but a part. "We must look at the population charts of Europe and Asia in 1850, 1870, and 1900," said Hitler, "and try to visualize what the map of 1945 will be."

Trouble from Providence

The Hitler of early 1944 was unlike the confident Führer who had set out for the Polish front in his train in September 1939. His animal energy and abnormal willpower remained unsapped, but his appearance had undergone a shocking change. Werner Best found him a tired, broken, and elderly man, dragging his feet and stooping so low that he seemed to bow. His features were sunken and lined with worry and anger. His eyes stared with an almost reproachful gaze. Hitler's secretaries noticed that sometimes his knees would begin to shake, or he had to grasp his trembling left hand with his right; the tremor when he had to lift a cup to his lips was too marked to be concealed. Yet he refused to take these symptoms seriously, and Dr. Morell loudly proclaimed his patient to be in the best of health. We know from his papers that for five months after September 1943 he continually urged Hitler to submit to a further electrocardiogram, without success. Not until September 1944 did Hitler agree: again the diagnosis of the electrocardiogram was "coronary sclerosis." It was the same with X-rays; several times Morell noted in his papers that his patient should be X-rayed, but there is no trace of any X-ray after 1940, with the exception of those of Hitler's head in September 1944. When Hitler's adjutants reproved Morell for his lackadaisical treatment of the Führer, his exasperated reply was invariably the same: "*You* try treating a patient like the Führer!"

For all his obesity—his weight hovered around 230 pounds—and hirsute repulsiveness, Morell retained Hitler's affections. Each evening at Hitler's midnight tea party, Morell would be snoring loudly within minutes of slumping into an armchair. Hitler's eyes were alive with sympathy and indulgence at this spectacle. "Without Morell I would probably have died long ago, or at least be incapable of working on. He was and is the only one who can help me." A secretary described the doctor thus: "With his podgy, hairy hands clasped across his potbelly, he fought back his sleepiness. In some strange way, his eyes closed from the bottom upward—it looked hideous behind his thick-lensed spectacles. Nor was he a good conversationalist. Sometimes Colonel von Below [Hitler's spry, elegant Luftwaffe adjutant] gently nudged him. Then he would wake up and chuckle, assuming that the Führer had told a joke."

Hitler's private milieu had also changed. He rarely came in contact with people from the world outside his headquarters. His horizon was the perimeter fence, with its guards and minefields. Schmundt and Schaub introduced what new faces they could to the evening conversation parties—the architect Hermann Giesler, the wives of the adjutants and headquarters commandant, and former members of Hitler's staff like Hans Pfeiffer and Hans Junge, both of whom would die shortly in France. Morell lamented in one letter that Julius Schaub had been injured in a Munich air raid, and the old familiar faces were gone. "Reichsleiter Bormann is mostly away on business in Berlin and Munich. Heini Hoffmann [Hitler's bibulous personal photographer and court jester] only puts in a guest appearance every four weeks or so. Scarcely anybody of the old clique is still here. The headquarters has outgrown itself, and most people are preoccupied with themselves. I for my own part have become a recluse, doing scientific research and working on my business undertakings in what time I can." Albert Speer had also vanished from Hitler's sight—at first recovering from a grave illness, then afflicted by a pathological fear that his colleagues were trying to usurp his powers; not until spring did Hitler see the armaments minister again.

Bormann's influence over Hitler was now immense. Rosenberg, Lammers, and the other Cabinet ministers rarely penetrated the Party secretary's protective shield around the Führer. In vain the finance minister, Count Schwerin von Krosigk, demanded to report to Hitler on the threatening inflation and the loss of public confidence in the Reichsmark. Hitler was told only what Bormann (and Himmler) wanted him to know about internal Reich affairs.

The long-delayed visit by Dr. Hans Frank, Governor General of occupied Poland—on February 6, 1944—provides a further significant example. The Russian army was now fighting on Polish soil, but Hitler—"exceptionally forthright and looking the picture of a healthy, dynamic, and active man" as Frank wrote that day—assured the Governor General that he would not allow the Generalgouvernement to become a battlefield. "Yes, my dear Frank, it *is* odd: previously we regarded the Generalgouvernement as something of a backwater; today it is our bulwark against the east." He applauded Frank's new policy, aimed at securing Polish assistance in the fight. Frank told him of the fortifications built along the frontier and showed him maps of Polish petroleum production, population distribution, forestation, and agricultural output. But even Hans Frank seems to have been pulling the wool over his Führer's eyes; in his eighteen-page diary record of the discussion—which Bormann also attended—Frank touched on the Jewish problem only once: "I said that getting rid of the Jews by getting them out of the Generalgouvernement[1] had taken a great load off the country's general situation."

Afterward Frank ran into Morell. "I asked him," wrote Frank, "about the Führer's health. He claimed it is better than ever before. His stomach pains are gone and his appetite has returned—a particularly good sign. He said he was proud of this achievement." Shortly after, Hitler's appetite failed again, however, though for a different reason. When Frau von Exner, the Viennese dietician recommended by Antonescu, became engaged to an SS adjutant at headquarters, it was learned that she had a Jewish great grandmother. Hitler had to dismiss her, after refusing to eat for many days. "You will understand that I must pay you off," he told her. "I cannot make one rule for myself and another for the rest." But he did order Martin Bormann to put her family papers in order—giving them full Aryan "clearance"—and his annoyance was intense when he learned many months later that Bormann, who had himself been rebuffed by the girl, had in fact resorted to petty persecution. Her relatives were ejected from the Party, a step which had severe financial effects on them.

In Italy, the Allies were being held at bay. Hitler's real fear was of the invasion threat looming in the west. "*If* only they would land half a million men," he reflected on December 30, "and then foul weather and storms cut them off in the rear—then everything would be all right!" Rommel's tour of inspection in Denmark was complete, and that day Hitler had instructed his representatives in Copenhagen to resort to criminal terrorist tactics to stamp out acts of sabotage and assassination by underground agents in Denmark. Since it was considered counterproductive to try and then execute these agents—and thus make martyrs of them—Hitler ordered Himmler's agents to strike back under cover against leading Danish opponents and their property. The next day an SS marksman gunned down a journalist, and a few days later the spiritual leader of the Danish resistance, Pastor Kaj Munk, was assassinated. "You can't smash terrorism by philosophizing," Hitler told his generals secretly on January 27, 1944; "you have to smash it by using even greater terror."

By early 1944, Rommel was confidently asserting his authority in preparing the defense of France. Hitler was cautiously optimistic; the Allies, he felt, had secured footholds in Africa and Italy only because of the Italian traitors. "But they won't find any here—they'll get the thrashing of their lives!" He also said,

[1]Literally, "*Die Beseitigung der Juden aus dem Generalgouvernement.*" In fact they had been got rid of *in* that domain; but the wording was in deference to Hitler's insistence on their deportation for forced labor in the east.

"I am convinced that when the time comes it will be a huge relief—just like Dieppe." Meanwhile Hitler applied his own mind to the Atlantic defenses. He insisted on digging in the scores of useless Panther tanks as gun batteries in France, since they had proved a liability on the battlefields of Russia. He ordered extra concrete pumped into the forward defenses. He commanded that pillboxes for three thousand new antitank and other guns were to be built by the end of April at the very latest. Most important of all, he gave Rommel's army group tactical command of the armies along the Channel coast. Rommel toured these areas from January until May and struck the fear of God into officers and men alike, rudely awakening them. Hitler knew that Rommel had many critics among the generals but he counted on the Desert Fox to light a bonfire under them—before the Allies could in the spring. On January 15, General Jodl reported to Hitler on his own tour of the Atlantic defenses. He was unimpressed by the pace of fortification activity; large sections of the defensive works were incomplete, and the Germans were fraternizing with the French coastal population. The Luftwaffe had not planned ahead at all.[2] He supported Rommel's contentions wholeheartedly.

For six weeks from January 12, Rommel stood in for Rundstedt as Commander in Chief West and began implementing tactical concepts strongly opposed to those of Rundstedt, who remembering the lessons of the Russian front had planned a flexible defense on French soil, with a powerful mobile reserve of panzer divisions in the rear. Rommel convincingly argued that the Allied invasion attempt must be defeated on the very landing beaches; the enemy, once ashore, could marshal such colossal and overwhelming material strength that he could never again be dislodged. Thus the panzer divisions must be brought right up to the coast; otherwise they would arrive on the battlefield too late—or not at all, if the enemy destroyed the road and railway links before them. This tallied well with Hitler's vision. "With every month the invasion is delayed the probability grows that we will get at least one squadron of jet aircraft. . . . The main thing is that the moment the invasion begins the enemy must be smothered in bombs—that'll force them to take cover, and even if there's only one jet airborne, they'll still be forced to take cover and this will waste them hour upon hour. But in half a day our reserves will be well on their way!" This delay would also enable Hitler to take stock: "Which is the decoy—and which is the real invasion!"

[2]"Yesterday," wrote Rommel on December 29, 1943, "I was in P[aris] again and spoke with Field Marshal Sp[errle, Commander in Chief Third Air Force]. The prospects here are not all that good. From what I had heard I expected a lot more from this Service." And Jodl wrote in his diary several days later: "How on earth is the air war against the invasion going to be conducted?" Not until August 1944 was Sperrle dismissed by Hitler.

Rommel's activity changed the whole face of the Atlantic defenses. With his Party backing and influence on Hitler, he was able to start fresh divisions moving to the west. He demanded millions of mines per month, to lay along the coast. He prepared to flood or swamp low-lying areas. He conferred with the Todt Organization's chief, Xaver Dorsch, on an ingenious arsenal of deadly gadgets to meet the invaders: submerged barriers of massive spikes designed to gash open the hulls of landing boats, and nutcracker mines supported on iron girders, staggered and echeloned along the beaches, some visible, some below the water's surface. Tempted by the cash rewards, the male French population willingly assisted, while their womenfolk made rush-matting for sand traps or helped to erect antiparatroop defenses. According to Rommel, they worked with a will and finished each day "singing lustily." All France knew, he said, what would happen to their towns and villages if Germany's enemies landed and made a battlefield of them.

From the Cicero documents Hitler knew that the Allies had scheduled the capture of Rome for the end of January 1944. All the indications were that this was the objective of the powerful offensive begun by a British corps in Italy on January 17. But wholly unexpectedly—and without even a hint from the German Intelligence services—on January 22 an American corps staged a sudden seaborne landing south of Rome at Anzio—to the rear of the German lines.

Misled by Canaris's assurances, Kesselring had denuded the Anzio coastline shortly before, and only two German battalions met the American troops debouched by three hundred ships along a twenty-mile stretch of shore. But both sides fumbled. Kesselring delayed his counterattack for a week, to allow further panzer divisions and heavy units to arrive in Italy. The Luftwaffe's Richthofen scornfully noted in his diary: "Thus we violate the cardinal rule of war accepted for many millennia—to lay into enemy beachheads with everything you've got immediately, so as to exploit the disorder always reigning in the first few days. In theory this decision has already cost us the battle for Rome." But the Americans were even more hesitant in consolidating their beachhead. "Politics play a big part," Hewel reminded Hitler. "No general over there can afford big defeats. Questions get asked, and if an over-risky gamble he's begun doesn't pay off, he gets hauled over the coals." Hitler realized that an American bloody nose at Anzio would be a big prestige boost after the dark months of 1943. He even said, "If we can wipe them out down there, then there won't *be* an invasion anywhere else"—Roosevelt could not take such a risk in a presidential election year. But Hitler's sixth sense urged caution on him too, telling him that Anzio was less a Battle for Rome—whatever the dramatic, purple prose he used in his messages to Kesselring[3]—than a sly enemy attempt to lure the high-grade German reserves like the brand-new 9th SS Panzer Division away from France into a peripheral war of attrition in Italy; and after the long-delayed counterattack by Mackensen's Fourteenth Army failed to throw the Americans back into the sea, he was content to see the beachhead merely contained.

"We were completely surprised by those few invasion operations they have launched so far," Hitler was to say in April. He asked Jodl to determine precisely why Intelligence had failed to predict Anzio. Kesselring claimed that the few clues that reached him in mid-January were dismissed by Admiral Canaris as erroneous. Early in February, the defection to the British of an important Abwehr agent in Turkey put the last nail in the admiral's long-prepared coffin. Erich Vermehren, a young junior-grade official in the Abwehr's main Middle East headquarters at Istanbul, had vanished with his countess wife, who was eight years his senior and a fervent Catholic. This blew the Abwehr in the eastern Mediterranean wide open and brought even Cicero's operations to an abrupt end. The Abwehr frantically tried to divert the blame to the SS or even to Ribbentrop's ministry, but Hitler had had enough of Admiral Canaris and told Himmler so at two meetings on February 9 and 11. Hitherto he had respected the OKW's sovereignty, but now he accepted the SS accusations. Canaris was disgraced and suspended from office. On February 12, Hitler signed the order for Himmler to set up a "unified German secret Intelligence service." But even now Canaris escaped arrest—shielded from criticism by his gullible superior, Keitel, and even put in charge of the OKW's economic-warfare unit outside Berlin.

On the Russian front, Hitler clung fanatically to his belief that Stalin's military strength was waning. Later in February, Zeitzler's staff produced estimates that over 18,000,000 of the 46,000,000 able-bodied men available to Stalin in 1941 had now been eliminated by battle casualties or loss of territory. Russian casualties were outnumbering German by seven to one. Stalin's manpower reserves had now shrunk to barely 2,100,000 men, according to Zeitzler. This was why Hitler still fought on, defending every centimeter of ground even though the Russians were still moving men and equipment into their battlefront faster than he himself could. And as that front moved ever closer to German soil, Hitler's willingness

[3]On January 28, 1944, Hitler radioed: "In the next few days the 'Battle for Rome' will break out. . . . It must be fought in holy wrath against an enemy who is waging a pitiless war of extermination against the German people, who shuns no means to that end, who is devoid of all higher ethical purpose, and who is intent only on the destruction of Germany and thereby of our European culture." The enemy must realize that his main 1944 invasion would be an undertaking that would choke on the blood of the British and American soldiers, the document concluded.

to permit operational retreats like the "Buffalo" movement of 1943 disappeared. From now on the German soldier would fight where he stood, holding out until the inevitable breach between East and West came to his salvation: such was Hitler's strategy.

In the north, Model's army group was preparing its final withdrawal to the East Wall (Panther) line. In the center, Busch had fought a series of successful defensive actions, and his line was still intact. But a gap of over 150 miles yawned north of Manstein's Army Group South, exposing it and Kleist's Army Group A to extreme danger. Since January 28, 54,000 German troops had been encircled at Cherkassy on the Dnieper River, and the same fate threatened the garrison of the Nikopol bridgehead. Hitler ordered a counterattack to cut off the Russians encircling Cherkassy; but snow and rain thwarted the operation, and after weeks of harrowing fighting Hitler reluctantly authorized the garrison there to break out as best they could, leaving most of their injured to the mercies of the enemy. The dramatic breakout began on the night of February 15—led by a silent phalanx of troops with fixed bayonets, followed by the artillery and heavier equipment; but instead of the Second Panzer Corps waiting to receive them in a designated position, they were greeted by heavily armed Russian units instead. The heavy gear was abandoned, but the men fought on to the westward. They were confronted by a river, sprang into the icy waters and forded it or were drowned. Only 30,000 of the 54,000 who set out reached the German lines. Transport aircraft had flown out 2,400 of the luckier injured men.

The Cherkassy pocket had irritated the Russians out of all proportion to its size. It was here that Stalin again employed his deadly psychological weapon, the League of German Officers—the organization of turncoat German prisoners in Russian hands. Seydlitz and his fellow generals broadcast appeals over Moscow radio to their encircled former comrades to lay down their arms. Officers in German uniform infiltrated into the pocket to commit acts of sabotage, issue conflicting orders, and deliver secret letters from Seydlitz to the generals still faithful to their Führer: each of the corps commanders in Cherkassy, Stemmermann, and Lieb received such letters; so did General Kruse. Their authenticity was beyond doubt. Elsewhere Seydlitz-letters were slipped into the hands of Field Marshals Rundstedt and Küchler, Generals Model and Lindemann. Some of Seydlitz's emissaries were captured, and revealed—before their execution—that they had been brainwashed and trained by the Russians at a special camp near Krasnogorsk. On hearing this Hitler cited Scripture: "Lord, forgive them—they know not what they do!" His revulsion toward the German officer corps as a whole was further increased by the revelations of corruption and debauchery at the highest level in the military government of Belgium, brought to light when members of military governor General von Falkenhausen's staff were put on trial in Berlin.

The Seydlitz and Falkenhausen affairs had a strange sequel. To restore Hitler's faith in his officers, General Schmundt took it on himself to secure every field marshal's signature to a declaration of personal loyalty to the Führer. Flying first to Rundstedt in France—most senior of Germany's serving soldiers—and satisfying him of the authenticity of Seydlitz's treachery, Schmundt then went on to Model, Rommel, Kleist, Busch, Manstein, and Weichs in turn (Kluge appears not to have signed the document). Weichs wrote in his diary: "Such a reaffirmation of our oath of allegiance seems unmilitary to me. An officer's loyalty ought to be taken for granted." But Weichs admitted that in the Party's history similar declarations of loyalty by the Gauleiters after various disgraceful affairs—like the alleged plot by Ernst Röhm in 1934—had succeeded in restoring Hitler's confidence in them. Perhaps it would work for the army too.

For a variety of reasons, Hitler decided it was time to leave the Wolf's Lair for a while. He planned to meet Antonescu (to ask him to his face about Romania's loyalty). He also wanted to be closer to the Italian front. "We have built headquarters in just about every other corner of the Reich," he wanly joked, "but never dreamed that we should one day need one near Italy!" Another reason for leaving was so that he could address the Nazi faithfuls at the Party Foundation Ceremony in Munich. But above all, the truth was that he could no longer take the risk of an enemy air raid on the Wolf's Lair, whose bunkers had been built only to withstand the pre-blockbuster type of bombs. The British bomber force had a month earlier dropped twenty-four hundred tons of bombs on Berlin in one night; both British and American daylight formations—currently blasting Göring's fighter-aircraft factories—had East Prussia well within their range. Sooner or later Churchill or Roosevelt might consider the Führer a worthwhile target. Thus he entrained for Munich on February 23, 1944, while the Todt Organization moved in to erect even stronger bunkers at the Wolf's Lair.

It is unlikely that he glimpsed the bomb-torn ruins of Posen, Cottbus, Leipzig, and Nuremberg as he passed through. He consistently and consciously avoided seeing the misery his enemies had wrought—a harsh but in retrospect a proper attitude, for an enraged mind cannot make sober and logical decisions. Besides, the blinds were drawn to shield his painful retinas. For two weeks now he had been troubled by a stabbing pain and increasingly opaque veil in his right eye, of such turbidity as to rend him virtually blind when he closed his left eye. As he was driven along the snow-swept autobahn toward Berchtesgaden that evening, the sirens were already sounding, searchlights were fingering the sky, and pathfinder flares were bathing the countryside in a hostile glare: a heavy British attack was beginning on Schweinfurt, and six hundred bombers were over Bavaria. The crack of the antiaircraft batteries was still echoing around the sleepy

Berchtesgaden valleys when Hitler arrived at the Berghof at 10:15 P.M., his driver having missed a turning in the deep snow and headed some distance in the general direction of Vienna by mistake. A staff stenographer wrote: "The war conference was slated to begin at 11:30 P.M. As we stood by in the anteroom the Führer came in with Reichsleiter [Martin] Bormann, Gruppenführer [Albert] Bormann, and the rest of his staff, having toured the air raid shelter tunnels built here in recent months. He welcomed us with a friendly grin. The conference began at 11:45 P.M. and ended at five past midnight."

Camouflage netting covered the Berghof, and at midday only a melancholy twilight filtered through the famous window of the Great Hall. On March 2 a leading Berlin eye specialist examined Hitler's blue-gray eyes, gently palpated the eyeballs, and peered into their recesses with an opthalmoscope and magnifying mirror. He diagnosed "minute hemorrhages in the vitreous humor," and Hitler heard him recommend to Morell that the Führer submit to two quarter-hour periods of complete relaxation every day with heat treatment by sunlamp if possible. He was to avoid all "unnecessary excitement, particularly during the period immediately before the night's rest." Hitler's nine-year-old spectacles were quite inadequate, and a new pair of bifocals were prescribed.

Everybody who saw Hitler was shocked by his physical transformation. Defeat —Manstein's army group was now in near flight from the Ukraine—was carving deep hollows in his features. Hungary was secretly negotiating with the Allies. The two German counterattacks at Anzio had failed to eradicate the American beachhead. The new German divisions would not be ready until May. The aircraft industry was in smoking ruins. Small wonder that when Eva Braun gently reproached him for walking with a stoop, he would reply, "That's because of the burden of worries I'm carrying all the time," or again, "It's the heavy keys I'm carrying in my trouser pockets," or, "It's so I suit you better: you wear high heels, and I stoop a bit—then we are just right for each other."

On March 5 the two armaments "dictators" Milch and Saur came to the Berghof —their respective bosses being indisposed: Göring on leave and Speer convalescing. Their report on future aircraft, tank, and gun production was optimistic despite the crushing blows dealt by the enemy bombers. A Fighter Staff had been created to mobilize industry for the defense of the Reich's airspace. Hitler agreed to make fighter aircraft production a top priority and demanded that the two planned bunker-factories—with seventeen-foot-thick concrete roofs—should each have at least seven million square feet of floor space, capable of housing everything needed for aircraft manufacture from the forging of the crankshafts and smelting of the steel down to the finished product. He released sixty-four miners to Saur from the gangs tunneling air raid shelters under the Berghof and advised him to train at least *ten thousand* more; he must not rest until Germany's entire war industry was underground.

At the Central Works underground factory near Nordhausen, Himmler's slave laborers were already tooling up the production lines for jet aircraft, A-4 rockets, and the Luftwaffe's V-1 flying bombs. At the Volkswagen's works, mass production of the flying bomb had at last begun in January, and the missile was now functioning flawlessly—covering 175 miles or more with barely any deviation in its Peenemünde trials. On March 5, Milch gleefully urged Hitler to begin the flying-bomb attack on England on April 20—Hitler's birthday—sending off fifteen hundred in the next ten days and the rest in May. "It will be the most evil torture you can imagine, just picture for yourselves a large high-explosive bomb falling on Berlin every half-hour and nobody knowing where the next will fall! Twenty days of that will have them all folding at the knees!"

Hitler, however, delayed the flying-bomb attack. Not until mid-May did he make up his mind on a date. Perhaps he had wanted all the "revenge" weapons to open fire simultaneously—A-4 rocket, flying bomb, "high-pressure pump," and Krupp's "Gustav" long-range guns, coupled with a saturation attack on London by the Third Air Force. He also wanted the attack to coincide with the Allied invasion. But the A-4 rocket was still far from ready. In January only 50, in February only 86 A-4s had left the underground Central Works—far short of the target figures. (In May, General Dornberger, chief of the rocket project, wryly reported: "Our main problem is getting the missiles to the target in one piece"; most of them were blowing up in midair. Of the 57 test-launched from the SS proving ground in Poland by mid-March, only 26 lifted off, and only 4 reached the target area intact.) In Speer's absence, loud criticism was voiced against this costly if spectacular weapon. The OKW pointed out that liquid-oxygen output alone would limit the rate of fire to about 25 A-4s a day. Even Saur, Speer's closest adviser, recommended on March 5 that Hitler consider converting the Central Works factory from A-4 assembly to fighter-aircraft manufacture: the tunnels were big enough to house a plant turning out a thousand planes a month. Hitler appeared to agree, but someone changed his mind again—perhaps it was Speer himself, whom Hitler visited two weeks later bearing a bouquet of flowers on the minister's thirty-ninth birthday. Or perhaps Himmler—by now a daily visitor to Hitler—may have tendered this advice.

Göring and Ribbentrop now counted for little in Hitler's esteem. He took to summoning low-ranking officers to the Berghof, knowing he could trust them to speak out openly. For several days he interviewed soldiers from platoon right up to divisional rank about the fighting at Anzio. They told him of the crushing enemy artillery superiority, of the slime and filth, of the inferior German radio gear and faulty hand-grenades. (As a consequence, Hitler ordered Kesselring to apply the lessons of 1918 trench warfare to Anzio; remorseless pressure must be put on the enemy by the long-forgotten techniques of storm-regiments and artillery bombardment.) A panzer general, Gerd von Schwerin, later described one such reception at the Berghof that March. Schmundt—who first privately expressed doubts as to whether Hitler's constant interference on the battlefield was really salutary—ushered him in. "I couldn't help feeling that while Hitler was trying to be sincere, his mind was elsewhere." Outside, Schwerin met Göring and Himmler, and he related how the Russians had kept their notorious wet-weather offensives rolling by rounding up thousands of women and making each one wade ten miles through the slime to the front lines with a shell on her back.

Schmundt, the general reported, told him laughingly that "nobody takes Göring seriously any more." Beside Bormann, the new force in Hitler's life was undeniably Grand Admiral Karl Dönitz. It was the admiral who had cajoled Hitler into preventing the earlier withdrawal of Army Group North to the Panther line (with grim consequences for Küchler's troops). It was Dönitz too who had demanded the retention of the Crimea. And now that Hitler's health was poor, it was Dönitz whom he sent to preside over the Memorial Day parade in Berlin and to address the ten thousand new officer-candidates in Breslau.

Ribbentrop was deeply wounded by Hitler's loss of faith in him and privately made an offer to Hitler which showed that he certainly made up in personal courage whatever he might lack in diplomacy. As Walter Schellenberg, chief of Himmler's foreign Intelligence service, later wrote:

> Ribbentrop told me he was very familiar with my special reports on Russia, and he had given the whole situation much thought. He had then gone to the Führer and told him frankly that their biggest and most dangerous enemy was the Soviet Union and that Stalin had as much military ability and statesmanship as Churchill and Roosevelt put together, if not more. The Führer shared this view and even mused out loud that Stalin was the only one he could find the necessary respect for, if one day he was going to reach a compromise peace with somebody after all. But he—Ribbentrop—had then put to the Führer the idea that everything possible should be done to liquidate Stalin, as the Soviet regime would then no longer be able to withstand the burdens of the war. Therefore he [Ribbentrop] had announced to the Führer his willingness to sacrifice his own life, if he could save Germany thereby. His plan was to do all he could to lure Stalin once more to the conference table; then he would gun him down. For a long time the Führer had turned this over in his mind, and then finally replied, "No. I don't like anything like that. It would be asking for trouble from Providence."[4]

[4]I have relied on Schellenberg's own handwritten text, rather than on the heavily "edited" published *Memoirs.*

At the end of February the Turkish foreign minister had confidentially warned Germany that unless the eastern front could be stabilized before the Russians crossed the Dniester River, the Balkans would disintegrate and Germany would eventually lose the war; Turkey would have to declare war too, if only to save her own skin.

The upshot was Hitler's dramatic meeting with Admiral Horthy, the Hungarian regent, on March 18. Hitler had reacted to Italy's defection in September by ordering contingency plans for the armed occupation of Romania and Hungary (code-named "Margarethe I" and "II") should either Antonescu or Horthy follow Badoglio's example. Antonescu had sworn continued loyalty, and Hitler believed him. Horthy, however, was something else. Hungary had not only refused formal recognition to the new Mussolini government, but had accepted legations from *both* the Badoglio and the Fascist regimes; and she had noisily demanded the return of her nine light divisions policing the rear areas on the Russian front—most recently in a letter from Horthy dated February 12—maintaining that she needed them for the defense of her own mountain frontier, the Carpathians, against the Red Army. In February, Ribbentrop received a long secret service report proving that Hungary was clandestinely dealing with the enemy. In mid-March Himmler learned from agents in Budapest that Prime Minister Kállay was advocating the sabotage of German military trains running through Hungary to Manstein's and Kleist's army groups. In short, the circumstances were almost identical to the situation in Italy the previous summer.

Originally, "Margarethe I" projected using Slovak, Croat, and Romanian troops as well as Germans for the invasion of Hungary. On March 8 Hitler selected Sunday the nineteenth as the invasion date but decided—probably on Kaltenbrunner's advice—to use only German troops; use of the hated satellites would provoke Hungarian resistance and destroy economic stability. Moreover, an attempt to secure Horthy's agreement to German demands would be made first; in particular Kállay's government must be replaced by an unambiguously pro-German one, under Béla von Imrédy for example. Göring believed Horthy would comply, but Hitler evidently did not. The OKW order for "Margarethe I" was issued on the eleventh; if the Hungarians did resist the German invasion, their army was to be disarmed and the ringleaders shot.

On March 15, after a fresh meeting with Himmler and Ribbentrop, Horthy was sent a loaded invitation to present himself at Klessheim castle near Salzburg in two or three days' time. Since Hitler offered in the invitation to deal with the military points raised in Horthy's letter of February 12—which he explained he had been unable to answer earlier because of illness—Horthy would probably bring his military chiefs with him; thus Hungary would be leaderless if "Margarethe" did result in a pitched battle. Horthy agreed to come with his generals on the eighteenth. On the day before, Hitler plotted with Ribbentrop, Jodl, and

Himmler the precise scenario for the confrontation: the regent's train would arrive at ten-thirty, and the talks would begin half an hour later. Every word spoken would be monitored by hidden microphones and recorded on disks in the castle's control room.[5] At twelve-thirty there would probably be a break for lunch; this would enable Hitler to decide whether or not the Hungarians would have to be disarmed. "If Horthy permits the invasion and there is no resistance, then we defer decision on disarming and demobilizing them," Jodl wrote in his diary. This time Hitler would accept no "lame excuses" from the slippery regent of Hungary.

Sure enough, Horthy objected next morning to the presence of Hitler's regular interpreter and insisted on talking with him in German and in complete privacy —or so he thought. Even so, the actual sequence of events is clouded by uncertainty; the disks must be presumed destroyed. Eyewitnesses saw Horthy suddenly burst out of Hitler's room, red-faced and protesting loudly, before vanishing into his own quarters, with Hitler hard on his heels in an attempt to preserve at least a semblance of protocol. Hitler had told him bluntly that he "was taking steps" to ensure he was not caught unawares by Hungarian treachery: he had insisted that Kállay be replaced by Imrédy as prime minister, and he had decided to send twelve divisions into Hungary to "assist" the new government; he demanded that Hungary's entire economy be geared to the war effort and that her numerous divisions mobilized against the Romanian frontier be sent to the Russian front instead. When Horthy lamely replied that then Hungary would be bombed just as Germany was being bombed, Hitler retorted, "This harsh certainty is better than any amount of uncertainty." Hitler hinted that the Romanians, Slovaks, and Croats would join the invasion—a particularly hateful prospect for the proud Hungarians. Believing perhaps that Hitler was still bluffing, Horthy had then charged out of the meeting room, exclaiming, "If it's all been decided already, there's no point in my staying!" At a given signal from Hitler, the air raid sirens sounded and a smoke screen was laid across the castle; Horthy was told that his train could not leave in the middle of an air raid. After lunch with Himmler and the generals, Hitler inquired loudly of Keitel whether the invasion could be postponed; Keitel replied that the troops were already on the move and could not be recalled.

Thus Horthy was left with an ultimatum calling for his consent to the invasion. The alternative was not spelled out, but it was clear to him that he had been ambushed. Toward 8 P.M. he accepted—a climb-down for which Hitler was

[5] "He's a cunning rogue," Hitler had told Zeitzler after the April 1943 meeting with Horthy. "Yesterday, I got him to agree to everything I wanted, in private. And today he comes back and says, 'You know, I'm very hard of hearing. It seems I only understood half of what you were saying yesterday.' "

totally unprepared. Evidently Ribbentrop's plain speaking to the Hungarian envoy Döme Sztójay in another room resulted in this volte-face. Horthy cabled coded instructions to his Cabinet in Budapest to permit the invasion. Hitler's only concession had been to agree not to occupy Budapest itself, apart from a "guard of honor" for Horthy. Now wreathed in smiles, the Führer conducted the aged regent to his train at nine o'clock; it was the last time he was to see him. The all clear had sounded. On Austrian soil, the train was unaccountably halted for several hours—since Hitler maintained telephone contact with SS General Kaltenbrunner, who was on the train, it appears that Horthy's safe return was dependent on his Cabinet's honoring the agreement. Four battle groups invaded Hungary concentrically at 4 A.M. No blood was shed, and now all Hungary—with its oil and vital raw materials—was in Hitler's hands. At the Citadel, Horthy's official residence, a German guard of honor, immaculate and ominous, was awaiting him when he arrived at eleven.

This, Hitler's last conquest, was truly an outstanding coup. Strategically, the cost of "Margarethe" had been high: the divisions had been subtracted from the Anzio battlefield and virtually every other front. But Hungary's industrial potential was well worth the cost. That very night of March 18, Hitler sent for Saur and instructed him to harness Hungarian industry to the war effort at once. The lower echelons of the Hungarian forces actually welcomed the invasion. Eventually the Hungarian contingent on the Russian front was doubled. Marshal Antonescu could also increase the Romanian contingent, now that he need no longer fear war with Hungary. Even so, it took a long time to dispel Hitler's doubts about Hungary. Field Marshal von Weichs, Commander in Chief Southeast, whose headquarters now transferred to Budapest, wrote after seeing Hitler on March 28: "The Führer mistrusts the Hungarians and particularly hates the regent, who no doubt equally loathes Germany. The links with the enemy powers still exist. Her defection is still to be reckoned with, a colossal danger for the eastern front. Thus as few Hungarians as possible are to be under arms, though it will be impossible to disarm the army completely."

Two other totally unrelated but interesting scenes took place that same Sunday, March 19, 1944, as German troops rolled into Hungary. The Führer sent his favorite secretary, Gerda Christian, to take flowers and champagne to his other secretary, Christa Schroeder, lying gravely ill in the hospital on her birthday; and he wrote her a rare handwritten letter of encouragement. The invalid was the most querulous member of his staff, but she was so touched that she wrote him an emotional reply and even promised to *give up smoking*—a minor triumph for the Führer, but a pleasing one. Hitler read her letter aloud to his fireside circle.

That same day Hitler had conferred at the Berghof with his leading field marshals—Rundstedt, Rommel, Kleist, Busch, and Manstein. Rundstedt stepped forward and read to an impassive Führer the declaration of personal loyalty all the field marshals had now signed; the field marshal then handed the document to him. Thus Seydlitz and his ilk were cast from the ranks (they were tried *in absentia* some weeks later, and condemned to death). The next day Hitler delivered to all the leading generals of the western front an unusually uninspiring and pallid speech. Salmuth, commanding the Fifteenth Army, was shocked at Hitler's personal appearance. "To my horror, it was an old, stooping man with an unhealthy, puffy face who came into the room. He looked downright worn-out, weary—I would even say ill." He spoke distantly of the new jet aircraft and submarines, without stating precisely *when* they would arrive. He warned the generals to be on guard against enemy parachute drops in the rear. The rest was a combination of rambling remarks and solecisms. "At tea afterward I sat at the Führer's round table," wrote Salmuth, "next to Rundstedt who was in a foul temper." Hitler conferred alone with Rommel—although the latter was technically Rundstedt's subordinate—and announced afterward that he was also giving Rommel control of the First and Nineteenth armies, as well as greater influence over the motorized divisions which were Rundstedt's only tactical reserve. Rundstedt saw little point in being Commander in Chief West, but stayed nonetheless. Now it was Rommel who was the optimist. "We have the utmost confidence that we'll get by, in the west," he wrote privately. Hitler had warned the generals, as the shorthand record of his speech shows, that he believed the enemy would establish their main beachhead in either Normandy or Brittany.

The Allied bombing of German cities continued, and now Budapest as well was the target of American bomber raids. When the Russians tried and executed as war criminals certain German officers—primarily from the SS—Hitler decided it was time to follow suit. On March 23 he told Hewel: "British and American war criminals must also be condemned to death and their confessions must also be publicized after their execution." Allied airmen accused of machine-gunning civilians, for example, were to be put on trial; he also wanted to punish captured American airmen who labeled their bombers "Murder Incorporated." Jodl suggested that since the enemy automatically executed all German agents, they should do the same with the plainclothes British and American agents and saboteurs who had fallen into their net in Hungary—some five hundred already, according to Kaltenbrunner. "The Führer mentioned that some had special assignments to murder and spread bacilli epidemics," Hewel noted.

On the night of March 24 the British again poured nearly twenty-five hundred tons of high explosives and incendiary bombs onto Berlin—though this time they lost over seventy bombers. No Geneva Convention protected the war's civilians;

the urge to punish the bomber crews was powerful, yet there was no legal way around the convention protecting prisoners of war. When the next morning Himmler announced at the Berghof that eighty Allied airmen had just escaped from a Wehrmacht prison camp at Sagan, and spoke of the millions of manhours the manhunt would cost, Hitler impulsively ordered all the escapees recaptured to be turned over to the secret police. "Himmler, you are not to let the escaped airmen out of your control!" (Jodl later claimed there was no word of "executions," just of "turning them over" to the SS; but Bodenschatz remembered Hitler asking those concerned to stay behind to see him after the war conference.) Fifty of the escapees were shot on Himmler's orders.

Many of Hitler's ministers wanted all captured bomber crews executed for attacking civilian centers—especially Ribbentrop. During May 1944, the enemy began machine-gunning civilian targets; Bormann initiated a campaign for Party officials and school teachers to advise the public, and school children in particular, on how to take cover when Allied fighters approached. Hitler asked Göring to select isolated cases of such machine-gunning and—where an accused airman fell into German hands—execute him. Jodl's staff suggested oral instructions be given to the commandant of the prisoner-collecting camp at Oberursel to turn such airmen over to the SD for "special treatment," but the technical problems—particularly of identification—proved insuperable. Kaltenbrunner had no such airmen in his cells. Keitel was opposed both to a regularized "lynch law" and to normal court-martial procedure. Göring, mindful of the hundreds of Luftwaffe airmen in enemy hands, suggested that clear cases of murder could be dealt with by the proper courts. The foreign ministry pointed out that the Geneva Convention required a three-month stay of execution of death sentences on prisoners of war. By this time it was late June 1944, and Hitler had more pressing problems on his mind.

By late March 1944 a seemingly irreconcilable difference emerged between Hitler and Manstein. At his noon conference on March 25, the field marshal was fighting for permission to withdraw General Hube's encircled First Panzer Army to the northwest before a second Stalingrad resulted.

Hitler insisted that Hube retain his existing battlefront between the Dniester and Tarnopol—a town he now declared a "fortified area." (He had just introduced this new fortress-like concept for key coastal towns in the west. They were to be commanded by tough, handpicked army generals who would not lose their nerve or honor when the enemy tide swept past their strongholds.) But Manstein said this would be impossible and demanded reinforcements for General Erich Raus's Fourth Panzer Army, whose task would be to mount a relief attack toward Hube's force; these reinforcements, suggested Manstein, could easily be spared from the armies which had occupied Hungary and from the western front. Hitler was adamant. "I can't release any strength to you so long as I have to reckon with an invasion in the west." He blamed Manstein for the present dilemma of the First Panzer Army: Manstein had tolerated one withdrawal after another, although Göring had reported that his troops were being put to flight by only a handful of Soviet tanks. Insulted by these remarks, Manstein told Schmundt afterward that he was quite ready to lay down his command. At that evening's conference, Hitler agreed to give him the reinforcements he wanted from Hungary, and the Second SS Panzer Korps from the west. With these units Raus's Fourth Panzer Army began its relief offensive on April 5, and the First Panzer Army fought its way out of the ring. It was the high point on the eastern front that spring; but Manstein was no longer in command.

Field Marshal von Kleist had followed him to the Berghof on March 27 to plead for the withdrawal of his Army Group A. Shortly after he had left, Hitler told General Zeitzler: "I have decided to release Manstein and Kleist." Zeitzler recognized from his tone of voice that arguing was no use; he asked to be relieved of office too, and when Hitler refused, he sent around an adjutant with a formal letter of resignation. Hitler sent for the Chief of Staff and rebuked him: "A general cannot resign."

The Führer sent his plane to fetch the two field marshals back to the Berghof on March 30. Probably Göring and Himmler lay behind Manstein's dismissal. Some weeks earlier General Scherff, Hitler's court historian, had warned a war correspondent not to mention Manstein by name in future dispatches; and a recent study of the field marshal in the Nazi weekly *Das Reich* had probably upset Hitler too. The famous Manstein interruption during Hitler's January speech to the generals was a further provocation. But when he told Manstein that evening, before the main conference, that what the southern front needed was a new name, a new slogan, and a commander expert in defensive strategy—he meant Model, who had just halted the rout in the north—he was probably speaking the truth. There was no bitterness between them. Hitler told an adjutant long afterward that should he ever come to mount great offensives again, Manstein would be their first commander; and in the autumn he donated a great estate to him. Manstein had after all been the only general to speak out for the Sedan breakthrough strategy in 1940—and that, Hitler reminisced now that he had steeled himself to sever their partnership, was something he would not easily forget.

Model and Kleist's successor, General Ferdinand Schörner—a Party faithful and personal nominee of Heinrich Himmler—were already waiting outside. Hitler offered Manstein his hand. The field marshal took it and said, "I hope for your sake your decision today turns out right for you."

The Most Reviled

Thus the Ukraine was lost—the fertile countryside for which Hitler had invaded Russia. The German invaders had been driven out by the Soviet armies and—not least—by the disappointed, deceived, and angry Ukrainians themselves. "If the rest of this war and its victorious conclusion should ever see these territories vouchsafed to us again," a Gauleiter wrote, "then there must be a radical change in our attitude to and treatment of the native population." Erich Koch had achieved the seemingly impossible in one year: converting the forty million Ukrainians who had greeted the German invaders with garlands and lauded them as their liberators from the hated Bolshevik yoke into a sullen, seething people, driven as partisans into the forests and swamplands of the north Ukraine.

In the early weeks of the Russian campaign, when Hitler's fifth Blitzkrieg victory seemed likely, Koch's brutal sledgehammer policies were arguably best suited to produce the maximum effect in the shortest time. But as one ugly surprise after another confronted Hitler that year, the same critical Gauleiter quoted above—Alfred Frauenfeld, governor of the Crimea—now pointed out that Hitler should have found the moral courage to replace Koch by someone with more elastic policies. It was not enough to draw on Britain's "brutal colonial policies" as an excuse. Koch had proclaimed the serfdom and inferiority of the Slavs with such raucous insistence that "even a disaster policy deliberately planned and paid for by the enemy could hardly have done more harm." Koch had frequently stormed, for example: "If I find a Ukrainian fit to sit at my table, I must shoot him!" Koch had closed down the schools laboriously reopened by the Wehrmacht, robbed the farmers of their last cows, dispensed with Ukrainian doctors and vets alike—without reflecting that diseases and epidemics were no respecters of the German occupation forces—and deported the able-bodied to Germany in a manner reminiscent of "Arab slave traders." When Hitler had instituted medals for bravery and hard work, Koch had waited nearly a year before unwillingly issuing any to the Ukrainians. In mid-April Koch was described to Himmler as looking like "an alcoholic on his last legs"—his face a pasty bluish-white, lined and pock-marked from one ear to the other. "He is incapable of orderly debate. Even the soberest instruction throws him into a rage, and he rejects it with a volley of oaths."

How far Hitler still sympathized with his raucous Gauleiter is uncertain. But his determination to *reconquer* these lost Russian territories—a prize glittering at the end of the coming bloody year—remained undimmed. He told the trusted Marshal Antonescu in March and Karl-Otto Saur in April that once the invasion threat had passed—either gloriously defeated by Rundstedt and Rommel or exposed as a shameless fraud—he would bring back his victorious armies from France to the eastern front and deliver the knockout blow. Instinct and intuition, those twin insidious sources of comfort to the Führer, assured him the Red Army was almost exhausted; he said as much to Kleist on March 30, when the dismissed army group commander advised him to make peace with Stalin. On April 8, a grim battle began to rage in the Crimea. Hitler would not relinquish his goal. In spite of Zeitzler's appeal that "thousands of German soldiers in the Crimea will be lost if you don't act now," Hitler refused to order their evacuation. "One thousand more or less are of no consequence." Manstein, inspired by Hitler's speech of March 19, shared this view; he admitted to Admiral Dönitz: "Perhaps the Führer is *right* in not yielding one foot of ground voluntarily." Antonescu, moved by Hitler's arguments, agreed that the Crimea must be held.

Hitler told his adjutants he would never let history reproach him for losing faith in final victory just when it was almost within his grasp—as had happened to Germany in November 1918. New secret weapons, new armies, were on the way. For the reconquest of Russia in 1945 he would need tanks and self-propelled assault guns above all. "The air force can't win wars," Saur told the Fighter Staff after a long talk with Hitler on April 7. "Its job is to protect the tank production lines and keep them working. The Russian campaign can only be ended with tanks. That's why the Führer said yesterday, 'If this tank production program is realized, then it will win the war for us.' But the prerequisite for this is that our Luftwaffe production targets are met one hundred percent, so that we can keep the enemy at bay and the tank factories rolling." Saur promised to increase aircraft production fivefold during 1944. A big new factory would be built in Hungary, turning out five hundred new fighters a month.

When Admiral Dönitz attempted on April 13 to obtain production priority for certain naval items, Hitler flatly refused. "Tanks and assault guns are my lifeblood too, but nonetheless we've got to put up a fighter umbrella over the Reich first of all. That is the alpha and omega of it."

He asked Göring what had become of the underground factories Speer's ministry had been ordered to build the previous autumn, and when Göring gave no satisfactory answer Hitler instructed Xaver Dorsch, chief of the Todt Organization, to present himself at the Berghof the next day. Dorsch pointed out that his organization did not operate within the Reich frontiers—the factories were the responsibility of Speer's own construction chief, Carl Stobbe-Dethleffsen. Hitler angrily retorted, "I've had enough of these petty squabbles! I want the Todt Organization to build the factories—at once!" The six-month-old blueprints were fetched from Berlin; Hitler passed them at once and ordained that in the future, Dorsch's organization was to construct all the major building projects in the Reich. Dorsch was embarrassed at this rebuff to his absent chief, Speer, and—after Bormann and the two obligatory stenographers had been asked to withdraw—he pointed out that it was Reichsminister Speer's will that the Todt Organization should not function within the Reich frontiers but only in the occupied countries. Hitler was unrepentant. On April 16 he ordered Dorsch to build ten mushroom-type bombproof hangars for the fighter squadrons, and a bombproof aircraft factory, the first of its kind, near Landsberg in Bavaria. Göring undertook to place the Luftwaffe's construction organization at Dorsch's disposal too. On Hitler's instructions, Göring summoned all the construction experts—except Speer and Stobbe-Dethleffsen—on the nineteenth. "I will brook no further delays," Hitler had told him.

Speer's reaction to this organized dismantling of his empire was immediate. On April 19 a voluminous and pained letter arrived at the Berghof, and its bearer—one of the minister's staff—orally added that Speer was minded to resign all his offices, a threat he had not however included in his letter. Speer's hypnotic command tended to dissipate in his absence. While it was unquestionably Speer who had achieved the production miracles—typified most sensationally by the launching on April 17 and 19 of Dönitz's first two Mark XXI U-boats six months ahead of schedule—it was Saur and Dorsch who were the frequent Berghof visitors, while Speer took a leisurely five-month convalescence in the Tyrol mountains. And it was Saur who stood beside the Führer as the brand-new armor rumbled past him at Klessheim castle on his birthday, April 20—the outstanding new 38-ton pursuit tank, and Vomag's heavy, fast, low-profiled hunter-killer tank, with its ultralong 75-millimeter gun. Once these birthday presents were in mass production, Hitler planned to turn the tide of battle on the eastern front decisively in Germany's favor. But that afternoon Field Marshal Milch begged him not to let Speer go, and he asked for some message of comfort with which to repair the minister's injured vanity. Hitler drummed his fingers absently on the windows, then curtly answered, "*Jawohl, gut!* Tell Speer from me that I am very fond of him. Is that enough?"

Milch returned from the Tyrol the next day, but Hitler was too grieved to notice him. That afternoon, he had received General Hube at the Berghof, decorated him for his First Panzer Army's magnificent fighting escape from the Soviet encirclement, and promoted him to four-star general. Hitler had mentioned to Schmundt and the other adjutants the previous evening the possibility that he would soon appoint the one-armed general Commander in Chief of the army. Hube had asked permission to fly back to Berlin that night for personal reasons; Hitler had agreed, although the general's pilot lacked night-flying experience. Now he regretted it, for the Junkers had flown into a mountain outside Salzburg. Hube was dead and the jovial Walther Hewel had received terrible burns and injuries.

A melancholy Führer welcomed Speer on the Berghof steps on April 24. Speer charmed him away from his previous designs; having realized that Xaver Dorsch now had Hitler's fullest confidence, Speer himself proposed making him overall director of Reich construction work—*inside* his ministry. Hitler told him to do as he thought best. It was the same with the A-4 projectile. On the twenty-fifth General Korten, the Luftwaffe's Chief of Staff, added his authority to the long-standing appeal by Saur, Milch, and Göring's technical adjutant, Colonel Ulrich Diesing, for A-4 production to shut down in favor of fighter—and now tank—production. ("We won't see the A-4 this year," Milch predicted.) Hitler refused. In the pilotless bombardment of England he saw an important means of striking at the morale of the enemy invasion troops—weren't his own soldiers in Russia sick with worry when the British bombed their home towns? Rommel—the only surviving candidate for army Commander in Chief now that Hube was dead—emphasized this psychological element of the battle that might now begin with any dawn. "The big air raids here probably mean the invasion preparations have already begun," wrote Rommel privately on the twenty-sixth. "Here at the front the damage is slight so far, and it's good that our troops get accustomed to this saturation bombardment. Morale in Britain is rock-bottom, one strike after another, the screams of 'down with Churchill and the Jews' and cries for peace are growing louder. Bad omens for such a risky offensive. . . ."

Before considering Rommel's preparations to meet the Allied invasion, we must first investigate what was for Hitler the most disturbing event of that spring—the premature and seemingly unnecessary loss of the Crimea. On April 10 the Sixth Army had been forced to abandon Odessa, the port through which the navy had been keeping General Jaenecke's beleaguered Seventeenth Army in the Crimea supplied; but the roots of the catastrophe went back much further—some would say to the "Crimea psychosis" induced by Jaenecke's furtive attempt to abandon the peninsula as early as October. Thereafter, both army and navy commanders in the Black Sea had contrived to keep Hitler, and even their own superiors, in the dark about developments. Thus, Zeitzler had sincerely assured Hitler that Nikolaev, the Russian naval dockyard, was in no danger—it was, in fact, overrun two days later. And Kleist had informed Hitler on March 27 that Admiral Helmuth Brinkmann had ordered the evacuation of the naval base at Odessa two weeks earlier—an arbitrary act of which even Dönitz was unaware when Hitler furiously telephoned him. Hitler had to resign himself to the loss of Odessa itself, consoled by the thought that at least there would be time for the demolition of its dockyards and the mining of its approaches. He dismissed Kleist three days later.

With General Schörner's appointment to Kleist's command, renamed Army Group South-Ukraine—a provocative hint at Hitler's undiminished plans of conquest—a fresh spirit swept through the troops. Schörner's Crimean orders were harsh and his methods unorthodox. He lured one Romanian division after another into the German lines and "intermarried" them irrevocably with German units so that Antonescu could not withdraw them if he wished. Now that the Seventeenth Army had fallen back on Sevastopol, the fortress harbor at the southern end of the Crimean peninsula, he ordered any troops abandoning their positions shot for cowardice; if Russian tanks—and over five hundred had poured through the breaches into the peninsula—broke through these last positions, they were to be knocked out in the rear and the lines themselves repaired. Any soldier destroying an enemy tank with a bazooka was to get an immediate three-week mainland leave.

Dönitz predicted that the loss of Odessa by Kleist's army group would make the eventual loss of the Crimea inevitable. Though the Seventeenth Army had enough food and ammunition to hold out for many months, the navy would then be able to ferry only about thirty thousand tons a month from Constanta, in Romania, to Sevastopol. Operating from Odessa, the Russians—ignoring the German minefields—would be in a position to interrupt the lighter coastal traffic; in addition, the route from Constanta to Sevastopol was far longer.

On April 3, Zeitzler confidentially informed the OKW that Odessa could not be held, but that lower echelons were not yet to be told; this time Dönitz and Hitler did learn in advance. Indeed, Zeitzler subsequently used Dönitz's own memorandum on the importance of Odessa for the Crimea to support his own argument for the peninsula's immediate evacuation. Dönitz responded pathetically that only the Führer could take in the whole strategic situation and that as soon as the invasion of France had been thwarted, the lost territories in Russia would be reconquered. Zeitzler rejoined that 180,000 troops were at risk in the Crimea—troops urgently needed for the defense of the South Ukraine and of Romania herself.

In spite of the points made in his earlier memorandum, Dönitz advised Hitler to hang on to the Crimea even if Odessa was lost. He telephoned the Berghof on April 8, emphasizing that the Seventeenth Army had supplies for a siege of five of six months. Recalling his own World War I experiences, he now argued that the Russians were unlikely to disrupt the German supply operations from Odessa and Nikolaev. Two days later, however, General Jaenecke ordered the evacuation of the Crimea to begin. He was acting on his own responsibility again, though with Schörner's subsequent approval, since a hundred Russian tanks were pouring southward following the collapse of the Romanian 10th Infantry Division on the northern front. But again Hitler had not been informed, and again he canceled Jaenecke's order—calling instead for an evacuation of the Kerch peninsula while the northern front was repaired.

But events were now moving faster than Hitler's orders, and the breach was too wide to repair. Even as Hitler was telephoning Dönitz that evening that not until the next day would he reach a decision on whether or not to abandon the Crimea, Jaenecke was informing the navy that his army was already in full flight toward Sevastopol. When the navy in turn put this startling news to General Jodl, he replied it was not an OKW concern—the Russian front was Zeitzler's affair. Hitler issued the only order possible on the twelfth—all nonessential personnel were to be evacuated from the Crimea. He added, however: "I have decided to hold on to the Sevastopol battlefield itself as long as humanly possible, to tie as many enemy forces as possible to that front." He feared that the loss of Odessa—which would bring Russian naval strength back to the western Black Sea again—and of the Crimea had already caused irreparable damage to Germany's political position. To stave off these effects, he ordered the army and navy to rush antitank guns, ammunition, bazookas, and above all food to Sevastopol. Dönitz promised that his navy would make every sacrifice necessary to keep the fortress provisioned, and he at least kept his word.

However, the effect of the Crimean debacle on Turkey was immediate. On April 20 she bowed to mounting Allied pressure, announced that she was no longer neutral but a pro-Allied country, and would cease the vital chrome deliveries to Germany within ten days. Privately the Turkish foreign minister apologized to Germany that his country had been threatened with war by Russia and with blockade by the Allies. It was a language Hitler fully understood, having employed it himself in more propitious circumstances.

Several days passed before the Russians began their all-out assault on Sevastopol—days during which they rebuilt the airfields and brought 27 divisions and some 200 tanks into position along the fortress's twenty-two-mile perimeter. Dönitz had evacuated 100,000 pioneers and nonessential troops to Constanta, leaving perhaps 35,000 manning the front line and 90,000 more in the rear—an imbalance which was the object of Hitler's later criticism. Their material position seemed hopeless: in the precipitous retreat into the fortress, Jaenecke had lost most of his army's guns and ammunition. He had 81 pieces of artillery, 36 antitank guns, and 9 tanks; their ammunition was low. Neither he nor his naval counterpart, Admiral Brinkmann, believed the siege could be withstood for long. Hitler disagreed: he ordered the war ministry to rush guns and ammunition to Sevastopol. Zeitzler even asked for Field Marshal Milch to be put in charge—for there were many similarities with Stalingrad. Hitler, however, left Zeitzler and his logistics generals in command, and this was a fatal error, for again they proved unequal to the task—whether it was premeditated treachery or incompetence we cannot tell.[1] At all events, Zeitzler shortly complained to Hitler that the navy's ships docking at Sevastopol to evacuate the prisoners, injured and "useless eaters," were arriving *empty* instead of bringing the army supplies Hitler had ordered; Hitler's inquiries revealed that those supplies had still not reached Constanta, so it was not the navy's fault. Dönitz now changed his tune, since he feared that a "sudden crisis" in the fortress might result in an equally sudden demand for the navy to evacuate its entire garrison in an impossibly short time. On April 24 he telegraphed to the Berghof—to put himself on record thus: "The Commander in Chief, navy, has never adjudged [whether Sevastopol could be held or not]; this is the army's concern alone." *Privately* he now accepted Zeitzler's view that the garrison was doomed; but the Führer must decide—the Führer must have his reasons for hanging on to Sevastopol.

Hitler in fact feared that the loss of Sevastopol would actually bring Turkey into the war and set off a similar chain-reaction in the other neutral lands. On April 25, Dönitz's two local commanders personally assured him at the Berghof that sufficient supplies for a hundred thousand troops could be convoyed to Sevastopol—provided they arrived at Constanta. Only Jaenecke spoke out against Hitler's decision to keep fighting; and even then his tongue failed him at the Berghof on April 29, and he had to speak his real mind in a carping five-page letter to Hitler the next day. He blamed Kleist's tactical errors for the loss of the Crimea; the imminent Soviet assault on the Seventeenth Army was bound to succeed. "Would it not be better to snatch this prey, over which the Bolsheviks are already crowing, from under their very noses and transfer the forces to Army Group South-Ukraine?" It was a tempting argument, but Hitler was a realist. The Sevastopol troops would arrive dispirited, exhausted, and virtually unarmed—useless as reinforcements for the main front; on the other hand, the twenty-seven Russian divisions presently besieging the fortress could immediately be thrown

[1]Both Eduard Wagner, the quartermaster general, and Zeitzler's general of artillery, Fritz Lindemann, were conspiring against Hitler; Hitler's adjutants particularly suspected Lindemann of active treason over the Crimea.

against the main front. The Führer had no use for an army general who could not see that, and he dismissed Jaenecke from his command. General Kurt Allmendinger replaced him. Some days later, Hitler ordered Jaenecke court-martialed in order to establish just why the fertile Crimea peninsula had been lost with such staggering speed.

The throttling of Germany's only chrome supplies put a time bomb under Hitler's strategy, though the fuse was longer than he at first feared: the OKW calculated that the Reich's chrome stocks—vital for the high-grade steels needed for Hitler's tank production—would last another eighteen months.

Parallel to this uncertainty about the war, or perhaps because of it, his health was worsening. His tremor was so pronounced by early May 1944 that his left leg shook uncontrollably even when he was in bed. While the Föhn mountain wind did not affect him, the incessant snow, sleet, and rain did. He needed Morell, but the portly doctor was unsettled by the rarefied air and lived down in Berchtesgaden itself, ascending the fifteen hundred feet to the Berghof only for two hours each midday. For weeks on end the whole mountainside was swathed several times a day in acrid smoke screens as enemy bombers approached, until Morell imagined he was suffocating and had to summon doctors to attend to himself. His Berlin assistant, Dr. Richard Weber, had to tend to Hitler; the jealous Morell would not trust his patient or consultation notes to either Dr. Brandt or his deputy, Dr. Hanskarl von Hasselbach.

Morell's consultation notes on two typical sessions with Hitler, on May 4 and 5, 1944, show that the Führer was no easy patient. Hitler's stomach spasms had returned. Morell had prescribed massage; Hitler had previously refused, and now refused again. The doctor advised an early retirement each night, but Hitler was already resting ten hours a day, and he refused to go to bed earlier. "That is impossible because of the British air raids!" He would not retire until the last bomber left German territory. Again Morell advised him to imbibe less liquid, less than two pints a day. "Fortunately drinking and smoking are not involved," he noted; in view of Hitler's heart condition he advised him to gulp down some coffee or take Cardiazol if he felt unwell suddenly, and meanwhile he ought to try breathing pure oxygen two or three times a day. He administered intravenous injections of glucose and of Testoviron—a sex hormone produced by a reputable Berlin firm.[2] In the following weeks he also injected Septo-Iodine, a recognized treatment for respiratory infections and heart condition, varying doses of Glyco-

[2]Hitler startled his secretaries by making sudden sexual allusions—completely out of character. When they told Morell, he smirked, and explained he had just given the Chief these injections.

norm and liver-extract, his own proprietary Vitamultin-Calcium preparation, and Tonophosphan, a tonic for Hitler's nerves and muscles. Hitler also continued to consume quantities of Dr. Koester's antigas pills. It was an incredible volume of medication for an intelligent man to submit to, but Hitler preferred it to the alternatives—spasms, fatigue, time-wasting exercise, and massage.

Since early April 1944 he had expected to be awakened in his ice-cold Berghof bedroom one morning with word that the Anglo-American invasion had begun. From December to April he had half hoped that the invasion clamor in the enemy newspapers was just bluff. "The whole show the British are putting on looks suspiciously like a charade to me," he had opined hopefully on April 6. "These latest reports of censorship and security measures over there—you don't go doing that if you are *really* up to something." Keitel had agreed: "No, you keep your mouth shut!" "I can't help feeling the whole thing will turn out to be a shameless charade," repeated Hitler.

This conformed with his estimate of the Allies' fighting ability—Kesselring was keeping them at bay in Italy with "his little finger," as Hitler put it. Enemy bomber superiority made no impact on German troops; in Italy, they had only slit-trenches for cover from the bombardment—but the Atlantic Wall fortifications were covered with concrete up to twenty feet thick. To thwart attempted airborne landings, Hitler had ordered virtually the entire light antiaircraft defenses of the Reich concentrated in France. He and Rommel were confident that the invasion—assuming it ever came—would end in disaster for the Allies. "From day to day we are growing stronger," Rommel wrote on May 6. "My inventions are coming into action. Thus I am looking forward to the battle with the profoundest confidence—it might be on May 15, or perhaps not until the end of the month."

Only the date was uncertain. While Rommel and Rundstedt believed the enemy would land on either side of the Somme estuary and thrust by the shortest route toward Paris, Hitler had long been convinced that the enemy's main invasion would occur far to the west—either in Normandy or Brittany—so that the Cherbourg peninsula could be made into a strategic bridgehead. He had said as much on March 4 and again to the western generals in his speech on March 20; he confidently repeated it to Antonescu on the twenty-third; he adhered to his opinion staunchly, despite the avalanche of contrary Intelligence reports from Foreign Armies West. "I am for bringing all our strength in here," he said on April 6, tapping the Normandy coastline on the charts; "particularly the forces we don't absolutely have to have anywhere else." As soon as Hube's army had fought itself free of the encirclement in Russia, Hitler ordered the crack "Das Reich" Division moved into Normandy. Rundstedt's and Rommel's papers reveal with what obstinacy they clung to their different appreciation of Eisenhower's intent. But on May 1 both of them were sharply reminded by Jodl's staff that Hitler expected the invasion in the Seventh Army's area, not the Fifteenth's; and on May 6, Hitler was again to have Jodl telephone Rundstedt's Chief of Staff that he "attached particular importance to Normandy."

In western Europe, a violent air assault on communications had begun—bridges, railway lines, locomotives, passenger trains, and canals were the targets. The French people suffered sorely: American aircraft killed 400 Frenchmen in Rouen on April 24 alone. Laval besought Hitler to try once more to win the French around to a combined defense of France, but Hitler—confident that another "Dieppe" fiasco was awaiting the Allies—refused to pay the price Laval demanded. The night bombing of Germany had temporarily ended in a clear victory for Göring's night fighters and the antiaircraft defenses.

Late on April 30, Saur telephoned Hitler with the latest tank and aircraft production figures; despite the almost total destruction of the factories in February and March, in April they had manufactured 1,859 new fighters and over 1,500 armored fighting vehicles. Hitler used the word "magnificent" in his reply. That his armaments workers were willing to work seventy-two hours a week indicated that morale was still high. Germany just had to hold out until the great East-West clash occurred—history books assured him that most great coalitions fell apart before five years were over. The bones of contention were already there: the oil of the Middle East, Russian aims in the North Sea, Soviet expansion toward India, the latent feud between Britain and the United States. "America is quietly and without much ado skinning Britain alive, pawning her into penury," he chuckled to Mussolini. "If we just sit tight and hold on without flinching, the big break between Britain and America is bound to come one day." When the British realize that the Americans are after their world position "then some Englishman *must* stand up against it." Politically, time was on Germany's side. What Hitler feared most was that he personally might not live to see the final victory—or that some military landslide might occur to snatch the political victory from his people's grasp.

With totally unexpected swiftness, the Russian armies now stormed and penetrated the Sevastopol fortress on the Crimea and wrote the end to the chapter Manstein had begun there so brilliantly two years before. The assault began on May 5. By late on the seventh, Schörner telegraphed to Zeitzler that the Seventeenth Army had lost 2,795 men; he was flying in all available reserves, 220-millimeter howitzer assault-guns, and heavy antitank guns, but few had yet reached the Black Sea from Germany; 120 heavy antitank guns had been promised to the army, but 40 were still en route by air to Constanta and the rest held up in railway transports on the Hungarian-Romanian frontier. Late on the eighth, Hitler conceded defeat and ordered the Seventeenth Army brought out by sea and air from Sevastopol—officers were to enforce order during the evacuation by the use of firearms if necessary. Only 37,500 German and Romanian troops were brought to the Romanian mainland before the enemy overran the last pocket of resistance five days later.

Hitler was furious at this fiasco. To shame the army, he ordered Zeitzler to transport these salvaged remnants of an army back to Germany, as they were fit only to work in the arms industry; as soldiers they were failures. Schörner—reporting to Hitler through the Reichsführer SS as well as through Zeitzler—bitterly blamed Kleist, his predecessor: the field marshal had allowed discipline to rot, his noncombat troops had worked a pleasant six- or seven-hour day, and the wines of the Crimea had done the rest. He praised Antonescu, but not the Romanian General Staff. Himmler told Hitler that in Schörner's view "radical solutions" were called for in Romania, *i.e.,* rooting out everybody—and particularly General Erich Hansen, the feckless German military attaché in Bucharest—except Antonescu himself. But Antonescu valued Hansen, so Hitler knew he could not recall him. Schörner's subordinates meanwhile demanded that the navy's Black Sea admirals—whom Dönitz now caused to be decorated with high medals—be court-martialed. Angry Seventeenth Army officers complained of navy cowardice; bloody and filthy from the carnage of Sevastopol, they had disembarked at Constanta and found naval officers in spotless uniforms sunning themselves, indifferent to whether their ships ran the gauntlet of the Russian defenses or whether they offered lame excuses for returning empty. But the real culprits were in the German General Staff, who had failed to supply the guns and ammunition fast enough. In the five-week battle for the Crimea, over seventy-five thousand Germans and Romanians paid for this failure with their lives.

An unnatural calm fell upon the whole eastern front until late June.

Parallel to the expanded tank output, Hitler still wanted a sizeable bomber production. The impact of the American raids on German industry and transport was an example of what the Luftwaffe should be capable of in the east. The Luftwaffe had executed its first hesitant strategic bombing raids in June 1943, when T34 tank factories, oil refineries, and ball-bearing plants in Gorki and Saratov were attacked on several nights running with great success. When General Karl Koller, a Bavarian, became chief of the Luftwaffe operations staff in September, he reassigned the Fourth Air Corps under General Rudolf Meister; its mission was to destroy Stalin's seven key electric-power stations. But in

February 1944 Hitler intervened and called on Meister to retrain his crews for a methodical attack on the Red Army's rear communications—bridges, railway junctions, and marshaling yards; as it happened, by April few worthwhile Russian industrial targets could be reached from airfields still in Luftwaffe hands.

Saur's fighter production program also made great inroads into the bomber factories. In February, March, and April the reeling aircraft industry had produced 567, 605, and 680 bombers, respectively. But the Fighter Staff's new program would cut the target to 550 bombers a month, which would support only 40 squadrons; this meant that eleven others would have to be disbanded. And if an even more radical plan was adopted, only 284 bombers would be assembled every month; this would mean that after October there would be sufficient support for only 26 squadrons. General Korten, Chief of the Air Staff, described this plan as the death of the bomber arm. Koller highlighted this danger in a report to Hitler on May 5 and on the nineteenth followed it with a persuasive study of the bomber strength needed to maintain German hegemony in Europe. At a conference with Göring on May 22, Hitler dismissed the planned targets as quite unacceptable, and the next day the Reichsmarschall announced to the Fighter Staff that he wanted an armada of at least twenty-six hundred bombers—which would require the manufacture of over eight hundred a month, including the four-engined Heinkel 177—in addition to nearly seven thousand fighter aircraft. Göring also gave Hitler a progress report on the Me-262 jet (unaware that three prototypes had crashed over the last few days for no apparent reason). Hitler—who was partly relying on these jet bombers to defeat the invasion—congratulated him. "Now they'll get there on time!" But a rude shock awaited him almost immediately.

It was May 23. Field Marshal von Richthofen had come up from Italy, where a troublesome enemy offensive had begun at Cassino on the twelfth—a patent attempt to lure German reserves and Luftwaffe units away from France; and that very morning a more serious thrust had begun from the Anzio beachhead. Richthofen wrote in his diary: "3 P.M. with the Führer. He's grown older, good-looking, very calm, very definite views on the military and political situation, no worries about anything. Again and again one can't help feeling this is a man blindly following his summons, walking unhesitatingly along the path prescribed to him without the slightest doubt as to its rightness and the final outcome. . . . The unpleasant military occurrences at Cassino and—since this morning—at the [Anzio] beachhead are contemplated by him quite calmly: as he puts it, we can be thankful that we are still fighting so far down. After all, last September we all thought, and he did too, that this summer would see us fighting in the Apennines or even in the Alps." Time was on their side, Hitler reminded the Luttwaffe commander; politically, Germany had won the war long ago.

At this moment Göring, Milch, Saur, and the aircraft specialists were ushered into the Great Hall. Hitler wanted to examine their aircraft production targets in person. He gazed out of the great picture window, listening absently, as the Fighter Staff's program figures were read out. When the Me-262 jet-fighter production was mentioned, he interrupted, "Jet *fighter?* I thought the 262 was coming as a high-speed bomber?" This, after all, was the order he had given last autumn. Milch replied, "For the time being it is being manufactured as a fighter!" Hitler persisted: "How many of the 262s already manufactured *can* carry bombs?" "None, mein Führer. The Me-262 is being manufactured exclusively as a fighter aircraft." An awkward silence followed, and then Milch explained that to carry a thousand-kilo bomb the jet would require an extensively strengthened airframe and undercarriage; the first one hundred being built were designed exclusively as fighters. Hitler lost his composure. The wonder aircraft on which —perhaps unrealistically—he had reposed his hopes of disrupting the invasion was not even being built. "Never mind!" he interrupted. "I only want one two-hundred-fifty-kilo bomb!" The aircraft was so fast that it needed neither cannon nor armorplate, noted Hitler. How much did they weigh? ("Who pays the slightest attention to the orders I give?" he complained. "I gave an unqualified order and left nobody in any doubt that the aircraft was to be fitted as a fighter-*bomber.*") Saur said the cannon, armor, and ammunition weighed over five hundred kilos. "Then it can all be taken out!" said Hitler triumphantly. Colonel Edgar Petersen, the chief of the Luftwaffe experimental station at Rechlin, nodded. "That can be done without any difficulty." In desperation Milch appealed to Hitler to think again, but he was subjected to a torrent of abuse. "Mein Führer," exclaimed the field marshal, "the smallest infant can see this is a fighter, not a bomber aircraft!" Hitler turned his back on him for the rest of the discussion. "*Aufschlagbrand!*" —crashed in flames!—whispered somebody: the reference was to Milch's career.

Hitler ordered the Me-262 to be manufactured solely as a high-speed bomber now. But there was a snag. Göring came the next day and confessed that his engineers had reminded him that the armor and cannon were all *forward* of the plane's center of gravity; to alter this would mean a major redesigning job, perhaps even changing the position of the wings. Because of the production pipeline, it would take five months to effect any change. "You gentlemen appear to be stone-deaf," Göring had raged at the Luftwaffe engineers on his return from the Berghof. "The lot of you! I referred again and again to the Führer's order. He doesn't care two hoots about getting the Me-262 as a fighter, but wants it only as a bomber. . . . And now suddenly it is impossible! The Führer says, 'For all I care you can put the fighters on a bonfire.' He wants an aircraft which can force its way through by virtue of its sheer speed, despite the enormous mass of fighters that will be guarding the invasion forces. What no civilian dares to do—simply ignore orders—you gentlemen dare time after time after time." In a further meeting, Hitler permitted the testing of the Me-262 fighter version to continue, but only the bomber version was to enter service as yet—attacking the enemy's embarkation movements on the far side of the English Channel, from a few thousand feet up, or bombing the disembarking mass of tanks and troops swarming around the invasion beaches. The Reichsmarschall personally promised that none of his staff would "go behind his back" again.

At Klessheim castle in March 1944, Horthy had assented to Hitler's demand that Hungary turn over her Jews to Germany. Working from Budapest, a task force under SS Colonel Adolf Eichmann deported four hundred thousand Jews over the next four months.

The motives of Hitler and Himmler still diverged, though the Führer's attitude had noticeably hardened. Hitler was primarily concerned that this potential Fifth Column be removed from the Balkans and was callous about their subsequent fate; but Himmler—however much he protested that he was not just "bloodthirsty"—was eager to see what he called an "uncompromising," an irrevocable, and above all a Final Solution. When Hitler instructed him in April to provide two 100,000-strong contingents of Hungarian Jews to work on Saur's bombproof tank and fighter factories in the Protectorate and elsewhere, the Reichsführer SS expressed unconcealed displeasure at this "singular" arrangement. But on May 24, Himmler assured an audience of generals: "Not one of them will in any way cross the German public's field of vision."

As part of the Nazi indoctrination project, during the spring he and Hitler separately made several secret speeches to groups of generals. Hitler's speech of April 26 has not survived. But Himmler's talk on May 5 to an audience including General Hans-Jürgen Stumpff and Hermann Reinecke (and a member of Hitler's own staff, Admiral Hans-Erich Voss) has: it was taken down by stenographers, stylistically improved, and like most of his main speeches retyped on a large-face "Führer" typewriter. Since only carbon copies are left in Himmler's files, Hitler *may* have been sent the top copies of each of Himmler's speeches. In theory he might therefore have found the passage in Himmler's seventy-page speech of October 6, 1943, where he bluntly disclosed to Albert Speer and the Gauleiters that he, Himmler, had decided to murder Jewish women and children as well as adult males. ("I took the decision that a clear-cut solution had to be found here too.") On May 5, 1944, however, Himmler tried a new version—or adapted it to his audience of generals. After revealing in now stereotyped sentences that he had "uncompromisingly" solved the "Jewish problem" in Germany and the German-occupied countries, he added: "I am telling this to you as my comrades. We are all soldiers regardless of which uniform we wear. You can imagine how I felt executing this soldierly order issued to me, but I obediently complied and carried it out to the best of my convictions." Never before, and never after, did Himmler hint at a *Führer* Order; but there is reason to doubt he dared show this passage to his Führer.[3]

Consider too Himmler's speech of May 24, in which again speaking before generals he explained his stance somewhat differently. He recalled how in 1933 and 1934 he had thrown habitual criminals into concentration camps without trial, and boasted, "I must admit I have committed many such illegal acts in my time. But rest assured of this: I have resorted to these only when I felt that sound common-sense and the inner justice of a Germanic—and right-thinking—people were on my side." With this in mind Himmler had confronted the "Jewish problem" too: "It was solved uncompromisingly—on orders and at the dictate of sound common-sense." One page later, Himmler's speech again hinted that Jewish women and children were also being liquidated.[4] The fact remains that in his personal meetings with Hitler, the Reichsführer continued to talk only of the "expulsion" [*Aussiedlung*] of the Jews, even as late as July 1944.

When the same generals came to the Obersalzberg on May 26, Hitler spoke to them in terms that were both more philosophical and less ambiguous. He spoke of the intolerance of nature, he compared Man to the smallest bacillus on the planet Earth, he reminded them how by expelling the Jews from their privileged positions he had opened up those same positions to the children of hundreds of thousands of ordinary working-class Germans and deprived the revolutionary masses of their traditional Jewish ferment:

> Of course, people can say, "Yes, but couldn't you have got out of it . . . more humanely?" My dear generals, we are fighting a battle of life and death. If our enemies are victorious in this struggle, the German people will be extirpated. The Bolsheviks will butcher millions upon millions of our intellectuals. Those who escape the bullet in the nape of the neck will be deported. The children of the upper classes will be taken away and got rid of. This entire bestiality has been organized by Jews. Today incendiary and other bombs are dropped on our cities although the enemy knows he is hitting just women and children. They are machine-gunning ordinary railroad trains, or farmers working in their fields. In one night in a city like Hamburg we lost over forty thousand women and children, burned to death. Expect nothing else from me, but that I do just what I think best suits the national interest and in the manner best serving the German nation.
>
> *(Prolonged loud applause.)*
>
> Kindness here as indeed anywhere else would be just about the greatest

[3]Page 28 of the large-face typescript, containing this pregnant sentence—for only Hitler was empowered to issue a "soldierly order" to Himmler—was manifestly retyped and inserted in the transcript at a later date, as the different indenting shows.

[4]This page alone was also retyped and possibly inserted at a later date in the typescript.

cruelty to our own people. If the Jews are going to hate me, then at least I want to take advantage of that hatred.

(Murmurs of approval.)

The advantage is this: now we have a cleanly organized nation, in which no outsider can interfere.

Look at the other countries . . . Hungary! The entire country subverted and rotten, Jews everywhere, Jews and still more Jews right up to the highest level, and the whole country covered by a continuous network of agents and spies waiting for the moment to strike, but fearing to do so in case a premature move on their part drew us in. Here too I intervened, and this problem is now going to be solved too. If I may say this: the Jews had as their program the extirpation [*Ausrottung*] of the German people. On September 1, 1939, I announced in the Reichstag, if any man believes he can extirpate the German nation in a world war, he is wrong; if Jewry really tries that, then the one that will be extirpated is Jewry itself.

(Spirited applause.)

In Auschwitz, the defunct paraphernalia of death—idle since late 1943—began to clank again as the first trainloads from Hungary arrived.

An oppressive uncertainty lay across the Obersalzberg. The invasion had still not come. On May 24, General Korten, the Luftwaffe's Chief of Staff, told Göring: "The invasion appears to have been postponed, otherwise we wouldn't be having these big [American] air raids on the Reich again." And Speer, who had now finally returned from sick leave, echoed this optimism. "If nothing has happened by July or August we can assume we will be left in peace all winter." The German command was even uncertain as to whether the invasion, when and if it came, would begin when dawn coincided with a high tide in France, or two hours after *low* tide as a recent Allied invasion exercise suggested. Rommel's fiendish underwater fangs along the possible invasion beaches relied on the former assumption. The field marshal was still confident, however. "Everything is going very well indeed and just as planned," he wrote on May 19. "Two days ago I telephoned the Führer for the first time. He was in the best of spirits and did not stint his praise for the job we have done in the west. I hope now to get on faster than ever. The weather meanwhile is still cold and at last it's raining. The British will just have to be patient a while." To his son Rommel wrote a shade more realistically. "These last months and weeks we have achieved the impossible, but we are still not as ready as I would have liked: more mines, even deeper submerged obstacles, better antiparatroop defenses, even more artillery, antiaircraft guns, mortars, and rockets!! So far their heavy bombing of the Atlantic Wall has not had much effect; damage and casualties have been slight."

It was time to begin wheeling the secret weapons out from under their elaborate camouflage. But what remained of them? Hitler had been deceived over the Me-262—Göring now told him that three and perhaps even six months would be needed before the bomber version reached the squadrons. The A-4 rocket had overcome its worst problems but would not be operational until September. The aircraft industry had delayed far too long over Hitler's recent demand for the 50-millimeter cannon—originally designed for tanks—to be installed in twin-engined fighters. The huge underground gun battery built near Calais for shelling London was ready, but the gun barrels themselves were still far from trouble-free—and the specially designed projectiles were still not capable of the necessary range. Only the Luftwaffe's pilotless flying bomb was standing by—its original ninety-six launching sites in France were admittedly in ruins, but these were only decoys now; still undetected by Allied aerial reconnaissance, the real catapults were well-concealed and awaiting last-minute assembly in a belt of countryside farther back. With these, Hitler assured Mussolini, he would "turn London into a garden of ruins" the moment the invasion began. (He also hinted that German chemists had developed a poison gas—in fact the first nerve gases—against which even German gas masks afforded no protection.)

In mid-May the Führer ordered the flying-bomb offensive to start with an all-out attack on London one night in mid-June, coupled with a fire-raising attack by Sperrle's bomber squadrons; thereafter, intermittent salvos were to be fired night after night—and by day too if bad weather hampered the British defenses. "Panic will break out in England," Hitler gloatingly told his private staff. "These flying bombs have such an unnerving effect that nobody can stand them very long. I am going to pay those barbarians back for machine-gunning our women and children and sacking our culture!" On about June 4 he decided that it was time to begin, and the flying-bomb regiment was instructed that by the tenth its prefabricated catapult equipment was to be moved from the hidden dumps up to the launching sites. In this way he would force the enemy's hand, he hoped: public outcry would leave Churchill no alternative but to launch a premature and hence disastrous invasion of France. "If the British came to us now with any kind of peace feelers," Hitler told Slovakia's Prime Minister Josef Tiso: "I would prefer to tell them to keep their feelers—until after the invasion." With the invasion defeated, he would revert to the conquest of Russia.

Hitler doubted that the invasion was imminent, but the waiting irritated him. He allowed Admiral Dönitz to go on leave on June 1 for the first time since war began. Rommel wrote with a trace of nervousness on May 29: "The nonstop Anglo-American bombardment is admittedly continuing. The French are suffering particularly cruelly—three thousand civilian dead these last forty-eight hours alone, while our own casualties are mostly low. Many decoy sites are being bombed."

In Italy, now that the Anzio forces had linked up with the main battlefront Rome itself could well become a battlefield, just as Stalingrad had. This produced another instance of Hitler's strange conception of morality. The same Führer who was indifferent to the fate of defenseless Jewish children was piously proud to have defeated Belgium without defiling Brussels, and France without attacking Paris—his enemies, it was noted, had just bombed the Rouen cathedral and attacked, quite pointlessly, the famous monastery at Monte Cassino. As early as February Hitler had turned down Kesselring's suggestion that in an emergency the Tiber bridges in Rome should be destroyed, as the river's steep embankments would check the most determined enemy's advance. In fact Hitler had reiterated that Rome's status as an "open city" must be strictly preserved. While he could jest to Mussolini: "You and I are the most reviled men in the world," he did not want to go into history as the man who caused Rome to be destroyed. Therefore, Wehrmacht troops had been forbidden to set foot there without special passes, and even during the fiercest fighting at Anzio all military transports had been tediously diverted around the outskirts of Rome.

This forbearance brought no Allied response. When Kesselring formally suggested to the enemy, through the Vatican, on June 3, that both sides continue to respect the "open city," they made no reply but instead appealed to the city's populace to join the battle. Sir Henry Wilson, the Supreme Allied Commander in the Mediterranean, broadcast the falsehood that the Germans were defending Rome, and the British and American tanks speedily penetrated to its very heart the next day. To impede further pursuit of his withdrawing army, Hitler should now have blown up the bridges, but he did not. Late the next evening, June 5, Roosevelt broadcast news of the victory. He attributed to the skill of his generals the fact that Rome had escaped damage.

It was after midnight when Hitler went to bed. The last Luftwaffe reconnaissance of southeastern England, a week before, had shown hardly any landing craft assembled at Dover—facing the Dunkirk-Dieppe coastline, where the latest saturation air raids led both Rommel and Rundstedt to believe that the invasion might eventually occur. The rest of Britain's south coast had eluded the Luftwaffe reconnaissance. Luftwaffe meteorologists forecast several days of poor weather. Thus Hitler did not suspect that five thousand vessels laden with the enemy were at that very moment bearing down upon the coast of France.

PART 5

THE WORMS TURN

Man with a Yellow Leather Briefcase

During the night the news of the parachute and glider landings in Normandy hardened, and ships' engines were heard offshore. But the Führer was not awakened; his adjutants consulted with Jodl, who pointed out that the situation would not clear up until daybreak anyway. It followed from this that until the full situation was put to him at the midday war conference, Hitler took no decision on the—increasingly frantic—appeals by Rundstedt to release the OKW panzer reserves to counterattack. By that time wave after wave of landing craft had disgorged tanks and men onto the landing beaches after annihilating naval and air bombardments, and the Seventh Army admitted that the Allies had already established west of the Orne River a beachhead some fifteen miles wide and two miles deep inland.

Thus by the time Hitler's war conference began, the Battle of France was already lost—if Rommel's dictum about the necessity for defeating the enemy on the very beaches had meant anything. The events of the next days disclosed that the movements of any German reserves by day were impossible, so overwhelming was the enemy's air superiority. That the enemy had not been defeated on the beaches was due in part to the weakness of the Atlantic Wall in Normandy—despite all Hitler's warnings since February 1944, the Wall was only 18 percent complete in the Seventh Army's sector, compared with 68 percent in the Channel sector commanded by Salmuth's Fifteenth Army—and in part to the sluggishness of German Intelligence, which had accurate evidence that the invasion would occur on June 6 or 7 but failed to alert all the echelons concerned—in particular General Friedrich Dollmann's Seventh Army.

Hitler subsequently ordered an investigation of this renewed Intelligence failure, which had resulted in Rommel leaving his French headquarters for Germany on the fourth, Dollmann being absent on a map exercise at Rennes, and Sepp Dietrich being in Brussels. Working in conjunction with the SS, the Abwehr in France had since early 1944 penetrated numerous Resistance "cells" in France;

thus they had learned that two lines of a Paul Verlaine poem broadcast by the BBC's French service would be the invasion-alert. On June 1 the first line was heard for the first time: *les sanglots longs des violons de l'automne.* This, Intelligence knew, indicated that the invasion was due in the first half of the month. At 9:15 P.M. on the fifth the BBC broadcast the second line: *blessent mon coeur d'une langueur monotone.* This was the prearranged signal for the Resistance to start sabotage operations for an invasion beginning within forty-eight hours of midnight. Salmuth's radio operators picked this up and alerted every lower echelon as well as the HQ of Army Group B—where Speidel was acting in Rommel's absence. Rundstedt's headquarters also subsequently claimed to have intercepted the signal and warned "all echelons concerned." But for some reason neither the OKW, nor the Berghof, nor the Seventh Army was warned—and it was Dollmann's army, in Normandy, that took the blow. This is all the more inexplicable as German Intelligence in Paris had analyzed the BBC secret messages—125 invasion-alerts were transmitted on the afternoon of June 1 alone—and found that nearly all 28 that were transmitted to cells penetrated by the Germans were in the Normandy–Brittany area. The results of Hitler's investigation are not known; the noisy tread of history approaching soon took his thoughts elsewhere, and if the culprits were either Colonel Georg Hansen, Canaris's successor as chief of military Intelligence, or Colonel Alexis von Roenne, chief of Foreign Armies West, both were shortly executed in another context.

Far more serious was the incorrect estimate of initial Allied strength in England. Hitler's last information was that 90 divisions and 22 brigades were under arms in the British Isles; the real number of divisions available for invasion operations was only 37. There is strong evidence that since early 1944 Zeitzler's faltering Intelligence branches had begun deliberately inventing "ghost" enemy divisions to frighten some common sense into Hitler; more recently a well-laid British deception campaign had fed substance into these phantoms—with success beyond the wildest dreams of the British, because throughout June Hitler dared not throw everything he had in France into the Normandy battle in case the enemy's "other" invasion army then appeared elsewhere. Thus while on D-Day morning Rundstedt cautiously adjudged the Normandy operation to be "quite serious after all," as the enemy's employment of three airborne divisions and paratroops at the root of the Cherbourg peninsula showed, his morning telegrams to Hitler stressed that he could not yet say with certainty whether this was the real invasion or only a decoy. Hitler released the meager OKW panzer reserves—two divisions—at about 2:30 P.M.; Rundstedt was instructed to destroy the beachhead by nightfall, as more Allied airborne and amphibious troops were probably on their way.

It is easy to smirk now, but this was the prevailing mood. Hitler and his generals were overconfident. In his unpublished memoirs, the Fifteenth Army's commander, General Hans von Salmuth, wrote of that invasion morning: "At 6 A.M., since it had been daylight for an hour and a half, I had my Chief of Staff telephone Seventh Army again to ask if the enemy had landed anywhere yet. The reply was, 'Fleets of troop transports and warships big and small are lying at various points offshore, with masses of landing craft. But so far no landing has yet taken place.' Thereupon I went back to sleep with a calm mind, after telling my Chief of Staff '—So their invasion has miscarried already!' " According to a manservant, Hitler's mood was equally cocky. "The news couldn't be better," was how he welcomed Keitel that morning. "As long as they were in Britain we couldn't get at them. Now we have them where we can destroy them." And to Göring: "They are landing here—and here: just where we expected them!"

The Luftwaffe High Command remained optimistic throughout the day. Although they too had been caught napping in France—in spite of the fact that a master plan drawn up in February and constantly updated since, had provided for nineteen squadrons of fighters to be rushed to the west the moment the invasion started—Göring and Korten, his Chief of Staff, retained their composure. On that sixth of June the Luftwaffe could raise only 319 sorties over France, compared with the enemy's 10,585, and only *12* fighter-bomber sorties were flown into the beachhead area itself (in which 10 of the pilots released their bombs prematurely); but the Luftwaffe assured Hitler that within three days they would reach maximum strength. On June 7, Richthofen wrote: "The Channel fighting is still assessed very optimistically by the Luftwaffe High Command."

Not until June 8 was Göring's optimism damped. By that evening he had only five ground-attack aircraft and ninety-five fighters operational against the invasion. He had eight hundred crews available for fighter squadrons, but not enough aircraft. The Allies' total air supremacy over the Normandy beachhead was a fact. Since even far inside the German-controlled area all daytime movement of men and materials was impossible, the immediate counterattack by the OKW reserves and the 21st Panzer Division failed. The artillery bombardment by offshore enemy warships guided by spotter planes was so deadly that when Göring announced the formation of a squadron of suicide-pilots willing to fly Focke-Wulf 190s laden with two-ton bombs (since no fuel load would be needed for a return flight) for several days Hitler considered dispatching them against these ships. Dönitz's U-boats could not get near them. General Guderian summed up the situation to Hitler a few days later: "Even the greatest bravery of the tank soldiers can't make up for the defection of two other Services." Gathering his forces, Rundstedt planned to mount an armored counterattack from under an impenetrable "wall of fire" put up by the Third Antiaircraft Corps west of Caen early on the eleventh; but on the evening of the tenth, he had to cancel the attack when an enemy tank assault disrupted the assembling forces, driving them to the defensive.

Thus by June 10 German optimism had evaporated. Dönitz conceded: "The invasion has succeeded. The Second Front has come." Loud recriminations began at the Berghof. When Göring blamed the navy for having assured everybody that the enemy would not risk his capital ships in a Channel invasion and for objecting to the earlier laying of the secret "pressure mines" off the French coast, Dönitz bridled: "Discussion of such matters does not seem opportune at this moment." It was obvious that the enemy planned to capture the deep port of Cherbourg next. If this could not be prevented, warned Rundstedt on June 11, the Führer might be confronted with a situation requiring "fundamental decisions." Rommel echoed this in a letter to Keitel the next day. Hitler now realized that his optimism had been misplaced, and belatedly ordered two high-grade SS panzer divisions (the 9th and 10th)—which had been standing by to attack a minor Russian salient near Kolomea—to entrain immediately for the Normandy front instead. "If I had had the 9th and 10th SS panzer divisions in the west," he grumbled at the end of August, "all this would probably never have happened." With these reinforcements Rundstedt was ordered to destroy the Normandy bridgehead piecemeal.

On the afternoon of June 6, 1944, the OKW had ordered the flying-bomb attack against London to begin. But first six days had to be spent in bringing up the heavy steel catapult rigs from their camouflaged dumps and transporting them to the sixty-four prepared launching sites along the Channel coast. The launching crews exchanged their Todt Organization camouflage for blue-gray Luftwaffe uniforms, and the regiment's command staff moved into its new bunker at Saleux; but on the eleventh it was clear that all was not well, as disastrous Allied bombing of the French road and rail networks had resulted in trains being split, catapult sections being delivered to the wrong sites, and vital components vanishing completely. Despite this—with none of the sites operational—the OKW insisted that day that the attack begin the next night.

How Hitler thirsted for the moment! Here at the Berghof he had joined the rest of Germany in the "front line" of the bombing war. By day he watched the American bomber squadrons glittering high overhead on their way from Italy to targets in southern Germany. By night the British flew the other way into Austria and Hungary, the Obersalzberg sirens driving the entire Berghof staff out the back door to the large steel portals masking the entrance to the tunnels now honeycombing the mountain. Hitler himself was loath to go down the sixty-five steps until the antiaircraft batteries began firing; he stood close to the tunnel exit, taking care that nobody tried to leave before the all clear sounded. Often the red glow of fires burning in Munich could be seen reflected in the skies. His housekeeper had begged him to move his town apartment's contents to somewhere safer, but he had refused. "Frau Winter, we must set an example."

His impatience with Göring's fighter defenses rose with each successful raid. In the raid on Munich on June 9, Eva Braun's close friend, Heini Handschuhmacher, the well-known actor, was killed with his wife. Eva and her women friends returned in tears from the funeral and pathetically described the misery caused by the raids. "Hitler listened with a mournful face," wrote a secretary later, "swore vengeance, and promised that he would repay everything onehundredfold with the Luftwaffe's new inventions."

The flying bomb—shortly christened V-1 by Goebbels—was one of the war's most terrifying weapons: a cheaply built pilotless plane with a one-ton warhead of high explosive, it was propelled so fast by its simple jet device that few modern fighter aircraft could engage it; its engine resonated with a deep organlike growl, awakening the whole countryside over which it passed—its sudden silence being the signal that it was about to impact. Göring proudly took the credit.

On the night of June 12 the flying-bomb attack on London began. The launching sites were still not ready, and the result was a fiasco: of ten V-1s catapulted, four crashed at once, two vanished without trace, one demolished a railway bridge in London, and the other three impacted elsewhere. Now Göring anxiously informed Hitler that Milch—the same field marshal who had deceived them over the Me-262 jet aircraft—was the author of the V-1. Two more days passed while the catapult rigs were properly adjusted. Late on June 15 the offensive was resumed; no fewer than 244 V-1s were launched against London by noon the next day; spotter aircraft reported fires sweeping the British capital.

The new campaign took the British completely by surprise. Though Hitler did not know it, Churchill had to order a complete redistribution of the British antiaircraft and fighter defenses: bombing of the V-1 sites now assumed a priority above the destruction of German cities, aircraft factories, and oil refineries. Göring retracted his earlier statement about the authorship of the weapon; but at 5:35 P.M. on the seventeenth Hitler telephoned Milch to congratulate him in person, and a few days later he jubilantly ordered Speer to throttle back A-4 rocket production to release manpower and materials to increase V-1 and jet-bomber production.

Surely the enemy would now have to launch their "second invasion" force against the Pas de Calais to neutralize this V-1 threat? Both Hitler and Jodl had recognized as early as the twelfth that defeating such a second invasion was now probably the only hope. Besides, the Russians were clearly winding up for a main offensive on the eastern front; war on two fronts, the nightmare Hitler had avoided in 1939, was about to become a reality.

Late on June 16 four Focke-Wulf Condors flew Hitler and his staff to Metz, while the entire fighter force along the route was grounded, and antiaircraft batteries forbidden to fire in order to avoid accidents. After dawn the next morning, while Luftwaffe fighters patroled the highway from Rheims onward, he drove to W2, the Führer's Headquarters built near Soissons, to confer with Rundstedt and Rommel and to congratulate the flying-bomb commander, General Erich Heinemann. The immediate purpose of Hitler's flight was to restore the two field marshals' confidence, shaken by the enemy's success in consolidating his bridgehead at Normandy. By the skillful use of airborne troops, the Americans had torn open the front and were bound to isolate the whole Cherbourg peninsula sooner or later. Hitler appears to have reproached Rommel, and Rommel evidently blamed the poor quality and equipment of the Normandy divisions —with some justice, for throughout the spring, Zeitzler had steadily drained away the best divisions to the eastern front. Hitler was also told of the crushing enemy air superiority.

Two aspects of the coming battle were discussed that day: the coming battle for Cherbourg and a future counterattack by four SS panzer divisions from west of Caen and Falaise—which was Hitler's own proposal. By 10 A.M., Hitler's first order for the defense of Cherbourg had been telephoned by Rommel's Chief of Staff Hans Speidel to the army group HQ. "The fortress Cherbourg is to be held at all costs. . . . A retreat in one stage only will not take place." The German troops were to make a fighting retreat into the fortress, delaying the enemy's advance by obstacles, minefields, and deception, while the time was used to stock up Cherbourg for a long siege and demolish the port facilities—starting immediately—so that the enemy could not use it. Before the SS counterattack, Hitler called for a clear Schwerpunkt in Normandy east of the Orne; this Schwerpunkt was to be established at the expense of the First and Nineteenth armies but not of Salmuth's Fifteenth Army in the Pas de Calais, where Rommel and Rundstedt both expected the "second invasion" to come. The navy and Luftwaffe would be ordered to concentrate on the enemy's warships and shipping tonnage; the new "pressure mines" would be used for the first time. Both field marshals were visibly impressed by Heinemann's report on the V-1 attack: all morning hundreds of enemy bombers had been bombarding the launching sites, though with scant effect. Hitler left Soissons—near the battlefield where as a corporal he had won his Iron Cross a quarter of a century before—late that afternoon.

Back at the Berghof the next evening, the news was that the Americans had, as feared, reached the west coast of the Cherbourg peninsula. At 11 P.M. he said accusingly to Jodl, "They are stating quite bluntly that they've got through. Now, have they or haven't they!" "Jawohl," conceded the general; "they got through."

The convincing details of the coming secret weapons probably account for Rommel's renewed exuberance. His next report exuded optimism again: the enemy had landed twenty-five divisions, but with heavy casualties; the local French population were still overwhelmingly on the German side. Admiral Friedrich Ruge, his naval aide, marveled at Rommel's new faith and surmised in his diary that Hitler must possess "sheer magnetism." Hitler seriously counted on the new secret mines to foil the second invasion; on June 18 he insisted that a barrage also be laid outside Le Havre—"so they can't stage a repeat performance there."

He had also spoken of the Messerschmitt jet bomber. Göring's propellor-driven fighter-bombers were being massacred in France, just as Hitler had feared. During June he closely followed the jet bomber's production progress and studied the photographs of the underground factories being built. General Korten appealed for the immediate appearance of twelve to fifteen Me-262 bombers at the battle front—whether piloted by civilians or officers was immaterial—and for three more to be used, despite Göring's misgivings, as high-speed photographic reconnaissance planes. Production of the Heinkel 177 heavy bomber was to be stepped up as well, with a corresponding cutback in medium-bomber (Junkers 188) production. On June 20, Hitler accepted Speer's proposal that all aircraft production be transferred to his armaments ministry. At last Hitler was taking a more personal interest in the Luftwaffe's equipment.

Since the Russians had overrun Sevastopol, little had occurred in the east. On June 10 they had attacked the Finns, and for several days Hitler had drawn political comfort from the significant failure of the Russians to assist the Normandy invasion by attacking German-held sectors of the eastern front instead. But Stalin would not postpone his summer offensive forever, and the question was, Where would the blow fall?

In May, Hitler had detected an enemy Schwerpunkt only at Kovel, which Model's Army Group North-Ukraine had relieved in April. Model had wanted throughout May to promote an attack here, and the Fifty-sixth Panzer Corps—with virtually all Army Group Center's tanks—had been transferred to him "temporarily" for this purpose. On June 11, however, Hitler canceled the Kovel attack when divisions had to be switched to the Normandy front. The upshot was that of his forty-five original divisions, Field Marshal Busch (Army Group Center) had only thirty-seven left in June to defend an eight hundred-mile perimeter should the Russians now attack it.

Almost complete radio silence had descended on the Russian front. Intuitively, Hitler suspected that Stalin would now go all-out for Army Group Center; the gathering storm-signs that reached him confirmed his view. But throughout May, General Zeitzler's eastern Intelligence expert, Colonel Gehlen, had scented the main Soviet Schwerpunkt opposite Model's Army Group North-Ukraine, consistent with what he called "the Balkans solution"; and even when Russian reinforcements were reported moving northward from there to the center—to Gomel and Smolensk—Gehlen would go no further on June 13 than to suggest that the Red Army might launch an initial attack on Army Group Center as a holding operation, albeit one with far-ranging objectives (even Minsk). The next day, both Zeitzler and his chief of operations, General Heusinger, reemphasized this view: the Soviet Schwerpunkt would for the first time come up against a German Schwerpunkt—Model's army group.

Zeitzler rejected all the conflicting evidence. On June 17, the OKL telephoned him directly to warn of evidence of an imminent Red Army offensive near Smolensk. A captured Russian cipher officer revealed that three corps of fighter planes, including one from the Crimea, had just arrived at Smolensk; over four thousand five hundred aircraft were suddenly confronting Army Group Center. Soviet reinforcements had been moved from Kovel, after the German attack had failed to materialize there, to Gomel and Smolensk, and they were confronting the Ninth and Fourth armies, respectively. On June 18 and 19, Hitler called for the Fourth Air Corps, the last great air reserve in the east, to bomb the Gomel armies, and he refused to transfer the corps to Normandy for minelaying operations for just this reason. As late as June 20, General Zeitzler was still obstinately maintaining that the real Soviet offensive would shortly come against Model's front. Hitler ignored his advice. From the Berghof, the Luftwaffe was informed the next day: "The general appreciation is that the expected attack on Army Group Center begins tomorrow." Once more, toward 2 A.M. on June 22, Hitler personally ordered the Sixth Air Force to stand by on full alert for that attack within the next few hours.

Before we record the catastrophe that now indeed befell Army Group Center, we must look briefly at two of Hitler's concurrent preoccupations—the bombing war and Finland.

On June 21, 2,500 American aircraft had attacked Berlin in broad daylight, releasing over 2,000 tons of bombs on the capital. Forty-four bombers were shot down, and in one of them was found a map revealing that 114 had flown on to Russian airfields in the Ukraine. Hitler ordered General Meister's Fourth Air Corps to raid them there that very night. Two-thirds of the bombers were destroyed and the rest crippled beyond repair. It was a satisfying and sudden end to the American "shuttle-bombing" raids.

Hitler's guest at the Berghof war conferences on June 21 and 22 was his favorite Bavarian general, Dietl, commander of the German Twentieth Army in Lapland. Since February Hitler had been aware of secret Soviet-Finnish armistice talks, but these had collapsed in March as the Russian terms were too harsh. Suspicious that this all-too democratic government might abandon the war at any moment,

Hitler stopped arms deliveries to Finland in April, and when Marshal Mannerheim promised him in May that the weapons would never end up in Russian hands Hitler privately dismissed this "platonic assurance" as quite valueless. Mannerheim's determined resistance to the Russian offensive of June 10 impressed him, however, and two days later Hitler decided: "As long as the Finns keep warring we'll support them; the moment they start jawing, the deliveries will be stopped." He ordered Göring to rush a fighter squadron to Helsinki and Guderian to supply a battalion of assault guns. At the evening conference on June 21 he nonetheless expressed disappointment that Mannerheim had withdrawn his troops so far. Dietl went red in the face, slammed his fist on the red marble map table, and dismissed Hitler's criticisms as typical of a "chairbound general" unencumbered by any expert knowledge of the terrain; he would fly back to Finland and support Mannerheim to the hilt. After the general left the Great Hall, Hitler turned to his gaping staff and exclaimed, "Gentlemen—that's the kind of general I like!"

Dietl and his corps commanders had spent two days listening to speeches by Keitel, Rosenberg, and Himmler at the SS training college at Sonthofen.[1] Himmler's speech—which again may have later been shown to the Führer—covered the familiar ground, though he no longer claimed to be murdering the Jews on *Hitler*'s orders. He conceded that ("at most") fifty thousand Germans were now in concentration camps, including some fifteen thousand political prisoners. He asked for the generals' sympathy in having had to eliminate the Jews: Germany could not have withstood the bombing terror if the Jewish germ had remained, he argued, nor could the front line have been held east of Lemberg (Lvov) if the big Jewish settlements had still existed in that city—or in Cracow, Lublin, and Warsaw. And using the familiar arguments he answered their unspoken question as to why the Jewish children had to be murdered too.

Next afternoon, on June 22, the same generals listened to a secret speech by Hitler on the Obersalzberg, on the nature of war and revolution. The shorthand record has survived in Bormann's files. To frequent storms of applause, the Führer expounded his philosophy that in war as in nature the weakest must go to the wall, and that a nation which failed to recognize this would as surely vanish from the face of the earth as had countless prehistoric species. "Nor can there occur a revolution in the Germany of today. The Jews have gone; and the born

[1]Of Keitel's speech on June 20, 1944, we know only that he had optimistically proclaimed that the Red Army would not attack until the Allies had scored major victories in the west and that its Schwerpunkt would lie in the south and not the center. This was not, of course, Hitler's view.

leaders I have already singled out long ago, regardless of their origins, for positions of authority." If any man now turned to the outside world against Germany, then a death sentence would be meted out to him. The generals fiercely applauded Hitler's image of the "little worm" of an infantryman in a slit trench, confronting ten or more Russian tanks with only a grenade in his hands, while democrats at home plotted his country's surrender. "How can one expect the brave little rifleman to die for his country on the battlefield, while at the same moment others at home are doing no less than plotting the betrayal of these men's sacrifices!" When people asked him, "How easy is your conscience now?" he could only respond that he could often not sleep, but that he never for one instant doubted that Germany would survive every danger. "I still have not made my ultimate appeal to the German nation," he reminded the generals, and they responded with frenetic applause and shouts of "Heil!"

The plane carrying Dietl and his generals back to Lapland crashed into the Semmering Mountain a few hours later, killing everybody aboard. Agonized by the fear that this loss might finally prompt Finland's defection, Hitler ordered absolute secrecy about the tragedy until Ribbentrop's mission in Helsinki—securing the Finnish government's unconditional agreement to reject any further Soviet peace proposals—was accomplished. Dietl's generals were quietly buried by the Party in Carinthia; Hitler himself attended the state funeral for Dietl at Salzburg on July 1.

The simultaneous loss of Cherbourg was not only bitter but also a mystery to Hitler. Jodl had spoken well of General Karl Wilhelm von Schlieben, the port's commandant, and Hitler had radioed him on June 21: "I expect you to fight this battle as Gneisenau once fought in the defense of Colberg." But that night the general called for urgent supplies to be airlifted to him, and Hitler caustically commented at the next day's noon conference: "Two years they've had to stock up Cherbourg, yet within two days of being cut off they are already clamoring for air supplies." Only now did he learn that far fewer German troops were in the port than he had supposed—and indeed ordered. Of the 77th Infantry Division only sixty men had arrived; the rest had either been wiped out or—against his orders—broken through the American line to the *south.* The low combat strength of the other divisions derived in part from Hitler's earlier order for every yard of the peninsula to be defended in a fighting retreat. He nonetheless asked some very angry questions of the Seventh Army that afternoon, and the answers supplied to him at the evening conference did not satisfy him. Although Cherbourg had in theory enough food and ammunition for an eight-week siege, its stock of antitank weapons was nonexistent. Rundstedt and Rommel claimed to have warned of this deficiency throughout their area for months.

Hitler considered desperate measures—a counterthrust into the rear of the American corps attacking the port, which Rundstedt rejected out of hand, or an airlift of three thousand paratroops. General Student was willing, but the OKL was not, unless a full moon could be provided. Hitler fumed: "It must be possible to put down three thousand troops in our own territory!" But given the Allied air supremacy, it was not; on June 25, 118 German fighter aircraft set off to support Schlieben, but all were beaten back. That afternoon an Anglo-American battle fleet appeared offshore and began blasting the port. At 7:32 P.M. Schlieben's radio operators faintly broadcast: "The final battle for Cherbourg has begun. General is fighting with his troops. Long live Führer and Germany." Then the sign-off prefix, and "Heil the Führer, Heil Germany!"

Far into the night Hitler debated with General Guderian and General Walter Buhle ways of providing Rundstedt with long-range artillery capable of engaging such enemy battle fleets from the shore. The next afternoon, June 26, Keitel ordered court-martial investigation of the negligence and omissions that had so weakened the Cherbourg garrison; everybody involved from Seventh Army downward was to be examined. Early on June 28, the Seventh Army's commander, Friedrich Dollmann, took poison. Hitler was told the general had died of a heart attack, believed it, and authorized a generous obituary.

"If people now say, 'Look, the British are in Cherbourg,' I reply, 'To you that is the beginning of their reconquest of France, but I look at it differently.' " Thus Hitler pacified his generals. "After all, we already hounded them out of France once; so Cherbourg is just the last ground they still hold. When war broke out, it was not we who were in France, but they . . . and the enemy was barely a hundred miles from Berlin, standing on our eastern frontiers." And in a way it was fortunate that the Germans were now hypnotized by the western front, for the events in the east were far grimmer.

The Russian offensive on June 22 had begun with deceptive mildness: company-strength infantry attacks on Army Group Center left two minor breaches torn temporarily on either side of Vitebsk. Zeitzler had continued to direct Hitler's attention to the apparent threat to Army Groups South- and North-Ukraine. But then great Russian tank formations had appeared, and poured through the breaches, while overwhelming operations by ground-attack squadrons had neutralized the German artillery, the backbone of the defensive system; the Sixth Air Force had only forty fighter aircraft operational that day. A month before, at the Berghof, Hitler had personally briefed Field Marshal Busch, summoned from Army Group Center headquarters at Minsk. He was to hold the present line and in particular defend the "fortified places" of Vitebsk, Orsha, Mogilev, and Bobruisk to the last man. By June 25, however, the Red Army was about to engulf the entire Fourth Army and most of the Ninth; moreover, the sheer scale of the Russian offensive only dawned slowly on the Germans. Believing that disaster could still be staved off, Hitler bluntly refused frantic appeals by Busch and Zeitzler to abandon the "fortified places" while there was still time; thus Busch lost six divisions tied down in their defense. When he came to the Berghof he appealed for Army Group North to be pulled back too, so that strength could be released to his own front. But now that Mannerheim had just pledged Finland's loyalty, Hitler refused to let him down like that. Himmler blamed this "incomprehensible collapse" on Busch. "In my view the army group's command was too soft and war-weary," he wrote on June 26. Hitler evidently agreed, for two days later, as a penalty for failure, he sacked the field marshal.

This was the only remedy he knew in such a desperate situation, and he applied it liberally. Others would follow Busch into the wilderness that same week, and at its end, Hitler—his determination to win through unimpaired—was even his own Chief of General Staff, for General Zeitzler had also disappeared, either sick or sickened by events.

Hostility toward Zeitzler had mounted at the Berghof. Early in May he had formally complained about General Guderian's disparaging comments on the attitude of the General Staff and tendered his resignation—an offer Hitler left temporarily unanswered. Some weeks later Göring slandered Zeitzler in earshot of the Berghof orderlies, remarking on the army's "cowardice." The final clash with Hitler came on June 30, with disaster threatening General Georg Lindemann's Army Group North in the Baltic states. Zeitzler appealed to Hitler to withdraw the army group to the shorter Dvina River line while there was yet time. Busch's successor—Model—and Lindemann supported Zeitzler from afar, but Hitler would not hear of it; to throw Finland into the arms of Stalin would deprive Germany of her last nickel supplies, with grave effects on arms production. "I bear the responsibility, not you," he acidly reminded Zeitzler. Undaunted, Zeitzler told him that now that the the invasion of France had manifestly succeeded, the war could not be won unless the much-publicized "total war" effort became a reality. He suggested the appointment of the Reichsführer SS Himmler as "dictator" to put teeth into the campaign. Total war alone would release the manpower the eastern front now needed. Hitler felt that Zeitzler's nerve had deserted him and commented spitefully on the defeatism of the General Staff.

Zeitzler left without saluting and suffered a complete nervous and physical collapse later that day. Hitler never saw him again. He managed without a Chief of General Staff for the following three weeks.

Rundstedt, the Commander in Chief West, was also a marked man. For several days—following June 26, 1944—Hitler had invited Field Marshal von Kluge as the heir-apparent to sit in on the Berghof war conferences and thus steep himself in Hitler's forced optimism.

He introduced Kluge to the murderous V-1 flying bomb and explained its strategic purpose. The enemy was already forced to keep 250 fighter aircraft on patrol against the V-1s; to add an element of confusion, Hitler had ordered them painted with the same black-and-white stripes as the Allied invasion aircraft. On June 26 he stepped up the V-1 saturation of London, still hoping to force the Allies to stage a disastrous second invasion in the Pas de Calais; and when the OKL suggested filling 250 V-1s a month with an extradestructive aluminized explosive, Trialen, Hitler responded by ordering ten times that number. He was ecstatic that England was suffering again, and by all accounts even worse than in 1940. "The all-out bombing attacks on our catapult sites are sufficient proof of the effectiveness of our weapons!" two officers of the V-1 regiment assured Hitler at the Berghof on June 29. Hitler proudly explained to Kluge that all the shells fired at Paris by Krupp's Big Bertha in World War I contained less explosive than one V-1. "We spare our men and our aircraft.—The V-1 is aircraft and bomb alike, and it needs no fuel for a return flight!" That night the two-thousandth flying bomb was launched against England.

The latest disheartening Intelligence forwarded by Rundstedt from Rommel's headquarters was that about thirty enemy divisions had already landed in Normandy and that at least *sixty-seven more* were standing by in England.[2] This phantom invasion army overshadowed Hitler's conferences at the Berghof that June 29, 1944. It meant that Salmuth's well-appointed Fifteenth Army, covering the Pas de Calais, still could not be weakened. Thus Hitler had to bow to the "painful verdict," as he called it, of Rundstedt and Rommel that no attack could be sprung on the American army in the Cherbourg peninsula, where isolated pockets of German troops were still fighting a fanatical last stand. On this day he finally accepted that Germany was on the defensive in France too. Rommel's primary concern had to be to prevent the enemy from breaking through into France's open countryside toward Paris, and the main counterattack on the beachhead—first proposed by Hitler at Soissons and subsequently enlarged at Guderian's suggestion to include the 2nd Panzer Division and the crack Panzer-Lehr Division as well as the four SS panzer divisions—was doomed to failure unless certain elementary requirements were first met.

These he spelled out on June 29, first to Rundstedt and Rommel and then that

[2]Only fifteen divisions were still in England, awaiting shipment to Normandy. It is not clear whether Hitler was being deliberately misled by German anti-Nazis or by the faulty intelligence of General Staff officers.

evening to Dönitz, Göring, and Sperrle, the Third Air Force commander in France. First, the enemy's offshore battle fleet had to be driven off or sunk, and his transport ships had to be prevented from reaching the invasion coast; Hitler proposed saturating the coastal waters with the new secret mines, sowing them with the same "bulldog tenacity" the enemy had shown in bombing the German ground-transport system. "It's far more effective to sink an entire ship's cargo than to have to deal with the troops and equipment piecemeal after they have been unloaded," he pointed out. He recommended the ruthless employment of every weapon available—circling torpedoes, submarines with snorkel breathing-tubes, radio-controlled launches packed with high explosives, and V-1 flying bombs manned by suicide-pilots.[3] The second requirement was for motor transport to match the enemy's immense mobility; if necessary, trucks and buses would have to be ruthlessly requisitioned from the French. Third, no proposed counterattack could survive long without logistics support; Hitler asked the Luftwaffe to establish certain "convoy highways" to the bridgehead, heavily protected by antiaircraft and fighter cover. The fourth requirement was for at least localized air superiority—an armada of fighters and fighter-bombers to keep the enemy bombers at bay.

While Göring called his generals together to examine Hitler's demand for the Luftwaffe to regain air supremacy in the west, Hitler himself asked Keitel to hint to Field Marshal von Rundstedt that he should take an extended leave. How often in later months—right to the end—Hitler bemoaned the fact that he had to occupy himself with even the most trivial matters; the fact that his Commander in Chief West had on his own initiative reached none of these relatively simple decisions was a persuasive argument against appointing a Commander in Chief East as well. Privately, Hitler blamed the women of France and the good food and liquor for softening his armies in the west. Rundstedt had done nothing to prevent this corruption of the Wehrmacht and erosion of its fighting spirit.

Rundstedt's fatalism was powerfully expressed on July 1, when he submitted to the OKW his own view that no counterattack would ever be possible and advised them to give up the bridgehead at Caen—the main enemy Schwerpunkt of attack—and withdraw the remaining front line beyond the range of the enemy ships' artillery. He enclosed a similar appreciation by General Leo Geyr von Schweppenburg, commander of Panzer Group West; Geyr suggested that there was a choice between tactical mending, which left the initiative with the enemy, and elastic warfare, which would give the defenders the initiative for at least some

[3]About a thousand V-1s with cockpits built in were found after the war at a depot south of Hamburg.

of the time. Precisely *how* he hoped to fight an elastic war with the panzer divisions immobilized by lack of fuel and motor transport he did not stipulate. Jodl soberly pointed out that the Rundstedt–Geyr proposals would be the first step toward a catastrophic evacuation of France. There were only two choices: either evacuation, or fighting this decisive battle where they stood at the first possible opportunity. Late that day Hitler signaled to Rommel that "the present lines are to be held. Any further enemy breakthrough is to be prevented by tenacious defense or by local counterattacks." Rundstedt was dismissed—Hitler sent one of his army adjutants, Colonel Heinrich Borgmann, to decorate him with the Oak Leaves and hand him the ominous blue envelope in person—and Kluge took his place. Geyr von Schweppenburg was also sacked, and Hitler nearly dismissed Blumentritt, Rundstedt's Chief of Staff, as well. For a time the energetic commander, fresh from the Berghof, brought new inspiration to the defense of France.

Hitler thus learned the hard way that the key to victory lay in the air defenses—just as the British had in 1940. In four months he hoped to recover air supremacy. The measures proposed by Reichsmarschall Göring to his astounded colleagues on the evening after the Führer's Berghof conference on June 29 were revolutionary. In the future only fighter aircraft would be manufactured—this was the "will of the Führer." Anybody disobeying would be stood before a firing squad.

Hitler's final discontent with the bomber arm had begun smoldering on the twentieth, while discussing with Milch and Saur ways of reaching the Me-262 production target of one thousand a month in the shortest time. But his real anger blazed up against the huge twin-engined Heinkel 177 heavy bomber a few days later: it was backward, plagued by faults, and suffered heavy casualties.[4] Its fuel consumption was so high that there was no future for it in a Germany clearly entering upon a crippling fuel crisis as one refinery after another was destroyed by enemy air raids. On June 25, at his midday conference, anguished by General von Schlieben's harrowing last appeals for the promised air support for Cherbourg, Hitler first remarked that mass production of fighters was more important than bomber production now. As for the four-engined version of the Heinkel 177, only now did he learn that the squadrons would not see it before 1946! But by then four-engined propellor-driven bombers would be in museums—rendered

[4]On June 27, 1944, General Karl Koller, the OKL chief of operations, was provided with statistics on the Heinkel 177: 179 conventional bombing sorties had been flown in the first four months of 1944, resulting in 26 planes lost. From November 1943 to June 1944, 192 sorties carrying remote-controlled bombs had resulted in 43 planes lost and only 3 destroyers and 5 merchant ships definitely sunk.

obsolete by mass-produced jet fighters like the Me-262. He telephoned Saur and asked him, "How many fighters can I build for one Heinkel 177?" Saur replied that "five thousand workers making two hundred Heinkel 177s a month could produce a thousand fighters more." That settled it. At the next day's war conference, Hitler reiterated: "What matters in our situation is to build fighters and still more fighters—and high-speed bombers too. We've got to get that air umbrella over our home base and our infantrymen! And if that means going without a strategic bomber force for years on end, then so be it!" At a midnight conference with Guderian two days later, Hitler happened to ask the general's Chief of Staff, Colonel Wolfgang Thomale, if he had seen the Luftwaffe in evidence in France that day. "No," the colonel replied. "That is, apart from two fighters between Paris and Chartres."

Such was the background to Hitler's final decision to scrap most bomber production, announced on July 1. General Koller forcefully argued that if only fighters were produced, there would be no minelaying, no guided bombs, no air launching of the V-1, and no Fourth Air Corps operations in the east—their only strategic bombing experiment; moreover, if the enemy began to use poison gas, the Luftwaffe would be powerless to reply. Thus Hitler's ax fell only on the Heinkel 177—but that decision was final. The next day he asked Saur on the phone how fighter production would now rise. "In June we turned out twenty-six hundred single- and twin-engined fighters," came the reply. "In July I hope to top the three thousand mark. In August thirty-three hundred, and then rising three hundred a month to forty-five hundred fighters in December. This will make our total aircraft output eventually sixty-five hundred, of which five thousand will be single- and twin-engined fighter types." As he replaced the receiver, Hitler recognized that the strategic issue was now this: could the bulging, straining battlefronts be kept from the Reich long enough for these figures to be attained? Much would depend on the courage and convictions of his field marshals.

The Führer lectured Kesselring on this when the field marshal came to the Berghof on July 3. After weeks of unremitting, hard-fought retreats, Kesselring had brought the enemy's advance in Italy to a standstill, still some way south of the as yet unfortified Apennine line. Kesselring depicted his plight in Italy—with insufficient troops, air cover, and civilian manpower—vividly. General Koller wrote that day:

> The Führer replied in great detail to all this, and explains just why we have to fight for every square meter of ground—because for us gaining time is everything now. The longer we can hold the enemy off at the periphery the better. Perhaps the individual soldier or NCO may not grasp why he is asked

to fight in the Abruzzi mountains instead of the Apennines, but his Supreme Commander must understand why and comply, because the interests of Germany's fight transcend those of the individual soldier.

Kesselring fears that he will be breached in his present position if he holds it too long, and he wants to fall back on the Apennine line early on. But the Führer wants that postponed as long as possible, as there is nothing else behind the Apennines, and if the enemy gets through there, the entire lowlands of Upper Italy will be lost; nor is that all, because the troops will find their escape cut off by the leapfrogging Allied tank formations. Another reason is that any withdrawal to the north increases the threat to the coasts of Greece, Albania, and Dalmatia.

Turning to the war in the air, the Führer again emphasizes how enormously different the situation would be if we still had the air superiority we used to. We are going to win it back—at least partially—but for that we need time, and we must not give up ground before then.

In the east, the catastrophic eclipse of Army Group Center was all but complete. At the midday conference on July 6, 1944, the Führer again rejected Model's view that four divisions could be extracted from Army Group North by ordering its withdrawal. It was an illusion, he said, to expect any savings; all that would happen was that the group would lose its fortified positions and its heavy guns and equipment. Turning to General Heusinger, Hitler quietly asked what the disaster had cost them so far in the Center and was told: "Twelve to fifteen divisions are encircled, but the overall losses will run to twenty-eight divisions."

Twenty-eight! Since June 22—in just two weeks—Hitler had lost 350,000 trained German soldiers to the Russians. Another might have lost his nerve, but Hitler's restless mind thought only of winning time for a few more months until the new Luftwaffe and the secret weapons reversed this trend. "I don't mind saying," he reminisced later, "it would be hard to imagine a graver crisis than the one in the east. When Field Marshal Model took over, Army Group Center was all gap. There was more gap than front—but then at last there was more front than gap." He had given Model a more realistic directive than had been given to his predecessor: the "fortified places" were only to be held long enough for a cohesive new front to be established farther back; but even this was a labor of Sisyphus, for by July 3, when Minsk itself had been overrun, the enemy had poured 126 infantry and 6 cavalry divisions with 45 tank brigades through a breach now over two hundred miles wide. Model had only 8 divisions worthy of the name!

At first the cause of this defeat was a mystery. Zeitzler's faulty strategic appreciation alone was not to blame; more serious was the Luftwaffe's virtual impotence—thrown into confusion by the sudden loss of its forward airfields and paralyzed by the first serious fuel shortage to affect the eastern front. Hitler's demands for an airlift to the encircled Fourth Army southeast of Minsk could not be fulfilled; the Messerschmitt 323 giant transport planes were grounded, and the entire Sixth Air Force was hamstrung by the lack of refined aviation fuel. Most ominous of the causes was the sudden unwillingness of leading army officers to continue the fight. As General Jodl put it soon after: "Practically the entire Army Group Center surrendered to the enemy this summer." There was evidence that Soviet-trained "Seydlitz officers" had infiltrated the battle zone, in German uniforms, and issued false orders to sabotage the army group's defense. Others seemed to have been active in Moscow's cause even longer. After the Fourth Army surrendered on July 8, Hitler was shown an order signed by General Vinzenz Müller of the Twelfth Army Corps[5] in which that army's soldiers were instructed to put an "end to the pointless bloodshed":

> The Russian command have promised (a) to care for the injured and (b) to let officers retain daggers and medals, and other ranks their decorations. All weapons and equipment are to be collected and handed over in good condition.

Two weeks later Müller and fifteen fellow generals of Army Group Center signed a long pamphlet attacking Hitler and denigrating their colleagues' continued defense of the Reich. Millions of facsimiles were scattered over the German lines. The text was personally broadcast by the generals on Moscow radio. Shortly afterward, the same generals, abetted by Paulus and Seydlitz, appealed to Army Group North officers to desert or disobey Hitler's "murderous orders" to stand fast. "Now," said Hitler, "I am beginning to understand how such frightful things could have happened in the Center."

The collapse had brought the Red Army to the very frontiers of East Prussia. Hordes of weary refugees had fled before them, swamping the province from White Russia. There were fears that if the enemy penetrated farther into Poland a general uprising would break out there. "When will the first task force of fifteen Me-262s begin operations?" the Führer impatiently asked on July 2.

He had still not abandoned hope. Somehow, however, the Soviet tide had to be stemmed before it engulfed East Prussia. Late on July 5 he decided to create new army divisions at an unprecedented speed to act as an emergency breakwater. He announced this to Himmler, Speer, Buhle, and half a dozen others at the Berghof the next day. Fifteen "blocking divisions" for the army would be raised

[5]Müller, fifty, was one of the little circle of dissidents around Hans Oster as early as 1939. After the war, he lived in the Soviet zone of Germany, where his memoirs, *Ich fand das wahre Vaterland (I Found the True Fatherland),* were published.

immediately from the navy and Luftwaffe; Speer's arms factories must contribute fifty thousand of their young workers. The Reichsführer SS would temporarily supervise the training of six such divisions. In addition, ten or twelve panzer brigades were to be created, each with perhaps fifty tanks. Hitler instructed Saur to institute a crash program to manufacture the necessary extra infantry equipment over the next weeks.

At this urgent conference, and an additional one called toward midnight, Hitler noticed the same one-armed colonel who had been at the Berghof a month before —a black patch on one eye, and two fingers missing from his one good arm; Schmundt had selected this officer, who seemed particularly fanatical, to be Chief of Staff to General Fromm, a man patently weary of his job as commander of the Replacement Army. This time the colonel was armed with a bulging yellow leather briefcase.

Very early on July 9, Hitler flew back to Rastenburg for a day of urgent talks there. With him he took Himmler, Keitel, Dönitz, Jodl, and Korten, while from the eastern front came Model, General Friessner (of Army Group North), and Greim. The Wolf's Lair was in a turmoil of noise and activity, for the strengthening of the bunkers was far from complete. Hitler again ruled against any weakening of Army Group North. He was seconded in this by Admiral Dönitz, who rehearsed the familiar strategic arguments against allowing Stalin free access to the Baltic Sea. The first new divisions were promised to Model by July 17, and Hitler explained how he intended to replace the Center's lost twenty-eight divisions: some of the new divisions would arrive in the second half of July, but the rest not before the end of August; three refurbished Crimea divisions would follow, joined by two from Norway and the 6th and 19th panzer divisions. Gauleiter Koch and the Party were to be put in charge of fortifying the East Prussian frontier. On balance, both Model and Friessner were optimistic about the Center and North; but within one or two days, Model warned, he expected the Russians to attack his other army group, North-Ukraine, at Kovel.

Hitler flew back to the Berghof that evening, his mind at peace. General Korten had informed him that during the night the first V-1s would be air-launched from Heinkel bombers against England and that the first four Messerschmitt 262 jet bombers would attack the invasion area within ten days. "The Allies only like advancing when air power is on their side," said Hitler. "That is why everything now depends on our fighter production. We must keep it top-secret and start stockpiling in a big way. Then just watch the enemy gape when we turn the tables on them four months from now—as far as air supremacy is concerned!"

Yet suddenly a mood of despair gripped the Führer and he decided abruptly to return to Rastenburg, even though the Wolf's Lair was still unready. The battle for Vilna, the last bastion before East Prussia, had just begun. He had already ordered the General Staff and OKL to stand by to evacuate their East Prussian headquarters to Potsdam "if need arose." But the cancer of defeatism he had discovered in the General Staff had deeply shocked him, and he felt that only his physical presence in East Prussia could prevent a rout. At the Berghof on the eleventh, the news was that both Model and Friessner admitted their assessments of two days earlier might have been overoptimistic. The colonel with the yellow briefcase had again come, to discuss the new blocking-divisions—now referred to as "grenadier divisions"; but as Himmler did not appear, the colonel left—his business uncompleted.

Hitler had asked Himmler to supervise all 15 embryo new divisions. He would trust the General Staff no longer.[6] On July 13 he personally addressed the generals and staff officers selected for these and the 10 panzer brigades, perhaps 160 men. Never again would he possess the physical strength to deliver such a speech, but of this, his last to his generals, there is no surviving record.

That morning Marshal Konev's attack on Army Group North-Ukraine had begun. East of East Prussia, Vilna had fallen, and Hitler was airlifting reliable SS troops to defend Kauen, the next town. The next morning he would himself fly back to Rastenburg. Desolately, he wandered through the Berghof rooms with the young wives of Dr. Brandt, his surgeon, and Colonel von Below, Luftwaffe adjutant, pausing affectionately in front of each familiar painting or tapestry as though taking leave of an old friend for the last time. One painting was of a rather plump young lady, whom Speer had always threatened to deflate with a knife. At last, the Führer bid the ladies courtly good night and kissed their hands. But shortly afterward he returned to the Great Hall and bid them farewell. At this Frau Brandt began to weep. Frau von Below said reassuringly, "But, mein Führer —you will be coming back in a week or two, won't you?"

Hitler did not reply.

[6]In Berchtesgaden on July 9, 1944, Speer had chanced upon the army's Quartermaster General Wagner—who had just reported to Hitler on the equipment lost in the Center—and Generals Erich Fellgiebel, Helmuth Stieff, and Fritz Lindemann, who were conniving in a luxury hotel. Zeitzler was also in the hotel, "convalescing." "The hotel ambience of coffee and cigarettes formed a distasteful contrast to the topic under discussion," recorded Speer's office chronicler; "—namely the divisions lost on the Russian front . . . [Wagner] makes the problems in the east all seem so trivial and it is hard to understand why his comments as Quartermaster General do not show greater concern, as he is responsible for the all-important military supplies. Inroads like these into the armaments sphere would have had the Minister [Speer] speaking in a very serious tone of voice. But this afternoon the generals were nonchalantly referring to the various eastern situations as mere trifles." (All were plotting, and suffered the consequences.)

"Do You Recognize My Voice?"

"We got back to the Wolf's Lair yesterday," wrote Martin Bormann on July 15, 1944. "With its twenty-two-foot-thick bunkers it is now really a fortress of the most modern kind." As Hitler's Condor touched down at Rastenburg airfield, fifteen minutes' drive away, thousands of Todt Organization laborers were still working on the strengthening of the Führer's headquarters. The old site used for "Barbarossa" was now barely recognizable: the mammoth concrete bunkers rearing up out of the trees had been expertly camouflaged against enemy reconnaissance; there was grass on the flat roofs, and both natural and artificial trees. It was an idyllic setting. "How beautiful it is out here," one of Hitler's stenographers noted in his diary. "The whole site is resplendent with luscious greenery. The woods breathe a magnificent tranquillity. The wooden hutments, including ours, have meantime been heavily bricked-in to afford protection against bomb-splinters. We all feel well at ease here. It's become a second home to us."

As Hitler's bunker proper was still incomplete, he moved into the former guest bunker in the heart of a top security zone compound which had been wired-off in the southwest corner of Zone I since September 1943. The noon war conferences were accordingly transferred to one of the gray-painted wood and brick hutments some forty yards west of this temporary home; at one end of the hut a forty-foot-long conference room had been created by simply knocking down two partition walls. The room thus had windows on three sides—it was light and airy and filled with the fragrances of the surrounding woods.

This peaceful setting belied the grimness of the dark crisis into which Germany was descending. For the first time Keitel and Fromm—commander of the Replacement Army—had plunged into discussions with Bormann and the Party chiefs on command relationships in the likely event that the Reich itself became a battleground. The trickle of refugees from the east had become a flood. At long last Hitler had bowed to pressure to *implement* the doctrine of total war. Some of this pressure came from Speer, but most came from Goebbels and Bormann.

On about July 15 Hitler instructed Bormann's three-man "cabinet"[1] to summon the principal ministers to find ways of stepping up the Reich's defense effort still further. On July 18, Goebbels sent Hitler a long letter protesting the continued underexploitation of the Reich's vast manpower resources. "At this moment, with East Prussia preparing to defend her soil as best she can, every mail delivery here in Berlin brings fresh invitations from every corner of the Reich to official receptions, to parties, to games, or to displays that today do more harm than good." Red tape was choking the Wehrmacht and civil service. Goebbels scorned the ability of any three-man committee to undo the damage that the failure to implement total war had done to public feeling, and he reminded Hitler that in October 1926 he had not suggested using a "committee" to capture "Red Berlin" for the Nazi party. "My suggestion is this: give absolute power to one man you can trust for every problem requiring a rapid solution. . . . Every time I see you, I look into your eyes and face to see what your health is like. When you came to Berlin by plane for the state funeral of General Hube—risking death from American fighter or bomber aircraft—I was shaking with fear, I confess. I dare not think what might have happened. You alone, mein Führer, are our guarantee of victory."

This was unquestionably true. No man possessed the affection of and authority over the German people that Hitler did, even at this gloomy pass in their fortunes. If he succumbed now, nothing would halt the Soviet avalanche—least of all his querulous generals. The Red Army would stand astride the Rhine within a month. Yet the Germans waited for Hitler's ultimate appeal, an appeal he seemed ashamed to issue. Goebbels besought him: "By calling all England to arms after Dunkirk did Churchill thereby condemn her to die? And Stalin—when he proclaimed during our advance on Moscow 'Better to die on your feet than live on your knees!'—did he imperil the whole USSR? On the contrary!" Joseph Goebbels, propaganda minister and veteran of the Party struggle since its earliest days, reminded Hitler he had always stood at his side in his hour of need.

"Our return was very timely," wrote Martin Bormann on July 15. "Surprisingly, this war has shown with increasing clarity that it is the Führer and his Party faithfuls who are inspired by a savage determination to keep fighting and resisting, rather than the military—among whom passion and intensity ought to have increased with their rank. The Führer has had to come here in person to stiffen the often shamefully weak-kneed attitude of the officers and hence their troops."

The optimism of the "Party faithfuls" was certainly limitless. Himmler, who

[1]See page 471.

visited Hitler that day, was soon writing to Kaltenbrunner: "How are we going to rule and pacify Russia when we reconquer large parts of her, as we certainly shall in the next years?" Jodl shared Bormann's criticisms of the army generals' defeatism. The German civilian public was showing far greater courage, though it had far worse to suffer. In East Prussia everybody from university professors to fifteen-year-olds had rallied to Gauleiter Koch's call to build defenses and fortifications. A dispiriting torrent of disorganized army units and refugee columns was making for the Reich frontiers, and Hitler had to issue stern orders before the rot became an outright rout. He ordered a new defensive line rapidly built along the entire eastern front, following the rivers San and Vistula to the Warsaw bridgehead, and then the Narev and a line forward of the Reich frontier to the Baltic; but it was touch-and-go whether there would be either the manpower to build it or the troops to man it before the Russian avalanche swept westward into Germany.

Fifteen new "grenadier divisions" ordered by Hitler were being raised in the Reich. The army had issued the first order over General Stieff's signature on July 8, but Hitler wanted more urgency, and a week later, on July 15, he summoned to the Wolf's Lair both General Fromm and his Chief of Staff—the colonel with the now familiar yellow briefcase. Most midday war conferences here were interminably long and the humid air was heavy with recriminations, as Hitler saw no way of checking the present trend until the autumn at least, when Germany might well regain fighter and U-boat supremacy. But this conference lasted only half an hour, from 1:10 to 1:40 P.M., as a special session on the reconstitution of the shattered eastern front followed until 2:20 P.M. Hitler cold-heartedly laid down that the refugee families were to be stopped east of the new line and the able-bodied members diverted to the fortification works. Nothing else could stop the Bolshevik hordes. "Things are pretty grim here," wrote Martin Bormann three days later. "The Russians are at Augustov near the East Prussian frontier, and if their armored units press on any farther, we've got nothing to stop them with for the time being. . . . The new divisions which are being formed still lack the necessary antitank weapons! . . . We have plenty of worries, and it's a good thing that the Führer is here." On July 19, Hitler ordered two East Prussian divisions raised from the province's elderly home guard. In this connection Fromm's Chief of Staff was detailed to report to Hitler the next day.

In France the Allies were mercilessly bombing and strafing the Germans containing the beachhead. For the first time napalm bombs were being used, and flame-throwing tanks of immense range were incinerating the inmates of the stubborn pillbox bunkers. Late on July 17, Field Marshal Kluge telephoned with the shattering news that Rommel's car had been strafed by an Allied plane; the driver had crashed into a ditch and Rommel's skull had been split; he would be in the hospital for many months.[2] The next day two thousand bombers hit the stronghold built by Rommel at Caen. Over two thousand French civilians were found dead in the ruins by British troops when they advanced on the nineteenth.

Hitler's world was thus beginning to crash. In Italy the German Fourteenth Army pulled out of Leghorn (Livorno). In Denmark Communist resistance cells were waging overt partisan warfare, and they aggravated the crisis by calling a general strike. Reich Commissioner Werner Best had ignored Hitler's instructions to deal with the terrorists *sub rosa,* as formal trial and execution just created martyrs; to Best and Ribbentrop the Führer grumbled, "You gentlemen always want to be smarter than I am!" When Best interjected, "May I say something?" Hitler replied, "I don't want to hear it. Get out!"

In Hungary too there were still ominous rumblings of distant thunder: a pro-German prime minister, General Döme Sztójay, had replaced Kállay in March, but Horthy and his advisers had maintained their clamor for Hitler to withdraw the German troops from Hungary. Horthy had still not kept his part of the Klessheim bargain—the total expulsion of the Jews from Hungary; moreover, after July 8 he refused to deport any more Jews, and a few days later he announced his intention of replacing Sztójay by a military regime. Ribbentrop telegraphed Hitler's furious reply to Budapest on July 17, after Hitler had consulted with Himmler again on the Hungarian Jews: "The Führer expects the Hungarian government to take action against the Budapest Jews forthwith and without further delay." Otherwise he would withdraw his approval of certain exceptions from the expulsion order—artists, musicians, and notably forty-six members of the Manfréd-Weiss industrial family, who had leased their important factory in Hungary to the Hermann Göring works in May in return for exit visas. But now Himmler's ghastly secret was coming out, for two Slovak Jews had escaped from Auschwitz extermination camp, and their horrifying revelations were published in two reputable Swiss newspapers early in July. Horthy refused to deport the Jews from Budapest; instead, he announced that a general would bring Hitler a letter on July 21.

The reasons for Hitler's discontent were therefore manifold. His irritation was such that on July 18 he dismissed one of his adjutants, SS Colonel Fritz Darges, transferring him to the eastern front because of a minor incident in the conference

[2]Rommel had been earmarked for a British assassination operation a few days later anyway. There are papers in secret British files on this.

hut.[3] He lunched in his bunker that day virtually alone, as always now, sharing the vegetarian repast with his secretary Fräulein Christa Schroeder. He was ill at ease, and he exclaimed, "Nothing must happen to me now, because there is nobody else who could take over!" He had premonitions of trouble; two days later he admitted to Mussolini that he had first experienced them during the flight to the Wolf's Lair on the fourteenth. At lunch with Fräulein Schroeder he commented uneasily, "There is something in the air."

There were several abscesses of opposition, but they were hard to identify and lance. Perhaps Hitler had learned through Himmler's agents of the current wave of rumors about an imminent attempt on his life. (On July 29 he was to say, "I admit I long expected an assassination attempt.") But from which quarter? He was cool toward the Prussian Junkers and the nobility, but they had served Germany well in the past. The field marshals or generals? Some, like General Fellgiebel, Chief of Signals, were conspicuous by their hostile remarks, but as Jodl was to note on the twenty-fourth: "The Führer always good-naturedly overlooked them and held a protecting hand over them." More likely assassins were the civilians—like ex-Mayor Carl Goerdeler of Leipzig, for whom the Gestapo had just asked Himmler to authorize an arrest warrant. Alternatively, the enemy might launch a paratroop attack right here, on the Wolf's Lair itself; Himmler discussed this very possibility with Hitler on the fifteenth. An entire battalion was concealed in the woods with tanks and both assault and antiaircraft guns; the very enticing green lawns of the Security Zones were in fact deadly minefields—but the possibility of enemy paratroop attack always remained.

Rommel's Army Group B now considered that the enemy had landed forty divisions in France and that about as many more were still available in Britain. By late on July 18 the enemy breakthrough east of Caen called for urgent remedial action. Three thousand Allied fighters and fighter-bombers were roaming the battlefield and supply roads as far as the Seine. Saturation bombing had taken a heavy toll of German tanks and men. Kluge telephoned early on July 19 to demand that the 116th Panzer Division be withdrawn from the Fifteenth Army and thrown into the breach. Hitler authorized this immediately, thus accepting for the first time that the Fifteenth Army was waiting for an invasion of the Pas de Calais that might never come. After a long talk that night with Schmundt and Keitel, he instructed Field Marshal Kluge to take permanent command of Rommel's army group as well, "as no other suitable person can be found." Kluge telephoned Keitel at noon: "Without doubt we've got a crisis here on our hands."

[3]The deeper reason was that Fritz Darges had broken off his relationship with Eva Braun's sister Gretl; she had then married Himmler's liaison officer, Hermann Fegelein, on June 3.

He said he was planning to address his senior commanders immediately behind the battlefront the next morning, July 20. "Good luck," said Keitel. "Take care of yourself!" Hitler trusted Kluge implicitly.

These were Hitler's principal worries that day, therefore: the threat to East Prussia and Silesia; the possible loss of France; the proclamation of total war designed to mobilize Germany's untapped resources; the seemingly unavoidable defection of Hungary. Nor were Germany's relations with Italy satisfactory: they were burdened by the continued internment of a million Italian troops and the annexation of the northern provinces. For political reasons Hitler had conceded to Mussolini the right to raise four new divisions of troops loyal to fascism. The first two, equipped with the best German weaponry, were at this very moment being inspected by Mussolini and Marshal Graziani in Germany, but on July 19, Hitler tentatively decided to disband all four divisions. On consideration, he felt that no good could come of them and that their German training personnel and equipment were badly needed for the new German divisions. He sent Bodenschatz to air this suggestion with Graziani: perhaps the Italian troops could be used for the antiaircraft defenses of key German factories instead. Mussolini himself was due to arrive at the Wolf's Lair after lunch on July 20. Bodenschatz reported to Hitler that morning that Graziani had not taken to the idea at all. Hitler replied, "Come and join the war conference with me."

The conference had been brought forward thirty minutes, to 12:30 P.M., because of the Duce's visit. Schaub arrived about 12:25 P.M. to tell him that the officers were assembled. As Hitler walked the forty yards to the gray conference hut, he saw Warlimont and various other officers waiting outside; the others were already in the oppressively hot conference room. General Heusinger, standing to his right, began briefing him on the eastern front. Shortly afterward, Keitel arrived, accompanied by General Buhle—who was an armaments expert—an adjutant, and Fromm's Chief of Staff, the colonel with the black eyepatch and yellow briefcase. "Mein Führer," Keitel announced, "this is Colonel Count Schenk von Stauffenberg, who is to brief you on the new divisions." He stepped back a pace to the left of Hitler, his customary position. Hitler shook the colonel's mutilated hand, then resumed his seat on a wicker stool, his back to the door, facing the open windows. Once he asked Buhle for a detail and the general suggested that Stauffenberg might reply; but to his evident chagrin the colonel had stepped outside. There were now twenty-four men in the room. From the other side of the heavy trestle table, the Luftwaffe Chief of Staff, General Korten, was just referring to an air reconnaissance report, and Hitler leaned across the maps, propping himself on his right elbow; there was a bunch of pencils in his right hand and in his left a magnifying glass with which to read the fine print.

For Hitler, this was the dividing instant of time between an old world and a new one. At that instant a blinding sheet of dazzling yellow flame engulfed him as two pounds of explosives detonated less than six feet away. His back was half turned to the blast, but his impression was that it came from just to the right of Colonel Heinz Brandt, Heusinger's chief assistant, who was waiting to lay out fresh situation maps. "The swine are bombing us!" thought Hitler as the blast wave caught him. He heard a distinct double-crack—probably the initial blast, and then the noise of his own eardrums bursting. Dense, opaque smoke filled the room. He found himself lying near the left doorjamb; he was covered with lathes and timbers from the ceiling, he could feel his hair and clothes on fire, and his right elbow was hurting savagely. As the choking fumes parted, his smarting eyes made out disheveled figures groping in the wreckage, and faces contorted by screams of pain which he could not hear. Perhaps an enemy paratroop attack had begun! If he tried to get out of the windows, he might blunder straight into their guns. He painfully extricated himself and stumbled into the corridor, beating out the flames on his ragged black trousers. He felt blood trickling down his legs and out of his ears. With his plaster-caked hair standing on end, he felt he must look like "a baboon"; but he was alive.

Supported by Keitel, who like a doused poodle had just shaken his towering frame free of debris, he limped out of the hut's middle exit as charred documents spiraled down from the sky and guards converged on him. Horribly maimed men were being carried out of the wrecked conference room and laid on the grass as Otto Günsche, his bodyguard, led the Führer back to his bunker. "Somebody must have thrown a hand grenade into the room," exclaimed Hitler; but the sentries had seen nobody. While a manservant ran for Dr. Morell, Hitler sat down unsteadily and took his own pulse—pleased at his self-composure. Then he thrust his injured arm inside his tunic, Napoleon-style, to ease the pain. His secretaries came in, and he grinned at them. "Well, ladies, things turned out well again!" Then he withdrew to his bedroom, walking taller and more cheerfully than he had for some time. Morell and the surgeon Hasselbach removed the shredded trousers, revealing that the skin on the lower third of both thighs had been badly torn by the explosions; altogether they removed over a hundred splinters of the fragmented oaken trestle from his legs. His face had been cut in a score of places by flying splinters, and his forehead was scarred by a falling roof timber. He began to mutter that this incident would give him the long-wanted opportunity of dealing with his critics, and the prospect evidently pleased him.

"It was the work of a coward!" he exclaimed, his mind still grappling with the identity of the perpetrator. "Probably one of the Todt Organization workmen installed a bomb." He sent guards out to search for the hidden fuse cable and for possible additional bombs. He instructed his press chief to telephone Dr. Goebbels, and he sent his Luftwaffe adjutant, Colonel von Below, bloodstained and deafened, to the telephone exchange a hundred yards away to summon Göring —who had stayed away that day as he could not abide Mussolini—and Himmler.

He ordered absolute secrecy about the incident. Below returned after having removed all the jacks from the telephone switchboard and forbidden the telephonists to go near them. But presently Hitler learned that the blast wave had evidently originated *above* floor level. Moreover, only a handful of officers had known that the war conference would be brought forward because of Mussolini's visit. And that yellow flame could only be from an English explosive. Whatever the truth, Himmler and the Gestapo investigators summoned with Kaltenbrunner from Berlin would find it out.

At about 1:15 P.M. he reemerged into the warm sunshine, wearing a fresh uniform over bandages covering all injuries but those to his head. To General Fellgiebel, the signals chief, whom he espied strolling deliberately up and down outside the security zone's perimeter fence, Hitler must have appeared unscathed. He sent for Colonel Ludolf Sander, his own headquarters signals chief, and asked for arrangements to be made for him to broadcast to the German people as soon as possible; but it would take several hours for the sound truck to arrive from Königsberg. Now Hitler learned of the carnage the explosion had caused. Those who had been on his right hand had suffered the worst: Colonel Heinz Brandt had lost a foot, the stenographer Heinrich Berger had lost both legs, Korten had been impaled by a jagged table fragment, Schmundt had ghastly leg injuries and an eye gouged out; nobody had escaped the burns and blast entirely. Stenographer Berger's colleague had been able to talk with him—Berger hoped he would survive but committed his wife and children to his friend's care if he should not. Hitler appointed Berger to a high civil-service grade forthwith, so that the widow could draw a pension—a provident gesture, for Berger died in agony that afternoon.

Hitler drew fresh energy from his narrow escape from death. Had he believed in God, he would have credited the Almighty with this miracle. His private secretary, Christa Schroeder, vividly recalled those hours, under later interrogation:

> I did not expect that July 20, 1944, to be called in for lunch with him after the assassination attempt. But nonetheless I was sent for to join him. I was astounded to see how fresh he looked, and how spritely he stepped toward me. He described to me how his servants had reacted to the news: [Heinz] Linge was indignant, Arndt had begun to cry. Then he said, verbatim, "Believe me, this is the turning point for Germany. From now on things will look up again. I'm glad the *Schweinehunde* have unmasked themselves!"
>
> I told him he couldn't possibly meet the Duce now. "On the contrary!" he retorted, "I must—what would the world press say if I did not!"

"Duce, I have just had the most enormous stroke of good fortune," Hitler said in greeting to the Italian dictator as he emerged from his train at 2:30 P.M. He had brought his entire staff to the local railroad station—Himmler, Keitel, Göring, Ribbentrop, and Bormann were all there. Security Zone I was packed with SS officers and armored vehicles which had crawled out of the woods. The Führer and the Duce drove to the shattered conference hut and inspected the gaping hole in the floor and the buckled floors of the adjacent rooms, where the blast wave had come up through the floor cavity. It was now that Martin Bormann brought to Hitler the corporal who had tended the telephone outside the conference room. This man had seen an officer leave in a hurry just before the explosion, a colonel with one arm; in fact he had left his briefcase, cap, and belt in the hut. The army officers had angrily rejected the corporal's implied libel on the worthy Colonel von Stauffenberg, but Bormann had taken him seriously. Stauffenberg certainly was nowhere to be found. Perhaps he had flown to Russia?

Suspicion against him hardened during the afternoon. The Gestapo investigators found shreds of the yellow leather briefcase embedded in the wreckage. Stauffenberg had bluffed his way past the cordons and left Rastenburg airfield at 1:13 P.M., ostensibly for Berlin's Rangsdorf airfield; but he had not arrived there. Moreover, shortly before four o'clock his chief, General Fromm, telephoned Keitel from Berlin and said that rumors were flying around the capital and ought he declare a state of emergency? "The Führer is alive. There is no cause whatever for that. Is Stauffenberg in Berlin?" Keitel rasped. Fromm, taken aback, replied, "No, I thought he was at Führer Headquarters." Keitel promised to keep him up-to-date. Almost at once the Wolf's Lair began monitoring the most extraordinary orders emanating from Fromm's Bendlerstrasse office to the territorial army commands *(Wehrkreise)*, proclaiming a state of emergency by the code word "Valkyrie." By telephone too the commands were being instructed that Field Marshal Erwin von Witzleben, Rundstedt's predecessor, was now Supreme Commander of the Wehrmacht and that he had appointed General Erich Hoepner commander of home forces.[4] These were names from the past indeed.

The emergence from obscurity of these forgotten, forcibly retired, or cashiered army officers could only mean that an army putsch was being attempted in Berlin. Hitler forthwith accepted Himmler's proposal that the Gestapo be given powers to arrest army officers. Since Fromm was *prima facie* one of the conspirators, Hitler neatly legalized the move by appointing Himmler his successor, thus giving the SS leader control over all army units in the Reich; a secretary typed the decree, Hitler signed it, and with this and Hitler's specific directive to restore order, Himmler and Kaltenbrunner took off by plane for Berlin at once. Himmler's mission was a delicate one. He felt he had been chosen not as the army's arch rival, that is, as Reichsführer SS, but "as the Führer's loyal thane, as a soldier,

[4]The conspirators had not realized that a special network fed all orders issued to the Wehrkreise to the Führer's headquarters automatically as well. This slip was crucial to the crushing of the putsch.

as a National Socialist, and as a *Germanic* German," as he put it; but would the army see it that way? Hitler had ordered him on no account to allow his Waffen SS to come into direct confrontation with the army; that would be the first step toward the ultimate tragedy of civil war.

Keitel's energetic countermeasures crushed the putsch in the provinces before it even began. At 4:15 P.M. his dramatic message went out to the Wehrkreise: "Most Immediate! . . . The Führer is alive! Safe and sound! Reichsführer SS new commander of Replacement Army, only his orders valid. Do not obey orders issued by General Fromm, Field Marshal von Witzleben, or General (ret.) Hoepner! Maintain contact with local Gauleiter and police commander!" Shortly afterward, General Helmuth Stieff telephoned Keitel on the orders of the army Quartermaster General, Eduard Wagner, at Zossen. Fromm's office was proclaiming that the army had taken power; at 4 P.M., said Stieff, Stauffenberg, and General Ludwig Beck—the army Chief of Staff Hitler had dismissed in 1938—had phoned Wagner from Berlin.[5] Beck was claiming to have "taken over"; Witzleben, the "new Supreme Commander," was said to be on his way to Zossen at that moment.

Toward five o'clock this was confirmed beyond doubt. A long telegram signed by Witzleben (and countersigned by Stauffenberg) was monitored, being transmitted to the Wehrkreis commands. It exploited the overwhelming loyalty of these officers to Hitler by suggesting that not they but Party malcontents were behind the putsch. The telegram was timed 4:45 P.M.:

> I. Internal unrest. An unscrupulous clique of combat-shy Party leaders has exploited the situation to stab the hard-pressed armies in the back and seize power for their own selfish purposes.
> II. In this hour of supreme danger the Reich government has declared martial law to preserve law and order, and appointed me Supreme Commander of the Wehrmacht with absolute executive authority.

Long, detailed instructions for the incorporation of the Waffen SS, the "elimination" of the Gestapo, and the ruthless breaking of any opposition followed. Accordingly, a warning was radioed by Hitler's HQ to Himmler's aircraft to divert to a Berlin airfield heavily guarded by reliable SS troops. Field Marshal Model, commanding Army Group Center, telephoned: he had received from Bendlerstrasse an order commencing "The Führer Adolf Hitler is dead"—but he had refused to obey it. Hitler sent for his press chief and ordered a succinct communiqué broadcast to the people. It would announce: "A bomb attack was

[5]Stauffenberg did not reach the war ministry in Bendlerstrasse until about 4:30 P.M., as he had cautiously landed elsewhere than at Rangsdorf airfield, only to find neither car, driver, nor gasoline waiting there for the drive into the city; this evidently cost him ninety minutes' delay.

made on the Führer today. . . . Apart from minor burns and bruises the Führer was uninjured. He resumed work immediately afterward and—as planned—received the Duce for a lengthy discussion."

The Italian visitors had been treated almost like embarrassments by their hosts. Hitler had subjected Mussolini to the usual impressive statistics of Speer's forthcoming production of tanks, guns, and ammunition, and had secretly confided that fighter-aircraft output would soon reach 5,000 per month compared with the 3,400 turned out by the Allies. The V-1 was a triumph, and soon there would be a V-2. He was resolved to "raze London to the ground"—and "after August, September, or October" the new secret U-boats would also enter service.

At five o'clock tea was served in the headquarters mess. Hitler began to brood; Ribbentrop began to blame the generals for Germany's plight; the generals blamed Ribbentrop and Dönitz, and somebody tactlessly referred to the Röhm purge of June 1934.

After a while Julius Schaub was called to the telephone. Hitler's personal adjutant, Alwin-Broder Albrecht, was calling from the Reich Chancellery: strange events were afoot in Berlin. A detachment of the Guards Battalion had just tried to occupy the Chancellery. Streetcars were rattling through the government quarter without halting. The whole area was being cordoned off by troops. Simultaneously, Joseph Goebbels telephoned on his private line from Berlin. The Party "commissar" attached to the Guards Battalion had just revealed to him that its commander, Major Otto Ernst Remer, had been instructed to occupy the government quarter. "Has the army gone mad?" the propaganda minister asked Hitler. At six o'clock the dissidents began issuing a new telegram to the Wehrkreise, this time signed by "General Fromm."[6] The commanders were being instructed to "secure" all radio and communications stations and arrest all ministers and leading Party and police officials. The concentration camps were to be occupied (but no prisoners were to be released as yet).

Hitler began to fear he was losing control of events in Berlin. He telephoned Goebbels to find out when the radio communiqué announcing his survival would be broadcast. Goebbels replied that he was sitting on it until he had composed a fitting commentary to go with it. Hitler exploded in anger. "I didn't ask you for a commentary. I just want the news broadcast as fast as possible!" At 6:28 P.M. the radio service was interrupted with the startling news flash. This dealt the first body-blow to the putsch, for a *live* Hitler's word was still law.

The awkward tea party with Mussolini continued until about seven o'clock.

[6]Fromm had not in fact signed the order.

Then the doors were opened and he was ushered out into the light drizzle. "The Duce's cloak!" ordered Hitler. Then they parted, never to meet again. Almost immediately, Goebbels was on the telephone again, this time with a highly suspicious Major Remer at his side—unable to discern whether his own army superiors or the wily propaganda minister was attempting to overthrow Hitler. Hitler was heard shouting into the telephone, demanding to know why Himmler had not yet arrived in Berlin. But with his ears deafened, the Führer could hardly hear the answers, so he asked to speak to Remer himself. "Major Remer, can you hear—do you recognize my voice?" Remer had spent forty-five minutes with him some months before, collecting the Oak Leaf cluster for bravery; once heard, Hitler's voice was unforgettable. "Major Remer," continued Hitler, "they tried to kill me, but I'm alive. Major Remer, I'm speaking to you as your Supreme Commander. Only my orders are to be obeyed. You are to restore order in Berlin for me. Use whatever force you consider necessary. Shoot anybody who tries to disobey my orders." This was the second, deadliest blow to the plot—for it enabled Hitler to use the army itself to put down the conspiracy.

Hours of suspense passed at the Wolf's Lair, while Keitel and Bormann telephoned and cabled orders to every command, canceling the plotters' moves. The injuries began to tell on Hitler's physique. He slumped into a chair, morosely consuming quantities of colored pastilles from a dish in front of him. "I am beginning to doubt that the German people is worthy of my genius," he exclaimed—a sullen outburst that provoked a clamor of loyal protestations. Dönitz reminded him of the navy's achievements. Göring could not match this, so he picked a quarrel with Ribbentrop, who retorted, "*I* am still the foreign minister, and my name is *von* Ribbentrop!" Göring brandished his marshal's baton at him. Hitler named General Guderian to succeed the ostensibly "sick" Zeitzler as Chief of the General Staff, and he assigned the youthful General Walther Wenck—a tough Chief of Staff from an eastern front army group—to take the injured General Heusinger's place. Martin Bormann meanwhile purveyed what scanty information he could to the Gauleiters, using his modern teleprinter linkup.[7] "The reactionary criminal vermin evidently staged the attack on the Führer and his loyal officers in conjunction with the National Committee 'Free Germany' in Moscow (General von Seydlitz and Count [Haubold von] Einsiedel). Should the attack succeed, the generals' clique comprising Fromm, [Friedrich] Olbricht, and Hoepner would take over power and make peace with Moscow; that this so-called

[7]This was another circuit the plotters had failed to immobilize. They had duly "secured" the Berlin radio building, but nobody had instructed this army detail as to what to do then—let alone interrupt the programs broadcast. These were the officers who criticized Hitler's generalship. "They should have gone to school with us Nazis," Hitler scoffed to Schaub. "Then they would have learned how to do it!"

peace would cost the German people their lives is obvious. That the attempt has misfired means the salvation of Germany, because now the hopes reposed in these traitorous generals have been smashed for good." And at 9:40 P.M. Bormann warned the Gauleiters: "A General Beck wants to take over the government. The one-time Field Marshal von Witzleben is posing as the Führer's successor. Of course no National Socialist Gauleiter will allow himself to be taken in by, or accept orders from, these criminals, who are just miniature worms in format."

Dining with his secretaries in his bunker that evening, Hitler voiced his anger at the assassins. "What cowards! If they had drawn a gun on me, I might still respect them. But they didn't dare risk their own lives." He snorted: "The idiots cannot even imagine the chaos there would be if the reins slipped out of my grasp. I'm going to make an example of them that will make anybody else think twice about betraying the German people. . . . These criminals! They don't realize that our enemies are planning to destroy Germany so thoroughly that she can never rise again." At the 10 P.M. war conference, Hitler began by expressing his regrets to the two duty stenographers over the death of their colleague. As a reaction to the murder attempt, he ordered a particularly violent V-1 attack on London during the night—to show that he was less inclined to compromise than ever.

The radio sound-truck from Königsberg had now arrived. Hitler's entire staff assembled in the teahouse at 11:30 P.M.—General Jodl with a white bandage around his head, Keitel with bandaged hands, others with sticking plasters; many men were missing. In a voice trembling with anger and emotion, Hitler recorded a fiery speech to the nation "So that you can hear my voice . . .":

> A minuscule clique of ambitious, unscrupulous officers of criminal stupidity has been plotting to get rid of me and to liquidate virtually the entire German Wehrmacht command staff at the same time. The bomb was placed by Colonel Count von Stauffenberg and exploded six feet away to my right. Several of my dear colleagues were gravely injured, one has died. I myself am completely uninjured apart from a few minor scratches, bruises, and burns. I regard this as a fresh confirmation of the mission given me by Providence to continue toward my goal. . . .

The speech was broadcast ninety minutes later. By that time Hitler had heard from a general who had escaped from the Bendlerstrasse building that Stauffenberg and Olbricht had locked Fromm in an office after he had refused to believe that Hitler was dead; Stauffenberg had sworn to the assembled staff officers that he "had seen the Führer's corpse being carried past on a stretcher."[8] Many

[8] "Keitel is lying," Stauffenberg assured Olbricht and Hoepner. He had seen an explosion like the impact of a 150-millimeter shell and doctors running over. "Hardly anybody can have survived!"—This emerged from the trials and interrogations.

idealists were eventually propelled to the hangman's noose by this easy lie, but Stauffenberg had nothing more to lose. Already the arrest-list was swelling: General Fellgiebel's very presence, uninvited, at the Wolf's Lair had compromised him; Keitel sent for him at midnight and arrested him. Hitler was mystified that the army's Chief of Signals had failed to gun him down when their eyes had met that very afternoon, as Hitler strolled with Schaub outside his bunker. "There he was, ambling up and down like a lamb, as though he'd had nothing to do with this conspiracy!" In Vienna and Prague the dissidents' orders had been largely carried out. In Paris the military governor had actually put the Gestapo and SS chiefs under lock and key, until Hitler's broadcast revealed the hollowness of Stauffenberg's claim. The position of Field Marshal von Kluge was ambiguous, for in an instant of black comedy the loyal General Hermann Reinecke, attempting to telephone General Fromm that evening, had found the doomed General Beck on the line, and Beck had imagined he had reached Kluge in France ("Kluge, is that you?"). Witzleben telephoned Keitel from his hideout during the night; the OKW chief kept him talking long enough to find out where he was, and then ordered his arrest too. A telegram from Fromm in the small hours spelled out the end of the putsch:

> Attempted putsch by irresponsible generals has been bloodily put down. All the ringleaders shot. . . . I have resumed control, after having been temporarily held under armed arrest.

Undeceived, Hitler ordered General Fromm's arrest as well. At 3:40 A.M. Martin Bormann circulated the triumphant teleprinter message to the Gauleiters: "The traitors' action can be regarded as at an end." Dizzy with euphoria, Hitler retired to bed.

Hitler saw the day's events as a temporary aberration, the product of a wayward clique of disgruntled army officers—a kind of blood poisoning which the army would get out of its own system. The perpetrators had been "shot by the army's own battalions," the press announced in special editions the next day—an infelicitous choice of words which caused many ordinary Germans to ask just how large the "minuscule clique" of traitors was? The Führer pushed the occurrence itself out of his mind, after emotionally sending the torn gray uniform jacket and black trousers to Eva Braun as a memento (they still exist). Himmler would no doubt see that the guilty did not escape unpunished.

Remarkably, the Allies had failed to exploit the hiatus in High Command operations; but the situation in France was already grave enough, and the bulging Normandy beachhead might burst into the rest of France at any moment. From Field Marshal Kluge's forward headquarters at La Roche-Guyon—Rommel's old HQ—a special courier arrived in the Wolf's Lair with two top-secret letters. The first was a letter from Kluge dated July 21; it endorsed the second—a strong recommendation by Rommel, written on July 15, that Hitler end the war. Rommel complained vigorously that although he had lost 97,000 men since June 6, he had been sent only 6,000 replacements; 225 tanks had been lost, but only 17 replaced. His infantry divisions lacked artillery, armor-piercing weapons, and above all bazookas. Given the enemy's harrowing air supremacy, their breakthrough into France was inevitable. "Our troops are fighting heroically all along the line, but the unequal battle is nearing its end. In my view you should draw the necessary conclusions. I feel bound as the army group's Commander in Chief to say this quite bluntly." Kluge's letter made its point in the words, "Unfortunately the field marshal's view is right." Nonetheless he had concluded a speech to his generals south of Caen the day before thus: "We must stand fast, and if there should be no way to turn the tide in our favor, then we must die honorably on the field of battle!"

Hitherto Hitler had worshiped Günther Hans von Kluge: physically and mentally alert, with an erudite high forehead, he was known through the army as "*kluge* Hans"—clever Hans. But evidently he and Rommel still did not appreciate, said Hitler a few days later, that this was Germany's fight for her destiny—"a struggle which cannot be discharged or disposed of by negotiation, by 'clever' politics, or by tactical sleight-of-hand." Obviously it was a temptation for Kluge to withdraw his hard-pressed armies from Normandy to some more distant line of defense, though such a line would certainly be far longer; but Hitler told Jodl on July 31: "If we lose France, we lose the basis of our U-boat campaign." Moreover, France was Germany's last source of tungsten—indispensable for high-grade steel manufacture and electronic equipment. It was pointless for his generals to calculate how they might better employ the Normandy divisions elsewhere in the west. Most were immobilized by lack of transportation; of the rest only a few would ever reach whatever new line the generals might propose to defend. Thus Kluge and his generals—Rommel, of course, was still hospitalized—must stand fast where they were until Göring had recovered at least partial air supremacy for the Luftwaffe in the west.

Nonetheless, Hitler also prepared for the worst. On July 23, spurred perhaps by these two letters, he ordered the West Wall fortifications which had been built in 1938 and 1939 to be readied for the defense of Germany. Two days later the Allied offensive began in Normandy. The British thrust toward Falaise was halted by a countermove of the First SS Panzer Corps, but late on the thirtieth the Americans managed to punch a dangerous hole through the line at the coastal town of Avranches. Hitler and Jodl now began secret deliberations envisaging the total loss of France, while resolved to insist that Kluge must defend the Normandy line to the utmost. The upshot was that Hitler instructed the OKW to prepare the Somme-Marne-Saône-Jura line for immediate occupation in the event of a collapse. (Hitler had ordered Rundstedt to reconnoiter this line ten months before.)[9] Hitler displayed the ability to reach hard decisions: if need be he would sacrifice the entire Balkans to recover enough military strength to defend Germany's last conquests elsewhere. Meanwhile he must inflict months of delay on the Allies; strong garrisons commanded by officers of proven courage and resourcefulness must be sacrificed to defend the main French ports and deprive the enemy of their use; the French railways must be destroyed down to the last freight car and track tie. On no account was any hint of these "horrific" strategic decisions to reach the army group headquarters in France, for who knew how many traitors still lurked there, waiting to pass the word to the enemy? After all, the military commander of France, General Carl-Heinrich von Stülpnagel, had made common cause with the putschists of July 20. "Let's be quite clear on one score," Hitler expounded to Jodl. "The tide in France cannot turn until we manage—even just for a short time—to regain air superiority." Meanwhile the French population watched and waited in the wings: now they began to rejoice at each enemy battle victory.

Hitler's ambition to regain the strategic initiative in the autumn was not pure fantasy. He had asked Göring to amass a great secret reserve of fighter aircraft, and he hoped some day to throw two thousand fighters into the struggle for France. Six new Mark XXI submarines had been delivered in July, and 144 were to have been built by the end of 1944. This was why the coming battles in the west must not go against Germany. Hitler himself would fly west to take command as he had in 1940—but his damaged eardrums made it impossible for him to fly anywhere for many days to come: the constant roaring and the pressure differences might provoke an inner-ear infection. "Obviously, if all the dams burst, I would do anything and wouldn't care—I'd go as gunner in a single-engined plane to get there as fast as possible. . . . Normally, I should have gone to bed for ten or fourteen days, but every day I've had to work at least eight hours not even counting the hours of reading of dispatches. . . . Apart from that the miracle is that the shock got rid of my nerve complaint almost entirely. My left leg still trembles somewhat if conferences go on too long, but previously this leg used to shake in bed. With this shock, that's vanished almost completely—not that I would recommend this kind of remedy."

The assassin's bomb had affected Hitler more than he liked to admit. On July 21 he suffered violent ear pains, and his right ear began to bleed. His eyes constantly

[9]A rare foresight by Hitler: see page 580.

flicked to the right (nystagmus); alone in his bunker, he kept thinking he was falling over to the right. That evening he went for a short walk in the twilight and twice found himself wandering off the path. There was a constant taste of blood in his mouth. An army ear-nose-and-throat expert, Dr. Erwin Giesing, was fetched; Hitler confessed that he could not sleep despite Morell's Phanodorm tablets, and Giesing noticed that his voice was unnaturally loud and that he was lip-reading replies. The next day Giesing cauterized a large rupture to Hitler's right eardrum, and on July 23, Professor Carl von Eicken—a specialist who had operated on Hitler's vocal cords in 1935—came to find out why the ear was still bleeding despite the hemostatic pills and injections being administered by Morell. Hitler joked: "Perhaps I'm just a natural bleeder!" The next day he asked Giesing to cauterize the ear again regardless of the pain. "I stopped feeling pain long ago," he observed. "Besides, pain exists to make a man of you."

He visited the army hospital at Rastenburg and talked with Schmundt and the other adjutants injured in the blast. "There are you," he remarked to Admiral Heinz Assmann, "seriously injured—yet you were not the one that was marked down for assassination. These gentlemen were after me and only me: yet I escaped entirely. Four times in this war my enemies have tried to take my life, and now the Almighty has stayed their hands once again. This can have only one historical interpretation, that Providence has elected me to lead the German people." Thus he had redoubled his resolve to lead them on, "not to final defeat but to victory." Two of the hospital beds were empty: Günther Korten, Chief of Air Staff, had died of his injuries on July 22; and Colonel Brandt—promoted to General to benefit his widow—had succumbed the same day. Korten would get a state funeral, but not Brandt: Scherff, Hitler's court historian, had shared his ward and reported that in his delirium the colonel had complained at Stauffenberg's callousness in placing the bomb at his feet when he, Brandt, was one of the conspirators himself; Brandt had even incriminated Heusinger, but the latter swore on oath that the colonel was lying and thus survived.

Each day revealed fresh names of conspirators. Himmler, who had decided to arrest even those who had only the most marginal association with the conspiracy, was appalled to find the eventual list totaling over six thousand. Zeitzler's adjutant was arrested and contritely confessed. Virtually every section head of the army General Staff except Reinhard Gehlen (Foreign Armies East) and Rudolf Gercke (transport) was involved. The implication of Colonels Hansen and Roenne, the Intelligence chiefs in the west, seemed to throw light on many otherwise inexplicable failures; so did the sudden suicide of General Eduard Wagner, the army's quartermaster general, and the disappearance of General Lindemann, the director of artillery. Hitler became convinced that General Fellgiebel's signals organization had instantly flashed his secrets to the enemy and was still doing so, as the accuracy of the British-controlled Soldatensender Calais transmitter showed. "Fellgiebel must confess," he raged, "if he has to be skinned alive!" Even Arthur Nebe, the Gestapo department chief—who had been a guard of honor on Heydrich's bier in 1942—had vanished without trace, as had Carl Goerdeler, twice appointed mayor of Leipzig and then provided with an abundant pension by the Führer. Goerdeler's papers were located in a hotel safe; they revealed that Goerdeler had been chosen to succeed Hitler, and they listed additional conspirators; these were arrested, and fresh chain reactions were established by their interrogation. On July 23, Admiral Canaris was picked up by the Gestapo, but since both Keitel and Himmler intervened on his behalf, his early imprisonment was more comfortable than that of his fellow conspirators. Franz Halder and Hjalmar Schacht, prewar governor of the Reichsbank, were also pulled in, as their opposition to Hitler was well documented.

Meanwhile Bormann began showing Hitler the lengthy interrogation reports compiled by Kaltenbrunner's staff. Kaltenbrunner clearly did not intend to spare the Führer's feelings. "I could not bear to watch this man running amok," one conspirator (General Stieff) had blurted out; "smashing his own great works by his obstinacy: we are defending Kirkenes and Crete, but we shall be losing Königsberg and Cracow in the process!" A physical revulsion took hold of Hitler as he realized the true scope of the plot; over half the traitors were army officers, but there were also trade-union officials, lawyers, civil servants, academics, and clergy. Even Count Wolf Heinrich von Helldorf, the pre-1933 brownshirt rowdy and Jew-baiter whom Hitler had made police president of Berlin, now confessed to being one of Stauffenberg's minions—not because he opposed National Socialism, but because he despised its plebeian aura and its creation of a nonaristocratic elite. None of the prisoners had much clue as to what system they were proposing in Hitler's place. The army generals, he reasoned, had failed to appreciate his *political* imperatives, and the politicians had criticized his generalship. They questioned his orders for the rigid defense of the Demyansk pocket, the Donets bend, the Dnieper line, the Nikopol bridgehead, the Crimea, the Narva line, the Vitebsk salient, and the Cherkassy pocket; one after another these positions had been lost until by July 1944 the core of the German army was destroyed. They blamed him for these military reverses; but there was a class element too, for he was the son of an Austrian customs official to whom the officer corps felt bound by neither blood nor brotherhood.

Gradually, the Gestapo investigators reconstructed the assassination attempt. The yellow briefcase was pieced together from its fragments. An English time-fuse had been used to detonate the explosive, evidently from Abwehr stocks. A second package of explosive was found where Stauffenberg's adjutant had jettisoned it from their car as they sped back to the airfield; had it also been used, their plot might have succeeded. Stauffenberg had also carried the assassination implements to the Berghof on July 11 and to Rastenburg four days later, but he had used neither those weapons then nor the second explosive charge on the twentieth. The riddles would remain unanswered, for General Fromm had invited Beck to put a bullet in his brains, and he had rushed Stauffenberg and his adjutant in front of a firing squad before the Gestapo could get at them. "He wanted to silence Beck before he unmasked him as his accomplice," Hitler aggressively declared.

Count von Helldorf's full confession was handed to Hitler as he was once again being treated by Dr. Giesing. Helldorf had blamed General Olbricht, who had advised him that Hitler's vaunted secret weapons were a myth and that even the A-4 rocket would not enter service before 1945. "Who would have thought Helldorf was such a rat?" asked Hitler. "That he was irresponsible was obvious enough from his gambling debts. How often I had to settle them for him—four or five times, and never less than one hundred thousand marks! A gambler like that was bound to fall into the hands of enemy agents, and the British secret service no doubt settled even bigger debts on his behalf. I'm sorry for his wife and pleasant children," he added, laying the report aside. "But I must clean out this Augean stable with an iron broom, and there can be no mercy. If I don't wipe out these traitors now, there may be more *Schweinereien* later, and the poor German soldier in the trenches has to pay for their stupidity with his life. How thankful I am to Remer [the Berlin garrison commander]. . . . A few more fine, clear-thinking officers like him and I wouldn't have to worry about the future. But this yellow gang sends me an even yellower Stauffenberg from Berlin—if he'd at least had the courage to stay there with his briefcase! But no! It was a pity to waste even one bullet on him. I keep asking myself what they were all after. To stop the war and start peace talks with the enemy—with *these* Tom Thumbs as the government? Because this gang had neither the guts nor the gumption to fight on. As though Stalin or Churchill or Roosevelt would have been bothered one instant by our sudden desire for peace! In eight days the Russians would have been in Berlin and it would have been all over for Germany—for good."

Hitler's escape had once more brought the entire German population together; for many weeks their fury against the plotters was said to be intense. It was reported that army generals in Berlin had to conceal their uniforms beneath raincoats to escape the people's indignation. Goebbels opened a fund to enable people and troops alike to express their feelings. "I just heard the frightful news," a Viennese widow wrote to Hitler on the evening of July 20. "Hatred—a deep, indelible hatred—fills me against these wretched creatures! Did nothing happen to you, really? Mein Führer—you are all that is left to me in this world. I had a child, but he died in action in Russia at Mayevka. He had passed his examinations and had a place waiting at technical college. I had been saving up for this, but now he'll never return, my darling child! Take my money, out of joy that nothing befell the Führer." A lock of hair and a picture of the boy accompanied the letter.

Goebbels himself arrived at the Wolf's Lair on July 22 and asked that semidictatorial powers be given him.[10] Goebbels was deeply moved by Hitler's appearance. "He was just coming out of his little headquarters bunker, not weary, but relaxed, not bowed, but with his head slightly sunk—a picture to melt the sternest heart. At that moment I wished the entire German people could have seen him; nobody in Germany would ever have doubted again." Two days earlier, he and Speer had vigorously informed an audience of government officials that despite total war and the efforts of Gauleiter Sauckel, manpower was still being criminally wasted: 500,000 women were working as domestics. While Speer had 6,000,000 armaments workers, another 3,200,000 men were being soaked up by office work in government and industry. A preliminary conference with Bormann, Speer, and Goebbels preceded the full session on July 23 with Hitler, Göring, and Himmler. Goebbels promised to procure half a million more men immediately for the war effort. Hitler ordered Göring to appoint the propaganda minister "Reich Commissar for Total War Mobilization" and announced—despite the misgivings of his doctors—that he would speak to the Gauleiters in one week's time.

The plot's side effects on government opinion in wavering countries like Turkey, Finland, Romania, and Bulgaria must have been grave, but the psychological damage to Hitler was also vast. Though he claimed the contrary, he now trusted nobody. Robert Ley's broadcast blaming "blue-blooded swine" for plotting Hitler's death brought Field Marshal von Richthofen in full-dress regalia to the Wolf's Lair formally protesting this slur on his fellow aristocrats who had unquestioningly obeyed their oaths of allegiance; Hitler pointed to his adjutants *von* Below, *von* Puttkamer, and Erik *von* Amsberg, as proof that he valued men only for their accomplishments. However, he himself would soon be heard mimicking an aristocratic general (General von Schlieben of Cherbourg) justifying a decision to choose dishonorable captivity to the hero's death he had demanded of his troops: "After all, what harm can possibly come to us? We'll be taken prisoner and get decent treatment—particularly we who are of noble families. We won't get put together with those frightful plebs." And although Hitler himself signed an order forbidding any intemperate criticism of the officer corps, the generals, and the nobility at large, in private he regretfully speculated that Stalin had been right to purge his regular officer corps in 1937, and that in 1934 he would have done better to opt for the SA against the Reichswehr. Every officer who now came

[10]As he had in his letter of July 18. See page 658.

to his headquarters was frisked for hidden weapons before being allowed into his presence. His food was tasted and tested for poison, and his medicines were purchased only from approved SS clinics in Berlin. Hitler trusted nobody; he even ordered the still-uniformed and bemedaled corpses of Stauffenberg and the others allegedly shot in Berlin to be exhumed, lest the army had deceived him about their execution.

Treachery and treason became the only explanation he could find for his defeats. While the Sixth Army, fighting in the Carpathians, had more than enough bazookas, the Seventh and Fifteenth armies in France had barely any. "Who issues these weapons?" asked Hitler angrily. Keitel shrugged his shoulders. "That was the quartermaster general, Wagner." "Aha!" Hitler said triumphantly. "The swine! He did well to shoot himself, otherwise I would have hanged him. In the open countryside of the Ukraine we have bazookas in abundance. And in the hedgerows of Normandy where our troops can only ward off the enemy's superabundance of tanks with such bazookas, we have none! He did it on purpose —it was treason!" He exclaimed, "These criminals won't go before a court-martial, because their accomplices will preside and spin the trials out. They will be thrown out of the Wehrmacht and tried by the People's Court. Nor will they die honorably before the firing squad, but like common criminals in the hangman's noose. . . . And above all, they'll get no time to make long speeches. Freisler will see to that—he's our Vishinsky!"[11]

Göring did what he could to restore Hitler's trust in the Wehrmacht. On July 22 a staff stenographer noted in his diary: "Before today's noon war conference, the Reichsmarschall delivered a short speech to the Führer proposing that as an outward token of gratitude for his miraculous escape the entire Wehrmacht should adopt the Hitler salute forthwith. The Führer signed the decree, whereupon there was a spontaneous ovation from everybody present." But all the raised hands in Germany could not erase the cancer of suspicion from Hitler's mind, and each fresh report from Kaltenbrunner started fresh tumors malignantly festering. By the end of July 1944 two names had cropped up that Hitler had never expected to see among his enemies: Field Marshals Kluge and Rommel. The allegation was so awesome that two weeks passed before Hitler could decide how to act on it.

[11]Roland Freisler was president of the Nazi People's Court; Andrei Vishinsky presided over the notorious Moscow Purge Trials.

He Who Rides a Tiger

August 1944 saw many of the intricate problems facing Hitler solved of their own accord, though not as he had wished. When September arrived, he no longer had to concern himself with Pétain's puppet government in France, for France was lost; nor with keeping Finland and Romania in the alliance, for both had defected; nor with impressing Turkey, for she had bowed to the enemy's pressure and broken off diplomatic relations with Germany. In Europe, Hungary alone remained an ally of any substance; but Admiral Horthy too regarded Germany as doomed, and had begun tactical maneuvering to regain his country's lost sovereignty—once again evoking from Hitler the warning that Germany and her allies were in one boat and there could be no disembarking in mid-tempest. Or as he put it in another context—reading Kaltenbrunner's reports on the renegades of July 20—"He who rides a tiger will find he can't dismount."

In France, the American breakthrough succeeded at Avranches. In the east the Red Army reached the Baltic on August 1, cutting off General Schörner's entire Army Group North from East Prussia. Russian troops were only an hour's drive from Hitler's headquarters. In Italy, the British occupied Florence. In Warsaw, a fresh uprising broke out.

Hitler fought a gigantic delaying action, but his health was now uncertain. General Heinz Guderian—the new Chief of General Staff—thus had a free hand. Hitler was disposed to accept this modern general's advice, for Guderian was born at Culm and it was his own homeland he was now defending; his forefathers had farmed West Prussian soil since the seventeenth century, and even now his wife was living in Hohensalza, close enough to hear the rumble of distant gunfire from the Warsaw front. "May the Führer's faith in you persist," she wrote him on July 30, "so that you really get the opportunity to go to work." "And so that you can save Germany's East," she added a few days later, "and our newfound ancestral homeland stays in our hands."

Guderian thrived on tough decisions. He was appalled at the neglect of the frontier defenses and issued dramatic orders for their renovation on July 27. "All eastern Germany must become a fortress in depth." Local Gauleiters and military commanders were to work together on the rapid construction of defensive positions—the Pilica line, the Narev-Bobr line, and the Vistula line from Warsaw northward to Danzig, with well-armed bridgeheads east of the most important cities along the river. Guderian signed these orders with Hitler's name; the Führer grumbled but allowed them to pass. A Russian invasion of East Prussia or the Upper Silesian industrial region would bring psychological disaster in its train. Indeed, now Hitler claimed to find positive advantages in the shrinking of his eastern empire—for it was the sheer distance of the eastern front of 1942 that had proved its undoing. Hundreds of thousands of men and women, young and old, began digging antitank trenches running southward from Stolp, across ripening harvest fields and farms. In Pomerania, seventy thousand women volunteered. Nothing had been done in the ancient fortresses of Königsberg and Lötzen; Guderian soon had them bristling with minefields and captured guns. Moreover, word of Hitler's presence in East Prussia was spread from mouth to mouth. Thus the miracle was achieved: the Red Army was halted at Augustov and Grodno, and Field Marshal Model's emaciated Army Group Center, with its fewer than forty divisions, undertrained and exhausted, withstood for a while the weight of one-third of the entire Soviet forces—143 rifle divisions, 19 rifle brigades, 12 cavalry divisions, and a host of armored brigades and regiments mustering over 2,000 tanks along its four-hundred-mile front line.

In Warsaw, astride the main access routes to Army Group Center, the Polish underground army rose in arms against the Germans as soon as the Russians showed across the river. Himmler came at once to Hitler. "Mein Führer," he orated with determined optimism, "the moment is an awkward one, but viewed historically what the Poles are doing is a blessing. We'll survive the next five or six weeks. But by then Warsaw, the capital, the brains, the nerve center of this former sixteen- or seventeen-million-strong nation of Poles, will have been wiped out—this nation that has barred our passage to the east for seven centuries and lain foul of us ever since the first Battle of Tannenberg." The Reichsführer ordered the total destruction of the city; it was to be burned down and blown up block by block. SS General von dem Bach-Zelewski fought a cruel battle against the partisans; but the Poles' commander, General Bor-Komorowski, was every inch his equal and rejected every demand to surrender, despite the around-the-clock bombardment of the city by 600-millimeter artillery and despite the dawning realization that the Russian relief attack across the river would not come in time. "I wish we had a multitude of men like General Bor," exclaimed Himmler on September 21, and when the last Polish insurgents finally surrendered ten days later, he ordered that Bor be treated well.

In Finland voices could again be heard in Parliament demanding an armistice.

The Red Army had reached Tukkum on the Gulf of Riga, thus cutting off Schörner's Army Group North. The importance the Russians attached to destroying Hitler's position in the north was clear from the appeals by Moscow radio urging his generals to defect while there was still time. It was to General Kinzel, the army group's Chief of Staff, that Stauffenberg and Beck had issued late on July 20 the "order" to retreat immediately. A catastrophe would have befallen the army group; bereft of artillery and ammunition it would have been devoured. But evidently the Berlin dissidents had failed to win any frontline commanders to their cause.

Hitler's major worry on this account was the German generals in Moscow. The OKW warned every headquarters of repeated cases in which unfamiliar officers in German uniforms and with valid identity cards had issued damaging orders to the troops. This became a standard explanation for each fresh reverse. "The Bolsheviks grow more useless every day," complained Schörner in a private letter to Hitler. "Recent days' prisoners range from fourteen-year-olds to old men. But what is astounding is the sheer hordes of human beings. . . ." Hitler had prepared calmly for the army group's temporary isolation: on July 12 he had already instructed the admiralty to coordinate the seaborne supplies to any such enclave. Schörner shared his confidence. He had ruthlessly stripped the entire command area of soldiers and packed them into the combat zone. "I am convinced the enemy is staking everything on one card," he wrote. "I am convinced that . . . what matters now is to survive this phase of the battle, then we shall have won." Guderian had planned a counterattack in August, confident that it would restore land contact to Schörner (and it did).

By early August, Army Group North-Ukraine had also weathered its crisis. The Soviet attack in mid-July had extended on the twenty-third to the sector of the First Hungarian Army, putting the headquarters unit to an unseemly flight which was only just halted forward of the Hungarian frontier. The Germans conceded that "German troops also gave way in places, which is attributed to the failings of individual commanders and the infiltration of panic-mongers and saboteurs from Russia." A few days later the army personnel branch recommended that in the future the families of German traitors should be punished, as a deterrent; Hitler approved the recommendation.

Farther south, Army Group South-Ukraine had been becalmed since the rout of April 1944, when it had fallen back on Romanian territory. At that time General Schörner had bitterly rebuked the OKW's General Erich Hansen—the military liaison to Marshal Antonescu—for the inadequate provision made to receive the struggling army group. The military chaos, the refugees, the abandoned equipment, and above all the added financial burden on the Romanian economy put a strain on German-Romanian relations. Hansen was nearly sixty and what Guderian described as "a man of General Beck"; but he had Antonescu's confidence, and thus Hitler refused Schörner's repeated recommendations for a replacement. As he later in August told General Alfred Gerstenberg, the Luftwaffe commander of the Romanian oil regions: "We are staking all we've got. If we lose the oil regions, we cannot win the war."

General Guderian had transferred six panzer and four infantry divisions away from Army Group South-Ukraine, and he had sent Schörner to Army Group North, where his particular skills were urgently needed. This brought Marshal Antonescu protesting to Rastenburg on August 5. Guderian—speaking French, for the marshal spoke no German—explained the military situation. Hitler spoke through his interpreter to Antonescu for hours on end, assuring him that the Stauffenberg putsch was of no importance, that impressive new German tanks and guns were under construction, that a new explosive "at the experimental stage" was capable of killing everybody within two miles of its point of impact, that he had failed to keep his promise about the Crimea and Ukraine because of "traitors" in the General Staff who had encouraged the decay of the lines of communication, and that pro-Soviet traitors had also procured the collapse of Army Group Center. But Antonescu was disturbed at the growing financial burden of enemy air raids on Romania—particularly now that the enemy might begin using Turkish airfields—and the discussion was sometimes heated. He assured Hitler that his army was completely loyal to him, that "he would remain at Germany's side and be the last country to abandon the Reich"; but Hitler mistrusted King Michael as he mistrusted every monarch.

It was a warm summer's day as Hitler took leave of Antonescu. He did not drive to the airfield with him, but as the column of cars moved off he suddenly stepped forward and called out in German, "Antonescu! Antonescu! On no account set foot inside the king's castle!" Antonescu had not understood him and stopped the car. Hitler repeated, "Don't go into the king's castle!" A sudden instinct had warned him that he might otherwise not see Antonescu again.

Before July was over, Himmler's drastic measures had provided the army with forty new reserve battalions, of which thirty were earmarked for Army Group North alone. The new divisions were divisions with a difference; they were now called *Volksgrenadier* divisions, for Himmler had obtained Hitler's approval to raise a People's Army which would eventually supplant and replace the army of Hans von Seeckt, Werner von Fritsch, and Walther von Brauchitsch—which he identified only with obstructionism, defeatism, and retreat. The Himmler divisions were designed to attract German youth untainted by the spirit of the older generation. Whereas General Fromm had grudgingly furnished Hitler with

60,000 new soldiers a month, by mid-August Himmler had already raised 450,000 new troops, and 250,000 more recruits were already in the barracks.

When Bormann assembled the Gauleiters at Posen on August 3, Himmler boasted of his prowess as the new de facto Commander in Chief of the army. He boasted too of having prepared since Stalingrad for such a putsch as the one on July 20, insisting for example on a separate training ground for the SS in Lausitz, near Berlin. But he could not explain how the rambling, ill-concealed Stauffenberg network had escaped his scrutiny. Speer then spoke of how future arms production would restore Germany's freedom of action and air supremacy by December. Production of the excellent MPi 44 submachine gun would increase fivefold to 100,000 a month; of tanks from 1,680 to 3,200; of V-1 flying bombs from 3,000 to 9,000; and of fighter aircraft from 2,927 to 4,800.[1]

Thus encouraged, the Gauleiters came to hear Hitler speak on August 4. He was still unwell—at times he felt dizzy and there was a ringing in his ears *(tinnitus aurium).* One diarist wrote: "The Führer walked in very slowly and stiffly, and proffered only his left hand; but later, when he began his speech, he loosened up and became more lively." No transcript has survived, but he evidently disclosed that he had set up an Army Court of Honor under Rundstedt to discharge the conspirators from the Wehrmacht so that they could be tried by the People's Court; those found guilty would be hanged. "What annoyed him most was that a clown like Goerdeler had been chosen to succeed him." Another diarist, Helmút Sündermann, the deputy press chief, wrote:

> The speech's beginning was delayed a bit as the Führer ordered the prepared desk to be removed; he had a small table and chair brought, sat down, and began to speak so softly at first that I had difficulty hearing from the back row. Then his voice rapidly rose. "I always knew that shots would be fired at me one day from this quarter; but I never dreamed the blow would be struck so far below the belt!" He said he was now "old and shaky," not because of his fight against Germany's enemies but because of the perpetual conflict with "this clique which always eluded me." This numerically small but highly influential group would have been totally incapable of any real political achievements, as they were wholly out of touch with the broad public. . . . Now we were in the position of somebody who had been poisoned—if we could surmount this crisis then we would not be dead, but in superb health. Although he had spoken virtually nothing of substance, his speech had an obvious impact on the Gauleiters. As the senior man present, [Konstantin] Hierl [leader of the Reich Labor Service] spoke a few words of thanks to the Führer: "There is only one kind of loyalty. There is no 'loyal, more loyal, loyalest.' There is only 'loyal,' and that says everything."

[1]Martin Bormann later warned Hitler that several Gauleiters had proof that Speer's figures were dishonest. Speer now admits that they were deliberately exaggerated, though justifiably so.

The Führer's insomnia had returned, and with it his nervous twitch. He scoffed at Stauffenberg's "bungling," but the injuries to his legs and arms were very painful, and Morell's treatment of his right elbow—a bandage soaked in acid aluminum acetate—had resulted in dermatitis and pruritis which left it so swollen that he could not sign state documents; when unsuspecting frontline generals heartily grasped his right hand he winced at the pain. Morell was also treating him with massive doses of Ultraseptyl, a sulfonamide-type drug (as Germany had no penicillin); the other doctors noted with concern that the Führer's health had begun to deteriorate. An oxygen bottle now stood permanently hissing in one corner of his bedroom, but still he could not sleep. One night, just after he had drifted off, the emergency lighting suddenly came on. "I had to clamber about like a monkey," he grumbled to his manservant. "I dragged a table over, but the fixture was right up in the ceiling, and then of course the bulb was so tightly screwed in that it was all I could do to unscrew it."

An unsettling predicament had confronted him since August 1. One of the confessed putschists, Lieutenant-Colonel Caesar von Hofacker, had convincingly implicated both Field Marshal von Kluge and the invalid Field Marshal Rommel in the July 20 plot. The degree of their involvement was uncertain, but neither had reported the conspiracy to Hitler. Both these officers enjoyed an immense popularity in the army—it would be unthinkable to stand them before the People's Court. Hitler decided to wait and see. He told Guderian: "Kluge is an accessory, but we cannot dispense with him." He sent for Jodl privately on August 1, showed him the Hofacker interrogation report, and indicated that as soon as Rommel had recovered, he would personally question him and then retire him from the army without fuss. As he said a few weeks later, "He has done the worst possible thing a soldier can do under such circumstances—sought for some way out other than the purely military."

The Allies had now landed a million and a half troops on the Normandy beachhead. The attempted British breakthrough from Caumont had been checked; but through the breach at Avranches on the coast, at the extreme southwestern end of the German containing line, American armor and troops were pouring into Brittany—General George S. Patton's Third Army. To Hitler it seemed that the Americans had suddenly mastered the German knack of exploiting God-given opportunities, but there was an obvious countermove: if German tanks struck through to the coast again, it would sever the one artery on which Patton's bold thrust relied. "We must strike like lightning," he announced. "When we reach the sea the American spearheads will be cut off. Obviously they are trying all-out for a major decision here, because otherwise they wouldn't have sent in their best general, Patton. That's the most dangerous man they have. But the more troops they squeeze through the gap, and the better they are, the better for us when we reach the sea and cut them off! We might even be able to eliminate their whole beachhead. We mustn't get bogged down with mopping up the Americans that have broken through; their turn will come later. We must wheel north like lightning and turn the entire enemy front from the rear." If Hitler's stroke of genius came off, the Allies would scarcely have time to beat a disorderly retreat to their artificial harbors off the Normandy beaches—and then he, Hitler, could turn his attention to Russia once again.

It was an intoxicating prospect, though with obvious fallacies. Hitler issued the order for the attack late on August 2. It was to be spearheaded by General von Funck's Forty-seventh Panzer Corps. Hitler planned to employ eight of his nine panzer divisions in Normandy, and a thousand fighter planes. He sent Jodl's deputy, General Warlimont, to "sit in" on Kluge's headquarters personally, and the generals there assured Warlimont that the attack might well succeed. During the sixth, Hitler drafted a powerfully worded message to Funck's troops:

> The outcome of the Battle for France depends on the success of the attack on the southern wing of the Seventh Army. Commander in Chief West [Kluge] will have a unique and unrepeatable opportunity of thrusting into a region largely devoid of the enemy, and to change the whole situation thereby.

While the spearheads were thrust boldly through to the sea, fresh panzer divisions were to follow in their wake and wheel north, where they would turn the enemy front in Normandy. "The utmost boldness, determination, and imagination must inspire every commander down to the lowest levels," Hitler's order continued. "Each man must believe in victory. The restoration of order in the rear areas and in Brittany can be left until later." But in a series of telephone conversations that afternoon General Jodl learned that Kluge was planning to start the attack before midnight, without waiting for the fighter squadrons to arrive. In addition, only four of the planned eight panzer divisions could be extricated from the battlefield in the north in time, and those that had arrived were still short of tanks and artillery. So far Funck would command only 75 Mark IV tanks, 70 Mark Vs, and 32 self-propelled assault guns. Kluge explained that the enemy had already detected their preparations, and he was prepared to take the responsibility for jumping off now even though understrength.

Hitler mistrusted Kluge's judgment. Above all, he wanted Kluge to wait for the right weather. He sent his best infantry general, Walter Buhle—whom he had earmarked as Zeitzler's eventual successor—by plane to France to influence Kluge, but it was too late: the half-cocked thrust toward Avranches had already begun by the time Buhle arrived. The first big town, Mortain, was recaptured by an SS panzer division, but then the fog lifted and a murderous enemy air assault began. Over a thousand Allied fighter-bombers roamed the battlefield virtually unchecked; the Luftwaffe could provide only 300 fighter planes, and by the next day, August 8, only 110 were still in action. Kluge's grenadiers unflinchingly faced slaughter by the enemy's strategic bomber squadrons, but the tanks themselves could proceed no farther. At eleven that evening Kluge informed Jodl that he had failed. When General Warlimont reported back from France that day, Hitler terminated his battle narrative with one rasping sentence—as ominous as the judgment the People's Court passed that same day on Witzleben, Hoepner, and their fellow conspirators: "The attack failed because Kluge *wanted* it to fail."[2]

Kluge's headquarters warned that the enemy's objective was becoming plainer every day: "Target Paris!"

At Hitler's headquarters the fiasco of Kluge's first counterattack was openly blamed on the Luftwaffe. But Reichsmarschall Göring had not been seen here since July 23, and he still had to introduce to Hitler a successor to the fatally injured Chief of Staff. Korten's deputy—an able Bavarian general, Karl Koller—officiated in their absence. Göring recognized that his own star was waning. After the July 20 putsch attempt, Admiral Dönitz had preceded him in a broadcast to the nation, and he was no match for the new Himmler-Bormann-Goebbels triumvirate; he had therefore retired to bed, surrounded by medicines. He eventually named Werner Kreipe as Korten's successor over the far more capable Koller, although Kreipe was many years the latter's junior. Until Göring had "recovered," Koller had to bear the brunt of Hitler's intemperate attacks. "At every conference the Führer goes on for hours on end about the Luftwaffe," lamented Koller in his fragmentary shorthand diary on August 8. "He strongly reproaches the Luftwaffe. The reasons are our lack of aircraft, technological shortcomings, and noncompletion of the replacement squadrons in the Reich, the Me-262, etc. . . . How am I to know what claims the Reichsmarschall and General Korten made, or undo the wrongs committed from 1939 to 1942 through the total absence of any planning? It's a hard lot to have to answer for these errors."

Six squadrons, each of sixty-eight fighters, had been transferred to the Reich for rehabilitation in July; now that Hitler ordered Kluge to prepare a second attack on Avranches, a tug-of-war began over these squadrons. He instructed Jodl late on the eighth to transfer four squadrons to the west by August 12. Kreipe was horrified and telephoned Göring and General Galland. "Both agree with me: the squadrons aren't ready, they will sink without trace in the chaos of the west

[2]The principal cause for the failure of Hitler's plan, here as elsewhere, was that OKW code signals were being deciphered by the British.

and then they are lost to the home defense." (This was sheer shortsightedness, because if the enemy overran France, his intensified bombing operations from French airfields would take more than four extra squadrons of fighters to prevent.) The next day Hitler increased his demand to six squadrons and ordered Kluge to be ready to attack Avranches again on the eleventh. "The Forty-seventh Panzer Corps attack failed because it was launched prematurely and was thus too weak, and under weather conditions favoring the enemy. It is to be repeated elsewhere with powerful forces." Kluge was to employ six panzer divisions in a more southwesterly direction than on the seventh; and General Hans Eberbach was to be in command instead of Funck (who had been on Fritsch's staff before the war and therefore could not be trusted).

General Kreipe was finally introduced to Hitler on August 11, and wrote in his diary: "The Führer has become very bent, with cotton wool in his ears, and frequently trembles uncontrollably; one must not shake his hand too violently. . . . First the Führer asked me about my career, then spoke at length on the origins of what he called the collapse and failure of the Luftwaffe—primarily the errors of the Reichsmarschall's technical advisers, who had made overhasty promises about the quality and quantity of new aircraft types. The air staff had probably also been deceived, and—through negligence or ignorance—made false statements to him on which he [Hitler] had unhappily based his decision. He mentioned Milch, Udet, and Jeschonnek in this context." Kreipe swore to speak only the unadulterated truth to him.

In France, meanwhile, the Goddess of Fortune had eluded Hitler's grasp and would not return. Suffice to say that events now overtook General Eberbach. The force he had assembled invited envelopment by the enemy, and the invitation was accepted. On the twelfth, the Allies captured Alençon in Eberbach's rear, and by late on the thirteenth the jaws closing on him—the British and Canadians from Falaise in the north, and the Americans from Argentan—were barely twenty miles apart. Desperate fighting ensued in the Falaise pocket to prevent the encirclement of the bulk of the German Seventh Army and Eberbach's Fifth Panzer Army. Small personal tragedies occurred, hurting Hitler deeply. Hans Pfeiffer, his one-time adjutant, died in a blazing tank in Normandy. Hans Junge, the young SS captain who had been his orderly, was struck down by a strafing Spitfire far behind the lines. Frau Traudl Junge was Hitler's youngest secretary—he kept the gloomy secret to himself until it was confirmed some days later, then broke it to her in person. "Ach, child, I am so sorry; your husband had a fine character." Bormann's private letters testify to Hitler's dejection over this one episode.

Field Marshal Kluge's tactics in Normandy, meanwhile, defied explanation. Despite Hitler's clear orders, he was still holding Eberbach's tank forces too far to the north, thus positively aiding Patton's encirclement operation. On August 14 Hitler again ordered Eberbach to attack the American Fifteenth Corps at Alençon; Kluge was to use the Nineteenth Army to defend the Mediterranean coast of France against the invasion now known to be imminent there as well.[3] Patton's tanks were already roaming across Brittany. The fortress commandant of Saint-Malo—a port Hitler had ordered strongly defended—radioed: "The enemy is putting German prisoners on his tanks so as to get close to our strongpoints." A Luftwaffe general attending Hitler's midday conference recorded: "Tense atmosphere. Fegelein [Himmler's liaison officer to Hitler] dropped hints that even more generals and field marshals are involved in July 20." That afternoon Heinrich Himmler, conferring alone with Hitler in the now restored conference barracks where Stauffenberg's bomb had exploded, arrived with still firmer proof that both Kluge and Rommel had been in the anti-Hitler conspiracy up to their necks. Late that evening, news reached Hitler's conference that the invasion of the French Riviera was underway.

Thus August 15, 1944, arrived. "The worst day of my life," Hitler subsequently admitted. It brought one of the war's great unsolved riddles. At the morning conference the news was that the Americans had started their big attack on the Falaise pocket, and the fate of Eberbach's panzer divisions was in the balance; but Field Marshal von Kluge had disappeared. He had ostensibly set out to confer with Eberbach on whether to abandon the panzer attack on Alençon. But he had not arrived, and an *enemy* radio signal was monitored asking where Kluge was! Was it coincidence that Major General Henning von Tresckow and so many other leading conspirators of July 20 had served under Kluge in Russia until 1943? The clouds of suspicion suddenly loomed up. As evening came, Hitler learned that Kluge's radio truck had been silent since last signaling at 9:30 A.M., and neither Eberbach, nor SS General Hausser, nor SS General Sepp Dietrich had seen him. Either he was dead, gunned down like Hans Junge by a strafing aircraft—or he was at that very moment secretly negotiating the surrender of the entire western front to the enemy. "To change our destiny by surrendering to the British and joining forces against Russia—what an idiotic notion!" Hitler scoffed a few days later. From his own sources he had long decided that Churchill had sold out the Balkans and all Europe east of the river Elbe—if not indeed the Weser—to Stalin.

[3]Largely by close surveillance of enemy ships passing Gibraltar, the German naval staff deduced that an invasion of southern France was imminent, although most of the evidence gained by German secret agents (*i.e.*, those leftovers of the Canaris era) pointed the other way. General Charles de Gaulle provided the necessary confirmation in a radio broadcast to France on August 7, boasting that "a mighty French army" (*i.e.*, that in North Africa) would shortly set foot in France.

He had recently described Britain's standpoint as *"Après moi le déluge*—if only we can get rid of the hated National Socialist Germany."

At 7:30 P.M. on August 15 Hitler ordered SS General Hausser to take over Army Group B and stop the enemy onrush threatening to envelope the Fifth Panzer Army. Kluge was still missing. Hitler spent a sleepless night, swallowed fresh sedatives to no avail at 6 A.M., and asked for a doctor again at eleven. He learned that Eberbach's HQ had reported Kluge's arrival late that night in the heart of the Falaise pocket; there was no explanation of where he had been all day.

Hitler could trust him no longer, and he radioed the order "Field Marshal von Kluge is to leave the danger area immediately for Fifth Panzer Army HQ, from which he is to direct the withdrawal movement." (From outside the pocket, Kluge could no longer secretly contact the Allies.) Field Marshal Model, to whom Hitler had only the day before pinned the Diamonds award for his magnificent reconstruction of Army Group Center, and who was already back at the eastern front, was now recalled to the Wolf's Lair and secretly appointed Kluge's successor. His instructions were to build up a new front in France as far forward of the Seine-Yonne line as possible, using to that end divisions evacuated from southern France step by step (any other line would mean the loss of the French coast and the V-1 launching sites).

Model was sent by plane to Kluge with a sealed letter ordering him back to Germany. He arrived unannounced at Kluge's headquarters late on the seventeenth and immediately issued orders which resulted three days later in the almost unhoped-for escape of the main German forces from the Falaise encirclement. Kluge returned to his native village—but in a coffin, having been killed on the nineteenth by a cerebral hemorrhage, according to the army doctors. Hitler, thwarted of his prey, ordered a second autopsy; but even Model's doctors again reported natural causes. According to his Chief of Staff, General Blumentritt, Kluge had been shocked by the failure of his counterattack on Avranches on August 7 and upset by Hitler's reproaches; he had sent his son into the Falaise pocket with the words "Let nobody accuse me of sparing my son and heir"; on the road to Nécy, the prearranged rendezvous with Eberbach and Hausser on the fifteenth, Kluge had seen four of his staff killed when their radio truck was strafed—hence, apparently, the day-long silence on his movements. Blumentritt had last seen him on the eighteenth, tapping a battle chart and moaning, "Avranches, Avranches! This town has cost me my reputation as a soldier. I'll go down in history as the Benedeck of the western front.[4] D'you know Count Moltke's book

[4]Ludwig von Benedeck commanded the Austrian army crushingly defeated at the Battle of Königgratz by General Helmuth von Moltke during the Austro-Prussian War (1866).

on Benedeck? I did my best, but that's fate for you." It seemed that an aged field marshal had faded away, his heart worn out by the burden of being both Commander in Chief West and Commander of Army Group B. Hitler allowed preparations for a state funeral to proceed; but mistrustfully he ordered SS doctors to stage yet a third autopsy, and meanwhile the death was to remain a state secret.

American forces had reached the Seine on August 18 and were only thirty-six miles from Paris. The German army was in full flight across the river, by barge, pontoon bridge, and raft, abandoning its heavy gear to the enemy in a panic-stricken scramble for the German frontier. Some German soldiers blamed the lack of fuel and motor transportation for the German defeat in France; others, the age and indolence of their commanders. The Luftwaffe's General Koller returned from Paris with grim reports on the moral decay of the army after four years of occupation and a carefree life as demigods.

Hitler had foreseen that all this would happen if the Normandy front collapsed; his generals had their "war of movement" with a vengeance. On the nineteenth he called in Keitel, Speer, and Jodl and soberly ordered them to lay the material foundations for a new western army, as he was planning a great counteroffensive in November when the enemy air forces would be grounded by bad weather. Twenty-five divisions must be raised and equipped for this. (Thus was born the Ardennes offensive of December.)

Martin Bormann steered most of the odium for the defeat onto the Luftwaffe. Göring was still malingering, and Hitler asked caustically how long the Reichsmarschall's illness might be expected to last; not until August 26 did Göring reappear at the Wolf's Lair, after an absence of five weeks. Meanwhile Bormann, aided by Goebbels, had initiated a "Luftwaffe Scandals" file to which the Gauleiters contributed profusely. Bombs had been shunted out of bombproof stores to make room for contraband from Italy and Greece. At Rechlin, the main experimental airfield, a technician tipped off Bormann that a villa was being built for the commandant at Lake Ammersee at Luftwaffe expense and that Luftwaffe workmen were flying down to Bavaria each weekend to finish the job. Göring's sacked deputy, Milch, was accused of having fostered bad aircraft and aeroengine projects for the sake of old Lufthansa business cronies. Gauleiter Hartmann Lauterbacher reported that four hundred flying instructors and pupils who had volunteered for an immediate special Reich-defense mission had been idle ever since. In Italy, General Maximilian Ritter von Pohl's staff had swollen while his squadrons had diminished; his officers were said to be idling in luxury hotels, with ample cigarettes, cognac, and coffee, or lazing on beaches with their female personnel.

Small wonder that Hitler unfavorably compared the Luftwaffe's squandering of manpower with the way that Himmler had conjured up new battalions for the army. Air Chief of Staff General Kreipe could not even find out how many men were in the Luftwaffe. Hitler began to think of dissolving the entire Luftwaffe and building up the antiaircraft defenses instead. On August 17 he had angrily telephoned Kreipe and instructed him to replace Field Marshal Sperrle, the fat Luftwaffe commander in France, by General Dessloch; it was typical of Hitler to have delayed this decision until now, when it was too late. The future of the Messerschmitt 262 jet was again debated. The first jet bomber squadron was still to enter service; Göring, Kreipe, Speer, and Galland all wanted the Me-262 used as a fighter after all. But now the enemy's bombing of the oil plants had reduced aviation fuel supplies to a trickle. The bombproof refineries would not begin operating until March 1945, but by December the OKW fuel reserve would have been consumed. Small wonder that Hitler began complaining of splitting headaches to his doctors; the ringing in his ears just would not stop.

On August 20, 1944, the Red Army launched its main offensive of the late summer on General Friessner's army group on the Romanian frontier—twenty-seven German and twenty Romanian divisions on a three-hundred-mile front from the Carpathians to the Black Sea. Within three days the Sixth Army would be all but encircled here, but Hitler's eyes were still on France. In Paris, armed partisan bands had risen against the German garrison. General Dietrich von Choltitz, the arrogant, feckless military commander Hitler had only recently appointed in place of General Hans von Boineburg—who had allowed the capital to decay into a rotten *Etappenstadt* of draft dodgers, malingerers, and army scroungers—asked the insurgents for a three-day armistice to prevent harm from coming to life, limb, or the capital. The insurgents agreed, Choltitz withdrew his pitifully few troops to the east bank of the Seine, and then, to his injured surprise, the uprising began again the next day. Paris, however, was vital both militarily and politically, and Hitler had emphatically demanded its defense in an order of the twentieth; and not just the city, but a cordon well outside the city. Every Seine bridge between Paris and the sea had been destroyed; Hitler ordered those intact in Paris heavily defended by antiaircraft guns. If, however, the bridges fell undemolished into enemy hands—and Choltitz had not even mined them yet—then the enemy could prise open Hitler's coastal defenses from the rear and rob him of his V-1 launching sites as well. "In all history the loss of Paris has meant the loss of France," Hitler reminded Model in an order on August 22. "Inside the city the first signs of revolt are to be harshly put down, *e.g.*, by blowing up entire street blocks, by public execution of the ringleaders, or by evacuation of any districts involved, as only this will stop things getting out of hand. The Seine bridges are to be prepared for demolition. Paris must not fall into enemy hands—or if it does, then only as a field of ruins."

Where previously he had relied on his army generals, now Hitler leaned increasingly on his trusted Party comrades—particularly on Martin Bormann and Heinrich Himmler, both of whom took to attending the regular war conferences. It was Bormann who mobilized the Gauleiters and Reich officials to construct deep frontier defenses in the west. When Hitler's two southeastern commanders, Weichs and Löhr, came for a conference on August 22, Himmler was also inexplicably hovering in the background. Weichs had brought news of a remarkable rapprochement between General Nedić, the puppet prime minister of Serbia, and Draža Mihajlovič, leader of the Četnik guerrillas, who proposed to unite in the face of the threat to the Serbs posed by Tito's Communist partisans; together they had offered to help Hitler in the Balkans if he would provide the necessary ammunition—three million rounds—and allow them to raise an army of fifty thousand men from the Četniks. Weichs admitted that these two men would have 90 percent of the Serbs behind them and proposed a modified acceptance of their terms—perhaps a quarter of a million rounds and six thousand troops at first. All Hitler's latent Austrian resentment against the Serbs welled up within him. "The Serbs are the only eternally consistent people in the Balkans," Jodl's diary quoted him as warning. "They alone have the strength and the ability to keep pursuing their pan-Serbian aims." Hitler's experiences in arming helpful friends and neighbors had chastened him; too often the ammunition had ended up in the bodies of German troops. He would therefore permit the new experiment proposed by Weichs on only the smallest scale.

Joseph Goebbels came the next day to confer with Hitler and Bormann. All Germany's erstwhile allies were scampering off the sinking ship. On August 17, Keitel had decorated Marshal Mannerheim with a high German award; but Mannerheim had pointedly responded that the Finnish people had made him president in place of Ryti because they objected to the latter's pro-German policies. This gave the marshal "a free hand."

On the southern Russian front, Marshal Rodion Malinovski's armies were pouring into Romania. Far into the night Hitler—his inflamed sinuses preventing sleep—conferred from his bed with Generals Guderian and Jodl. He trusted Marshal Antonescu, but not the Romanian army; indeed, only recently he had secretly authorized General Friessner to withdraw Army Group South-Ukraine to the obvious best line—from Galatz on the Danube to the Carpathians—the instant the Russians attacked. But to say that the Romanian divisions were failing would be a euphemism. Friessner's Chief of Staff wrote: "It was obvious they were deliberately not fighting, so as to shorten the war." As Friessner fell back, Hitler obviously felt he could defend the new line and the vital oil fields, for on August

22 he ordered experts to find out if a seventy-foot-wide canal could be excavated immediately—using hordes of slave laborers—from the Danube to the Black Sea at Constanta; because if the Russians could blockade the Danube at its delta, the strategic implications would be vast. Rumors multiplied—for instance from the air attaché in Hungary—that a coup d'etat was imminent in Romania, but the German envoys in Bucharest itself reassured Hitler that all was well. Hitler rebuked Kreipe on August 21: "Your air attachés shouldn't poke their noses into what doesn't concern them. The SS report the opposite." Nonetheless Hitler at last decided to replace General Hansen as his military representative in Bucharest.

Again he was overtaken by the rudeness of events. He was having tea with his staff in his bunker late that day, August 23, when his Wehrmacht adjutant, Amsberg, called him to the telephone. A voice announced that Marshal Antonescu had just been arrested after seeking an audience with his king. Hitler replaced the receiver and commented to Amsberg: "Why on earth didn't he listen to me! I knew this would happen!" Shortly afterward, Romanian radio broadcast a proclamation by King Michael: "The Romanian government has accepted the armistice offered by Russia and the United Nations." The Allies had promised to restore Transylvania to Romania, to guarantee her independence, and to fight side by side with her against the Hungarian dictatorship. The king ordered his forces not to open hostilities with the German Wehrmacht, however. This was cold comfort for Hitler, for much of his current oil requirements were met from the Romanian wells. But his men in Bucharest were not men of action—indeed, as in Warsaw and Paris, the German agencies were scattered throughout the capital of Romania and the surrounding country with a blithe disregard for a potential emergency such as this; the embassy's radio station was in a distant suburb, which left Hitler reliant on the ancient Romanian telephone service. Kreipe wrote that evening: "Telephone conversation with Ambassador [Manfred] von Killinger, and Gerstenberg [the Luftwaffe attaché] in Bucharest. Both trapped in the legation, Killinger a complete wreck, sends greetings to the Führer. Gerstenberg suggests dive-bomber attack and using the [German] antiaircraft division at Ploesti to seize the city! I phone Hitler several times, he approves Gerstenberg's proposals, demands the arrest of the king. Contact established with Bucharest once more, then interrupted."

From 9:45 P.M. until far into the night Hitler's headquarters issued orders to Friessner's army group and General Hansen—still the German military representative in the Bucharest legation. Friessner was to prepare for a German takeover of the oil fields and plan means for getting the oil to the Reich. Every German serviceman in Romania was placed at his disposal. Hansen was to put down the putsch, the Fifth Antiaircraft Division at Ploesti was to occupy the capital as Gersternberg had suggested, and Admiral Brinkmann was to seize the

Black Sea harbor of Constanta. A pro-Nazi Romanian general was to be appointed head of the government. Friessner promptly dismissed Hansen and commanded Gerstenberg to execute Hitler's orders.

Hitler began his delayed evening war conference at 2 A.M. and afterward again discussed the wholly altered Balkan situation with Field Marshal von Weichs. He had decided to abandon Greece to the enemy the moment they attacked, particularly the Peloponnesus.[5] He would shift his Schwerpunkt to northern Greece. This made it vital to prevent the Bulgarians—whose defection was clearly only hours away—from seizing the railway line from Nis to Skoplje for the Allies, as this was the only link with Greece.

At 3:30 A.M. Gerstenberg radioed from Ploesti to Hitler's headquarters: "Fought my way out and took command in Ploesti together with SS General Hoffmeyer." But both Hansen and Killinger had already given up hope. Their telephone message reached East Prussia an hour later: "This is no putsch by some court camarilla, but a well-laid coup d'etat from above with the complete backing of the army and people." Not one Romanian general sympathetic to Nazi Germany could now be found. The Romanians controlled the means of communication. "Given the balance of forces, there is at present no prospect of a military or political success." However, Hitler repeated his orders and detailed Ribbentrop to broadcast a proclamation to the Romanians; Horia Sima, the leader of the Iron Guard which had with Heydrich's clandestine backing unsuccessfully attempted to overthrow Antonescu in January 1941—after helping him to power in 1940—would be brought out of German exile, where he had languished then on Antonescu's insistence, and appointed his successor.

Hitler had ordered Gerstenberg to advance on Bucharest at 6:30 A.M., and five hours later the two thousand antiaircraft troops were at the city's northern outskirts. Gerstenberg emphatically disowned Hansen's gloomy assessment and called down three bombing attacks on the city center. But he was outnumbered 4 to 1; the Romanians had mined the approach roads and they were bringing up tanks and artillery. Gerstenburg captured the radio station, but without proper combat troops he could proceed no farther. Hitler ordered more troops in. "War conference with the Führer," a Luftwaffe general wrote at midday. "Everyone busy with Romania. Hitler very optimistic, curses SS Intelligence service and foreign ministry, mimicks Ribbentrop.—Goebbels and Bormann also present." But the new troops were slow in arriving, and the Romanians were master of their capital still.

The midday conference next day was long and acrimonious. "Ribbentrop

[5]This and his recent secret order to General Friessner (page 691) again refute the postwar legend that Hitler never voluntarily abandoned territory when it was strategically desirable that he do so.

pleads extenuating circumstances, is sure Killinger and Gerstenberg will restore the situation. Hitler accepts this view." Using the bombing attacks as an excuse, the Romanians declared war on Germany on the twenty-fifth. Hitler transferred General Stahel, the Luftwaffe troubleshooter-general who had had served him well in Sicily and more recently in Vilna and Warsaw, to take command in Bucharest. But within four days of his arriving in Romania he and Gerstenberg were captives of the Red Army now debouching into the country. Baron Manfred von Killinger committed suicide as his legation was stormed.

With the now hostile Romanians in the rear, Friessner's army group collapsed; sixteen German divisions were wiped out in the debacle. Finland and Bulgaria trembled, and from Hungary too came sounds of an imminent earthquake that needed no seismograph for Hitler to detect.

To his war staff Hitler still radiated confidence and dynamism. A young SS captain, fresh from the street-fighting in Warsaw, who now joined the conferences as Fegelein's adjutant, jotted down his first impressions on August 27, 1944:

> After supper at 10 P.M. work goes on until 3 A.M. or even later. Every day I see the Führer for several hours and stand only a pace or two away; each day it is the same great experience anew, one I will never forget. I am filled with the most ineffable admiration of him; he is unique as a man, as a politician, as a military commander. He radiates such a comforting calmness. But more than once I have heard him speak harshly—and each occasion was when on purpose or sometimes out of ignorance less than the full and brutal truth had been spoken, or even an outright lie. He seems to sense it at once; it is enormously impressive for me. . . . The Führer is never angry if, as I have myself found several times, you tell him you have to make an immediate inquiry before you can answer a question or questions. What astounds me again and again is the radiance emanating from the Führer: I have seen the highest ranking officers come to report laden with problems and worries. They always leave his presence full of new confidence and hope.

Yet the secret image of Hitler was not always what the public then believed or history has come to accept of him. The sequel to July 20 provides many examples. He was revolted by the newsreel film of the People's Court hearing against Field Marshal Witzleben and the other putschists, and he sent a sharp rebuke to Roland Freisler over his melodramatic and insulting behavior as the judge. "He is behaving like a ham actor, instead of getting the trial of these common criminals over as quickly as possible," Hitler told Schaub. The hangings were also filmed, but Hitler refused to see the films; when Fegelein produced photographs of the naked corpses, Hitler irritably tossed the pictures aside. Helldorf—on his instructions—was required to witness his fellow-conspirators' execution before his turn came. Hitler ordered their property sold to benefit the "frontline troops" they had betrayed. Most remarkable was his instruction to Himmler at the end of August to provide proper monthly subsistence payments to the next-of-kin of the hanged men "to spare them the worst hardships as in the case of the next-of-kin left by those shot after [the Röhm purge of] June 30, 1934."

About 140 people were executed after July 20, and perhaps 700 more arrested. Investigations still continued.

Choltitz's feeble surrender of Paris on August 25 now made it impossible to build a Somme-Marne position in time. Warsaw, Paris, and now Bucharest had seen disgraceful scenes of German officialdom—and above all Wehrmacht officers—in full flight. Hitler issued an angry order to his viceroys to prevent any recurrence by evacuating their main staffs immediately from the biggest non-German cities:

> Our military and civilian authorities are often living irresponsibly and opulently without the slightest warlike preparations, sometimes even surrounded by their families and female employees. Defeats at the front coupled with uprisings in the cities result in their being paralyzed the moment a crisis breaks out. The upshot is that our troops are witness to a panic-stricken headlong flight, encumbered by a disgraceful load of German and alien womenfolk and their own or other people's ill-gotten goods, streaming across the countryside.
>
> Nothing is more likely to tarnish the image of these German authorities and thus of the Reich in the eyes of our troops and foreign populations. When their escape is cut off and the German authorities are trapped by the enemy or insurgents, moreover, it is the combat troops who have to go in and risk their own lives to protect them or rescue them from their luxurious quarters.

Shameful word reached Hitler of the scenes of rout and degradation in France. In one area, five chaotic columns—two of them out in the fields—belonging to five different divisions streamed eastward down the same road toward Belgium or the West Wall. In another, officers forced their cars past bridge bottlenecks at pistol point, or Luftwaffe trucks laden with furniture and loot pulled out of bases in which irreplaceable radar gear or artillery or ammunition would fall intact into enemy hands. All the while enemy aircraft leisurely strafed the columns from a hundred feet up with cannon and machine-gun fire.

Scapegoats were sought in Rommel's old headquarters most of all. General Speidel, the Chief of Staff, was indicted by several of the putschists as an accomplice, but Model demurred at his release, and two weeks passed before Speidel was turned over to the Gestapo. Hitler assumed that all Rommel's associates had become infected by the spirit of July 20.

Kluge's mortal remains were still at his village church, awaiting burial while rumor and speculation spread. On August 28, General Burgdorf, chief of army personnel, showed Hitler the long-awaited report on the third autopsy, by SS doctors—and with it a long, penciled letter Kluge had addressed to his Führer. Martin Bormann noted triumphantly in his diary:

> On the evening of August 28, SS General Fegelein disclosed to me that analysis by the RSHA [Reich Main Security Office] has established that Field Marshal Kluge poisoned himself with cyanide! And that Kluge wrote the Führer a farewell letter, which General Burgdorf handed to him.
>
> Kluge wrote that as a soldier he has drawn the consequences of his defeat, which he had predicted and dreaded all along. In Kluge's view Germany's defeat is inevitable; hence the Führer should realize this and act accordingly.

The letter was a strange amalgam of Nazi fanaticism, personal asseverations of loyalty, and defeatism. The next day cross-examination of Kluge's nephew in the People's Court elicited clear proof that the field marshal was linked with the plotters—evidence so damning that a stunned Judge Freisler adjourned the trial to send for Kluge, not realizing that he was long dead. To Speidel's successor, General Hans Krebs, Hitler vented his bitter disgust thus: "Twice I personally promoted him, I gave him the highest medals, a big cash gift to buy an estate, and a supplement to his field marshal's pay. . . . Maybe he just slid in, I don't know; maybe he saw no other way out: he saw one officer after another being arrested, and feared what they might testify."

Hitler ordered a quiet funeral, with military pallbearers but no other honors. Now he could interpret the army's reports on that "blackest day"—August 15—more certainly: obviously Kluge *had* tried to contact the enemy, only to have a chance fighter-bomber destroy his only radio truck. Why else had he stopped halfway and sent off his staff officer, Major Behr, to go on alone to the alleged rendezvous planned with Eberbach and the other generals? "It was the purest chance that his plan was not carried out," Hitler marveled on August 31. "The army group's entire actions are explicable only in this light." But all of this was only of academic interest now.[6]

Kluge, at sixty-two, had given up the fight; Hitler, at fifty-five, would fight on. "We shall fight on, if need be on the Rhine. Where, matters not the least to me.

[6]I know of only one clue to the mystery on the Allied side. In American files is a reported statement of Lieutenant Colonel George R. Pfann, secretary of General Patton's Third Army General Staff, in 1945. Pfann explained that Patton had vanished from Third Army HQ for an entire day in mid-August, 1944; when he returned, he stated he had been out to try to make contact with a German emissary, who had not, however, shown up at the appointed place. On the German side is the CIC interrogation of Kluge's son-in-law, Dr. Udo Esch (of the German army medical corps), on July 27, 1945. It was he who had supplied Kluge with the cyanide. Kluge, said Esch, discussed with him the possibility of surrendering the entire western front. "He went to the front lines but was unable to get in touch with the Allied commanders."

Come what may we will keep fighting this fight until—as Frederick the Great once said—one of our accursed enemies tires of the struggle, and we can get a peace assuring the German nation's livelihood for the next fifty or a hundred years—and above all a peace that does not drag our honor in the mire as happened in 1918."

Rommel Gets a Choice

"I have always said," remarked Hitler as autumn 1944 approached, "the time is not ripe for a *political* decision. I think I may say I have shown often enough in my life that I know how to score political triumphs; I need hardly add that I won't let a suitable opportunity pass. But obviously it is infantile and naïve to look for a favorable political initiative at a moment of grave military defeats. There may be such initiatives once one has the upper hand again. . . ." The outburst was directed as much against Foreign Minister Ribbentrop as against Field Marshal Kluge. The day before, August 30, Ribbentrop had submitted a memorandum asking for authority to put out peace feelers; it began with a quotation from *Mein Kampf*: "The job of diplomatists is to ensure that a people does not founder heroically, but survives. Any means to this end is justified; to spurn such means can only be termed a contemptible crime."

But Hitler was waiting, yearning for a wholly different event—the moment when the differences between East and West finally brought the Russians into open conflict with their allies. He hinted to a French diplomat on September 1 that this was one hidden blessing of the German retreats: when the Bolsheviks filled the vacuum, their true brutal nature was not concealed for long. Was this perhaps the secret reason for Hitler's new readiness to evacuate his troops from the Balkans—to provide bait for his enemies to squabble over? One remarkable episode suggests that it was.

On September 2, Field Marshal von Weichs cabled Hitler's headquarters that British officers had asked for a meeting in which to coordinate Germany's step-by-step withdrawal from Greece with the British advance, so as to leave no such momentary vacuum for Communists to fill. Weichs reminded Jodl that the Führer had disclosed his intention of abandoning southern Greece.[1] But captured

[1]See page 693.

documents clearly betrayed the Communists' intentions of seizing the key posts there before the British could take over. Dr. Hermann Neubacher, the foreign minister's special envoy to the Balkans, supported Weichs's appeal for permission to meet the British. But Hitler—his eye now on more distant aims—refused. Already the Russians were south of Bucharest, thrusting toward the Danube—probably, in Hitler's view, racing for the Aegean Sea and the Dardanelles before the British could get there. As the great German withdrawal from southern Greece began, the British took no action to disrupt it—another sign, in his view, that Stalin had laid claim to the entire Balkans. "It is politically desirable to foment trouble between Communists and nationalists in every region we abandon," quoted Jodl in his diary.

Besides, Hitler had another card up his sleeve. By way of Japan, loud and unmistakable hints reached Hitler late in August that Stalin was reluctant to destroy Germany, as Russia would need all Germany's industrial expertise in the coming conflict with the West. "Stalin is evidently willing to conclude a peace treaty even with a National Socialist Germany under Adolf Hitler," the telegram from Tokyo read. This was why the Soviet offensive had stopped short of Russia's 1940 frontiers, and this was why Stalin had not emulated his western allies' terror-bombing of German cities. General Guderian agreed with Hitler that Germany still held some trump cards. If only Germany could survive the next months—"and that means holding the eastern and western fronts at all costs"—her military and political position could only get better.

Not sharing Hitler's strategic motivation, Finland and Bulgaria shortly followed Romania's distressing example. On August 21 a German counteroffensive by the Third Panzer Army had restored contact with Schörner's isolated Army Group North, and he came to see Hitler six days later to plead for permission to abandon Estonia. On this occasion Hitler's silence alone persuaded Schörner to withdraw his request. But a few days later the political situation altered, for Hitler learned that Finland had begun armistice talks in Moscow. On September 2, General Kreipe wrote in his diary: "The Finns jump overboard. At war conference [Führer] swears about Mannerheim, takes immediate decisions." Himmler warned Hitler the same day of secret reports that Hungary was also planning to defect. Bulgaria too was unmistakably steering a course out of the war, and Hitler had to rule against any armed German intervention in Sofia; on the eighth the Bulgarian government formally declared war on the Reich. Finally, in Slovakia, smoldering partisan troubles blazed into open rebellion late in August, obliging Hitler to send in security forces and disarm the Slovak divisions.

All these diminutions of Hitler's empire produced one certainty: that within months his arms factories would no longer have the oil or raw materials to manufacture the weapons the Wehrmacht would need. It was a trend which did not take Hitler by surprise, for in August he had instructed Albert Speer to analyze just how long the war could be protracted, given a "minimum economic region." These instructions anticipated the German evacuation of Finland, Norway, and all southern Europe as far as the Alps in Italy, the Sava River in Yugoslavia and the Tisza River in Hungary. With France overrun by the enemy, all the machine tools and materials sent to the French factories by Speer were lost.[2]

The Reich had lost Ukrainian manganese, Turkish chrome, Portuguese and Spanish tungsten, Romanian petroleum, Balkan ores, southern France's bauxite, and probably the Finnish nickel of Petsamo. How long Sweden would supply iron ore was uncertain. On September 3, Speer had assured Dönitz he already had enough iron ore for the whole of 1945. But later, his experts' final verdict on Hitler's "minimum economic region" came to a very different conclusion: "If the present production of special steels is continued, chrome supplies will be exhausted by January 1, 1945. Then armament production will come to a complete standstill." Assuming this bottleneck could somehow be surmounted, steel output would end by August 31, 1945. This prognosis reached Hitler on September 5, 1944. "Hitler suddenly began talking of the war," a doctor treating him at this time recalled. "He said the British and American gentlemen had made a huge miscalculation. They had not been able to meet their invasion deadline. And he still had all the raw materials he needed to last one year; we even had enough gasoline stockpiled for eleven months." And his experts had talked of a new electrosteel process for hardening armor plate which would make them independent of foreign chrome and tungsten.

Even so, "one year" put a very clear deadline on any breach between East and West—if such a breach was to avail Hitler's Germany.

Under Albert Speer and Karl-Otto Saur, arms production was still soaring. A new peak had been reached in August 1944. With trembling and barely legible handwriting Hitler put the finishing touches and signature to a document commending his arms manufacturers.

His arm was still far from healed. He jokingly said to his secretaries, "Before the bomb I had this shake in my left leg; now it's in my right hand. I'm glad it

[2]Martin Bormann observed in an uncharitable memorandum of August 17, 1944: "This shows again how wrong Minister Speer's agreements with the French economics minister [Jean] Bichelonne [in October 1943] were. It would have been far better to follow Sauckel's demands to fetch as many [French] workers as possible into the Reich. . . . Now we have lost both the machine tools and the materials Herr Speer sent over to them."

hasn't reached my head yet. It'll be a bad day when I can't keep my head from nodding!" Worse, he had caught a head cold from his barber—for he still couldn't shave himself—and now sinus headaches kept him awake all night. His head felt as though it was bursting, and Morell's treatment did not improve it. Another doctor elicited the fact that Morell was using a sulfonamide drug, Ultraseptyl—preferring this to the more usual I. G. Farben sulfa drug Tibatin because it was made by a Budapest firm in which Morell had a controlling interest. At the end of this Ultraseptyl treatment, Hitler was almost paralyzed by stomach pains and lay awake with dreadful nightmares. On August 18, Professor von Eicken had examined him and recommended a different drug; but Morell sharply rebuked him: "Out of the question—the Führer is allergic to anything else." The army doctor, Erwin Giesing, tested the drug on himself and experienced the same side effects after five days. To ease the sinus pains, he began cocaine treatment of Hitler, using a 10 percent solution supplied—like everything else—by the SS pharmacy in Berlin. Hitler sensed an immediate relief, though the cocaine reaction often brought out a sweat; on one occasion Giesing suspected it had brought on a mild heart attack, because Hitler felt giddy, things went black in front of his eyes, and for a full ninety seconds he had to lean heavily on the table in order not to fall over.

Over the next weeks the Führer began begging—indeed, importunately imploring—the army doctor to prolong the cocaine treatments; and in return he obediently found time to sit hunched over inhaling apparatus or in front of shortwave radiation equipment. He began to take a morbid interest in his own body, borrowed medical lexicons from Giesing, and experimented on his orderlies with Giesing's mirrors and instruments after the doctor had gone. He came to look forward to the cocaine and once said admonishingly to the doctor, "I hope you are not making an addict out of me." No longer did he have to salute with his left arm; no longer was his pillow bloodstained when he awoke each morning. But his memory was fading, he noted with concern; he forgot names and faces too easily. "But what does my health matter, when the entire nation's existence is at stake?" he would hoarsely ask the doctor.

At war conferences with his generals, Hitler awkwardly fumbled with vitamin and other unlabeled tablets and consumed them in seemingly random quantities.

He trusted only Martin Bormann, and he spent many hours alone with him. But July 20 had left him increasingly irritable and snarling. Emerging from his bunker to walk to the conference hut, he found his six-foot SS adjutant, Schulze, waiting to escort him. "Herrgott!" Hitler burst out. "Must somebody always follow me? Can't I ever go alone!" Everybody was suspect, new or old: the new Luftwaffe Chief of Staff, Kreipe, was under telephone surveillance, but SS bloodhounds were also following every movement of Rommel now that he had risen from his sickbed.

To be out of Hitler's favor was to be persona non grata with his staff as well. General Blumentritt related how he reported to the Wolf's Lair on September 13 with a cloud over his head after being replaced by General Siegfried Westphal in Hitler's housecleaning of Kluge's and Rommel's staffs. Guderian cut him dead outside the hut with a loud rebuke: "You dare come *here*—after what happened in the west?" But then Hitler approached through the woods, with slow and weary steps, escorted by five or six men, and greeted Blumentritt most courteously. At this the other generals were also nice to him, and Keitel invited him to tea.

In the west, at Keitel's suggestion, Hitler had reappointed Field Marshal von Rundstedt as Supreme Commander; his loyalty was beyond reproach. Model had tactical command, as commander of Army Group B; Rommel was formally relegated to the "Führer-reserve." On September 3, Brussels fell, and the next day the Allies captured the port of Antwerp with hardly any resistance; almost no effort had been made to destroy the port installations. Thus a huge breach was torn in the German line from Liège to the North Sea, through which a determined enemy might well sweep forward into northern Germany or encircle the Ruhr. Model reported that the Allies had two thousand five hundred tanks; the entire German tank strength in the west was less than one hundred. Without air cover he was helpless. The first Me-262 jets had still not arrived.

The V-1 flying-bomb organization in northern France had been overrun but on September 3, Hitler ordered air launchings of the deadly weapon from Heinkel launching-aircraft to continue. Production had just reached 3,419 a month. The damage inflicted on London had been enormous—in one suburb during August over 20,000 houses a day had been severely damaged by flying-bomb explosions. The British government now conceded that 450 aircraft with 2,900 flying personnel had been lost in the fight against this weapon. And now Hitler opened fire with what he called V-2—the army's fourteen-ton A-4 rocket designed at Peenemünde. Launching sites for the V-2 were in Holland, and to ensure that all went well the Führer appointed one of Himmler's best SS generals, Hans Kammler, to direct the V-weapon attack. The rocket had overcome its chronic "air burst" problem, and 374 had been manufactured by slave labor during August in an underground factory in the Harz Mountains. The initial attack on Paris was called off after two launchings miscarried on September 6, but two evenings later the first missiles slammed into Central London without warning. Hitler triumphantly ordered Himmler to decorate Wernher von Braun and his chief engineers, and he instructed Speer to step up V-2 output to 900 a month. (In

September and October, 629 and 628 were produced, and in November 662.)

Hitler angrily forbade any discussion of the Me-262 as a jet fighter but grudgingly conceded that every twentieth Me-262 manufactured could be supplied to the fighter squadrons. His discontent with the Luftwaffe was almost pathological. After General Kreipe set out the fuel situation on September 3—it was now so grave that all bomber and some fighter and dive-bomber operations would have to be curtailed—he stunned the Chief of Staff by remarking: "I am considering disbanding the air force altogether and tripling the antiaircraft artillery instead." He repeated his attack on the Luftwaffe when Göring again deigned to appear at the Wolf's Lair on the fifth. Kreipe's diary recorded:

> Führer spoke first: a tirade against the Luftwaffe. No good, gets worse year after year, he was lied to permanently about production figures and also about aircraft performances. Absolute collapse in France, ground staff and signals troops had left their airfields in headlong flight to save their own skins instead of helping the army to fight.
>
> Again the question of Me-262 operations was ventilated. The same arguments as to why only "high-speed bomber" can be considered. In milder form he again developed his idea of manufacturing only Me-262s in the future, while tripling the antiaircraft instead. . . . Our fighter designs were all wrong. What we need to fight the four-engined bombers are heavy twin-engined fighters with large-caliber armament. At the Reichsmarschall's request, Colonel [Hans] Boehm-Tettelbach, who had commanded a fighter squadron, was called in. From his own experience he explained why even heavy fighter aircraft with fighter escorts were not the best way of combatting heavy bombers. Boehm-Tettlbach was rudely sent away.
>
> For about ten minutes Hitler and Göring then talked privately. Then I was called in again. The Führer promoted me very cordially to full general and said I had been an excellent representative of the Luftwaffe these last weeks. . . . Afterward I sat a long time with Göring, who was extremely pleased with himself and said the idea of disbanding the air force was a dead duck. He promised to get Himmler to stop tapping my telephone.

Göring had provided Hitler with the means to plug the yawning breech between the Seventh Army on the German frontier and the North Sea: his paratroop regiments, training or reequipping under General Kurt Student in Germany. On September 4, Hitler ordered Student to establish a new army, the First Parachute Army, along the Albert Canal in Belgium—a meager force with twenty-five tanks and thirty-five batteries of 88-millimeter antiaircraft guns to defend a sixty-mile line from Maastricht to Antwerp; the line from Antwerp to the sea would be taken over by the remnants of the Fifteenth Army struggling over the Scheldt Estuary.

Farther south the rout was also halted, after Hitler, Keitel, and Bormann issued draconian orders to the commanding generals and the Gauleiters. Squads of military police separated even the highest-ranking officers from their truck-loads of chaises-longues and French women, and caught deserters fleeing from their units. When the Gauleiters warned Bormann that the military headquarters were moving into luxury hotels and chateaux inside the German frontier, Hitler stepped in with an order to his generals to house their staffs in the most humble quarters practicable; in one case a general had even tried to take over a military hospital. All along the western frontier women and children, young and old, were digging hastily improvised fortifications, an operation for which Gauleiter Koch's achievements in East Prussia served as an example. To halt the Allied invasion, the factories were turning out bazookas by the hundred thousand, in addition to the extra tanks, artillery, and ammunition Hitler had ordered for his great winter counterattack—the "great opportunity" that "fog, night, and snow" would afford him, as he prophesied on September 1.

Hitler's first plan had been to counterattack from Lorraine into the inviting flank of the American thrust toward Belgium. The Allies were short of fuel, as the best and closest French ports were still denied them by determined German garrisons. But Jodl argued against launching any attack until November 1, which would allow for time to replenish the divisions concerned; besides, Himmler's Volksgrenadier training program and Speer's special arms production effort were geared to the November 1 date Hitler had set in mid-August.

Hitler accepted Jodl's advice. The hours of inactivity forced on him by his doctors gave him time to think. As he gazed for hours on end at the ceiling of his shabbily furnished bunker bedroom, hearing only the hiss of the oxygen bottle in the corner, a far more adventurous campaign took shape in his mind. On about September 12 he sent for Jodl, who fetched a map which they spread out on the white bedspread. Together they sketched the direction of the attack and its necessary breadth and depth. Hitler had decided to strike again through the Ardennes—scene of his 1940 triumph—and seize Antwerp as soon as winter closed in. That day he established a new SS panzer army in Germany and transferred the robust SS General Sepp Dietrich from the Fifth Panzer Army to command it, camouflaging the move's importance by telling General Hasso von Manteuffel, his successor, that he felt better use could be made of Dietrich at home than in the field.

The Sixth SS Panzer Army was to be the spearhead of Rundstedt's Ardennes campaign. But Dietrich's skills were at best questionable. So, why the SS? The answer lay in the regular army's unencouraging record in the west. Besides, the Gestapo reports on the army's renegades—remorselessly fed to Hitler by Bormann and Fegelein—laid bare the moral decay into which most army generals had apparently relapsed: Beck, an amiable procrastinator, an Olympian academic, and embittered ponderer; Witzleben, the pessimist whose only reading was schoolgirl books from his wife's library; Eduard Wagner, a bureaucratic empire builder of pathological vanity; Tresckow, whose rebellion had been initiated when Schmundt had rebuffed his ambitions to succeed Heusinger as chief of operations in the General Staff. In a Germany bomb-blasted and rationed, these army plotters had lived the easy lives of grand gourmets. In Olbricht's cellars investigators found a thousand bottles of wine. A champagne orgy lasting far into the night had been their reaction to news of Hitler's "death." Fromm had flown regularly by plane on private hunting parties, sending his empty Mercedes on ahead by road. While the armies cried out for troops, the conspirators had squandered able-bodied soldiers on petty household jobs or on guarding their damaged homes. Because of the fuel crisis, teams of oxen were now having to haul the Me-262 jet aircraft onto the runways of German airfields. But according to Gestapo reports Stauffenberg had had his army chauffeur drive him a hundred miles a day or more on private excursions—in addition, his home was said to have been full of black-market alcohol and other scarce goods.

These reports must have made some impression on the prudish and ascetic Hitler in September—although it was he himself who had initiated the army's decline by leaving it leaderless when he dismissed Brauchitsch in December 1941.

After the regular war conference on September 16, Hitler asked certain men to remain behind—among them Jodl, Guderian, Buhle, Fegelein, and Hewel. Kreipe's diary records that Jodl began by stating that some fifty-five German divisions at present confronted ninety-six enemy divisions in the west, and that ten more Allied divisions were en route from England; the enemy's main strategic reserve—an airborne army—was still in Britain. The German divisions were short of heavy guns, ammunition, and tanks. "The Führer interrupts Jodl: he has resolved to mount a counterattack from the Ardennes, with Antwerp as the target." He considered that the German defensive position was strong enough to outweigh the enemy's numerical advantage. "The present front can easily be held! Our own attacking force will consist of thirty new Volksgrenadier divisions and new panzer divisions, plus panzer divisions from the eastern front. Split the British and American armies at their seam, then a new Dunkirk!" But with Antwerp in German hands, this time the encircled enemy armies would have no port from which to escape. "Guderian objects because of situation on eastern front," Kreipe's diary adds. "Jodl refers to enemy air supremacy and fears of parachute landings in Holland, Denmark, and northern Germany. Hitler demands one thousand five hundred fighters by November 1!" Kreipe's reasoned objections were overruled. "Acid comments. That's why our offensive will begin in a bad-weather period, when the enemy air force is grounded too. Von Rundstedt will take command. All preparations by November 1. The Führer sums up his decision in a lengthy speech." On pain of death, he ordered them to keep this secret to themselves and their most trustworthy staff officers.

American troops were now standing on German soil, and a bloody fight for Aachen, the first big German city, had begun. The Party ordered the city evacuated, but the German divisional commander, General Gerd von Schwerin, rescinded the order and provided a city official with a letter in English commending the citizens to the American troops' mercy. Schwerin was relieved of his command at once. Hitler issued the following secret message to his commanders, instructing them to pass it on to their troops by word of mouth.

> The fighting in the west has now spilled over onto German soil. German towns and villages will become battlefields. This fact must instill fanaticism into our fight and spur on every able-bodied man in the combat zone to make a supreme effort, so that every pillbox, every city block, every village becomes a fortress against which the enemy bleeds to death or which entombs its defenders in the man-to-man fight.
>
> No longer will this be a war of movement, but a choice between holding the line or annihilation. . . .

On the Russian front, the Red Army had begun a new stubborn attack on Schörner's Army Group North: twenty Soviet armies (equivalent to German corps) were pitted against Schörner's Sixteenth and Eighteenth armies. The Narva line was breached, and on September 16, Guderian and Schörner both came to Hitler to appeal for permission to abandon Estonia and withdraw Army Group North to a bridgehead at Riga. With Finland now out of the Nazi coalition, the political arguments no longer weighed; but Hitler was still reluctant, as Schörner's thirty-three divisions were tying down over a hundred of the enemy—the familiar "Crimea" argument. Besides, he disclosed to the generals, he had to keep some pawns in hand, as the Russians were currently extending feelers to him. One of Ribbentrop's staff had passed this news to him; this time Hitler authorized his minister to put out counterfeelers—but the Russian intermediary never showed up at the rendezvous. Perhaps an overeager agent had misinterpreted a sign. When some weeks later Frau von Ribbentrop wrote to Hitler suggesting that she should unofficially contact the Soviet ambassadress in Stockholm, Madame Kollontay, Hitler forbade her to. "Probing the Soviet attitude," he reflected, "is like touching a glowing stove to find out if it's hot."

On September 17, 1944, German speculation about the Allies' next move in the west was dramatically terminated. Instead of attempting a direct frontal assault on the West Wall, the Allies launched a sudden airborne attack on key river bridges in Holland; the attack was designed to capture a succession of important crossings from Eindhoven as far as the Rhine bridge at Arnhem, fifty miles to the north. British and American armored spearheads plunged northward along the corridor thus created toward the Zuider Zee; their mission was to cut off all Hitler's troops in Holland and destroy the V-2 rocket-launching sites near The Hague. If the Arnhem bridge was captured, the Allies could circumvent the billion-Reichsmark West Wall altogether. Small wonder that Hitler's heart sank at the news. His Luftwaffe chief recorded in his diary: "Nonstop telephoning and issuing of orders for the defense. Führer telephones. Afternoon, to see him and Jodl again. Quite a flap on."

The bold assault took the Germans completely by surprise, even though their Intelligence had been watching the enemy's airborne army for some weeks. Over fifteen hundred Allied troop transports and five hundred gliders had taken part. The Luftwaffe flew six hundred and fifty sorties against the airborne landings that day.

Arnhem was not even in the German combat zone—for the first hour only the proverbial cookhouse parties could defend the town. The town commandant had been killed in an air raid that morning, leaving only his elderly operations officer, one Major Ernst Schleifenbaum, in charge—an unlikely Horatio to hold the bridge. But for some reason the British paratroops had been set down five miles west of the bridge, at Oosterbeek (by chance the very place where Model had his army group headquarters); and this gave Schleifenbaum time to raise an emergency force for Arnhem's initial defense. In one unit were men of twenty-eight different commands, World War I veterans every one; each was given a captured gun and twenty rounds, and sent out to defend Arnhem against ten thousand enemy paratroops until help arrived. Schleifenbaum was to write some weeks later: "When Field Marshal Model came on the telephone and said, 'You are responsible to me for holding Arnhem!' I felt quite faint, until the old Siegerland nerves came to my aid. . . . We old fellows still have something in us yet." Undetected by the enemy, the Second SS Panzer Corps was only fifteen miles away and licking its wounds after defeat in France. Of these two divisions, Model threw Colonel Walter Harzer's 9th SS, the "Hohenstaufen" Panzer Division, into the fight. Moreover, the entire Allied battle plan was captured from a wrecked glider that same day. Although the Allies threw in fresh airborne forces the next morning, September 18, Arnhem and the bridge remained in German hands—after Aachen, the second defensive triumph for Hitler following a long run of defeats in the west. When the exhausted British fell back toward Nijmegen, they left over 1,000 dead and 6,450 prisoners at Arnhem.

Hitler did not at first recognize it as a tactical success. He thundered at the "idiocy of allowing the enemy to capture bridges [at Nijmegen] undestroyed"; and although the Luftwaffe's General Student deserved much credit, it could not offset the Party's campaign against Reichsmarschall Göring. Gauleiter Lauterbacher had just detected nine hundred Luftwaffe troops idling at Güstrow airfield; another one thousand five hundred at a camp near Flensburg wondered why they still had neither uniforms nor work. In addition, the British night raids had begun again. Ancient Königsberg was now in ruins, and one recent saturation attack on Darmstadt's center had left twelve thousand civilian dead in half an hour. The Me-262 jet had been unable to intervene at Arnhem, as its home airfield at Rheine had been plowed over by night raids. In consequence of all this, Hitler began to consider replacing Göring—at least *de facto*—by a real Luftwaffe commander like General von Greim; Richthofen, alas, had undergone a brain operation and might not live much longer.

The gathering storm is clearly described in Kreipe's diary on September 18—a day already made grim for Hitler by a painful headache which had allowed him no sleep. "During the Führer's conference," wrote Kreipe, "there are fresh reports of airborne landings in Holland. The Führer loses his temper and rages at the Luftwaffe's failure; he demands to know immediately what fighter sorties were flown in Holland to engage the enemy. I telephone Luftflotte 'Reich' and find out that because of the weather hardly any sorties were flown today. The Führer takes my report to this effect as an excuse for the most biting criticism. 'The entire air force is incompetent, yellow, and leaving me in the lurch. I've had fresh reports that numerous Luftwaffe units are retreating across the Rhine.' I inform him that under General Putzier we have set up an organization along the roads and at the Rhine crossings to catch them. I asked for concrete examples for me to follow up. Hitler retorted, 'I have no desire to speak with you again. Tomorrow I want to talk to the Reichsmarschall—no doubt you can arrange *that!*' " Göring still refused to see the danger signals. "When I warn him the whole witch-hunt is aimed at him, he just scoffs," wrote Kreipe the next day. "The Führer's war conference follows: icy atmosphere. I am ignored completely. At its end Göring sees Hitler. He tries to take me too, but Hitler indicates that he wants to speak with him alone. About 8 P.M. the Reichsmarschall comes back from the Führer, absolutely broken and washed up. After a long silence he tells me the Führer doesn't like me, as I have no faith in him, I am a typical staff-officer type and calculating machine, defeatist and unreliable; I am just full of objections and contradictions. . . . I responded that he must realize that the whole campaign is really directed against himself. Göring shot up and angrily rejected this. 'The Führer has expressly assured me of his confidence in me!' "

Shortly after midnight Fegelein informed General Kreipe that Hitler had forbidden him to set foot within the Wolf's Lair again. For the next two months the Luftwaffe had no Chief of Staff, and Göring kept a safe distance between himself and Hitler.

Deep-rooted factors contributed to this arbitrary and irrational behavior. One was that on the eighteenth he had just authorized Schörner's army group to abandon Estonia on the Baltic after all. Many thousands of Estonians who had fought to keep out the Red Army would be suffering now. Another factor was his own failing health, and the unspoken fear that with each cumulating illness since July 20 his own life was slipping inconclusively away as surely as was that of his beloved General Schmundt, who was dying of his wounds at Rastenburg hospital two miles away.

With his splitting headache undiminished, he drove to the hospital for head X-rays to be made on September 19. The X-ray department was searched for bombs, and guards were posted on every exit. After three X-ray photographs had been taken—all of which were found by the Allies in 1945[3]—he shook hands with the Catholic nursing sisters, then asked his doctor, Hasselbach, to guide him around the wards where the victims of July 20 lay. Schmundt was now in high fever (his wife wrote in her diary: "Afternoon: Führer here again, works like medicine"); at his bedside Hitler began to weep, because the doctors had advised him his adjutant had not long to live: gangrene had set in. "I was called in too late," Morell had gravely assured him that morning. "Otherwise I could have saved him with my penicillin." (In fact his "penicillin"—analyzed by Giesing—proved quite valueless.)

Word of Hitler's presence had spread, and when he rejoined his car he found several hundred people thronging outside, who burst out cheering as they recognized him. Half were civilians from Rastenburg town, the rest were invalid troops—including many cripples, many on stretchers, and many without an arm or leg, whose emotion at this, their first encounter with their Führer at such close quarters, could be seen glistening in their eyes. Even now his very proximity still infused many Germans with the certainty of eventual victory. A few days before, one of his SS staff had written privately: "Never have I been so confident as to our war position. Up here one gets a far broader view, you see things with a different eye. . . . With our Führer, nothing can possibly go wrong for Germany or any of us; he is quite simply *wunderbar.*"

[3]I obtained these X-rays in 1967; they do indeed show a cloudiness of the left maxillary sinus, needing irrigation. In 1968 the Soviet author Lev Bezymenski published good photographs of the jaw taken from a corpse found in the Chancellery garden in Berlin in 1945. As I first demonstrated in *Die Zeit* (Hamburg) on January 14, 1972, this jaw was identical to that in the X-rays *and* to that sketched from memory by Hitler's dentist, Professor Blaschke, under American interrogation in 1945. More recently the Norwegian-born dental expert Dr. Reidar F. Sognnaes, of the section of oral biology at the University of California, confirmed this at a symposium on forensic medicine in Edinburgh.

Over the next week Hitler's dimly lit bunker rooms seemed crowded with doctors. Professor von Eicken came from Berlin to perform the sinus irrigation. Giesing and Hasselbach were treating his other injuries. A fresh electrocardiogram was made to test the progress of his coronary sclerosis. His stomach spasms had returned, and even Dr. Koester's antigas pills were failing to exorcise them—Hitler's valet, Heinz Linge, showed the little black pills to Giesing at his request. In the daylight more than one of Hitler's staff thought his skin and eyes were turning an unhealthy yellow. General Nikolaus von Vormann, the retiring commander of the Ninth Army, visited him on September 26; he has described how he was frisked for hidden weapons, then led into a small room some ten feet square, with a small round table and some chairs.

> Through a curtain, Hitler came in alone from the next room; it was a tired, broken man who greeted me, then shuffled over to a chair, his shoulders drooping, and asked me to sit down. Without waiting to find out my business, he began to speak of our coming final victory and the new secret weapons. When I tried to tell him of the impossible situation on the Vistula and in Warsaw, from whence I came, he interrupted me, "Your successor [General Smilo Freiherr von] Lüttwitz will get help." He spoke so softly and hesitantly it was hard to understand him. His hands trembled so much he had to grip them between his knees. This was not the same Hitler I had last seen at war conferences on July 15 and 18—before the murder attempt of the twentieth.

Later that day, September 26, Heinrich Himmler arrived with a bulging briefcase of things to discuss. The real blockbuster was noted on his agenda simply as "Treason since 1939." In a locked safe at Abwehr headquarters outside Berlin Gestapo investigators had found documents proving that Mayor Goerdeler, General Oster, General Beck, and above all Admiral Canaris—the slippery former chief of Intelligence—had been plotting Hitler's overthrow since 1939 at least. More revolting still for Hitler was the proof that it was Canaris and his men who had deliberately betrayed the plans and dates of his 1940 western campaign ("Yellow") to the enemy. These documents extended only to mid-1940. They had been assembled by two of the admiral's staff—General Oster and Hans von Dohnanyi—with a view toward someday prosecuting Brauchitsch, then the army's Commander in Chief, for refusing to aid the anti-Hitler plotters. Hitler could only speculate on the harm Canaris had done to Germany since then. From General Muñoz Grandes, who had commanded Spain's contingent in Russia, he had learned some time ago that Canaris had personally warned Franco against bringing Spain in to the war on Hitler's side; but this clue had not been followed up.

It was all of only academic interest now, with the Russians poised to invade East Prussia and the Allies massing on the West Wall. Since his arrest in July, Canaris had told ingenious tales to save his neck, but those who had rejected the

Third Reich—Oster and Dohnanyi—betrayed their friend Canaris as their accomplice under Gestapo questioning and in a face-to-face encounter. General Alexander von Pfuhlstein, former commander of the "Brandenburg" (Commando) Division, was arrested on September 4, and he had strongly implicated Canaris in the murder plot as well: the admiral had once discussed using the division to storm the Wolf's Lair. (Canaris hotly denied it: "I only discussed with you using the division to protect Abwehr buildings if such a revolution should break out!") Pfuhlstein told his interrogators that Canaris had confidently predicted Germany's defeat for December 1943. Colonel Georg Hansen advised his questioners to search for Canaris's diaries, and these other damning documents had been found in the locked safe of another Abwehr colonel who had succumbed to the suicide epidemic after July 20.

The documents showed that the plotters had sent the then Colonel Georg Thomas—another of Keitel's department heads—to win Halder and Brauchitsch over in November 1939. Halder had refused: Brauchitsch would never join in, the German army would not rebel, and besides Britain's fight was against Germany, not Hitler. A 1939 "study" by Oster dealt explicitly with a coup d'etat. There were voluminous memoranda by General Beck, and scattered pages of the fabled Canaris diary throwing a revealing new light on the 1943 Black Chapel case and Abwehr dealings with the Vatican.[4] In April 1940, the documents indicated, Thomas had shown Halder a message from one Dr. Josef Müller—a Bavarian lawyer friendly with the Pope: the Vatican was willing to intercede with the British and French provided Hitler and Ribbentrop were first eliminated. On being informed of this approach, Brauchitsch had proposed to Halder that Thomas be arrested. The same Josef Müller had betrayed the date of "Yellow" to the Vatican—evidently on Abwehr instructions, since when Abwehr investigations of the leak led to Müller, Canaris ordered the affair hushed up. This explained how the Belgian envoy to the Vatican had been able to telegraph a coded warning to Brüssels, as Hitler had learned from the Forschungsamt in May 1940.[5] Oster had also warned the Dutch directly. This must explain why the "Brandenburg" agents detailed to capture the Meuse bridges in Holland had been massacred and why the bridges were blown before the Germans could make use of them. Hitler grimly informed Jodl of the news Himmler had brought. The facts about Admiral Canaris were so terrible that he could not make them public until the war was over; then there would be a state trial at which the German people could take their revenge.[6]

[4]See page 503.

[5]See page 106.

[6]After months of investigation, in November 1945 a British Intelligence report concluded that the Abwehr under Canaris had opposed Hitler only because of its jealousy over the inroads made into their domain by Himmler's agencies. "The role of Admiral Canaris has never been entirely clear, but

A personal catastrophe was about to fall upon Hitler, immobilizing him for two weeks.

First, Martin Bormann secured from him one last signature on September 26, 1944, ordering the Party to raise a people's army, a *Volkssturm,* by public levy on every able-bodied man between sixteen and sixty for the defense of German soil. The original idea was Guderian's. Alarmed to see his siege-defense troops in the east drained off to the West Wall, he had proposed a local territorial reserve *(Landsturm)* for temporarily plugging any breaches in his eastern defenses. Guderian had suggested Wilhelm Schepmann, chief of the SA, as their leader, because since 1934 the army had always got on well with the paramilitary Brownshirt organization. Bormann, however, could point to the results the Party had achieved in the west; Rundstedt had highly praised him. On the twenty-third the field marshal had sent four thousand sets of the necessary army blueprints to the seven western Gauleiters, and already the Party had half a million men erecting tank obstacles, bunkers, and fortifications. Hitler trusted Bormann, and the Party got the job of raising the Volkssturm—to mobilize "the people" just as Stalin had mobilized the factory workers of Moscow and Leningrad in 1941.

During the night Hitler was attacked by stomach cramps of such intensity that he had to bite back his need to scream. The next morning he refused to get up; wearing a gray flannel dressing gown over his shapeless army nightshirt, he lay with empty and expressionless eyes on his bed. A loaded revolver was on the night table. He refused to eat that day or the next. Morell was summoned, diagnosed only the old intestinal troubles, and gave him liver-extract injections; but the pains got worse. The fat doctor was seen leaving the bunker pale and sweating, for his medical experience had its limitations. Professor von Eicken arrived on the twenty-seventh from Berlin, but Morell sent him back without allowing him near his patient. Martin Bormann, sick with worry, remained constantly in the bunker for three days. Doctor Giesing recognized a case of jaundice, but Morell angrily denied it and attributed Hitler's yellow color and spasms to a gall bladder blockage caused by nervous worry; he began dosing his agonized patient with castor oil at one end and warm camomile-tea enemas at the other in the hope of

---

it is now demonstrable that he drew into the Abwehr men whom he knew to be engaged in anti-Hitler activities and on several occasions took steps to defend them. The fact that his attitude concerning the war seems from the first to have been strongly defeatist provides the only clue to the behavior of one of the most obscure figures in the history of the Nazi period."

unblocking the intestinal tracts. The pain got worse, and between September 28 and 30, Hitler lost six pounds. Blood tests and urinalyses were taken, but Morell refused to show them to his fellow doctors.[7] The Wolf's Lair was paralyzed. The war conferences were canceled for days on end. Admiral Puttkamer, recovering from his bomb injuries, hobbled in on crutches to read to Hitler the daily notes on the war situation. But for days Hitler just lay there with no comment or reaction at all.

By October 2 he had begun to dress again but still stayed in his little bedroom, where Blondi and her new puppies lay in a big wooden box in the corner. On the night before, General Schmundt—his chief adjutant since 1938 and one of the organizing architects of the Wehrmacht—had died of his injuries from Stauffenberg's bomb. Richard Schulze, his SS adjutant, found Hitler sitting on the edge of his bed in black trousers, collarless shirt, and suspenders. It was Schulze's thirtieth birthday. Hitler summoned up a smile and handed him the obligatory Glashütte gold watch. "I don't suppose I'll be presenting any more of these!" he exclaimed. Three days later, Puttkamer ushered in Schmundt's widow. Hitler was still frail and ill, and began to weep as she came in. "It is you who must console me," he sighed, "for mine was the greater loss."

Frau Schmundt then explained that the Gestapo were harrying her for access to Schmundt's secret diaries. She begged Hitler to take them into his personal custody. "Jawohl," agreed Hitler after some reflection. "Will it suffice if they are locked up in the Chancellery safe, and you have one key and Puttkamer the other?"

During Hitler's illness, Giesing sampled the little black antigas pills himself and suffered the same testiness, aversion to light, thirst, loss of appetite, enhanced sense of taste, and stomach cramps that had afflicted Hitler; it might even explain his jaundice too. From the Latin label it seemed that the quantities Hitler had consumed since Stalingrad must have *cumulatively poisoned* him with strychnine and atropine. Hitler somberly thanked Giesing; he had thought them just charcoal tablets for absorbing stomach gases.

All Morell's rivals—and they were many—closed in for the kill. Professor Brandt, Hitler's surgeon since 1934 and a staunch adviser of Speer's ministry, hurried from Berlin and accused Morell of criminal negligence. But Bormann was now out for Speer's blood, and he knew of Hitler's irrational affection for Morell as the only doctor who had helped him earlier. "Every other German has the right to choose his own doctor," Hitler confirmed. "I have chosen Morell." Morell,

[7]The reports are in Morell's papers. The urine tests revealed the presence of bile pigments and increased amounts of urobilinogen and urobilin—both consistent with an attack of jaundice.

pale and frightened, apologized profusely for his oversight. Bormann dismissed both Brandt and Hasselbach—using the latter's indiscreet revelations on the pills affair to Hitler's adjutants during the journey back from Schmundt's funeral at Tannenberg as a formal pretext. On October 9, Giesing too was paid off. Even Himmler was cold and unsympathetic to the doctors. He was next seen heading toward Hitler's bunker with his own personal doctor in tow—the thirty-six-year-old orthopedic surgeon, Dr. Ludwig Stumpfegger, a tall slim SS major with a brilliant reputation for bone and muscle surgery. Morell remained Hitler's doctor, but the consumption of the antigas pills was stopped. And Stumpfegger, Himmler's nominee, replaced Brandt, Hasselbach, and Giesing on Hitler's staff.

Hitler's irrational and often infuriating loyalty to his old faithfuls saved Göring as it had saved Morell.

Enraged by the Luftwaffe record, he had sacked Kreipe and determined to get rid of Göring too. On September 21 he interviewed General von Greim, commander of the Sixth Air Force, from the eastern front and asked him to become Göring's "Deputy Commander in Chief"; it would be a new position, and Greim discussed it thoroughly with Himmler, Fegelein, and Bormann over the next two weeks before Göring rebelled and sent him back to the east. The Reichsmarschall then sent for General Kurt Pflugbeil, commander of the First Air Force, and offered him Kreipe's job; Pflugbeil took one look at the situation at Luftwaffe headquarters and fled back to his own command. Göring gave up. In mid-October he went hunting on Rominten Heide, and here, he remarked, he proposed to stay —"keeping a strict eye on Himmler and Bormann" nonetheless, for the Reichsführer had now demanded air force squadrons of its own for the SS. At the Wolf's Lair, General Eckhard Christian alone represented the Luftwaffe when Hitler's war conferences resumed.

Fortunately, Hitler's adjutants remarked, the war stagnated during his two-week illness. Ominous rumblings still came from Hungary; the auguries of an East-West split became louder; planning for the Ardennes offensive continued; in Warsaw the Polish uprising collapsed; in northern Norway, Hitler authorized the Twentieth Army to fall back on the Lyngen Fjord–Narvik line; in the Balkans he ordered all Greece, southern Macedonia, and southern Albania abandoned to the enemy.

A melancholy report reached him on the last days of German rule in Estonia, too. Schörner had allowed ten days for the evacuation starting on September 18. In seventy ships the German navy had snatched the last Germans from the Baltic ports and evacuated a hundred thousand Estonian refugees as well. The oil-shale works were demolished, and the last Germans embarked in Revel (Tallin) on September 21. The local population could hardly believe that the Germans were letting the Russians return, and many announced that they would vanish into the forests and wait for the Germans to come back, as come they surely must. "On the twenty-first, knots of civilians gathered in the streets of Revel, armed with rifles. The last Germans to sail out could see a huge Estonian flag unfurled from the tower of the ancient Teutonic castle, 'Lanky Hermann,' and the German war ensign flew alongside—a sign that there were still Estonians minded to put up a fight, however hopeless, against the Bolsheviks. As far as we know," the report concluded on the twenty-eighth, "the Bolsheviks have liquidated all Estonians suspected of collaboration with the German administration and transported the able-bodied as slaves."

On October 7 a big Russian attack began, and the news that East Prussia itself was threatened brought Hitler out of his sickroom and back into the conference hut again. The generals urged him to leave the Wolf's Lair, but his answer was always the same: "The East Prussians would say I was leaving them to the Russians, and they'd be right. However secret we kept it, they'd still find out. The wretched people here have already had one taste of the Russian reign of terror in 1914 and 1915. I want to spare them a second dose."

In mid-October one problem could no longer be shelved: the future of Erwin Rommel. The field marshal, Hitler's favorite until recently, the first commandant of his HQ (in 1939), had recovered from his crash injuries at the family home near Ulm. The agents shadowing his movements reported that he went for walks "leaning on his son"; but local Nazi officials reported that Rommel was still uttering mutinous remarks. If any one popular hero could persuade the Germans to call a halt to the war, it was Rommel. The evidence against him seemed also complete: Lieutenant Colonel Hofacker had before his execution testified in writing that Rommel had assured the putschists that they could count on him if the plot succeeded.

Hitler showed Keitel the Hofacker document. Keitel sent for Rommel, but the field marshal declined to come. This left only a direct appeal to Rommel's sense of dignity.

At Hitler's dictation, Keitel wrote Rommel a letter advising him to come to see the Führer if he considered himself innocent or to behave as an officer should if he did not; otherwise he would be arrested and put on trial by the People's Court. General Wilhelm Burgdorf—Schmundt's burly successor as Hitler's adjutant and chief of army personnel—and his deputy, General Ernst Maisel, took the letter and the Hofacker statement in person to Rommel's home at Ulm, using a small unmarked Mercedes from Schaub's motor pool; the autobahns were closed to prevent Rommel's escape. At the evening war conference on October 14, Hitler was informed briefly that Rommel had just "died of his injuries." His only comment was an expressionless "There goes another of the Old Guard." He ordered no press announcement for the moment. Burgdorf returned to the Wolf's Lair with the field marshal's cap and baton and reported to Hitler and Keitel. Rommel had asked him if the Führer was aware of the Hofacker statement and then asked for time to think. Burgdorf had asked him to choose poison rather than the conventional pistol, to avoid causing public speculation. The Führer had, he said, promised a state funeral with full honors to preserve Rommel's popular reputation. The alternative would be trial and—if found guilty—dishonor, and execution.

Secret and promise were well kept. Even Hitler's adjutants did not find out. On October 15 or 16, Colonel von Amsberg drafted the usual obituary announcement for the *Army Gazette.* For a field marshal only the Führer himself could sign; Amsberg left it on Hitler's tray. Days passed, until Amsberg inquired whether the wording ought perhaps to be altered in some way. Hitler bit his lip and virtuously exclaimed, "I will not sign this obituary. I will not lie!"

On the Brink of a Volcano

On October 15, 1944, the day after Rommel's sudden death, Hitler's agents deposed the Hungarian regent, Admiral Nikolaus Horthy, and brought "a thousand years of Hungarian history" to an end.

The Nazi coup in Budapest had its origins in July, when Horthy had stopped the deportation of Hungarian Jews to Germany and sent his then adjutant General Béla Miklós to Hitler with a letter announcing his intention of appointing a military government; Hitler had received the general on July 21, claimed to be entitled to interfere in Hungarian affairs given the country's key position in the Balkans, and evidently also made some promise about the Jews, because four days later Himmler ordered the deportations to cease until further notice. He had already started talks with Allied intermediaries on an alternative means of disposing of the Jews—by barter, in exchange for goods or foreign currency from the Allies; on July 20, Ribbentrop had advised Edmund Veesenmayer, his representative in Budapest, that according to the BBC the Allies had rejected the barter proposal as an impudent attempt at weakening them. As his own penciled notes for the discussion reveal, at about this time Himmler debated with Hitler the "transfer of the Jews abroad." "Setting them free against foreign currency, [while retaining] the most important as hostages" was the proposal—to which the Reichsführer added his own comment: "Am against it"; as he subsequently checked the proposal, with the proviso that the currency must come "from abroad," Hitler evidently overruled him. By the end of July, Adolf Eichmann had left Hungary, and his task force was disbanded soon after. The first 318 Hungarian Jews were released from Bergen-Belsen camp and transferred to Switzerland to prove Germany's intention of keeping the bargain; but Himmler's intermediaries were asking for trucks in exchange ("to be used only on the eastern front"), and although further consignments of Jews were allowed to leave—1,355 in December and 1,100 in February 1945—the deal collapsed.

In October 1944, Himmler ordered the extermination of the Jews to stop. What led to this order is uncertain. SS General Ernst Kaltenbrunner, chief of the Reich Main Security Office, stated in his closing speech to the Allied tribunal at Nuremberg two years later that he had received a stunning report from an investigating judge he had appointed in 1943 to prosecute corruption at top level in the concentration camp system: this lawyer, Dr. Konrad Morgen, had been drafted into the SS for the purpose, and his early inquiries at Buchenwald convinced him that illegal murders of witnesses of the commandant's corrupt practices had occurred. Morgen had secured the execution of the commandant, Karl Koch, and eventually procured indictments in two hundred other cases. Late in 1943 he had realized that a systematic mass murder was proceeding at two camps—Auschwitz and Lublin. The commandant at Lublin, a former Stuttgart lawyer named Wirth, told him "they were destroying the Jews on the Führer's orders," and he was running altogether four extermination camps in the eastern Generalgouvernement of Poland, including Majdanek near Treblinka, in which five thousand Jews were themselves operating the machinery (before being systematically liquidated themselves). Shortly after telling him this, Morgen later reported, Wirth vanished from Lublin, having been instructed to raze his extermination camps to the ground. Late in 1943, he continued, while following up a major gold-smuggling racket, he stumbled on the truth about Auschwitz, where one Rudolf Hoess was commandant. Believing at that time that Hitler himself had ordered all this, Morgen felt powerless to intervene. He began a merciless prosecution of the camp officials over the "lesser" murders, however—outside the general massacre program, hoping in this way to ventilate the whole issue. But an investigating judge sent to scrutinize the files of the Reich Main Security Office itself—under whose Departments IV and IVb the massacre had begun—found that no general order for the massacre had ever been received or issued. Morgen himself was the target of harassment; his staff's barracks were burned down one night, with all their files, but he fought on and eventually laid the dossier before Kaltenbrunner.

Kaltenbrunner stated (in August 1946) that he was "stunned by the report." He himself had been interested only in the Intelligence side of his office. He sent the document by special courier that October 1944 day to Hitler. Hitler sent for him in person next day, and after a long discussion agreed to call Himmler and Oswald Pohl, chief of the concentration camps, to account for their actions. In Kaltenbrunner's presence—as he described at Nuremberg—the Führer ordered SS General Fegelein to ensure that Himmler reported to him immediately. (According to the manservant's register, Himmler came on October 17, and then again on November 7.) Hitler gave Kaltenbrunner his word, as they shook hands and parted, that he would put an immediate end to the massacre. (We have only Kaltenbrunner's account of all this; he himself was hanged at Nuremberg, and his widow possesses none of his personal papers which might have thrown light on the truth. Morgen, now a respected lawyer in Frankfurt, supports only part of the SS general's account, while motivated by an obvious and understandable antipathy toward him.)

The following scene is, however, independently testified to. On October 27, 1944, news reports reached Hitler that the Russians claimed to have found a former concentration camp, Majdanek, near Lublin, at which 1,500,000 people had been liquidated; according to Heinz Lorenz, his press officer, Hitler angrily dismissed the reports as propaganda—just as German troops had been accused of "hacking off children's hands in Belgium" in 1914. When Ribbentrop pressed him for an answer, the Führer replied more revealingly, "That is Himmler's affair and his alone." He betrayed no flicker of emotion.

There was no act of violence Hitler was not prepared to commit to keep Hungary—his only remaining petroleum supplier and a large foodstuffs exporter—within his domain, his "minimum economic region." From the end of August 1944, when Horthy openly courted Hitler's disapproval and announced that he had appointed General Geisa Lákatos to head a military government in place of the ailing and pro-German Döme Sztójay, one alarm signal after another was reported to Hitler indicating that the regent was plotting to follow Romania's—or even better—Finland's path out of the war while there was still time.

Initially, Hitler fought to win time, hoping for a spectacular military victory in the defense of Hungary by General Friessner to restore the Hungarian Cabinet's flagging spirit. When on September 7 Horthy issued a semi-ultimatum demanding five fresh German panzer divisions within "twenty-four hours" or he would ask the enemy governments for an armistice, Hitler ordered Guderian to accept the demand insofar as possible; and the first divisions began moving into Hungary the next day. But the next morning, the eighth, the German air attaché telephoned urgent warnings from Budapest about "goings-on similar to Romania." Hitler took him seriously, since this general, Cuno Heribert Fuetterer, had also provided the earliest alert of the coup in Bucharest. This warning gave him five weeks' clear notice to stage in Hungary a countercoup of the kind he had tried and failed to achieve in Romania in August.

After Antonescu's overthrow in August, the Hungarian and German general staffs had agreed to launch an offensive from Klausenburg to capture the Romanian half of Transylvania and then to hold and fortify the general line of the Carpathian Mountains. But the German troops movements, two hundred trainloads, would take ten days, and the Romanians and Russians reached and blocked the passes first. When the offensive began on the fifth, it rapidly fell apart—leaving Guderian no option but to abandon the easternmost tip of Hungary and fall back on the Maros River. What unsettled Hitler was that the Hungarian

Lakatos regime suddenly stopped the invasion of Romanian Transylvania at the eleventh hour without consulting him—evidently for political reasons. This excited his distrust. When General Janos Vörös, Guderian's Hungarian counterpart, pleaded for more military assistance on the twelfth, the Führer told him to his face: "I have no faith in your Lakatos government." This evoked from Vörös an assurance, given with Hungarian flamboyance and feeling, that Horthy would remain loyal and would fight at Germany's side until the end of the war. Hitler again promised to send the rest of the five panzer divisions, and at that night's war conference he outlined to Vörös his plans for a great new offensive to reconquer all of Romania.

He suspected Admiral Horthy of plotting a Badoglio-type betrayal. The admiral wanted high-grade German troops moved to eastern Hungary; then he would sign a sudden pact with Stalin—the British and Americans having evidently given him the cold shoulder—and deliver these now isolated German divisions to the enemy sword. East of the Tisza River Hitler had evidently already written off Hungary; but if he was not to lose western Hungary as well, he had no option but to take just that risk of treachery and pack every good division he had into the front line.

Together with SS Major Otto Skorzeny, Hitler began plotting ways of eliminating Horthy's now baneful influence on his generals. Horthy and his entourage lived ensconced in the Citadel at Budapest. Immediately after Antonescu's overthrow, the SS commander in Budapest, SS General Otto Winkelmann, had investigated the layout and security organization of the Citadel. Now Hitler spent hours each day poring over the original building-plans of the Citadel and its labyrinthine underground tunnels, plotting Horthy's capture and overthrow with all the Machiavellian attention to detail that had accompanied his planning for the Dirschau bridge and Eben-Emael fortress operations in 1939 and 1940.

Hitler's strategy in Hungary in September 1944 had derived from the comforting conviction that having digested Romania, the Red Army would wheel south to realize Russia's historic ambitions in the Dardanelles—and to reach the Balkans before Britain and the United States. The planned German offensive from Klausenburg had been a product of this belief: the Red Army was assumed to be leaving only covering forces along its Carpathian flank. The Russian offensive from this very region, spilling out *northward* into the Hungarian lowlands and capturing Arad, proved the falseness of Hitler's assumption—and this was the very eve of his debilitating two-week illness.

Immediately, on September 23, fresh alarms began sounding at the Wolf's Lair. German Intelligence networks evidently learned that Horthy was putting out increasingly urgent feelers to the western Allies in Italy and Switzerland, because

Hitler ordered the Luftwaffe to keep a close watch on all Hungarian airfields to prevent Horthy from sending his family out to safety in Switzerland. The Führer also discussed with Jodl the possibility of using three or four paratroop battalions to arrest the regent if he tried to move into the Hungarian army headquarters; some days later the plan was amended to include Skorzeny and five hundred Waffen SS troops in gliders. The scale of these operations was inevitable, because Winkelmann had learned that the Hungarian commandant of Budapest, General Bakay, was already plotting a large-scale military operation to round up every major German sympathizer. It was an undeclared war, in which Hitler was determined to keep the initiative. On September 25 he designated all Hungary a German "operations zone," thus bringing it under unified German General Staff control to avoid the clashes of interest that had hamstrung the German counter-coup in Bucharest.[1] Ferenc Szálasi, the extreme right-wing Hungarian General Staff major and Fascist leader, declared his willingness to take over the government. Millions of Hungarian pamphlets were printed in Vienna and transported to Budapest in sealed police trucks ready for the coup.

But Hitler was now ill, and the coup was postponed day after day—whether because of this or because he wanted Horthy to make the first move, we cannot tell. He must have found out that early in October Horthy had at last sent a team of negotiators to Moscow, because on October 3 he ordered the fight for Hungary's defense to continue even though "we are standing on the brink of a volcano." Some facts spoke for themselves. Although the Red Army had long been ready at Arad, it was still postponing its offensive, so evidently somebody was negotiating somewhere.[2] On the sixth—without any authority from Hitler or Himmler—Winkelmann decided to force Horthy's hand, because (as he later explained to the Reichsführer) "you can't just keep on postponing a putsch that's all ready and waiting." He ordered four top Horthy men kidnapped, including General Bakay and Horthy's own son and heir, who was believed to be dealing with the enemy himself. Bakay was netted at dawn on October 10. Later that day Himmler, Winkelmann, and probably SS General von dem Bach-Zelewski as well reported to Hitler for further orders; Bach-Zelewski—who had just cruelly put down the Polish uprising in Warsaw and was now ordered to raze the entire city to the ground—was directed to take his giant 650-millimeter mortar to Budapest

[1]Romania had been partly an OKW and partly a General Staff theater; operational control was shared by General Gerstenberg, General Friessner, General Hansen, and Admiral Brinkmann.

[2]They were indeed. The severe armistice terms dictated by Molotov to the Hungarian delegation on October 8, 1944, required the Hungarian armies not only to declare war on Germany "immediately," but to commence hostilities against them at the same time—just as Hitler had feared. Horthy cabled his acceptance of these terms on the tenth, as the secret Hungarian telegrams show. After the war, however, Horthy frequently denied he had ever accepted.

and help Skorzeny's operation. He arrived on the thirteenth. The same day Hitler directed Rudolf Rahn, one of Ribbentrop's best troubleshooting ambassadors, to follow him to Budapest and supervise the political aspects of the anti-Horthy coup, which was code-named *Panzerfaust*—"Bazooka."

To put teeth into their political pressure on Horthy, the Russians launched a big offensive on October 6 from the area between Arad and Klausenburg, across the plains toward Debrecen and Szolnok, which is on the Tisza. If this push had succeeded, it would have trapped Friessner's army group in the Carpathians, but at Debrecen Hitler had assembled three panzer divisions and on the tenth began a four-day tank battle which resulted in the destruction of several Soviet armored corps. This triumph should have stiffened Horthy's resolve to fight on; but he had already crossed the political Rubicon and secret orders had been issued to the First and Second Hungarian armies to retreat—the first phase of the betrayal of his erstwhile ally. Friessner was bewildered. His operations officer later wrote: "A major crisis occurred when on October 13 a section of the Hungarians—in fact the very ones who had been most effusive in their friendship toward us gullible soldiers—changed to the enemy side in mid-battle, no doubt in the misguided hope of a better future."[3]

During the following night, the first instructions were telegraphed to Veesenmayer in Budapest. The next morning, October 14, the crisis reports from Budapest multiplied. But Rudolf Rahn had now arrived there, and so had forty-two Tiger tanks which were being conspicuously unloaded at one of the main stations. It was the day of Rommel's sudden death; Goebbels, Speer, and Keitel were visiting the Wolf's Lair. Hitler himself attended his war conference ninety minutes after midnight; at a quarter to four in the morning he sent for his two secretaries and gossiped with them until five, when he went to bed. The news from Budapest was that Horthy had demanded to see Veesenmayer at noon the next day, and that the regent's Cabinet was meeting at ten; this probably meant that the hour for Hungary's defection had arrived. During the night the Hungarian General Staff telegraphed a threat to Guderian to withdraw the Hungarian troops from the front because Germany had not kept her promises. Guderian sent his deputy, General Wenck, flying to Budapest with his reply—an ultimatum to the Hungarians to stop meddling with the Hungarian divisions in Friessner's army group, as all Hungary was a German theater of operations now; and to rescind within twelve hours the orders to the First and Second Hungarian armies to

[3]His manuscript continued: "At the end of September we had transferred our army group headquarters to a picturesque but modern sanatorium for railwaymen in the Matra Mountains north of Gyöngyös. The accommodation and surroundings could not have been more beautiful. I refused to be robbed of my daily midday ride on Yutta through the brightly colored autumn beech forest. In the evening the deer were calling!!"—The general was a passionate huntsman.

retreat, failing which the Reich would take such measures as seemed necessary to attain her objectives. As this ultimatum was being delivered at 10 A.M., Skorzeny's team in Budapest was kidnapping Horthy's son—luring him to an ambush by telling him that an emissary from Marshal Tito was waiting for him.

Thus by the time Hitler was awakened by his staff on October 15 at half-past noon, the die had been cast; Horthy's son, the pawn in Hitler's hand, had been rolled—bloodstained and senseless—into a carpet and bundled into a plane bound for Vienna. At that very moment, unaware that at noon "Panzerfaust" had begun to roll, the regent was receiving the German envoy, Veesenmayer. Let us hear Winkelmann's coarsely worded narrative of that day, in his proud report to Himmler:

> Veesenmayer showed up at Horthy's punctually at 12 noon; Horthy immediately launched into a violent tirade, complaining we had kidnapped his son—we'd ambushed him. The old fellow said he had always warned him, but his son had refused to listen. He demanded that we release his son from custody, etc.
>
> Veesenmayer stood up to him like a man and didn't have to wheel out the biggest gun we had agreed on, namely to tell the old chap that if there was the least whiff of treachery we would stand his son up against a wall. Horthy threatened to quit the war, but did not commit himself positively as to when. Shortly afterward, his radio broadcast the foul proclamation.
>
> Meantime Ambassador Rahn had driven over to Horthy to appeal to his conscience. Horthy was crying like a little boy, kept clutching Rahn's hand and promising to call everything off, running to the telephone and then not speaking into it, and in general acting like somebody demented.

Horthy's armistice announcement had been broadcast at 2 P.M. Almost immediately the radio building was seized by a German police lieutenant and a handful of men—even before Bach-Zelewski's Tigers had arrived. A proclamation was broadcast, apparently signed by General Vörös, declaring Horthy's announcement of an armistice null and void and ordering the fight against the Red Army continued. Hungarian and German march music was broadcast, and then came Ferenc Szálasi's pronouncement that he had assumed power. Horthy's own troops in the capital deserted him. He and his dwindling supporters retreated into the Citadel; other Hungarian ministers, "pale and evil-smelling" in SS General Winkelmann's words, sought German protection. The Citadel was well guarded, and its approaches were mined; but Hitler had twenty-five thousand men in the city and more than forty Tigers—and he had the seventy-two-year-old statesman's son as hostage. The deal was put to the regent during the evening hours: at 6 A.M. the Citadel would be stormed; alternatively, if the regent would resign, legally transfer power to Szálasi, and leave the country, his son would be restored to him. Horthy's prime minister, General Lakatos, acted as the go-between. Horthy must have heard the Tigers raising a horrendous clatter as they pawed their way around the inclines to his Citadel.

Hitler canceled the midnight war conference and retired to his bunker at 1:15 A.M. to gossip with his secretaries Frau Christian and Fräulein Schroeder. Shortly before 4 A.M. Budapest telephoned: General Lakatos had told Veesenmayer that his government would resign, and that Horthy would abdicate the next day. Horthy was asking in return for asylum in Germany for himself, his family, and some friends, and for promises that the Reich would not blacken his name over the events of the previous day and would prevent any civil war in Hungary. Hitler agreed, and went to bed at four.

Thus Hungary remained in his *Festung Europa,* such as it now was, with Ferenc Szálasi as the constitutionally appointed head of state; Stalin's hopes of trapping Friessner's Army Group South were crushed. Horthy's orders to his First and Second armies—of which Hitler seemingly never learned—had been squashed before they even left the Budapest ministry.[4] General Miklós, commanding the First Army, deserted with a handful of his staff to the Russians. General Lajos von Veress, commanding the Second Army, was arrested by Friessner for ordering his army to retreat. A second great tank battle was fought by Friessner at Debrecen, and a new defeat inflicted on the Red Army. A brief respite was thus granted the Nazis in Hungary.

In anticipation of the battle for East Prussia, Hitler had moved over into Bunker Eleven, a monstrous rebuilt complex of dormitories, operations rooms, and offices for himself and his principal minions; there was even space for his own diet kitchen in it. It would be proof against the heaviest known bombs, and against poison-gas attack, since it had its own compressed air and oxygen supplies and a U-boat air-conditioning plant in case all else broke down.[5] On the day of Arnhem, Hitler had ordered a realistic reassessment of the Wolf's Lair's defenses against mass paratroop attack. "We can't afford to take rash risks any longer. . . . If a *Schweinerei* happens here—then myself, my entire High Command, the Reichsmarschall, the OKH, the Reichsführer SS, and the foreign minister, we are all sitting ducks! What a catch we would be! If I could get my hands on the entire

[4]Upon receiving a certain code message ("Carry out order of March 1, 1920"), Generals Veress and Miklós were to contact the Russians and turn their guns immediately on the Germans instead; the Third Army's General Heszlény was not trusted enough to be taken into Horthy's confidence. Horthy issued the code message on October 15, but the Hungarian defense ministry officers were suspicious and refused to transmit it.

[5]The air-conditioning plant installed by the Dräger firm had poison-gas filters; should these filters perish, canaries in the bunker rooms would provide an early warning. But Hitler declined to have canaries in his own rooms.

Russian High Command at one fell swoop, I would risk two paratroop divisions for it immediately!" On the day the Russian attack on Memel had begun, he had demanded twelve heavy antiaircraft batteries for his headquarters' defense immediately.

Here on the eastern front, Hitler, now tired and ailing, had long lost the initiative in the face of the baffling Russian superiority; his only strategic prerogative was to decide which towns to defend and which to abandon. An avalanche of enemy tanks had again swamped across Army Group North and reached the Baltic coast in the second week of October. Memel was surrounded, but Hitler ordered this ancient port fortified and held. Along the Memel River, the northern border of East Prussia itself, he managed to establish a new front line on the twelfth, while the long-range guns of the German battle fleet held the enemy at bay. But Schörner's attempts to drive a fresh corridor through to East Prussia failed, and the twenty-six divisions of his Army Group North were again cut off —this time in Kurland, a fifty-mile-square promontory into the Baltic. Hitler accepted Dönitz's arguments that the port of Libau, at its closest end, was more important than Riga, and the latter port was abandoned on the fifteenth. In this pocket the army group remained, attracting a disproportionate number of Russian divisions away from the main front—a controversial appendix of Hitler's "Barbarossa" campaign until the war was over, surviving six bloody battles undefeated.

On October 16, 1944, the day of Horthy's abdication, as Göring, Ribbentrop, and Goebbels joined in Hitler's noon war conference, the Red Army suddenly stormed into East Prussia itself, with two big armored spearheads thrusting into the eastern flank of the province toward Gumbinnen and Goldap, evidently making for Königsberg itself. Refugee columns began streaming past Hitler's headquarters. The German divisions were outnumbered 4 to 1. Gumbinnen fell, burning from end to end. By the twenty-second many of Hitler's staff considered East Prussia already lost. At Hitler's noon conference that day Keitel pleaded with him to leave for Berlin. Martin Bormann privately instructed the stenographers to begin packing for the move to the Chancellery and ordered the transcription section to make the transfer in three days.

Why did Hitler not tour the nearby battlefield now? He was far from well. Half the evening war conferences were canceled so that he could retire to bed, swooning with nameless pains against which neither Drs. Morell nor Stumpfegger, nor Eicken, summoned again from Berlin, could effectively prescribe. Morell thought it was an inflammation of the nasopharyngeal area. His dentist, Professor Hugo Blaschke, X-rayed the jaw, found an agonizing defect to the second bicuspid about which Hitler had kept silent, and after days of pleading was allowed to extract it.

An atmosphere of imminent defeat lay heavily in his private rooms—an air which no conditioning plant could dispel. One secretary wrote: "It made us despair to see the one man who could end all the misery with a stroke of his pen lying apathetically in bed, gazing at us with weary eyes, while all around us all Hell was loose. It was as though the Flesh had suddenly realized the futility of the efforts of his Will and had just gone on strike; and Hitler, who had never run into such disobedience before, was caught unawares by it."

Dr. Theo Morell gloomily wrote on October 23, "It's real autumn here, with dense fogbanks everywhere." Hitler's secretaries sat each evening gossiping at his bedside. At midnight an adjutant—Puttkamer, Below, or Major Willi Johannmeyer—would bring the brief war report. Sometimes Colonel von Amsberg, his Wehrmacht adjutant, spent the day touring the battlefields, where the Russians had now broken into Rominten Heide. Other times he would stand dutifully at the foot of Hitler's bed listening to the Führer ruminating on the errors he had committed in the past. In the darkness, after the secretaries left at four or five, Hitler made up his mind to stay at the Wolf's Lair and to die fighting for the Reich's frontier, rather than return to Berlin.

Then the miracle happened—Hitler believed it was just because his riflemen knew that he was still there. General Hossbach's Fourth Army halted the Russian onslaught and launched a courageous counterattack; first he deliberately accepted the risk to Goldap and concentrated on the enemy spearhead west of Gumbinnen. Here the Russians were put to flight and Gumbinnen recaptured. As Hossbach then swung south to deal with the Goldap spearhead, the devastation and carnage left by the Russian General Galizki's Eleventh Guards Army were witnessed for the first time. General Kreipe, touring the combat zone, wrote in his diary: "Visited 'Hermann Göring' Panzer Corps, in combat at Gumbinnen. Gumbinnen ablaze. Refugee columns. In and around Nemmendorf women and children crucified on barn doors and shot. I order photographs taken as evidence." The Gumbinnen atrocities made a deep impression on Hitler. The same secretary wrote: "Gone was his good temper. When we arrived at night for tea, he looked grim and careworn and he had to make an effort to put these pictures and reports from the eastern front out of his mind: women raped, children massacred, men mutilated . . . He swore revenge for them. 'They aren't human,' he said. 'They're the beasts of the Asiatic steppes. The war I am waging against them is a fight for the dignity of European man. No price is too high for victory. We must be harsh and fight with every means at our disposal.' "

On October 25, Hitler told Bormann he would definitely not consider leaving the Wolf's Lair until the crisis in East Prussia was over. "We would prefer rather more safety for the Führer," Bormann wrote nervously that day. "After all, forty or fifty miles are nothing for modern tanks to cover. Besides, we would prefer a more congenial place for the Führer to convalesce. But the Führer commands, and we obey." His secretaries asked if they ought to learn to handle pistols. Hitler loftily excused them from this need. "No, thank you, ladies: I have no desire to die at the hands of one of my secretaries!"

Amsberg, leaving to take up a frontline command, reported for one last time to the Führer in his bunker living room and asked what he ought to tell the officers of his new unit. "I know what I must not say, but not what I should." With a sigh of resignation Hitler told him: "You know for yourself how black things look. Tell them I am thinking and fighting all day and night for the German people and that my thoughts are always out there with my troops. I did try—and I will keep trying—to bring this war to a happy conclusion yet. But you know the way our Luftwaffe is, and there's no point in concealing it."

Sepp Dietrich, raising the new SS Sixth Panzer Army for the Ardennes offensive, visited Hitler and lectured him: if there was no Luftwaffe available even for reconnaissance, then the most heroic fight the infantry or U-boats could put up would be in vain. Göring called the criticisms libel and bitterly resented Bormann's daily rapid teleprinter reports submitted by the Gauleiters direct through him and Schaub to Hitler; these Party chiefs had no praise for the Reichsmarschall. By day and night the most devastating rain of fire in history was eating out the heart of Hitler's war industry. A five-thousand-ton deluge of bombs dropped on one city center within twenty minutes was a commonplace; nine thousand tons of bombs cascaded on Duisburg in one October day. With France lost, the Luftwaffe had no early-warning systems; conversely the enemy had stationed radar guidance systems in France enabling them to pinpoint towns as small as Bonn despite the most adverse weather. These saturation raids began to cause severe shortages throughout the German economy. By October all medical supplies—drugs, serums, bandages, anesthetics, and analgesics—were scarce or even unobtainable, as the factories had been destroyed. But the American daylight raids were a rapier thrust to the heart; synthetic rubber production was hit, and this alone limited the number of the new secret Mark XXI submarines Hitler could build. The loss of synthetic gasoline was so severe that a vicious cycle set in: by October over three thousand day fighters were available, but their fuel supplies were low; the refineries were inadequately defended; and those pilots that did engage the enemy had been undertrained because of the lack of gasoline.

Four times in the last two weeks of October Hitler taxed Göring in person about the Luftwaffe. Göring told him he had agreed with Adolf Galland and Albert Speer on a policy of conservation; he had now saved up three thousand one hundred fighter aircraft to throw en masse against the enemy bombers on a day when the weather was good enough. To Hitler it seemed a strategy designed to conserve only the pilots. He again began considering supplanting Göring with Greim. On November 1 he had another ninety-minute talk with the general. Greim had suggested appointing a chief of air warfare—namely himself—with operational command over the entire Luftwaffe. Göring came to the Wolf's Lair on November 3 and again on the fifth, and talked Hitler out of it. Evidently the price Hitler demanded in return was that Göring must appoint General Karl Koller, the Bavarian who had worked his way up from the ranks, as Luftwaffe Chief of Staff. Göring told Koller that day about the fight being waged against him by the SS, the army, and the Party. "He talked about the situation and declared that he is just fed up," wrote Koller that day. "He wished he were dead. He would like to join the paratroop army and fight with it at the front, but the Führer won't let him go and has told him that only he can rebuild the Luftwaffe."

Be that as it may, Hitler's consultations with Göring about major Luftwaffe policy were now only pro forma. He had just ordered Speer to triple antiaircraft artillery production at the expense of aircraft production, and he had decided that antiaircraft batteries should be concentrated on the defense of the steel industry, major factories, and railway centers; Allied airmen described the German batteries as their deadliest enemies. And it was thanks to Hitler that the Me-262 was in service as a jet bomber—though five months later than he had planned. As he had predicted, the Me-262 was proving an unwieldy disappointment as a fighter—it was vulnerable to enemy fighters during its takeoff and landing. But the bomber version was performing well against the large enemy troop assemblies around Nijmegen. Hitler accepted Speer's advice and ordered the rapid design and mass production (without trial) of a single-jet fighter, the Volksjäger; Heinkel's design was accepted, and the new plane was incorporated in the special production decree Speer asked Hitler to sign on October 12, concentrating aircraft production capacity on the new high-performance planes.

Meanwhile the devastation continued. General Galland kept delaying his fighters' *Grosser Schlag*—the Grand Slam. Finally Hitler lost patience, calculated for himself that Galland's arithmetic was full of fallacies, and announced at a war conference on November 6: "It's pure madness to go on turning out new aircraft all the time just so that the Luftwaffe can juggle with figures." On the twelfth, Galland claimed he had three thousand seven hundred fighter aircraft ready, but that same day an episode in Norway dealt the death blow to his plan. A small force of British heavy bombers attacked the crippled battleship *Tirpitz* at anchor in Tromsö Fjord. The local Luftwaffe fighter squadron was given more than adequate warning of the attack, and the Lancaster bombers, each carrying a ten-ton earthquake bomb, would have made easy targets; but—as Admiral Dönitz furiously telegraphed to Hitler—the fighters arrived too late. After eight minutes it was all over, and the huge battleship suddenly capsized, entombing one thousand sailors in the hull. Hitler angrily ordered Galland to surrender his hoard of fighters for his own Grosser Schlag—the coming top-secret Ardennes offensive—instead.

After the *Tirpitz* incident, he did not spare Göring's feelings even in public. Some days later, Göring showed him a memorandum. Hitler tossed it contemptuously aside. "There's no point in my reading that, it's all a pack of lies!"—and he turned his back on him. Galland was also on the way out.

To balance his grudges, Hitler showed special favor to some. Only recently he had ordered Bormann to find a suitable estate to present to Field Marshal von Manstein, and he did not take it amiss when Rundstedt asked for the services of Manstein, Leeb, or Kleist on the western front; he hinted to his staff that if ever Germany began great military offensives in the east he would again send for Manstein to command. Even Field Marshal von Brauchitsch—whom one officer claimed to have seen riding through Berlin in full field marshal's uniform on July 20 and whose conduct in 1939 and 1940 was not above reproach, as the Oster/Dohnanyi documents revealed—was restored to Hitler's favor. On August 3 he had written Hitler a letter offering his services and dissociating himself from Stauffenberg and the putschists; and now that Hitler's secret order creating the Volkssturm under Himmler had been made public, the elderly field marshal wrote again offering his life for Germany. Brauchitsch was given high marks in Hitler's book for having fostered Peenemünde and the V-2 rocket project: the V-1 flying bomb was still in action against the port of Antwerp, to which the enemy had now forced access by clearing the Scheldt Estuary, but only the V-2 rocket could still reach London. Every day he asked Jodl for the latest V-2 launching figures. Twenty or thirty times a day the missiles hit the British capital, each time with a one-ton warhead and the dynamic force of an express train. "No population can hold out under such an uninterrupted bombardment," Hitler gloated to his secretaries. "Their nerves won't stand it, because there is no warning from the sirens. The bomb can impact at any instant. Sheer panic will grip the masses and drive them out into the open countryside. But just imagine what that means—for the millions of people of a city almost twice as big as Berlin to swarm out to where there is neither roof nor rafter to accommodate them. . . . It will be an avalanche of misery and suffering, because even when the people get there, the local villagers will regard them as a plague. What parliamentary government can survive that! There will be such a storm of protest and war-weariness that the government will be overthrown. And that will mean peace at last."

By early November the British government had still not admitted that London was under enemy missile attack. But the repeated appeals to the evacuees not to return to the capital, and the lengthening obituary notices in London newspapers, gave all the confirmation Hitler needed.

From his two-week illness onward, Hitler, who had avoided as much contact with the civil affairs of the Reich as possible since 1939, concerned himself exclusively with military command decisions.

Dr. Hans Lammers, chief of the Reich Chancellery, had secured his last conference with him on September 24, 1944. That day the Führer signed his last law into the statute book (a minor item permitting Wehrmacht members to belong to the Nazi party).

In the east and west, in the Balkans, in Italy and in Norway, he was having to yield ground to the enemy which he might have been able to defend with his new strategic reserves but for his unshakable decision to concentrate those reserves in a great new counteroffensive in the Ardennes. Every day saw him in secret consultation with the handful of associates he had taken into his confidence —Fegelein, Himmler's liaison officer; Jodl, his chief strategic adviser; Buhle, who was scouring the Reich for every available piece of artillery. But even the military burden was now proving too much for him. He could seldom muster enough strength to hold his evening war conference. Several times he lay awake all night, sick with worry about the future—and about an aching throat which stirred in him the same cancer fears that had led to an operation in 1935. After supper on October 29, for example, he received Fegelein, Puttkamer, and Dr. Franz von Sonnleitner—Hewel's stand-in—for their reports on SS, Wehrmacht, and foreign affairs, then he sat sipping tea until 3:30 A.M. But he could not sleep: Dr. Morell was fetched at 6:10 A.M.—no doubt with sedatives—and again after breakfast eight hours later. Even the most vital evening conferences were transferred to this shabby, semidarkened bedroom. There was room for only one stenographer. "10:50 to 11:21 P.M.: took down conference of General Buhle and SS General Fegelein in Führer's bedroom," noted the stenographer Karl Thöt, on the thirty-first. "The Führer was lying in bed, but no less vigorous than usual. I sat behind his two visitors at a round table with a lamp."

His Ardennes gamble depended on the eastern front remaining stable until then. Here the war gods aided Hitler. Although fierce fighting would rage all winter in Hungary, elsewhere the Red Army was evidently exhausted. General Guderian predicted that Stalin would delay his main offensive until the frost—probably later than usual this year. Thwarted in East Prussia by Hossbach's counterattack, the Red Army had stormed Schörner's army group in Kurland on October 27, again hoping for a quick victory. But again they lost heavily. On the eleventh day of this fierce battle General Wenck said triumphantly to Hitler, "We have already knocked out five hundred twenty-two tanks." When Hitler soberly pointed out that the Russians had "huge numbers of tanks," Wenck continued, "—against which our own material losses are only three 75-millimeter guns, seven light field-howitzers, nine 122-millimeter Russian guns, and one 150-millimeter." "Slight losses indeed!" conceded Hitler. "When we stand fast! All our losses have come from our 'glorious' retreats—the kind of retreat one makes to 'regain one's tactical freedom.' "

By November 5 the Red Army had also been thrown out of the East Prussian town of Goldap, leaving a battlefield strewn with so much equipment in comparison to the meager haul of Russian captives that Hitler concluded—probably rightly—that the Red Army's "divisions" were of only regimental troop strength. "They are staking everything on their artillery," he pronounced. "Their 'divisions' are all understrength, just conglomerations of a few thousand men." Wenck agreed; it was remarkable, he pointed out, that they had scraped reinforcements together from quite far afield to try to save their foothold in Goldap. Hitler tried to read Stalin's mind. Where would it be best to launch the great winter offensive? In East Prussia or in Poland? "He must have had his doubts," commented Hitler, reflecting on the barely-hoped-for German victory in East Prussia. "He has always been wary of sending his troops into a highly developed area, as they would be bound to realize the absurdity of bolshevism after seeing it. So it is possible he'll move them into here"—indicating the Vistula bridgeheads in Poland—"and that up here [on the Baltic] he'll say he's got what he wanted by snapping off this thing," meaning Army Group North. Some minutes later, after hearing of an aircraft reconnaissance report on the menacing Soviet bridgehead across the Vistula at Baranov, Hitler again postulated: "That's where we must be on the lookout. Everything he's doing up here is just a diversion. . . . Besides, he must sense that up here on German soil [*i.e.*, East Prussia] he'll have to shed a lot of blood—a lot."

The Führer felt he had good reason to expect an early clash between Russia and her Allies. Throughout the autumn the unnatural three-year-old alliance between the capitalist democracies and the Bolshevik dictatorship had been closely examined in Berlin for signs of "metal fatigue."

Hairline cracks were already appearing. Stalin had given British and American military delegations twenty-four hours to get out of Bulgaria. His invasion of Romania and Bulgaria, and the spread of Communist subversion in the Balkans, flagrantly violated the Teheran agreements of 1943—as the Cicero documents showed. Stalin's annexation of eastern Poland was causing uproar in London and Washington if the foreign press dispatches and code intercepts were to be trusted: Hitler and Ribbentrop soon believed they could name their own price—once the "East-West war" began. On October 10, Himmler had shown Hitler a strong clue that Stalin was again putting out oblique feelers to him.

Foreign Minister Anthony Eden admitted in Parliament that relations with Stalin were strained, but he advised Goebbels not to fasten any hopes on it. However, actions spoke louder than words. Neither Stalin nor Hitler could fail to see that the British were still purposefully allowing the Wehrmacht to escape unhindered from the southern Balkans to the battlefields in Hungary. "It's obvious the British could have done something here, given the position we're in," Jodl commented to Hitler. "They only had to invade somewhere along here"—indicating the Adriatic coast of the Balkans—"and they would have cut us off completely down there." In the United States meanwhile, the Hearst press quoted Washington officials' predictions of an early outright conflict. In Iran, British and American oil interests had already provoked a government crisis over their dispute with the Russian oil interests. In Greece the government appointed by the British military commander had disbanded the Communist guerrilla units—on paper, if not in fact. Most encouraging of all for Hitler was the Luftwaffe's discovery that an entire British tactical air force wing had vanished from the Italian front despite Field Marshal Sir Harold Alexander's warning that the Germans were not weakening. At the same time German Intelligence had reported *Russian* troops and tanks appearing on Bulgaria's frontier with Turkey, only a hundred miles from the coveted Dardanelles. A tactical air force needed prepared bases—like those airfields the British had demanded of Turkey last winter. Hitler speculated:

> Perhaps they have disengaged a tactical wing to be on the safe side. Because for all the polite phrases they are swapping, the tension seems to be building up. Perhaps they are disengaging it to transfer it to Greece or to *here*—

and at this point Hitler's finger must have tapped eastern Thrace, that is, northern Turkey.

> It's quite definite that the Russians will attack there. I estimate it'll take them two to three weeks to deal with that. And when you're on one shore of the Dardanelles you don't just stop there, because you've got to occupy the other shore as well. You can only use the waterway if you control both shores. So he'll have to take the second bit as well [southern Turkey].

"And that," concluded Hitler logically, "will start the whole structure toppling. . . . My view is the British are standing by, because vital interests are at stake." A few weeks later Ribbentrop summarized Hitler's current strategy as follows: "If we are asked whether we would consider a political settlement, we reply that we are intent only on fighting on, and are not thinking of any political settlement—because this stance in itself might bring such a political settlement that much nearer."

Meanwhile the OKW instructed German military attachés not to discuss the coming East-West conflict at all.

With Hitler's last European ally gone, and the German nation nevertheless unbowed by bombing or military reverses, the Allies could only hope for a speedy victory if the Führer was ill or a power struggle broke out. Rumors abounded in the foreign press that he was ill, exhausted, in an asylum, or even Himmler's captive. "According to this one," Hitler guffawed, reading one news report aloud to his staff, "I'm a prisoner in my own house, my own 'residence' on the Obersalzberg!"

No doubt his increasing dependence on doctors and specialists caused some of the rumors. Morell had temporarily abandoned him—pleading a heart complaint—and was now far from the autumn fogs and military alarms of East Prussia. His assistant, Dr. Richard Weber, proved equally acceptable; on some days he was called to Hitler's bunker three or four times, and on November 13, Hitler was examined by the dentist, Blaschke, and by Major Stumpfegger as well. His throat was very sore, and he was finding it difficult to eat. He postponed the necessary X-rays, fearing they might reveal a malignancy.

The preparations for his top-secret counterattack in the Ardennes were nearing completion. Rundstedt had capably fulfilled Hitler's main requirement—that the western front be stabilized until the attack was launched. At Arnhem, Aachen, and now Antwerp, a series of costly battles had been forced on the Allies: Antwerp had fallen into enemy hands in early September, but for three months Hitler had prevented any convoys reaching the port. Aachen, the westernmost town of the Reich, had barred Lieutenant General Omar Bradley's advance across the West Wall. For purely prestige reasons he had begun a heavy attack here on October 2, but Hitler had ordered the town defended house by house, as Stalingrad had been, and when the Americans poured artillery shells into it he repeated his Paris order—that on entering, the enemy was to find only a field of ruins. When Aachen was finally encircled and overrun on October 21, the Allies found to their chagrin that Hitler had used the vital respite to rebuild the West Wall line to the east. Every ton of equipment and supplies that the enemy moved to the Aachen area for the later drive to the Ruhr pleased Hitler more—for then the booty from the Ardennes attack would be bigger. He told his staff he would not be tempted to divert reinforcements from his own Ardennes buildup "even if the enemy pushes through to Cologne."

This *was* General Eisenhower's main objective for early November: the British and American armies would exploit the Aachen gap to reach the Rhine on a one-hundred-mile front; they would then envelope the Ruhr industrial region from north and south. But Rundstedt launched a strong spoiling attack on

October 27, and Eisenhower's plans were delayed by two weeks. Meanwhile General Patton, south of the Ardennes, had assured his superiors that he could reach the Saar in three days—with a quarter of a million troops, his Third U.S. Army outnumbered the Germans 3 to 1 in that sector—and then "easily breach the West Wall." Patton's attack began on November 8, but confronted with pouring rain, mud, and minefields he advanced only fifteen miles toward the West Wall in eight days before the elastic tactics of General Hermann Balck and the stubborn defense of the city of Metz finally halted him.

Hitler had not lost his nerve. In his secret order for the Ardennes attack signed on November 10 he expressly accepted all the risks inherent in his Ardennes buildup "even if the enemy offensive on either side of Metz, and the imminent attack on the Ruhr region, should create major inroads into our territory or fortifications." It was a calculated risk, but one largely justified by events.

Hitler had provisionally ordered the Ardennes attack to begin on December 1. The eastern front was still quiet, with the exception of Hungary. But on November 14 the Allies began a renewed assault on the Alsace region; two days later the delayed American attack through the Aachen gap also began, while bombers devastated the minor towns between there and the Rhine: 2,703 tons were dropped on Düren in one attack—leaving it 95 percent wiped out—1,917 tons on Jülich, and 1,020 tons on Heinsberg. A steady drain on the German fuel and ammunition resources buildup for the Ardennes attack began. Thus Keitel and Jodl had a powerful case for Hitler to transfer his headquarters to the west. Moreover, his throat had now been X-rayed, and on the eighteenth it was again examined at Karlshof hospital (near Rastenburg) by Eicken, Morell, Stumpfegger —who had transferred his loyalties completely from Himmler to the Führer— and Dr. Brandt; a laryngeal polyp, not a malignant tumor, had been found on the anterior third of his left vocal cord, but Eicken would have to operate on Hitler's throat in Berlin at once.

The Führer's departure from East Prussia was kept secret. The special train would have to arrive in Berlin in the dark small hours for that reason. At 3:15 P.M. on November 20, while the noise and clatter of the construction gangs working on the last bunkers still continued, Hitler left the Wolf's Lair for Görlitz station and boarded his train. After tea he slept for a while, and then he invited his private staff to dine with him at 8:30 P.M. An SS orderly iisted those at dinner as Martin Bormann, Dr. Morell, the dietician Fräulein Manzialy, Julius Schaub, the impresario Benno von Arent, and two secretaries. One of the latter wrote evocatively of the journey:

> I had come to love the forest life and East Prussia's landscape. Now we were leaving them forever. Hitler probably knew that too. And although he ordered

the construction work continued as though he intended to return one day, he too was in a farewell mood. Had he not always maintained that so long as he personally commanded any sector it had never been abandoned? His carriage windows were blacked out. He sat in his compartment with the light switched on . . . a twilight like a mausoleum.

I had never seen Hitler as dejected and distant as on this day. His voice barely rose above a whisper. His eyes were rooted to a spot on the white tablecloth. An oppressive atmosphere crowded in on the narrow, swaying cage around us.

Hitler suddenly began to talk about an operation and about his confidence in Professor von Eicken's skill. "It's a great responsibility for him, but he's the only one who can do it. An operation on the vocal cords isn't dangerous, but it may leave me with no voice . . ."

At 5:30 A.M., the train arrived at Berlin's Grunewald station. The usual station, the Silesian station, had been damaged in an air raid. With the car's headlights picking out only ruins to the right and left, Hitler was driven back to his Chancellery.

His sojourn here lasted three weeks, as circumstances obliged him to keep postponing the Ardennes attack. Fräulein Eva Braun joined him, and lunched and dined with him almost every day. Eicken operated on him on November 22; the pathologist confirmed that the polyp—a piece of flesh the size of a millet seed—was quite benign, more commonly referred to as a "singer's knot." The morphine injection Eicken used to anesthetize the Führer proved an alarming overdose, however, for he was knocked out by it for nearly eight hours; the professor had failed to take into account Hitler's total abstinence from alcohol and nicotine in calculating the dose. Gradually Hitler's voice returned, although by early December he could still only whisper; soon the entire Chancellery was talking in whispers too. He remained out of sight, kept company only by Eva and the three older secretaries; an adjutant brought him the war reports. When Albert Speer came for a conference on the twenty-eighth, it was obvious Hitler had recovered.

During Hitler's fresh physical incapacity, the enemy inflicted an unexpected defeat on General Balck's Army Group G. It was of little strategic significance, but a further blow to German morale. On November 23, American tanks pushed into Strasbourg and reached the Upper Rhine, after the German First and Nineteenth armies had been put to flight. On the twenty-sixth Hitler put Himmler himself in command of this Upper Rhine sector, with control over all army, Waffen SS, and even Luftwaffe units in his area.

On December 10, Hitler left Berlin at 5 P.M.; ten hours later, in pitch darkness, he switched from his train to a car and drove on to the Eagle's Nest, the bunker headquarters built in 1940 at Bad Nauheim near the western front. That afternoon and the next he forcefully addressed two audiences of twenty senior generals whose divisions would begin the Ardennes attack on the sixteenth (his voice was not strong enough to command a larger audience). He suggested that evil forces had blocked Germany's unification ever since the Treaty of Westphalia in 1648. Peoples suffered the hardships of war bravely, but only so long as victory was still possible. If that hope was now suddenly removed from the enemy, their people must turn against the war. "Whatever they do, they cannot expect me to surrender. Never, never!" He reminded his audiences of how Frederick the Great had fought on in the Seven Years' War although all his generals and even his own brother had lost hope. "His state presidents, his ministers, turned up from Berlin in droves to beg him to stop the war because it could no longer be won. But the tenacity of that one man made it possible to fight on until finally the tide miraculously turned. To suggest that if the throne hadn't changed hands in Russia the tide would not have changed, is quite beside the point; because if they had stopped the war in the *fifth* year a throne change in the seventh year would have been neither here nor there. It is that moment we have to wait for!"

Never in history had heterogeneous coalitions such as existed between East and West in 1944 survived long. The enemy powers were already almost at each other's throats. "If you sit at the center of the web, like a spider, and follow this trend, you can see how from hour to hour the contrasts between them grow. So if we throw in a few really powerful punches, we may at any moment see this entire artificially erected common front suddenly collapse with a mighty clap of thunder."

The Ardennes offensive began at 5:30 A.M. on December 16. The weather was perfect for the attack.

PART 6

ENDKAMPF

The Gamble

It was a calculated risk that Hitler was taking, but he and his military advisers recognized that they had no choice.

Hitler himself reflected early in December 1944 that his own life was virtually spent in any case: before World War I he had been too impoverished to enjoy it; during that war itself he had been consigned to the Flanders battlefields; afterward, he had committed himself body and soul to his fight for power. Now a new war, more terrible than the first, had robbed the former infantryman turned Führer of the fruits of success. This is how Hitler viewed his career in retrospect. He insisted that now his one aim was to fight the war through to a victorious conclusion that would make fresh passages of arms impossible in Europe for at least a century. "Frederick II earned his title 'the Great' not because he was victorious, but because he did not despair in adversity; equally, posterity will come to recognize me because I too will never have surrendered after grievous misfortunes."

Hitler had commenced an order to his commanders on November 25 as follows: "This war will determine the survival or extinction of the German people. It demands the unqualified commitment of every individual. Even seemingly hopeless situations have been mastered by the blind courage and bravery of the troops, the stubborn steadfastness of all ranks, and by calm, unyielding leadership."

This was not just a war to decide frontiers or systems of government; it was a war against the destruction of the German race. In his view, the enemy had made their purposes quite plain. Whether Germany was defeated or surrendered "unconditionally," the Americans planned to convert Germany into "a country primarily agricultural and pastoral in its character"; the plan drafted by Henry Morgenthau, U.S. Secretary of the Treasury, to that end had been secretly initialed by Churchill and Roosevelt in mid-September. The American press had obtained and published it—a gift to Goebbels's anti-Semitic propaganda.[1] He and Hitler proclaimed that the enemy leaders were agreed on the extermination of forty million Germans, for such would be the necessary outcome of the plan. The resumption of the saturation bombing and firestorm raids seemingly added authority to the claim. Over 2,200 tons of fire bombs were dropped by night on ancient Heilbronn, massacring 7,147 civilians within ten minutes. On December 15—the very eve of the Ardennes gamble—Churchill announced in Parliament his approval of Stalin's demands on eastern Poland; the Poles could in return have all East Prussia and much of eastern Germany, from which the Germans would be expelled—"Because expulsion is the most satisfactory and lasting means, so far as we are in a position to judge." "Earlier," Hitler reminded his generals, "that kind of thing would have been dismissed as a propaganda slogan, as a propaganda lie. Here we have it from the horse's mouth, but even so it falls a long way short of reality, because if Germany collapses, Britain has no hope whatever of making a stand against bolshevism anywhere." From Guderian's eastern Intelligence branch Hitler knew that Russian deserters had reported that Stalin had recently ordered that while the Red Army was to behave properly in Poland, in German territory the troops might loot and rob and "do as they pleased." The whirlwind Hitler had sown in 1941 was approaching.

To surrender on terms like these would be a betrayal of the three million Germans who had now been lost in battle or enemy air raids. He had not invested billions of Reichsmarks in this war[2] just to see ten million Germans cast onto the winter roads of East Prussia and Silesia as refugees, while the unindustrious Poles confiscated their neat farms and homesteads.

But Hitler saw sound political and strategic reasons for launching his big winter counterattack, and in the west rather than the east. The British and Americans were obviously experiencing supply problems; their armies were thinly spread along the five-hundred-mile western front; they were low in fuel and ammunition, and experiencing manpower shortages. Keitel on the other hand planned to raise half a million new German troops by February 1945. "Our position is no different from that of the Russians in 1941–42," Hitler comforted his generals. "They too were in the most straitened circumstances, but then they began to launch isolated offensives along our long battlefront—on which we ourselves were on the defen-

[1]The full Morgenthau Plan approved by "F.D.R." and "W.S.C." provided for any people trying to flee Germany's frontiers to be gunned down by armed guards; a long list of categories of officials was to be summarily executed. A photocopy of the thirty-page document is in my possession.

[2]The German finance minister's papers reveal that Wehrmacht costs from September 1, 1939, to November 30, 1944, had totaled 398,760 million Reichsmarks; a further 199,700 million had been spent on the civil sector. Against this, the Reich had raised only 288,550 million Reichsmarks by direct and indirect taxation and by occupation charges.

sive—and slowly maneuvered us back again." Once the German public saw this process start there would be a great sigh of relief, and the young would volunteer enthusiastically for battle. "And this I must say—our nation is as decent as one could ask for. It would be impossible to find a better people than the Germans." He did not mention the difference between Russia in 1942 and Germany now: that the ticking time-bomb left by the raw-materials crisis gave him only a limited number of months in which to succeed.

Recognizing that General Eisenhower's command abilities were questioned by the British, Hitler hoped for most *political* gain by puncturing the enemy front where it was held by the U.S. First Army—which had already suffered heavy losses in the battle for Aachen. In any case, the Americans had left only four or five divisions to hold a one-hundred-mile Ardennes front. In his view, the United States was such a potpourri of inferior races, a country with so little tradition of heroic national sacrifice, that a great bloodletting here would invite fundamental political controversies across the Atlantic. In short, the demeaning label applied by Goebbels and Rommel to the American troops in North Africa—"the Italians" of the western alliance—had stuck in his mind. And what Stalin had done to the Italians at Stalingrad, Hitler would repeat with the Americans here in the Ardennes. "If we succeed," he explained on December 2 to Generals Hasso von Manteuffel and Sepp Dietrich, the two panzer army commanders involved, "we will have knocked out half the enemy front. Then let's see what happens!" Most probably, he would then transport his spare divisions back to the eastern front in time to buttress it against the coming big Soviet offensive.

This meant a further gamble within the main one. The chief of Guderian's operations branch, Colonel Bogislaw von Bonin, was confident about the strength of certain sectors of the eastern front—notably East Prussia, Warsaw, and Cracow—but Hitler knew that Stalin would not forever postpone the big offensive he was clearly preparing in the Vistula bridgeheads from Warsaw to Cracow.[3] The gamble was, how long did Hitler have? On December 2, Army Group A predicted the Soviet attack within one week and asked that the moment the offensive began

[3]Hitler emphasized this to the new Hungarian leader, Ferenc Szálasi, when they first met on December 4.

The General Staff's insouciance of early December about the eastern front is understandably muted in postwar memoirs. But in captivity in August 1945 Major General Burkhart Mueller-Hillebrand was overheard telling a fellow general how Guderian had summoned the chiefs of staff of the eastern armies to an OKH conference at Zossen on December 5: "First there was a tremendous grubfest with enough food to burst, and then a binge. Guderian stayed until 2 A.M., by which time they were standing on the tables. I was revolted." Every evening the OKH, including the operations branch, were drunk as lords, he said.

the navy, army, and air force destroy the numerous wooden bridges erected by the Russians over the Vistula. Guderian believed the attack would be in mid-December, when the first frosts hardened the ground. Russian prisoners gave "December 20" as the date. Had the Ardennes offensive begun in mid-November as originally planned, the risk would have been less; but it had already been delayed nearly a month by logistics problems. It was due to begin on December 16. Guderian was sure Stalin would march westward the moment Hitler had committed his strategic reserve in the Ardennes. But Hitler was equally convinced of the opposite—that while Stalin was not bluffing, he would wait until Germany and the Allies had exhausted their reserves in the west, just as he had waited in vain in 1940.

Hitler's conviction proved correct. Not until mid-January 1945 did Stalin show his hand. Hitler also won his second extraordinary gamble, on concealing his Ardennes intentions for three months from the enemy. He had ordered absolute radio silence before the attack; no preparatory orders were to be conveyed by plane or transmitted even in code by radio; special war diaries were to be kept for the preparatory phase; potentially unreliable troops, like those born in the Alsace, were to be withdrawn from the front line; reprisals were threatened against the next-of-kin of any deserters; and any hint that the enemy had wind of the attack was to be reported immediately.

No hints came. In the first twelve days of December 1944 there were only five known or probable desertions from the western front. Hitler's security measures proved almost perfect; besides, the renegades who had betrayed his moves in the past were now in Himmler's custody awaiting trial. Not until the second day of the actual offensive did an enemy aircraft suddenly sight "thousands of vehicles" massing in the mountainous Eifel plateau. Hitler concluded that Eisenhower, Bradley, and General Bernard Law Montgomery had been living only in their own dreamworld of future campaigns. "Perhaps," he was to say, "there was also the belief that I might already be dead, or at least suffering from cancer somewhere—unable to drink or live on much longer, which would rule me out as a danger."

The only order known to have fallen into enemy hands was one for the formation of a special reconnaissance unit in the west—about two battalions of volunteers with one common qualification: an ability to speak American; captured American uniforms and equipment were also to be sent in. Hitler—with his predilection for the adventuresome—had sent for SS Colonel Otto Skorzeny on October 21, told him that three captured German tanks flying German colors had been put to devastating use by the Americans in the fight for Aachen, and directed him to build up a phony "American" task force to seize key bridges across the Meuse River between Liège and Namur when the Ardennes attack began. Other American-uniformed units were to spread alarm and confusion behind the American lines.

The rapid seizure of bridgeheads across the Meuse would be vital. At a tightly restricted late October conference, Hitler had revealed his Ardennes plan to the chiefs of staff of Rundstedt and Model (Generals Westphal and Krebs) and informed them that the strategic object of the offensive would be to destroy enemy forces, not capture territory as such. Model and his generals were urging that the knife be plunged in only as far as the Meuse, to excise merely the American forces massing for the attack on the Ruhr. However, if the knife was forced right through to the coast at Antwerp, it would also trap the British armies in the Netherlands. Göring had promised two thousand planes for the attack. Model and Rundstedt accepted this, but warned that they were not strong enough to reach Antwerp. They favored the more limited solution—turning at the Meuse instead. Throughout November the tactical controversy raged until Hitler, on the twenty-fifth, insisted that his own decision to go for the "big solution" was final. The small solution might prolong the war; the big one might end it—at least in the west. To use the General Staff's own jarring phrase, it was time for a *Ganzer Entschluss,* a "total decision." Therefore the Meuse must be forded by the second day and Antwerp itself captured by the seventh, for no bad-weather period could be relied on to last longer and keep Allied planes grounded.

Hitler jealously watched over the planning, from the infantrymen's winter boots and blankets to the deployment of the formidable Jagd-Tiger tanks with their 128-millimeter guns. He had remorselessly herded artillery units into the western front. During November, 1,349 tanks and assault guns were sent to Rundstedt, and 1,000 more would follow before Christmas. Snow-clearing troops were put on standby. Special tanks had to be built to spread sand on the icy mountain roads. Victory was certain: he began drafting orders to ensure that this time no German soldiers set foot inside Paris—the germ center of the recent Wehrmacht defeat. A special SS squad was detailed to round up and execute civic and Party officials in towns and villages that had surrendered too readily to the enemy. Hitler dictated orders for the initial artillery bombardment to concentrate on the enemy-occupied villages and headquarters. It was to be followed by a further one-minute barrage and by a saturation bombardment of the enemy artillery positions. "There must not be one gun barrel that does not join in this artillery preparation!" During lulls in the bombardment, the troops were to simulate infantry assaults ("Shouts of 'Hurrah,' and machine-gun bursts") to get on the American defenders' nerves. Hitler had learned a vital lesson from the Russian June 1944 offensive against Army Group Center: to conserve his tank strength, the initial breach in the enemy line would be made by the *infantry* with assault-gun support. The panzer divisions would not follow until the following night; these were the "thousands of vehicles" the Allied spotter aircraft had sighted massing in the Eifel district. On November 26, Hitler set December 10 as the first possible date; and at a conference with Model, Dietrich, Manteuffel, and Westphal on December 2 zero hour was fixed at 5:30 A.M.

Twice more the attack was postponed briefly, while the last supplies arrived. The requested stockpile of 3.8 million gallons of gasoline had been built up, and more than the 50 trainloads of ammunition. The morale of the troops was high. Some 170 bombers, 90 ground-attack planes, and nearly 1,500 fighter aircraft were standing by. Twenty-eight German divisions were about to fall upon only 5 American divisions. At 3 P.M. on December 15, Hitler held a final war conference with Himmler and Rundstedt's Chief of Staff, General Westphal. Model wanted another postponement, but Rundstedt's advice was to go ahead before their intentions were unmasked. Hitler agreed, and at 3:30, Westphal telephoned the Führer's decision to Rundstedt's command post nearby. The Luftwaffe meteorologist forecast poor weather for several days. The enemy air force would be virtually grounded. Hitler telegraphed once more to Model forbidding him to turn the knife before crossing the Meuse. He assured him that "if you comply with all these basic operational guidelines, a great victory is certain." The Führer dined with his secretaries, sat talking with Bormann or Hewel, went briefly with Bormann to hear the latest war report from Colonel von Below and Major Johannmeyer at 1:10 A.M., and retired to bed at five—half an hour before the artillery barrage began—satisfied that no ugly surprises were in store.

By the time he was awakened, at 11:30 A.M. on December 16, the American front had been engulfed at many places along a seventy-mile sector between Monschau and Echternach, and the German infantry was already eight and ten miles inside enemy territory. Jodl confirmed that they had taken the Americans completely by surprise. A glow of confidence warmed the bleak bunker headquarters. After Hitler had been tended by Drs. Morell and Blaschke for an hour, he went for a casual stroll with Bormann's younger brother and lunched with the secretaries. The thunder of gunfire could clearly be heard. One of his staff stenographers wrote in his diary: "When [Stenographer Ewald] Reynitz and I went over at 3 P.M. for the war conference, an imposing number of German fighter planes swept low overhead, and Major Büchs [a Luftwaffe adjutant] . . . turned to all of us as we excitedly watched our fighters roaring past after so many months of German air inferiority, and said challengingly, 'Who dares say anything against the Luftwaffe now!' . . . When we reached the conference room the Führer was already there, contrary to his custom. It was only too evident how delighted he was at the first magnificent news of our offensive. Even before the conference the Reich press chief, Dr. [Otto] Dietrich, told us: 'Well—now at last you're going to get something cheerful to take down!' And so it was." To Hitler the battle was already as good as won. That day he ordered the German navy to do everything possible to prevent British ships escaping from Antwerp before—and after—Sepp Dietrich's SS Sixth Panzer Army got there.

It will serve no purpose to follow here the next month's events on the Ardennes battlefields. It is more interesting to see how opinion at the Eagle's Nest, inspired by Hitler's hardy optimism, persistently failed to grasp the harsh realities of the campaign. Hitler's tanks never recaptured Antwerp—perhaps he had deliberately set his armies' sights too high. Worse, they never even saw the Meuse, let alone crossed it.

What caused this tactical defeat? Some factors came as a shock to Hitler: the Americans had established an unexpected main line of defense two or three miles behind their battle front; and they fought with inexplicable bravery. But other factors should have caused less surprise. The Luftwaffe radio operators newly transferred to man Sepp Dietrich's tanks were unfamiliar with battle procedures. The battalion of superheavy Jagd-Tiger tanks—each weighing seventy-two tons and equipped with 128-millimeter guns—sent by Hitler to block the roads on the northern flank against American forces concentrated around Aachen was not even deployed; Hitler learned twelve days later it had never crossed the Rhine. "They must be insane!" he announced. "If the enemy attacks our defenses with ten or twelve heavy tanks, there's enough screaming to bring the house down; but when we've got twenty-four of the heaviest tanks in the world, they aren't even used!" Those tanks that did attack ran out of gasoline too soon, as they churned in low gear through the narrow, twisting valleys and defiles. The fuel shortage was aggravated by the overmotorization of attacking divisions. Convoys of empty trucks were following so they could be stuffed with booty. The roads were blocked by blown bridges and by obstacles the Germans themselves had created in their retreat some weeks earlier. Gasoline tankers could not get through, as immense traffic jams built up in the narrow roads leading to the battlefields. Finally, although General von Manteuffel's Fifth Panzer Army broke through first, Hitler continued to attach the Schwerpunkt to the SS Sixth Panzer Army—perhaps for political reasons.

Despite all this Hitler kept his eye on the strategic blessings of his counterstroke. He betrayed no signs of disappointment at the offensive's slow progress. Within five days 25,000 American prisoners were taken and 350 enemy tanks claimed destroyed; the Allied air force was still grounded by the weather. The Luftwaffe and paratroop support operations were rolling like clockwork. Skorzeny's "American" units were spreading consternation behind the lines. There were signs among the Americans in Belgium of the same sort of panic that had gripped the Germans after the enemy breakthrough at Avranches that summer. By December 22, Eisenhower had had to call off his attacks along the rest of the western front, and he even relinquished hard-won bridgeheads along the Saar. Sixteen to twenty enemy divisions were estimated to be bearing down on the

Ardennes battlefield, but Hitler's slow advance on the Meuse had not yet been checked, and the weather was still against the Allies. At a war conference Hitler chuckled: "Mr. Churchill, now *you* must make a *Ganzer Entschluss!*"—and he mimicked the British prime minister's speech impediment as he did so.

With an offensive against East Prussia and Silesia now, Stalin could immediately have disembarrassed his western Allies. But apart from the continuing struggle in Hungary he made no move.

In Italy, France, Belgium, and Britain Communist underground movements were stirring at Moscow's command. Reports reached Hitler of open warfare between the pro-Stalin elements in Greece and the British troops. After a luckless attempt to bring the warring factions to heel, Churchill flew out of Athens "with his tail between his legs," mocked Hitler. "And now he wants people to believe him capable of stopping the tide of bolshevism into Europe as a whole!" Meanwhile Churchill's frank Poland speech in Parliament had evoked a response which promised a storm to come. At his Washington press conference Roosevelt was asked whether the Atlantic Charter—which Stalin's annexation of eastern Poland so flagrantly violated—had ever existed in writing, and if so where; he replied that it had not. This lie did nothing to still the Polish exiles' discontent. The Soviet attack on Schörner's army group in Kurland, resumed on December 22, did not cause one German division to be withdrawn from the west. (Nor was it any more profitable than the Red Army's previous two attempts to capture this rump of northern Latvia.) The Intelligence now reaching Hitler was that Stalin had attached outrageous political demands to the unleashing of his big offensive. December 20, the date given by interrogated Russian prisoners as the one set for launching a Soviet offensive, had now passed. Hitler slapped the map table at the Eagle's Nest and crowed to his staff: "You see, perhaps we've made it after all!"

On the seventh day of Hitler's offensive, December 23, the skies cleared. By day and by night the Allied air force regained control of the Ardennes battlefield. The knife had now plunged forty miles into the enemy front; but the railroad stations in the German rear, at Koblenz, Gerolstein, and Bingen, were devastated, and Allied fighter-bombers created havoc on the roads. General Patton's Third Army had begun a counteroffensive on Rundstedt's southern flank. The 2nd Panzer Division was only five miles from the Meuse. Hitler stood outside his blockhouse impassively watching as two thousand enemy bombers swarmed eastward over his head, glittering solemnly in the weak winter sun, spelling the end of his hopes of an easy triumph in the west. Over lunch, his sharp-tongued secretary Christa Schroeder challenged him. "Mein Führer, we *have* lost the war—haven't we?" He stonily replied that they had not.

He had begun rereading the *Collected Letters* of Frederick the Great, and found one letter written in the fifth year of what was to be a seven-year war:

> I first went to war with the finest army Europe ever saw. I now have a rabble; I have no commanders left, my generals are incompetent, the officers can't lead, the troops are hopeless.

Yet Frederick had finally won through. And it was this obdurate tenacity that alone assured victory: "When all goes well people are on top of the world," Hitler explained to a panzer general at 2 A.M. one morning. "But when everything starts going wrong they just fold up and give in." So if Hitler's troops now asked him, Why all this sacrifice? he would answer, "The war cannot last as long again as it has already lasted. Nobody could stand it, neither we nor the others. The question is, Which side will crack first? And I say that the side that lasts longer will do so only if it stands to lose everything. *We* stand to lose everything. If the other side announces one day, 'We've had enough!' no harm will come to them. If America says, 'Cut! Stop! No more American boys for Europe!' it won't hurt them. New York remains New York, Chicago remains Chicago, Detroit remains Detroit, San Francisco remains San Francisco. Nothing changes. But if we say today, 'We've had enough, we're packing up'—then Germany will cease to exist."

This was the "cornered tiger" logic into which Allied insistence on unconditional surrender had forced him. But it was not illogical, for cracks kept appearing in the monolithic enemy front. Hitler learned secretly that Stalin was willing to negotiate with him now, before beginning his main eastern front attack. But Hitler was no more inclined to throw in the towel than Stalin had been in 1941. When Ribbentrop gamely offered to fly with his family to Moscow now, as a surety for Germany's honest intent, Hitler begged him not to. "Ribbentrop, don't pull a Rudolf Hess on me!" Stalin's offer seemed to confirm that the Red Army was exhausted; and had not the General Staff proclaimed its confidence in the strength of the main eastern front?[4]

Surviving documents indicate that both Guderian and Hitler were preoccupied with Hungary in December 1944, rather than with the rest of the Russian front. Without Hungary there would be neither aluminum to build aircraft nor aviation fuel to fly them. "This is why Hungary is so vital," agreed Guderian. Late in November Stalin committed two army groups to the fight for Budapest and western Hungary—the cornerstone of Hitler's "minimum economic region"; Hitler's strategy was to force Stalin to throw even more weight into Hungary. Now that Hungary was at stake, it did not occur to either Hitler or the Hungarians to declare Budapest an "open city": on December 4, Ferenc Szálasi sanctioned the house-by-house defense of the beautiful city in return for an undertak-

[4]See the statement of Colonel von Bonin, chief of the General Staff operations branch, as quoted by the navy on December 1, 1944 (page 741).

ing by Hitler not to make a deal with Stalin at Hungary's expense. Throughout December the Soviet pincer attack continued. General Friessner moved seventy thousand German and Hungarian troops into the city's defenses. On the twentieth the final Russian offensive began. When Guderian arrived that day for two days of talks and a privileged invitation to tea at Hitler's headquarters, Hungary was the first point on his agenda, followed by the need to reshuffle divisions southward along the eastern front; the other sectors in Poland, East Prussia, and Kurland were relegated to points 7, 10, and 11 of Guderian's agenda. But Hitler's Hungarian strategy began to fail. The Soviet thrust bypassing the city to the west met so little German resistance that Hitler dismissed Friessner and the Sixth Army's General Fretter Pico on December 23; by the twenty-fourth, Budapest was totally invested by the enemy.

It was Christmas Eve 1944, but at the Eagle's Nest near Frankfurt—where Hitler was still directing the Ardennes battle—there was little respite.[5] Not until December 26 did Guderian again arrive from Berlin. Jodl's diary and General Staff records show that Hitler agreed to move what meager forces he could to the Second Panzer Army holding the "Margaret line," in Hungary, between the Drava River and Lake Balaton, in defense of the vital petroleum fields at Nagykanisza; an infantry division would be moved from the west to Budapest. Two more would follow to the main eastern front. In particular, Guderian had sent out an order late on December 24 for the Fourth SS Panzer Corps, commanded by the redoubtable Herbert Gille, to entrain from Warsaw (Army Group A) to Hungary—where its two panzer divisions, "Death's Head," followed by "Viking," would begin a counterattack on New Year's Day to relieve the besieged city of Budapest. As Guderian wrote on December 31 to his Hungarian counterpart: "By deliberately taking a very grave risk on the rest of the eastern front we have done everything possible to restore firm contact with Budapest."[6]

[5]The manservant's duty-register shows that on December 24, 1944, Hitler lunched with his two middle-aged secretaries, invited Keitel, Jodl, Burgdorf, Buhle, Scherff, Bormann, and Fegelein to tea, slept three hours, then dined with the same secretaries and his dietician until the midnight war conference. An SS major wrote the next day: "After a short break, we worked on during the night. Supper last night was quite good. Field Marshal Keitel made a speech, short and sweet, then we all sat around a candlelit Christmas tree for a while before going back to work. This morning I ran into the Chief [Hitler]. He shook my hand, asked about the family, and even remembered that we have two children and that the daughter was born the day I joined him. I could do and sacrifice anything for this man."

[6]I have seen no documentary evidence that Guderian expressed concern for the main eastern front comparable to his concern about Hungary until early 1945. The General Staff's subsequent failure to prevent the Soviet invasion in mid-January resulted in many durable postwar legends; aided by Jodl's little-known diary, by the fragmentary stenograms and Admiral Voss's digests of Hitler's daily conferences, and by the manservant's visitors' record, I have done my best to untangle these legends. There is no contemporary evidence to support Guderian's 1951 version, which has him at the Eagle's Nest on December 24 for the sole purpose of pleading with Hitler to transfer the defensive Schwer-

---

In the west, Model now estimated that 38 of Eisenhower's 70 divisions were battling to contain the Ardennes bulge. Hitler was cock-a-hoop. "We have knocked out at least six or seven hundred enemy tanks; about six or seven divisions have presumably been completely destroyed." In the tank battle between Vaux and Grandmenil on December 27, Manteuffel destroyed 62 enemy tanks and captured 8. But General Patton's counterattack into the flank south of the bulge was causing concern; with the failure to reach the Meuse, Hitler lifted his prohibition on dealing with the tough American pocket of forces contained at Bastogne; and to ease the logjam in the Ardennes, he began plotting with Rundstedt a series of rapid blows along the denuded American front further south.

The first would be "North Wind"—an attack by eight divisions from the Saarbrücken region, designed to take from the rear the Americans advancing through northern Alsace. The second would be toward Metz, to restore Germany's iron-ore position. "The purpose of all these attacks," Hitler theatrically announced to his generals, "will mainly be to eliminate the Americans south of our [Ardennes] entry point—to destroy them bit by bit, to eliminate [*ausrotten*] them division by division." This would damage Eisenhower's plans and reputation, and it would cost him heavily in fuel for regrouping and ammunition—all of which Eisenhower had to bring up over greater distances than Hitler.

If these body blows succeeded, then Manteuffel and Dietrich could resume their attack in the Ardennes. "If not," Rundstedt's war diary recognized, "it will mean the end of our offensive operations and a transition to a defensive war of attrition. But no matter what, the important result remains that for the time being we have rid the Rhine and Palatinate of the threat of an enemy offensive."

One other strategic success of these weeks should not be overlooked: as Field Marshal von Weichs, Commander in Chief Southeast, wrote in his diary on December 30 1944: "The auspicious return of our troops from Greece . . . is akin to a great battle won." The soldiers of General Löhr's Army Group E had force-marched up to a thousand miles from the torrid heat of the Mediterranean to the midwinter snowstorms of the Croatian mountains and had still managed to fight off the Russians, Bulgarians, and Communist partisans harrying their flanks. Had Hitler delayed his secret oral order to Weichs to evacuate Greece in

---

punkt from west to east and Hitler snubbing him—"The eastern front must manage with what it's got." Not until January 14—two days *after* the Soviet invasion began—did Admiral Voss report from Hitler's conference that "[Guderian] has now asked the Führer to transfer the war's Schwerpunkt to the eastern front."

August, or had Löhr shown less resolution in adversity, the entire army group would have been lost.

Crossing this last high plateau of his fortunes, Hitler still radiated determination, the nameless energy of a Messiah, to his visitors: Szálasi noticed it; Bormann cultivated it; Guderian succumbed to it. But he had aged: his back was bent, his spine had lost its symmetry (Scoliosis); his face was haggard and his voice quavered; his hair was gray, and the famous moustache—which he clung to as he did to his "postman's cap" in spite of all Eva Braun's remonstrances—was snow-white. Admiral Heinz Assmann wrote: "His handclasp was weak and soft, all his movements were those of a senile man; only his eyes retained their flickering gleam and penetrating look." His "midday" conference rarely began before 5 P.M.; after that his doctors ordered him to sleep three hours each day. He went for frequent strolls in the snow around his bunker. Wieland Wagner, the composer's grandson, found the convalescent Führer's manner "even tamer and kindlier than before"; Blaskowitz, conferring with him about "North Wind" on December 28, observed that his left shoulder drooped and his hand was shaking; Baron von Steengracht felt he "still put a brave face on, but he was frail and his hand trembled." Indeed, Hitler could now hardly write; since December a trusted civil servant had had to forge his signature on official citations and awards. All this worried Martin Bormann badly. Professors Eicken and Morell, and the SS doctor, Stumpfegger, examined Hitler on the thirtieth and found him medically recovered from his operation; and his throat was well enough for him to prerecord that day his radio speech for New Year's Eve. But the speech itself lacked the wit and bite of his earlier annual addresses. Goebbels may have told him later that the public missed any references to the new weapons or campaigns which might yet bring them the promised victory.

This was as well, for at the end of the plateau there was an abyss. Göring's Luftwaffe delivered its grand slam attack on January 1, 1945, with 1,035 fighters and fighter-bombers attacking the enemy airfields in the Low Countries. Five hundred planes were claimed destroyed, but Göring also lost 277 planes, nearly two-thirds of them to his own antiaircraft guns, which had not been warned. Hitler was unimpressed. In 1944 Allied heavy bombers had dropped a hundred times more bombs on Germany than Göring had on Britain in 1940. This proved what he had all along said about the value of the four-engined bomber. The Luftwaffe's aircraft were powerless against them. The 217 rocket-propelled Me-163 interceptor aircraft built and launched had claimed only 5 bombers; Hitler ordered Me-163 production canceled. Antiaircraft artillery alone could defend Germany now. Meanwhile the devastation of the railway and canal system was resulting in crippling coal, steel, and munitions shortages. At a meeting with Hitler on January 3, Speer blamed Göring and the Luftwaffe; but others blamed Speer himself. Martin Bormann brought to Hitler's attention convincing reports that Speer had misled both the Gauleiters and Hitler on the real output figures of the arms and aircraft factories.

The transport, munitions, and fuel crises were directly affecting Hitler's strategy. Coal was piling up in the Ruhr pitheads, but the railroads could not carry it to the factories. The loss of France, Lorraine, and Belgium had cut German steel output by the autumn from 3,100,000 to 2,000,000 tons a month; but the colossal air attack on German transportation since mid-October had cut Ruhr production alone from 700,000 to only 400,000 tons in November. There were frustrating side effects on the new secret weapons Hitler had relied on to turn the tide in the eleventh hour: prefabricated sections of the secret Mark XXI submarine could not be brought to the assembly points because of wrecked canals. In November only 9 instead of 17 had been assembled, and in December only 18 instead of 28, because now air raids had stopped submarine-battery production too. How right Hitler had been to press his "lunatic" demand late in 1939 for keeping Germany's air frontiers as far apart as possible! "Herr Beck and his memoranda!" he scorned. "Those gentlemen wanted to fight in the pre-airpower age!" He could not even strike back equally at Eisenhower's transportation. "We can't rely on the V-1 or V-2 bombardment alone."[7] On January 8 he again insisted on equipping the Me-262 jet aircraft with 500-kilo bombs to disrupt the enemy's railroads and dockyards behind the western front.

Hitler's counterattacks were also failing. "North Wind" caused Eisenhower momentary alarm—he abandoned hard-won ground and even contemplated evacuating Strasbourg after Himmler, commanding Army Group Upper Rhine, succeeded in throwing a bridgehead across the fast-flowing Rhine north of the city; but the enemy sidestepped fast enough to escape encirclement in Alsace. In Hungary, Gille's relief attack slowed to a halt six days later, still short of Budapest. On January 3—even as Hitler was debating the transportation crisis with Speer, Goebbels and Dr. Albert Ganzenmüller, the transport minister—Britain's Field Marshal Montgomery began his carefully planned offensive on the northern flank of the Ardennes bulge; Patton was still relentlessly attacking it from the south. Hitler—whose generals had now claimed to have destroyed 1,230 Allied tanks in the battle and captured 400 guns and 24,000 American prisoners—decided to cut his losses. At a conference with Hitler and Göring on the seventh, Rundstedt asked the Führer to authorize Model's request to pull back the westernmost attack spearhead, the Forty-seventh Panzer Corps; Hitler agreed, and decided that if he was not to lose the initiative entirely, he must also pull out Sepp

[7]Allied-held Antwerp had been under continual rocket attack and flying-bomb bombardment since October 1944. Damage was severe. On December 17 one V-2 rocket killed seven hundred people in the packed Rex cinema, half of them soldiers.

Dietrich's SS Sixth Panzer Army to establish a tactical reserve while he could, for there was no knowing what the enemy might do with the divisions he could now release from the Ardennes battlefield. This order—Hitler's tacit admission that he had lost the Ardennes gamble—was issued from the Eagle's Nest at 2 A.M. on January 8, 1945.

Deep snow drifts blanketed Hitler's headquarters. It was 20°F. In Poland, the ground had frozen, but Stalin had still not begun his big push from the Vistula bridgeheads toward Berlin. On January 3 the General Staff's eastern expert, General Gehlen, announced: "Various signs indicate that the attack has again been postponed to mid-January."

When General Guderian came to Hitler's headquarters on January 9, the Führer speculated: "If the Russians aren't attacking, then it's for political reasons." Guderian seconded that: "It's because of the British." But he now expressed extreme alarm about the eight-hundred-mile front between the Carpathian Mountains and the Baltic, where the Russians—ignoring Hitler's attempt to lure their reserves south into Hungary—had built up an immense superiority in tanks, artillery, and troops. Guderian had just visited General Josef Harpe—commanding the army group astride Warsaw—and now fearlessly put to Hitler Harpe's proposals for the army group to fall back on a "given word" from the winding Vistula River line to a more economical one; this would create two strong groups of reserves for a counterattack after Stalin's big offensive began. Guderian's adjutant later wrote a dispassionate account of the heated argument that followed:

> Guderian was very spirited and waded in with gusto. His program was in effect that we should give up and move the forces farther west. Guderian showed on the map how critical Harpe's situation at Cracow was. . . . The Baranov bridgehead salient was being continually reinforced by the Russians; reconnaissance planes had sighted innumerable tanks and aircraft. For twenty miles the front line was stretched to breaking point. . . . From the mountains up to as far as Warsaw the army group had only six divisions. That was far too few, they could never halt a serious attack. . . .
>
> A "given word" had therefore been prearranged, upon which the troops in the German salient were to be pulled back to a shorter chord line. . . . Hitler was curt and skeptical, and belittled everything. He kept repeating that the Russians didn't have much—their formations were exhausted, they hadn't any tanks, and to talk of superiority was nonsense. He minimized the Russian enemy and exaggerated our own strength in a most irresponsible manner. He began to tear the general's arguments to shreds. When he raised his voice, the others fell silent. Guderian explained the situation and again mentioned the

> "given word" plan. After a few words Hitler interrupted: "Out of the question. Where a German soldier is, there he stays!" Guderian tried to talk him around, but in vain.

Guderian's object had been to win the entire Sixth SS Panzer Army from the west for the eastern front, but Hitler would grant him only two divisions. "The others present listened in silence," concluded the adjutant's account. "Only Göring butted in once or twice."

Hitler's reasons for rejecting Guderian's appeal on January 9 are plain from the fragments of stenographic record. Firstly, if Stalin's attack was due in mid-January, it was too late to begin rethinking their strategy; secondly, he believed that with nine panzer and three panzer-grenadier divisions (sited north and south of Cracow, southwest of Warsaw, and in East Prussia) Guderian already held sufficient in reserve to stave off the threat; thirdly, he was inspired by the fortifications dug by the Gauleiters and east Germans over the last months; and fourthly, as he admitted in private to his own adjutants the next day, "I always shudder when I hear talk of 'withdrawing here' in order to be able to 'operate there'; I've been hearing that tune for two years now, and every time it's been a disaster."

Guderian's statistics failed to impress Hitler either. The German army already had 3,000 tanks and assault guns in the east; by Hitler's reckoning, Stalin would need a 3 to 1 superiority to begin an offensive (although his own superiority in the Ardennes had fallen far short of that in December). "At any rate, they don't have nine thousand tanks." As for artillery, if Stalin really had "150 guns per kilometer" he must have 20,000 in his bridgeheads altogether, which was absurd. The hordes of Soviet divisions listed by the General Staff reminded Hitler of "Chinese divisions": each probably had only a few thousand men. Here Guderian could retort that his own panzer divisions each had only 70 or 80 tanks compared with 250 in June 1941. When the general bewailed the crippling ammunition shortage—"If only we could get the ammunition now, we could put up a tremendous showing!"—Hitler lectured him: "Now you see what nobody wanted to see at the time: the potential harm of our retreats in the east. From our factories down there"—pointing to the Donets Basin—"we would probably already be supplying the eastern front with two or three million shells a month. But people told me, 'What's the point, just for a few iron-ore mines!' And the front line was shorter then than it is now."

That evening, January 9, an army adjutant gave Hitler the first *documented* hint that Stalin's attack was imminent. "Over the last few days there have been continued heavy movements into the Baranov bridgehead [across the Vistula]. The impression there is that they are going to start soon after all."

Over the next two days the warning signs multiplied: "ice-bridges" were being laid; minefields were being cleared; and radio monitoring posts heard of reinforcements being moved up. Prisoners confirmed that the offensive would begin between the eleventh and sixteenth. The Russian artillery was in place, and the infantry had taken up its assault positions. So Hitler learned on the eleventh; before he fell asleep at 4:20 A.M. the next morning, he probably had word that an all-out hour-long Russian artillery bombardment had just taken place in the Baranov bridgehead; and when he rose at noon, Jodl's adjutant, Colonel Heinz Waizenegger, came almost at once to announce that after a further hour-long barrage between 7 and 8 A.M. Stalin's great offensive had begun. At the Eagle's Nest they now wondered, Was this the Russians' last desperate exertion? Or would still further attacks follow?

Hitler was still on the western front. Two of his secretaries—the young but widowed Frau Junge and the elderly Frau Wolf—had just returned from leave and lunched with him at two. Frau Junge had hitched a truck ride through Munich the morning after British bombers had blasted the city with two thousand tons of bombs, and her emotional description made his blood boil. "In a very few weeks this nightmare will suddenly stop," he pronounced. "Our new jet aircraft are now in mass production. Soon the Allies will think twice about flying over Reich territory."

One anecdote remained in Frau Junge's memory of that day, and it illustrates Hitler's bantering manner with his immediate entourage. His dog Blondi urgently needed to go out, and sprang delightedly through the bunker door with the manservant summoned for the purpose. "Amazing what little things can please a dog," Frau Junge remarked, at which Hitler laughed, adding: "Not to mention us human beings too! I was once on the road for hours on end with my men, and I had to go on to Magdeburg to open the first stretch of autobahn there. But when my convoy of cars was spotted, more and more cars would fall in behind. It was often quite impossible to make an urgently necessary stop in some wood or other and be alone. And when we reached this autobahn there was almost a calamity. Hour after hour we drove on, dying for a break, but everywhere they were lining the autobahn—Hitler Youth, League of German Girls, Brownshirts, SS, the lot —I had no idea the Party had so many formations. I felt at that moment it was too many. Brückner and Schaub sat petrified with masklike faces next to me. I had to keep standing, too, with a fixed grin. Then Brückner suddenly reminded us: 'Mein Führer, I had your special train sent to Magdeburg station!' How glad we were to see that train."

Julius Schaub cupped his hand over one ear and grunted in appreciation of the story. "Mein Führer, do you remember The Elephant at Weimar!" "Ja," Hitler laughed. "That was an old-fashioned hotel prewar, but well managed. My regular rooms had running water but no bathroom or W.C., so I had to walk down this long corridor and vanish into the little room at the end. It was sheer purgatory every time, because when I left my room word spread around the hotel like wildfire, and when I emerged from the awkward closet they were all waiting to cheer me and I had to give the Hitler salute and a rather embarrassed smile all the way back to my room. Later on I had that hotel rebuilt." As Frau Junge afterward wrote, it was as though there was no war and Hitler had no cares. "But those who, like us, knew him well, recognized that he had recourse to such small talk as a kind of anesthetic to distract him from the losses of territory, equipment, and human life of which every hour brought fresh report."

At Hitler's main war conference that day, January 12, the news was that Marshal Konev's powerful infantry and tank forces had swept through the three German divisions containing the Baranov bridgehead and had already advanced ten miles westward. By the next day they had advanced twenty miles; nothing was halting the onrushing enemy. The German panzer divisions had been split up and mauled, and now after a two-hour artillery barrage by 350 batteries a new deluge of tanks and infantry hit the eastern flank of East Prussia. On the fourteenth the two other Vistula bridgeheads also debouched into southern Poland south of Warsaw, and a second offensive began against East Prussia, this time on the southern flank. The deadline for the offensive here was known, and the Germans drenched the massing Russian forces and artillery with shells, briefly throwing Marshal Rokossovski's forces off balance. But although 245 enemy tanks had already been destroyed, by the fifteenth the whole eastern front was ablaze, and it was clear that the enemy had achieved his strategic breakthrough. Kielce in southern Poland fell. Warsaw, still in German hands, was bypassed to the north and south. Hitler, aghast at the sudden collapse after his armies in Kurland and East Prussia had held off the enemy so well before, admitted to Colonel von Below, one of his most trusted adjutants: "We have no hope." Only a miracle could save Germany now.

Stalin had committed 180 divisions to his front in Poland. Hitler had 133 in the east, but 30 were in the Kurland and Memel pockets and 28 were in Hungary. Stalin's "divisions" had barely more than 4,000 men, but his superiority in aircraft, tanks, and guns was overwhelming. On the fourteenth, Guderian at last cabled an appeal to Hitler to transfer the war's Schwerpunkt to the eastern front. Hitler held a last conference with Rundstedt and Model on January 15, instructing them to hold off the Allies for as long as possible. At 6 P.M. he drove with his staff to the station and boarded his special train. At 7:15 P.M. he held another war conference. Five minutes later Guderian again telephoned, appealing for "everything to be thrown into the eastern front." (In fact, Hitler was to order over forty divisions moved to the east over the next six weeks.) As the train gathered speed toward Berlin, one of his staff—the SS colonel who was later to fulfill Hitler's last and hardest order—remarked within his hearing: "Berlin will be most practical as our headquarters: we'll soon be able to take the streetcar from the eastern to the western front!"[8] Hitler laughed wanly at this witticism, and the rest of his staff joined in.

[8]This was SS Colonel Otto Günsche. See page 822 below.

Waiting for a Telegram

When he awoke at 9 A.M. on January 16, 1945, his train was approaching the capital. Snowdrifts concealed Berlin's cruelest injuries. Forty minutes later he was being driven from Grunewald station to the Reich Chancellery.

The old wing, scene of his prewar political triumphs, had suffered unmistakably, and he could make out snow-filled craters in the gardens. A rectangular concrete slab elevated some feet above ground level marked the site of the deep shelter which Albert Speer had built for him. It looked an inhospitable place. Hitler decided to sleep in his usual first-floor bedroom for the time being—a hurricane seemed to have blasted through it, but it had been repaired—and to continue holding his war conferences in the ornate study overlooking the ravaged Chancellery gardens.

No stenograms of the next conferences survive, but they were clearly charged with high drama. General Harpe's Army Group A had collapsed; since Schörner's army group had fought brilliant defensive actions in Kurland, Hitler send for him that afternoon, awarded him the Diamonds, and appointed him Harpe's successor. He also instructed the navy to embark two panzer and two infantry divisions at the Kurland port of Libau immediately and to bring them by sea to reinforce the main eastern front. In Poland and East Prussia he designated several cities as "fortresses," to be held as breakwaters and buttresses, slowing down the swirling enemy advance.

Postmortems on the catastrophe in Poland began. Hitler learned that the Twenty-fourth Panzer Corps (General Nehring), stationed southwest of Kielce—much too close to the Russian Schwerpunkt—had received telephone orders from Harpe to hold Kielce as a "hinge," without counterattacking, although that was what panzer divisions were for. Now that the front line had been overrun so "unexpectedly rapidly," the corps was engulfed. Seething with anger, Hitler ordered Harpe to report to him in person. The general calmly produced a Führer Order explicitly reserving these divisions—the 16th and 17th panzer divisions—

to Hitler's whim. Hitler had never seen the order before, and concluded that Guderian's staff was responsible.

The loss of Warsaw produced another example of the General Staff's waywardness. Hitler had ordered the Polish capital defended as a fortress, but when Guderian next appeared at the Chancellery he told the startled Führer that the city had already fallen to the Russians, and he had redrawn the situation map accordingly. But even as they were conferring, a radio message arrived from the German battle commandant in Warsaw: he was still holding out, though enveloped on all sides. Hitler ordered the city held at all costs—like Budapest, which was still surviving the Soviet onslaught. However, it was now too late, as Guderian's earlier order to the contrary had been obeyed.

Asked for an explanation, Guderian blamed his chief of operations, Colonel Bogislaw von Bonin, for the inaccurate report (the same officer had expressed the General Staff's confidence in the eastern front's defenses in December). Hitler ordered Bonin arrested, and when Guderian guiltily objected, Hitler retorted, "I'm out for the General Staff's blood. This General Staff clique has got to be stamped out!"[1] On the eighteenth he instructed Jodl to draft a firmly worded order that in the future no commander was to commence any attack or retreat without first having informed the Führer in sufficient time for the order to be countermanded; any future inaccurate reports submitted to him—"whether by design or through negligence"—would be severely punished. The order was issued three days later.

Faced with this Soviet invasion, Hitler skeptically authorized Ribbentrop's first cautious feelers to the western powers. His mind was clear on the general terms. (Once he had said he would fight on until "a peace that is honorable, acceptable to Germany, and will safeguard the life of her coming generations becomes possible; because I need hardly add how distasteful I find this war.") Failing that, Ribbentrop's feelers might still drive a wedge into the enemy alliance. Sources strongly suggested that it was falling apart. Both Roosevelt and Churchill refused to accept Stalin's "Lublin Committee" puppet government and his proposed frontiers for Poland. Hitler confidently expected the alliance to founder on this rock—a misjudgment as monumental as his Dunkirk error five years before.

Whereas then, in 1940, Hitler had assumed that Churchill could not honorably

[1]Bonin stayed in prison until the end of the war. Subsequently he was involved in strange dealings with the Soviet occupation authorities in East Germany in the 1950s. As for Hitler's remarks about the General Staff, several officers present testified later that General Jodl (one of the General Staff's most illustrious products) coldly informed him that it was small wonder that "the spirit of July 20" was prevalent if Hitler cast its officers into prison on such flimsy pretexts.

abandon the French in battle, now in 1945 he could not believe that Churchill would bring himself to abandon Poland to bolshevism; after all, Britain had gone to war over Poland's integrity in 1939. Surely the British would now see that Germany was central Europe's last bulwark against the hordes of Asia? "There must be people in Britain who can see what it is they are demolishing!" he exclaimed in exasperation to his adjutants.

On January 2, German Intelligence sources reported that Moscow's Comintern had ordered anti-British agitation to begin. With his Ardennes offensive still causing acute embarrassment to the Allies, Hitler authorized Ribbentrop—probably that same day—to draw up proposals for the western governments; the form of these proposals was to be such that they could not be attributed to Hitler himself. By the nineteenth, when Ribbentrop brought the document to him, the political climate seemed even more propitious; London and Washington could surely find little comfort in the Red Army's immense offensive. The document proposed that Germany retain her national frontiers and renounce both her economic autarky and her ambitions to a hegemony over Europe; that she cooperate in her foreign policy and in economic affairs; that freedom of religion would be restored and the Jews resettled somewhere in an international community. The proposals were stated to be the views of "authoritative sources in Berlin including the foreign minister." Hitler approved it. Ribbentrop signed it and sent one of his most experienced diplomats, Dr. Werner von Schmieden, who had a distinguished League of Nations record, to Switzerland to make contact with a Mr. Allen Dulles—Roosevelt's Intelligence chief there—and an equivalent British official. Now Berlin could only wait for the reply.

Hitler confidently prepared fresh military undertakings in the east meanwhile. His health must have improved, for his doctors only rarely visited him. But his milieu changed. Martin Bormann—who returned from a two-week leave on January 19, bringing Eva Braun to Berlin with him—held regular morning conferences with Hitler. Goebbels and Ley were frequent guests. Admiral Dönitz attended the war conferences almost daily—for his warships were to evacuate hundreds of thousands of civilians from the threatened eastern provinces. On January 20, the admiral offered Hitler twenty thousand naval troops for the land battles. That same day Hitler conferred with Speer and Saur on ways of restoring the Luftwaffe's supremacy; Göring, Messerschmitt, and other experts crowded the Chancellery study. Hitler ordered—once again—the heaviest cannon, and air-to-air missiles like the R4M rocket, to be mass-produced for the fighter squadrons. Jet-fighter development was to continue at top priority, and the Führer called for a long-range heavy bomber to be designed using the jet-engine principle. Göring was ignored. General Galland was not present—having been replaced that day in disgrace by Colonel Gollob as commander of the fighter force.

This long-term industrial planning showed that Hitler still expected a Seven Years' War. Jodl's staff had formulated a new master plan to stave off an earlier defeat: by weakening the western front to the utmost degree compatible with safety, an assault army would be built up in the east before the end of February 1945; this would head off the Russian invasion. Meanwhile the western enemy would be harried by more aggressive warfare from Hitler's Atlantic "fortresses" —Lorient, Saint-Nazaire, La Rochelle, and North Gironde—and their long lines of communication would be disrupted by U-boat, minelaying, midget-submarine operations, and Luftwaffe attacks. On January 19, Dönitz endorsed Hitler's delaying strategy. One hundred and seven of the secret Mark XXI electro-U-boats were already fitting out, and the first were to begin operations in March.

Before the eastern front had caved in, Hitler had ordered the powerful Sixth SS Panzer Army disengaged from the Ardennes battlefield as a tactical reserve for Rundstedt. Late on January 19, Hitler began to consider transferring the army to the east instead, and the next day he ordered its First Panzer Corps to Berlin before heading for the eastern front as rapidly as possible. But events were rapidly overtaking him, and he knew that weeks had to pass before the panzer army could complete its transfer. Martin Bormann, who saw him at 1:45 P.M., wrote in his diary: "Midday: situation in the east growing increasingly menacing. Evacuation of the Warthe Gau. Tank spearheads approaching Kattowitz, etcetera." Hitler blotted from his mind the almost audible sounds of the battle approaching Berlin, and he tried to envisage the Wehrmacht's plight several weeks hence. He concluded that the *strategic* danger to the Reich lay in Hungary and Austria, where Stalin was preparing with an army of inferior troops and Balkan allies to capture the last remaining petroleum fields south of Lake Balaton and in the Viennese region. On January 20, Hitler confided to press chief Otto Dietrich: "I'm going to attack the Russians where they least expect it. The Sixth SS Panzer Army's off to Budapest! If we start an offensive in Hungary, the Russians will have to go too."

His plan was for a rapid pincer attack, launched from both ends of the fifty-mile-long Lake Balaton to unhinge the southern end of the Russian front. On January 21 he cabled Weichs, the Commander in Chief Southeast, to investigate the feasibility of a simultaneous thrust by three or four divisions from Croatia across the Drava into southern Hungary; Weichs replied the next day in terms of conditional approval. Hitler forthwith ordered the Sixth Panzer Army sent to Hungary. When Guderian, exhausted by poor health, protested that he needed the army to defend Berlin, Hitler caustically replied, "You intend operating without gasoline. Fine! How far do you think your tanks will get!" The counter-offensive in Hungary must come first. But it took longer to prepare than Hitler had calculated.

In Poland, Cracow and Lodz were overrun. To release a corps for East Prussia, Hitler ordered Memel abandoned and its dockyard destroyed; on January 21 he authorized General Hossbach's badly mauled Fourth Army to fall back on the line of lakes on either side of the well-provided fortress town of Lötzen. The Russians had torn a huge breach between the German armies fighting in East Prussia—Army Group Center—and Schörner's Army Group A; now virtually nothing stood between them and the Baltic. At a conference with Guderian and Jodl on January 21, Hitler announced that the Reichsführer SS, Himmler, would take over command of a new Army Group Vistula to plug this gap and thereby prevent the enemy from breaking right through to Danzig and Posen and even isolating East Prussia; Himmler was also to "organize the national defense on German soil behind the entire eastern front." When Guderian proposed that this would be an ideal assignment for Field Marshal von Weichs instead—he had an army group staff available and Himmler had not—Hitler rejected the suggestion. Himmler's unorthodox talents had impressed him during the Reichsführer's brief command on the Upper Rhine front; he hoped for a ruthlessness and tenacity from the Reichsführer that was lacking in the elderly, worn-out army generals.

Two days later the Russians reached the coast at Elbing (Elblag), cutting off East Prussia. On the twenty-fourth Hossbach withdrew the Fourth Army to the west and abandoned the Lötzen fortifications without a fight. Hitler's permission was not asked—in flagrant violation of an explicit order; he was not even told. Confronted with this fresh *fait accompli* Hitler exploded: "Hossbach and the Russians are hand in glove!" The general and his entire staff were dismissed immediately; and the same rough justice was meted out to the army group commander, the badly injured General Hans Reinhardt, who was replaced by General Rendulic. To Jodl, Hitler privately compared the Lötzen "treachery" with the August 1944 "Avranches affair" which had presaged the fall of France.

Russian tanks were now rolling into Upper Silesia—the industrial province to which Hitler had evacuated his most precious war factories. The Oder was reached and bridged by the enemy at Steinau. Auschwitz was overrun. The fortress of Posen was encircled, and on January 27 the long, hard fight for possession of the city began; comparable in ferocity with the battles for Stalingrad and the Alcázar of Toledo, it would end only one month later with the death of its commandant and surrender to the Russians after they had threatened to massacre the injured Germans in their hands. Millions of Germans began fleeing westward before the advancing Russians. In East Prussia there were 2,000,000: the navy would evacuate 450,000 from the port of Pillau over the next weeks; 900,000 more set out on foot despite sub-zero temperatures, along the forty-mile causeway to Danzig or across the frozen lagoon known as the Frisches Haff. Behind them the invading Russians—incited by Stalin and by an order signed by Marshal Zhukov himself[2]—raped, pillaged, burned, and plundered. Gehlen's Intelligence branch confirmed that the Russians were shooting civilians quite indiscriminately. "Refugee columns overtaken by Soviet tanks are often machine-gunned and then crushed beneath them."

Every road to Berlin, Dresden, and the west was choked with fleeing refugees. All Germany listened on January 30 to Hitler's radio broadcast, the last he would ever make. His private adjutant, Alwin-Broder Albrecht, wrote the next day: "From all sides the response to the Führer's speech has been indescribably positive, however gloomy the omens may be. . . . What moved me most deeply was one telegram that arrived today from a refugee column trekking from the east. It just read: 'Führer, we trust in you!'—signed, 'A column passing through so-and-so.' " And a few days later Albrecht wrote from Hitler's Chancellery to a querulous mother uncomfortably billeted in Schleswig-Holstein: "It should be sheer ecstasy to hear children noisily playing and shouting. Imagine what a mother feels when her children freeze to death and must be left at the roadside, as happens in countless cases now." Hitler ordered Berlin's buses to rush bread to the refugee columns.

The war he had started had bred inhumanity. To exploit the refugee chaos in Berlin, the Americans sent over nine hundred heavy bombers at noon on February 3. Hitler was awakened in time and took shelter as two thousand tons of bombs rained down, but it was a near thing: his dining room collapsed onto his staff's prepared luncheon table, and the city's casualties were immense. But on the eastern front the slaying of prisoners—an atrocity rare in the west—was commonplace, as neither belligerent had the protection of the Geneva Convention. On February 16, Himmler's Chief of Staff signaled his army commanders: "Führer Order: When villages are captured, and particularly during assault-troop raids, the prisoners are not to be slain near the front line as the civil population has to pay for it afterward." The world's newspapers shortly reported what the Russians had found at Majdanek and other concentration camp sites.

Ever westward and northward the Russians swept, across frozen rivers and frosted fields, exploiting the Polish and east German railroads and autobahns

[2]Zhukov's long Order of the Day fell into German hands. It was headed, "Death to the Germans!" and announced in uncompromising terms that the hour had come for the Red Army to wreak revenge on "Hitler's cannibals." "We'll take revenge for all those burned to death in the Devil's furnaces, poisoned in the gas chambers, shot and martyred. We'll take cruel revenge for them all. . . . Woe betide the land of murderers! . . . *This time we will destroy the German breed once and for all.*"

which the withdrawing armies had not had time to destroy. On January 27, Schörner had to order the Upper Silesian industrial region abandoned. Two days later Königsberg, capital of East Prussia, was isolated by the enemy, and on the thirtieth the Russians reached and bridged the Oder on both sides of Küstrin (Kostrzyn)—only fifty miles from the center of Berlin. The German command structure in the east had collapsed. Hitler had lost contact with entire armies; he did not know which cities had fallen and which were still in his troops' hands. He instructed Guderian: "Over the next few days I must be told everything that is known about the enemy's movements and the most likely directions of attack and assembly areas, because our own countermeasures will depend on them." "Jawohl," answered Guderian.

One thought consoled Hitler: the Soviet avalanche must be causing concern in London and Washington. What was claimed to be a captured directive of the Allied "combined chiefs of staff" showed this concern quite clearly. The Allies' strategic air forces were shortly to begin a series of annihilating attacks on east and central German railway centers, ostensibly in aid of the Russians but in fact designed to hinder their westward progress.[3] The Berlin raid was clearly the first. Hitler instructed Ribbentrop to feed to the British Intelligence networks a phony report that Stalin was raising an army of two hundred thousand German Communists; under General Paulus and other captured German officers, this "army" was to march westward and set up a puppet government, for example in Königsberg. "That'll shake them—like being jabbed with a cobbler's awl!"

A dialogue between Hitler, Jodl, and Göring on January 27 illustrates how firmly rooted their daydreams had become. Hitler mused, "I don't know—do you think the British can still be watching this entire Russian development with a thrill of excitement?" "No, definitely not," replied Jodl. "Their plans were quite different. . . ." "They certainly never bargained for us standing firm in the west and letting the Russians conquer all Germany meanwhile," seconded Göring. "If it goes on like this we'll be getting a telegram in a few days' time. . . . They went to war to stop us moving east, not to have the east coming right up to the Atlantic!" "Absolutely right!" said Hitler. "It doesn't make sense. The British newspapers are already bitterly asking, What's the point of this war?"

It was in this mood of *Schadenfreude* that Hitler conducted two lengthy conferences with Ribbentrop early in February 1945, and then on the seventh with SS General Karl Wolff—his chief police representative in occupied Italy—as well. No note survives, but Wolff later described having drawn Hitler's attention to the

[3]The directive, dated January 24, 1945, was claimed by Luftwaffe Intelligence to have been captured, together with two others issued by General Carl F. Spaatz, the American bomber force commander; in fact they were forgeries, concocted by the Luftwaffe's Intelligence branch.

military stalemate in Italy and to the western Allies' "increasingly concrete peace feelers extended via Switzerland," coupled with similar offers of mediation by the Vatican. Hitler took note of his remarks and pointedly refrained from forbidding him to pursue these channels to the West. Ribbentrop notified Wolff that Hitler's reaction was thus one of guarded approval. Wolff then began secret talks in Switzerland with the same Mr. Dulles whom Herr von Schmieden had been sent to contact.

At the Reich Chancellery the broadcast of Hitler's January 30 speech was followed by the premiere of Goebbels's most ambitious color film ever, *Kolberg:* the story of one of the most stirring battles in the Seven Years' War. Hitler never saw it, but throughout his rapidly shrinking domain the film revived failing spirits; it was even dispatched by fighter aircraft to inspire the German garrisons of the remaining Atlantic fortresses. "These times require lionhearts," wrote one of his adjutants after seeing *Kolberg,* "so it is salutary to be reminded of what previous generations suffered in the fight for our nation's survival. . . . The film matches present history so well that its originators—and work began on the film in 1942 —must have had clairvoyant powers." History in the besieged Baltic port of Kolberg would indeed soon be repeated.

Two weeks had passed since the Soviet invasion. Schörner's army group had now claimed 1,356 enemy tanks and the army group in East Prussia an equal number; but the enemy losses were being replaced with equal rapidity. The fortress city of Posen—where German-speaking officers in German uniforms had infiltrated the lines—was still holding out; but other strongholds were being engulfed one after the other. Chelmno, Thorn, and Marienwerder (Kwidzyn) had to be relinquished by Himmler's makeshift army group; Hitler and Guderian authorized these painful retreats. Hitler's day ended later and later: on January 30–31 it was five-thirty before he retired, only to be awakened at noon by Martin Bormann with the alarming news that Russian tanks were approaching Krossen and had just crossed the frozen Oder River between Küstrin and Wriezen.

The Oder was the last major river before Berlin. Its western banks were defended only by the Volkssturm battalions rushed into position from the capital itself, from central Germany, and even from Austria. These elderly soldiers—the ill-armed home guard which the Party had been organizing since autumn—slowed down the Russian onslaught and without support manned the Oder line, fighting off the Red Army for the whole first week of February until regular army reinforcements arrived. Meanwhile Hitler directed that over three hundred heavy antiaircraft batteries be transferred from the Reich's air defense to the Oder line to provide a formidable if immobile antitank defense. All fighter planes were committed to the Silesian and East Prussian battlefields, because most could now carry bombs—as Hitler had always demanded. Thus the crisis was overcome, though it took stamina: even Himmler had called his army group staff together one evening and announced that there was no hope of withstanding the Russian pressure any longer. ("But then it began to drip outside," he recalled later. "The thaw had come—we had been saved as though by a miracle. Now we would have time to build up the Oder defenses after all. Since then I have never doubted we'll win the war.") Ten weeks would pass before the Russians could recover the impetus they had lost so close to their final objective—Berlin.

In weakening the Reich's air defenses to keep the Russians at bay, Hitler perhaps hoped the Allied bombers might be called off—just as those still German-occupied islands in the Aegean were very obviously being left unmolested by the British. ("So that the British do not need to defend them against the Russians or any other usurpers," the German naval staff observed.) This fear was borne out by evidence that the British were fortifying the isles of Lemnos and Chios which the Germans had evacuated; in addition, the German commandant of the eastern Aegean had received a secret British offer to carry supplies to the German-held islands on British steamships. From February 5 onward the Americans in the Saar began appealing by loudspeaker to the opposing German troops to concern themselves with the Russians, their common enemy, and make common cause with the Allies; this was a particularly worrying form of propaganda for the German High Command. But against all these auguries Hitler had to set one new hard fact: since early February, somewhere in the world, Churchill, Roosevelt, and Stalin were meeting to settle their differences.

Almost all Silesia had been overrun. In Breslau, the capital, 38 Volkssturm battalions had been raised from the city's quarter-million population and from the surrounding countryside. With these 15,000 men and 30,000 regular troops, Breslau defied air and artillery bombardment and ground attack in a long siege that was not ended until a week after Hitler himself had perished. Here Bormann had a more than usually fanatical Gauleiter—Karl Hanke, Goebbels's former state secretary and an intimate friend of Albert Speer. "Hanke's a devil of a fellow," said Hitler approvingly. "He's a Silesian himself." Hitler knew, however, what the loss of the Silesian coal would mean, now that the Ruhr was virtually isolated by the rail and canal destruction. Germany's economic collapse seemed inevitable. Japan was in a similar plight. The enemy blockade of her seaways to the south—now that the Philippines had been retaken by the United States—would deprive her of rice, oil, bauxite, and iron ore; Hitler's attaché in Tokyo warned that Japan could not fight on longer than another year.

This was the economic background to his "nod" to Karl Wolff and Ribbentrop early in February—the go-ahead to contact the western Allies. The oil crisis had already forced on Hitler a strategic choice between East and West anyway. In January the bomb-battered refineries had produced only 50,000 tons of gasoline and 12,000 tons of aviation fuel; the latter figure represented only 6 percent of the May 1944 output. It was unlikely that the new U-boats and jet aircraft—145 Me-262 jets had been produced in January alone—would get the diesel and J-2 kerosene they needed. Because of the fuel shortage, the air war against Antwerp was now restricted to single-engined fighter-bombers. At the end of January Hitler ruled that in the future the western front must go short of fuel and ammunition to aid the eastern front: Rundstedt had to forfeit fuel to replenish the Sixth SS Panzer Army before its departure for Hungary, although at any moment Eisenhower might begin his new offensive toward the Ruhr and Rundstedt lacked the fuel to move up his own reserves accordingly.

Along the Oder the ice was still thawing. Hitler ordered ice-breakers and explosives used to speed up the process. By February 8, the immediate danger to Berlin had passed. During the previous week the OKW had taken forceful action to prevent a panic-stricken flight from the capital; but important Wehrmacht command posts were ordered to leave, and provision was made for the ministries to follow if a new crisis should develop. For Hitler himself Bormann began preparing an emergency headquarters at Stolpe, in his own earlier stamping-ground, Mecklenburg.

The ruinous American daylight raid had left Berlin's government quarter a shambles. The railroads and stations were obliterated. Bormann wrote: "The Reich Chancellery garden is an amazing sight—deep craters, fallen trees, and the paths blotted out by rubble and debris. The Führer's residence was badly hit several times. Only fragments remain of the Winter Garden and the Banquet Hall walls. . . . Vossstrasse is pitted with enormous craters, and the houses opposite in Hermann-Göringstrasse have been completely burned out." Hitler's residence and Bormann's Party Chancellery lost all telephone contact with the outside world. An adjutant wrote on the fifth: "Some twenty-five bombs fell on our district. There's no water, no heat, no electricity. . . . By roundabout route water reached the main points again after twenty hours, but we'll have to wait another two weeks for heat—unless the visitors return in the meantime—for which possibility we are steeling ourselves."

Every night the sirens wailed in Berlin. The Russians had captured 130 airfields since mid-January, nearly all intact, and Soviet bombers joined the British and American campaign. Many cities like Dresden had lost all their antiaircraft guns to the eastern front. With the fighter squadrons still committed to the Oder battlefront, the big cities were defenseless. Not one aircraft had climbed to the defense of Berlin on February 3 for this reason. Every sea or land disaster was now laid at the Luftwaffe's door. When a Soviet submarine sank the liner *Wilhelm Gustloff,* drowning five thousand refugees from East Prussia, and when the hospital ship *Steuben* was torpedoed some days later, drowning nearly all the twenty-five hundred casualties and one thousand refugees aboard her, Dönitz blamed the Luftwaffe for failing to provide antisubmarine patrols. Hitler—confined to his air raid shelter yet again by a small raiding force of Mosquitoes—received from the Ninth SS Panzer Corps in the heart of beleaguered Budapest the radio message familiar ever since Stalingrad: the Luftwaffe airlift was letting them down. The Luftwaffe war diary shows that Hitler strongly attacked Göring for the failure, without even checking on the justice of the allegation.

In vain the anxious Reichsmarschall signed strings of belated death sentences on Luftwaffe officers—including a full general, Waber, his commander in the northern Balkans—for offenses ranging from desertion, cowardice, slackness, espionage, corruption, and loose living to precipitate flight from airfields and depots, and allowing new aircraft, fuel, and bomb dumps to fall into enemy hands. For every sin that Göring punished, Bormann could always prove the commission of ten more.

When Lammers ventilated the delicate matter of Hitler's heir, Bormann contemptuously advised him that Göring was out of the running. Hitler openly ridiculed the Reichsmarschall's visit to the Oder front, and no word of it reached the press. Göring's very presence in the cramped air raid shelter revolted the Führer, since both the Reichsmarschall and his adjutant Dr. Ramon Ondarza made liberal use of conflicting perfumes, with which the shelter's air purification system could not cope. Eventually Hitler loudly commanded Göring: "Tell your man Ondarza that he stinks like a cesspit, and he's not to perfume himself when he comes visiting again!" Göring fully understood Hitler's characteristically oblique hint.

No word had yet come from the western powers—no "telegram." Nor was there word of Stalin's meeting with the western leaders, except that it was somewhere on the Black Sea. In Bulgaria, King Boris's successors had just been shot by the new Communist regime. In Poland, Stalin's new satellite government proclaimed the forthcoming annexation of Silesia and East Prussia.

The very simultaneity of action in east and west suggested there was a disconcertingly high degree of collaboration between the enemy powers after all. On February 8, Marshal Konev attacked from the Steinau bridgehead across the Oder with the obvious aim of encircling Breslau. On the same day a big Allied offensive developed between the Rhine and the Meuse.[4] Far into the night Hitler sat talking with Bormann, Speer, the latter's fellow architect, Professor Hermann

[4]Rundstedt had asked permission to make local tactical withdrawals where necessary. Hitler granted this but forbade the surrender of any fortifications or city. "The enemy may well be able to storm the ruins of a bunker line or city, but they are never to be evacuated—except on the Führer's orders."

Giesler—who had replaced Speer as Hitler's principal confidant on city planning —and Eva Braun, who was returning to Munich the next day now that the immediate danger to Berlin had passed. Toward morning Hitler was informed that the British had destroyed the Pölitz synthetic refinery, the Luftwaffe's last gasoline source. It had been defended by 429 guns, but Hitler shortly learned that a nameless Luftwaffe officer had ordered its entire searchlight defenses removed. With the Luftwaffe's dwindling fuel stocks now down to only 6,000 tons, it would receive only 400 more tons in February.

Professor Giesler had come to Berlin for a specific reason. Late on February 9 he unveiled to Hitler his model for the reconstruction of the bomb-desecrated city of Linz—where Hitler had first heard Wagner's *Rienzi* and decided to become a statesman. Hitler had decreed that Linz must replace Budapest as the Danube's fairest city; it was to have fine Party buildings, a concert hall seating thirty-five thousand, and a bell tower five hundred feet high—with Hitler's parents entombed in a crypt at its base—on the north bank, and a major replanning of the old city on the south. A wide ceremonial mall was to extend from the railroad station to the city center, flanked by opera houses, theaters, a museum, library, and immense art gallery. Now in Giesler's model it all took shape before Hitler's eyes. At 4 A.M. that morning he again stole into the shelter where the model was laid out, and he returned at 3 A.M. the morning after.

When SS General Kaltenbrunner came with alarming reports of declining public morale, Hitler took the Gestapo chief, himself a native of Linz, into the model room. For many minutes Hitler described how Linz would arise anew when victory was theirs—how he would be the art gallery's principal benefactor, and he would found a medical academy there as well. When the ponderous general himself warmed to the theme, Hitler challenged him with his haunting eyes. "My dear Kaltenbrunner, do you imagine I could talk like this about my plans for the future if I did not believe deep down that we really are going to win this war in the end!"

In their advance toward Berlin, the Russians had been held off about seventy miles from the Pomeranian coast by Himmler's army group, leaving an inviting three-hundred-mile flank for the Germans to attack. Since early February Guderian had been planning to exploit this, to relieve the pressure on Berlin. But the rate of buildup for this counterattack was slow, partly because only one bridge was available across the Oder at Stettin. Hitler's enthusiasm waned; the odds were heavily against them, and Himmler expressed a marked reluctance to risk his forces. At one meeting Hitler was stung into rebuking Himmler: "Now you too have turned defeatist!"—and showed him the door. On February 10 he called both Guderian and Himmler to the Chancellery. Guderian pleaded for the attack to be brought forward—"We can't wait until every last can of gasoline has arrived!" —and demanded a capable army general for Himmler's command staff. He suggested his own deputy, General Wenck. According to Guderian the argument lasted two and a half hours. Eventually he got his way, because Hitler smiled wearily and instructed Himmler: "Wenck will be attached to your staff." The attack would be brought forward to the fifteenth.

In the event, the operation, from south of Stargard, was a failure. On the third day Wenck was injured in a motor accident. Perhaps because of this the attack lost all further impetus, and Hitler called it off.

Guderian's star began to wane as rapidly as Zeitzler's had after the failure of "Citadel" in 1943. When Hitler learned that the general had recently advised Ribbentrop that the war was lost, he made a terrible scene at the next war conference. "In a situation like this any sign of defeatism is open treachery. That is just what General Guderian's recent discussion with Ribbentrop amounts to. I expect every one of my colleagues to stand by me—the greater the peril, the more your tenacity. It must be clear to everybody, if I throw an ordinary workman who mutters defeatist remarks in an air raid shelter into a concentration camp or hang him, or if the same thing happens to a soldier who loses his nerve and runs away, that I must expect at least as much from you. This kind of sedition has got to stop."

The outcome of Stalin's meeting with Churchill and Roosevelt at Yalta, in the Crimea, had produced this shift in Hitler's stance. The mere fact that the Allied and Soviet military staffs were also conferring there had persuaded him that the western leaders were blind to Stalin's ambitions. He cannot have been surprised when Werner von Schmieden now returned from Switzerland having failed "for technical reasons" to contact Allen Dulles. From Yalta the enemy leaders announced on February 13 that Hitler's Reich was to be destroyed and carved up between the victors as "occupation zones." The Yalta communiqué—sent in to Hitler page by page as it came over the teleprinters—produced a hoot of triumph from him. "So much for the drivel talked by our coffeehouse diplomats and foreign ministry politicos! Here they have it in black and white: if we lose the war, Germany will cease to exist. What matters now is to keep our nerve and not give in." He dictated to his press officer his own brutal response, deliberately burning any bridges that might still exist. He would never surrender; nor would he allow his people to.

That evening, February 13, 1945, to distract himself with dividers and magnifying glass from the ugly world of war outside, Hitler again walked down to view the models for the rebuilding of Linz. He dined at eight with two secretaries, then slept until it was time for the midnight war conference.

Here the news was that since midday Breslau had been totally encircled by the Soviet armies and that three hundred heavy bombers had just set the ancient heart of Dresden—alive with a million homeless refugees—on fire. A firestorm like that in Hamburg had broken out there. Before the conference was over, word arrived that a new attack, heavier than the first, had begun on Dresden. The city had had no antiaircraft guns; and only that day the Luftwaffe had decided that jet-fighter and ground-attack operations in the east and west must take precedence over Reich defense, so no fighters had operated. Fire brigades were converging on Dresden from all over Germany. From the city itself there was a merciful silence, as all the telephone lines were down. It was 6:15 A.M. before Hitler retired to his cramped bunker bedroom. At 1 P.M. he was awakened with the news that the American bomber forces were continuing the carnage in Dresden which the British had left incomplete the night before; huge fires were still raging in the city.

After the all clear sounded in Berlin, Hitler was surprised to meet in the Chancellery hall the army doctor who had treated his ear injuries after July 20; Dr. Giesing had been visiting an adjutant in the Chancellery when the alert sounded. He wrote some weeks later: "Hitler and I sat down on a corner bench in the big hall upstairs. Now that I could see his face better by daylight, I was astounded at the change. He looked older and more bowed than ever. His complexion was as pale as before, and there were pronounced bags under his eyes. His speech was clear but very soft. . . ." Twice the Führer asked the doctor where his family was; twice he replied, "They are in Krefeld, mein Führer." Hitler seemed distant; he looked exhausted. His hands were white and his fingernails devoid of blood. Twice he asked Giesing which hospital he worked at, and twice the doctor told him.

Then Hitler suddenly turned to the war. "Germany is in a tough spot, but I'll get her out of it. The British and Americans have miscalculated badly. . . . In no time at all I'm going to start using my Victory weapon *(Siegwaffe)* and then the war will come to a glorious end. Some time ago we solved the problem of nuclear fission, and we have developed it so far that we can exploit the energy for armaments purposes *(Rüstungszwecke)*. They won't even know what hit them! It's the weapon of the future. With it Germany's future is assured. It was Providence that allowed me to perceive this final path to victory."[5] His gaze remained

[5]Hitler had already hinted at atomic bombs in his last talk with Antonescu in August 1944. Giesing in fact wrote his account of this conversation with Hitler from memory on June 21, 1945—six weeks before Hiroshima! The origin of Hitler's optimism is puzzling. Scientists under Professors Werner Heisenberg and Carl-Friedrich von Weizsäcker had been studying nuclear fission and atomic bomb physics since 1939, and they had started building an experimental atomic pile at Haigerloch in 1944; in December the Reich chief of nuclear research, Professor Walther Gerlach, appealed to Bormann for exemption for them from Volkssturm service and speciously mentioned their "atomic bomb" research as justification. I suspect that Bormann was Hitler's source.

rooted to the floor. All at once he again asked the doctor where his family was. "In Krefeld, mein Führer." "Nothing can happen to them there, that's for sure," Hitler replied. "The West Wall will stand fast and then our *Siegwaffe* will decide the war in a very short time. . . . And if the war should go against us, then we must all die bravely. I shall remain at the head of my forces and die in action. But Providence has brought me this far unscathed, and I shall continue along this prescribed path undeterred by whatever may befall me."

The night's death toll in Dresden was estimated at a quarter-million. Hitler was intrigued that the British bombers had not instead been employed against Himmler's armies, which were winding up for a counterattack in Pomerania. "They flatten the Dresden opera house and wipe out refugees—but Stettin harbor, which is jam-packed with troop transports, they leave alone!" At 7:15 P.M. on February 14, Hitler discussed Dresden for forty-five minutes with Goebbels. The propaganda minister suggested retaliating with the Luftwaffe's huge stocks of top-secret nerve gases, but without a bomber force this was impossible.

Goebbels's alternative proposal was to execute one Allied prisoner for every German civilian killed in air raids. It would invite reprisals against German prisoners in Allied hands, but to Hitler this was not without its attractions. Since the renewed British offensive in the west, German desertions had assumed epidemic proportions; not without reason the German infantryman was attracted to the carefree prison-camp existence and the Allies' humane treatment of prisoners. "This constant sniveling about humanity will cost us the war," Hitler complained. "Neither the Russians in the east nor these hypocrites in the west stick to the Geneva Convention—just look at their attacks on the civilian population!" According to the staff stenographer present, Heinz Buchholz, Hitler emphasized that the Russians had demonstrated what could be achieved by ruthlessly punishing enemy airmen. "Our airmen couldn't be persuaded to fly over Moscow or Leningrad for their lives, after the Russians began executing Luftwaffe airmen. They just published that 'enemy paratroopers had been found and exterminated.' "

The idea of dropping the Geneva Convention appealed to Hitler, but not to the Party or the Wehrmacht. Keitel, Jodl, and Dönitz opposed it (the latter recommended that at least they should not announce publicly that they were going to disregard the convention). Ribbentrop—summoned by his horrified liaison officer Walther Hewel—ultimately talked Hitler out of the idea during a forty-minute stroll with him in the blitzed Chancellery gardens on February 21. But their conversation also revolved around Ribbentrop's latest clandestine peace approach to the Allies—four days previously Ribbentrop had sent a sixteen-page telegram to certain German ambassadors outlining arguments to use in favor of an armistice. Germany proposed to fight on until her enemies realized she could not be defeated; Stalin's aim was to rule Europe; he would abide by none of his solemn undertakings—already he was raising a Soviet German army. Ribbentrop argued that this was Europe's last chance to unite against Stalin. But on February 21, after his talk with Hitler, he had to recall the telegram and tell his ambassadors to ignore it.

Hitler had seen the photographs of Dresden. In heaps of five hundred at a time, the city's air raid victims were now being publicly cremated on makeshift grids of steel girders in the ruined town center. The pictures showed the thousands of men and women and children, still in their Mardi Gras fancy dress costumes, being stacked like rotting cabbages onto the bonfires. Where was the justice in history if an enemy could vanquish Germany by means such as these? This was the mood that impelled Hitler now.

Two vivid descriptions of Hitler in late February 1945 exist. One was by a General Staff officer who had last seen him in 1941 and was now brought by Schörner to the Chancellery on February 19. "—Older, stooping, an unhealthy pink tinge in his bloated face. But his eyes were as clear and calm as ever, though harsher than I recalled them. His voice was still gruff and self-possessed. He asked his questions calmly and listened patiently until I finished." A clammy, oppressive heat gripped the bunker under the Chancellery—the central heating had been restored two weeks after the Berlin raid. "What repelled me was the atmosphere and the attitude of what we called 'the scum' in the anterooms. Well-dressed and handsome young adjutants, many with the highest medals—which they unquestionably had once deserved—some of them SS officers, lolling around with bored expressions and criticizing everything. . . ."

The second description was by a Gauleiter, summoned along with other Party dignitaries at short notice to the Chancellery at 2 P.M. on February 24. On the previous day the Americans had unexpectedly begun their big offensive across the Roer River east of Aachen—even though the flood waters Rundstedt had released by breaching the Roer dams on the eighth had not subsided. North of this, the Canadian First Army had already penetrated deeply into Germany west of the Rhine. On this February 24, the Red Army had just begun an equally unexpected attack on Himmler's thin line defending Pomerania. Only in Hungary had a modest success been achieved, with the destruction that day of a Russian bridgehead across the Gran River after days of arduous fighting.

When Hitler entered one of the few still undamaged Chancellery halls, followed by Bormann, he found sixty or seventy of the Gauleiters and officials lined up around three sides. He shook hands with each of them, then invited them to a simple luncheon—stew, followed by real coffee. Afterward he made a speech, sitting at a small table on which he had spread out his notes—an old man, his back bent, his left hand shaking so violently that his entire frame trembled. His voice gained in strength as the customary climax was reached, but the sensational news his Party faithfuls had all anticipated was not forthcoming; no mention here of "nuclear fission." He talked of a forthcoming counterattack in the east, an operation which had been delayed by the losses of heavy weapons. He referred wistfully to the deceased General Hube and wished he had more generals "carved of the same oak." He asked for a supreme final effort from the Party so that the war might still be won—they must bring out a *furor teutonicus* in the people. If the people now gave up, this would prove they had no moral worth: they would deserve annihilation.

He lavished praise on the West Wall, the new U-boats, and the jet aircraft. Politically, he now expected Britain to hold out to the end, unshakable in her alliance with Russia; but he predicted the day when serious conflict would arise between Russia and the United States.

In conclusion Hitler mentioned to the Gauleiters his own declining health. Frederick the Great, he said, had also returned from his wars an ill and broken man, and now he too felt this burden. At one stage he tried to convey a glass of water to his mouth, but his hand trembled so much that he abandoned the attempt. Perhaps it was an act of showmanship, for he concluded with a smile: "I used to have this tremor in my leg. Now it's in my arm. I can only hope it won't proceed to my head. But even if it does I can only say this: my heart will never quaver." Over the next few weeks, he warned them, he might be forced to adopt some harsh measures which they might not understand; he asked the Gauleiters not to misjudge him.

Six to eight thousand Russian tanks had been claimed destroyed since mid-January. Still the General Staff's belief was that the Red Army's next move would be the assault on Berlin—regardless of the danger from Himmler's army group. General Ritter Bruno von Hauenschildt was designated commander of the Berlin district. He attended Hitler's daily war conferences. The city's antiaircraft batteries were regrouped into tight clusters situated where they could also command the main approach roads.

The very day of Hitler's speech to the Gauleiters proved Guderian's experts wrong. Instead of continuing westward toward Berlin, Marshal Zhukov turned north against Himmler's army group in Pomerania. Gehlen conceded the new situation in a belated appreciation the next day. On the twenty-seventh, Zhukov achieved a massive breakthrough in Himmler's lines; two enemy tank armies which Gehlen had believed on the Oder front preparing to exploit the Küstrin bridgehead now emerged far to the northeast, racing toward Köslin and the Baltic coast. At a conference that day Hitler promised immediate reinforcements to Himmler for a counterattack, and he ordered the historic rail and road corridor

—cause of the 1939 dispute with Poland—held at all costs. Meanwhile all manner of deception was to be used to persuade the Russians that between the Oder front and Berlin a deep and impregnable defense had been established. Phonograph records of moving tanks, marching troops, and construction work were to be played over loudspeakers toward the enemy lines. Unless Himmler's counterattack succeeded, the loss of East and West Prussia seemed inevitable.

Germany's military reserves were long since exhausted. On February 27, Jodl showed Hitler a telegram from Rundstedt, forcefully complaining that of the 52,215 soldiers promised him in February, only 11,902 had come. Martin Bormann believed that over 500,000 deserters were concealing themselves in the Reich, and he had campaigned since mid-February for action against this "epidemic of cowardice." His staff proposed public hangings of such men under the slogan Gauleiter Karl Hanke had recently found effective in his fanatical defense of Breslau: "Death and dishonor to those who fear an honorable death!" Hitler proposed to Himmler two radical solutions designed to shame the deserters back into their units: to attain "a suitable effect on the men's attitude" the Reich women's leader, Frau Scholtze-Klink, should be consulted on the creation of a women's battalion. Secondly, 6,000 youths of fifteen were to be recruited to reinforce Himmler's rear lines of defense. Bormann acidly observed to his staff in a memorandum: "This means that we are now calling up women and fifteen-year-olds to strengthen the front."

Turkey, Egypt, Finland, and a host of South American countries now declared war on Germany. Turkey gave one week's notice; Finland backdated her declaration to September 15, 1944, there being nothing in the rules against such an action.

In the west, the Americans broke out of their Roer bridgehead on February 28 and began advancing with tanks on the Rhine between Düsseldorf and Venlo. Hitler ordered every available jet- and propellor-driven aircraft to engage them. American tanks flying German colors tried to rush the Rhine bridges at Düsseldorf and Uerdingen, but these—and every other bridge from Duisburg down to Koblenz—were destroyed in the nick of time. The apathy of the German people west of the Rhine shocked Hitler. Weeks of terror-bombing, which had lately extended to even the smallest villages, had reduced the people's former defiance to a simpering servility. White flags waited for the enemy. Local farmers attacked German troops with pitchforks when they tried to blow up minor bridges to hamper the enemy invasion; other gangs of farmers removed tank obstacles. At Bingen the citizens refused to complete tank obstacles. The deputy mayor of Ingelheim was publicly hanged for advising his citizens to let the enemy in. At Trier the Volkssturm melted away; other Volkssturm units were reported throwing their bazookas, machine guns, and ammunition into lakes and rivers. At

Remagen, American troops entering the town were astonished (and delighted) to find the railway bridge across the Rhine still intact and flung an immediate armored bridgehead onto the eastern shore. Most of Cologne was overrun. The crisis developed so suddenly that Hitler voiced to the OKW a lingering suspicion that Rundstedt might be secretly dealing with the western powers; why else had his headquarters at Ziegenberg still not been bombed?[6]

By March 8 the situation in the east was also worse. Pomerania seemed lost, and with it Hitler's faith in Himmler was finally destroyed. Pleading angina, the Reichsführer SS had abandoned his command staff for a health clinic at Hohenlychen; his staff described as "utopian" Hitler's orders to seal the breach torn by Zhukov in Pomerania's defenses. On March 4, General Hans Krebs—deputizing for the injured Wenck—quoted to Hitler the blunt objections telephoned by General Kinzel, Himmler's operations officer: "This war is being fought on paper, it's quite divorced from reality!"

A year before Hitler would not have tolerated such criticism; but now he had to swallow it, because each military defeat eroded his authority. He decided on a more limited eastward counterattack from Stettin instead. General Erich Raus's Fourth Panzer Army would receive the necessary reinforcements by March 6. Shortly afterward his Third SS Panzer Corps (under General Martin Unrein's command) announced that it was ready, or at least had enough ammunition for the first two days' attack. Hitler, cautious ever since Avranches, sent an SS adjutant to Stettin to check. SS Major Johannes Göhler reported back that the divisions had no ammunition at all. "On the drive up to Stettin," wrote Göhler privately, "we passed endless columns of refugees who had set out weeks ago. A shocking sight. It was freezing cold and the roads were like glass. The roads were jammed again and again, so I had time to speak with many of them. I can scarcely comprehend their faith in victory. As for the troops I spoke with, everybody from corps commander downward wanted to know about the Führer's health, about how things are on other sectors of the front, and more than anything about whether we can hope for further V-weapons. What could I say? I radiated what optimism I could. How young are the faces one sees among the soldiers, and what devotion! Among the divisional commanders I found frequent skepticism but also a fierce determination to stand fast and do their duty. Don't ask me my own thoughts—I'd often like to believe in miracles."

On the afternoon of March 8, General Raus came in person to the bunker to explain his army's defeat in Pomerania. He pointed out that his army's 8 divisions —with only 70 tanks among them—had held a line 150 miles long against 8 Soviet

[6]Hitler replaced Rundstedt by Kesselring as Commander in Chief West two days after the Remagen incident; however, he stressed that Rundstedt still enjoyed his "fullest confidence."

armies and 1,600 tanks. Hitler interrupted nigglingly: "*Fourteen* hundred!" Raus had built dense thickets of tank obstacles with the help of the Party and local authorities. The Volkssturm had manned positions at every village entrance. The battle for Pomerania was illuminated by countless acts of bravery by puny defenders against Stalin's armored invaders. Naval personnel armed with antitank weapons had wrought particular havoc. Out of 34 tanks attacking the naval-held bridgehead at Divenow on March 7 only one had escaped destruction; and this very morning the same naval troops had fearlessly charged across open country and wiped out all 36 attacking Russian tanks—though not without heavy loss to themselves. In the battle for Pomerania, 580 enemy tanks had been knocked out —360 by bazooka at close range. But Hitler was unimpressed by Raus and sent him from the room. "Where does he come from—Berlin? East Prussia?" he inquired. Guderian replied, "He's one of your fellow countrymen: an Austrian!" Hitler decided to dismiss Raus. "He's too nondescript, bogged down in petty details." Manteuffel would replace him. That day, March 8, 1945, Guderian predicted that since the Pomeranian threat to the Red Army's northern flank had now collapsed, Stalin's main attack on Berlin would begin "in about one week."[7]

How high Hitler set his chances we do not know. On March 13 he lightly assured Hindenburg's wizened old state secretary, Otto Meissner, that he was to stay on to enjoy Germany's peacetime reconstruction. "I can't let you retire until you're seventy"—in 1950. Two nights later Hitler was inspiring Kesselring, Rundstedt's successor, with promise of a great "defensive victory" coming in the east, after which Germany's main tank output would revert to the western front.

His new master plan must not fail: a sudden northward thrust from the Ninth Army's narrow bridgehead at Frankfurt-on-Oder would destroy Zhukov's forces massing at Küstrin and thus disrupt the big offensive for weeks to come. In conference with Himmler, Göring, and Guderian on March 15, Hitler instructed them to deceive the Russians into expecting the thrust to turn south, not north. That day he drove to the corps headquarters in the Frankfurt bridgehead to inspect for himself the unit strengths and their stocks of ammunition. Refugees swirled past his car windows in anonymous multitudes; ten million were now fleeing the Russian tanks and guns.

On the road back from the Oder River to his capital, Hitler remained sunk deep in thought.

[7]The General Staff misjudged again. Not until mid-April 1945 did the Soviet attack on Berlin begin.

Hitler Goes to Ground

What intangible forces sustained Hitler during these last dark weeks and in turn allowed him to sustain others? Schopenhauer identifies a certain rare character whom Fate has raised from total obscurity to eminence and who ever afterward believes that the same forces will never wholly desert him in his hour of misfortune—that no abyss is really bottomless, but that when he has plumbed its depths he will once again be lifted to the heights. Such a man was Hitler. He had been tutored, years before the war, by Lloyd George, too. The elderly British statesman had revealed to him in conversation that only the Armistice of 1918 had saved the Allies and dashed the cup of victory from Germany's lips—a perhaps ill-considered remark which the Führer never tired of quoting.

While in Italy the stalemate continued, the "race for Berlin" between East and West convinced Hitler that the two world hemispheres must within months be at war with each other, a war from which Germany would emerge as the *lachender Dritte.* His analysis was correct in all but one essential detail: the time scale. Had his war lasted the full seven years, he might have reaped the Cold War rewards that fell to his successors. Yet Hitler had good reason to expect them to come sooner. Until the very last days of his life his Intelligence experts nourished his beliefs with evidence of the coming conflict—evidence of the most concrete kind. For example, a group of Soviet agents parachuted into Templin on the night of April 7–8, 1945, admitted under interrogation that their mission had been to find out what plans the Allies had made for attacking the Russians; if the Allies reached Berlin first, the agents were to destroy their papers and lie low, "on no account revealing themselves as agents."

If Stalin himself expected such a clash, then Hitler intended to keep his Reich in existence—however battered and however diminished—until then.

Since late February 1945, and a further ruinous American air raid on Berlin, Hitler and his staff had spent their nights in the Reich Chancellery's shelters. Albert Speer had begun building the main deep shelter for Hitler in mid-1944, and now it lay becalmed and impregnable—compared by Julius Schaub to "a U-boat prowling the depths below Berlin's sea of houses and ministry buildings." Such was the scene of this final chapter of Hitler's life, with its narrow concrete passageway and cell-like rooms, the constant hum of air-conditioning machinery, the glare of artificial light, the throng of military and Party officials—some curious, some concerned, but most clinging to Hitler and his infectious belief that this crisis would be overcome.[1] The Führer's shelter was entered down a short flight of steps and through gas-tight doors from the older, weaker shelter built in 1938 beneath the Chancellery's ceremonial hall. Right of the passageway after the machine room was Martin Bormann's office with the main telephone switchboard and his teleprinter units; the office was wallpapered with maps of Germany and Berlin, each covered with a celluloid sheet on which a five-man unit marked in blue chinagraph pencil the progress of each enemy bomber-stream hour by hour. Here Hitler spent the hours of the big alerts, watching with tired eyes the arrows approaching Berlin; each week the tracks grew more complex, for now the British bombers attacked from behind "screens" of radio-jamming and electronic countermeasures, feinting first toward one city, then another, while "fast raiding forces" mounted diversionary attacks far from the main targets of the night. Since the holocaust of Dresden, British bomber forces had cascaded incendiaries and explosives into Chemnitz (Karl-Marx Stadt), Duisburg, Worms, Kassel, ancient Würzburg—the list was endless.

The Americans too had begun attacking area targets. Nuremberg and Munich were laid waste. But by day the tide was beginning to turn, as the Me-262 jets with the heavier armament and air-to-air rockets joined the squadrons. The grim pages of the Luftwaffe High Command's war diary reported: "Four Me-262s shot down four bombers. . . ." But as the Luftwaffe's fuel stocks ran out, this last hope expired. General Peltz (Ninth Air Corps) and Colonel Hajo Herrmann (Ninth Fighter Division) had secured in February Göring's permission in principle for a mass attack by suicide pilots on American bomber formations. Originally 600 Messerschmitt 109s were set aside for this, but the Chief of Air Staff, General Karl Koller, objected that since the Me-109 was ceasing manufacture and only 1,800 still survived, the suicide attack ("Werewolf") would accelerate the end of piston-engined fighter operations and tactical reconnaissance missions until the improved Ta-152 fighter arrived.

[1]Thus Admiral Dönitz advised his commanders on March 3, 1945: "Let us place our trust unconditionally in Adolf Hitler's leadership. Believe me, in my two years as Navy Commander in Chief I have found that his strategic views always turned out right."

The suicide operation—almost overlooked by history—was vivid proof of the anger and bitterness fomented by the bombing war. After weeks of hesitation Koller made available 180 Me-109s with high-performance engines on April 3; 150 pilots were released, but far more, 184, volunteered and flew in "Werewolf" four days later—emptying their cannon into the bombers at point-blank range and then ramming them. The battle took place west of Hanover on April 7, 1945. Of the "suicide" Me-109s, 133 were lost after destroying 23 American bombers; 77 pilots were killed; the escorting jet fighters claimed 28 more American bombers that day.

Left of the red-carpeted main passageway in Hitler's shelter—with its incongruously lavish decor of priceless paintings and furniture rescued from the Chancellery upstairs—were his private rooms: a bedroom with army bed, wardrobe, chest of drawers, and a safe; and a tiny, low-ceilinged living room with desk, table, and hard upholstered sofa; a portrait of Frederick the Great hung over the desk. Between the bedroom and passageway was the small conference room, filled with a map table surrounded by a wooden bench. Through the doors at the passageway's far end a spiral staircase led up into the Chancellery gardens.

A filtration system protected the shelter against poison-gas attack. Recently it had been improved after fumes were detected during a war conference; inquiry revealed that Göring's chauffeur had parked his car near the air-intake duct and had left its engine running to keep warm! In February 1945 Hitler was also fitted with a gas mask in case of emergencies.

This bunker was connected to the Voss Bunker under the Chancellery, which could house two thousand people. In 1939 Hitler had opened it to Berlin's hospital and welfare services, and many an "Adolf" had first seen the light of day here, the birth being marked by flowers for the mother and a bankbook with a hundred marks for the child. During April 1945 an SS Life Guard battalion moved in, as did Bormann's staff and a field hospital, and the maternity clinic was moved to a shelter underneath the Reichstag. Every evening a line formed in the street for access to the Voss Bunker. Hitler ordered a concrete shelter built for those waiting, but weeks later his order had still not been carried out. "I have to attend to every minor detail myself," he exclaimed angrily at lunch to his secretaries. "And yet there's nobody suitable as a successor. Hess went off his rocker. Göring's lost the public's sympathy. Himmler is unacceptable to the Party." Fräulein Schroeder, the sharpest of his secretaries, pointed out: "But Himmler's name is often mentioned by the people." "The man's got no artistic sense at all!" retorted Hitler, to which Fräulein Schroeder tartly replied, "In our present straits artistic sense hardly matters!" Hitler stopped eating and angrily stalked out. "Carry on—rack your brains to think of a successor!" Some days later he repeated this injured challenge. "Why not Admiral Dönitz?" Julius Schaub suggested. Hitler did not reply.

The Luftwaffe's impotence against the air raids began to corrode his mind. A million people in Germany's domains had been slain by the enemy's bombers or machine-gunned to death in fields, streets, and trains. He was obsessed by the idea that those responsible were escaping unpunished.

One day early in April Bormann read to Hitler an Allied newspaper report that German troops had saved an American bomber crew about to be lynched by angry townsfolk after a raid. Hitler was furious and looked around at General Koller, standing to the left of his chair. "These are the men who are murdering German women and children! It's incredible!" Since Kaltenbrunner was hovering in the background, Hitler turned to him too. "I order that all bomber crews shot down these last few months or in the future are to be turned over by the Luftwaffe to the SD at once and liquidated." This sweeping order was greeted with hostile silence by the officers present in the cramped conference room. Koller pointed out that the enemy might then simply take reprisals against their Luftwaffe prisoners; Hitler retorted that they could arrest one hundred thousand French civilians in Germany and hold them hostage to prevent such reprisals.

In the passageway outside, Keitel, Kaltenbrunner, and Koller agreed that the order should be ignored. But Hitler buttonholed Koller a few minutes later and appealed to him. "You must help me—we can't go on like this. Our air defenses have failed. What am I to do against this nightmare terror-bombing and the murder of our women and children?" Koller urged patience. "When our jet squadrons get stronger the war in the air over Germany will turn in our favor again." Hitler replied, "I cannot wait until then. If these airmen realize that in the future they will be liquidated as terrorists, they'll think twice about whether to fly over." Koller replied that neither the Luftwaffe—into whose officers the laws and articles of war had been painfully drummed—nor the SD would lend themselves to such an order; he also pointed out that Luftwaffe pilots would themselves suffer in enemy hands. Hitler replied without emotion, "In other words the Luftwaffe is afraid. Fair enough, but I am in charge of the German people's safety, and I know no other way."

The failure to execute this latest order showed again that as the end approached Hitler's authority was crumbling. Yet another instance was his ministers' unauthorized peace feelers to the enemy. Since Yalta, Hitler had emphatically opposed all such feelers, but Ribbentrop persisted nonetheless. He sent his English affairs expert, Fritz Hesse, to Stockholm, and when the Swedish press exposed Hesse's mission on March 15—earning for Ribbentrop a thunderous rebuke from Hitler—a few days later the foreign minister again sent Werner von Schmieden to

Switzerland and Consul Eitel Friedrich Moellhausen to Madrid, to contact Allen Dulles and the American ambassador, Robert Murphy, respectively, about terms for a halt to the "frightful bombing and carnage"; but Schmieden was still waiting for an entry visa to Switzerland when the war ended, and Murphy had evidently just left Madrid for Washington before Moellhausen could get to see him. Reichsmarschall Göring referred to Hitler's stubbornness in a private conversation late in March; General Koller noted that when he complained to Göring about the lack of clear directives from Hitler "the Reichsmarschall agreed—he is just as much in the dark. F[ührer] told him nothing. Nor is it permissible to make the slightest political move, for example, the attempt of a British diplomat in Sweden to contact us was strictly rebuffed by F. The Führer flatly forbids Reichsmarschall to make any use of his own comprehensive contacts abroad . . .[2] Again and again the foreign minister [Ribbentrop] submits fresh possibilities to F., but he just turns them down." Thus nobody knew how long a war still to plan for: another year or longer? or just a few last desperate months?

By the date of Göring's remarks, March 28, 1945, Germany's position was militarily hopeless. Asked by Hitler ten days earlier to comment on the loss of Saar coal and its effect on their arms production, Albert Speer had answered in one sentence, "It will speed up the general collapse." When Gauleiter Forster had arrived from Danzig late on the nineteenth with word that "four thousand" Russian tanks were converging on that city, Hitler had still confidently sworn that Danzig would be saved. But in the west a catastrophe had already occurred. All attempts at destroying the Remagen bridge across the Rhine failed until too late; by the time the German naval frogmen and jet bombers had between them brought it down, the Americans had another bridge in service and the enemy bridgehead had swollen to unmanageable proportions.

Kolberg had fallen in mid-March after holding out against the Polish and Russian enemy—some in German uniforms—long enough for sixty thousand of the port's civilians to escape by sea. The civilian evacuation of Königsberg and Danzig was in full swing. In Hungary and Pomerania the counterattacks in which Hitler had vested his hopes had failed dismally. In the west one disaster overtook another. On the night of March 22, American amphibious tanks had sprung a surprise bridgehead across the Rhine at Oppenheim at a cost of only eight

[2]Some words are missing from Koller's note, as his papers decayed during the postwar years of burial and concealment. Count Lutz Schwerin von Krosigk also noted in his unpublished diary a talk with Goebbels on April 9, 1945, in which Goebbels described how Germany had put out cautious peace feelers. The Russians and Americans had reacted positively, but the British had rejected them out of hand.

casualties. At 3 A.M. on the twenty-fourth, Montgomery's main Rhine crossing began at Wesel. By March 28 it was clear that the Ruhr was about to be encircled. Whole companies of German troops were throwing away their weapons and deserting. There were reports that German civilians had actually helped the Americans cross the Main near Frankfurt and were dancing with them in the streets at night. General Koller confided to Göring: "My own faith in our army commanders and in our striking power is exhausted." He regarded the southern American operation as strategically the most dangerous: it was the old French interwar strategy of thrusting eastward astride the Main toward Czechoslovakia so as to slice Germany in two.

The speed of events in the west stunned Hitler, who had been confident that in the east a great German defensive triumph lay in store. On March 25 he told Gauleiter Fritz Sauckel that for the first time he feared the war was lost. But as General Jodl explained to Allied interrogators: "For our leaders there was no alternative but to fight on to their last breath; your propaganda itself fostered this attitude." American troop indoctrination manuals had reached the Chancellery; as one Führer adjutant wrote: "The implacable hatred preached in them against the entire German nation seems little short of the Old Testament language to me." Early in April, Hitler was shown a captured British manual ominously code-named "Eclipse": evidently the end product of the Morgenthau Plan, it named numerous categories of Germans for "automatic arrest" and contained maps of the ultimate dissection of Germany and Berlin into occupation zones. At the same time army Intelligence secured a copy of Stalin's infamous "Order Number Five": "The German people is to be destroyed. All German factories and property are to be laid waste. The German animal must be battered to death in its hovels." Brief German reconquests of ground in East Prussia brought fresh reports on the fate of the Germans who had not escaped in time. "It shall not be! These illiterate brutes shall not inundate all Europe!" Hitler raged. "I am the last bulwark against this peril. If there is any justice, then we shall emerge victorious. One day the world will see the moral of this struggle!"

Defeat seemed certain to all but the most blindly loyal. The hours Hitler spent with them increased, for they alone still displayed the kind of caged fanaticism that might even now see Germany through her misfortunes. He rewarded their loyalty well. When Goebbels late in March abused the Reich press chief, Dr. Otto Dietrich, for his overconservative press policies toward the Allies, Hitler sent for Dietrich and told him: "I'm sending you on six weeks' leave. By then it will all be over one way or the other." Dr. Robert Ley, leader of the Labor Front and previously the butt of many cruel witticisms in Hitler's milieu, was now like Goebbels favored with many hours of Hitler's private conversation. He left Berlin inflated with new courage and conviction, to organize an "Adolf Hitler" Free Corps in Austria—tank-killer teams trained and equipped to operate behind the

Russian lines. "The Führer was head and shoulders above us all," wrote Ley after the war. "And we were too puny for this Titan." Hitler's earlier sycophants discreetly bowed out or were impatiently dismissed. As the end approached, old scores were settled all around—by Goebbels against Ribbentrop, by Bormann against Speer, by Speer against Göring, and by Ley against "that petty and pitiable" Heinrich Himmler. On March 20, Hitler relieved the Reichsführer of command of Army Group Vistula. "The Führer saw through Himmler," wrote Ley. "I had a long talk with the Führer at the time, in which he bitterly complained of Himmler's disobedience, dishonesty, and incompetence."

Fundamental to Hitler's predicament was that many of his generals and ministers were already secretly preparing window-dressing for the war crimes trials they regarded as inevitable: Gotthard Heinrici, the mild-mannered, church-going general Hitler was forced to appoint as Himmler's successor—for want of any better commanders—lacked the wholehearted commitment of a Schörner or Model: Model held out with Army Group B in the encircled Ruhr pocket until his guns had fired their last ammunition; he then took his own life to cheat the enemy. This was the bold spirit which had saved Stalin's Russia in 1941 and 1942. But Hitler's lieutenants lacked even the will to cheat the enemy of the spoils of war: the arms factories of Upper Silesia had fallen intact into Russian hands and were now adding to the arms and ammunition stockpiles being built up on the eastern bank of the Oder. Speer had not hesitated to order the destruction of Hungarian oil refineries in January—a premature destruction that the OKW was just able to stop in time. But by March he was planning less for Germany's defense than for his own.[3]

Speer's character was ambivalent and complex, and Hitler evidently changed his mind about him; after a half-hearted attempt at dismissing him late in March he cut him out of his political testament entirely one month later. He was disappointed by the failure of Me-262 jet aircraft production to reach Speer's predictions, and he appointed SS General Hans Kammler—already special commissioner for V-weapons—to take charge. Another of Speer's projects—codenamed "Iron Hammer"—had also fallen short of expectations: 82 special aircraft, arranged in tandem, had been built for a daredevil attack on the main Soviet power stations, producing between them 1,904,000,000 kilowatts for Stalin's tank and arms factories. Since February, Göring had strongly backed the project, and enough fuel had been set aside while the bomber and Pathfinder crews were trained. But on March 18, Speer had advised Hitler to divert nearly half the special

[3]Perhaps Speer was exaggerating when he claimed under Allied interrogation a few weeks later that he "had counted up all the acts of high treason which he had committed from the end of January onward and had arrived at a total of over sixty."

aircraft to destroy the Soviet bridges across the Oder or Vistula rivers the moment the big enemy offensive began. Hitler was torn between the two alternatives but reverted in Speer's absence on March 26 to his order for an attack on the Soviet power stations. "Imagine what it would have meant for us if the enemy had attacked all *our* power stations simultaneously! It is just the same for the enemy. I'd rather forgo the attack on the Vistula bridges—we can do them sometime later." But when the full moon came, the weather conditions were wrong and "Iron Hammer" had to be postponed indefinitely.

Hitler did not even resent Speer's uncomfortably frank March 15 memorandum on the economic situation. He told Guderian he had stuffed it, "unread," into the man-high safe at the foot of his bed. It bravely exposed Speer's conviction that the war was hopelessly lost: the enemy air raids, and the loss of the coal-bearing regions, made Germany's "final economic collapse" inevitable within four to eight weeks. "*After this collapse the war cannot even be militarily continued.*" Speer's memorandum urged Hitler to remember the government's obligation in the coming hours of trial to aid its people; and he demanded strict orders prohibiting the destruction of factories and bridges, as this could now only harm Germany. Hitler turned a deaf ear on Speer when he again argued these points, in person this time, late on the eighteenth. Speer was an intellectual foreign to the dictates of strategy; and it was the minister's fortieth birthday next day. But his indulgence toward Speer cooled when he learned a week later through Party channels that Speer had secretly driven to the west to sabotage Hitler's orders for a scorched-earth policy to slow down the enemy advance. Hitler had issued these orders on March 19, after Keitel's orders issued in January had failed to prevent the scandalous events of Upper Silesia and the Saar, where entire industries had fallen intact into enemy hands. Hitler's emphatic directive called for the destruction of all military installations and transport-, communications- and public-utility equipment "insofar as they may be of use to the enemy in the furtherance of his fight."[4]

Both Speer and his energetic deputy, Karl-Otto Saur, shuttled between Berlin and the Ruhr, but Hitler soon learned that their purposes were very different. Saur admitted that further production in the Ruhr was hopeless, but he bitterly criticized the response of the General Staff officers there to his own expressions of optimism. Speer on the other hand had spread despondency and gloom, infecting everybody he had met and urging them to turn their factories over to the enemy intact. Meanwhile the American spearheads were plunging deeper and deeper into Germany. At Hanau and Aschaffenburg two more key bridges fell undemolished into their hands. Probably only Speer's friendship with Hitler and

[4]In his memoirs Speer omits the words I quote.

Eva Braun now spared him from an unkinder fate. Late on March 28 the Führer coldly received him and instructed him to stand down as armaments minister, giving the customary ill-health plea as an excuse. Speer clearly lacked the necessary faith that the tide could still turn in their favor, the Führer pointed out. Speer flushed and protested, but Hitler challenged him outright. "Do you still hope for a successful continuation of the war, or is your faith shattered?" When after twenty-four hours Speer had still not given him a straight answer, Hitler virtually sacked him, although he continued to value his presence at the Chancellery as a friend. Meanwhile, Jodl and his military staff attempted to put Hitler's defense doctrines into practice—instilling into the western army group commanders the need to bring home to the enemy that they were plunging into a Germany "fanatical with fighting spirit." Only this would enable the western front to be stabilized. "This is not the time or place for considering the civilian population," the OKW order concluded.

Bormann added his own characteristic warning to his Gauleiters: "Devil take the one who deserts his Gau under enemy attack except with express orders from the Führer, or who does not fight to the last breath in his body—he will be cast out as a deserter and dealt with accordingly."

Hitler spent the last week in March 1945 purging his followers of the faint of heart. Hans Lammers, his chief of Chancellery, came for the last time on the twenty-seventh and mentioned his high blood pressure; Hitler sent him to Berchtesgaden on sick leave. On March 29 he dismissed General Guderian too, fearing that when the crisis came his poor health would produce a breakdown similar to his collapse in the Moscow winter of 1941. General Hans Krebs, a young and tough idealist strongly reminiscent of Zeitzler in his heyday, took over as Chief of the General Staff. Heinrich Himmler had also fallen from grace, for the SS Sixth Panzer Army in Hungary under SS General Sepp Dietrich had not only failed in its big counterattack north of Lake Balaton, but had been routed and thrown back onto the Austrian frontier. Nothing could stop the Russians from pouring into Vienna; the Hungarian oil fields were lost. "If we lose the war, it will be his fault!" Hitler raged, and ordered that as a punishment Sepp Dietrich's principal divisions were to be stripped of their brassards and insignia for three days. Himmler was packed off to Vienna to issue a stern reprimand to his Waffen SS generals.

Guderian's dismissal resulted from a similar defeat just east of Berlin. Hitler had clung to the ancient city of Küstrin to deny its important Oder bridges and road junctions to the Russians; since mid-March he had been preparing a limited counterattack toward Küstrin from his own Frankfurt bridgehead, hoping to destroy the enemy assault forces massing for the attack on Berlin. But before General Theodor Busse's Ninth Army could begin the counterattack, the Russians struck and encircled Küstrin completely; Busse's own attack on March 22 failed, but Hitler insisted that it must be repeated immediately. General Heinrici, Himmler's successor as army group commander, came to the bunker in person on March 25 to argue for Küstrin to be abandoned to the enemy so that he could conserve what ammunition and gasoline he had for the big defensive battle looming ahead. But again Hitler insisted on a policy of attack. A purely defensive stance would allow the Russians to pounce at will—the German reserves would be tied down in hasty repair jobs, and then Heinrici would begin clamoring for new reserves all over again. "Since the enemy will always be stronger than us," Hitler wearily reminded him, "they will then ultimately break through and that will be your downfall." Their only hope was to throw rapid punches at the enemy before they were ready to attack, delaying them week after week while Hitler stockpiled ammunition for the major battle. Most Russian strength was massing south of Küstrin—particularly artillery. Hitler admitted that a renewed counterattack here would be a gamble, but with the necessary faith, he insisted, it would succeed.[5]

The new attack began on March 28. The German tanks reached Küstrin's outskirts, but once again the infantry failed to follow through and the tanks were brought back. Against Hitler's explicit orders the Küstrin garrison then broke out to the west, knifing through Russian lines which Heinrici and Busse had described as impenetrable. Hitler summoned General Busse to the bunker and informed him of his displeasure. Guderian loudly and intemperately defended him, purpling with rage. Hitler cleared the bunker conference room and advised Guderian: "You need sick leave. I don't think your heart can stand the strain. Come back in six weeks."

Along the Oder, Marshal Zhukov had assembled over 750,000 troops for the offensive; farther south along the Neisse Marshal Konev had 500,000 more under his command. Additional Soviet forces were approaching from the battlefields of East and West Prussia, but Hitler believed that the attack might begin without them, because the Russians were determined to reach Berlin before the Americans.

On the day after Guderian's dismissal Hitler issued a clear-sighted appraisal of the situation "now that we have failed to shatter the enemy preparations by counterattack." He demanded a fanatical defense effort by Army Group Vistula, from General Heinrici himself right down to the youngest recruit. In particular Hitler ordered Heinrici to construct a "main battle line" two to four miles behind

[5]Cornelius Ryan omitted mention of this conference of March 25, 1945, in *The Last Battle* (New York, 1966) and—relying on an alleged "diary" of General Heinrici—refers to a conference on April 6 as the first with Hitler. The war diaries of Army Group Vistula and the OKH operations staff establish the correct date as the fourth.

the present front line—a bitter lesson he had learned from the Americans on the dawn of his own Ardennes offensive. The moment the Russian offensive was seriously anticipated, Heinrici was to fall back on this second line; the huge enemy artillery bombardment would then fall on the empty trenches of the original front line. Heinrici was also ordered to resite his artillery farther back, where it could saturate the countryside between the present front and the "main battle line" when the Russian attack began.[6]

Thus his malevolently brilliant brain was still functioning logically and flexibly, even though his physical frame was a palsied shadow of the Hitler that had sprung this war on central Europe in 1939. His doctors were unanimous in agreeing that his sanity remained intact until the end, even though he could not walk more than thirty paces without gripping something firm for support, and his bloodshot eyes became so poor that he had to put on his spectacles even to read documents typed on the special big-face typewriters. His hair had turned an ashen gray, and Morell observed in Hitler for the first time now *fetor ex ore*—the clinical description of bad breath. But when frontline commanders were brought down to the shelter, his willpower and perseverance appeared undiminished—the central powerhouse, coordinating and commanding, that alone seemed to enable Germany to withstand the onslaught of the whole world in indignant coalition against her. A year before he had dominated all Europe from the North Cape to the Crimea and the Spanish frontier; now millions of enemy troops were only an hour's drive away, east and west of his capital, and his headquarters was this shelter. Yet the admiration of his strategic advisers was unimpaired. "Looking at the whole picture," General Jodl unashamedly told his interrogators, "I am convinced that he was a great military leader. Certainly no historian can say that Hannibal was a poor general just because ultimately Carthage was destroyed." Admiral Dönitz, himself no simpleton, unreservedly echoed this judgment on Hitler.

For Hitler the spring had brought encouraging signs for the future, which blinded him to the remorseless approach of the enemy armies. Hundreds of the new jets were now reaching the squadrons. Jet reconnaissance planes had reopened the skies over England and Scotland. On March 17 the first Mark XXI submarine—capable of voyaging submerged to Japan—had set forth, bound eventually for the east coast of the United States. Underground oil plants were being built by the SS. He and the General Staff believed that Stalin could be held off, for Soviet tank losses were outrunning production: in February, Stalin had lost 4,600, against a monthly output of only 2,300; in the first twenty-two days of March no fewer than 5,452 Soviet tanks were claimed destroyed. "The enemy's

[6]Unaware of this Hitler Order of March 30, 1945, Cornelius Ryan in *The Last Battle*, pages 299, 342, and 351, gives Heinrici the credit for this stratagem.

reserves will shortly be exhausted," the General Staff assured the Führer. Stalin had been provoked into launching a sixth attack on Hitler's besieged army in Kurland; again he had suffered a bloody defeat, and he made no further attempts. In the beleaguered fortresses of Breslau and Königsberg German garrisons were still holding out. "And as long as I have Königsberg I can still claim to the German people that East Prussia is not lost," Hitler explained in private. On the Czech frontier, the tough General Ferdinand Schörner fought a grim twenty-day defensive battle for the industrial city of Moravian Ostrau (Ostrava) which ended on April 3 in a convincing victory for his Army Group Center. Hitler appointed him field marshal.

During the first week of April 1945 this optimism was severely shaken. On April 2 the Reich surgeon general, Dr. Karl Brandt, privately warned him that one-fifth of all essential medical items was already unobtainable, and that stocks of two-fifths more would run out completely in two months. This put the shortest time-fuse yet on Hitler's strategy: without medicines disease and epidemic would cut his people down. Now that the Ruhr and Saar arsenals had been overrun, crippling production shortages in weapons, small arms, ammunition, and explosives made a mockery of his efforts to raise fresh divisions from the Hitler Youth or Reich Labor Service battalions. Virtually all aircraft production had ceased; the ground-attack and air-transport squadrons were already running out of replacement aircraft. An airlift to Field Marshal Model's Army Group B, encircled in the Ruhr pocket, was out of the question. The Breslau garrison was barely surviving, but in Königsberg—despite Hitler's repeated instructions that the fortress was to be held to the last man—the commandant, General Otto Lasch, surrendered to the Russians on April 9; during the following night Hitler ordered a message sent to all surviving command posts and radio units at Königsberg: "General Lasch is to be shot as a traitor immediately."

But which generals heeded Hitler's orders now? His authority was waning, and they were beginning to act arbitrarily, in disregard and ignorance of the central strategy laid down in Berlin. "Blomberg always told me that obedience stops short at generals," Hitler was to recall a few days before the end. At his midday war conference on April 1, Hitler had expressly laid down: "Anybody retreating in Austria is to be shot!" But now every day Martin Bormann submitted sheafs of telegrams from the angry and bewildered Gauleiters reporting the Wehrmacht's headlong retreat from across the Hungarian frontier. During the afternoon of April 5, General Otto Wöhler's Army Group South retreated *fifty miles;* Bormann jotted in his diary: "*The Bolsheviks are outside Vienna!*" But Hitler merely sacked the general and replaced him with Lothar Rendulić, the gritty general who had just thwarted Stalin's last assault on the Kurland army group. One of Bormann's Party officials had telephoned that night: "None of the army group gentlemen"—meaning Wöhler's staff—"has the slightest faith in their ability to hold off the enemy penetration into the [Zisterdorf] petroleum fields;

nor in fact, and this I must state plainly, do they believe we can still win. The Luftwaffe blew up all Vienna's searchlight sites on the night of April 3 without a word to the army group. In the Lower Danube Gau the Wehrmacht rout goes on."

Zisterdorf, outside Vienna, was Hitler's only remaining source of petroleum. On April 6 he ordered its defense until the last possible moment. Vienna itself seemed bent on suicide. From there SS Colonel Skorzeny reported on the tenth that while the tank brigades were running out of gasoline, retreating Luftwaffe units were passing through with truckloads of "girls and furniture"; a handful of tough SS commanders could stop the rout—he himself had just ordered three traitors hanged from a bridge. Three days later Vienna was overrun.

Warily—because he knew Hitler's loathing of astrologers—Dr. Goebbels had sent for the Führer's horoscope, which the Gestapo kept filed away. Two separate horoscopes came to a remarkably unanimous conclusion—and both could be interpreted as having already predicted the outbreak of war in 1939, the victories until 1941, and the hammer blows of defeat since then; the hardest blows, they prophesised, would fall in this first half of April, while the second half would temporarily give Germany the upper hand again. A period of stalemate would follow until August 1945, in which month peace would return. After three cruel years, the horoscopes concluded, Germany's ascent to greatness would be resumed in 1948.

Stalin's big Oder offensive might begin any day now. General Theodor Busse was confident that his Ninth Army could stop it from reaching Berlin. In the west, Hitler planned to launch in mid-April a counterattack against the long exposed American flank as they thrust eastward. Goebbels strove to persuade Hitler not to lose hope, for he was sure the clash between Russia and the West must come within the next three to four months—by August 1945, in short. Early in April he came to the shelter and, in his melodious and theatrical voice, read aloud to Hitler from Carlyle's fine description of the darkest hours of the Seven Years' War. It was a moment in which Frederick the Great saw no way out, his generals and ministers were convinced of imminent defeat, and Prussia's enemies already gloated over its fall. With an uncertain future stretching darkly before him the great king wrote one last letter to Count Finckenstein proclaiming that if the tide had not turned by a certain date he would accept defeat and swallow poison.

Here Carlyle apostrophized:

> Brave King! Tarry awhile, because your days of travail will soon pass. Already the sun has risen behind the clouds of your misfortune, and soon it will shine forth.

Three days before the king's deadline, the Czarina Elizabeth died, the accession of Peter III took Russia out of the war, and thus the House of Brandenburg was saved. Goebbels saw tears starting in Hitler's eyes as he laid the book aside.

Putting himself in Stalin's now enviable shoes, Hitler himself believed the buildup before Berlin was only a feint and that the real Russian offensive would first be toward Prague. Stalin must surely intend to embrace the important Czech industrial region before his American rivals could reach it—just as Hitler had striven for the Donets Basin and the Caucasus in 1941. Hitler had chided General Guderian: "The Russians won't be as stupid as us. We were dazzled by our nearness to Moscow and just had to capture the capital. Remember, Guderian —*you* were the one who wanted to be first into Moscow at the head of your army! And just look at the consequences!" Whether this was intuition or on General Staff advice the records do not disclose, but at this crucial juncture, he impulsively ordered General Busse to relinquish four SS panzer divisions to Schörner's army group defending Czechoslovakia.

In early March, Schörner had commanded 413,000 troops, and 527,000 more were under Heinrici's command; since then Hitler had moved strong reinforcements to the Oder and Neisse fronts. The Soviet forces were not so overwhelming in terms of troop strength as they were in purely *material* strength: tens of thousands of Russian guns and rocket launchers waited mutely on the Oder's higher eastern bank overlooking the German positions; the Luftwaffe was powerless to interfere. Against the enemy's frightening tank superiority, Hitler could set only his own antitank and antiaircraft batteries, and the bravery of individual tank-killer squads equipped with hand-held bazookas. Yet he was confident of a swift victory. He summoned General Heinrici to the shelter again on April 4 and subjected the Oder defenses to a mile-by-mile scrutiny. He reminded Heinrici of the need to lay down deadly minefields at the obvious Schwerpunkt positions; he ordered the Ninth Army to drive tunnels into the strategically crucial Seelow Heights—which commanded the marshy valley west of Küstrin through which the Russian attack must advance—to protect the army's reserves from enemy artillery. He gave Heinrici control of all army and Luftwaffe antiaircraft batteries and warned him against "Seydlitz officers" infiltrating in German uniforms. Behind the main front line, thousands of trees were being felled and antitank trenches dug. Evidence of Russian occupation methods, seen by General Busse's officers and troops in villages they had recaptured, determined them to keep Soviet forces from advancing one more yard into Europe.

By April 11 American forces had reached the Elbe at Magdeburg—only sixty miles from Berlin. Hitler was told that a Russian deserter had revealed that the Oder offensive would begin in four days' time, but he suspected it might come even earlier, as the Russians would want to reach Berlin before the Americans. Again he asked for a complete report on Heinrici's army group. He was assured that no other sector in Germany was so powerfully manned with troops and artillery. He congratulated Heinrici's officers. "The Russians are going to suffer their bloodiest defeat ever!" But late on April 12 he admitted to his staff that he was uneasy about the sector east of Cottbus—where Schörner's and Heinrici's army groups met at the junction of Oder and Neisse.

One thing was certain: he could not fight a long battle of attrition because his stocks of aviation fuel would keep the Luftwaffe airborne over the Oder battlefield for only a few days, and—as the quartermaster general warned explicitly on April 15—all German munitions supplies would shortly cease. Their munitions factories and dumps were almost all in enemy hands. "There may shortly occur the most momentous consequences for our entire war effort," the general had warned.

As American troops advanced across Thuringia, Hitler was confronted with the problem of the concentration camps. Göring advised him to turn them over intact and under guard to the Western Allies, who would sort out the criminals from the foreign laborers and Russian prisoners, thus preventing hordes of embittered ex-convicts from roaming the countryside and inflicting additional horrors on the law-abiding. Hitler did not share Göring's trust in the enemy. Sitting casually on the edge of the map table after one war conference, he instructed Himmler's representative to ensure that all inmates were liquidated or evacuated before the camps were overrun.

Nor had he forgotten his special collection of prominent prisoners—among them his star defendants for planned postwar trials. On April 8 prison officials loaded them aboard prison vans for transfer to the south. There was a kaleidoscope of famous names: the Schuschnigg family, General Thomas, Dr. Schacht, General Halder, Molotov's nephew, Captain S. Payne Best (a British Intelligence officer kidnapped in Venlo, Holland, in November 1939), and Colonel Bogislaw von Bonin. Behind them at Flossenbürg camp they left Admiral Canaris and General Oster. A few days before, General Buhle had stumbled by chance on the long-sought secret diaries of Canaris, and they sealed the Abwehr chief's fate. He and General Oster were hanged after a summary court-martial on the ninth. The surviving VIPs were moved to Dachau, near Munich. A vague notion of continuing the war from the easily defended mountain region of Bohemia, Bavaria, and northern Italy had begun to crystalize in Hitler's brain. When Gauleiter Franz Hofer came from the Tirol on April 9 and urged Hitler to abandon most of northern Italy—arguing that the only arms production of any significance came from the South Tirol—the Führer pointed out that virtually the entire arms effort now relied on electrosteel supplied by northern Italy. Late on April 10 he ordered Karl-Otto Saur—Speer's *de facto* successor as armaments minister—to investigate the possibility of creating an independent arms industry in the Alps.

If the remaining Reich was cut in two by the American and Russian spearheads, military governments under Admiral Dönitz and Field Marshal Kesselring would rule the northern and southern Reich respectively—a curious but significant rebuff by Hitler to the Party's ambitions. He briefed Kesselring at length late on April 12. Kesselring ever after recalled the Führer's radiant optimism. "I'd even say, in retrospect, he was a man possessed by the idea that he might yet be saved—he clutched at it like a drowning man at straws." Hitler talked of the coming great victory on the Oder, of his new secret weapons, of the Twelfth Army he was raising under General Wenck to defeat the Allies on the Elbe, and of the coming rupture between the Russians and the West. General Busse, commanding the Ninth Army on the Oder, shared Hitler's confidence. "If need be, we'll stand fast here until the Americans are kicking us in the arse," he said, earthily expressing his strategic convictions to Goebbels that evening; and the propaganda minister assured Busse's more skeptical staff that if there was any justice, some miracle would surely save the Reich, just as the House of Brandenburg had been saved in 1762. With gentle irony an officer inquired, "Which Czarina is going to die, then?" All along the Oder, a troublesome Russian artillery activity had just begun.

The news of President Franklin Delano Roosevelt's sudden death on April 12 in Warm Springs, Georgia, reached Hitler only a few minutes after an American news agency announced it that night. Goebbels telephoned, his voice shrill with excitement. "Mein Führer, I congratulate you! Now Roosevelt is dead! It is written in the stars that the second half of April will be the turning point for us. This *is* the turning point!" All Hitler's ministers agreed that God had wrought a swift and terrible Judgment on their hated enemy. Speer and other doubting Thomases were fetched. Hitler brandished the news agency report at them. "Do you *still* say we have lost the war!"

The next morning he began dictating his famous proclamation to his soldiers on the eastern front—to be released the moment Stalin's offensive began:

> For one last time our mortal enemies, the Jewish Bolsheviks, are throwing their weight into the attack. They are attempting to shatter Germany and annihilate our people. You soldiers in the east already know full well the fate awaiting German women and children. The older men and children will be murdered,

women and girls will be debased to barrack-room whores. The rest will go on foot to Siberia.

We have been expecting this attack, and since this January everything has been done to build up a strong front. A mighty artillery is waiting to greet the enemy. Our infantry losses have been made good by innumerable new units. . . . This time the Bolsheviks will meet the old fate of Asia—they must and shall bleed to death at the gates of the German Reich's capital.

Whoever fails in his duty now is a traitor to our people. The regiment or division that abandons its position will be a disgrace to the women and children who have withstood the bombing terror in our cities.

Again Hitler warned them to be on guard against German traitors in the pay of Stalin and perhaps even wearing German uniforms. "Berlin stays German! Vienna"—which the Russians had overrun that very April 13—"will be German again. Europe will never be Russian."

He issued the proclamation to the army groups that night. It closed with a reference to Roosevelt. "At this moment when fate has carried off the greatest War Criminal of all times from the face of this earth, the war's turning point has come."

Hitler seemed to have shut his eyes to the possibility that Berlin itself might become a battlefield; but late on April 13, 1945, when Ribbentrop spoke with him, he gave permission for the nervous diplomatic corps to leave the capital for southern Germany. The next day the shelling of Busse's positions increased, and two hundred Russian tanks launched attacks of up to regimental strength; ninety-eight tanks were destroyed. April 15 brought a lull. According to a Russian prisoner, the attacks had been for reconnaissance purposes.

It was on this day that Eva Braun unexpectedly arrived back in Berlin. Some of those who knew Hitler intimately found the decision to remain at his side comparatively easy. The last letter from one of his adjutants to his wife admitted, however: "It is certainly hard for us men to stand in our last battle far from our families, knowing that our wives and children will later have to face the trials of life alone. But hundreds of thousands of others have found the strength, and I am trying to set an example, however humble, to all my compatriots."

During the night General Wenck's new army succeeded in destroying one American bridgehead on the Elbe south of Magdeburg and in reducing another. But a Russian prisoner taken south of Küstrin revealed that the big Oder offensive would begin the next morning, April 16—he spoke of a colossal artillery barrage and of mighty new tanks and howitzers standing by, and he reported that the Red Army troops had been ordered to tidy up their uniforms and wash and shave every day "to make a cultivated impression" from now on. This had the ring of authenticity; Hitler ordered Busse's Ninth Army pulled back during the remaining hours of darkness into the secret second line of defense (a line which, he now learned, Heinrici had built without much enthusiasm). At his midnight conference Hitler learned with stabbing misgivings of a puzzling request by General Heinrici—for permission to transfer his army group HQ to a new site which Hitler found, after much searching on the map, to be to the *rear* of Berlin and thus *behind* the Führer's own headquarters.[7] He flatly forbade such a transfer and again ordered General Krebs to telephone instructions to the army group to build up its rear positions as fast as possible.

Too late, these afterthoughts. At 5 A.M. the next morning, April 16, a mighty Russian artillery barrage began all along the Oder and Neisse rivers. Nearly half a million shells thundered down on the—now virtually abandoned—German forward positions. At 6:30 A.M. Zhukov's tanks and infantry began pouring across both sides of the Frankfurt-on-Oder strongpoint still held by Busse's Ninth Army; an hour later the main assault on the Fourth Panzer Army defending the Neisse front began. Savage battles developed between tank and gun, while overhead two thousand Russian planes bombed and harrassed the defenders; the German air force threw all it had into the battle. Sixty planes manned by suicide pilots crash-bombed the Oder bridges across which the enemy was flooding westward. By nightfall, although a five-mile-deep breach had been torn into the front near Wriezen, held only by the ill-experienced 9th Paratroop Division, there was no doubt in the Chancellery that a resounding defeat had been inflicted on the enemy.

Christa Schroeder asked quietly whether they would now be leaving Berlin. Hitler answered almost resentfully, "No. Calm down—Berlin will always be German!" The secretary replied that she was not afraid and regarded her life as spent already. "But I can't quite see how it's all going to end, with the Americans coming closer every day on one side and the Russians on the other."

"Time!" explained Hitler. "We've just got to gain time!"

[7]In defiance of the orders he had accepted from Hitler, Heinrici had secretly decided that if his Oder front collapsed, he would abandon Berlin to the enemy without even the pretense of a fight. He did not inform Hitler of this—although the decision affected not only his own two armies, but also the defenders of Berlin and the capital's three million civilian inhabitants. Albert Speer claimed to have brought about Heinrici's remarkable decision in a secret conference with him on April 15, 1945.

"Eclipse"

Hitler recognized that the end of what he envisioned as his lone fight against bolshevism was approaching, and there are clues in the documents as to how long he believed he could postpone it: for example, he had ordered the General Staff to provide the Berlin area with logistics sufficient for three divisions to hold out for twenty days, should the city be surrounded. If open conflict had not broken out between Stalin and the Americans by then, Hitler realized, his gamble had failed; it would be his "Eclipse," to use the code name assigned by his victorious enemies to the postwar carve-up of the Reich. By April 15, 1945, the document outlining this plan—captured from the British in the west—had been fully translated and was in the hands of Hitler, Himmler, and the military authorities; its appended maps revealed that Berlin was to be an enclave far inside the Russian occupation zone, divided like Germany itself into British, American, and Russian zones.

What encouraged Hitler was the fact that the American spearheads, in reaching the Elbe, had already encroached on Stalin's zone, while the Russians had duly halted at the demarcation line on reaching Saint-Pölten in Austria late on April 15. A clash seemed inevitable, and Hitler's General Staff toadied to this desperate belief. Colonel Gerhard Wessel, the new chief of Foreign Armies East, reported with emphasis on the fifteenth[1] that Russian officers were apprehensive that the Americans were preparing an attack ("We must drench the Americans *'accidentally'* with our artillery fire to let them taste the lash of the Red Army"); Wessel also disclosed that the British too were adopting a dangerous new propaganda line to subvert German security forces in Slovenia. "Britain is shortly going to start fighting the Soviet Union herself, and with better prospects than the Reich; Britain has already begun raising Russian units for this purpose." Over

[1]He succeeded General Gehlen in 1968 as chief of the West German Intelligence service.

and over during the next two weeks Hitler restated the belief that sustained him: "Perhaps the others"—meaning Britain and the United States—"can be convinced, after all, that there is only one man capable of halting the Bolshevik colossus, and that is me." This was the real point of fighting an otherwise hopeless battle for Berlin.

Since Roosevelt's death, Foreign Minister Ribbentrop had secretly circulated to German diplomatic channels abroad a fourteen-page memorandum designed for Allied consumption—a forbidding and not wholly inaccurate prophecy of Stalin's postwar position as the cruel and authoritarian ruler of both a Soviet Union of proven "biological strength" and of three hundred million non-Soviet eastern Europeans too. German technicians and factories captured by Stalin were already working to expand Stalin's power; could England, asked the memorandum, afford to abet this menace to her traditional routes to the Middle East and India, particularly once the United States had withdrawn her forces from western Europe as one day she must?

So far the British had been blinded by their hatred, but the Americans suddenly proved more amenable. On the night of April 17, SS General Fegelein—Himmler's representative—adroitly informed Hitler that the secret talks between SS General Wolff and Allen Dulles in Switzerland had resulted in principle on terms for an armistice on the Italian front. The Americans were still talking of unconditional surrender, but that was a minor problem if thereby the enemy alliance could be torn asunder. At 3 A.M. the Führer sent for Wolff and congratulated him. "I hear that you and your skill have managed to establish the first official contacts to top Americans." He asked Wolff not to leave Berlin until the next evening, to give him time to think it over. "I am grateful that you've succeeded in opening the first doorway to the West and America. Of course, the terms are very bad—there can be no talk of unconditional surrender, obviously." But by 5 P.M. his mood had hardened again. Strolling with Wolff, Kaltenbrunner, and Fegelein in the Chancellery garden, Hitler enlarged on his own hopeful theories. "I want the front to hold for eight more weeks. I am waiting for East and West to fall out. We are going to hold the Italian fortress at all costs, and Berlin too." This was the message Hitler gave Wolff to pass on to General Heinrich von Vietinghoff, Kesselring's colorless successor as Commander in Chief in Italy.

Hitler took harsh action against every vestige of defeatism. After consultation with Bormann, he ordered the arrest of his handsome former staff surgeon, Dr. Brandt, for sending his wife and family to Bad Liebenstein, where they would fall into American hands; on April 18, Brandt was summarily condemned to death for the offense.[2] Similar sentences would follow.

But entire armies could not be court-martialed for losing heart. Zisterdorf fell to the Russians. On the seventeenth Gauleiter August Eigruber cabled from Linz that "the petroleum fields are in jeopardy"; by the next day General Hans Kreysing's Eighth Army had already abandoned them precipitately, after prematurely destroying the installations. Himmler reported to Hitler that in Austria the army's tendency was to retreat everywhere even though "Ivan is obviously both wary and weary of fighting."

This was Hitler's second motive for making a last stand in Berlin: to set an example to his generals and thereby restore his personal authority over them.

Great slaughter had been inflicted on the Russians, but by early April 18 alarming fissures were appearing in the defenses. On the sixteenth Busse's Ninth Army had destroyed 211 tanks—and 106 more the next day—on the Oder front; while General Fritz Gräser's adjacent Fourth Panzer Army had knocked out 93 and 140 tanks on the Neisse front. Busse's front was still intact, though mauled and buckled by the sheer weight of Zhukov's onslaught; at Wriezen in particular a deep wedge had been hammered into the main German line. But southeast of Berlin Marshal Konev's army group had thrown two bridgeheads across the Neisse on the very first day—in fact just where Hitler had foreseen the Russian Schwerpunkt, though angled differently. Russian tanks were already approaching Cottbus and the Spree River at Spremberg: Konev's objective, like Zhukov's, was obviously Berlin and not Prague. This gave Hitler less time than he had thought.

Counterattacks by Heinrici and Schörner failed to restore the old battle line. On April 17, Hitler ordered the autobahn bridges blown up and every available aircraft, including the Messerschmitt jets, thrown in to stop the enemy from reaching Cottbus. At his midday conference he proclaimed: "The Russians are in for the bloodiest defeat imaginable before they reach Berlin!" But the failure of the counterattacks unsettled him. He sat brooding far into the night with Eva Braun and his secretaries, trying to convince them and himself that the wedge at Wriezen was just the natural luck of the attacker, but that such luck would not hold for long. Now he had to agree to pull troops out of the German bridgehead east of Frankfurt-on-Oder to strengthen the fortress's flanks. He began to blame General Heinrici for the sudden plight of the Oder front—calling him "a plodding, irresolute pedant lacking the necessary enthusiasm for the job."

[2]Himmler and Speer together prevented Brandt's execution by a series of maneuvers. He survived the war, only to be hanged by the Americans at Landsberg.

During the eighteenth a furious battle was fought for Seelow, the high plateau commanding the Russian assault area. By evening it was firmly in Zhukov's hands, and Hitler learned that only the SS "Nederland" Division—a volunteer unit of Dutch mercenaries—had been thrown into a counterattack. Perhaps this was the cause of his petulant outburst to General Karl Hilpert, the new commander of the Kurland army group, that day: "If the German nation loses this war, that will prove it was unworthy of me." A further eruption came when he learned that Goebbels had sent five battalions of wholly unsuitable Volkssturm troops to the Oder front—although Hitler had insisted that such troops were only to be used as a last resort in defense of their own towns and villages. There were enough able-bodied airmen and sailors who could have been sent—if only they had had the guns and ammunition.

From now until the end, Hitler slept only fitfully and irregularly. The long days were punctuated by an unending series of ill tidings, each one bringing the end much closer than its predecessor. Restless and pallid, Hitler rambled around the shelter, took brief strolls upstairs, then sat in the telephone exchange or machine room—where he had never set foot before—or visited his dogs in their makeshift kennels behind the lavatories; he took to sitting in the passageway with one of the puppies on his lap, silently staring at the officers passing in and out of the shelter.

He had news that separatist movements were stirring in Württemberg, Bavaria, and Austria. Late on April 19, Saur reported back to Hitler from the south, where he had conferred two days earlier with Gauleiter Hofer and SS General Kammler on the possibility of establishing an "Alpine Redoubt." In one of the Chancellery's few remaining rooms, Saur laid the unpalatable news squarely on the line: there was not enough time left to start large-scale arms production in the Alps; the most they could count on would be small factories for re-machining captured ammunition to fit German weapons. It was an uninspiring end to the armaments empire Speer had created. As Hitler accompanied Saur to the exit, he talked nostalgically of Speer's deceased predecessor. "Who knows—if Todt hadn't been killed, the war might have gone very differently!" He gave the stocky arms expert his hand, and he prophesied: "Within the next twenty-four hours we shall have won or lost the war."

This echoed the latest dispatch of Heinrici's army group: at Müncheberg, due east of Berlin, and at Wriezen, farther north, the Russians had finally broken through into open country between 5 and 6 P.M. Immense tank forces were pouring through the two breaches; at Müncheberg alone tank-killer squads and aircraft destroyed 60 tanks during the next few hours, while the Ninth Army's total that day was 226 Russian tanks knocked out. "The battle," Heinrici's army group reported that evening, "is about to be decided." A stabbing headache assailed Hitler as this news reached his bunker. He weakly called for a servant to fetch Dr. Morell, and at his behest the physician crudely drained a quantity of blood from Hitler's right arm until it blocked the hypodermic needle and Morell had to force a somewhat larger needle into the veins. The servant blanched as the blood ran into a beaker, but wisecracked: "Mein Führer, all we need do now is mix the blood with some fat and we could put it on sale as Führer blood sausage!" Hitler repeated the unpleasant witticism to Eva Braun and the secretaries over tea that evening.

Midnight would bring his fifty-sixth birthday. Bormann wanly observed in his diary that it was "not exactly a birthday situation." Hitler had asked his staff to refrain from ceremony, but Eva Braun cajoled him into stepping into the anteroom and shaking hands with the adjutants who had gathered there. Saur had brought a perfect scale-model of a 350-millimeter mortar for Hitler's collection. Hitler spoke for a while with Goebbels and Ley about his determination to defend the Alpine Redoubt and Bohemia-Moravia in the south, and Norway in the north; then he retired to drink tea with Eva in his low-ceilinged drawing room-cum-study.

All night after that he lay awake, until the knocking of Heinz Linge, his valet, told him it was morning. General Burgdorf, the chief Wehrmacht adjutant, was outside the door. He shouted that during the night the Russians had broken through Schörner's army group on both sides of Spremberg; the Fourth Panzer Army was trying to repair the breaches by a counterattack. Hitler merely said, "Linge, I haven't slept yet. Wake me an hour later than usual, at 2 P.M."

When he awoke Berlin was under heavy air attack—a birthday bombardment that continued all day. His eyes were stinging, but the pain subsided after Linge administered cocaine eyedrops.[3] Morell gave him a glucose injection, then Hitler fondled a puppy for a while before lunching with Eva and the two duty-secretaries, Johanna Wolf and Christa Schroeder. There was no conversation. After lunch they picked their way along the duckboards into the Voss Bunker, to steal another look at the model of Linz; he identified to them the house where he had spent his youth.

[3]A desk calendar later found in the shelter shows that Linge had to administer eyedrops at an ever-increasing rate—rising from one a day on April 16 to thirteen on April 28, the last page with entries.

Wrapped in a gray coat with its collar turned up, he climbed the spiral staircase to the Chancellery garden followed by Goebbels. The Berlin air was thick with the dust and smoke from a hundred fires. A short line of fresh-faced Hitler Youths awaited decoration for bravery against enemy tanks on the Oder front. The once well-tended lawns and paths were now pocked with holes and craters and strewn with branches and empty canisters. The perimeter wall was punctuated by dug-outs and piles of bazookas at the ready. Near the music room a small parade of troops from the Kurland battlefield awaited inspection. Himmler saluted, and Hitler—stooping and shuffling—passed along the line. They crowded around in a semicircle. He apologized for not being able to speak very loudly, but he did promise that victory would be theirs and that they could tell their children that they had been there when it was finally won.

At about 4 P.M. that afternoon, April 20, 1945, he retraced his steps into the shelter, having seen the sky for the last time.

Before the main war conference began, he allowed his principal ministers in singly to proffer formal birthday greetings. Ribbentrop stayed about ten minutes, the others—Göring, Dönitz, Keitel, and Jodl—rather less. Keitel dropped a broad hint that it was time for Hitler to leave Berlin, but Hitler interrupted: "Keitel, I know what I want—I am going to fight in front of Berlin, fight in Berlin, and fight behind Berlin!" With this Clemenceau-like utterance he extended his trembling hand to the field marshal and sent for the next well-wisher.

The main conference began immediately. Both north and south of Berlin the Russians had indeed decided the battle, and armored spearheads were dashing westward. Unless Schörner's counterattack succeeded, the last main road out of Berlin to the south would be cut off in a matter of hours. Göring echoed Keitel's feeling that it was time for a far-reaching military decision on the future of Berlin. General Koller pointed out that the truckloads of OKW equipment and documents would have to leave Berlin for the south immediately—certainly there was neither the fuel nor the fighter escort for the OKW to evacuate Berlin by air. Hitler authorized an immediate splitting of the command: Dönitz and part of the OKW staff were to leave for northern Germany; another part were to leave at once for the south. He gave the impression that he would in due course follow. Bormann left the room at once to organize sufficient armored transport and omnibuses for the transfer. Göring—whose own truckloads of property were already at Karinhall waiting for the word to go—inquired, "Mein Führer, do you have any objection to my leaving for Berchtesgaden now?" Hitler was dumbfounded that Göring could so casually desert him but did not betray his disappointment; he frigidly granted Göring's plea.

At 6 P.M. Spremberg fell to the Russians; they were now only a few miles from the vital autobahn from Berlin to the south. At 9:30 P.M., as a new air raid started, Hitler sent for the two older secretaries with whom he had lunched. Christa Schroeder wrote a few days after:

> Pale, tired, and listless, he met us in his tiny shelter study where we had eaten our meals or had tea with him of late. He said that the situation had changed for the worse over the last four days. "I find myself compelled to split up my staff, and as you are the more senior you go first. A car is leaving for the south in one hour. You can each take two suitcases, Martin Bormann will tell you the rest." I asked to stay in Berlin, so that my younger colleague could go as her mother lived in Munich. He replied, "No, I'm going to start a resistance movement and I'll need you two for that. You mean the most to me. If worse comes to worst, the younger ones will always get through—Frau Christian at any rate—and if one of the young ones doesn't make it, that's just Fate." He put out his hand to stop any further argument. He noticed how downcast we were, and tried to console us. "We'll see you soon, I'm coming down myself in a few days' time!" Absolutely numbed, my colleague and I left his room, to pack the two suitcases permitted us in the Voss Bunker where we four secretaries had shared a bedroom for some time. The hall outside was packed with pedestrians who had taken refuge from the air raid outside. In the midst of our packing the phone rang. I answered it—it was the Chief. In a toneless voice he said, "Girls, we're cut off"—we were going to drive down through Bohemia —"your car won't get through there now. You'll have to fly at dawn." But soon after he phoned again. "Girls, you'll have to hurry. The plane's leaving as soon as the all clear sounds." His voice sounded melancholy and dull and he stopped in mid-sentence. I said something, but although he still had not hung up, he made no reply.

The Russians had now reached Baruth—just ten miles south of OKW and OKH headquarters at Zossen, south of Berlin, and still more tanks were pouring through the big gap between the Fourth Panzer and Ninth armies. Schörner's counterattack had begun, but when Hitler called on Heinrici to attack, in order to close this gap, the army group commander demurred, demanding permission to pull back the Ninth Army's right flank instead, as it seemed in danger of encirclement. But Heinrici could give Hitler no assurances that this would not cost the flank corps its entire artillery, so Hitler—after hours of deliberation—ordered the line held where it was. Heinrici dramatically telephoned the General Staff half an hour after midnight to protest that Hitler's order was "unrealizable and hopeless." "I ought to declare: 'Mein Führer, as the order is against your interests I request you to relieve me of my command . . . then I can go into battle as an ordinary Volkssturm man with a gun in my hand!' " General Krebs drily pointed out: "The Führer expects you to make a supreme effort to plug the gaps as far east as possible, using everything you can scrape together, regardless of Berlin's later defense." Again Hitler ordered every available jet to attack the Russians south of Berlin.

In fact General Heinrici had already decided to "override" Hitler's order to stand fast. The Ninth Army, he felt, should withdraw westward while it still could. Thus the breach which must eventually seal Berlin's fate—and Hitler's too if he stayed for the capital's defense—was further widened. But at the time Hitler believed that his orders were being obeyed.

That night he resolved not to leave Berlin.

Cramped with his two remaining secretaries in his study he had explained, "I'd feel like some Tibetan lama, turning a useless, empty prayer wheel. I must force the decision here in Berlin or go down fighting." Hardly anybody arrived for the night conference—most of his staff, like his secretaries, were packing feverishly. Kreb's operations officer brought the grim news that the breach in the Fourth Panzer Army had widened still farther. Hitler calmly blamed this on that army's "betrayal." The general challenged him. "Mein Führer, you often talk of your betrayal by your commanders and troops. Do you really believe so much has been betrayed?" Hitler cast him a pitying look. "All our defeats in the east are solely the result of treachery"—and he spoke with deep conviction. At 1 A.M., Hitler dismissed the two stenographers, Kurt Peschel and Hans Jonuschat, so that they too could catch that night's plane south. As the general also departed, Ambassador Walther Hewel stuck his head around the door. "Mein Führer, do you have any orders for me yet?" Hitler shook his head. Ribbentrop's representative exclaimed, "Mein Führer, the zero hour is about to strike! If you still plan to achieve anything by political means, it's high time now!" Hitler replied with an exhausted air, "Politics? I'm through with politics. It sickens me. When I'm dead you'll have more than enough politics to contend with."

Outside, the all clear was just sounding. Puttkamer—his naval adjutant since 1935—was leaving, evacuating too General Schmundt's dangerous diaries in a suitcase; Saur joined him on the plane, with orders to organize in the Alps what arms production he could. About eighty other staff members and their families flew south that night. But in the early hours Martin Bormann cabled to the Berghof: "Wolf [*i.e.*, Hitler] is staying here, because if anybody can master the situation here, it is only he."

The next morning, April 21, 1945, there was a hammering on Hitler's bedroom door. Linge shouted that Russian artillery had begun pouring shells into the heart of Berlin. Hitler shaved rapidly—"I can't stand anybody else hovering near my throat with an open razor," he used to say—and stepped into his study. General Burgdorf announced that the Russians had evidently brought up a heavy battery by rail across the Oder. Hitler telephoned orders to the OKL to identify and attack the battery at once; General Koller assured him: "The Russians have *no* railway bridges across the Oder. Perhaps they have captured and turned around one of our heavy batteries." Soon after, Koller came on the phone again; the offending Russian battery had been spotted from the observation post atop the towering antiaircraft bunker at the zoo. It was just eight miles away—at Marzahn.

Throughout the day, as the rain of shells on Berlin continued, a growing sense of isolation gripped Hitler's bunker. Koller was unable to brief Hitler on the Luftwaffe operations south of the city because of communications failures. Nothing had been heard from General Helmuth Weidling's Fifty-sixth Panzer Corps, due east of the city, since 8 P.M. the previous evening. According to one incredible report, Weidling himself had fled with his staff to the Olympic village *west* of Berlin; his arrest was ordered. The jets had been prevented by enemy fighter patrols from operating from Prague airfields against the Russian spearheads south of Berlin. Hitler angrily phoned Koller. "Then the jets are quite useless, the Luftwaffe is quite superfluous!" Infuriated by a Saar industrialist's letter with further disclosures about the Luftwaffe, Hitler again angrily called up Koller. "The entire Luftwaffe command ought to be strung up!" and he slammed the phone down. Heinrici—ordered to report in person to the shelter that day—asked to be excused as he was "completely overburdened." He successfully avoided having to look his Führer in the eye ever again.

During the afternoon Hitler began planning a last attempt at plugging the widening breach torn in Heinrici's front between Eberswalde and Werneuchen, northeast of Berlin. An *ad hoc* battle group under the bullet-headed SS General Felix Steiner must—like a sliding door—push south during the night from Eberswalde to Werneuchen; if Steiner succeeded, Zhukov's advanced forces north of Berlin would be cut off. But north of Eberswalde the Soviet Marshal Rokossovski had now breached the Oder front sector held by General von Manteuffel's Third Panzer Army, and Hitler's detailed order to Steiner, issued about 5 P.M., had an hysterical undertone:

> Any officers failing to accept this order without reservations are to be arrested and shot at once. You will account with your life for the execution of this order. The fate of the German capital depends on the success of your mission.

Krebs repeated this to the over-busy Heinrici by telephone, but Heinrici was also preoccupied with salvaging his right flank—the Ninth Army's flank corps—from Russian encirclement at Fürstenwalde. "All I can manage now is to pull it back *south* of the string of lakes southeast of Berlin," Heinrici warned. This was tantamount to abandoning Berlin. As for the Steiner attack, if the Führer insisted on it, then Heinrici asked to be replaced as Steiner's superior.

Hitler insisted, but did not replace him; perhaps Krebs did not report the conversation to him, for Hitler now pinned all his hopes on Steiner's attack. At 9 P.M. he learned that a battalion of the "Hermann Göring" Division was still defending the Reichsmarschall's abandoned stately home at Karinhall. He ordered the force handed to Steiner, and when Koller plaintively telephoned at 10:30 P.M. to ask where Steiner was, the Führer snatched the phone from Krebs's hand and rasped, "The Luftwaffe is to transfer every man available for ground fighting in the north to Steiner. Any commander holding men back will have breathed his last breath within five hours. . . . You yourself will pay with your life unless every last man is thrown in." Krebs confirmed this. "Everybody into the attack from Eberswalde to the south!"—and then hung up.

What orders Heinrici now issued to Steiner we do not know. But even Steiner was no fool, and to attack Zhukov's flank with a motley collection of demoralized, ill-armed, and undermunitioned troops would be courting disaster. He stalled while ostensibly girding himself for the attack.

The SS general's inactivity—to put the best possible interpretation on it—was the last straw for Hitler after Sepp Dietrich's fiasco in Hungary. In the narrow confines of his bunker, the Führer suffered an apparent nervous breakdown on April 22, as the Russians closed in from the east, north, and south on Berlin's outer ring of defense. Little now stood between Berlin and a seemingly inevitable defeat. Although crippled by 90 percent power failures, Daimler-Benz, Alkett, and the other arms factories were still sending their remaining tanks and assault guns straight to the nearest front line. But fuel and ammunition were running out, and there was already heavy street fighting in the suburbs. The Russians were in Köpenick and approaching Spandau. By evening they might well be fighting in the government quarter itself. This was the military position as Krebs finally secured Hitler's authorization for the garrison at Frankfurt-on-Oder to abandon that city to the enemy as well.

The war conference on April 22 began routinely at about 3 P.M. First Goebbels telephoned, and later Ribbentrop; but then Hitler asked about the operation which had obviously been in the foreground of his mind all night—Steiner's counterattack in the north. An SS authority assured him the attack had begun well, but Hitler mistrustfully asked the Luftwaffe to check; within the hour General Koller came on the phone with word that Steiner had not yet begun his attack and would not begin before nightfall. This betrayal and deceit by the SS, of all people, shook Hitler to the core.[4] He asked if the Luftwaffe troops had duly come under Steiner's command; General Christian replied that they had still not received any orders from Steiner. Hitler straightened up and purpled. He suspected a *fait accompli,* to force him to leave Berlin. His eyes bulged. "That's it,"

[4]Steiner wrote in postwar memoirs that he had decided against the relief attack as it was pointless.

he shouted. "How am I supposed to direct the war in such circumstances! The war's lost! But if you gentlemen imagine I'll leave Berlin now, then you've another think coming. I'd sooner put a bullet in my brains!" Everybody stared. Hitler abruptly stalked out, while the adjutant Otto Günsche started after him, calling out, "But, mein Führer . . ." Walther Hewel telephoned Foreign Minister Ribbentrop in extreme agitation: "The Führer's had a nervous breakdown—he's going to shoot himself!"

Hitler ordered a telephone call put through to Goebbels. When the propaganda minister's voice came on the line, he dictated to him an announcement: "I have decided to stay to the end of the battle in Berlin." He ordered Goebbels to bring his family to the shelter and sent for Julius Schaub, his lifelong factotum. By the time Schaub hobbled in, Hitler had recovered some of his composure. "Schaub—we must destroy all the documents here at once. Get some gasoline." He fumbled with his ring of safe keys, handed them to Schaub, and went into the tiny bedroom. While Schaub opened the small safe at the foot of the bed and stuffed its contents into a brown suitcase on the bed, Hitler took his lightweight 6.35-millimeter Walther pistol from his trouser pocket and exchanged it for the more lethal 7.65-millimeter Walther from the bedside table. The bulging suitcase was carried upstairs; from the upstairs safes more suitcases were filled, and then emptied into a crater in the garden. For a while Hitler stood with Schaub, watching his collection of memoirs, memoranda, and secret letters from world statesmen consumed by the flames. "Richelieu once said, give me five lines one man has penned!" Hitler lamented afterward. "What I have lost! My dearest memories! But what's the point—sooner or later you've got to get rid of all that stuff." He indicated that Schaub must leave for Munich and the Berghof and destroy the papers there too.[5] But first there was something he wanted to dictate—evidently something for posterity.

Hitler's anguished staff realized that he intended to remain in Berlin and brave the coming storm. "I have been betrayed by those I trusted most," he declaimed. "I'm going to stay here in Berlin, the capital of our crusade against bolshevism, and direct its defense myself." Goebbels, Bormann, Keitel, and Jodl begged him to reconsider. Dönitz and Himmler telephoned. Ribbentrop arrived, but was not even given a hearing. Keitel cornered Hitler alone but was interrupted almost at once. "I know what you're going to say: It's time to take a *Ganzer Entschluss!* I've taken it already. I'm going to defend Berlin to the bitter end. Either I restore my command here in the capital—assuming Wenck keeps the Americans off my

[5]I have reason to believe that Schaub did not complete this latter task but sold Hitler's papers to a former magistrate now living on Lake Starnberg in Bavaria. This gentleman has so far proved unapproachable.

back and throws them back over the Elbe—or I go down here in Berlin with my troops fighting for the symbol of the Reich." He felt that if he had stayed in East Prussia in November, the Russians would never have got through there. That was why, he disclosed to the furious field marshal, he had just ordered his decision to stay in Berlin announced to the people; he could not change his mind now.

Jodl joined the argument and pointed out that if at the last moment Hitler committed suicide in Berlin, the German army would be leaderless. (He also candidly explained that given the Führer's trembling hands he was too infirm to handle a rifle or bazooka in the street fighting and that in any case there was the danger that he might be captured.) Hitler called Martin Bormann in, and ordered him, Keitel, and Jodl to fly to Berchtesgaden that night to continue the war with Göring as acting Führer. All three refused. Somebody objected that there was not one German soldier who would be willing to fight for the Reichsmarschall. Hitler retorted, "There's not much fighting left to be done. And when it comes to negotiating, the Reichsmarschall will be better at that than I."

It was nearly 5 P.M., and the Russians had now taken the Silesia station. The Führer's bunker vibrated with the distant echoes of exploding shells. His petrified staff was clustered in the passageway, many of them expecting to hear pistol shots announcing that Hitler had abandoned them. In a private aside to Eva Braun, General Burgdorf put their chances now at only 10 percent. But Jodl argued on—pointing out that Hitler still held powerful trump cards in the form of Schörner's undefeated army group and the armies on the Elbe and in Norway. He reminded Hitler of the demarcation line shown on the captured "Eclipse" maps and suggested that now they should swing Wenck's Twelfth Army around from west to east and use it to relieve Berlin. Hitler shrugged. "Do whatever you want!" Secretly he may have been relieved, like a convict granted a last-minute reprieve. Perhaps, as Jodl argued, *now* the Allies would take his anti-Bolshevik intent seriously. Keitel announced that he would drive in person to give the necessary orders to Wenck that night. Hitler ordered a hearty meal prepared for the field marshal before he set out.

Hitler was not appalled at the prospect of imminent death. At an August 1944 war conference he had told his generals he was almost looking forward to it, just as an artisan savors the coming of the evening, when he can set his gnarled hands to rest; in death Hitler looked for "a release from my sorrows and sleepless nights and from this nervous suffering. It takes only the fraction of a second—then one is cast free from all that and rests in eternal peace." Ever since World War I he had lived on borrowed time. Besides, as he told Schörner, his death might remove the last obstacle preventing the Allies from making common cause with Germany. If Model could find the courage to take his own life, so would he; he, Hitler, was no Paulus. "Did not Varus command his slave: 'Now kill me!' " he noted in a comparison to the Roman general who had led three legions to their destruction.

He gruffly instructed Eva Braun and the two remaining secretaries to get changed and fly south. "It's all over—it's quite hopeless." Eva took both his hands in hers. "But you know I am going to stay here with you!" Hitler's eyes glistened, and he did something nobody had seen him do before—he kissed her lightly on the lips. Frau Junge chimed in, "I'll stay too!" and Frau Christian echoed her. "I wish my generals were as brave as you," Hitler replied.

Despite a telephone call from his liaison officer, Hermann Fegelein, Himmler had failed to show up at the shelter, evidently fearing from what Fegelein told him that he would be arrested for SS General Steiner's passivity; Fegelein was sent to meet him halfway but failed to return. Instead Himmler's doctor, Karl Gebhardt, a potbellied, bespectacled Bavarian, arrived about 11 P.M.; he pleaded with Hitler to leave or at least to let the women and children sheltering in the adjacent Voss Bunker escape under Red Cross cover. Hitler learned that Himmler had a battalion of six hundred SS troops for his own safety outside Berlin; he invited Himmler through Gebhardt to contribute them to the defense of the Chancellery. Some time after, Himmler's chief lieutenant, General Gottlob Berger, arrived. Hitler repeated to him his reproaches about the SS's disloyalty and asked Berger to go to Bavaria to crush the dissident and separatist movements stirring there and in Württemberg and Austria. "Everybody has deceived me! Nobody has been telling me the truth! The Wehrmacht has lied to me! Even the SS has left me in the lurch!" His last instruction to Berger before the latter flew south was to round up as many British and American officer-prisoners as possible and transport them under guard to the Alpine Redoubt—as hostages; though for what purpose even Hitler did not seem clear.

Under cover of darkness, still more of his staff left Berlin. General Koller flew to Bavaria. Morell came to the shelter, clutching his heart and gasping that he needed a change of climate; he offered Hitler a last injection before he left, a morphine pick-me-up, but Hitler suspected that a plot might be afoot to drug him and evacuate him from Berlin by force. He contemptuously dismissed the gaudily bedecked professor. "You can take off that uniform and go back to your practice in the Kurfürstendamm!" Morell chose Munich instead and flew out that night. Hitler sent out the remaining two staff stenographers as well; their orders were to take the last shorthand records to the "outside world."

Hitler's press officer, Heinz Lorenz, was instructed to take down the remaining historic war conferences as best he could. His fragmentary notes—which begin with Keitel's exhausted return with Jodl from the battlefield at 3 P.M. on April 23—reveal the growing desperation at Hitler's shelter. East of Berlin the Fifty-sixth Panzer Corps had vanished without trace, as had General Weidling, its commander. "It is all so abominable! When you come to think it over, what's the point of living on!" exclaimed Hitler. Steiner had made no discernible move with his 25th Panzer-Grenadier and 7th Panzer divisions at Eberswalde, north of the capital. The Russians had swarmed across the Havel River between Oranienburg and Spandau—unless the Havel lakes could be defended, the city would be completely encircled at any moment.

The situation on Germany's other fronts no longer occupied Hitler. With tanks swarming as far as the eye could see toward the heart of Berlin along the Landsberg Chaussee from the east—and the new "Stalin" tanks at that, virtually impregnable to German shells—the bunker conferences devolved only on the defenses of Berlin. Hitler's last stratagem began unfolding. At noon Goebbels's ministry released the news. "The Führer is in Berlin. . . . Our leadership has resolved to remain in Berlin and defend the Reich capital to the end." Perhaps if Stalin knew that Hitler was still in Berlin, his armies might overreach themselves and suffer the same kind of defeat Hitler himself had suffered at Moscow. Lorenz recorded Hitler's belief thus: "The enemy now knows I am here. They will do all they can to concentrate on us. That gives us an excellent opportunity of luring them into an ambush. But this depends on all our people realizing the importance of this hour and genuinely obeying the orders they get from above; they must be honest about it! This business up here"—indicating Steiner on the map—"was downright dishonest! Steiner had too many nagging doubts about the defenses confronting him." General Krebs interjected, "I believe we still have four days' time." "In four days we'll know the outcome," agreed Hitler.

The "ambush" to which Hitler referred was the plan Keitel and Jodl had proposed—for the army on the Elbe and Mulde fronts, facing the Americans, to be turned around, to link up south of Berlin with Busse's Ninth Army and then strike northward toward Potsdam and Berlin, mopping up the elite Russian troops they thereby cut off. Wenck's objective would be the autobahn at Ferch, near Potsdam. At the same time the Forty-first Panzer Corps—commanded by the reliable General Rudolf Holste, an old regimental comrade of Keitel's—would be brought back across the Elbe, to counterattack between Spandau and Oranienburg; Steiner was to turn over his mechanized divisions (the 25th Panzer-Grenadiers and the 7th Panzer) to Holste, northwest of Berlin.

The realist in Hitler whispered that defeat was inevitable, and he made no secret of this to his intimates, even if he felt constrained to put on a braver face to his generals. Eva Braun wrote that April 23: "The Führer himself has lost all hope of a happy ending. But while we still live all of us have hope, including me."

Later she added: "At present things are said to be looking up. General Burgdorf who gave us only a 10 percent chance yesterday has raised the odds to 50–50 today. Perhaps things may turn out well after all!" Hitler drank chocolate with Goebbels's five little girls and son Helmuth, who had now moved into Morell's quarters. Helmuth read aloud his school essay on the Führer's birthday. Helga squawked, "You stole that from Papa!" "You mean Papa stole it from me!" retorted Helmuth, to the delight of the adult listeners. The children seemed oblivious of the fate their parents planned for them.

Before Keitel returned to Wenck's headquarters, he came in to see Hitler and quietly inquired whether any talks at all were proceeding with the enemy. Hitler replied that before he could start talks he must win "one more" victory—the Battle for Berlin. He disclosed that he had opened up one channel to the Allies through Italy and that he had asked Ribbentrop to discuss further steps with him that evening. Ribbentrop's only proposal of substance was to have top Czech industrialists flown that night to France, where they would attempt to persuade the Americans to protect Bohemia and Moravia from the Bolsheviks. "The Führer has agreed to this," Ribbentrop informed Karl-Hermann Frank by letter. For the first time Hitler now admitted to Ribbentrop that the war was lost—but he insisted that he had been right all along, that Britain would have done better to have fought at his side and not against him. He dictated to Ribbentrop four secret negotiation points to put to the British if he got the chance, points vital to the future of Europe. If the Continent was to survive in a world dominated by bolshevism, then somehow London and Berlin must bury the hatchet between them. He instructed Ribbentrop to write secretly to Churchill in this sense. "You will see," Hitler predicted. "My spirit will arise from the grave. One day people will see that I was right."

When Ribbentrop left—eventually attaching his diplomatic staff to General Wenck's Twelfth Army staff—an adjutant announced that Albert Speer had just arrived in the Chancellery, having made a venturesome landing by light plane on the East-West Axis across the Tiergarten after a flight escorted by a whole fighter squadron from Rechlin. Eva Braun, who like Hitler had been troubled by the recurring rumors of Speer's inexplicable behavior, greeted him warmly. "I knew you'd return—you won't desert the Führer!" Speer grinned. "I'm leaving Berlin again tonight!" According to Julius Schaub—who also left that night—when Hitler asked his friend's opinion on his decision to fight the battle for Berlin to its end, Speer's almost brutal advice was that it was better to die there than in his weekend cottage on the Obersalzberg, that is, if the Führer attached any importance to the verdict of history. The remark reveals much about Speer's own motives. Hitler, unaware that Speer had secretly arranged with Heinrici for Berlin to be abandoned to the Russians, agreed.

After the war conference, Bormann brought to Hitler a startling telegram just received from Göring at Berchtesgaden. Göring, it seemed, was seizing power.

> Mein Führer!
>
> In view of your decision to remain in the fortress of Berlin, are you agreed that I immediately assume overall leadership of the Reich as your Deputy, in accordance with your decree of June 29, 1941, with complete freedom of action at home and abroad?
>
> Unless an answer is given by 10 P.M. I will assume you have been deprived of your freedom of action. I shall then regard the conditions laid down by your Decree as being met, and shall act in the best interests of the people and Fatherland.
>
> You know my feelings for you in these the hardest hours of my life. I cannot express them adequately.
>
> May God protect you and allow you to come here soon despite everything.
>
> Your loyal Hermann Göring.

Bormann no doubt read this aloud to Hitler in tones worthy of a public prosecutor. But that Ribbentrop and Speer, Göring's other archenemies, were by chance also in Hitler's bunker was a double misfortune for the Reichsmarschall. Ribbentrop had received from Göring a telegram asking him to fly down immediately unless ordered to the contrary by 10 P.M. Keitel also heard from Göring. Somehow Hitler learned that Göring's plan was to fly to the American supreme commander, General Eisenhower, and ask for peace terms. Hitler immediately cabled Göring that he alone would decide when the Decree of June 29, 1941, took effect; Göring was forbidden to undertake any steps in the direction he had hinted at. The Führer then ordered Göring and his staff on the Obersalzberg placed under house arrest. The shelter was in an uproar over Göring's "treachery." Speer undoubtedly fanned the flames, for that same day he wrote to General Galland, now a jet-fighter squadron commander in Bavaria, enclosing a copy of Göring's telegram to Ribbentrop. "This telegram is clear. The Führer has reacted to it accordingly and ordered Göring's arrest. I request you and your comrades to do everything to prevent an airplane flight by Göring as discussed."[6]

Thus with characteristic hesitancy and with prodding from Bormann, Hitler took the decision with which he had been grappling since September 1944—

[6]Speer does not refer to this in his memoirs. The only acceptable explanation is that if Göring tried to fly to Eisenhower, Galland was to have him shot down. Speer evidently feared Göring would get the credit for peace moves, leaving high and dry his own hesitant preparations—which included a radio speech prerecorded at Hamburg ordering the German people to stop fighting.

dismissing Göring. But even then he spared his feelings, telegraphing the Reichsmarschall: "Your actions are punishable by the death sentence, but because of your valuable services in the past I will refrain from instituting proceedings if you will voluntarily relinquish your offices and titles. Otherwise steps will have to be taken." Göring hastened to comply. Hitler meanwhile ordered General Robert von Greim from Munich to Berlin; Koller was also instructed to return, and the Luftwaffe's General Josef Kammhuber was sent for as well. Greim's take-off was, however, prevented by an air raid; Koller pleaded ill-health, and Kammhuber also avoided coming to the capital. The Luftwaffe was in chaos anyway. General Galland's fighter squadron had somehow amassed ninety-five new Me-262 jets on its Munich airfield, but the squadron had only twenty pilots; on the other hand, the crack jet-fighter wing JG.7 had only twenty Me-262s left and could not obtain replacements. Nothing had prevented the British bomber squadrons from executing a precision attack in broad daylight on the Obersalzberg early on April 25, leaving the Berghof a smoking ruin.

The last week of Hitler's leadership was plagued by the crumbling communications system. From April 24, 1945, onward, it is difficult to relate the orders emanating from his bomb- and shell-shattered Chancellery building to either the war information reaching him or the actions of his commanders in the field. On April 24, Hitler himself contributed to the command chaos by an order upending the existing command structure and subordinating the General Staff's eastern front to the OKW operations staff. But three days later Hitler's only radiotelephone link with Jodl's headquarters was silenced, and Hitler could communicate with the outside world only via a telephone to the admiralty's still-functioning signals room. Jodl's clear instructions to the armies were repeated by Hitler on April 24: Generals Holste, Wenck, Schörner, and Busse were to speed up their relief attacks toward Berlin, from northwest, southwest, and south, respectively, and "restore a broad land contact with Berlin again, thereby bringing the Battle of Berlin to a victorious conclusion." But apart from Wenck and Schörner, Hitler's commanders no longer even paid lip service to his authority—they were driven only by the compulsion to escape the Russian grasp themselves before the final collapse came.

Apart from word that part of the Ninth Army had been encircled southeast of Berlin, there was no news of the army until Weidling, the "missing" commander of its Fifty-sixth Panzer Corps, whose arrest for desertion Hitler had ordered, reached Berlin's outskirts and the public telephone; he then stormed into the Chancellery to establish his innocence. On April 24, Hitler willingly appointed this fiery general battle-commandant of Berlin.

Weidling set about reorganizing the capital's defenses, laying down new signals networks and dismissing indifferent sector commanders; but his task was nigh impossible. Hitler and Goebbels had optimistically sacrificed the capital's resources of men, ammunition, and gasoline to the forward defenses on the Oder, and little now remained for Berlin. According to Keitel, a decamping army commandant had blown up Berlin's last major ammunition dump at Krampnitz. Weidling would have little infantry, no artillery, and hardly any tanks. Apart from the shattered remnants of his own corps, the coming street battles would be fought between trained, professional Russian combat troops with the glint of final victory in their eyes, and a few thousand antiaircraft soldiers, Volkssturm men, and police armed with captured rifles, broken-down tanks, or makeshift rocket-launchers. About 2,700 youths—hardly more than children—had been mustered into a "tank-killer brigade"; Hitler assigned this Hitler Youth offering to the defense of the bridges across which the relief armies must march into Berlin. Late on April 24, Hitler appealed to the navy for troops; from Flensburg, Admiral Dönitz promised to airlift 2,000 of his best sailors and fortress troops into Berlin in the next forty-eight hours and to put 3,500 more of his most cherished fleet personnel—including crews trained to operate the new secret U-boats—on standby for the fight; unless Berlin won this last battle—which Hitler described to Dönitz as "a battle for Germany's whole future" outranking all other theaters in importance—those U-boats would never operate.

Dönitz kept this promise—unlike Himmler, who had eventually parted with only half his personal security battalion. (According to stenographer Ewald Reynitz, in these last days of his life Hitler refused to speak to Himmler even over the telephone and flatly forbade Himmler to participate in the war conferences.) Even Ribbentrop courageously requested permission to take up arms in Berlin. But Hitler forbade this: Ribbentrop knew too many secrets to be allowed to fall into enemy hands; and Walther Hewel—whom Hitler urged with the rest of his staff to take poison before the Russians could capture them[7]—telegraphed the foreign minister in Mecklenburg: "The Führer appreciates your intentions but has turned you down. Until the ring encircling Berlin has been broken open or until you receive further instructions, you are to stand by outside the combat area." Hewel added significantly: "I have no political information whatever." Schörner, whose army group had just recaptured Bautzen and Weissenberg, south of Berlin, inflicting heavy losses on the Russians, also began moving northward toward the capital. "The attack by Schörner's army group proves," Dönitz was signaled by Hitler's staff on April 26, "that given the will, we are still capable of beating the enemy even today." These distant victories glowed faintly through the thickening gloom of the communications breakdowns besetting Hitler's shelter.

[7]Hewel, Krebs, Burgdorf, the Goebbels family, and many others followed Hitler's request.

"The British and Americans along the Elbe are holding back," Hitler observed. ". . . I think the time has now come when out of a sheer instinct for self-preservation they must act against this bloated proletarian Colossus, this Bolshevik Moloch. . . . If I can win through here and hang on to the capital, perhaps hope will spring in British and American hearts that with our Nazi Germany they may after all have some chance against this entire danger. And the only man capable of this is me. . . . But I am only Führer as long as I can really *lead.* I can't lead if I go south and sit on some mountain, but only if I have authority over armies and those armies obey me. Give me one victory here—however high the price—and then I'll regain the right to eliminate the deadweights who constantly obstruct. After that I will work with the generals who've proved their worth." Later he again digressed on this theme. "First I must set an example to everybody I blamed for retreating, by not retreating myself. It is possible that I will die here, but then at least I shall have died an honorable death." Hitler proclaimed that this Battle of Berlin was as important as the 1683 Battle of Vienna, which had turned the tide of the Turkish conquest of Europe.

The first battalion of Dönitz's naval troops arrived, and Weidling threw them straight into the fight. The makeshift hospital in the Voss Bunker next to Hitler's bunker filled with casualties. The streets were strewn with burning vehicles and tanks. The government quarter was under nonstop bombardment by artillery and bombers. But Weidling reported to Hitler that it was proving difficult to demolish bridges—for example along the Teltow Canal defense line—because Speer's staff had decamped with all the bridge plans. Speer had also fought tooth and nail against the dismantling of the bronze lampposts along the East-West Axis, as Hitler had ordered, to prepare an emergency landing strip. (Speer had protested to Weidling's predecessor: "You seem to forget I am responsible for the reconstruction of Berlin.")

During April 26 spirits soared in Hitler's bunker, as the news of Wenck's approaching army and Schörner's successes trickled in. That evening General Greim limped into the shelter with a female admirer, having been shot in the leg as he piloted his light plane to the East-West Axis and made a crash-landing on the boulevard. His injuries were tended, then he was put to bed in a room opposite Hitler's conference room. For many hours Hitler sat at his bedside, morosely describing Göring's "ultimatum" and the history of the Luftwaffe's failure—only General Koller had dared tell him the truth about the technical inferiority of German planes. At 10 P.M., German radio broadcast Greim's promotion to field marshal and his appointment as Göring's successor. Hitler urged suicide capsules on Greim and his woman friend, and instructed them—if worse came to worst—to arrange their own cremation so that the Russians would find nothing. "I firmly believed that Berlin could be saved on the banks of the Oder. Everything we had here was moved forward to that position. You must believe me—when all our efforts there failed I was the most stunned of all," he mused. But Wenck was now approaching Berlin. "If he can relieve Berlin, we shall fall back to a new line and fight on." He ordered his new Luftwaffe commander to concentrate the Messerschmitt jet squadrons around Prague.

At night Hitler was kept awake by the shell fire and by his own vivid memories. This was Stalingrad all over again, but this time the miracle would happen. "Imagine! Like wildfire the word spreads throughout Berlin: one of our armies has broken through from the west and restored contact with us!" How could Stalin hope to reduce a great city of four million people with only four hundred tanks, especially if fifty were being knocked out each day? "The Russians have already exhausted their strength in crossing the Oder, particularly the northern army group [Zhukov's]."

Against this Hitler had to set his own virtual helplessness and lack of precise information on the battle. Schörner's forces were approaching, and within one day this pressure should begin embarrassing the Russians in the south. According to Keitel, General Holste's battle group in the northwest had gained ground at Nauen and Kremmen and would gather its last reinforcements for its main attack early on the twenty-eighth. Hitler impatiently told Krebs, "It's high time they got a move on!" General Wenck's relief offensive from the southwest—three well-fueled divisions under General Karl-Erik Koehler—had already reached the Schwielow lake, and during the morning the Party announced that it had reached Potsdam, thus attaining the tactical objective laid down four days before. But a tough ring of Soviet troops still barred the way to Berlin.

Hitler realized that time was running out fast. At 5 A.M. on April 27 a big Russian push along the Hohenzollerndamm Boulevard had begun. As Goebbels nervously put it: "I keep getting this nightmare picture: Wenck is at Potsdam, and here the Russians are pouring into Potsdamer Platz!" "—And I'm here at Potsdamer Platz, not Potsdam!" agreed Hitler uneasily. His eyes were transfixed by the colored arrows marking the relief armies on the map. He recognized the problem his dwindling authority was causing. Wenck had the drive, the gasoline, and the loyalty to get to Potsdam, but he lacked the tanks to smash the Russian armor. General Busse's Ninth Army—encircled southeast of Berlin—had the tanks, but its westward movement seemed designed to *bypass* Berlin to the south. Hitler was puzzled by this defiance of his orders.[8] Late on the twenty-sixth he had

[8]Busse had decided to drive with his army remnants toward the American lines—unaware at that time of Hitler's plan to denude the Elbe battlefront in favor of Berlin.

radioed to Jodl: "Make it clear to Ninth Army that it is to wheel sharply north with Twelfth Army to take weight off Battle for Berlin." Throughout the twenty-seventh he speculated on this puzzle. "I just don't understand the direction of its attack. Busse's driving into a complete vacuum." "If he had pushed northwest instead, and covered as much distance as he has now, he would have accomplished much more." "Wenck and the Ninth Army would already have linked up." And, late that day, it occurred to him at last why the Ninth Army had pleaded its radio failure. "If there's a long radio silence, it is always the sign that things are going badly." "It's impossible to command if every plan that's drawn up is adapted by every army commander as he sees fit." "What's happened now is just what I predicted: they've been encircled."

North of Berlin, the generals' disobedience to orders was even more blatant. Heinrici's remaining Oder sector, south of Stettin, had collapsed under the weight of Marshal Rokossovski's attack. Since noon on April 26, Heinrici had begged Jodl to allow General Steiner's two armored divisions to repair the damage. But Hitler and Jodl mistrusted Steiner, and these divisions had been ordered to support Holste's more promising relief attack instead. This order was ignored. Heinrici assured Keitel he was holding a line from Angermünde to Ückerheim, but when the field marshal set out on a surprise visit to the battlefield he found the front line only a few miles away, in the midst of what was a well-prepared retreat; and the 5th Light Infantry Division—although its troops were still eager for combat with the Russians—was being pulled back westward because "its officers have decided not to fight any longer." Keitel telephoned Hitler about Heinrici's deceit. Far from holding the line, Heinrici and Manteuffel—commanding the Third Panzer Army on the breached Oder sector—were deliberately herding their troops across Mecklenburg toward the haven of the Allied lines. At about 5 P.M. Jodl radiotelephoned his grim decision to Hitler: Steiner's two armored divisions would have to be thrown northward—away from Berlin—into the southern flank of the Russian spearheads pursuing Manteuffel's troops.

Up to now Hitler had been sustained by the hope of relief. "If we can just hold on two, three, or four days more here, Wenck's army may arrive and perhaps even Busse's too," he had said. Admiral Voss had assured him: "Wenck's coming, mein Führer! The only question is—can he manage by himself!" And Hitler had responded, "I'll sleep a bit better tonight. I don't want to be awakened unless a Russian tank's outside my sleeping cubicle. Then I must be given time to do what has to be done." But the new hysterical atmosphere created by Jodl's radiotelephone message can be judged from the words Martin Bormann jotted in his diary:

> The divisions marching to relieve us have been halted by Himmler and Jodl! We shall stand by and die with our Führer, loyal unto death. If others think

they must act "out of superior judgment," then they are sacrificing the Führer. And their loyalty—Devil take them!—is no better than their sense of "honor"!

A premature dusk had fallen over Berlin outside the shelter, as smoke clouds and mortar dust blotted out the sun. Gatow and Tempelhof airfields had been cut off. Junkers transport planes were redirected to the Axis landing strip, but the Russians had strung out antiaircraft batteries along the flight path and many planes were lost. A hundred of Dönitz's crack troops had been sent to the Chancellery for Hitler's personal protection. Camouflaged by swastika pennants, four enemy tanks had reached Wilhelms Platz before they were detected and destroyed. "Identification regulations are to be strictly obeyed!" Hitler ordered. The Russians announced that they were bringing up 406-millimeter and 370-millimeter mortars to reduce the last citadel of Hitler's capital. Hitler handed his adjutants more of the brass-encased cyanide capsules, to use if absolutely necessary. When the time came he would order a general breakout toward Wenck's army at Potsdam. He disclosed privately to Colonel von Below, his Luftwaffe adjutant ever since 1937: "Only my wife and I will stay behind." He compared Eva Braun's loyalty with the gross disloyalty displayed by Göring and Himmler—whom he intuitively blamed for Steiner's disobedience.

At the late night conference, General Krebs reassured Hitler that the battle lines in Berlin itself were stable again. Hitler Youth units were holding a big bridgehead south of the Pichelsdorf bridge in anticipation of Wenck's arrival; isolated trucks from Wenck's army had already broken through. But the first Russian snipers were roaming Potsdamer Platz and Hitler pointed out: "The subway and streetcar tunnels are a source of danger." Transport planes with more troops were standing by, but one had just crashed and was blocking the Axis Boulevard. Colonel von Below announced that the first air drops of ammunition had begun.

A ticking clock coming over the radio loudspeakers warned that enemy bombers were still over Germany. Hitler brooded on the evening's bulletin that Benito Mussolini had just been captured alive by Italian Communist guerrillas. He could hear the distant singing of the Goebbels children in sixfold chorus as they prepared for bed. During the evening he had unpinned his own golden Party medallion and bestowed it on their red-eyed mother, Magda. She wrote: "Our children are wonderful! . . . Never a whimper or word of complaint. The thudding of shells is getting even on my nerves, but the little ones soothe their younger sisters, and their presence here is a boon to us because now and again they manage to prise a smile from the Führer." They told "Uncle Hitler" they were longing for the day when the new soldiers he had promised would come and drive the Russians away. For their sake Hitler hoped too, though he himself had long decided to stay.

"In this city I have had the right to command others; now I must heed the commands of Fate. Even if I could save myself here, I will not do so. The captain too goes down with his ship."

At 3 A.M.—it was now April 28—Krebs telephoned Keitel at the OKW's field headquarters. "The Führer is most anxious to know about the relief attack west of Oranienburg. What's the news? Is it making any headway? The Führer doesn't *want* Steiner to be commander there!! Hasn't Holste taken over there yet? If help doesn't reach us in the next thirty-six or forty-eight hours, it'll be too late!!!" Keitel replied that he was going to see Steiner in person. Some hours later Hitler learned that a small separatist uprising had begun in Bavaria; a Munich radio station had been seized, and it was broadcasting seditious proclamations to the local workers and foreigners.

It is unlikely that Hitler slept that night. The Chancellery was under direct and heavy shellfire. The Munich separatists had been bloodily suppressed by local forces, but in Berlin the Russians had now penetrated the last lines of defense. The Führer restlessly paced the bunker passageways, gripping a Berlin street map that was disintegrating in his clammy hands. Over three hundred Russian tanks had been destroyed in the street fighting. Busse's Ninth Army had at last linked up with General Wenck's Twelfth, but both were beyond the limits of exhaustion. Moreover, by 4:30 P.M. General Krebs had learned from Jodl the full extent of Heinrici's disobedience north of Berlin: Keitel had discovered the southern flank of Manteuffel's Third Panzer Army retreating across the Schorf Heide in compliance with secret *orders* which Heinrici had concealed from both the OKW and Hitler. Steiner was covering this illicit retreat and doing nothing to seal off the breach at Prenzlau. Keitel was apoplectic with anger and instructed Heinrici and Manteuffel to meet him at a lonely crossroads to account for their actions. One thing was certain: Berlin's northern defenses were wide open.

Hitler had hardly seen Himmler's liaison officer SS General Fegelein, or the Gestapo chief, Müller, this last week. But on April 28 his staff began receiving erratic and surreptitious telephone calls from Fegelein. Hitler suspected he was absconding, and he debated with Greim the possibility that the Reichsführer SS was condoning this—which might have sinister implications. Late that afternoon Bormann showed him yet another stunning news report: Allied radio had proclaimed that Himmler had contacted the United States and Britain and guaranteed them Germany's unconditional surrender! But the Western Allies were insisting on including Russia in the surrender terms.

This bombshell caused a furor. Bormann sneered, "I always said *loyalty* has to be stamped on your heart and not on your belt buckle!" Fegelein's effects were searched and papers relating to Himmler's treachery were found, along with two money belts of gold sovereigns and other enemy currencies. Eva Braun, whose sister had married Fegelein, mournfully noted: "The Führer is spared nothing. With his life drawing to a close even the SS and his trusted Fegelein are deserting him." Fegelein's adjutant stated he had last seen him changing into civilian clothes at his Kurfürstendamm apartment; Bormann sent men out into the inferno to search for him. He cabled his Party headquarters in Munich at 8 P.M.: "Instead of spurring on the troops to fight us free with orders and appeals, just silence from the top men. Loyalty apparently yielding to disloyalty. We remain here. Reich Chancellery already in ruins."

Two hours later General Weidling, the city commandant, reported that the Russians were hammering Wenck's relief army into the ground. The situation in the city was desperate. Food and medical stores were exhausted. He read out an appeal by Professor Ferdinand Sauerbruch, of the Charité hospital, to consider the plight of the injured. Finally Weidling outlined his plan for a mass breakout by the remaining troops, but Hitler replied that he would not himself leave the Chancellery. His naval liaison admiral radioed to Dönitz: "We are holding on to the very end." At midnight Keitel's telegram arrived. At the crossroads rendezvous Heinrici had suavely promised to obey orders, but at 11:30 P.M. he admitted he had in fact ordered a further retreat; Keitel had dismissed him and his Chief of Staff General Ivo-Thilo von Trotha, who appeared to be equally guilty.[9] At about the same time Eva Braun was phoned by Fegelein. "Eva, you must abandon the Führer if you can't persuade him to leave Berlin. Don't be stupid, it's a matter of life and death now!" Within the hour he had been brought back to the bunker, still in civilian clothes. Hitler told Bormann to hand him over to SS General Wilhelm Mohnke, to help the fight for central Berlin; but Bormann and Günsche—Hitler's personal adjutant—pointed out that Fegelein would just run away again, so the Führer ordered him summarily court-martialed and executed.

"Our Reich Chancellery is reduced to rubble," wrote Bormann in his diary. "*'On dagger's edge the world now stands'!* Treason and treachery by Himmler—unconditional surrender—announced abroad. Fegelein disgraced—the coward tried to clear out of Berlin in civilian clothes!" Hitler, reeling with suspicion, saw this as the origin of Steiner's failure too. Perhaps at this very moment Himmler was plotting to kill or kidnap him? Suddenly he mistrusted the cyanide capsules supplied by the SS's Dr. Stumpfegger. He sent for Professor Werner Haase from the Voss Bunker operating theater and ordered him to test a sample capsule on Blondi—the largest animal available in the shelter. The dog's jaws were forced

[9]It is hard to fault Dönitz's opinion that Heinrici and Trotha "should have been court-martialed, not just dismissed"; Keitel was surprised to find that Trotha gravitated to Speer's staff on his arrival in Flensburg.

open and an ampoule was broken inside them with pliers; a bitter almond smell wafted toward the expressionless Führer; the dog howled briefly and then stiffened. A short council followed on the best methods of suicide; then Hitler handed ampoules to the rest of his staff, apologizing for being unable to offer them no kinder farewell gift.

More Russian tanks were reported massing south of Potsdamer Platz for the assault on the Chancellery. Hitler was informed that Wenck's guns were already shelling the Russian positions here. While Eva Braun, Goebbels, and Hewel hastily wrote last letters to their relatives, a chalk-faced Hitler slumped on Field Marshal Greim's bed. "Our only hope is Wenck. We must throw in every plane we've got to cover his breakthrough." An Arado training plane had just made a brilliant landing on the shell-cratered Axis; Hitler ordered the injured Greim to betake himself and his female admirer to Rechlin air base to command the Luftwaffe attack—and to arrest Himmler, if his treason were found to be proved. The woman became hysterical, and both begged to stay and share Hitler's end. The Führer dismissed them with "God protect you." Bormann and Krebs signed a joint appeal to Wenck to break through as soon as he could, so as to furnish Hitler with a basis for political maneuver. But Hitler himself was already writing finis: Himmler's treachery and the failure of the relief divisions left him with no desire to live on.

With the shelter's concrete membranes reverberating under the blast of Russian shells, and a table being laid for eight in his small study, he sent for his youngest secretary—the widowed Traudl Junge. "Perhaps I can just dictate something to you now." For a while Hitler stood at his usual midtable place, leaning on the now bare map-room table with both hands and staring at her shorthand pad. Suddenly he barked out: "My Political Testament" and began dictating without notes—part *pièce justificative,* part paean of praise for his brave troops' accomplishments against such odds. "From the sacrifice of our soldiers and my own comradeship with them unto death, we have sown a seed which one day in Germany's history will blossom forth into a glorious rebirth of the National Socialist movement and thus bring about a truly united nation." Even dictated under stress, and without notes, the document betrayed, at least in its drafting and construction, no trace of any mental disequilibrium. Hitler formally expelled Göring and Himmler from the Party and appointed Dönitz as his own successor; Speer was also sacked. Field Marshal Schörner—"the only man to shine as a real warlord on the entire eastern front," Hitler had sighed a day before—was appointed Commander in Chief of the German army.

It was about 2 A.M., April 29, 1945. Another notable event lay ahead, and this was at the forefront of Hitler's private testament, that he now dictated. "During my years of struggle I believed I ought not to engage in marriage; but now my mortal span is at its end I have resolved to take as my wife the woman who came to this city when it was already virtually under siege, after long years of true friendship, to link her fate with my own. It is her wish to go with me to her death, as my wife. This will make up for all I could not give her because of my work on behalf of my people." Hitler bequeathed his effects to the Party; or if it no longer existed, to the state. With neat realism he added that should the state also have been destroyed "further dispositions on my part would seem superfluous." He asked Martin Bormann as his executor and most loyal henchman to take care of his next of kin, his private staff and secretaries, his housekeeper, and Eva's mother.

Elsewhere in the shelter the small wedding party had assembled. A city official had been fetched from Goebbels's ministry as registrar, a slight, quiet-spoken man in Party uniform and a Volkssturm armband. Hitler signed with his most legible signature in months; Eva—wearing the black silk afternoon dress that was Hitler's favorite—signed more nervously. From time to time during the funereal wedding supper Hitler left to discuss with Goebbels and Bormann the constitution of the Cabinet with which Dönitz must carry forward the war against "the poisoner of all nations, international Jewry." Goebbels was included as Reich Chancellor, but Goebbels warned Hitler that he would not leave Berlin. Most of the rest were "moderates" like Seyss-Inquart, Schwerin von Krosigk, and Backe. Gauleiter Karl Hanke, still defending his embattled Breslau, was to replace Himmler as Reichsführer SS and chief of police.

Bormann, the new Party minister, was still transmitting strongly worded messages to Dönitz at Flensburg. "Foreign press reports fresh treason. The Führer expects you to strike like lightning and tough as steel against every traitor in north zone. Without fear or favor. Schörner, Wenck, and rest must prove their loyalty to the Führer by fastest relief of Führer. Bormann." In his diary he recorded Himmler's treason, Hitler's wedding, and the dictating of the political and private testaments. "The traitors Jodl, Himmler, and Steiner are abandoning us to the Bolsheviks! Yet another heavy barrage! Enemy reports state Americans penetrated Munich." By 4 A.M. Frau Junge had finished typing the testaments in triplicate (Hitler wanted to make certain that one copy reached the outside world). Hitler himself was still reminiscing softly with Goebbels about the exhilarating struggle for power and empire which was now approaching its end. Death would be a merciful release—and all the easier now that he had been betrayed by so many of the living.

Hitler's conferences over the next thirty-six hours were irregular and brief, for a Stygian information blackout was descending: his armies were silent and for days he had seen no diplomatic cables. The street fighting in Berlin could be followed only by ringing up telephone numbers at random. Often Russian voices answered. During the night, rain had grounded the OKW's aerial-carrying balloon, so VHF radiotelephone contact was interrupted. At noon on April 29, Jodl reported briefly that Wenck was at a standstill, but at 12:50 P.M. the VHF channel again went dead.

From now on the enemy news bulletins provided Hitler's main information on his own armies. Italian radio was monitored describing the scene as the corpses of Mussolini and a dozen other Fascist leaders "shot in the back" were strung up at the Standard Oil station in a Milan square. Admiral Voss signaled from the shelter to Dönitz at 4 P.M.: "All contact with army authorities outside cut off. Urgently request information on fighting outside Berlin via naval signals channel." Hitler's now idle liaison staff began edging toward the exits. Krebs's aide, Captain Gerhardt Boldt, suggested that he and two fellow officers attempt to contact the Twelfth Army. Hitler willingly dispatched them. "My regards to Wenck—and tell him to hurry, or it'll be too late!" The three sets of testaments were entrusted to three other hardy souls who were ordered to smuggle them out to Dönitz, Schörner, and to the Berghof. General Burgdorf wrote to Schörner: "The testament is to be published as soon as the Führer so orders or his death is confirmed."

Heavy fighting was going on at the Anhalt railroad station. With the tattered street map in his hand, Hitler spoke to his chauffeur, Erich Kempka, who had driven him on so many historic journeys since 1933. Kempka told him his motor pool was ferrying supplies to the troops guarding the Chancellery, from the Brandenburg Gate to Potsdamer Platz: "Their courage is exceptional. They're waiting for General Wenck's relief columns to arrive." Hitler calmly responded, "We're all waiting for Wenck." In his study he wrote a last letter to Keitel: the fight would soon end, he would commit suicide, and Dönitz would succeed him as Reich President; Keitel was to support the admiral to the end. "My people and Wehrmacht have given their all in this long hard struggle. The sacrifice has been immense. Many people have abused my trust in them. Disloyalty and betrayal have undermined our resistance throughout this war. This was why it was not granted to me to lead my people to victory." He refused to believe that such great sacrifice could have been in vain. "The aim must still be to win territory in the east for the German people."

The Russians were pushing down Saarlandstrasse and Wilhelmstrasse and were nearly at the air ministry. At 7:52 P.M. Hitler signaled five urgent questions to Jodl. "I am to be informed at once: 1. Where are Wenck's spearheads? 2. When do they attack? 3. Where is the Ninth Army? 4. In which direction is Ninth Army breaking through? 5. Where are Holste's spearheads?" Hours passed without any answer. Bormann issued two signals. The first reflected the ugly atmosphere of the bunker and read: "Our own impression is increasingly clear that for many days the divisions in Berlin battle zone have been marking time instead of hacking-out the Führer. We only receive information supervised, suppressed, or doctored by Teilhaus [Keitel]. We can only transmit via Teilhaus. Führer orders you to take rapid and ruthless action against all traitors." The second signal was briefer: "The Führer's alive and directing defense Berlin."

At the last battle conference on the twenty-ninth, General Weidling announced that there was heavy fighting at the nearby Potsdam Station. There were no bazookas left. Tanks could no longer be repaired. He predicted that the fighting would end within twenty-four hours. A long silence followed this. Hitler wearily asked Mohnke, the Citadel commandant, if he agreed; Mohnke said he did. With great effort, Hitler lifted himself from his chair and turned to go. Weidling asked what his troops should do when their ammunition ran out. Hitler replied, "I cannot permit the *surrender* of Berlin. Your men will have to break out in small groups." He restated this in a letter to Weidling and Mohnke during the night. Soon after, he received Keitel's telegram replying to his questions. It left no hope whatever that Berlin would be relieved. "1. Wenck's spearhead is stalled south of Schwielow lake. 2. Twelfth Army is therefore unable to continue attack to Berlin. 3. Bulk of Ninth Army encircled. 4. Holste's Corps forced onto defensive."

At Eva's suggestion, all the women in the Chancellery shelters—refugees fleeing the Russians, nurses from the Voss Bunker hospital, cooks, and officers' wives—were brought to one of the passages. His eyes bleary and unseeing, Hitler went and shook hands with them and spoke a few words in a low voice to each. One of the nurses began a hysterical speech, insisting that the Führer would bring them victory after all, but Hitler brusquely silenced her. "One must accept one's fate like a man." He knew he had taken a deliberate gamble by staying in Berlin; his gamble had failed. By morning, on April 30, 1945, he had decided to die at 3 P.M.

He shaved and dressed as punctiliously as ever, donning the olive-green shirt, and black shoes, socks, and trousers for the last time. Eva was pale but composed; she wore a blue dress with white trimmings and a favorite gold bracelet set with a green jewel which "meant a lot" to her. The Russians were now fighting in the subway tunnels under Friedrichstrasse and Vossstrasse; they were at Weidendamm bridge and on the edge of Potsdamer Platz, where a counterattack had begun.

Hitler sent for Bormann and then for Otto Günsche, his personal adjutant. He told them he and his wife would commit suicide that afternoon; Günsche was to ensure that both were really dead—by delivering coups de grâce if necessary—and then burn both bodies to ashes. "I would not want my body put on display in some waxworks in the future." His shelter was to remain intact. "I want the Russians to realize that I stayed here to the very last moment." Choking with emotion, Günsche replied, "Jawohl, mein Führer. I will see to it." Frau Goebbels sank to her knees and pleaded with him to stay, but he gently raised her and explained that his death was necessary to remove the last obstacle in Dönitz's path, if Germany was to be saved. His female staff was assembled, and a last lunch was taken together. When he walked through the bunker for the last time to say farewell, accompanied by Eva, he probably noticed a handful of officers of his escort waiting with two stretchers near the exit staircase.

It was about three-thirty when Hitler and Eva withdrew into the little green-and-white tiled study. Hitler closed the double doors, leaving Goebbels, Krebs, Burgdorf, and Bormann in the conference room. The doors sealed out all sounds but the murmur of the ventilation plant and the echoing explosion of shells. Eva sat on the narrow couch, kicked off her shoes, and swung her legs up onto the faded blue and white upholstery beside her. Hitler sat next to her, with his mother's photograph to his right and the portrait of Frederick the Great frowning down in front of him. They unscrewed the brass casings—like lipstick containers—and extracted thc thin glass phials with their amber liquid content. Eva bit the glass and sank her head on his shoulder. Her knees drew up sharply in agony. Controlling his trembling hand, Adolf Hitler raised the heavy 7.65-millimeter Walther to his right temple, clenched his teeth on the phial in his mouth, and squeezed the trigger.

A Select Bibliography of Published Literature on Hitler

ABETZ, OTTO. *Das offene Problem* (Löln, 1951).
ADÁM, MAGDA (ed., with G. Juhász, L. Kerekes). *Allianz Hitler–Horthy–Mussolini. Dokumente zur ungarischen Aussenpolitik* (Budapest, 1966).
ALFIERI, DINO. *Deux dictateurs face à face* (Paris, 1948).
ANFUSO, FILIPPO. *Roma–Berlino–Salò* (Italy, 1950).
ASSMANN, HEINZ. *Deutsche Schicksalsjahre* (Wiesbaden, 1951).
AUSWÄRTIGES AMT, Berlin. *Weissbuch Nr. 3—Polnische Dokumente zur Vorgeschichte des Krieges* (Berlin, 1940).
______. *Weissbuch Nr. 4—Dokumente zur englische-französischen Politik der Kriegsausweitung* (Berlin, 1940).
______. *Weissbuch Nr. 5—Weitere Dokumente zur Kriegsausweiterungspolitik der Westmächte. Die Generalstabsbesprechungen Englands und Frankreichs mit Belgien und den Niederländen* (Berlin, 1940)
______. *Weissbuch Nr. 6—Die Geheimakten des französischen Generalstabes* (Berlin, 1940).
______. *Weissbuch Nr. 7—Dokumente zum Konflikt mit Jugoslawien und Griechenland* (Berlin, 1941).
______. *Weissbuch Nr. 8—Dokumente über die Alleinschuld Englands am Bombenkrieg gegen die Zivilbevölkerung* (Berlin, 1943).
BAUR, HANS. *Ich flog Mächtige der Erde* (Kempten, 1956).
BAYLE, FRANCOIS. *Croix gammée contre caducée. Les experiences humanies en Allemagne pendant la deuxième guerre mondiale* (Berlin & Neustadt/Pfalz, 1950).
BEST, S. PAYNE. *The Venlo Incident* (London, 1950).
BEZYMENSKI, LEV. *Der Tod des Adolf Hitler* (Hamburg, 1968).
______. *Die letzten Notizen von Martin Bormann* (Stuttgart, 1974).
______. *Sonderakte Barbarossa* (Stuttgart, 1968).
BLAU, GEORGE E. *The German Campaign in the Balkans, Spring 1941* (Washington, 1953).
______. *The German Campaign in Russia, Planning and Operations (1940–1942)* (Washington, 1955).
BOELCKE, WILLI A. *Kriegspropaganda 1939–1941* (Stuttgart, 1966).
______. *Deutschlands Rüstung im Zweiten Weltkrieg* (Frankfurt, 1969).
______. *Wollt Ihr den totalen Krieg?* (Stuttgart, 1967).
BOLDT, G. *Die letzten Tage der Reichskanzlei* (Hamburg, 1947).
BONDY, L. W. *Racketeers of Hatred. Julius Streicher and the Jew-Baiters' International* (London, 1946).
BOR, PETER. *Gespräche mit Halder* (Wiesbaden, 1950).

BORMANN, MARTIN. *The Bormann Letters* (London, 1954).
BRITISH AIR MINISTRY. *The Rise and Fall of the German Air Force (1933–1945)* (London, 1948).
BROSZAT, MARTIN. *Nationalsozialistische Polenpolitik 1939–1945* (Stuttgart, 1961).
BUCHHEIM, HANS. *Anatomie des SS-Staates* (Freiburg i.Br., 1965).
BULLITT, ORVILLE H. *For the President* (Boston, 1972).
BURDICK, CHARLES. *Germany's Military Strategy and Spain in World War II* (Syracuse, N.Y., 1968).
BUTLER, J. R. M. *Grand Strategy,* Vol. 2 (London, H.M.S.O.).
CAVALLERO, UGO. *Diario* (Rome, 1948).
CHURCHILL, W. S. *The Second World War,* Vols. 1–6 (London, 1948–54).
COLLIER, BASIL. *The Defence of the United Kingdom* (London, H.M.S.O., 1957).
CSIMA, JANOS. *Adalékok a Horthy hadsereg szervezetének és haborús tevékenységének tanulmányozásához 1938–1945* (Budapest, 1961).
DEAKIN, F. W. *The Brutal Friendship. Mussolini, Hitler, and the Fall of Italian Fascism* (New York, 1962).
DETWILER, D. S. *Hitler, Franco und Gibraltar* (Wiesbaden, 1962).
DIETRICH, OTTO. *Zwölf Jahre mit Hitler* (Köln, 1955).
DILKS, DAVID (ed.). *The Diaries of Sir Alexander Cadogan 1938–1945* (London, 1971).
Documents on British Foreign Policy (London, H.M.S.O.)
Documents Diplomatiques Français 1932–1939, Vols. 3–6 (Paris, 1968–70).
Documenti Diplomatici Italiani (Rome, 1954 *et seq.*).
Documents on German Foreign Policy (London, H.M.S.O.)
DOMARUS, MAX. *Hitler—Reden und Proklamationen 1932–1945,* Vols. 1, 2 (Neustadt and. Aisch, 1962–63).
DÖNITZ, KARL. *Zehn Jahre und Zwanzig Tage* (Bonn, 1958).
ERICKSON, JOHN. *The Soviet High Command* (London, 1962).
FABRY, PHILIPP W. *Die Sowjetunion und das Dritte Reich* (Stuttgart, 1971).
FENYO, MARIO D. *Hitler, Horthy and Hungary* (New Haven, 1972).
FOOT, M. R. D. *S.O.E. in France* (London, H.M.S.O., 1966).
Foreign Relations of the United States (Washington, D.C.).
FRANK, K. H. *Confessions of Karl-Hermann Frank* (Prague, 1946).
FRIESSNER, HANS. *Verratene Schlachten, die Tragödie der deutschen Wehrmacht in Rumänien und Ungarn* (Hamburg, 1956).
GOEBBELS, JOSEPH. *Tagebücher aus den Jahren 1942–1943* (Zürich, 1948).
GÖRLITZ, WALTER (ed.). *Generalfeldmarschall Keitel—Verbrecher oder Offizier* (Göttingen, 1961).
GREINER, HELMUTH. *Die Oberste Wehrmachtführung 1939–1943* (Wiesbaden, 1951).
GROSCURTH, HELMUTH. *Tagebücher eines Abwehroffiziers 1938–1940* (Stuttgart, 1970).
GUDERIAN, HEINZ. *Erinnerungen eines Soldaten* (Heidelberg, 1951).
HAGEN, HANS W. *Zwischen Eid und Befehl* (München, 1959).
HALDER, FRANZ. *Kriegstagebuch 1939–1942,* Vols. 1–3 (Stuttgart, 1962–64).
HASSELL, ULRICH VON. *Vom andern Deutschland, Tagebüchern 1938–1944* (Frankfurt, 1964).
HEDIN, SVEN. *Ohne Auftrag in Berlin* (Buenos Aires, 1949).
HEIBER, HELMUT (ed.). *Hitlers Lagebesprechungen, Die Protokollfragmente seiner militärischen Konferenzen 1942–1945* (Stuttgart 1962).
———. *Reichsführer! Briefe an und von Himmler* (Stuttgart, 1968).
HESSE, FRITZ. *Das Spiel um Deutschland* (Munich, 1953).
HILGER, GUSTAV. *Wir und der Kreml* (Frankfurt, 1956).
HILL, LEONIDAS E. (ed.). *Die Weizsäcker Papiere 1933–1950.*
HILLGRUBER, ANDREAS. *Staatsmänner und Diplomaten bei Hitler 1939–1941* (Frankfurt, 1967); Vol. 2: 1942–1944 (Frankfurt, 1970).

———. *Hitler, König Carol und Marschall Antonescu* (Wiesbaden, 1954).
HITLER, ADOLF. *Hitlers Zweites Buch* (Stuttgart, 1961).
———. *Mein Kampf* (Munich, 1936).
HOENSCH, JÖRG K. *Die Slowakei und Hitlers Ostpolitik* (Cologne & Graz, 1965).
HOFFMANN, PETER. *Widerstand, Staatsstreich, Attentat* (Munich, 1969).
HUBATSCH, WALTHER. *Hitlers Weisungen für die Kriegführung 1939–1945* (Frankfurt, 1962).
———. *Weserübung. Die deutsche Besetzung von Dänemark und Norwegen* 1940 (Göttingen, 1960).
JÄCKEL, EBERHARD. *Frankreich in Hitlers Europa* (Stuttgart, 1966).
JACOBSEN, HANS-ADOLF. *Fall Gelb* (Wiesbaden, 1957).
KEHRIG, MANFRED. *Stalingrad. Analyse und Dokumentation einer Schlacht* (Stuttgart, 1975).
KEHRL, HANS. *Krisenmanager im Dritten Reich* (Düsseldorf, 1973).
KEMPKA, ERICH. *Ich habe Adolf Hitler verbrannt* (Munich, 1948).
KESSELRING, ALBERT. *Soldat bis zum Letzten Tag* (Bonn, 1953).
KLEE, K. *Das Unternehmen Seelöwe* (Göttingen, 1958).
KLEIST, PETER. *Zwischen Hitler und Stalin 1939–1945* (Bonn, 1950).
KLINK, ERNST. *Das Gesetz des Handelns. Die Operation Zitadelle 1943* (Stuttgart, 1966).
KOLLER, KARL. *Der letzte Monat* (Mannheim, 1949).
KOTZE, HILDEGARD VON (ed.). *Es spricht der Führer* (Gütersloh, 1966).
KRAUSE, KARL-WILHELM. *Zehn Jahre lang Tag und Nacht Kammerdiener bei Adolf Hitler* (Hamburg, 1949).
KRECKER, LOTHAR. *Deutschland und die Türkei im Zweiten Weltkrieg* (Frankfurt, 1964).
Kriegstagebuch des Oberkommandos der Wehrmacht (Wehrmachtführungsstab) 1940–1945, Vols. 1–4 (Frankfurt, 1965, 1963, 1963, 1961).
LASCH, OTTO. *So fiel Königsberg* (München, 1958).
LIDDELL HART, SIR BASIL (ed.). *The Rommel Papers* (London, 195).
———. *The Other Side of the Hill* (London, 1948)
LOSSBERG, BERNHARD VON. *Im Wehrmachtführungsstab* (Hamburg, 1949).
LÜDDE-NEURATH, W. *Regierung Dönitz* (Berlin, 1964).
LUTHER, HANS. *Der französische Widerstand gegen die deutsche Besatzungsmacht und seine Bekämpfung* (Tübingen, 1957).
MACARTNEY, C. A. *October Fifteenth, a History of Modern Hungary 1929–1945*, Vols. 1–2 (Edinburgh, 1956–57).
MANSTEIN, ERICH VON. *Verlorene Siege* (Bonn, 1955).
MARTIN, BERND. *Deutschland und Japan im Zweiten Weltkrieg* (Göttingen, 1969).
———. *Friedensinitiativen und Machtpolitik im Zweiten Weltkrieg 1939–1942* (Düsseldorf, 1974).
MEISSNER, OTTO. *Staatssekretär unter Ebert–Hindenburg–Hitler* (Hamburg, 1950).
Militärgeschichtliches Forschungsamt: Operationsgebiet östliche Ostsee und der Finnisch-Baltische Raum 1944 (Stuttgart, 1961).
MILWARD, ALAN S. *The German Economy at War* (London, 1965).
MOELLHAUSEN, EITEL FRIEDRICH. *Die gebrochene Achse* (Alfeld, 1949).
Monatshefte für Auswärtige Politik, Bd. VII (1940).
MÜLLER, KLAUS-JÜRGEN. *Das Heer und Hitler* (Stuttgart, 1969).
NEUBACHER, HERMANN. *Sonderauftrag Südost 1940–1945* (Göttingen, 1956).
NEVAKIVI, JUKKA. *Apu jota ei pyydetty* (Helsinki, 1972).
ORLOW, DIETRICH. *The Nazis in the Balkans. A Case Study of Totalitarian Politics* (Pittsburgh, 1968).
OVEN, WILFRIED VON. *Mit Goebbels bis zum Ende*, Vols. 1–2 (Buenos Aires, 1949).
OVERSTRAETEN, GENERAL VAN. *Albert I–Leopold III* (Brussels, no year).
PAPEN, FRANZ VON. *Der Wahrheit eine Gasse* (Munich, 1952).

PHILIPPI, ALFRED (FERDINAND HEIM). *Der Feldzug gegen Sowjetrussland 1941–1945* (Stuttgart, 1962).
PICKER, HENRY. *Hitlers Tischgespräche im Führerhauptquartier 1941–1942* (Stuttgart, 1963).
PLATEN-HALLERMUND, ALICE. *Die Tötung Geisteskranker* (Frankfurt, 1948).
Der Prozess gegen die Hauptkriegsverbrecher vor dem Internationalen Militärgerichtshof Nürnberg, 14. November 1945–1. Oktober 1946 (Nürnberg, 1947–49).
POULSSON, E. *Lehrbuch für Pharmakologie* (10.Aufl., ? Berlin, 1934).
PUTTKAMER, KARL-JESKO VON. *Die unheimliche See—Hitler und die Kriegsmarine* (Munich, Vienna, 1952).
RAEDER, ERICH. *Mein Leben,* Vol. 2 (Tübingen, 1957).
RAHN, RUDOLF. *Ruheloses Leben* (Düsseldorf, 1949).
Reichsgesetztblatt, Teil I (published in Berlin).
REINHARDT, K. *Die Wende vor Moskau. Das Scheitern der Strategie Hitlers im Winter 1941–42* (Stuttgart, 1972).
REITLINGER, GERALD. *Die Endlösung, Hitlers Versuch der Ausrottung der Juden Europas 1939–1945* (Berlin, 1956).
RIBBENTROP, JOACHIM VON. *Zwischen London und Moskau* (Leoni, 1961).
RINTELEN, ENNO VON. *Mussolini als Bundesgenosse* (Tübingen, 1951).
ROOSEVELT, F. D. *Nothing to Fear. The Selected Addresses of F. D. Roosevelt 1932–1945* (New York, 1961).
ROSKILL, S. W. *The War at Sea,* Vols. 1–3 (London, H.M.S.O., 1960).
ROTHFELS, HANS. *Die deutsche Opposition gegen Hitler* (Frankfurt, 1958).
SALEWSKI, MICHAEL. *Die deutsche Seekriegsleitung 1935–1945* (Frankfurt, 1970).
SCHENCK, ERNST-GÜNTHER. *Ich sah Berlin sterben* (Herford, 1970).
SCHEURIG, BODO. *Free Germany* (Middletown, Conn., 1970).
SCHMIDT, PAUL. *Statist auf diplomatischer Bühne 1923–1945* (Bonn, 1949).
SCHRAMM, E. (VON THADDEN). *Griechenland und die Grossmächte im Zweiten Weltkrieg* (Weisbaden, 1955).
SCHRAMM, PERCY ERNST. *Das Ende des Krieges* (Cologne, 1965).
SCHRÖDER, JOSEF. *Italiens Kriegsaustritt 1943* (Göttingen, 1969).
SERAPHIM, HANS-GUNTHER (ed.). *Das politische Tagebuch Alfred Rosenbergs* (Göttingen, 1956).
SIEGLER, FRITZ VON. *Die höheren Dienststellen der Deutschen Wehrmacht 1933–1945* (Munich, 1955).
SKORZENY, OTTO. *Geheimkommando Skorzeny* (Hamburg, 1950).
SPEER, ALBERT. *Erinnerungen* (Berlin, 1969).
STEINER, FELIX. *Die Freiwilligen* (Göttingen, 1958).
STOCKHORST, ERICH. *Fünftausend Köpfe—Wer war was im 3. Reich* (Velbert, 1967).
SÜNDERMANN, HELMUT. *Deutsche Notizen, 1945–1965* (Leoni, 1966).
A Szálasi-per [*The Szálasi Trial*] (Budapest, 1946).
TANNER, VÄINÖ. *Olin ulkoministerinä talvisodan aikana* (Helsinki, 1950).
TANSILL, CHARLES C. *Back Door to War* (Chicago, 1952).
THOMAS, GEORG. *Geschichte der deutschen Wehr-und Rüstungswirtschaft* (Boppard am Rhein, 1966).
TREVOR-ROPER, HUGH. *The Last Days of Hitler* (London, 1947).
———. *Hitler's Table Talk* (London, 1953).
TURNEY, ALFRED W. *Disaster at Moscow. Von Bock's Campaigns 1941–42* (London, 1971).
U.S. ARMY. *The German Campaign in Poland 1939* (Washington, 1956).
U.S. Strategic Bombing Survey: The Effects of Strategic Bombing on the German War Economy (Washington, D.C.)
VÖLKER, KARL-HEINZ. *Die deutsche Luftwaffe 1933–1939* (Stuttgart, 1967).

———: *Dokumente und Dokumentarfotos zur Geschichte der deutschen Luftwaffe* (Stuttgart, 1968).

Völkischer Beobachter, Berlin or Munich editions, 1939–1945.

VORMANN, NIKOLAUS VON. *Der Feldzug in Polen 1939* (Weissenburg, 1958).

WAGNER, EDUARD. *Der Generalquartiermeister, Briefe und Tagebuchaufzeichnungen* (Munich, Vienna, 1963).

WAGNER, GERHARD (ed.). *Lagevorträge des Oberbefehlshabers der Kriegsmarine vor Hitler 1939–1945* (Munich, 1972).

WARLIMONT, WALTER. *Im Hauptquartier der deutschen Wehrmacht 1939–1945* (Frankfurt, 1962).

WEBSTER, SIR CHARLES (NOBLE FRANKLAND). *The Strategic Air Offensive against Germany 1939–1945* (London, H.M.S.O., 1961).

WEIZSÄCKER, ERNST VON. *Erinnerungen* (Munich, 1950).

WILMOT, CHESTER. *The Struggle for Europe* (London, 1952).

WOODWARD, SIR LLEWELLYN. *British Foreign Policy in the Second World War* (London, H.M.S.O., 1962).

ZIEMKE, EARL F. *The German Northern Theater of Operations 1940–1945* (Washington, D.C., 1959).

ZOLLER, ALBERT. *Hitler privat. Erlebnisbericht seiner Geheimsekretärin* (Dusseldorf, 1949).

Notes

ABBREVIATION USED IN NOTES

AA Auswärtiges Amt, German foreign ministry. For a listing of Serials against NA microfilm numbers, see George A. Kent, *A Catalog of Files and Microfilms of the German Foreign Ministry Archives 1920–1945*, Vol. III, pages 525 *et seq.*

ADI(K) British Air Ministry's Assistant Directorate of Intelligence, interrogation and captured documents section.

AL/ File number assigned by CO Enemy Documents Section; document now in IWM

BA Bundesarchiv, the German federal archives, based on Koblenz (civil agencies) and Freiburg (military)

BDC Berlin Document Center (of U.S. Mission, Berlin)

—C A Nuremberg Document Series (*e.g.*, 100–C)

CAB Cabinet File (in British Public Records Office)

CCPWE U.S. Army Interrogation series (now in NA)

CIC Counter intelligence Corps of the U.S. Army

CIOS Combined Intelligence Objectives Survey

CIR Consolidated Interrogation Report (U.S. army)

CO Cabinet Office files

CP Cabinet Paper (British)

CSDIC Combined Services Detailed Interrogation Center (these British reports are still top secret)

D— Nuremberg document series

DBFP *Documents on British Foreign Policy*

DDI *Documenti Diplomatici Italiani*

DGFP *Documents on German Foreign Policy*

DIC Detailed Interrogation Center (*see* CSDIC)

DIS Detailed Interrogation Summary (U.S. army)

EC— A Nuremberg Document series

ED— An IfZ document series

ETHINT European Theater Interrogation (U.S. Army series)

F— An IfZ document series

FA Forschungsamt, literally Research Office: Göring's wiretap agency

FD— Foreign Documents, a British series of unpublished captured documents, currently held by Imperial War Museum, London

FIR Final Interrogation Report (U.S. Army interrogation)

FIAT Field Intelligence Agency, Technical

FO Foreign Office, London

FRUS *Foreign Relations of the United States*

GB— British documentary exhibit at Nuremberg

GRGG CSDIC document series

II H— German army document, in BA, Freiburg

IfZ Institut für Zeitgeschichte, Institute of Contemporary History, Munich

IIR Interim Interrogation Report (U.S. Army interrogation)

IMT International Military Tribunal: *Trial of the Major German War Criminals at Nuremberg*

KTB Kriegstagebuch, war diary of a German operational unit

Kl. Erw. Kleine Erwerbung, a minor accession by BA, Koblenz

L— A Nuremberg document series

46—M Interrogations at Berchtesgaden, 1945, now in library of University of Pennsylvania

MA— IfZ microfilm series

MD Milch Documents, original RLM files recently restituted by British government to BA, Freiburg; microfilms of them are available from Imperial War Museum, London, and soon from NA too. (The citation MD 64/3456 refers to Vol. 64, page 3456.)

MGFA Militärgeschichtliches Forschungsamt, German defense ministry historical research section in Freiburg

MI Military Intelligence branch (British)

MISC Military Intelligence Service Center (U.S. Army interrogations)

ML— NA microfilm series

N *Nachlass,* the papers of a German military personage, now held by BA, Freiburg

NA National Archives, Washington, D.C.

ND Nuremberg Document

NG— A Nuremberg document series

NCA *Nazi Conspiracy and Aggression* (U.S. publication of selected Nuremberg documents)

NO— A Nuremberg document series

NOKW— A Nuremberg document series

NS— Collections of Nazi documents in BA, Koblenz

OCMH Office of the Chief of Military History, Washington, D.C.

ONI Office of Naval Intelligence

O.QU. *Oberquartiermeister,* Quartermaster

OUSCC Office of U.S. Chief of Counsel (IMT)

P— MS series of U.S. Army: postwar writings of German officers in prison camps (complete collection in NA)

PG/ Files of German admiralty, now held by BA, Freiburg

PID Political Intelligence Division of the FO

PRO Public Record Office, London

—PS A Nuremberg document series

R— A Nuremberg document series (*e.g.*, R–100)

R Collections of Reich documents in BA, Koblenz (*e.g.*, R 43II/606)

REP Document series of Bavarian State Archives, Nuremberg

RGBl. *Reichsgesetzblatt*, the Reich government gazette

RH German army document in BA, Freiburg

RIIA Royal Institute of International Affairs, London

RIR Reinterrogation Report (U.S. Army)

RLM Reichsluftfahrt-Ministerium, Reich air ministry

SAIC U.S. Seventh Army Interrogation Center

SAO C. Webster and N. Frankland, *The Strategic Air Offensive against Germany*, 4 vols (London, 1961)

SS— BDC document series

T NA microfilm series. (The citation T78/300/1364 refers to Micropcopy T78, roll 300, page 1364.)

USNIP U.S. Naval Institute *Proceedings*

USFET U.S. Forces, European Theater

USSBS U.S. Strategic Bombing Survey

VB Völkischer Beobachter, the Nazis' national newspaper

VfZ *Vierteljahrshefte für Zeitgeschichte*, quarterly published by IfZ

WR *Wehrwissenschaftliche Rundschau*, German military science monthly journal

X— OCMH document series, now in NA

X—P DIC interrogation series (prisoners' conversations, recorded by hidden microphones, as at CSDIC's)

ZS— *Zeugenschrift*, collection by IfZ of written and oral testimonies

ZSg.— Zeitungs-Sammlung, newspaper cuttings collection in BA, Koblenz

Notes On The Text

4 TOTAL WAR

Trauma and Tragedy

p. 453 My chapters on Stalingrad are largely based on the records of the Sixth Army, of Gehlen's Intelligence branch, and the diary of the chief of army personnel; on the personal diaries of Richthofen, Milch, Manstein, and Generals Fiebig and Pickert (CO's of the Eighth Air Corps and the Stalingrad antiaircraft division, respectively); on the notes, letters, and manuscripts of staff at Hitler's HQ (Captain Junge, Below, Greiner, Engel, Scheidt); on Zeitzler's manuscripts written in about 1951 (N63/79, 80, and 101) and interrogations of Heusinger, Göring, Christian, and others; and on fragmentary documents like Hitler's war conference stenograms and Jodl's staff talks with the Japanese (naval staff war diary, annexes, Part C, Vol. XV). I was also fortunate to find among Milch's private papers the only copy of Major Werner Beumelburg's official manuscript on Stalingrad, dated June 8, 1943, and "based on official files and individual testimony."

p. 454 On the Heim affair, see Kehrig, *op. cit.*, pages 133 *et seq.*, citing the war diary of The Forty-Eighth Panzer Corps. Weichs dealt with it in his manuscript (N19/12). Heim's own version—in *Der Feldzug gegen Sowjetrussland* (Stuttgart, 1962)—is justifiably bitter. See also the war diary of the chief of army personnel, November 26, 1942, July 28, August 16, and September 23, 1944. By September 25, 1944, Heim was talking freely to his British captors about secret events at Hitler's HQ (CSDIC report SRGG 1063C, top secret).

p. 455 For the recriminations between the German and Romanian commanders over the collapse, see Greiner's unpublished notes of December 8 and 11; and Hitler's war conference on December 12, and talk with Antonescu on January 10.

p. 455 Hitler's signal was repeated by Weichs' Army Group B to the Sixth Army at 3:25 P.M., November 21 (BA file 75167/6). Richthofen noted in his diary that day: "Sixth Army thinks it can be kept supplied in its pocket by my Luftflotte. Trying all I can to prove to them it won't work out." See in general Colonel Johannes Fischer's semiofficial study of the Stalingrad airlift decision in *Militärgeschichtliche Mitteilungen*, 1969, pages 7 *et seq.* —which however relies heavily on the since-discredited "Engel diary" for its dates.

p. 456 According to Milch's diary, Colonel Artur Eschenauer—Jeschonnek's supply adviser—described to him how he had warned Jeschonnek that the so-called 1000-kilo supply container could only carry 500–680 kilograms of supplies, and the "250-kilo" container only 170 kilograms; their names derived from their *shapes* only. Göring refused to pass this fact on to Hitler (diary, May 21, 1946). See also Hitler's conference with Speer, January 18, 1943. The first reference to a "transport Schwerpunkt with the Fourth Air Force" is in the air ministry files on November 24, 1942 (MD17/3390).

On February 10, 1943, Göring admitted to Richthofen (diary) that "at the beginning of the Stalingrad episode he had played the optimist and supported the Führer in his decision to stand fast there." But when Richthofen asked Hitler the next day, Hitler replied that "he had promised [Sixth Army] the five hundred tons [daily], apparently without the Reichsmarschall's knowledge." In a speech to Luftwaffe generals on February 15, (Koller diary) Göring defended the Stalingrad decision. "Initially there was no reason to evacuate [Sixth Army], as there was justification for the view that the strong forces could hold out until they were relieved. But then fuel ran out in Stalingrad. 'Well, they could still have evacuated on foot!' But there was still the hope that Stalingrad could be relieved. Then the Italian front caved in, and with the breakthrough at Kolnikovo the front was torn wide open for hundreds of miles and was beyond repair. If we had fought much harder—in Stalingrad itself too—we would still be in Stalingrad today and it would not have surrendered. Paulus was too soft, didn't make a fortress out of this Stalingrad."

p. 456 From his comments to his doctors in 1944, and even as early as the war conference on December 12, 1942, it is clear that the twenty-four hour incommunicado train journey became a standby-alibi to Hitler for his defeat at Stalingrad. Linge's diary shows that an identical train journey, in November 1943, did indeed last from 4:30 P.M. on the ninth to 6:50 P.M. on the tenth; added to which, while Hitler arrived at the Wolf's Lair in the small hours of November 24, 1942, the OKW operations staff train did not arrive until a day later (according to the diaries of Greiner and one of the stenographers).

p. 457 An air force table of airlift sorties to the Sixth Army, November 24, 1942, to February 3, 1943 (microfilm T321/18/8846 *et seq.*), suggests that Greiner's figures are on the low side. Greiner's note on the food situation at Stalingrad echoes an entry in General Martin Fiebig's diary, November 26. "The Sixth Army does not take an unfavorable view of its tactical position, if it can get 300 cubic meters [about 210 tons] of gasoline and 30 tons of tank ammunition a day; food is said to be adequate for one month."

p. 458 Initially Hitler's optimism about Stalingrad was widely shared. The OKW diarist Greiner wrote in a private letter on November 27, 1942: "The Russian offensive still gives us fewest headaches, as we are entitled to the confident expectation that the situation can be cleared up in a short time. . . . Far worse is our situation in North Africa: everything depends on hanging on to Tunis and western Libya and Tripoli at least, and that's not going to be easy against the onrush of superior British and American forces from east and west." Jodl echoed this attitude to the Japanese on December 4. "Russian attackers will soon be deadlocked. Manstein is on the way. Perhaps next Russian attack on Italian army. German forces standing by. Situation in Russia indubitably more difficult. We now assume Soviet Union has some thirteen thousand aircraft and three thousand tanks; quality declining." (The naval staff queried whether "*thirteen thousand*" should not read "——— *hundred*"*!*) And the unusually well-informed Weizsäcker wrote in his diary, December 9: "From the eastern front too our military HQ is emitting favorable noises. Even Stalingrad, where some two hundred thousand men are cut off, no longer impresses our command: the view is that the eastern front won't suffer any grave strategic collapse this winter." On December 11, Ribbentrop cabled to all his missions instructions to refute enemy propaganda claims that Germany was badgering Japan to attack Russia in the Far East; until January 20, 1943, this was in fact true.

p. 458 Manstein's situation appreciation of November 24, 1942, is in BA file 39694/3b and in the war diary of Manstein's Army Group Don (N507/1). Under OCMH interrogation on September 10, 1945, General Heusinger confirmed that Manstein was initially of this view, that the Sixth Army's withdrawal from Stalingrad was *not* necessary. Major Engel's "diary" entry of November 26 ("Long discussion on Manstein's appreciation of situation, proposal to withdraw Sixth Army . . .") is further reason to treat this source with extreme caution—as Colonel Manfred Kehrig, the official West German historian (*Stalingrad,* Stuttgart, 1974), has also recently warned. Kehrig's history also uses the diaries of Count Johann von Kielmansegg, who headed Group East of the General Staff operations branch, and Major Thilo, who dealt with Army Group B affairs in that branch; but Kehrig did not procure either the *original* Richthofen diary or Greiner's papers, both of which I have used.

p. 459 A typed narrative of Rommel's meeting with Hitler and Göring is in the war diary of Panzer Army Africa (T313/472/1016ff); the shorthand record by his adjutant is in his papers (T84/259).

p. 461 On Abwehr subversive operations in North Africa, I used Greiner's record of Warlimont's conference on December 6, 1942; a memo by Canaris of December 14 (Ritter's AA files, Serial 1105); Lahousen's diary, December 21; and Canaris's memos for Keitel, dated December 9, and talk with him on December 11 (AL/1933). According to newspaper reports, U.S. courts-martial sentenced 174 Arabs to death for sabotaging railroads.

p. 462 Bormann's memo on Hitler's conversation with Anton Mussert on December 10, 1942, is in BA file NS–19/*neu* 1556. Keitel made similar remarks to Canaris on December 20 (AL/1933).

p. 462 Himmler's own handwritten agenda for discussion with Hitler on December 10 survives (T175/94/5330); against Item 3, "Jews in France," Himmler put a tick and the word *abschaffen*—dispose of. In his subsequent memo to the Gestapo chief, Müller, however, he used the milder words *verhaftet und abtransportiert*—arrested and transported away (T175/103/5558).

There are other illuminating references to the "Jewish problem" in Himmler's files at this time. On October 2, 1942, he wrote to Pohl, Krüger, Globocnik, and Wolff about his determination to extract the Jews from their protected status within important arms factories in Poland too. "It will then be our aim to replace these Jewish workers by Poles and to merge most of these Jewish concentration-camp workshops into a very few big Jewish concentration-camp factories, as far as practicable in the east of the Generalgouvernement. But there too the Jews must one day, in accordance with the Führer's wish, disappear [*verschwinden*]" (T175/22/7359). On November 30, Himmler sent to Gestapo Chief Müller a "very interesting [press] announcement about a memorandum written by Dr. [Stephen F.] Wise [President of the American Jewish Congress] in September 1942," and commented: "Given the scale of the Jewish migration, I'm not surprised that such rumors crop up somewhere in the world. We both know there's a high death rate among the Jews who are put to work. But you are to guarantee to me that at each location the cadavers of these deceased Jews are either burned or buried, and that nothing else can happen with the cadavers wherever they are. You are to investigate at once in all quarters to find out whether there have been any such abuses as the—no doubt mendacious—rumors disseminated around the world claim. All such abuses are to be reported to me on the SS oath of honor" (T175/68/4325). This letter was the purest humbug, and Himmler's suave reaction to two specific Allied press reports on the extermination of the European Jews proves it. On November 24, 1942, *The Times* (London) published a dispatch from the Jewish Agency in Jerusalem on the holocaust, partly fanciful but with an unmistakable hard core of truth. Himmler's office obtained it from Sweden and forwarded it with a noncommittal letter to the SS Reich Main Security Office in Berlin "for your attention" (T175/68/4406). On February 14, 1943, the same newspaper published a report received by the British Section of the World Jewish Congress from Central Europe, claiming that the extermination of Jews was being accelerated: Bohemia-Moravia was to be "*judenrein*" by March 31, deportations from Germany were continuing, and the mass exterminations in Poland were proceeding, in one place at the rate of six thousand daily. "Before being massacred, the Jews are ordered to strip and their clothes are sent to Germany." Rudolf Brandt, Himmler's adjutant, sent the news report to Kaltenbrunner's office. "On the instructions of the Reichsführer SS I am transmitting herewith to you a press dispatch on the accelerated extermination [*Ausrottung*] of the Jews in Occupied Europe" (T175/68/4398).

p. 464 Hitler's thought processes can be reconstructed from the stenogram of his war conference on December 12, 1942, and from Greiner's unpublished note of the same date. By this time, according to the diary of the Eighth Air Corps commander, Fiebig (December 11), Paulus's casualties were increasing at the rate of 1,000 a day; he still had 270,000 men, of whom 40,000 were infantry combat troops.

p. 466 I used both German and Italian accounts of the conference: the latter are in *comando supremo* files (T821/21/951 *et seq.,* and T821/457/409 *et seq.*). On December 19, 1942, Greiner noted: "Italians had urged some kind of arrangement with Stalin, but this is rejected by Führer out of hand, as even without weakening eastern front there is enough strength for the southern." As Weizsäcker commented (diary, December 25), it was hardly surprising that Ciano got this reply: "Talk like this can only be direct and without witnesses, and between the Duce and the Führer—not by Duce to General von Rintelen, Duce to Göring, Ciano to the Führer."

p. 467 Zeitzler nervously retorted to Richthofen: "But you were one of the first to advise us to hang on to the Volga.!" Richthofen denied this in his diary *("Impertinence.!").*

For Hitler's order to raise two SS divisions, see his adjutant Pfeiffer's teletype to Himmler, December 19, (T175/145/2277); Greiner's note, January 23; Wolff's memo, January 13 (IfZ, MA-333, page 8079); Himmler's letter to Bormann, March 13 (T175/70/6813), and speech, October 6, 1943.

Retreat

p. 471 From the diaries of Goebbels and Bormann, and Speer's Chronik (FD-3037/49) it is possible to reconstruct the origins of the formidable three-man cabal established by Keitel, Bormann, and Lammers late in 1942, to extract every last ounce of effort out of the nation—and in particular "one million new soldiers" (as Goebbels secretly announced at a ministerial conference on January 5). Goebbels was however given only a consultative role by Hitler's formal decree setting up the Council of Three on January 13, 1943 (IfZ, MA-470, pages 4910 *et seq.*) See also Speer, *Erinnerungen,* pages 265 *et seq.,* and the diary of Colonel Gerhard Kühne of the OKH.

p. 472 Despite the apparent entry in Engel's "diary" for December 29, 1942, there is no proof that Hitler ordered the Taman bridgehead held until one month later (see Greiner's note of January 23). According to the stenographer's diary, the special conference at which Hitler presumably planned the Kharkov offensive lasted from 10 to 11:45 P.M. on New Year's Eve.

p. 472 The number of transport aircraft on hand always vastly outnumbered those that actually flew, as Milch's records show. From January 1 to 14 the daily availability of Junkers 52s and Heinkel 111s was: 481, 473, 482, 485, 480, 467, 464, 437, 466, 470, 472, 466, 498, 539, to which were added 20 four-engined FW 200s and 28 big Heinkel 177s on January 9; but over the same period the sorties actually flown were only 78, 0, 97, 145, 53, 29, 63, 76, 102, 102, 95, 51, 69, 74.

p. 473 The cassette was handed to Göring on his splendid fiftieth birthday, January 12, 1943, by Keitel.

Hitler's private sources of Intelligence—like the letter from Winrich Behr to Colonel von Below quoted—must not be underestimated. Hewel will certainly have shown him the letter he received, dated January 9, from an arms specialist attached to Army Group Center. "The fighting is hard, perhaps harder than ever before, but even so the feeling is that the Russians are also at the end of their tether; it is a war of annihilation in which the one who keeps his nerve in the last quarter-hour will emerge victorious—and that will be us" (Hewel's private correspondence, AA files).

p. 473 On the Arctic fiasco, I used the naval staff war diary (especially January 23 and March 10, 1943) and the report in Raeder's personal file (PG/31762); and material from Puttkamer and Junge. For Speer's campaign against Raeder and the admiral's resignation, I used manuscripts in Raeder's files, Speer's note on his discussion with Hitler on January 3–5 (Point 78: Speer "reported in detail to the Führer the worries of the U-boat people that, owing to Admiral Dönitz's partly bad standing with the naval staff, he could come to harm"), and his frank postwar admission to Milch that he had caused Raeder's downfall (Milch diary, July 13, 1947). In fact, as Raeder wrote reminding Hitler on January 14, 1943, he had "thrice given Admiral Dönitz preferential promotion" during the war. See also Krancke's memo of February 13, 1943 (PG/31747).

p. 474 A month after Hitler's remark to Antonescu, Göring also privately admitted that while he was not worried about the situation "it's not quite clear to me how we are intending to end this war" (Weizsäcker diary, February 17, 1943).

p. 476 Dönitz's visit to Hitler on January 25, 1943, is confirmed by Bormann's diary and Puttkamer's memoirs; there exists no transcript, but his "connivance" at the scrapping of the capital ships emerges from a telephone call recorded in the next day's naval staff war diary.

The appointment of Milch to manage the Stalingrad airlift is described in his diaries, in an OCMH interrogation of Göring, July 20, 1945, in Greiner's note for January 16, 1943, and in Milch's unpublished manuscript memoirs. Speer announced to Central Planning on January 26 that Milch would be "away in the east for probably six to eight weeks" (MD 47/9236). A few days earlier, Hitler had ordered mass production of airdrop containers on the biggest scale.

pp. 476–77 Göring is quoted in Koller's diary, February 15, 1943.

pp. 477–78 On Hitler's new propaganda directive to Goebbels after Stalingrad see Goebbels's ministerial conference on January 24, 1943; Gottlob Berger's letter to Himmler, January 29, (T175/124/9596); naval staff diary January 24, Weizsäcker's diary February 12, and Goebbels's diary March 9, 1943.

p. 479 Allied "plans to invade Portugal" were presumably misinformation fed deliberately to Hitler. They are mentioned in the naval staff diary, February 4, and Hitler's meeting with Dönitz on the ninth, and in Canaris's diary February 9 (AL/1933), and a memo of the tenth in naval file PG/31747. Canaris admittedly saw no reason to believe them, but pointed toward Spanish Morocco (naval staff diary, February 13). Finally, on April 25, 1943, the naval staff diary sarcastically asked what had happened to the invasion so confidently predicted by the OKW in Portugal for the February 22.

p. 480 Traudl Humps, who had joined his staff in November and in April 1943 married SS Lieutenant Hans Junge, his manservant, she kindly made her unpublished memoirs available to me. The army doctor mentioned was Dr. Erwin Giesing.

p. 481 The material on Hitler's foreign policy comes from Ritter's AA file on Japan (Serial 1028), with its notes on Oshima's meetings with Hitler and Ribbentrop; from Weizsäcker's diary, January 27–30, and February 6, 1943; and from Ribbentrop's memoirs, page 263.

p. 481 Rosenberg's querulous conferences with Hitler are dealt with in Himmler's files, in Etzdorf's note of February 23, 1943, and in Goebbels's unpublished diary, February 16.

p. 482 The Russian document—originating from General Krupennikov, 1941–42 deputy chief of Soviet replacements—is in naval files, PG/32602–3; the statistics are quoted by Greiner in an unpublished note of January 8 and January 23; by Hitler to Antonescu on April 12, and by Gehlen's department to the war academy in a lecture on April 16 (BA file H3/319).

The quotation on Hitler's speech, February 7, 1943, is from Frau Ursula Backe's diary, February 8. There are similar words in a letter by an SS captain on Hitler's staff, writing on September 7, 1944, about the present trials of German fortitude. "On this point even the Führer yesterday said, 'Those who don't want to fight don't deserve to survive.' "

p. 483 Hitler's remarks are quoted in Milch's conferences soon after (MD35/4685 and /3226, and MD18/4735).

pp. 483–84 Richthofen was disappointed when Manstein told him the outcome of his talk with Hitler (diary, February 8, 1943). "Führer was calm and composed, Manstein visibly bucked up. Naturally no discussion whatsoever of another kind of command or command-organization, although this was just what Manstein was there for." (Manstein humanly gives the opposite impression in his postwar memoirs.) Richthofen advised the field marshal to keep a tighter grip on the panzer divisions, with short sharp forays, leaving behind their "dead wood" and carving up the enemy front piece by piece—copying Russian tactics; Manstein replied that his commanders would not oblige. Richthofen wrote: "I told him quite cheerfully that in my far-off youth I had once heard a rumor that in military affairs it was possible to issue *orders.*"

On Kluge's similar trip to Hitler, I used Schlabendorff's August 1944 testimony under Gestapo interrogation (NS–6/41), Zeitzler's manuscripts (N63/80 and 101), and Engel's notes.

p. 485 The quotation is from Hitler's secret speech on June 22, 1944 (NS–26/51).

p. 486 The late Fritz Todt—Speer's predecessor—had described the power radiated by Hitler thus, in a private letter to a professor dated September 30, 1933, which I found amongst Todt's personal effects: "The most beautiful thing about my work is that it takes me close to the Führer. I am convinced that any man who can spend ten minutes a week with the Führer achieves many times his normal output of work."

Strychnine

p. 489 The medical details are from interrogations of Morell, Giesing, and Gebhardt; Professor Ernst-Günther Schenck identified Prostakrinum for me from the 1939 *Gehe Codex* as a product of Morell's own firm, Hamma A. G., used to combat a hypertrophied prostate and general sex-hormone insufficiency in the male.

p. 489 The appointment book kept by Hitler's servants Hans Junge and Heinz Linge from March 22 to June 20, 1943, lay in a waterlogged condition in 1945, and ended up in the Hoover Library, California; it was restored at my request in 1965. I have deposited a transcript with the IfZ.

p. 490 The panzer Lieutenant General Karl Eibl (Twenty-fourth Panzer Corps), holder of Germany's second highest medal, lost his leg in the blast and died under the subsequent emergency operation (performed without anesthetic). Hitler did not tell Mussolini of the incident until April 23, 1944.

p. 490 Hitler's anxiety to spare his allies' feelings is plain from his order to Eighth Army, February 14, 1943 (in its war diary appendices, file 36199/9); from Ritter's memo to Ribbentrop, March 20 (Serial 1006); and from Scherff's letter to Jodl, June 25 (T77/1035/7945).

p. 492 Professor Charles Burdick wrote a convincing account of the German planning for an invasion of Spain, 1942–43, in *WR*, 1964, pages 164 *et seq.;* I also used the unpublished diaries of Greiner and Canaris (especially February 9, 1943: AL/1933) and of Richthofen, and Junge's memo on Hitler's conference of February 10 (PG/31747). Burdick does not mention the German-Spanish secret protocol of February 11, 1943; it will be found on AA microfilms of Ribbentrop's office files, Serial F3, page 0355.

p. 494 Hitler made his remark about Rommel at the conference on August 31, 1944 (Heiber, page 614); Goebbels quoted Göring similarly on March 2, 1943. Canaris also reported at length on Tunis after a visit there on February 27, 1943, is in file AL/1933.

p. 494 On the fighting in Tunis: Goebbels's unpublished diary, February 1943; war conference stenogram, March 4; Rommel's private letters (T84/R274); Kesselring's memoirs; the war diaries of the naval staff and OKW, and Greiner's handwritten draft for the latter; correspondence between Hitler and Mussolini (T586/405), and Ritter's AA files, Serial 5757. On March 15 Richthofen entered Jeschonnek's observations in his diary: "Rommel very low, nerves finished too. For the first time Kesselring's fixed grin was wiped off his face. Only the Führer is still optimistic. What's certain is that in the long run Africa can't be held for supply reasons."

p. 498 The undeniable restoration of the generals' faith in Hitler that spring emerges from Greiner's unpublished note of March 14, and from an entry in the anti-Hitler conspirator Hassell's diary two weeks later. "The generals are enough to drive you around the bend," Etzdorf had told him in despair. "Now that everything's going better again, everything's apparently okay: 'The Führer has turned out right again.'—Hopeless!"

My footnote is based on security documents in the BA Schumacher Collection, file 487, and Canaris's journey report (AL/1933). On the fabled assassination attempt at Smolensk, see Fabian von Schlabrendorff, *Offiziere gegen Hitler* (Zürich 1946), and Peter Hoffmann, *Widerstand, Staatsstreich, Attentat* (Munich, 1969), Chap. IX. In the conspirators' earlier accounts—*e.g.*, the British Consolidated Interrogation Report "The Political and Social Background of the 20 July Incident" (Secret, September 10, 1945) and the USFET interrogation of Baron Rudolf von Gersdorff himself (OI-IIR/34, dated February 18, 1946)—there are irritating discrepancies. Was their alleged bomb disguised as brandy (round) or Cointreau (square) bottles? Was the Abwehr explosive that Canaris mentioned used? or British-made Clam explosives with magnetic fastenings? Was the packet handed to Colonel Heinz Brandt to carry—he and Tresckow, the other main conspirator, died in 1944—or did Schlabrendorff himself "place it under Hitler's seat"? We can only speculate—particularly since Brandt in fact *never* flew in Hitler's plane, according to Schaub's manuscripts.

p. 500 The effect of strychnine and atropine is described in E. Poulsson's *Lehrbuch für Pharmakologie* (10th ed., 1934); it is only proper to point out that from the composition of "Dr. Koester's Antigas Pills" as described in the 1937 *Gehe Codex*, Professor Schenck —whom I consulted—doubted whether Hitler could have imbibed enough to have a serious effect. Hitler's doctors, going by the figures printed on the pillbox, thought differently.

p. 503 For the Abwehr Intelligence failures see Eberhard's diary, September 28, 1938; Colonel Ulrich Liss's remarks in Groscurth's diary, October 5 and 10, 1939; Tippelskirch's diary, September 19, 1939, etc.; but also Canaris's spirited self-defense in Goebbels's diary, April 9 and 11, 1943—he claimed that he had predicted everything in good time, but the truth had been withheld from Hitler. Not so.

p. 503 Canaris sardonically quoted Keitel's remark in a memo of October 23, 1941 (AL/1933). Lahousen heard Keitel say much the same that spring, as he recalled under interrogation. There is evidence that the Army's chief judge advocate, Karl Sack—one of the conspirators—gulled Keitel into believing that the SS was out to undermine the OKW's Abwehr, thus persuading him to stifle the Gestapo investigations.

p. 503 (footnote 6) Himmler's report on population movements dated January 20, 1943, is in BA file R 43 II/1411a. A major statistical study by his analyst, Dr. Richard Korherr, on the Soviet manpower reservoir definitely went to Hitler as well; it was retyped on the "Führer typewriter" and shown him in May 1943 (Himmler files, T175/54/6437 *et seq.*).

p. 503 Himmler had ordered Korherr to make a statistical analysis of the Final Solution, by letter of January 18, 1943 (T175/18/1557) explaining that Kaltenbrunner's office "lacked the necessary expert precision." The draft and shortened final reports, and Himmler's related correspondence, are on microfilm T175/103/5017 *et seq.*). As the ribbon copy of the shorter version is still in Himmler's files, it may not even have gone to Hitler. Nor did several letters which at about this time reached Dr. Hans Lammers alleging that Jews were being methodically exterminated in Poland (ND, NG–1903). At the Nuremberg war crimes trials, Lammers stated that he followed up these reports by asking Himmler. "Himmler denied that there was any authorized killing going on and told me—making reference to the Führer's orders—'I have to evacuate the Jews and in such evacuations there are . . . obviously fatalities. Apart from those, the people are being housed in camps in the East.' And he fetched a mass of pictures and albums and showed me how the Jews were being put to work in the camps on war production, in shoe factories, tailors' shops, and the like. Then he told me: 'This job comes from the Führer. If you think you must put a stop to it, then go and tell the Führer' " (IMT, Vol. XI, page 62).

Clutching at Straws

p. 508 For the contingency planning for an invasion of Sweden, see Wolf Junge's manuscript; the naval staff plans in its war diary annex, Part C, Vol. III; the naval staff war diary, October 23, 1943; and the OKW war diary.

p. 509 According to the manservant's register, Hitler saw Horthy three times: at 5:30 P.M. on April 16, and at 12:10 and 5 P.M. on the 17th; three corresponding records exist, by interpreter Paul Schmidt, but as both Horthy and Schmidt claim in their memoirs that the interpreter was absent during at least the first meeting, it is probable that as in 1944 (see Jodl diary, March 17, 1944) the conference room at Klessheim was bugged with hidden microphones.

p. 509 On the deportation of Hungary's Jews, see the AA's letter to Bormann, March 9, 1943 (Serial 5231 pages E310707 *et seq.*), and the Abwehr's security objections—in a letter to the AA—against allowing large units of Hungarian Jews to come near German military movements (*ibid.*, K206893). According to Schmidt's notes, Ribbentrop went even further than Hitler in one outburst to Horthy, exclaiming "that the Jews must either be destroyed or put in concentration camps—there is no other way" (a wording which caused Ribbentrop some discomfiture in the witness box at Nuremberg). Horthy copied the wording into his 1953 memoirs (page 254) but put them in Hitler's mouth! Secret Hungarian records do not echo the wording in such bluntness. In a draft letter to Hitler on May 7, Horthy included a sentence—later deleted—"Your Excellency further reproached me that my government does not proceed with stamping out Jewry with the same radicalism as is practiced in Germany." And in his discussion with the Hungarian envoy Sztójay a few days later Ribbentrop went no further than to remind him that Hitler had (in the summer of 1942) decreed that "by the summer of 1943 all Jews of Germany and the German occupied countries are to be moved to the eastern, *i.e.*, Russian, territories." Ribbentrop added that for security reasons Germany required her allies to conform—Mussolini had, for instance, just undertaken to intern the Jews in Italy (documents in National Archives, Budapest).

p. 510 Many sources exist highlighting the Rosenberg-Koch squabble over policies in Russia: the Goebbels diaries and Himmler files (T175/124 and /171); BDC file SS 981; Richthofen's diary, May 24, 1943; the stenogram of Hitler's conference with Keitel and Zeitzler on June 8; Etzdorf's note of April 13; Ribbentrop's memo on the Vlasov operation, April 6 (Etzdorf's file, Serial 1247); Bormann's memo of May 19 (BA file R 58/1005); Gehlen's files, containing Hewel's memo of May 24 (T81/219/9474 *et seq.*); the diary of Colonel Heinz-Danko Herre, of Gehlen's staff; Kluge's conference with General Reinhardt of the Third Panzer Army, June 17 (in the Army's war diary, annexes, H 12–33/5); Etzdorf's teletype to the AA, June 17 (Serial 364), and Lahousen's diary, June 21, 1943.

p. 512 The best history of "Citadel" so far is unquestionably the German official historian Dr. Ernst Klink's *Das Gesetz des Handelns* (Stuttgart, 1966); it supersedes earlier studies by Generals F.W. Hauck and Gotthard Heinrici in *WR*, 1965, and by Eike Middeldorf, *ibid.*, 1953. Klink kindly read and commented on my own "Citadel" narrative, which benefits from a number of sources not available to him—notably the Richthofen diary and the manservant's diary, which helps, for example, to pinpoint the date of Zeitzler's visit as April 21, 1943.

p. 513 On Model's visit: Ninth Army war diary, April 27–28, (BA, 34739/2) and annexes, Vol. VIII (35212/2); Model's appreciation, April 25 (35939/12); Junge diary, April 27, 1943; war conference, May 18, 1944 (stenogram); and Guderian's manuscript, March 1949 (IfZ, ZS–57).

Hitler's order of April 29 is mentioned in the OKW war diary, July 5; the resulting OKH order of April 30 is in the Fourth Panzer Army's war diary, annexes (34888/23) and the Ninth Army's war diary, annexes (34890/1); for the Luftwaffe view, Richthofen's diary contains an appreciation dated May 1, 1943.

p. 513 Guderian's notes on his tank conferences with Hitler are on microfilm T78/622. I also used Saur's testimony (FD–3049/49).

p. 514 Richthofen glued a lengthy memo on Jeschonnek's account of the May 4, 1943, Munich conference into his diary, May 25. On the fifth Richthofen himself wrote: "Rumor has it that some kind of conferences between Guderian and the Führer and Zeitzler have brought an element of uncertainty into opinions. Perhaps—and the interpolation of Guderian indicates this—it is hoped that minor technical improvements will result in major military changes. Of course this is pure rubbish—they haven't resulted in decisive victories in any war yet, but again and again they are tried for by us." On May 24, Richthofen flatly told Jeschonnek that the Russians would build far more by way of defensive positions in six weeks than the Germans could hope to increase their striking power.

There is no evidence that either Guderian or Manstein opposed the delay. In 1958 correspondence with Zeitzler, General Theodor Busse loyally quoted Manstein as telling Hitler, "The attack will be tough, but I think it'll succeed." But Kempf clearly recalled in 1958 telephoning Zeitzler three days later, furious at the delay; Zeitzler had replied that the general's call was "grist to his mill. He [Zeitzler] had desperately opposed any further postponement of 'Citadel,' but only Field Marshal von Kluge had supported him" (N63/12). This is supported by Kempf's memo on the telephone conversation in the Eighth Army war diary (36188/20).

p. 515 Hitler's words to Warlimont are quoted in a naval staff memo on Hitler's Berghof conference, May 1, 1943 (PG/31747).

p. 515 On Hitler's speech of May 7, 1943, I used the diaries of Junge, Bormann, Himmler, and Goebbels.

p. 516 From May 1943 onward, a diary, kept by Rommel, exists in British hands—as far as I know I am the first to have exploited it (AL/1708). For Rommel's fierce anti-Italian feelings, see also the Goebbels diary, May 10–13, and Rommel's letters of May 10–13 (T84/R274).

p. 517 Connoisseurs of British Intelligence operations will find the complete file on the corpse and its documents in German naval archives, PG/33216; they should also read the naval staff diary, May 1943, and microfilm T78/343. On May 25, Goebbels wrote in his diary that Canaris "energetically refuted" his hypothesis that the documents were deliberately planted. The duty stenographer who noted that Hitler shared Goebbels's skepticism —initially—was the late Ludwig Krieger, who described the scene in his private papers in 1945 and to me in a 1972 interview.

p. 518 Dönitz's famous admission to Hitler on May 14, 1943, that his U-boat offensive had collapsed, caused a sensation at the Wolf's Lair; see Goebbels's diary, and Rommel's diary and private letters (T84/R275/0324).

For Hitler's plan to strengthen the Balkans, see his war conference on May 20 (Heiber, pages 238 *et seq.*); the date of this is now firmly established by the manservant's diary.

p. 519 Captain Wolf Junge's handwritten account of Hitler's conference of May 15 is in naval archives (PG/31747). Rommel's diary also refers to it. "Following the situation report the Führer speaks on probable developments in Italy and Greece. There are prospects for my early employment."

p. 520 An early meeting with Mussolini was probably the topic raised by Hitler with Prince Philip of Hesse at 4:45 P.M. on May 20, 1943; the prince—who had married Princess Mafalda, daughter of the king of Italy, in 1923—was frequently used by Hitler as a special courier to Rome.

p. 520 Hewel's memo for Ribbentrop, June 25, 1943,is in Ritter's AA file (Serial 1462). See also Scherff's letter to Jodl, June 25 (T77/1035/7945), and the naval staff's indignant protests at aspersions cast by Hitler on German shortcomings in supplying North Africa (war diary, June 29 and August 5). Hitler even summarily deleted three pages of Goebbels's proposed speech of June 5 because they referred to North Africa (NS–6/129).

p. 521 The quotations are from Hitler's conference with Konstantin von Neurath—son of the famous pre-1938 foreign minister—on May 20, 1943 (Heiber, pages 220 *et seq.*); see also Rommel's diary. Winston Churchill alleged with his characteristic attention to accuracy (*The Second World War,* Vol. V, page 29) that "Neurath, the foreign secretary," was present.

p. 522 The Berghof menu is pasted into Eva Braun's album (NA, 242–EB–22–33a). In his unpublished diary Goebbels wrote on June 25 after a day with Hitler: "Little is left of the physical fitness we always used to marvel at in him."

pp. 522–23 Canaris's record of his talks with Warlimont and Rommel's chief of staff General Alfred Gause is in the Canaris diary file AL/1933, which unfortunately ends at this point; see also the Lahousen diary, June 4.

Correcting the Front Line

p. 526 Guderian's note on his June 16 conference with Hitler is in BA file H16/236. According to the naval staff war diary, June 25, the General Staff expected tank production to increase from four hundred to one thousand three hundred a month by autumn. Zeitzler's naval liaison officer emphasized the uncertainty being injected into the eastern front by the Mediterranean situation. But "the troops' morale is high, offset only by the bad news reaching them on the effects of enemy air raids at home" *(ibid.).* According to Goebbels's unpublished diary, June 25, Zeitzler had visited Hitler on the twenty-fourth —no doubt to agree to the final postponement of "Citadel."

p. 528 On the dispute between Frank and the SS, I relied on Nuremburg trial documents NG–3556, 2233–PS, NO–2202, and 437–PS; see also Hassell's diary, May 15, 1943, with its authentic detail by Frank's administration chief on the SS mass extermination of Jews in Poland. On Frank's meeting with Hitler on May 9, I used the diaries of Goebbels, Frank, and Bormann, and the latter's memo of May 11 (BA, Schumacher Collection, file 371). On May 31, Frank called a big security-conference in Cracow; Himmler agreed to send representatives, apologizing in a letter to Frank on May 26: "The evacuation of the last two hundred fifty thousand Jews, which will doubtless cause unrest for some weeks, must be completed as rapidly as possible despite all the difficulties" (T175/128/4157 *et seq.*).

p. 529 Himmler's talk with Hitler, June 19, 1943: see his files, T175/94/5096 *et seq.*, T175/40 and T175/76; and T175/94/5098.

p. 529 On the Schirachs' last visit to the Berghof (June 1943) I collected testimony from both Schirachs, Otto Günsche, secretary Christa Schroeder, Marion Schönmann—whose wording I have followed—Traudl Humps (who learned about it from her husband, Hans Junge), and the cameraman Walter Frentz; also from the Goebbels diary, June 25, 1943, and Table Talk, June 24 (evening).

Traces of Hitler's "scalepan" argument recur in Table Talks on September 14 and November 5, 1941, and in Goebbels's diary, May 23 and 30, 1942.

pp. 530–31 Professor Ernst Heinkel describes the aircraft designers' conference with Hitler on June 27, 1943, in his memoirs, pages 459 *et seq.* I also used Bormann's diary, Speer's notes, Messerschmitt's interrogations and personal papers (FD–4355/45, Vol. 6), and Wolf Junge's manuscript.

p. 531 The "Hektor" and "Josephine" reports (see pages 572–73) will be found in Baron Gustav Adolf Steengracht von Moyland's AA file, Serial 98. Controller of these alleged "agents" was Counsellor of Legation Karl-Heinz Kraemer, at the Stockholm legation; he has declined to identify them.

p. 532 Envoy Hans Thomsen's telegram of June 21, 1943, is in Steengracht's file, Serial 191. The "gentleman" was Peter Kleist (see his book *European Tragedy,* pages 144 *et seq.*) Subsequently the Russians claimed that Alexandrov—a former counsellor of their Berlin embassy, by June 1943 head of the German division of the Soviet foreign ministry—was in Australia in June 1943 (see *Izvestia,* July 29, 1947). Not so. The June 22, 1943, announcement was made in *Pravda.* The July 1 article was by N. Malinin in *Voina i rabochnii klass* (War and the Working Class).

p. 532 General Hans Friessner (Twenty-Third Corps) wrote the manuscript record of Hitler's speech which I quote. I found it in his personal papers, BA file H 14–23/1, pages 121–9. In his diary, Rommel wrote: "Evening, big conference in outbuilding [of General Staff HQ]. Every field marshal and field commander present, and some corps commanders.

Führer gives picture of the situation and the planned operations. Afterward a gettogether until 2:50 A.M." A short verbatim extract of the speech (pages 55 to 61 only) is on microfilm T77/778/0773 *et seq.* See also Manstein, pages 495 *et seq.*

The panzer general von Knobelsdorff was overheard on May 14, 1945, describing the evening to a fellow prisoner thus: "Hitler promised us the world there. . . . Naturally we never got it. Hermann [Göring] sat next to him, wilting more and more from one quarter-hour to the next until his face looked downright sheepish—a complete dullard. He kept eating pills and then perked up for a while. . . . We sat together with the Führer for a while, but Hermann went off with his Luftwaffe men" (X–P4).

p. 534 In fact about three *thousand* Allied ships were involved. Rommel's diary states, July 10, 1943: "Noon war conference with Führer. British and Americans landed on Sicily with paratroops and landing craft. Three hundred ships.—9:30 P.M. to 1:40 A.M. discussion with Führer."

p. 535 The view at Hitler's HQ was that Stalin's July 12, 1943, counteroffensive was a last desperate fling. Milch—who saw Hitler the next day—reassured his staff on the nineteenth: "The Russians have *got* to attack. They have no option. They have such ghastly domestic problems, and so little hope that things will get better, that they say, 'If we don't finish the war this summer and winter at the latest, then for me it'll be all over.' The Russians will not survive this winter as a fighting force—and that's definite" (MD22/6076). And see the food minister Herbert Backe's remarks, quoted by his wife in a letter to Heydrich's widow on July 25: "He says it's very important for us not to have a bad harvest in this critical year. America's harvest has failed; Russia is starving. Besides this, my husband thinks it good that the Russians are attacking—it's a sign of their weakness: they *have* to." Richthofen's words, written after Hitler's noon conference on July 28, are very similar (diary), as are Goebbels's that same day.

pp. 535–36 The captured letters are analyzed in a report of July 7, 1943, shown to Hitler (H3/644).

p. 538 Rommel's diary, July 13, 1943, encapsulates Germany's growing military plight. "Noon, Führer's war conference; ditto evening.—"Hermann Göring" Division has not met desired success in attack [in Sicily]. Syracuse occupied by British. Two battalions of enemy paratroops landed west of Catania destroyed by our own paratroops. Field Marshals von Kluge and von Manstein report to Führer, evening General Guderian too. Russians staging counterattacks. Model's [Ninth] Army can't keep up."

p. 540 There is a record of the talk with the Italian ambassador in Milch's files (MD53/1116 *et seq.*)

p. 540 Rommel's diary on July 16, 1943, reads: "At noon conference. Göring wants General Stahel as Commander in Chief [Sicily] and not Hube. I get Hube accepted and suggest General Bayerlein as his Chief of Staff. The Führer acquiesces.—Heavy tank losses on eastern front. The breach at Bryansk [Second Panzer Army] has been sealed off.—Phoned General Bayerlein, didn't reach him. Went over to Führer's evening conference. Hube is called on to operate offensively." And the next day Rommel continued: "At noon conference with Führer. Ambassador [Hans George] von Mackensen [Rome] with Führer. General Bayerlein expected in afternoon.—Situation in east for a time at crisis point, eases again. Russian attacks beaten back. Italy: British air raids. . . . 4 P.M.: summoned to Führer. Initially Admiral Dönitz, Field Marshal Keitel, General Jodl, and myself present; later General Bayerlein. Bayerlein not taking on new job as still ill. Colonel Kriebel is then proposed. I suggest von Bonin instead and he gets the job.—To Führer's evening conference."

On Hitler's mid-July strategy prior to Mussolini's overthrow, see his remarks to the Bulgarian leaders on October 18, 1943.

pp. 541–42 This fragment of Mussolini's diary, dated August 19, 1943, is in secret AA files, Serial 715, pages 263729 *et seq.;* for the official Italian record, see Mussolini's papers (T586/405/394 *et seq.*) and the records of the *comando supremo* (T821/251/955 *et seq.*).

p. 543 Himmler's Intelligence report to Bormann, July 19, 1943, is in the Reichsführer's files (T175/53/7178ff).

p. 543 For the Abwehr's mistaken belief that the Allies would soon invade the Balkans —which culminated in Hitler's directive of July 26, 1943—see the naval staff and OKW war diaries, July 28.

pp. 543–45 My narrative of events at Hitler's HQ is based on Milch's diary, on Admiral Krancke's reports (in naval staff diary), on Goebbels's diary, and on the stenograms of Hitler's dramatic war conferences on July 25.

"Axis"

p. 546 I drew on signals in the naval staff war diary's annexes, Part C, Vol. XIV (PG/32216), the diaries of Rommel, Richthofen, the OKW, and other sources complementing Josef Schröder's authoritative history *Italiens Kriegsaustritt 1943* (Göttingen, 1969).

p. 547 Himmler's telephone log shows that he telephoned R.S.H.A. chief General Kaltenbrunner at noon on July 28: "Reports from Italy.—Grab all dissidents.—Morale [after raids on] Hamburg."

p. 548 Rommel's diary expands on Richthofen's dramatic record of July 26, 1943. "12 noon land at Rastenburg [on return from Greece]. Drive to Wolf's Lair immediately. . . . Situation in Italy still confused. No news yet on how Mussolini's overthrow happened. On king's orders Marshal Badoglio has taken office as head of government. It's to be expected that despite pronouncements by king and Badoglio Italy will drop out of the war, or at least that the British will undertake fresh major landings in Upper Italy. . . . I'm hoping to be sent into Italy soon." See also the record of Hitler's conferences with Admiral Dönitz over these days.

Skorzeny himself described (in a 1970 interview) how he was picked by Hitler. Richthofen did not think much of General Student. "He's personally an absolute fool and hasn't the faintest idea of how to get on with his ('somewhat fantastic') mission, or what it's consequences may be" (diary, July 27). Captain Wolf Junge—Jodl's naval staff officer—also wrote fully about this episode in his unpublished manuscript memoirs.

p. 550 Junge described the huge relief created at Hitler's HQ by Churchill's gloating speech. The naval staff war diary commented, on July 27, that it was ideal for German purposes, and added the next day: "In comments on Churchill's speech the Italians point out that it has unmasked as pure hypocrisy the British claim to be fighting only fascism."

p. 550 On the German-monitored Churchill telephone conversation, see OKW war diary July 29 and August 3, 1943; and Himmler's telephone call to SS General Gottlob Berger at 11 P.M. on July 29 ("Churchill-Roosevelt conversation"). According to Sir Alexander Cadogan's diary, there had been a meeting of the Defence Committee at 10:30 P.M. that July 28: "Discussed armistice terms and Ike's mad idea of broadcasting a bowdlerized version. PM got Pres[ident] on the telephone and squashed latter idea. But Ike authorized to put out a proclamation. PM mainly preoccupied about our prisoners." Knowledge of this intercept was undoubtedly behind Admiral Hans-Erich Voss's warning from the Wolf's Lair to the naval staff on July 30 that the situation toward Italy was more acute "as there is further evidence that the Italian government is playing a double game." See also Rommel's diary, August 4, 1943.

The Americans were alarmed at Churchill's foolish noncompliance with telephone security rules. General Marshal advised Harry Hopkins that U.S. Army censors had listened in to one such recent conversation; while Hopkins had tactfully kept urging Churchill to guard his tongue, "the prime minister cited names and places in such a way as to create possible danger for himself and others." The U.S. Army warned that the Germans were known to be able to unscramble the radiotelephone (NA, letter from J. McCarthy to Hopkins, October 12, 1943, in Hopkins Papers, Box 136, Winston Churchill file.) Unfortunately no British or U.S. recordings of the actual conversations seem to exist, so we can only speculate on precisely what secrets were compromised.

p. 551 Rommel wrote with relish on July 30, 1943: "I'm going to enjoy this new job far more than the Southeast command. . . . We can guess what the Italians have up their sleeve now that Mussolini's resigned: they'll change sides, lock, stock, and barrel. Question is—will they find the actual courage to take the plunge."

For the faulty Intelligence on Italy, see the war diaries of the OKW, July 30–31, and August 3 and 5, 1943, and of the naval staff, July 29. On Canaris's role: Lahousen diary, July 29–August 3, 1943, and Walther Huppenkothen's 1945 manuscript "Canaris und Abwehr" in BDC files.

p. 551 Ribbentrop described his telephone call to Hitler in a later (December 30, 1944) talk with Ambassador Filippo Anfuso (in AA files). The Italian records of the talks with Keitel and Ribbentrop on August 6 are in *comando supremo* files (T821/251/777 *et seq.*).

pp. 552–53 Professor Hermann Giesler's record of the Führer's conference with Ley and himself on August 20, 1943, is in the present files of the Munich city planning bureau.

p. 554 Rommel commented on the Stalin rumors in his diary, August 9, 1943. "If they are founded on truth, they open up undreamed of new possibilities to us." Hitler's reflection is quoted from his conference with Dönitz a few days later.

p. 555 Rommel's letter commenting on Mussolini's departure from the European stage was written on August 6 to his wife (T84/R27/0352).

p. 556 Rommel's diary contains a complete account of the August 15, 1943, meeting at Bologna. (The Italian map was later published in *Das Reich,* October 10; and see the *Völkischer Beobachter,* October 23–24.) On August 16, Rommel noted: "General Jodl reports by phone from Sicily that by tomorrow provisionally 90 to 95 percent of the German troops will have been withdrawn." The evacuation was completed by 6:30 A.M. the next day, including all trucks and guns, despite the huge Allied superiority (see naval staff diary, August 20).

p. 556 Helmut Heiber wrote a fine study of King Boris's mysterious decease in *VfZ,* 1961, pages 384 *et seq.* The three German doctors are all dead—Eppinger and de Crinis as 1945 suicides and Seitz (as my researches in Madrid established) of natural causes there some years ago. The HQ stenographer Krieger recalled—in a postwar letter—that Hitler issued strict instructions to Raeder, Keitel, and the other prominent guests at the funeral in Sophia "on no account to accept food or drink offered to them there, but to feign stomach upsets and only eat the food they had brought with them from the Führer's HQ."

p. 557 Nonetheless Prince Philipp of Hesse retained his admiration for Hitler, despite his subsequent incarceration. He described under American interrogation (July 21, 1945) how Hitler had treated him almost like a son, spending hours every night talking with him of his plans for the reconstruction of Germany. Philip—who was Oberpräsident of Hesse-Nassau province—"had realized that he was probably in some sense a prisoner [at Hitler's HQ], and his urgent requests to return to his post when Kassel came in for heavy air attacks [on July 28 and 30, 1943] had been refused."

p. 558 The quotation is from Himmler's speech to Reich propaganda officials, January 28, 1944 (T175/94/4784 *et seq.*).

p. 559 The code name "Baroque" figures in Himmler's agenda for discussion with Hitler about March 17, 1943 ("Overall 'Operation Baroque' ") and in several telephone conversations, *e.g.,* with Kaltenbrunner on November 2, 1943 (T84/25). Himmler laughingly revealed the whole story in his speech to the Gauleiters on August 3, 1944 (see *VfZ,* 1953, pages 375 *et seq.*). Under CIC interrogation the Gestapo officials Walther Huppenkothen and Willi Litzenberg testified to Hitler's knowledge of the Himmler-Popitz rendezvous (which is also noted in Himmler's pocket diary, August 23, 1943). As Dr. Franz Reuter related in his monograph, "Der 20. Juli und seine Vorgeschichte" (in British secret files), Popitz spoke less than Himmler, who "seemed not satisfied at all with the outcome of the conversation." See also Goebbels's diary, September 23, 1943, and the Hassell diaries.

p. 560 The agent's message was cabled by Himmler's staff to Fritz Darges, Bormann's adjutant at Hitler's HQ, late on August 25, 1943 (T175/117/2393).

p. 561 In addition to the AA record of Hitler's talk with Antonescu, a Romanian version exists in Antonescu's files, "Conversatia dintre Domnul Maresal Antonescu si Fuhrerul Adolf Hitler" (ND, USSR–235).

p. 563 For the events of September 8, 1943, I used the diaries of Linge, Goebbels, the naval staff (and the latter's annexes, Part C, Vol. XIV), and the OKW. Hitler and Ribbentrop described the events—with Badoglio's and Roatta's manifold protestations of loyalty—frequently afterward, *e.g.*, to the Bulgarian envoy Sagoroff on October 6 (AA Serial 68, pages 49298 *et seq.*); to Saffet Arikan, the Turkish ambassador, on October 7 (AA Serial 5452, pages E366598 *et seq.*); and in Hitler's secret speech on January 27, 1944 (BA Schumacher collection, file 365). The actual timing of the Italian announcement clearly took Hitler by surprise. Himmler—as his diary shows—had flown away on leave to Bavaria that morning, only to be recalled by a telephone call from Hitler's HQ at 8:20 P.M., the very moment that Jodl's order was being cabled to the various HQ's: "Marshal Badoglio has confirmed accuracy of Allied radio broadcasts about Italian capitulation. Code word 'Axis' takes effect immediately" (T77/792/1641). For Field Marshal Kesselring the first sign that the betrayal was imminent was that morning's air raid on his HQ at Frascati, outside Rome: in a crashed Allied bomber were found target maps showing his and Richthofen's HQ's in such detail that official Italian collaboration was obvious. Besides, Rome's fire brigade was waiting outside Frascati just before the attack began—which did not prevent the villagers from losing many dead (the Germans alone lost ninety killed). See also Jodl's version of events, in his notes for a speech to Gauleiters on November 7 and in staff talks with the Japanese on September 29, 1943.

p. 564 The prince's arrest is described by Goebbels; and by Baron von Steengracht in an overheard conversation with Papen on June 27, 1945 (X–P 18); and by the prince himself under interrogation by the U.S. State Department.

Feelers to Stalin

pp. 565–66 On the East Wall controversy I relied on Speer's records of conferences with Hitler, and his Chronik; on Führer decrees in file FD–3049/49; on the naval staff war diary, July 19, 1943; on OKW staff papers on the wall's positioning, on microfilm T77/778; and on Field Marshal von Küchler's memo on his conference with Hitler on September 11, 1943 (Army Group North, war diary).

p. 567 Vice Admiral Wilhelm Meisel first recorded Hitler's hopes for an East-West split at the Führer's evening war conference on August 28, 1943.

p. 568 A report by Likus on Soviet feelers, addressed to Ribbentrop on August 9, 1943, is in AA files (Serial 146, pages 130779 *et seq.*). Kleist describes his contact with Edgar Klauss in *Zwischen Hitler und Stalin,* (Bonn, 1950). From Klauss's original documents now in possession of my friend and colleague Dr. Bernd Martin of Freiburg there can be no doubt that Klauss's Soviet contacts were genuine. Significantly, it was not until late September that these indirect German approaches were reported by the Soviet legation in Stockholm to their U.S. colleagues (see Mr. Herschel Johnson's telegram from there to Washington, September 29, 1943, in *FRUS,* 1943, Vol. III, pages 698 *et seq.*).

p. 569 Hitler's decrees carving up northern Italy will be found in file FD–3049/49.

p. 571 A number of entries in Himmler's telephone notes relate to problems with the Ciano family. After Himmler and Kaltenbrunner visited Hitler on September 15, 1943, the two SS potentates talked about "Situation in Rome. Commun[ists]. Italian guests; villa for Musso family. Jewish Question [in Italy]." And at 6 P.M. Himmler telephoned Hewel at Hitler's HQ: "Edda Ciano telephone [conversation] with Mussolini." On September 20, after talking with Kaltenbrunner about "Ciano family's behavior," Himmler jotted on his agenda for discussion with Hitler that evening, "Journeys of Countess [Edda] Ciano: smashing up furniture."

p. 573 (footnote) The air staff report exposing these phony "star agents" is dated December 14, 1944 (BA file RL2/547).

pp. 573–74 The narrative of the air offensive is based on unpublished documents in Milch's files, volumes 31, 39, 51, 53, 62, and 63; on Milch's secret speech to the Gauleiters on October 6 (T175/119/5054 *et seq.*); on Speer's notes on Führer conferences; on Hitler's war conference of October 4 and his remarks to the Bulgarian regents on October 18, 1943.

p. 575 The telegram from Consul Eitel Friedrich Moellhausen, October 6, 1943, is ND, NG–5027; Hitler's negation of the SS order is in Franz von Sonnleitner's teletype dated October 9, 1943. For the SS report on the roundup of Rome's Jews, October 17, see T175/53/7133.

pp. 575–76 At one stage in his speech of October 6, 1943—according to the wire-recording archived in Washington (NA, 242–299)—Himmler directly addressed himself to "You, Herr Reichsminister," which indicates that Speer was a listener. Few generals later admitted that they had known; perhaps they did not realize the enormity of what they were being told in such dry sentences. Field Marshal Weichs frankly told interrogators of the U.S. Seventh Army on May 30, 1945, that Himmler had once visited him in the Balkans and confirmed that the rumors were true—that the (unspecified) victims were loaded into railroad trucks without knowing that a sudden, painless death awaited them. "They are just criminals of whom we must rid ourselves," was Himmler's explanation.

p. 577 The fragmentary record of Hitler's remarks—in the war conference of October 27, 1943—was found by my Soviet colleague Lev Bezymenski in Moscow archives. Hitler had just had a long talk with Himmler, who had seen Schellenberg during the afternoon. Schellenberg's report on "MacEvan" is in AA file Serial 1755, pages 404620 *et seq.*

p. 578 Rommel himself wrote to his wife on October 26, 1943: "Anyway, he hasn't signed the order for the new job. . . . Perhaps I didn't inspire much hope that the position could be held. Perhaps my hesitation whether to take over the command was cause enough. Perhaps there are quite different groundss. So K[esselring] stays for the time being" (T84/R275/0379). And Richthofen added his own comment (diary, October 21): "Apparently Rommel's not getting overall command in Italy after all. Evidently made a bad impression during his report to Führer, from which he came back yesterday—an impression which doesn't surprise me."

p. 579 The case history of the Melitopol-Zaporozh'ye Line needs examining in detail, as it shows how justified Hitler's suspicions of his field commanders were. Kleist's Sixth Army had withdrawn to this line, which Manstein described as a "well-built position," but in *Verlorene Siege,* pages 537 *et seq.,* Manstein himself admits that Kleist was thrown out of the line "surprisingly rapidly" by the Red Army in October 1943. At the end of the year Hitler fulminated, "That was the spirit then—*Retreat!*... Everybody lost their nerve, even Kleist. *Everybody, retreat!*" In the same war conference (December 28) he scoffed "Nobody's going to maintain that this line here [forward of Melitopol] would have been tougher than that [the new line] or the entire front we have now [December]. But now from here down we have to hold this whole line now; while there we only had this little bit to defend. Then we wouldn't be having our Crimea difficulties either." Over the months that followed, Hitler learned the truth. Luftwaffe General Karl Kitzinger, an expert on lines of fortification, had offered to take over the job in 1943. The army had indignantly refused, saying that only Manstein's army group could do it. "The upshot was," snarled Hitler on July 31, 1944, to Jodl, "that nothing—nothing whatsoever—was done. Not one shovelful. The positions they claimed to have built from Melitipol to Zaporozh'ye were a lie from start to finish. They told me downright lies. They cheated me. There was nothing." (See Heiber, page 605.)

Hitler's letter to Antonescu, October 25, 2943, is in the marshal's papers (ND, USSR–240).

p. 581 Hitler's order to Rundstedt to reconnoiter a *rear* line in France was cabled by Jodl to the Commander in Chief West on October 31 (T78/317/1448); see too the OKW war diary. The teletype is entered under November 2 in the war diary of Commander in Chief West, but was not forwarded by Blumentritt to the army and corps commanders concerned until the eleventh. See too Hitler's conference with Jodl, July 31, 1944 (Heiber, page 594).

"And So It Will Be, Mein Führer!"

p. 583 On the Balkan situation: Weichs's appreciation of November 1, 1943, is in naval staff war diary, annexes, Part C, Vol. XIV (PG/32217); I also used the OKW war diary, Weichs's private diary (N 19/3), and the files of the German envoy at Zagreb, Kasche (AA Serial 1770), and interrogations of Dr. Hermann Neubacher, who later published an erudite history, *Sonderauftrag Südost 1940–45* (Göttingen, 1958).

p. 584 Much has been written about "Cicero." I have relied only on the contemporary records, in Cabinet Office file AL 2656, secret AA files (Serial 1553), and Steengracht's AA file on Turkey (Serial 61). There are cautious references to his work in the naval staff diary (*e.g.*, November 12) and Ribbentrop's discussions with Dobri Bozhiloff, the Bulgarian Prime Minister, and Oshima, and in Goebbels's diary, November 13 and 20, 1943. As the summary in Jodl's diary, February 1944, shows, the authenticity of Cicero's documents was accepted at every level right up to Hitler.

p. 585 On Hoth's dismissal: war diary of chief of army personnel, November 3, 1943. On January 7, 1944, Hitler remarked to Keitel, on the army's poor political record. "I hear hideous reports on this score. Worst of all, I don't mind saying, was how it was in Hoth's army: in his generals' presence Hoth constantly criticized all the *Weltanschauung*-measures. This is why the Fourth Panzer Army has made the worst showing" (NS–6/162).

p. 586 In Central Planning on March 1, 1944, Milch recalled: "On March 5 [last year] I stated to the Führer that there was already enough manpower in the army, air force, and navy for them to mobilize the necessary combat troops from within. In November the Führer ordered a census and found out that there are only 265,000 combat troops permanently at the eastern front. . . . Remember, I had that job at Stalingrad [directing the airlift to the Sixth Army in January 1943]: at Taganrog [far to the rear] there were 65,000 army troops, while every kilometer at the front was being held by one lieutenant and six men, who would have been delighted to get twenty or thirty men to help them" (MD 48/9983 *et seq.*).

p. 587 I used an investigation by U.S. authorities of the underground Central Works factory in May 1945 (FD–3268/45), its production records (held in London), and the excellent reports made by the special mission of Colonel T. R. B. Sanders on the V-weapon sites in France, February 21, 1945, top secret; also a manuscript by Colonel Eugen Walter (MS B–689) of the "Sixty-Fifth Army Corps" set up to control the V-weapons, and Milch's documents and Jodl's diary.

p. 589 On the planning of the Luftwaffe's winter attack on London see Goebbels's diary, December 7, 1943; Koller's files (T321/90/0413 *et seq.*), and the annexes to the OKL war diary on T321/10. Hitler is quoted from his war conference on January 28, 1944.

p. 590 The original FO telegrams to Ankara are in PRO files, *e.g.*, FO 371/37478–9.

p. 592 Küchler's account of his meeting with Hitler is an annex to the war diary of Army Group North (T311/79/2814 *et seq.*). See also Admiral Heinz Assmann's letter to the naval staff, December 29, 1943 (PG/31747), which I quote at length on pages 592–93.

p. 593 There is a file on the *Scharnhorst*'s end in naval staff war diary annexes, Part C, Vol. II. I also used the entries for December 2 and 23–28, 1943, and January 8, 1944, and Dönitz's conference with Commander in Chief Naval Group North (PG/31747).

p. 594 A Colonel Lersner's record of Hitler's speech on October 16, 1943, is on microfilm T77/1039/2937 *et seq.* On Nazi indoctrination proposals, see the papers by Waldemar Besson, Gerhard L. Weinberg, and Volker Berghahn published in *VfZ,* in 1961 (page 76), 1964 (page 443), and 1969 (page 17), respectively. General Schörner's correspondence is in British files (AL/2831).

p. 594 See the stenogram of Reinecke's discussion with Hitler on January 7, 1944, in Party files (NS–6/162). I also used interrogations of Reinecke and Göring by OCMH.

p. 596 Many sources on the January 4, 1944, conference exist: by Lammers, (ND, 1292–PS) and a circular (T84/175/4886 *et seq.*); by Sauckel, (1292–PS) and memo (T175/71/8037 *et seq.*); by Speer, in his Chronik; references in Central Planning meetings on February 16 and March 1, 1944 (MD48/10066 *et seq.*, and 9953 *et seq.*), and in the diaries of Milch and Himmler.

p. 596 Edda Mussolini's letters are in AA files Serial 738, pages 267674 *et seq.*

p. 597 Encouraged by Cicero's reports, Hitler began withdrawing forces from the Balkans in December: see Jodl's diary for December 23, 28, and 29, 1943, and February 10 (?), 1944.

pp. 597–98 The shorthand record of Hitler's January 27, 1944, secret address is in the BA Schumacher collection, file 365. It is referred to also in the diaries of the naval staff, Jodl, Weichs (March 3, 1944), and Salmuth (March 27, 1946), and of the chief of army personnel (Schmundt), January 27, 1944: Hitler had "delivered a speech in very grave tones," during which "Field Marshal von Manstein made an interruption. In connection with this interruption and the various tensions of late the question of retiring Field Marshal Manstein is again debated."

p. 599 Bormann's record of Hitler's remarks on January 27–28, 1944, is on IfZ microfilm MA–340.

Trouble from Providence

p. 600 Walter Schellenberg, who saw Hitler that spring, wrote in his manuscript memoirs: "His eyes—once the dominating feature of his face—were now tired and lusterless; his left arm shook so strongly that he almost constantly had to clutch it with his right hand; he made a conscious effort to conceal his clumsy movements, which began not with the limbs but with the body itself."

p. 602 Dr. Werner Best quoted Hitler's remark of December 30, 1943, in his manuscript (ZS–207/1)

p. 603 A file of Rommel's daily diarylike reports is held by the OCMH in Washington (X–501). Salmuth was to write (on March 18, 1946): "Whether Rommel was really a great commander in the European theater—as opposed to the African—I will not comment." Salmuth was irritated by Rommel's "unpleasant manner" of shouting at officers and men alike on these inspection tours, and by his "highly superficial and abrupt tone." Nonetheless Salmuth was the first to recommend to Rundstedt that Rommel's Army Group B should assume tactical command of both the Seventh and the Fifteenth armies (Salmuth, private papers).

p. 604 Rommel reported in detail on his anti-invasion measures on April 22, 1944 (AL/510/1/4).

p. 605 Telegrams from Istanbul, Ankara, and Sofia relating to the damaging defection of Erich Vermehren are in Steengracht's AA files, Serial 61, pages 41960 *et seq.* The rest of the story, resulting in Canaris's dismissal, is built up from the naval staff war diary, February 19 and 22, and March 2, 4, and 7; Himmler's diary, February 9 and 11; a memo by Wagner, July 1, 1944 (Bobrick's papers, Serial 738, pages 267624 *et seq.*); Hitler's order of February 12 (file H3/1539); and Walther Huppenkothen's 1945 manuscript (BDC files). Canaris was appointed "Chief of the Special Staff for Economic Warfare and Measures" as of July 1, according to the naval staff war diary, July 10; twelve days later he was arrested for high treason.

p. 606 On the operations of the turncoat German officers in the Cherkassy pocket: CSDIC interrogation of Lieutenant General Kruse; and the diaries of the chief of army personnel and of Weichs, March 3, 1944, and of Ulrich von Hassell, February 23.

p. 608 Professor W. Löhlein's record of his examination of Hitler's eyes on March 2, 1944, is in American files (OI-CIR/4); I also used Dr. Erwin Giesing's manuscript.

p. 610 Count Gerd von Schwerin wrote a note on his personal impressions of Hitler at Nuremberg on November 12, 1945.

p. 610 Schellenberg recorded his conversation with Ribbentrop in his handwritten manuscript (IfZ files).

p. 611 The preparations for the occupation of Hungary are described from the diaries of Jodl, Weichs, and the OKW; and OKW files (T77/791) and Steengracht's file on Hungary, Serial 99.

p. 612 Of descending value on Hitler's confrontation with Horthy are these sources: Captain Assmann's report to the naval staff (war diary, March 19, 1944); Jodl's diary, March 18; Horthy's account to his Crown Council in Budapest, March 19 (in the Horthy papers). The version in the OKW war diary, Vol. IV, pages 200 *et seq.* and 230, is marred by inaccuracies. See particularly the OKH attaché section's lengthy "Report on the Journey with [Hungarian] General Homlok to Salzburg from March 17 to 20, 1944" (T78/451/6889 *et seq.*): Hitler reproached Horthy for the attitude of the Hungarian press. He would be forced "to clear things up" and asked Horthy to agree in writing that the German troops which would invade on March 19 were doing so "at his request"; Horthy refused, as this would be unconstitutional. I also used postwar interrogations of Horthy, Ribbentrop, Carl Rekowski, Edmund Veesenmayer, and General Greiffenberg; and Zeitzler's manuscript (N63/117).

p. 613 Jodl also took a lengthy note of Hitler's March 28, 1944, conference.

p. 614 General Alexander von Falkenhausen, military governor of Belgium, also observed Rommel's extreme optimism when the field marshal visited him early in March 1944 in Brussels. "Our views on the political and military situation could not have been more divergent. But when I repaid the visit on June 1, 1944, at La Roche-Guyon [Rommel's HQ] he had changed and wholeheartedly adopted my view" (U.S. Army, MS B–289).

p. 614 On the proposed execution of Allied airmen, see the OKW file on film T77/778; Hewel's memo of March 24, 1944 (NG–4059); Milch's diary, February 23–24, 1946; Bormann's circular of May 15, 1944 (BDC file 182); and a memo by Ribbentrop's bureau, July 17, 1944 (Ritter's files, Serial 6530).

p. 616 Below and Günsche both told me of Hitler's affection for Manstein. I also referred to Backe's letter to Manstein of October 17, 1944, and Hitler's remarks in the noon war conference on March 2, 1945: "Manstein has in my eyes the greatest talent for operational strategy. No doubt about it. I'm the last person to deny that."

The Most Reviled

p. 617 Gauleiter Frauenfeld's study on the administration of the occupied east, dated February 10, 1944, is in Himmler's files (T175/125/0419 *et seq.*).

p. 618 For Hitler's military policies in southern Russia, see his conversation with the Romanian General Garbea on March 29, 1944 (T78/366/8829 et seq.).

p. 618 Saur reported Hitler's remarks to the Fighter Staff on April 8 (MD5/2388 *et seq.*); I also use Göring's version of the Führer's conference with Dönitz on April 13 (MD64/6480 *et seq.*).

p. 620 In addition to the better known materials on the evacuation of the Crimea—like the OKW war diaries, and papers by Baron von Weitershausen and by H. D. von Conrady in *WR* in 1954 (pages 209 *et seq.*, and 327 *et seq.*) and in 1961 (pages 312 *et seq.*, respectively)—I used the naval staff war diary and the hitherto unknown diaries of the army liaison officer to Dönitz (T608/1/529 *et seq.*) and the army's special evacuation staff under General Lindemann (T78/269/7187 *et seq.*); further documents from the naval side will be found in OKW files (T77/778) and in Schörner's papers (AL/2831/2).

pp. 622–23 General von Trotha, Schörner's operations officer, flew into Sevastopol at this time. In his 1946 manuscript he described: "As our plane approached we could see the waves tinged red at one place. There were high cliffs there, on top of which our troops had shot hundreds of horses and thrown them over into the sea, so they wouldn't fall into enemy hands."

p. 623 That Jaenecke's tongue had failed him is eloquently shown in the opening words of his letter to Hitler the next day, April 30, 1944: "At yesterday's conference there were one or two points I unfortunately omitted to make . . ." (AL/2831/3).

p. 625 German Intelligence had obtained a proof copy of Eisenhower's still-secret Proclamation to the French people, announcing the disembarcation of French and Allied troops in France; see the naval staff war diary, April 13, 1944, and file PG/33399 for a full translation.

p. 625 According to Army Group B's war diary, on May 1 and 6 Hitler again stressed his belief that the invasion would strike Normandy and Cherbourg and demanded close scrutiny of the readiness of General Erich Marcks's Eighty-Fourth Corps, defending that sector; Rundstedt's war diary records that Jodl telephoned on May 9 that the Führer expected the invasion in mid-May—perhaps on the eighteenth—and that the main effort would be against Normandy, followed by a subsidiary push into Brittany. On May 27, Hitler repeated this to the Japanese ambassador, Oshima; anything other than the invasions of Brittany and Normandy would be "just diversions."

p. 627 The final report of Admiral, Black Sea, is in naval staff war diary annexes, Part C, Vol. XIV.

p. 628 Koller's studies on the shrinking Luftwaffe bomber force are in his private papers (in my possession) and in OKL war diary annexes (T321/1) and Milch's papers (MD53/706 *et seq.*). What follows is also based on Göring's conferences (MD64) and on a memo in Bormann's files on the Me-262 jet (NS–6/152).

p. 630 Horthy's assent is implicit in Ribbentrop's telegram to Veesenmayer some weeks later, on July 16—after Horthy had just stopped the transports of Jews—protesting that this was a departure from "the measures agreed on at Klessheim" (AA Serial K789). Himmler's views are evident from his handwritten speech notes, *e.g.,* for his speech to field commanders at Posen on January 26, 1944." Jewish question. In the General gouvernement [Poland] huge calmdown since Jewish problem solved. —Racial struggle.—Total solution. —Don't let avengers arise to take revenge on our children" (T175/94/4835 *et seq.*). His May 5 speech is on microfilm T175/92/3475 *et seq.,* and that of May 24, T175/94/4609 *et seq.* That Himmler only talked of "expulsion" of Jews *(Aussiedlung)* to Hitler is clear from his handwritten agenda of July (or August) 1944 (*ibid.,* page 5065).

pp. 631–32 Hitler's speech is recorded in Himmler's files (*ibid.,* 4972 *et seq.*). He used similar language to Sztójay on June 7, 1944.

p. 632 Korten's optimism (MD64/6998) and Speer's in Central Planning the next day (MD55/2170) are echoed in a letter written by the food minister, Herbert Backe, on May 17, 1944. "Apparently the invasion's got to be taken seriously after all. There's talk of May 18—that means tomorrow. I won't believe it until they are actually ashore. . . . Our generals are very optimistic, without exception. . . . Immense preparations have been made on our side. I am not particularly worried about it. Here everybody is longing for it to start" (Backe's private papers).

p. 633 Not only had Dönitz gone on leave—see the naval staff diary of June 6, 1944, and his interrogation on August 6, 1945—but Salmuth (Fifteenth Army) went on a two-day hunting party, and Rommel returned briefly to Germany

5. THE WORMS TURN

Man with a Yellow Leather Briefcase

p. 637 Little is known of the actual events at the Berghof during the night of the invasion. I have pieced them together from statements of Hitler's adjutants, of Keitel, Jodl, and Zeitzler, and from the times recorded in the war diaries of the naval staff, Commander in Chief West, and the OKW. What is certain is that Chester Wilmot's version in *Struggle for Europe* (pages 248 and 287), which has Hitler "forbidding" Jodl at 4 A.M. to release the OKW reserves, is pure fantasy. The situation crystalized far too slowly for even the OKW to be blamed for delaying this decision.

Hitler probably stayed awake until 3 A.M. (Milch diary, May 7, 1947, quoting Speer). Twenty minutes earlier (according to the naval staff diary) the "Admiral, Channel Coast" had telephoned the OKW tersely: "Advance report: from 2 A.M. on, large number of paratroops and gliders, east coast Cotentin peninsula and east of Trouville." Not until 3:45 A.M. was this enlarged upon. By 5:45 A.M. Naval Group West believed the invasion had begun—but neither Rundstedt's staff nor the OKW shared this conviction. At 7:30 A.M. Naval Group West convincingly reported: "Invasion area extends from Saint-Vaast to Deauville, main efforts evidently Quistreham and Saint-Vaast. North of Barfleur major invasion force heading south. Cargo ships with the invasion forces . . ." At 8:15 A.M. this was forwarded to Jodl's staff at Berchtesgaden by telephone, and they now agreed that their earlier skepticism seemed misplaced. At 9:30 A.M. Reuter officially confirmed the invasion, and a string of intercepted Allied wireless messages reached the Berghof: "No details so far, but we are ashore." "Front line overrun." "Situation on Red Beach isn't too good."

p. 638 The SD report that the BBC invasion-alerts had been monitored was forwarded by Kaltenbrunner to the OKW on June 1; thence to Foreign Armies West on June 2, 6:50 P.M. (T78/451/6880 *et seq.*). Under Nuremberg interrogation, Walter Schellenberg blamed the military for failing to appreciate the significance of this scoop. This seems justified, for on the very eve of the invasion—June 5, 1944—Rommel's much-praised Chief of Staff, General Hans Speidel, sanguinely dismissed the invasion-alert signals which the BBC had broadcast with increasing frequency since June 1 as "not providing any evidence of an imminent invasion" (Army Group B, weekly report, T311/3/2156 *et seq.*). See also the war diaries of the Fifteenth Army, which independently monitored the BBC messages and warned Speidel. Note that the war diary of Commander in Chief West was *retrospectively* written up—one forms a different impression altogether of the army's readiness and alertness from sources like the naval staff diary of June 11, 1944. The admiralty was certainly warned on June 2 (see file PG/33399), and on June 3 the naval staff noted: "Foreign Armies West regards June 5 to 13 as favorable invasion date."

In later months the naval staff painstakingly analyzed all the Abwehr agents' reports on the coming invasion. Of the 173 received prior to June 6, 1944, only 8 percent had been right; 14 percent had been partially correct; the rest had been wrong or worthless (diary, March 23, 1945). What is a staggering indictment of German army Intelligence methods is the treatment of the Operational Plan of the U.S. Fifth Corps—*i.e.,* of the entire American sector in Normandy—which fell into the hands of the German 351st Infantry Division on June 7, 1944, and can thereafter be traced (through postwar statements) up to the Eighty-Fourth German Corps (General Marcks) and thence to Seventh Army, which forwarded it to Rommel's HQ on June 11. Blumentritt—Rundstedt's Chief of Staff—believes in manuscript B637 that he saw it and sent it up by courier on June 12 to the OKW. Had this document ever reached the OKW or Hitler it would have left no doubt that Normandy was *the* main invasion area. Having been seized from the corpse of an American officer killed in a gunfight, an enemy trick was ruled out. But there is no mention of the document in the files of either the OKW or Commander-in-Chief West.

p. 639 Salmuth's March 1946 manuscript on the invasion is in his private papers. Not until 9:12 A.M. did the German naval commandant in Normandy forward from the big gun battery at Marcouf to the naval staff the pregnant signal: "Very many landing craft are approaching under cover of battleships and cruisers."

p. 639 The hardy optimism of the Germans in the face of the colossal invasion is evident wherever we look in their records. Hitler's personal adjutant, Alwin-Broder Albrecht, wrote on June 9: "Anyway, everybody here's breathing a sigh of relief." Hitler told Sztójay that they had been looking forward to it, because it would end with the defeat of the British. And the naval staff recorded on June 7: "As for the invasion operations in the west, the Führer and Field Marshal Rommel view the situation positively and confidently, in anticipation of the success of our countermeasures." These included the laying of the new top-secret German "pressure mines" off the invasion coast, which Hitler authorized at his noon conference that day.

p. 639 There are sparse references to the "suicide pilot" project in General Koller's papers, among which I found a sequence of daily air staff reports. Speer heard of the project, because on July 28, 1944, he wrote to Hitler: "The endeavors to throw these men into action against the enemy invasion fleet are to be condemned, as long as using them against Russian power stations would be capable of procuring quite different results in the long run."

p. 640 The war diary of Colonel Max Wachtel's "Antiaircraft Regiment 155(W)"—the V-1 flying-bomb launchers—has survived intact.

p. 642 Schramm's account of Hitler's visit to Soissons on June 17, 1944 (OKW war diary, Vol. IV, pages 316 *et seq.*), is unreliable. Koller's papers make it plain that Hitler went on his own initiative. My account depends on Heinz Assmann's description (naval staff diary), on Jodl's diary, on signals in the war diaries of Rundstedt and Army Group B (T84/281), and on the typed narrative of the conference in the volume of appendices to Army Group B's war diary (T311/278).

pp. 642–43 Rommel's exuberance is clear from a diary entry of Admiral Friedrich Ruge and from Rommel's own weekly report of June 19: "Despite the enemy's vast superiority in air power and ships' artillery and ruthless expenditure of troops and equipment in repeated heavy attacks, they have gained no successes, but actually lost ground at Caumont. . . . Our Intelligence and captured documents show that the enemy has not reached one of his far-flung objectives, but has had to throw in considerably more forces than originally intended. . . . In the fighting so far the enemy has lost over five hundred tanks and over one thousand planes. . . . The population in the combat area is friendly toward us; there has been a perceptible decrease in the sabotage and other resistance activity that sprang up in the first postinvasion days" (Army Group B, war diary, annexes).

p. 643 In August 1944 Hermann Gackenholz wrote a full report on the disastrous collapse of Army Group Center for its war diary; the war diary is in OCMH files. Gackenholz kept the report and published it in *VfZ*, 1955, pages 317 *et seq.* The faulty appreciations of Stalin's intentions by Gehlen's branch of the General Staff can be followed in this, in the naval staff war diary, and above all in Koller's daily reports.

p. 644 General Student described on September 22, 1945, to fellow generals how in his presence, two days before the Russian offensive began, "Zeitzler explained his reasons for expecting the main enemy effort to come in the south. He considered a big attack in the center quite improbable. Hitler thought otherwise and at the last moment ordered reserves sent to Army Group Center" (General Kurt Dittmar, diary).

p. 645 Himmler's speech of June 21, 1944, is on microfilm T175/93/3950 *et seq.*; Hitler's of the next day is on microfilm T580/871.

p. 647 Hitler later learned from Allied press reports that General von Schlieben's surrender had been somewhat inglorious. "A braggart," Hitler complained to Jodl on July 31. "He issues a defiant proclamation . . . and then waits for the others [the Americans] to arrive, whereupon he immediately runs up a white flag. When they ask him, 'How can you square issuing such a proclamation with your own honor?' he just shrugs."

p. 647 Dollmann's Chief of Staff, Max Pemsel—who hitherto has always denied this—admitted to me for the first time that it was indeed suicide; Dollmann had retired for the first time to Pemsel's vacant bed and was found in it the next morning.

p. 648 Even if Hitler had authorized the withdrawal of Army Group North, its divisions could not have reached the crisis area of Army Group Center in less than four weeks (see Hitler's conference with Dönitz, July 9, 1944).

p. 648 Zeitzler described his last row with Hitler in various postwar manuscripts (N63/1, /80, and /96); his adjutant Günther Smend described it to the Gestapo on August 1, 1944 (T84/22/4535 *et seq.*) By July 1 he was—according to Gackenholz's report—already "off sick."

p. 649 The quotations are from the war diary of Antiaircraft Regiment 155(W). See too Rommel's appreciation, dated June 26, 1944, on the internal situation in France." The population affected continues to be embittered by the Allies' ruthless mode of warfare, especially by their use of air power, while otherwise the population is reserved. Coastal population in Belgium is tending to migrate away. Combat operations by the new weapon [V-1] against England evoked interest and in some parts satisfaction." For Rommel's conference with Hitler on June 28, see the note taken by his adjutant (Appendix to Army Group B war diary, T311/278).

p. 651 Koller's formal record of Hitler's remarks on June 29, 1944, is in his papers; he also jotted down a shorthand record of both these and Göring's subsequent outbursts about "the cowardly fighter pilots."

pp. 652–53 Again I quote Koller's lengthy record, but equally explicit accounts of Hitler's speech are to be found in both Jodl's diary and the naval staff war diary of July 3, 1944.

p. 653 Koller noted Hitler's question to Heusinger; his later reminiscence is quoted from his conference with Generals Siegfried Westphal and Hans Krebs on August 31, 1944 (Heiber, page 615). He had said the same to Antonescu on August 5.

p. 654 General Vinzenz Müller's order of July 8, 1944, will be found on microfilm T77/1038/0780 *et seq.*, together with other similar documents emanating from the renegades. See also the war diary of the chief of army personnel, July 27.

pp. 654–655 This war diary (see note for page 654, above), together with Koller's, Speer's, Thomale's, and Himmler's papers, was used to trace the origins of the fifteen "blocking divisions" *(Sperrverbände)*—out of which the *Volksgrenadier* divisions were born.

p. 655 With the exception of Peter Hoffmann, no historian noticed that Hitler undertook this lightning one-day visit back to the Wolf's Lair on July 9, 1944. From the records of Jodl, Dönitz, and Koller there can, however, be no doubt. It is also referred to by Major General Peter von Groeben in his study "The Collapse of Army Group Center" (U.S. army manuscripts, T31). It was here too—as Himmler wrote to Rosenberg on July 14—that Hitler ordered every available man in Estonia to be recruited into the SS (T175/125/0532).

p. 656 According to the stenographer's diary, Hitler's July 13, 1944, secret speech lasted from 10:22 to 11:40 P.M. Eighteen days later, his health shattered by the bomb attempt, Hitler admitted to Jodl: "Obviously I can stand up and even speak for a certain length of time, but then I suddenly have to sit down again. I would not trust myself to speak to ten thousand people today. Nor would I trust myself to make a speech like that one I recently did on the Obersalzberg, because I might suddenly faint and collapse" (Heiber, page 608). Its content was evidently the familiar litany. On April 11, 1945, General Fellgiebel's adjutant told British interrogation officers that General Stieff—chief of the OKH organization branch—had privately muttered, 'If I hear that phonograph record played once more I'll go crazy!"—to which Fellgiebel, a fellow-conspirator, replied with heavy irony, "Well, Stieff, that was the last time."

"Do You Recognize My Voice?"

p. 657 On the implementation of total war, see Lammers's letter to Keitel, July 17, 1944, and subsequent correspondence (T175/71/7972 *et seq.*). Only the French text of Goebbels's letter survives in British files, AL/1904/4; the original may be in France.

p. 659 The infantry general Edgar Röhricht mentions Stieff's order of July 8, 1944, in his March 1946 study "Himmler's Struggle for Military Power" (in IfZ files). Significantly, when Stauffenberg returned from Hitler's HQ on July 11 or 15, 1944, and exclaimed that the whole HQ ought to be blown sky high, Colonel Georg Hansen—Canaris's successor and a fellow-conspirator—"attributed this exclamation to Stauffenberg's very powerful irritation that the fifteen new divisions being raised were to be subordinated to the Reichsführer SS [Himmler]" (Gestapo interrogation of Hansen, July 29, 1944, T84/19/0257).

p. 661 See the verbatim interrogation of Fräulein Schroeder at Berchtesgaden, May 22, 1945.

p. 661 See the brief record of Hitler's speech to Nazi indoctrination officers on July 29, 1944 (T78/80/0603 *et seq.*); Jodl's speech of July 24 (T77/1432), and Himmler's speech of August 3, 1944, about Fellgiebel's defeatist utterances.

p. 661 These first withdrawals from the idle Fifteenth Army are referred to in the diaries of the OKW, Kluge's staff, and the naval staff, July 20, 1944, and their strategic importance is underlined in Jodl's diary.

pp. 662–63 Percy Schramm wrote several annexes to the OKW war diary on the July 20, 1944, bomb incident, based on Warlimont's verbal information; they were not published, but are on T77/1432/0620 *et seq.* I also used the diary of one staff stenographer, the version in Schmundt's official diary, and above all Peter Hoffmann's excellent study in *VfZ*, 1964, pages 254 *et seq.*, and his full-length book, *Widerstand, Staatsstreich, Attentat* (Munich, 1969), Chap. XI. In addition I assembled a voluminous collection of statements and interrogations of the officers in the hut, largely from secret British files.

p. 663 Hitler related his personal impressions on several occasions: on August 15, 1944, to the envoy Siegfried Kasche (whose record is in his papers, AA Serial 1770, pages 405808 *et seq.*); to the staff stenographer Ludwig Krieger; to his ENT-specialist Erwin Giesing; and to the Gauleiters on August 4. The wife of Food Minister Herbert Backe wrote in a diary on August 7, 1944: "Herbert came straight from the Führer conference. At lunch he was only three places away from the Führer. Gauleiter Giesler [of Munich] asked the Führer. 'What did you feel at the moment of the blast?' The Führer said, 'I thought I had heard three detonations and suspected hand grenades had been tossed in from outside. The generals jumped out of the windows. But I thought I would then be running right into the killers' arms. I went out through the door, putting out the flames in my hair. . . .' "

p. 663 On Hitler's injuries I used manuscripts or testimony of Morell, his wife, Hasselbach, Brandt, and Giesing.

p. 665 Keitel's alacrity is evident from the documents. The Berlin conspirators had begun issuing their "Valkyrie" signals a few minutes before 4 P.M.—misusing Fromm's signature and making reference in them to Witzleben and Hoepner. Just *fifteen* minutes later Keitel was already issuing the first teletypes from Hitler's HQ overriding these spurious signals. By 4:05 P.M. the OKH General Staff already had evidence that Stauffenberg had failed, for staff at Zossen monitored a telephone conversation between Hermann Fegelein (Himmler's liaison officer at Hitler's HQ) and SS General Hans Jüttner on the explosion's failure—it had been "similar to Munich [in November 1939], but Führer safe and well."

pp. 665–66 Himmler emphasized the delicacy of his role in speeches on July 21 and 26, 1944 (T175/93/3904 and 4146). See also Keitel's memoirs, page 222.

p. 666 Eduard Wagner's role is an enigma. He wrote on July 21 to Zeitzler: "I swear to you on my word of honor that I had nothing to do with the events of July 20," and enclosed a full account of the events at Zossen as he remembered them (IfZ file, ED–95).

p. 666 A complete sequence of the key July 20, 1944, telegrams was captured by British Intelligence in the files of the Nazi party office in Schleswig-Holstein. This particular one omitted the first sentence: "The Führer Adolf Hitler is dead." But it is included in the later versions—e.g., in naval staff war diary, 8:05 P.M.; and Kluge's Paris staff received by teletype at 8:10 P.M. an assurance that the 6:28 P.M. radio broadcast (page 666) was a lie and that the Führer *was* dead and that all steps were to be taken as swiftly as possible.

p. 667 I used Schaub's unpublished manuscript, and a private letter by the adjutant Albrecht dated July 22, 1944.

p. 668 See the report by Dr. Hans Hagen on his visit to Goebbels (T84/19/0022 et seq.). The propaganda minister had a direct telephone line to Hitler, unknown to the plotters (OCMH interrogation of General Wilhelm Arnold, OKH signals chief, August 25, 1945).

p. 668 The interpreter present, Eugen Dollmann, gives a spirited account of Hitler's conversation with Mussolini, Göring, and Ribbentrop in a prison-cell conversation monitored by the British on July 22, 1945 (CSDIC/CMF/X194).

p. 669 The engineer General Werner Kennes—Fromm's armaments expert—had slipped out of the Bendlerstrasse building at midnight. Generals Hoepner and von Thüngen were also witnesses to Stauffenberg's bland assurance that he had seen Hitler's corpse; so was another—anonymous—officer, of whose testimony before the People's Court only the sound recording survives.

p. 671 Rommel's "Observations on the Situation," dated July 15, 1944, are in Army Group B's war diary annexes (T311/3/2241 *et seq.*); Kluge forwarded the document with a letter to Hitler dated July 21 *(ibid.)*. They are mentioned in his war diary, but the annexes referred to are missing. Professor H. A. Jacobsen and other historians have uncritically quoted from the erroneous text given (from memory) by General Hans Speidel in *Invasion 1944*. Note that Rommel's letter was *not* addressed to Hitler.

p. 672 The quote is from Hitler's talk with Jodl on July 31, 1944 (Heiber).

p. 673 Eicken's treatment notes on Hitler survive (NA special microfilm, ML–125 and 131). He was also interrogated by the British.

p. 673 At Christmas 1944 Himmler told Admiral von Puttkamer: "If only we'd known the scale right from the start, we'd have proceeded quite differently; then we'd have differentiated more—we wouldn't have hanged people just because they had heard talk of something."

p. 674 Helmuth Maurer—Canaris's pianist neighbor, who wrote a long unpublished manuscript on the Abwehr chief—had been with him on the afternoon of July 20, 1944. About 3 P.M. Stauffenberg telephoned that the Führer was dead. Canaris knew his phone was tapped and responded, "Was it the Russians?" Maurer says that the admiral's nerves went to pieces over the next three days until his arrest. According to the SS investigator Horst Kopkow (under British CSDIC interrogation), Canaris pressed Schellenberg to know whether that "petty staff officer" Hansen hadn't been jotting down pettifogging notes again. Only Canaris's most recent diary was immediately found, and that was not incriminating.

p. 675 Reinicke described the Berliners' indignation under OCMH interrogation in July 1945. The diary of the Catholic Field Marshal von Weichs mirrors the fury of the unimplicated officers. "*21 July.* Putsch. Frightful situation—this internal unrest too. Success would have produced chaos. Madness to think a rapid peace can be achieved by such means. A stab in the back like 1918, but worse as it comes from a quarter from which one might have expected the opposite. Horrifying, the names that participated in this revolt. How will the army sit this terrible upheaval out, now that its officers and generals will forfeit every shred of confidence in them? How will our allies take this blow?" And on *22 July:* ". . . because even if the assassination had worked, the putsch would still have collapsed, as not one soldier would have accepted orders from these leaders."

p. 675 A bulky collection of letters to Hitler after the plot is in Goebbels's files (BA, R55DC/145).

p. 677 Rommel had warned Hitler of the bazooka shortage at his mid-March 1944 conference; the Seventh Army needed 5,190 but had only 644; the Fifteenth Army needed 6,228 but had only 781 (war diary, Army Group B, quartermaster, annexes). Wagner in fact shared responsibility for distribution with Kluge's quartermaster, Colonel Eberhard Finkh—who was one of the conspirators and was sentenced to death on August 30, 1944. According to the naval staff diary, August 9, the OKW noted: "Despite adequate supplies of ammunition, weapons, and equipment at home Commander in Chief West keeps reporting shortages of specific types, particularly armor-piercing ammunition and bazookas."

Historians dissatisfied with Schramm's summary treatment of the war's theaters in the OKW war diary will find excellent daily reports on Hitler's war conferences as submitted to the naval staff by the attending admiral (usually Voss) from August 1944 to January 1945 (PG/32122b); and from December 1944 to April 7, 1945 (PG/31742).

He Who Rides the Tiger

p. 680 A minute on Stauffenberg's telephone call to Army Group North at 7:55 P.M., July 20, is in German army files (T78/352/2592); Beck himself took the phone, declaring, "To let yourselves be shut in—just as in Stalingrad—that is no way to lead an army!"

p. 681 In addition to the German record of Hitler's meeting with Antonescu there exists the marshal's own account, published on January 15, 1953, in *La Nation Roumaine* in Paris. I also used Guderian's manuscript (ZS–57), the army conferences with General Garbea (T78/366/8704 *et seq.*), and—with caution—Professor Andreas Hillgruber's study of the last months of the German-Romanian alliance in *WR*, 1957, pages 377 *et seq.*: Hillgruber relies perhaps too heavily on Erik Hansen as a source. Hitler's warning was witnessed by his adjutant Colonel Erik von Amsberg, whom I interviewed in 1971; and Hitler himself later referred to it, according to Wolf Junge's manuscript.

p. 682 The diarist was Herbert Backe's wife. I also used the account written by Hitler's deputy press chief Dr. Helmut Sündermann—at the time, according to his son.

p. 683 See Jodl's diary, August 1, 1944. "5 P.M.: Führer has me read Kaltenbrunner's report [dated July 30] on the testimony of Lieutenant Colonel Hofacker about discussions with K[luge] and R[ommel]. Führer is looking for a new Commander in Chief West. Plans to question R[ommel] after he's better again and then to retire him without further ado."

Kluge appears to have remained on the sidelines as an interested observer of the conspiracy and little more. At an emergency conference late on July 20 with Stülpnagel, Hofacker, and Blumentritt he had dissociated himself from the deed, but he had noticeably failed to report these meetings to the Gestapo investigators. Salmuth later wrote: "It became clear to me that Kluge had known what was planned on July 20 when I paid a visit to him the next day, because when I asked him for his view he only answered, 'Well, it didn't work out!' and these few words told me enough."

p. 684 On Hitler's and Jodl's attempts to prevent Kluge launching the Avranches counterattack prematurely, see the war diary of Commander in Chief West, annexes. That the panzer divisions were unready is clear from the telephone log of the Seventh Army (AL/528/1).

p. 685 General Werner Kreipe's diary (transcribed by the Americans as MS P–069) and Koller's papers provide extensive information on Hitler and the Luftwaffe at this stage.

p. 687 Of 192 agents' reports, only 15 accurately predicted the Allied invasion of southern France. See the naval staff war diary, August 8, 10, 13, and 15, 1944; and its annex, "Investigation of the Value of R.S.H.A. Intelligence on Enemy Invasion Plans," October 16, 1944 (PG/32218).

p. 687 Blumentritt stated under British interrogation that Keitel had told him of the intercepted enemy signal to Kluge. Guderian told much the same to Milch (diary, October 28, 1945). "Kluge tried in France to contact the enemy to surrender, but this misfired. . . . Moreover Kluge is to blame for the false use of the tanks—he seems to have deliberately tried to lead the tank units into the pocket at Falaise!!" Salmuth also heard of this story from Gauleiter Greiser in January 1945—but dismissed it as "a rumor probably spread by the Party on orders from above." I also used a conversation between General Eberbach and Blumentritt on August 19, 1945, recorded by CSDIC, the diary of chief of army personnel, and Blumentritt's letters to Jodl (AL/1720) and Burgdorf (X–967).

p. 689 Jodl recorded Hitler's meeting of August 19, 1944, in his diary; Buhle—also present—told the OKH artillery branch of Hitler's intention to raise fourteen new artillery brigades on August 24: "By these means a concentration of one thousand guns is to be achieved for a decisive job in the west." And, "The armament of the twenty-five divisions demanded is to be German" (T78/269/7521 *et seq.*)

p. 689 Martin Bormann's file on "Luftwaffe Scandals" is in the BA Schumacher collection file 315.

p. 690 According to the unpublished manuscript of the Abwehr colonel Friedrich-Wilhelm Heinz on "Canaris and Nicolai" (NA special film ML–690), a trusted crony of

Canaris's placed on Choltitz's staff persuaded the general to turn over Paris intact to the enemy. Hitler's order to the contrary (page 690) is in the annexes both of Army Group B's war diary and of Commander in Chief West's war diary.

pp. 691–92 Hitler's startling—but short-lived—project for a canal is reported by Admiral Voss in the naval staff war diary.

pp. 692–93 My narrative of Antonescu's overthrow—and Hitler's attempted countermeasures—relies on the naval staff diary (which is far preferable to the OKW war diary here); General Hans Friessner's memoirs, *Verratene Schlachten* (Hamburg, 1956); and a report by the Fourth Air Force on events in Romania in 1944, dated February 11, 1945.

p. 693 Hitler's immediate decision to abandon Greece is recorded in Weichs's private diary, August 23–24, 1944. The formal OKW directive followed on August 26; see also OKW war diary, Vol. IV, page 681.

p. 694 Hitler's rebuke to Freisler is confirmed by Schaub's unpublished manuscript, by interviews of Heinz Lorenz and Otto Günsche in 1967, and by a U.S. Seventh Army interrogation of Dr. Immanuel Schäffer of the propaganda ministry in June 1945. British files contain an account by one of the guards at Plötzensee, describing the hangings; Helldorf's grim treatment is described by the Gestapo official Dr. Georg Kiessel in his account of "The Plot of July 20, 1944, and its Origins," August 6, 1946 (British files), and by SS Captain Otto Prochnow under CSDIC interrogation, March 1946. The rest is based on Himmler's letters to Thierack, November 7, 1944 (BDC, SS–4465), and to Lammers and SS General Franz Breithaupt, August 27, 1944 (BDC file 242). British files list 81 such executions at Plötzensee prison after July 20, 1944; a separate list of 130 names altogether also exists. Kiessel puts the final figure at 140. There is no support for the figure of "4,890" put about by the Allies in 1945, nor for the *New Statesman*'s "official estimate" of "over twenty thousand executed."

p. 696 The original page in Bormann's handwriting is in OCMH files, Washington (X–967). Kluge's penciled letter to Hitler is in London files (MI.14/7). The version published in the OKW war diary, Vol. IV, pages 1574 *et seq.*, is only a translation of an English translation.

p. 696 On the Kluge mystery, see the memo by Colonel Hugh M. Cole, historical officer attached to the U.S. Third Army, in OCMH file X–967 (and *Time* magazine, June 25, 1945). According to the CSDIC interrogation of Blumentritt, Kluge's first reaction to the spurious word of Hitler's death on July 20, 1944, had been: "If the Führer's dead, we ought to get in touch with the people on the other side right away." So the idea was not anathema to him. And note his curious words on the telephone to Blumentritt at 11:55 A.M. on August 16, after his miraculous return from his "vanishing act" the day before: "Pass word up to the top that I'm now 'back from abroad' again and that I didn't let the reins of government out of my hands for one instant" (war diary, Commander in Chief West, annex 1450).

Rommel Gets a Choice

p. 698 Ribbentrop's description of his peace proposal is partially confirmed by an entry in Kreipe's diary on September 13, 1944. After telling Göring bluntly how hopeless the Luftwaffe situation was, he inquired whether it was not time for the Reichsmarschall to make a political intervention. This question "was answered with bitter criticism of Ribbentrop—he [Göring] was the last person who should now make the Führer feel uncertain."

p. 698 Weichs's telegram to Hitler's HQ, and the reply, are in Ritter's AA files, Serial 1487, pages 368686 *et seq.;* the fieldmarshal also referred to this after the war (N 19/12), as did Hermann Neubacher—under U.S. State Department interrogation—who stated that the British local commander, General Sir R. M. Scobie, had contacted both himself and the German Commander in Chief, Northern Greece, the mountain corps general Hubert Lanz. Ribbentrop confirmed the "bait" strategy in a conversation with the Belgian Fascist leader Léon Degrelle on December 8, 1944 (AA Serial B 16): see also naval staff diary, September 6 and 14, and Jodl's diary, September 14, and directive to Weichs (AA Serial 1487); and OKW war diary, Vol. IV page 719.

p. 699 Two Japanese admiralty officers informed the German naval attaché of Stalin's alleged views on August 25; Ambassador Heinrich Georg Stahmer's telegram from Tokyo reporting this reached Ribbentrop's train on August 26 (AA, Ritter's files, Serial 1436, page 363344). Most probably this was connected with the recent return of the Soviet ambassador Jakob Malik to Tokyo from Moscow. A few days later the Japanese foreign minister, Mamoru Shigemitsu, visited Stahmer in the same connection. Finally, on September 4, Ambassador Oshima came from Berlin to the Wolf's Lair to put the same proposals directly to Hitler. (Ribbentrop's report on this talk to Stahmer two days later is in Ritter's file, Serial 1436.) Hitler however painted an optimistic picture of Germany's sound strategic position—a coming counteroffensive with fresh divisions, new fighter aircraft, new submarine types, and adequate raw materials for two years—and emphasized that there was so far not the slightest sign that Stalin wanted peace. Only a military impasse would convince Stalin; for the time being Hitler asked the Japanese to refrain from such steps. Thus the Japanese attempt to mediate between Hitler and Stalin failed. On this whole episode see also naval staff war diary, September 5, 1944, and Speer's testimony at Nuremberg, Vol. XVI, page 533. That Guderian shared Hitler's view was reported by his liaison officer to the naval staff (diary, September 17).

p. 700 Speer's prognosis on the nickel supply was also inconsistent. On September 13, 1944, the naval staff noted Speer's clear announcement that the Petsamo nickel supply was no longer of great importance to Germany's arms industry—a view the naval staff diary strongly disputed five days later.

pp. 703–704 See Keitel's draconian order to the infantry General Hans-Karl von Scheele on September 10, 1944, ordering immediate court martialing and public execution of deserters (T77/869/5928 *et seq.*)

p. 704 The plan for a western counteroffensive began to crystalize in Hitler's order of August 29, 1944: "There is only one possibility, and that is to wade into the American right flank and thus endanger the enemy's advance into Belgium itself from the rear" (Army Group B, war diary annexes); the plan took clearer shape in his order of September 3 to Rundstedt (*ibid.*, and war diary, Commander in Chief West). Kreipe's diary of September 11 shows that Hitler was still half-looking at the Vosges offensive idea, but then he switched attention to the Ardennes. See the ETHINT interrogations of Jodl and his staff officer Major Herbert Büchs.

p. 704 Kaltenbrunner's damning reports are in BA file N6/41.

p. 706 Schörner's visit is recorded in Jodl's diary, September 16, 1944. When Dönitz heard of the plan to abandon Estonia, he hurried to Hitler but could not change his mind; on the eighteenth the evacuation began (naval staff diary, September 15; and see Schörner's teletype to Keitel, September 9, in film T77/778).

p. 706 Frau von Ribbentrop confirmed the episode of Madame Kollonti to me. Both Ribbentrop and Colonel Bogislav von Bonin—of the General Staff—reported Hitler's "pawn in hand" argument under interrogation in 1945. Interestingly, on September 12, 1944, Himmler jotted down as Item 9 on his agenda for discussion with Hitler the words "Britain or Russia"; and as Item 10, "Russia—Japan." Both items are endorsed "dealt with" (T175/94/5062).

pp. 706–707 On the Arnhem operation I used General Kurt Student's account in the journal *Der Frontsoldat Erzählt*, 1952; Schleifenbaum's letter to a Herman Giesler, January 11, 1945 (T81/122/4665 *et seq.*); an unpublished letter by Colonel W. Harzer to *Quick* magazine, December 1955; and entries in the naval staff war diary.

p. 710 Himmler's visit to Hitler on September 26, 1944, is reconstructed from his handwritten agenda (T175/94/5056); from Bormann's letter to his wife that day; from Kaltenbrunner's interrogation of Canaris and Pfuhlstein, September 21, (NS–6/41); the war diary of the chief of army personnel, September 4; manuscripts of Jodl, 1944 (T77/775) and Huppenkothen, 1945 (BDC), and Kiessel and Georg Thomas; and interrogations of Jodl, Lahousen—who privately confirmed in Nuremberg on November 12, 1945, that Canaris and Oster had betrayed the date of "Yellow," but declined to say more as both were now dead—and of Huppenkothen, Kopkow, and Thomas.

p. 712 Hitler's confinement to bed with jaundice is testified to by Giesing, Hasselbach, and Brandt; it is referred to in Bormann's letters of September 30 and October 1 and 4, in the manuscripts of the secretary Traudl Junge and Assmann, and in my 1965 interview with Saur and Puttkamer. After visiting him on October 5, 1944, Schmundt's widow wrote in her diary: "With Puttkamer this afternoon in the Wolf's Lair. Führer bedridden. Said he had lost his finest man."

p. 713 As Professor Morell wrote on October 23, 1944: "The last few weeks have not been too pleasant for me. There was a lot of trouble. But the Führer was so charming to me that this more than makes up for it."

pp. 714–15 Alfred Rosenberg's report to Hitler on the evacuation of Estonia, dated September 28, 1944 (NG–1094).

pp. 715–16 A primary source on Rommel's suicide is the testimony of Julius Schaub's chauffeur, Heinz Doose, who drove the car in which Rommel swallowed the poison. When Doose handed the field marshal's cap and baton in to Schaub, the latter went pale. "I didn't know about this . . . I want nothing to do with it!" The rest of my narrative relies on interrogations of Keitel and Jodl; my interviews of the adjutants Günsche, Amsberg, and Göhler; written statements of the staff stenographers Buchholz and Krieger; and a handwritten note on Keitel's talk with his son in the Nuremberg cells on September 21, 1946.

On the Brink of a Volcano

p. 717 In Himmler's files is a teletype report from SS Colonel Kurt Becher dated August 25, 1944. The fact that "three hundred items [Jews] had unconditionally crossed the frontier" would amend the other side's opinion that "we only want their agreement to exploit it for propaganda purposes" (T175/59/4473 *et seq.*). See too in this connection Schellenberg's interesting explanation noted by Count Schwerin von Krosigk in his diary on April 15, 1945: the treatment of the Jews had been worse than a crime—it was a folly, he said, as two thirds of all Jews lived outside the German domain. Quite wrongly the Reichsführer was being blamed for what "admittedly occurred in his name, but not at his behest." Therefore they had now allowed one thousand two hundred Jews to go to Switzerland, with the object of improving the Reichsführer's image abroad.

On April 19, 1945, Himmler himself claimed to Krosigk "that for two years nothing else has happened to the Jews still left in Germany—we need them as a pawn for all the coming negotiations."

p. 718 Kaltenbrunner's closing speech is in IMT, Vol. XXII, pages 431 *et seq.* His widow, now living in Linz, Austria, was unable to provide me with any further documentary support for his—on the face of it, implausible—account. I traced Dr. Konrad Morgen, now a respected Frankfurt attorney; he displayed understandable animus toward Kaltenbrunner, but his replies to my questions largely supported the SS general's claim. Morgen himself had reported voluntarily to the U.S. Seventh Army on September 22, 1945, and was regarded by them as a reliable witness on SS atrocities (SAIC report PIR/313); but when Kaltenbrunner's defense counsel applied for Morgen's appearance at Nuremberg, the Americans denied knowledge of his whereabouts until July 1, 1946, when they admitted that he was being held at Dachau. Thus Morgen's testimony came too late for Kaltenbrunner to be cross-examined on it (IMT, Vol. XX, pages 532 *et seq.*). Kaltenbrunner made his claim about showing the Morgen report to Hitler in his Closing Speech at Nuremberg, August 1946 (IMT, Vol. XXII, pages 431 *et seq.*). I also used his testimony earlier (Vol. XI, pages 306 and 338). Dr. Konrad Morgen's testimony is in IMT, Vol. XX, pages 532 *et seq.*: and I corresponded with him in 1974. Heinz Lorenz several times described how Hitler reacted to the Majdanek reports (*e.g.*, in CSDIC interrogation); and see Helmut Sündermann's diary, October 27, 1944.

In Himmler's files are only faint echoes of Morgen's long investigations; thus on January 29, 1944, Martin Bormann asked him "please to read for *yourself*" a horrifying report on conditions at Lublin concentration camp. Himmler replied suavely that the commandant concerned, SS Major Hermann Florstedt, was already under arrest: "The abuses are being ruthlessly remedied [*ausgerottet*] and redressed by a sweeping judicial process" (T175/53/7290).

p. 719 On Hungary's preparations for defection: OCMH and U.S. State Department interrogations of Greiffenberg and Veesenmayer; Kasche's note on Hitler's talk with the Croat "Poglavnik," September 18, 1944 (AA Serial 1770); and naval staff diary, September 26–28.

p. 720 For Hitler's remarks to Vörös, see Greiffenberg's telegram to Berlin on his talk with Geisa Lakatos, the Hungarian Prime Minister, September 15, (T77/869/5914).

p. 720 SS General Winkelmann's sometimes hilarious account of events in Budapest, dated October 25, 1944, is in Himmler's files (T175/59/4489 et seq.). Even Otto Skorzeny deprecates Winkelmann's choice of words.

p. 721 I adopt the word "shameful" used by Professor C. A. Macartney in his publication of the secret Hungarian telegrams in *VfZ*, 1966, pages 79 *et seq.* From Lakatos's testimony in the trial of Szálasi we know that in the decisive Budapest government meeting of October 10, 1944, he had spoken in favor of accepting the Soviet terms—and even proposed they invite the Red Army to halt briefly outside Budapest to give Béla Miklos's First Army time to withdraw "so that we can really attack the Germans properly."

p. 722 The appointment book kept by manservant Heinz Linge for the Führer from October 14, 1944, to February 28, 1945, was found by British Intelligence officers on September 10, 1945, in the ruins of the Chancellery (T84/22); with it was Hitler's desk appointment pad of April 1945 (AL/1488/4).

p. 724 Hitler kept his promise not to blacken Horthy's name. See the D.N.B. (German News Agency) dispatch of October 17, and Helmut Sündermann's diary of the same date. Editors had been instructed, "No attacks are to be made on the former regent."

p. 724 A folder of documents on the bunker's air-conditioning plant is in the BA, file R 58/1057.

p. 726 Hitler told Keitel and Jodl, in conversation on April 22, 1945, that he had resolved to die at the Wolf's Lair.

p. 726 Jodl's note on the Führer's war conference of October 25, 1944, survives. "Russian atrocities during occupation of East Prussian territory must be publicized by Wehrmacht propaganda branch. Photographs, eyewitness accounts, documentary reports, etc., for this" (1787–PS).

p. 728 On the decline in Göring's role: interrogations of Göring and Galland; Speer's chronicle, October 7, 1944; the Kreipe diary; and Koller's note on a talk with Göring, November 5.

p. 728 The disappointing performance of the Me-262 jet as a fighter is highlighted in Messerschmitt director Fritz Seiler's papers (FD–4924/45)—a report by Ludwig Bölkow dated October 25—and a memo in Bormann's files, dated October 21 (NS–6/152). The first Heinkel 162 "Volks" fighter flew on December 6, 1944; it was an aerodynamic disaster.

p. 733 The quotation is from Hitler's war conference on November 6, 1944 (Heiber, page 711). See the *Neue Zürcher Zeitung* November 14, and Himmler's files (T175/524) for such rumors. Hitler also mentioned them during lunch with Szálasi on December 4. Baron Gabriel von Kemény, the Hungarian foreign minister, later reported: "The Führer said with a laugh that the enemy camp has repeatedly proclaimed him dead—crediting him with a complete nervous breakdown or rumoring a cancer of the throat" (T175/130/6884).

PART SIX: END KAMPF

The Gamble

p. 739 Hitler's reflection that his life was already spent: see his conversation with the Hungarian Fascist leader Szálasi, December 4, 1944.

p. 740 (footnote) The figures are from a financial survey of the previous five and one quarter war years prepared by the finance ministry on November 30, 1944 (T178/16/2913 *et seq.*).

pp. 740–41 The quotation is from Hitler's secret speech of December 28.

p. 741 According to the invaluable naval staff diary, December 1, 1944, Colonel von Bonin expressed great confidence in the German defensive strength along the eastern front, "especially in the areas of East Prussia, Warsaw, and Cracow."

p. 743 On the planning of the Ardennes offensive, I used interrogations of Westphal, Jodl, Keitel, Koller, Manteuffel, and Büchs; the diaries of Jodl, Commander in Chief West, the OKW, and the naval staff; Jodl's notes on Führer conferences (1787–PS); Wilhelm Scheidt's manuscript and various published monographs.

p. 744 On the gasoline allocation for the offensive, see Jodl's diary, November 10 and December 18. From the OKW diary, January 4, 1945, it is clear that in fact *more* that the amount requested was supplied; but the actual consumption was higher than foreseen. It was precisely with this fear in mind that Keitel—who was responsible for fuel allocation—had ordered Rundstedt and others on December 7 to take stern action against unauthorized motorization of the troops (T77/778). The effect of the emphasis on the western front was grave in the east. From the draft General Staff war diary (T78/339) we learn that General von Greim's Sixth Air Force had only enough fuel reserve for about three major combat days by January 5, 1945.

p. 745 The excessive gasoline consumption is mentioned in the naval staff diary as early as December 17, 1944—Day Two of the offensive. See Hitler's postmortem account of their errors on December 28, 1944 (Heiber, page 746); SS General Bach-Zelewski, who attended the speech, stated that Rundstedt thanked Hitler for the "harsh but just" criticism (U.S. Army manuscript B-252: "Fourteenth SS Corps in Nov.–Dec. 1944").

p. 746 The navy's Captain Wolf Junge heard Hitler's mocking words to Churchill and mentions them in his manuscript.

p. 747 The quotation is from Hitler's talk with General Wolfgang Thomale, December 30, 1944 (Heiber, pages 779 *et seq.*).

p. 747 Under CSDIC interrogation on May 23, 1945, Milch said, "Hewel, the representative of the foreign office with the Führer, told me of Stalin's offer of negotiations fourteen days before the Russians staged their offensive on the Vistula front" (SRGG 1255C).

pp. 747–48 In addition to the German version of Hitler's talk with Szálasi and Baron Kemény's version in Himmler's files, two Hungarian versions exist (T973/1 and /14).

p. 752 Gehlen's Intelligence report of January 3, 1945, is in file H3/179.

pp. 752–53 For Guderian's visit to Hitler on January 9, 1945, I used—with caution—his own memoirs and the IfZ file ZS–57, and with greater confidence the fragmentary remarks by Hitler in his war conferences later that day and on January 10 and 27, and a manuscript by Colonel Freytag von Loringhofen (Guderian's adjutant) found among the general's papers for me by his son.

p. 753 For Germany's overconfidence in the eastern fortifications, see *e.g.*, Jodl's speech to allied military attachés in Berlin on January 13, 1945, 4 P.M. (T77/775/0754 *et seq.*) and the OCMH interrogation of Bonin.

p. 754 The conversation is recorded in Traudl Junge's manuscript.

p. 755 Gehlen assessed Stalin's attack strength at: 225 rifle divisions, 22 tank corps, 29 other tank formations, and 3 cavalry corps. But at Yalta Stalin—who surely had no reason to play down his contribution—stated he had only 180 divisions in Poland. Were

Guderian and Gehlen hoodwinked by the Russians? And as far as the Soviet divisions' strengths are concerned, General S. M. Shtemenko wrote in the Russian history, *The General Staff in the War Years* (Moscow, 1968): "At the time our divisions averaged only about four thousand men each."

p. 755 Guderian's cable to Hitler, dated January 14, 1945, is in the war diary of the General Staff operations branch (annexes, T78/305/6032 *et seq.*). He reported that Army Groups A and Center were fighting desperate defensive battles and that the enemy had now succeeded in making a strategic breakthrough from the western part of the Baranov bridgehead. "I therefore request the immediate transfer of several panzer and further infantry divisions from the west to the eastern front." And see naval staff war diary, January 14 for Admiral Voss's account.

pp. 755–56 Jodl records Guderian's phone call in his diary. It was followed by a telegram at 7:30 P.M., dictated by telephone to Hitler's train at 2:25 A.M., repeating the demand for reinforcements for Army Group A. Traudl Junge recorded Otto Günsche's witticism.

Waiting for a Telegram

pp. 757–58 Dönitz's adjutant, W. Lüdde-Neurath, described the scene with Harpe on January 19, 1945, in his book *Regierung Dönitz* (Berlin, 1964).

p. 759 Dr. Werner von Schmieden described his mission under OCMH interrogation; I also used the testimony of Fritz Hesse, interpreter Paul Schmidt, and Ribbentrop's colleague Fräulein Blank.

p. 759 The new OKW master plan is summarized in the naval staff diary, January 19, 1945, but is not mentioned at all in Schramm's OKW war diary.

p. 760 On the withdrawal of the Sixth SS Panzer Army to Hungary—instead of the eastern front—I used the annexes to the General Staff operations branch war diary (T78/305), the OKW war diary, and Jodl's notes after Führer conferences (1787–PS); see also Helmut Sündermann's diary, January 20, 1945, and Hitler's conference with Dönitz three days later, which clearly puts the Hungarian and Viennese oil fields foremost among their defense priorities.

p. 761 The conference leading to Himmler's appointment is in Jodl's diary, January 21, 1945. Hitler's resulting order was sent by Bormann to the Gauleiters (IfZ file ED–36) and to Himmler himself; see the war diary of Army Group Vistula, T311/167/8516 *et seq.*, and the General Staff war diary, T78/305/5979.

p. 762 Zhukov's order is appended to Gehlen's report of February 22, 1945, "Red Army's Behavior on German Soil" (T311/168/0014); a copy in big typescript for Hitler is in General Staff files (T78/304/5627).

p. 763 The ostensibly captured directive of the Allied Combined Chiefs of Staff is retranslated into English as an Appendix to a British Intelligence report on the achievements of the German Intelligence branches (Appendix III to ADI(K) Report 395/1945). It begins: "The Soviet Union has achieved successes in the east to an extent not expected by the Anglo-American command. In the event of any further rapid advance towards the West, a situation may thus develop which would be extremely unwelcome to the Anglo-American Governments and Commands. Experience has shown that the Soviet Union does not release—except under strongest military pressure—any territory it has occupied. . . . *Our military measures must therefore be such as to permit the Germans to reinforce their Eastern Front, a reinforcement they can mainly achieve by weakening their Western Front. . . .*" The directive lists ways of deceiving the Russians as to this shift in Allied aims —by cunning propaganda techniques, for example. Its authenticity seems vouched for by the subsequent realization of much of the directive: "Maximum 'terror' effort to shake the war morale of the German people . . . The bombing of the communications system should receive the first priority. . . . The preparation of a strong 'terror' mission against Berlin of some 1,200 four-engined bombers in several streams. . . ." As stated, the document was a Luftwaffe forgery.

pp. 763–64 I used Karl Wolff's testimony at Nuremberg, December 1, 1947, and in IfZ file ZS–317. He evidently saw Hitler on January 6 or 7, 1945 (Linge and Bormann diaries).

p. 764 See Hans Kissel's study of the Volkssturm 1944–45 in *WR,* 1960, pages 219 *et seq.*

p. 764 On the transfer of antiaircraft batteries from the Reich to the Oder front see Jodl's note on Hitler's conference of February 1, 1945, and the war diary of the OKL operations staff (T321/10/6799 *et seq.*).

pp. 764–65 Himmler recalled the crisis in conversation with Schwerin von Krosigk on April 19 (diary); and see the Reichsführer's order of February 1, 1945: "The thaw which has begun at this precise stage in the conflict is a gift of Fate . . . The Lord God has not forgotten his worthy German people" (T78/304/5774).

p. 767 For Göring's punitive measures, see his order of January 16, 1945 (T177/3/5007 *et seq.*). Lammers quotes Bormann's advice in a letter of April 24 (T580/265).

p. 768 I corresponded with Professor Hermann Giesler on his model for Linz; Hitler's plans are described by the local Gauleiter, August Eigruber, in a speech there on November 25, 1942 (T175/124/9670 *et seq.*); I also used Linge's diary, February 9–10, and Sündermann's, February 14, 1945, and Wilhelm Scheidt's manuscript.

p. 769 On Ribbentrop's last peace attempt, I used Guderian's testimony, and an overheard conversation of Ribbentrop's state secretary, Steengracht, on July 14, 1945: "So Guderian came to Ribbentrop and told him, 'It's all over. The game's up. Their tank superiority is one to eight, their aircraft one to sixteen.' Then Ribbentrop went to Hitler and told him that. Hitler retorted that he would not allow the foreign office to concern itself with such criticism. 'Secondly the figures are all wrong, and thirdly the soldiers don't know what they're talking about anyway' " (X–P–18).

p. 771 On the proposal to kill Allied prisoners in reprisal, I relied on the testimony of Ribbentrop, Scheidt, Steengracht, Sündermann, Jodl, and the stenographer Krieger—who particularly recalled Keitel's opposition. Also, Hitler's talks with Dönitz, February 19–21, and a memo by Jodl (ND, 606–D). Linge's diary of February 21 actually records: "3:15–3:55 P.M. [Hitler] strolls with foreign minister." The other main topic was clearly Ribbentrop's unauthorized peace feelers, for that same day according to the Weizsäcker diary, Ribbentrop urgently canceled his previous instructions to ventilate armistice proposals through neutral channels.

p. 772 The first description is by General von Trotha; the second is by Gauleiter Karl Wahl, under U.S. Army interrogation, June 1, 1945.

p. 773 Gauleiter Friedrich Rainer also described the "glass of water" scene. And see the account in Helmut Sündermann's diary, February 25, 1945. "He [Hitler] spoke with a firm voice, and particularly moved the Gauleiters with one sentence: 'You may see my hand tremble sometimes today, and perhaps even my head now and then; but my heart —never!' " Herbert Backe, who had scribbled notes on his shirtcuff during the speech, quoted the identical words to his wife for her diary on March 10, 1945.

p. 774 Bormann's memorandum is in the BA Schumacher collection, file 368. The women's battalion is also mentioned by Göring under interrogation on May 24.

p. 775 There is an invaluable file of telephone conversations between the General Staff and Army Group Vistula in the latter's war diary annexes (T311/167–169); I also used General Erhard Raus's postwar manuscript, "The Pomeranian Battle and the Command in the East" (D-189).

p. 776 Meissner related this under U.S. State Department interrogation, August 31, 1945.

p. 776 The conference is in Jodl's diary. General Eberhard Kinzel telephoned Army Group Vistula afterward that Hitler had ordered the Third Panzer Army to revert to the defensive at once, as "the imminent attack on Berlin" would necessitate the disengagement of various panzer and panzer-grenadier divisions for that front sector (T311/169/0913).

Hitler Goes to Ground

p. 777 See *e.g.*, the teletype from Foreign Armies East to the General Staff on April 16, 1945 (T78/304/5405).

p. 778 Copies of Admiral Dönitz's notes to his commanders are in Bormann's files (T81/5/2954 *et seq.*)

pp. 778–79 On "Operation *Werewolf*"—the Luftwaffe kamikaze attack—see the OKL war diary, March 18 and April 3, 6, and 7, 1945. It is not even mentioned in Schramm's OKW war diary.

p. 779 In generally describing life in Hitler's Berlin bunker I used the manuscripts or testimony of Schaub, Christa Schroeder, Speer, Puttkamer, Göhler, Below, Scheidt, Guderian, Saur, Jodl, Keitel, Günsche, General Erich Dethleffsen, and others.

p. 780 The outburst is described by General Koller in a letter to the Nuremberg lawyer Professor Franz Exner dated March 25, 1946, and independently by the attending staff stenographer Gerhard Herrgesell, July 19, 1945. A few days beforehand, Professor Giesler's mother had been killed on the road from Stuttgart to Ulm by an Allied fighter plane, which may have influenced Hitler.

pp. 780–81 Schmieden's failure is related in his interrogations. Fritz Hesse went to Sweden on February 17 with Ribbentrop's peace proposals; but on March 15 the Swedish journalist Arvid Fredborg compromised them in a *Svenska Dagbladet* article, "Nazistis fredstrevarė gjordes via Stockholm?"—which, according to Karl Wolff, Kaltenbrunner at once reported to Hitler. See Sündermann's diary, March 18, on this.

Ribbentrop described the Moellhausen mission in some detail, but the diplomat touches on it only barely in *Die gebrochene Achse* (Alfeld/Leine, 1949), page 280. An interrogation of Dr. Ernst Jahr, chief of the ecclesiastical affairs branch of the Gestapo, stated on May 3, 1946, that Ribbentrop had also sent Bishop Heckel—director of the foreign affairs section of the German Evangelical church—to Stockholm during March 1945 to open up ecclesiastical channels to London.

p. 781 The quotation is from General Koller's diary, March 28, 1945. See too Göring's OCMH interrogation, July 20, 1945.

p. 781 At Hitler's conference on March 8, 1945, after the Remagen bridge scandal, Sündermann noted in his diary: "The Führer also plans to send in flying courts-martial to stamp out these signs of dissolution. I have noted down two of his angry outbursts: 'Only Russian methods can help us now,' and 'If we lose the war the Germans will be exterminated anyway—so it's a good thing to exterminate some of these creatures now.' " The Remagen culprits were executed.

pp. 782–83 Among Robert Ley's papers I found a long manuscript he wrote about Hitler in August 1945. It is among the files of the American prosecutor Justice Robert H. Jackson, who recommended that Ley's papers should be destroyed after his Nuremberg suicide.

pp. 783–84 For my account of "Iron Hammer" I used Koller's papers, the OKL war diary, Gehlen's files (H3/653), and a teletype from Himmler to Fegelein, March 13, 1945 (T311/169/0831).

p. 785 Speer gives his version of his talk with Hitler in a letter to him dated March 29, 1945—but he never delivered it. His Allied interrogators recorded that although Speer had hoped to withhold the letter from them because of its "purely personal" language, they "found it nonetheless." But there can be no doubt that Speer did put up a tough fight against the destruction orders. On April 3, 1945, Milch noted in his diary a session of the transport staff Hitler had set up under Speer in mid-February: "Speer relates his battle with F[ührer] over demolitions."

p. 785 Bormann circulated the OKW order (signed by Jodl) to all Gauleiters on March 30, 1945 (T81/5/3034 *et seq.*).

p. 786 In addition to Heinrici's notes—appended to the war diary of his army group

(T311/169)—a valuable source is General Theodor Busse's article on the Ninth Army's operations in *WR*, 1955, pages 159 *et seq.* I also used the daily notes written by Guderian's and Krebs's adjutants after Hitler's conferences (T78/305).

p. 787 In an OCMH interrogation of July 21, 1945, Admiral Dönitz echoed Jodl's words to the USSBS on June 29: "Despite the defeat at Carthage the people admired Hannibal, didn't they? And despite our German defeat the people still admire Hitler." The admiral added, "Hitler was a man with an abundance of good nature. His mistake was that he was *too* noble. He persisted too much in his loyalty toward people who didn't deserve it." This trait in Hitler was also referred to by Göring—of all people (OCMH interrogation, July 23).

p. 787 The first Mark XXI submarine (U-2511, Captain Adalbert Schnee) put out on March 17, 1945, but was delayed in home waters by air raids and did not finally commence operations from Bergen until April 30—only to be recalled almost immediately by Dönitz upon Hitler's death.

pp. 788–89 There is a folder of the Gauleiters' teletype reports to Bormann during April 1945 on microfilm T580/43; I also used his diary, which was found on a corpse—presumably his—in Berlin early in May.

p. 789 Goebbels related all this to Schwerin von Krosigk; see the latter's diary, April 15, 1945.

p. 790 Hitler's erroneous supposition that Stalin would first drive into Bohemia is clear from the adjutants' notes on his war conferences from March 28 to April 6 (T78/305).

p. 791 Quartermaster general Alfred Toppe's letter to Keitel, April 15, 1945, is on microfilm T77/778.

p. 791 One of the participants in the conferences where Hitler ordered the liquidation of the convicts gave me the information; himself an SS major, he asked for his identity not to be divulged.

p. 792 Busse's words are quoted by Goebbels in the Schwerin von Krosigk diary.

p. 793 On the evacuation of the diplomatic corps, see the memo of May 1, 1945, in the Ribbentrop papers (T580/266). The adjutant quoted is Albrecht. After his letter of April 9, his wife heard no more of him—he was presumed killed in the defense of the Chancellery.

p. 793 The prisoner interrogations were reported by Colonel Gerhard Wessel on April 15, 1945 (T78/305).

p. 794 After the war Speer made little secret of his part in persuading Heinrici to abandon Berlin to the Russians without much fight. See his CIOS interrogation, June 1, 1945, and his conversation with Milch shortly before his departure to Spandau prison (diary, July 1947). "Hitler stayed in Berlin to organize the resistance. This Speer thwarted with General Heinrici and his Chief of Staff Kinzel, who sacrificed Berlin at his request. Only thus could be prevented the large-scale demolition of Berlin bridges and factories which Hitler had ordained should the battle come." In his recent *Memoirs,* Speer rather identifies Heinrici himself as the mastermind. The general had disclosed: "There won't be any fight over Berlin." Speer: "So Berlin will be swiftly captured?" Heinrici: "Well, there won't be any real resistance." There is a record of Speer's visit to Heinrici's HQ on April 15, 1945, in the army group war diary (T311/169/1719), but it is vague on this point: Speer was against any battle for Berlin because of the civilian casualties—a sound argument—and because of the destruction of vital industrial and traffic bridges Hitler had ordered. The record then states that should Army Group Vistula's front be breached, it proposed to "pull back Ninth Army on both sides past Berlin." (Hitler, of course, was never told this.) However, Hitler himself had on April 4, 1945, personally instructed Heinrici that "a commission must immediately be set up to prepare and supervise the demolition of bridges in Greater Berlin," but that *on no account* were the principal traffic bridges to be so prepared (General Staff diary, annexes, T78/305/6931 and 6945). In the circumstances it is difficult to understand Albert Speer's meddling in purely military affairs.

p. 794 The words are from Fräulein Christa Schroeder's shorthand notes written in May 1945 and transcribed at my request.

"Eclipse"

p. 795 My narrative of the last battle for Berlin is largely based on the war diaries of the General Staff (T78/304) and its annexes (*ibid.,* and T78/305), and of Army Group Vistula (T311/169 and /170); on the private diaries of Martin Bormann, of the Luftwaffe General Karl Koller (ADI[K] Report 348/1945), and of Jodl; on numerous interrogations and interviews of those concerned; and on the fragmentary shorthand notes of Hitler's last staff conferences, salvaged by Heinz Lorenz in 1945 and published in *Der Spiegel,* No. 3, 1966 (their authenticity is established beyond doubt by official British papers I have seen).

p. 795 A German translation of the British 21st Army Group's *"Eclipse"* folder, typed on Hitler's large-face typewriter, is in General Staff records (T78/434/5864 *et seq.*). Keitel initialed it on April 15; I find no evidence to support Cornelius Ryan's contention in *The Last Battle* that the document was captured as early as January.

p. 795 Wessel's report of April 15, 1945, is on microfilm T78/304/4862.

p. 796 Ribbentrop's renewed feelers: the memorandum is on film T77/775/1439 *et seq;* from its contents, it was written between the capture of Vienna (April 13) and the Soviet attack across the Oder (April 16)—and not in mid-February 1945 as Reimer Hansen surmises in *Geschichte in Wissenschaft und Unterricht,* 1967, pages 716 *et seq.*

p. 796 On dealings with the British and Americans: Schwerin von Krosigk diary, April 15, 1945, and interrogations of Karl Wolff in December 1947. Wolff's appointment with Hitler "before staff conference" on April 18 is in fact noted on Hitler's desk pad, in British Cabinet Office files.

p. 797 Hitler's remarks in private were recalled under Soviet interrogation by his staff —Heinz Linge and Otto Günsche; their manuscript is in my possession—and by his secretary Traudl Junge in her manuscript memoirs.

p. 800 Axmann described Hitler's short speech under interrogation on January 14, 1946.

p. 800 Bormann certainly gained the impression that Hitler would leave for the south soon; see the manuscript by Bormann's secretary, Ilse Krüger, in British files. So did Jodl: his wife wrote in her diary that April 20: "A[lfred] told me this evening that we may fall back briefly to the north, but that F[ührer's] intention is to go to the south." (Cornelius Ryan's version of this entry—in the opposite sense—must be a misunderstanding.) Milch, who met Speer the next day, noted in his own diary Speer's "good impression of Führer, bad impression of 'that dodger Göring.' "

p. 801 Quoted from her May 1945 shorthand note.

p. 803 Weidling died in Soviet captivity, but fortunately wrote a long account of the battle for Berlin first which was published in *Voennoistoricheskii Zhurnal,* Moscow, October–November 1961.

p. 804 The tumultuous events of April 22, 1945, are described by the diaries of Koller and Jodl April 22–23; by memos of Koller, and Lieutenant Volck, April 25; in interrogations of Keitel, Jodl, Christian, Freytag von Loringhoven, Below, Colonel von Brauchitsch, Lorenz, and the stenographers Haagen and Herrgesell; and in written manuscripts of Günsche, Linge, Ilse Krüger, Traudl Junge, and Keitel.

p. 804 Felix Steiner, *Die Freiwilligen* (Göttingen, 1958), pages 324 *et seq.*

p. 806 An important private letter by Eva Braun to her sister, dated April 23, 1945, describes the contemporary mood.

The decision to turn round the Twelfth Army to fight the Russians—no less than an invitation to the Allies to take Berlin—was made by 5 P.M., for at that time Krebs telephoned it to Heinrici (T311/170/2182 *et seq.*).

p. 808 German Radio broadcast Hitler's decision to stay in Berlin at 12:40 P.M., April 23, 1945 (BBC Monitoring Report). Among the papers of Ribbentrop's Nuremberg defense counsel I found an eleven-page account by the foreign minister of the last days of Hitler (Rep. 502 AXA 132). He describes arriving at Hitler's shelter after the regular war conference on April 23: "While I was there I learned that it was by no means certain whether the Führer would be leaving for southern Germany, even temporarily. I thereupon spoke to Fräulein Eva Braun and asked her to influence the Führer to go to southern Germany, because if he was cut off in Berlin he could no longer lead and then the front lines might easily just cave in. Fräulein Braun told me she couldn't understand either—the previous day the Führer had been talking of probably flying down south; apparently somebody had talked him around to the opposite view."

p. 809 Ribbentrop's secret letter to Churchill was circulated as a memorandum, CP (45) 48 to the British Cabinet. It is in PRO file CAB 66/66. Ribbentrop swore in it that both he and Hitler had always striven for rapprochement with Britain; Ribbentrop "had always regarded England as my second home." Churchill sent the letter to Stalin on July 12, 1945—"I assume its content may be of some interest to you, although it is exceptionally long and tedious."

Ribbentrop described his last meeting with Hitler in several interrogations, in Rep. 502 AXA 132, and his memoirs. In his other manuscript, Rep. 502 AXA 122, he proposed repeating the four main points of the offer to the British prosecuting counsel Sir David Maxwell-Fyfe, since he had had no reply from Churchill or Eden. According to an overheard conversation of his state secretary, Steengracht, on July 14, Ribbentrop told him after that April 23, 1945, meeting: "You know, the Führer has proved right after all. The last thing he told me was, 'I actually came to power ten years too soon. Another ten years and I would really have kneaded the Party into shape.' . . . I wrote that letter to Churchill because I had to. In our last discussion the Führer—he was quite calm—told me he had never wanted any harm to come to Britain. The big handshake with 'Germanic' England—that had always been his goal" (X–P 18).

p. 810 The telegram draft was found in Göring's possession as a prisoner (DE 426/DIS 202). I also used an interrogation of Below, and the manuscripts of Ilse Krüger and Hans Rattenhuber (in Russian archives); and Koller's secondhand version (diary, April 23). Göring's telegram to Ribbentrop and Speer's letter to Galland are on microfilm T77/775. In Donitz's last diary (T608/1) we find a telephone call from Bormann on April 23, after which—at 10:45 P.M.—the admiral phoned General Stumpff, the Luftwaffe commander in Germany. "I have the following Führer order for you: 'The Reichsmarschall who's down in the south has off his own bat ordered that the Reich government elements that fell back to the north are to fly down to the south. The Führer does not want that at all. It is to be prevented at all costs. You [Stumpff] are to see to that. Have you understood that?' "

p. 810 Göring certainly found little support at the Chancellery. On April 25, 1945, Koller explained to the new Luftwaffe Commander in Chief Greim: "He hadn't one friend there. He was just surrounded by enemies who fought him and the Luftwaffe in the most malicious manner these last two years and more, instead of helping" (diary). And Göring's personal assistant Dr. Fritz Goernnert told American interrogators on May 12: "He [Göring] realized more and more that [the Luftwaffe's decline] was no accident. The Luftwaffe depended entirely on raw material allocations. You just couldn't get them for the Luftwaffe. Reichsminister Speer played the biggest part against Göring, because that's just the way he was—highly ambitious. He thought that in this way he could satisfy his ambitions still further" (46M–8).

This is my own view too, after having intensively studied the interplay of Luftwaffe and German army arms production (which was Speer's domain, along with raw material allocations). On the basic question as to whether Speer deliberately obstructed Luftwaffe production as a means of humiliating Göring and obtaining control over it himself, see Göring's USSBS interrogation of June 29, 1945; Milch's resignation speech of June 30, 1944, (MD56/2701 *et seq.*); and the air ministry study of the reasons for the huge increase in aircraft production from March to June 1944–i.e., from the moment Speer's ministry took over (FD–4439/45).

p. 811 Hitler's order of April 24, 1945 (evening), is in OKW files (T77/775/1198 *et seq.*). Koller inadequately summarized it in his diary two days later, which text is unfortunately adopted by the OKW diary, Vol. IV, page 1590.

p. 813 A long U.S. DIC interrogation report on Hanna Reitsch—Greim's female admirer—is in my possession.

pp. 816–17 Transcripts of the last letters written by Joseph and Magda Goebbels to their surviving son—by her first marriage—Harald Quandt, on April 28, 1945, are also in my possession.

p. 817 The texts—not always accurate—of the last days' signals from the Chancellery are in the war diaries of the OKW command staffs north and/or south.

p. 817 The BBC Monitoring Report of April 28, 1945, noted that a "Freedom Action Bavaria" began broadcasting at 5:50 A.M. to workers to protect their installations against "Nazi sabotage"; Gauleiter Paul Giesler quickly broadcast his counterattack at 9:56 A.M., and at 4:48 P.M. he announced that the "traitors" had been "summarily dealt with."

p. 817 The BBC Monitoring Report noted the first Allied report of Himmler's surrender offer at 1:55 P.M. About 5 P.M. Dönitz asked if the OKW was aware of this report. Himmler denied it, and Schwerin von Krosigk—Ribbentrop's successor—repeated this dementi in a telegram to Ambassador Stahmer in Tokyo on May 6, 1945. Precisely how far Himmler did in fact go is uncertain. Reporting an earlier meeting between him and Count Folke Bernadotte, the British envoy in Stockholm cabled London on April 13 that Himmler had refused to consider a surrender as he was bound by his oath to the Führer, to whom he owed everything and whom he could not desert; Hitler was now interested only in the future architecture of Germany's cities, according to Himmler. (The telegram is in British files.)

p. 818 Bormann's cable to Munich is quoted in Dönitz's files, T608/1; so is Admiral Voss's radio message.

p. 818 In an order to Heinrici and Manteuffel that April 28, 1945, Keitel refused to cancel the dismissal decision and put General von Tippelskirch (Twenty-First Army) in command of the army group (T77/779/5697; and T77/1432/0025).

Dönitz's opinion is cited by W. Baum in his study of the German military collapse, *WR*, 1960, page 251. Keitel's view is in his *Memoirs.*

p. 819 To his stepson Harald Quandt, Joseph Goebbels wrote: "Germany will survive this frightful war but only if our people have vivid examples before their eyes upon which to righten themselves. We want to set such an example. . . . One day the lies will collapse and truth will again triumph over them. The hour will come when we shall stand above them all, pure and immaculate, just as our faith and endeavor have always been. Farewell, my dear Harald! Whether we shall ever meet again is in the hands of God. If not, then be proud to have belonged to a family that was loyal to the Führer and his pure and holy mission even in misfortune." Frau Goebbels wrote in the same vein. Hanna Reitsch read the letters and decided not to forward them; the farewell letter of Eva Braun ("With the Führer I have had everything. To die now beside him completes my happiness") she tore up—no doubt out of jealous pique.

p. 819 The letter to Wenck read as follows: "Esteemed General Wenck! As can be seen from the attached dispatches, the SS Reichsführer Himmler made the Anglo-Americans an offer which would have surrendered our nation unconditionally to the plutocrats. Only the Führer—and he alone—can bring about a turning point. The prerequisite to that is the immediate establishment of contact between the Wenck Army and ourselves, so that the Führer regains freedom of action for domestic and diplomatic moves. Yours, Krebs, Chief of the General Staff. Heil Hitler, yours, M. Bormann."

p. 819 For Hitler's coming suicide the generals blamed the Party, and vice versa. General Wilhelm Burgdorf wrote on April 29 to Schörner that Hitler had signed his will "today under the shattering news of the Reichsführer's treachery." Bormann emphasized the failure of the generals in his letter to Dönitz: "As our position seems hopeless because of the nonarrival of every division, the Führer last night dictated the enclosed Political Testament."

p. 821 Hitler's last letter to Keitel was destroyed by the courier, Colonel von Below, on May 2, 1945; but he reconstructed it under CSDIC interrogation in March 1946.

pp. 822–23 My principal witness is Otto Günsche himself, who tape-recorded many hours of his recollections in 1967 and again in 1971 for me. Furthermore, I used interrogations of Kempka—who helped in burning the bodies—the secretaries Gerda Christian, Traudl Junge, and Ilse Krüger, and Goebbels's adjutant Günther Schwägermann. Contrary to the otherwise reliable account of Lev Bezymenski, *Der Tod des Adolf Hitler* (Hamburg, 1968)—based on Soviet documents—there is not the least doubt that Hitler shot himself as well as took poison, as in fact Artur Axmann privately told Milch in prison on March 1, 1948 (diary). Fragments of the cyanide phial were found in Hitler's jaw. And *Life* magazine published in July 1945 William Vandivert's excellent photographs of the bunker room and couch, on which the blood stains are clearly visible. Both Kempka and SS Brigadier Hans Rattenhuber (manuscript dated May 20, 1945, Moscow) noticed the bloodstains on the carpet too. The Walther pistol with which Hitler killed himself is now in private German hands.

According to Goebbels's telegram to Admiral Dönitz, May 1, 1945, Hitler died at 3:30 P.M., April 30, 1945.

Index

Publisher's Note

This index covers both volumes of Hitler's War and has been printed in both books. Page references 1–450 therefore apply to *Hitler's War 1939–1942* and page references 451–823 to *Hitler's War 1942–1945*.